SOCIAL STRUCTURES

SOCIAL STRUCTURES

John Levi Martin

PRINCETON UNIVERSITY PRESS   PRINCETON AND OXFORD

Published by Princeton University Press, 41 William Street,
Princeton, New Jersey 08540
In the United Kingdom: Princeton University Press, 6 Oxford Street,
Woodstock, Oxfordshire OX20 1TW

Library of Congress Cataloging-in-Publication Data

Martin, John Levi, 1964–
Social structures / John Levi Martin.
p.   cm.
Includes biographical references and index.
ISBN 978-0-691-12711-8 (cl.)
1. Social structure. 2. Social networks. 3. Social interaction.
4. Social institutions. I. Title.
HM706.M37 2009
305—dc22   2009003738

British Library Cataloging-in-Publication Data is available

This book has been composed in Times Roman typeface

Printed on acid-free paper. ∞

press.princeton.edu

Printed in the United States of America

10 9 8 7 6 5 4 3 2 1

Contents

Acknowledgments

PORTIONS of the research in chapter 4 were funded by the National Science Foundation and the Rutgers Office of Sponsored Research Projects; portions of the research in chapter 5 were made possible by a research leave from Rutgers University; portions of the research in chapter 8 were made possible by course reduction supported by the Graduate School of the University of Wisconsin, Madison.

This book was largely inspired indirectly by Kate Stovel, who, when we were both being recruited by Rutgers University, told Eviatar Zerubavel her idea of teaching a course on social structures. It was the first time I had ever heard the term used in the plural in such a way. Eviatar himself urged me toward such a project when I first came to Rutgers and had expressed interest. Eviatar repeatedly exhorted me to ignore the "practical" concerns that I had as a young faculty member and follow my instincts, which of course was eminently practical advice. In addition to continual intellectual dialogue and friendship, he read, and offered helpful comments on, the first drafts I made of the introductory framework. Other colleagues at Rutgers gave important feedback: Karen Cerulo gave advice on the initial framing of the project; Paul McLean read and commented extensively on chapter 6; Ann Mische on chapters 1–3; and Chip Clarke on chapter 7.

Peter Bearman not only read and gave comments on most of the chapters but helped guide the book toward its current form. The influence of his own work is apparent throughout but is even larger than it appears. This book would not exist were it not for him. David Gibson and Mustafa Emirbayer read the first two chapters and made valuable suggestions that dramatically increased the readability of this book. Adam Slez and Ivan Ermakoff read and made valuable comments on chapters 7 and 8; Karen Streir on chapter 4. Jan Fuhse read the entire manuscript and made many valuable suggestions; he has been a welcome interlocutor. Other people whose support was of great help at this time include Ron Breiger, Stanley Lieberson, James Montgomery, Dr. Daniel Mondrow, and Erik Olin Wright. A number of readers for Princeton University Press, as well as editor Tim Sullivan, made valuable comments on the manuscript. In particular, Scott Boorman saw the central thrust at a time when there were confusions and pointed me to research that would bolster the arguments here. His influence runs throughout this work.

I am also grateful for Harrison White's support in many ways for many years and regret that I have repaid him here by misusing his own terminology. I hope that I can make up for that by dedicating this work to him, in part as person, and in part as a knot in a web of ties.

Preface

From Big Structures to Small

> Now the smallest Particles of Matter may cohere by the strongest
> Attractions, and compose bigger Particles of Weaker Virtue; and
> many of these may cohere and compose bigger Particles whose
> Virtue is still weaker, and so on for divers Successions.
> —ISAAC NEWTON, *Opticks*

THE BIRTH of the modern social sciences took place sometime in the eighteenth to nineteenth centuries, when a number of European thinkers became convinced that there was some sort of order to the social life around them, an order that came neither from God nor from prince but was inherent to social life itself. The first metaphor that was used to describe this order was an organismic one—an old metaphor to be sure, but the new sociologists took this metaphor far more seriously than had earlier political philosophers. In particular, Herbert Spencer (e.g., 1896 [1873]: 56–60) proposed that just as an organism had organs, or structures, that met its functional needs, so society had "social structures" that carried out social functions.

The term *structure* here meant the same as "organ," just as Hobbes's earlier discussion of social "Systemes" also meant organs (see Hobbes 1909 [1651]: 171). In particular, Hobbes saw that the prominent organizations that comprised the modern nation-state met functions just as surely as did the organs in a body. While the social scientists, understanding this metaphor to be more than a figure of speech, refrained from some of the excessively detailed allegories made by Hobbes (such as spies being the "eyes" of the realm), they too suggested that the most visible social structures, namely, the organizations making up the nation-state, existed because they fulfilled certain functions. The army defended against enemies; the executive branch of the government was, as Durkheim (1933 [1893]: 132) also suggested, a social brain.

Nowadays the organismic context for the idea of social structure has receded into the background, and "social structures" are loosely taken to indicate almost any form of regularity or constraint in social life. Yet part of the nineteenth-century legacy remains—a belief that analyzing such structures requires that we begin by looking at the big picture, as big as we possibly can.

And yet even the big social structures that inspired the reverent study of the first sociologists historically arise as a concretion of previously existing smaller structures. Over time, they change and their original form is smoothed

over, but in periods of social dislocation we have the opportunity of redis-
covering the elemental fact that big structures are put together out of smaller
pieces (Simon 1962: 473; Gould 2003: 151).[1]

Most recently, the collapse of state socialism in Eastern Europe has brought
this home, as we have been able to witness new patterns of regular social
interaction develop by necessity. It was first assumed by many that the introduction of market society would smash apart all preexisting ties that had been
part of the authoritative mechanism for the interfirm transactions of state socialism. Evidence of widespread survival of such ties was frequently taken as
a sign of corruption or a sullen refusal to go with the flow. But those who have
interviewed economic actors find these interpretations ungenerous. In
the midst of confusion and chaos, new sets of exchange relations had to be
pieced together, and starting from scratch would mean trading with people
whom one had no particular reason to trust. It certainly made more sense to
trade with those one knew, even if this is, according to some textbooks, not
the most "efficient" choice (see recently Keister 2001: 337; Stark 1996).[2] Thus
the new structures of market-based economic interaction were composed by a
reassembling of surviving components of the former large-scale structures of
state socialism.

More generally, the structures we see around us—up to and including the
state organizations that first inspired analogies to organismic structures—in
most cases also developed from smaller components. These components in
turn may be residues of a shattered former large-scale structure, or, more interestingly, they may have been generated from even smaller units, namely interpersonal relationships.

Could we reconstruct the process, at least analytically, whereby individual
relationships combine to form structural units, and these structural units then
aggregate to form large-scale structures? And could we do this without relying
on a tendentious evolutionary history such as that of Spencer? We might, if
different sorts of relationships naturally lend themselves to certain structural
forms. And it is precisely this—that certain relationships have inherent structural potentials—that I will attempt to demonstrate here. With this correspondence between type of relationship and structural form, we can begin with
types of relationships and find the forms that are likely to arise in the absence
of other disturbing factors. In certain circumstances, these structural forms

---

[1] Spencer had such a conception of tracing large structures back to smaller components, but he
proposed a simple historical progression that proved untenable. Also see Park (1974: 141) for a
recognition of the importance of local structures for large scale political structures.

[2] Recently, Hanley, King, and János (2002) have taken issue with Stark's description of Hungary, but the difference may simply be due to changes that have occurred since around 1990 (see
2002: 135 and n.5 for complications in judging ownership patterns). This would actually support
the interpretation of Stark's work made here.

may comprise the building blocks of larger structures. This book is thus an attempt to begin an analysis of the structural tendencies inherent in certain forms of relationships, and their eventual consequences up to and including some of the structures that first impressed Spencer and the other organismic thinkers. I begin by proposing a way to think about structure, and then survey the simplest forms of structure that tend to arise in social interactions.

SOCIAL STRUCTURES

1 ────────────────────────────

Introduction: Social Action and Structures

> The large systems and the super-individual organizations that custom-
> arily come to mind when we think of society, are nothing but imme-
> diate interactions that occur among men constantly, every minute,
> but that have become crystallized as permanent fields, as autono-
> mous phenomena. As they crystallize, they attain their own existence
> and their own laws, and may even confront or oppose spontaneous
> interaction itself.
> —GEORG SIMMEL, *Fundamental Problems of Sociology*

The Dialectic of Institutionalization

We set out, then, to determine where structures such as those impressing the
early social theorists (for example, the army) "come from." In any strict historical sense, our answer will of course be "other structures." And so on, all the
way down. This seems a dead end, and so there is pressure to replace the
historical interpretation of this question with an analytic one. The functionalist
approach, which so enthralled the early social theorists, did just this. Although
the results of this effort were less than satisfying, the idea of an analytic response is not intrinsically a poor one.

The functionalist approach basically turns the "where" question into a
"why" question: *why* does society *have* an army? But one can pose an analytic
"where" question if one were to make two assumptions: first, that we can
conduct some sort of analysis whereby we identify *components* of structures,
and second, that it is *noncontradictory* to propose that the structure can be
produced via the aggregation of these components. Neither of these assumptions is always reasonable. Regarding the first, not all things are susceptible to
analysis because not all things have separable parts. Regarding the second, in
some cases parts cannot be imagined to exist separate from the whole (for
example, we cannot say a body "comes from" organs because we cannot imagine the organs existing independently). But structures like the army are composed of things that do exist separately, and hence we may pose an analytic
frame to our question.

Indeed, there is in sociology one extremely general, and extremely satisfying, answer along these lines, and this is that structures "come from" the
crystallization of relationships. The most elegant formulation of this idea was

made by the theorist Georg Simmel. In contrast both to the methodological individualists such as Weber who did not speak of "society" as a thing, and to the collectivists such as Comte who considered society akin to an organism, Simmel saw society as a web of crystallized interactions. While there is no "society" as a thing in itself but only persons and their action (and so Weber was technically correct), these interactions themselves have a tendency to reify, to become thinglike, and even to guide spontaneous action (and so Comte was on to something). What we mean by society, then, is simply the set of permanent interactions, "crystallized as definable, consistent structures," that is, institutions. An institution may remain even after the sentiment or purpose that gave rise to it is gone; indeed, it can even (in the words of Marx) appear as an "alien power" that hangs over the heads of the persons whose interactions comprise it (Simmel 1950 [1908]: 9f, 41, 96, 380f).[1]

Interestingly, Simmel's archenemy Emile Durkheim, would-be dogmatic founder of a functionalist school largely in the Comtian tradition, frequently agreed. Durkheim occasionally proposed that social institutions, rather than being explicable in terms of what Comte called social statics (the functional organization of the social body), must be understood as the emergent effects of the dynamics of social action. "Certain of these social manners of acting and thinking acquire, by reason of their repetition, a certain rigidity which on its own account crystallizes them, so to speak, and isolates them from the particular events which reflect them" (Durkheim 1938 [1895]: 45).[2]

Both Simmel and Durkheim, then, help us understand what often seems paradoxical: how society can seem like a thing outside us and frequently opposed to us, when it is nothing but the aggregate of our own actions. This understanding is left largely as intuition or vision—a general answer to the

---

[1] For Simmel, the story does not end here, for "sociation continuously emerges and ceases and emerges again." The basic relationship between the impulse toward sociation (social interaction) and these petrified forms is understood by Simmel to be dialectical in the Hegelian/vitalist sense of a dynamic interplay between the *content* of sociation—our desire to enter into relationships—and the particular structural *form* that may emerge. This version of the dialectic was formulated by Hegel (1949 [1803]) and the implications for the estrangement, whereby our actions become things oriented against us, basically introduced via Feuerbach (1983 [1843]), Marx and Engels (1976 [1845–46]: especially 47f), and Marx (1906 [1867]: 81ff). On Simmel's balancing of form and content, see Simmel (1955 [1922]: 172).

[2] The only difference between this formulation of Durkheim's and Simmel's version is that while Simmel somewhat romantically stressed the potential for estrangement of the living essence in this petrification, Durkheim welcomed the process of crystallization as it eased the task of the analyst who would find herself totally at sea were she surrounded by a host of uncrystallized relations. "Social life consists, then, of free currents perpetually in the process of transformation and incapable of being mentally fixed by the observer, and the scholars cannot approach the study of social reality from this angle. But we know that it possesses the power of crystallization without ceasing to be itself" (Durkheim 1938 [1895]: 45).

question of "what is society" but not generative of empirical understanding.[3] It expresses how we can *conceive* of the generation of patterns of social interaction without necessarily making any focused claims as to the nature of empirical processes of institution formation. While a number of recent approaches to the nature of social order build on this general insight (specifically those of Giddens 1984; Bourdieu 1984 [1979]; and White 1992),[4] they tend to supplement their account with specific substantive claims that are not inherent to the basic understanding of the relation between action and institution suggested by Durkheim and Simmel. The fundamental vision put forward by all these authors may be formulaically put as follows: social interactions, when repeated, display formal characteristics; and this form can then take on a life of its own, ultimately leading to institutions that we (as actors) can treat as given and exogenous to social action for our own purposes, though at any moment (or at least at some moments) these institutions may crumble to the ground if not rejuvenated with compatible action.

We have perhaps as a discipline spent too much time in taking turns at giving a somewhat more elegant phrasing to this insight as opposed to determining whether it is amenable to empirical elaboration. Because this understanding is, as noted above, a form of dialectic, it is somewhat resistant to being put in the form of directed graphs of arrows between variables that have so enamored social scientists. But there is a possible foothold for analysis, as we see two moments in this process. In the first, certain patterns of interaction recur with sufficient regularity among different sets of persons that we (as analysts) can recognize formal characteristics that are independent of the individuals involved. Most important, there are conditions under which interpersonal interactions tend to align and structure themselves. Structure emerges, perhaps, out of unstructured interactions quite like the emergence of crystalline structure in a seeming fluid. From a single seed, it is possible for structure to spread, at least if there is no external force jarring the components.[5]

In the second—just as Simmel argued—there comes a point when such structure seems to take on a life of its own, something that can be referred to by persons as if it existed apart from the myriad interactions that compose it. Instead of simply noticing that there are recurrent patterns, we can make reference to these patterns as independent entities that make predictable demands on us. It is at this point that we speak of an institution.

[3] I have previously (Martin 2001) argued that this form of social theory is necessarily "weak" and not generative of sociological research, a claim that I now partially repent.
[4] White (1992: 127, cf. 136) puts it more graphically: "Social organization is like some impacted, mineralized goo. . . ."
[5] It is worth emphasizing that the word *structure* will here be used only in the sense of patternings of relationships, without prejudice to other possible forms of regularity that some might wish to term "structural."

An institution exists when interactants subjectively understand the formal pattern in terms of the *content* of relationships. Marriage as an institution has particular structural characteristics: it (in the simplest conventional monogamous version) divides both men and women into two classes each, the unmarried and the married. The married are paired with one and only one member of the married class of the opposite sex. When navigating the world structured by such relations, however, people tend to focus on the content of the institution of marriage as opposed to these structural features. Here they are focusing not on the content of any *particular* marriage (happy or unhappy in its own way), but on the content of the *institution* of marriage. This content may be seen as the translation of the formal characteristics of marriage as a set of dyads into a subjective sense of what marriage "is all about": trust, commitment, exclusivity, and so on (Swidler 2001). For actors to focus on the content seems a wise choice, as this is easier to translate into action imperatives in any situation than are purely structural principles.[6]

This is not to say that relationships lacked all content before such a development of structure. But it is reasonable to suggest that their content is changed and perhaps elaborated by structural formations and, even more important, persons can get a different *conception* of the content of the relationship when they abstract general principle from concrete structures. Second, we may propose as a thought experiment arranging persons into structures and finding that the experience of traversing such formations induces subjective understandings of the "content" of these relationships. (Such an experiment was done to surprising success by Breer and Locke [1965]). Finally, it is worth emphasizing that in no way does this approach deny that the structure of relationships is in part a function of their content. But this is hardly surprising. What is more interesting is that the reverse may also be the case and in fact that attention to this process gives us analytic purchase in understanding the development of large-scale structures from small.[7] Demonstrating this point, however, awaits substantive examinations.

Such examination is the goal of the following pages. This book traces the emergence of structure up to but not quite including the point at which cultural understandings become detached from concrete patterns. Starting from the simplest elements of interpersonal interaction, we examine the forma-

[6] We may also propose that the contents of relationships, when sufficiently strong and generalized, become detachable from any particular structural form and can be connected in *fields* in which the alignment of content, and not of form, is of paramount importance. Casual inspection suggests that the bulk of social action is best explained by reference to these overarching cultural fields and not to isolated institutions nor to concrete and necessarily local structures. Yet to understand these fields, we may need to trace them back to the simplest structures.

[7] As Jad Fair has pointed out, it is no news if a dog bites a man. But man bites dog—front page!

tion of obdurate patterns of organization, and their potential alignment into larger structures.

If we refuse to entertain any explanation of the regularities in social life that does not end up with an arrow pointing one way and not the other we are unlikely to get very far in the current project. We cannot begin here with the sort of "theory" from which testable hypotheses may be derived. But it may well be for the very reason that it lacks a formally elegant and logically integral structure that this understanding escapes what the Buddhists call "the stage of playwords"—a stage of unproductive obsession with terminology that for sociological theory is frequently terminal. Since we cannot get very far simply juxtaposing theoretical terms, we must begin looking very carefully at how social structures actually form. In this chapter, I lay out the understanding of structure that will be used, its relation to persons, and to their subjective conceptions.

What Might We Mean by Social Structure?

Social Structure as Position and Expectation

The arguments given above imply that we begin our attempt to understand social life by examining the forms that repeated interactions tend to take. We might reasonably call this the formation of social structure, or perhaps better, of social structures in the plural. Unfortunately, the term *social structure* is used by social scientists in a number of different ways. Many of these are unpardonably vague, basically meaning "anything that makes people do something they don't want to do." Others are implausibly specific, especially those that attempted to synthesize the classic structuralism of the Levi-Strauss variety with more intuitive understandings of the sets into which people seemed to be clumped, especially social classes. In practice, however, this vision was difficult to distinguish from the functionalist one mentioned in the preface.

This functionalist idea of social structure, coming from Spencer, was based on an organismic analogy. Just as organs and bones are structures of a body, so there are structures in society. This vision, while generative and profound, offers little for the current investigation, because structure is necessarily defined in relation to the properties of the transcendent whole, society. We, on the other hand, are attempting to trace the generation of transindividual consistencies in action and cannot assume the existence of what we set out to derive.

But there is another coherent approach to social structure coming from anthropology, especially the work of Linton (1936). Here social structures are understood as agglomerations of statuses and their action-counterparts, roles. The family is therefore a social structure, since it has a set of predefined roles that shape interaction. This account has the seeming virtue of emphasizing the importance of subjective expectations, which the theorists agree, play a crucial role in the development of structure. Yet, as we shall see, for the very reason that the Lintonian approach makes this link central ab initio, despite its real insights, it may make a poor starting place for theoretical investigation.

To Linton, the anthropologist's job of mapping out societies would lead to a conception of the structure of the society in question as the anthropologist learned the various "slots" into which persons could be fitted: for an example of kinship structure these could include mother, brother, mother's brother, wife, husband, mother's husband. Linton called such a slot a "status," a "collection of rights and duties." That is as much as to say that it is a set of expectations: rights are what we may expect from others, duties are what others may expect from us. The point is that every slot in the social structure that has a name— that is socially understood as a meaningful category—has attached to it these expectations. And that is why society functions so smoothly. When we interact with one another, chances are good that we are not simply interacting as two unique individuals, but as two statuses, so that what we can expect from one another is remarkably clear. Since every status has its "dynamic aspect"—a role—one knows what the status calls on one to do.

The confusing thing is that social structure—regularities in interaction— then turns out to be at base a matter of shared expectations. This, in turn, implies that the fundamental ordering principles of societies are *cultural*. Talcott Parsons (1968; Parsons and Shils 1956) followed this line of theorizing to its logical conclusions. Consequently, despite the common division of "variables" into the trinity of cultural, structural, and personality in the Parsonian world, culture always trumps structure and personality, for the ultimate cultural values are the "topmost controlling component of the social system." Structure is the embodiment of culture as expectations, and personality is the introjection of culture via socialization.

Consequently, it was difficult to propose that there was any analytically useful distinction between culture and social structure—between the subjective conceptions of actors and the action patterns that an analyst might uncover. To call status and role structural, when there was a one-to-one mapping between structure and normative considerations that were ultimately tied to cultural values, was as much as to call the front end of a dog culture and his tail end social structure. To steal a phrase from the great Jim Stockinger, we might say that in the American functionalist tradition culture—more specifically, *values*—gobbled up social structure.[8]

This same paradox haunted Parsons's approach to institutions: it was never clear whether institutions were about *knowing* what to do, or in doing it, since

---

[8] Even when Parsons (1960: 19f, 22) turned to the analysis of organizations, which might seem to be the perfect site for a purely structural analysis, the two possible points of view he proposed were the cultural-institutional, based on values, and the "group" or "role" point of view, which also assumed normative expectations.

Parsons defined away in advance the possibility that regularities in action could arise without shared expectations. Consequently, despite its evident plausibility—indeed, it is because of it—this line of theorizing collapsed structures, culture, and institutions, when there are good theoretical reasons for keeping these distinct. There is no reason to forbid, at least for analytic purposes, a difference between regularities in interaction (structure) and those institutions that appear as givens for individuals engaging in interaction. Many of the formations considered to be "structures" in the Lintonian understanding (such as the family) are better thought of as "institutions." In other words, any useful definition of social structure has to allow for regularities in interaction that are *not* institutions, and that do *not* arise because interactants understand their normative responsibility to act in a certain way.

To preserve such a distinct sense of "structure," I propose that we begin by considering social structure simply as regular patterns of interaction, and leave to the side the question of why these patterns exist. In particular, we should leave open, at least for a while, the relation between such patterns and large-scale cultural expectations. The nearest attempt to formulate a theory of social structure along vaguely Lintonian lines minus the emphasis on subjectivity was made by Nadel (1957), an approach now being resuscitated by theorists such as White (1992).[9]

It is indeed hard to imagine how structure could arise and "guide behavior" (as Nadel says) in the absence of such rules. But as Turner (1994) has demonstrated, with closer attention, it is hard to say how rules can guide behavior at all—that is, how "structure" can be something outside us forcing us to do things. Frederik Barth (1981: 22, 32, 34–37, 48), building on Nadel, made a radical simplification by divorcing structure (or form) from culture and making the degree of connection an empirical question rather than definitionally true. He argued that there could be a study of forms of regular interaction without assuming that these are "causes" of action. In place of such a causal frame, he argued that we must examine the "constraints and incentives" that "canalize choices," some perhaps cutting a channel deep enough to be considered an institution. Seen in this light, it becomes apparent that investigations of social structure have been derailed by the fantastic belief that social structure is something that *causes* regularities in action, when social structure is simply what

---

[9] White and his colleagues (White, Boorman, and Breiger 1976; Boorman and White 1976) used—and to some degree fused—Nadel's (1957) idea of treating networks as interlocks of mutually dependent relationships, and his idea of role systems as restricted sets of possible combinations of roles. This produced a conception of structure as sets of regularities in the ways in which relationships can aggregate. But Nadel himself actually never relinquished the idea of a role as primarily a *normative*, and hence subjective, construct (1957:16, 24). Indeed, while White was able to find the presence of roles simply on the basis of observed regularities, Nadel (1957: 140f, 147f) refused to accept that there could be a form of orderliness that guided behavior that was not formulated as rules with sanctions.

we *call* regularities in action. As Barth (1981: 63) was to conclude, what we want then is not to examine the "effects" of such structures, but rather how they "grow."

To do this we need not develop an elaborated theoretical terminology; we only need a minimal vocabulary for understanding the nature of such interactional patterns. And this brings us back to Georg Simmel, the widely acknowledged founder of the formal analysis of social life.[10]

Pitfalls of Formal Analysis

Simmel's idea of a wholly formal sociology has been one of the most intriguing ones in social theory, although until recently, there were few attempts to carry it out. There are three extremely good reasons for this reticence. The first has to do with the paucity of generative propositions introduced by Simmel that could be foundational for a serious study. Dated generalizations were supported by appeal to either the classical education that would form the cultural capital of any scholar of his time, or to obviously personal experience (e.g., the nature of love). For every claim of Simmel's that is of serious importance in beginning an understanding of the formal properties of social action, there is another that seems to be pulled out of thin air.

The second reason for the abandonment of formal sociology was that, as this book will try to make clear, we are unlikely to find everyday social life to be obviously marked by the presence of such structures—instead, simple formal structures are rare. Our investigation will help demonstrate why this is the case, and why it is more common for action to be coordinated by the cultural logic of institutions than by structural imperatives. Third—and perhaps most important—there is something deeply flawed in the idea of a "formal" sociology that seeks to come up with wholly general propositions about the effect of form regardless of content in the first place.

In recent years, network analysts have gone rather far in carrying out a Simmelian program, to great success (though, as Davis [1979] admits, Simmelian justifications, tacked on to increase the prestige of the endeavor, were not originally the motivations). However, there have been serious weaknesses due to a lack of attention to the content of relationships and to a recurring idea that social network structure could be an alternative to institutional or other structural theories of society (e.g., Lawler, Ridgeway, and Markovsky 1993; cf. Somers 1993: 95). In contrast, I shall argue that forms of repeated interaction amenable to network representation—social structure as it shall be called here—have an analytically central position in our understanding of social organization, but that attention to structures of interpersonal relationships

---

[10] As Levine (1985; 1991a: 109; 1991b: 1103) in particular has stressed, the view of Simmel as wholly a formalist is to some degree a caricature, but one that Simmel brought on himself.

is only a starting point of such analysis and not an independent "theory." To facilitate making this start, I go on to lay out the bases of an understanding of social structure.

An Approach to Formal Analysis

Social structure is here considered to refer to recurring patterns of social interaction, where the patterning is in regards to concrete individuals (and not roles or classes). It is a type of social organization that does not make reference to roles (though one may speak of certain structural positions *as* roles), and hence is analytically prior to institutions.

For purposes of clarity, it will be helpful to give definitions of the few terms used—in all cases these are conventional definitions and carry no theoretical baggage.[11] We will be interested in social action, and by action we mean consciously intended behavior by one person, the actor in question. If this action has a different individual as consciously intended direct or indirect object, we consider this action to be "social" action (cf. Nadel 1957: 86). For an example with a person as the direct object, if I attack a person, that would be considered social action for analytic purposes, though the psychologically inclined might consider such action quite antisocial. For an example involving a person as indirect object, if I dig a ditch for my employer, we must also consider this social action.

For purposes of brevity, I will frequently refer to "social action" simply as interaction but want to emphasize that action copresence is not always necessary. That is, if we are examining patronage relationships, we can decompose these into a set of social actions, but many of the acts of patronage are not interactions between a patron P and a client C. Instead, many are social actions between the patron P and others O outside the structure, but these actions hold the client as the indirect object of the action, and not an actual interactant (such as when P solicits O on C's behalf). For analytic purposes, as a first approximation it is permissible to fold such P-O interactions that have C as the indirect object into the P-C relationship.

As a consequence of this definition, many formal patterns that do not involve social interaction between the individuals who compose them are not treated here. For example, a set of officeholders in a corporation may be connected by a vacancy chain (White 1970), but they do not necessarily know about one another's existence, and while this structure does affect their action, it is not itself a pattern of repeated interaction. Furthermore, the patterns that are treated here tend to be rather simple; many network analysts will be disappointed that

---

[11] This approach is very close to that laid out by the ethologist R. A. Hinde (1979: 296, 299, 310), who nests interactions in relationships and relationships in social structure, and who also emphasizes the need for attention to the content of relationships.

aesthetically pleasing structures are given no attention because they are too delicate to appear in a sufficient variety of circumstances to warrant attention in this context. Relatedly, I have tended to forebear from repeating discussions that may be found elsewhere, and have thus given short shrift to certain social structures that are perhaps the most widely studied, namely kinship exchange structures. Aficionados of such structures will again find the treatment here far simpler and less elegant than that given by others; in particular, no use is made of the advanced mathematics that have recently been used to unify a large number of complex kinship structures as special cases. But the theoretical implications of the complex structures are perhaps more obscure for the questions of interest here than are those of simpler structures where we can posit (with moderate chance of success) those subjective principles that might actually guide action.

In sum, the focus on structure here will be structures of interaction. It would of course be possible to speak of "relations" or "ties," as is commonly done in network analysis. But relations can be established without any social action whatsoever. Many people are deeply in love with performers whom they have never met and never will, and while these are meaningful relations for a network analysis (for example, determining the attractiveness of various popular idols), they are not necessarily structurally meaningful.

Further, it is helpful to distinguish between structural analysis as intended here and social network analysis. Whether it is a good thing or a bad thing, network analysis (one hardly notices when the "social" is dropped) has emphasized examining structural features of networks considered quite generally— that is, sets of relations that can be formalized as a graph or as a matrix. In some cases these are relationships between persons, but in other cases they are between organizations, or between persons and organizations (as in the relationship of "member") or internal to an organization, a text or even a self. In contrast, I am proposing to study only those forms in which the relations established are mutually acknowledged relationships that guide social action on the part of *persons*. While it may be that some of the analyses will also prove relevant to the relationships between autochthonous corporate bodies,[12] I do not assume that this is the case. The structural similarity between interpersonal and interorganizational or intergroup relationships is an empirical question, and one that should not be decided on the basis of methodological preferences. Many formal network analysts are not interested in the properties of nodes and edges, and consider all data, once it has been turned into a graph, to be basically comparable. There is a beauty and vision to this, and it is still

---

[12] To the extent that a group has unified decision-making power, relationships between groups may follow the structures found here. But in such cases, we are so likely to find a single individual at the helm that there is little reason not to consider the relationships established relationships between individuals.

important to pursue this logic as far as it can go, to determine to what extent there can be a pure science of the organization of actors.[13] But for studying social structure, the nature of nodes and edges can make quite a difference. When nodes are persons, and edges are interactions, we can quite quickly map out a great deal of the range of possible structural forms that are likely to arise.

Relations, then, are not as important for the analysis of simple structures as is interaction (cf. Nadel 1957: 90). Interactions themselves are too particular and disparate for structural analysis; consequently, the focus here will be on "relationships," by which is indicated the possibility of a specific type of inter-action. In other words, even though interactions are fleeting and tend to be distributed spottily in time with great areas of blank canvas in between, we can collapse over some section of time and declare a relationship to exist when action of a certain type is plausible (see Nadel 1957: 128). If between January 1, 1985, and December 31, 1985, Ronald could drop by George's house and spend the afternoon playing, and George could drop by Ronald's house, we might say that in 1985 the two "were" friends, though there were many times during 1985 when the two were not together. For purposes of simplicity, then, we will define a relationship in terms of the particular actions appropriate to it—which I shall call an "action profile"—without being troubled by the fact that we allow the relationship to persist during periods in which none of these actions are taking place. Like persons watching a movie, we shall construct a continuous mental image from discrete actions and consider this repeated though not uninterrupted interaction to constitute a relationship between two persons. In contrast, a "relation" will indicate any property of a dyad, whether or not it involves action. Thus "mutual ignorance" is a conceivable relation, although it is not a relationship.

I have argued that purely formal analysis of structures is seriously limited: we cannot ignore the content of the relationship when thinking about the struc-tural forms that connected sets of relationships may take. This does not, how-ever, mean that generalizing is limited, or that the content of any relationship must be understood in all its richness (see Nadel 1957: 113, 122). Instead, it is possible to focus on certain aspects of the content of the relationship that are most pregnant with structural implications—tendencies for *sets* of relation-ships to possess certain formal properties.

That is, we will consider the content of some relationship to have an implicit "structural tendency" when certain patterns of aggregating relationships would be subjectively understood as dissonant with this content. First, let us now define "structure" to involve the "concatenation" of relationships (cf. White

[13] Recently White (2002: 202, 205) has suggested ways in which different forms of ordering may be embedded in one another.

1992).[14] Two relationships are concatenated by sharing at least one person. Two friendships, for example, may be joined if they only involve three persons total—Amy is friends with Beth, and Beth is friends with Christine. Structures may similarly be concatenated to form larger structures.

But not all paths of concatenation are equally plausible given the content of some relationship. For an extremely simple example, the content of the relationship of "best friends" is (in principle) one that does not fit with a concatenation of relationships in which two relationships "share" a single person— more simply, that someone has two "best friends." Rather than go through all possible relationships and assess their structural tendencies, we may be able to group relationships on a priori grounds and focus on only some of the aspects of their content, those aspects that may be most relevant for structure. In particular, we may focus on the *directionality* of the relationship—a simple aspect of its content that is clearly of structural relevance.

A relationship may have three forms of directionality. First, it may be symmetric, or mutual, in that the action profiles for both parties are identical. This is true for the relationship of spending time together: if *A* spends time with *B*, *B* must spend the same amount of time with *A*. Second, the relationship may be antisymmetric, in that it requires that the two parties have *different* action-profiles. For example, kickback schemes aside, an employer cannot employ another employer who in turn also employs the first, but must employ an employee. Finally, the relationship may be directed, or asymmetric, such that one party has a particular action profile vis-à-vis the other, which may or may not be reciprocated.[15] While this is not an especially rich understanding of the content of relationships, it is, I hope to show, of inestimable importance in understanding how structure develops.[16] We will attempt to examine the devel-

[14] Concatenation is thus one form of aggregation; there may be other accounts of the formation of large-scale structures out of small that rely on forms of aggregation *other* than concatenation, but they are not explored here. Concatenation is to be preferred to a term like *spread*, which tends to imply that we start with a single "seed."

[15] In what follows, I will denote a symmetric relationship with a line with no arrow tips, an asymmetric relationship as a line with an arrow pointing away from the person who is initiating the action in question, and an antisymmetric relationship as one with an arrow tip at one end and an arrow tail at the other.

[16] More generally, the prefixes a- and in- will mean "not necessarily, but neither necessarily not" while the prefix "anti-" will mean "necessarily not." Thus "intransitive" will mean not necessarily transitive, and " antitransitive" will mean definitely not transitive. This usage is somewhat idiosyncratic, since "asymmetric" is often used to mean antisymmetric (e.g., Hage and Harary [1983: 71]), with ungainly terms such as *nonsymmetric* coined for the case in which symmetry is empirically open. Unfortunately there is no clearer term, and clarity is of some importance here, as there have been a number of structural discussions that have foundered at this point. Thus Hage and Harary (1983: 72) criticize Levi-Strauss's claim—which will be supported in chapter 3—that there can be a close connection between the vertical orderings of pecking orders and the circular ones of generalized exchange, but do so by assimilating "intransitive" to "antitransitive."

opment of structure from analytically prior relationships considered in isolation. As a result, the first structure that is to be examined in all cases is a small one, or what I will follow other analysts in considering "local" structure.

Local Structure

I have distinguished the structural investigations proposed here from social network analysis as commonly understood. At the same time, social network analysis emerged as a faith in the possibility of rigorous empirical investigation along the lines of classic structuralism à la Levi-Strauss (1969 [1949]). In particular, much of the excitement came from the idea that observed structural regularities in social networks could empirically generate the statuses and roles of anthropological theory à la Nadel (1957) (especially Lorrain and White 1971; and White, Boorman, and Breiger 1976). The techniques initially proposed, however, fell short of such a goal because the type of equivalence first implemented ("structural equivalence") only equated persons with identical patterns of ties to the same others. Thus two line workers with different foremen would not be seen as equivalent, because they did not share the same foreman (Faust 1988: 336).

Because of this limitation, other forms of equivalence were introduced that were algorithmically more difficult to uncover, but corresponded better to this intuitive understanding of equivalence (e.g., Everett and Borgatti 1994). But there were a few (see Breiger and Pattison 1986; Breiger 2000; and especially Pattison 1994: 88) who held on to the idea of distinctly *local* structuring and proposed that there were theoretically different principles behind the two approaches, and that the principle lying behind structural equivalence was, to say the least, as important as that lying behind the more intuitively pleasing forms of equivalence ("regular" and "general" equivalence).[17] This neglect of the importance of the concrete *individuals* who anchor any relationship came perhaps from a general tendency for network researchers, who focus on ties, to downgrade the importance of persons. It was believed, and quite reasonably so, that individuals are to some nontrivial extent really the

---

[17] This theoretical emphasis on studying global structure in terms of local pieces has been shared by other of White's first- and second-order students in addition to Breiger and Pattison, notably Bearman, Chase, Mische, and Gibson; my debt to their approach will be made clear over the course of this book. Boyd and Jonas (2001: especially 122) recently demonstrated that the nonlocal assumption of regular equivalence may lead it to necessarily diverge from actual data in a way that structural equivalence does not (for example, due to the exceptional popularity of certain concrete persons). Faust (1988: 334) also found this method of structural equivalence that focused on concrete ties to do better at uncovering structure in data from a naturally occurring informal group than methods based on general equivalence. Recently, Boyd (2002: 323, 329) has gone so far as to conclude that the concept while mathematically elegant is sociologically flawed—"nature abhors regular equivalence."

intersections of relationships, and so one could attempt to focus on relationships in themselves and bracket the question of what these relationships were between. Whatever one may think about the theoretical niceties of such questions, for the development of local structure, it is necessary to treat persons as nonproblematic and fixed, although this assumption may be relaxed in succeeding stages of investigation.[18]

The vision of Simmel's dialectic of institutionalization that inspires this work implies that it is at such a local level that we may see social action being shaped by distinct principles we would rightly call structural.[19] When things have developed to the extent that regular equivalence guides action—that is, when one may interact with any of a set of for-all-purposes-equivalent actors— then we are looking at *institutions*, not structures as I here use the term. Thus a structure is a pattern of interaction that links a person to *particular* others, as opposed to classes of others.

The importance of such local or particular structures has been downgraded by a sociology that arose in the context of European political economy, which presupposed the division of persons into functionally equivalent classes. Sociology (exceptions such as Simmel aside), far from challenging the preexisting tendency of social thought to ignore the particular elements of social life, associated itself with the strong theoretical claim that such particularism was doomed to extinction anyway ("modernization" theory). Certainly, from a functional perspective, great parsimony is gained by treating sets of persons and indeed whole social structures (in both the Spencerian sense and the sense introduced here) as functionally equivalent. That is, it does not matter that one officer has a relationship over here with an enlisted man, and another officer has a relationship over there with a different enlisted man. All that matters is the overall relationship between officers and enlisted. But the parsimony of considering persons interchangeable representatives of categories comes at a cost: we are likely to be left with a misleading picture of the generation and stabilization of actually existing social structures and institutions by ignoring the importance of ties that connect specific persons.

---

[18] Some network theorists in effect declare that the relations themselves, and not the persons, should be the units of analysis. Now this is the kind of change that must be justified on analytic grounds: there is no general philosophic reason for such a preference. This is because if relations become the units, then the relations are connected to one another by the (former) units, which then become the relations! A determination to stand "on the side of relations," however earnest, must only lead to wild catapulting back and forth. For the case of social structures, I do not believe that there are sufficient analytic grounds to treat relations—in this case, interactions—as the things, as opposed to the persons. But only successful explication can prove this point, so it must be considered deferred for now. More generally, it strikes me that there is nothing so analytically distasteful about people that we must bend over backward to remove them from our theories, when our theories are, when the day is done, only by, of, and for people—whatever they may be.

[19] Incidentally, it is only at this level where we would be likely to require empirical analysis of sociograms to uncover such structure—no one should need to blockmodel an organization to discover that line workers are line workers and foremen are foremen.

It is not simply that for analytic purposes it is best to consider structural patterns as involving concrete persons of particular types; it is more generally that the approach that looks for functional equivalence tends to assume as preexisting the categories and imperatives of social action that we perhaps should first try to explain. Certainly, *given* the division between officers and enlisted men, it is "functional" that the enlisted generally do what they are told and do not turn their weapons on each other nor on their commanders. But why *are* we given these categories? As a first approximation—it is certainly simplistic, but not too misleading on the general level at which the statement is made—we may say that the relationship between what now appear as classes of functional equivalents was originally a derivation from personalistic relationships between landowners and their dependents, and this *before* there was any organization of the landowners into a single army. In other words, before there was any whole for the categorical divisions to be functional *for*, there were particular relationships between particular persons. We are able to generalize—landowners were similar in their relationships to their dependents— but the relationships were still particular in that no dependent would have a relationship with someone *else's* landowner.

The general indifference of sociological theory to the particularities of small structures leads it to prematurely account for local structural patterns by reference to the larger ones. We have somehow managed to almost entirely avoid the fact that large structures, including institutional structures such as organizations, are generally concretes of smaller structures, and even more important, the larger structures tend to be the result of historical processes in which small structures were progressively aggregated. Such smaller units may be bought, rescued, coordinated, or coerced, but fewer large structures are constructed from scratch than are adapted from existing (even if damaged) elements.

The implications of this are stark: social life may be "seen" in terms of functions or systems, but the fundamental assumption of such theoretical schemes, namely the preexistence of a higher-level unit with regard to which we are to analyze the development of subunits, is indefensible as a statement of fact. Only a series of happy accidents (or an extraordinarily long evolutionary time) would lead the set of structures that have developed through the concatenation of smaller structures to take on a form that would be explicated by the complicated systemics of, say, Luhmann (1995 [1984]).[20] I will empha-

---

[20] This is not to deny the possibility, indeed probability, of systemic characteristics developing through autopoietic processes in social life. There is, however, no reason to imagine that large-scale social structures like the army have any role in such processes, as there is no reason to connect the systemic processes that reestablish equilibrium with the human needs of a set of individuals. For example, one can see a system in a set of processes whereby people stop working and instead wastefully rob their neighbor of accumulated surplus whenever their neighbor's stock rises above a certain amount. The total surplus will stay within certain bounds just as the temperature does in a thermostatic system. But the system processes producing this equilibrium serve no functions for the set of *persons*.

size below that the priority I give to social structure—that is, beginning with the aggregation of relationships into structure, then structure into institutions— is justified if only on the basis of analytic convenience. At the same time, it is true that in certain situations, this analytic priority translates to a temporal priority. In particular, when existing institutional structures or fields are radically disrupted, new ones grow from the more obdurate local structures that have survived. The importance of such particularistic structures has been recently noted in economic sociology, in part because of the radical changes in European economic structures (mentioned in the preface) and in part due to a more fundamental awakening of concern with the importance of interpersonal trust (Williamson 1985; Granovetter 1985; Silver 1985). But we shall see that the phenomenon is more general—large structures can only be quickly assembled using strong preexisting components with certain structural properties.

Our task, then, is to begin to understand how patterns of relationships between particular others form and what their structural tendencies are. To simplify this task, here I will consider only "single stranded" structures—that is, regular patterns of interactions where the interactions are guided by a single qualitative relationship. Thus while the interaction profiles that constitute friendship may involve spending time together, talking on the phone, and loaning money, we can analyze friendship while considering all these subsumed in a single sort of relationship. A business, on the other hand, involves some persons working together in a room, some persons giving orders to others, some persons cutting paychecks for others, and in this case we would not subsume all of these interactions into a single relationship, but instead analyze a multistranded structure involving relations of co-working, authority, and so on. While many such multistranded structures may turn out to be homologous to some of the structures examined here, a full treatment is too complex.

The single-stranded, local structures I will examine are clearly of the greatest simplicity. Yet even so, it is unlikely that such structures would continuously reappear as forms of regular interaction were the people in question unable to *understand* the formal principles of these structures in some subjective terms. It is not necessary that people be able to visualize or define the structure as we shall do here, but it is necessary that they understand how structurally consistent ties are formed and the relationships they should have with those who are indirectly tied to them. I will call such subjective understandings "heuristics."

Heuristics

Structures are not actual—we cannot touch them or push them around as such. They are an analytic construct, and they are an analytic construct that actors may not necessarily recognize. But structures should not be an arbitrary analytic construct, for we may posit a fundamental duality between the bird's-eye view of structure that will occupy us here, and the lived experience of actors. This brings us back to Simmel's understanding of the duality between the form and content of relationships, and the sense that one should be able to transform an account in terms of form into one in terms of content and vice versa. I suggest that an account in terms of content must be one that makes reference to the subjectively understood action imperatives associated with a relationship: what it calls on us to do, especially in regard to the formation or cessation of other relationships. When there is consensus or at least organized disagreement about what some relationship entails, we are seeing those sorts of expectations that were pivotal for the Lintonian/Parsonian understanding of structure. For example, instead of conceiving of marriage in structural terms (a set of dyads), it may be understood as what one relationship implies about forming—or in this case, not forming—other relationships, as in "to forsake all others."[21]

If indeed there is a duality between culture and structure then at least in the abstract it is only a matter of analytic convenience whether we treat the pure form of some regularized set of interactions as structure or as "culture" in the sense of shared subjective orientations. (At least, this may be true in a case of stability; we explore change in the succeeding chapters.) To take the example of patronage structures studied later, we may understand these relationships in cultural terms by examining the intersubjective rules of proceeding of which all parties are aware: that a patronage relationship links an inferior and a superior by demanding loyalty and support from the subaltern and patronage and/or protection from the superordinate. This implies that the client follows the rule "get a patron who has more X than you; do not have more than one patron" (or that the patron follows the rule "get a client who has less X than you; do not share clients"), where X is anything the separates people into those with more and those with less. But in structural terms, this may also be understood as action channeled within relationships that are antitransitive, antisymmetric, and irreflexive. These relationships, when tied together or concatenated, will form a tree.

It is important to emphasize that while there is a *duality* between structure and culture—between the objective pattern of relationships and the subjective understandings guiding relationship formation—this is not equivalent to the *fusion* proposed by the Lintonian/Parsonian perspective. While the Lintonian approach *defines* structures in fundamentally cultural terms, the approach laid out here sees the two forms of organization as *reaching out* to one another: certain cultural understandings will, if left undisturbed, generate certain structural forms; certain structures will, if sufficiently clear and extensive, induce

---

[21] One may compare Levi-Strauss's (1969 [1949]: 410) understanding of the duality between relation and class.

certain subjectivities or relational strategies. But it is certainly possible for the two not to match up perfectly.

For example, Levi-Strauss (1969 [1949]: 98–101) demonstrates that the presence of dual exogamous moieties has a clear relation to cross-cousin marriage, since (a) if a male ego comes from same moiety as his father but the opposite from his mother, then his mother's brother's daughter (as well as his father's sister's daughter) will always be in the opposite one; (b) pursuing cross-cousin marriage exclusively produces two exogamous moieties. Yet it is possible for a preference of cross-cousin marriage to exist without dual organization, and it is possible for dual organization to exist without cross-cousin marriage.

Such dislocation between structural pattern and subjective understandings is likely to occur at the stage of institutionalization: once persons are able to come up with subjective representations of the logic of structure, and hence strategies for navigating these structures, there is nothing to prevent them from mixing and matching such strategies semi-independently of the structural context. Indeed, the frequent complaint of field workers that Levi-Strauss's elementary structures were never found in their pure form, and that the subjects of study might for good reasons do the opposite of what the structural model implied (e.g., Kasakoff 1974: 159), is as much as to say that the patterns of interaction had become institutionalized, such that participants could subjectively understand them as heuristics and for this reason violate the form to better express the content (e.g., alliance).

For the purposes of first analysis, then, we can examine the subjective representations that would most directly correspond to structural imperatives without claiming that it is impossible for the structures to exist without the subjective understandings, or vice versa. Since the structures that will be examined here are simple, the imperatives for action that constitute their subjective correlatives are also simple; I shall refer to such subjective understandings as "heuristics."[22]

A heuristic is a rule that could be induced by an observer as a guiding principle of action on the basis of observed regularities in this action. In general, heuristics are very simple instructions that, by interacting with the wider social order in a reasonable way, allow for the production of insightful or complex behavior. For example, "buy low, sell high" is an extremely simple heuristic that, given a market economy with imperishable goods, can lead to rational profiteering.[23] Heuristics work well because they are "ecologically ra-

---

[22] I believe that this point—the duality of structural form and subjective representation—was made by Harrison White (1992) regarding "types of tie."

[23] The insight underlying this view is due to Simon (1962: 51–54), who pointed out that the behavior of an ant walking on a beach is objectively quite complex, although the ant's subjectivity is probably quite simple. The complexity enters because of the structuring of the ant's environ-

tional" in that they make use of predictable features of the natural or social environment to simplify otherwise daunting processing tasks (see Gigerenzer et al. 1999: 13, 24f). The phrase "ecologically rational" should not be understood as implying strong claims about the efficiency of thought, or any other properties. Instead, the point is that to understand the operation of the cognition, we must understand the structure of the environment.

As the example "buy low, sell high" makes clear, heuristics are frequently consciously held. But they need not be in order to have analytic value. It may be that in many cases people employ more complex cognitive processes, or hold more diffuse senses of what is "proper" to some given situation, but that these can be adequately summed up in a simple heuristic, even if the actors would protest that they do nothing so simplistic and base. For example, the heuristic, "drop a tie to a friend with few ties to other friends" may in fact objectively describe the formation of friendship patterns, when the children (let us say) in question would insist that they do nothing of the kind. Instead, the pattern of relationship formation may actually be due to the combination of three things: first, a process "see my friends' friend regularly"; second, the affective pattern "embrace as a friend anyone you see regularly"; and third, a limitation to the number of others that one can simultaneously hold as friends. While the children do not deliberately drop those who have few friendships with their other friends, they might as well.

Thus heuristics provide efficient rules of thumb for navigating social structure; while they may diverge from empirical subjectivities in that they are overly parsimonious, an actor who understood the heuristic would successfully anticipate the actions of others. Further, it may not matter *whom* we see as holding the heuristic. That is, what appears as a heuristic followed by one person can, in some cases, also be seen as due to actions on the part of this person's interactants. Thus the client's heuristic "only have one patron" may also (and equivalently) be seen as the patron's heuristic "drop any client with another patron." But since both clients and patrons need to understand the structural principles involved, we do not need to agonize over which one of these scenarios to put forward.

These simple heuristics are effective guides to navigating the social realm because they are ecologically rational—they fit the structural tendencies associated with the content of certain relationships. Consequently, there are pressures on actors to adopt these heuristics, because *given* the existence of a relationship with structural implications, failure to do so may mean failure to maintain relationships. Those who attempt to have two patrons may find themselves dropped by both; those who think they can be spiteful to their

---

ment. So, too, our apparently complex behavior may be deceptive, and we may have simpler understandings than we would like to believe.

friends' friends may find themselves friendless. More often than not, we will find explicit confirmation that these heuristics are widely acknowledged as principles of action, and where they are challenged, we are likely to see structural degradation.

It is for this reason that we may speak of a "structural tendency" inherent in certain relationships. Such a tendency should be defined, not tautologically in regard to the probability of future development, but substantively in regard to the felt difficulty of living in certain types of worlds. In other words, the subjective correlative to a structural tendency is the tension, unhappiness, or confusion experienced by someone torn between two best friends. While the person need not hold the heuristic that the analyst can induce, she cannot (or so we postulate) hold the *contrary* heuristic without suffering.

When we can translate a structural principle into a plausible heuristic, we can understand how it comes to be that local structures are aggregated to form big structures. As units are formed, persons understand what the structure "implies" vis-à-vis a consistent arrangement of the parts. It is this aggregation that is of greatest interest to us here; I close by foreshadowing the argument to be made about the nature of structure.

Formation of Structure

In the following chapters, I will attempt an empirical examination of the processes outlined by Durkheim and Simmel whereby patterns of interaction take on a structure that then can confront actors as an objective fact. Although this basic process may be postulated to occur for complex relationships as for simple ones, and for large structures as for small, I propose to begin the investigation with local structures. Precisely because local structures are simple, and rarely appear in their purity, they are a fitting place for sociological study. Just as some biologists trek to Taylor Valley in the Antarctic precisely because it is, in the words of one scientist, "the simplest ecosystem on earth,"[24] and physicists go to great pains construct chambers that can produce a perfect vacuum because it is not the complicated environment we normally find, so too it may prove greatly advantageous for sociologists to carefully scrutinize those simple structures that do arise even in complex societies.

Thus I propose that we begin by close empirical attention to such cases, and from there work our way to institutions which in turn can be patterned. While this analytic order should not be understood as a rigidly temporal order, there are continual *tendencies* toward the emergence of structure in certain situa-

[24] The words are those of Andrew Parsons, quoted in the *New York Times*, February 3, 1998. Scott A. Boorman (personal communication) has pointed out that the opposite is also argued— that richer ecosystems may have simpler patterns (see MacArthur 1972: 199).

tions, *tendencies* toward the induction of structural form into intersubjective cultural understandings of action, *tendencies* toward the detachment and transportation of these cultural understandings once they have formed, and *tendencies* for these understandings to align themselves in cultural terms. Consequently, it is analytically preferable to trace things starting out from structure. Then we are in a position to understand the more prevalent cases in which local structure is shaped, deliberately or not, by institutions, with their categories, connections, and imperatives. Before beginning this analytic project, let me summarize the introduced terminology and argument.

A relationship indicates the possibility of repeated actions of a particular type between two persons; each person is said to have an "action profile" corresponding to the relationship. When the relationship is symmetric, both parties have the same action profile; when the relationship is asymmetric, one party has at least potentially an empty action profile; and when the relationship is antisymmetric, the two parties have different action profiles.[25] For example, Reinhardt and Reinhardt's (1981) classic investigation of social relationships between cattle found three types of relationships. One, dominance, is intrinsically antisymmetric—the relationship must involve an act of dominance and an act of submission, and these must be delegated to different cows. Licking, on the other hand, is asymmetric—one cow may return the licks received, or she may not. Finally, spending time together is inherently symmetric. Interestingly, Reinhardt and Reinhardt found these relationships to take on different structural forms; further, the form of each relationship seems to be an interpretable function of its content (also see Coleman 1960: 72; Skvoretz and Faust 2002 for similar thoughts).

In the chapters that follow, I will attempt to investigate how the content of relationships leads to certain structural forms by focusing on paradigmatic cases of the different types of relationships. For example, mutual or symmetric relationships by their very nature assert the interchangeability of persons. While many relationships may be symmetric (for example, "eating lunch with"), the relationships of *friendship* and *alliance* highlight this interchangeability, and hence are given special attention. Asymmetric relations distinguish the two interactants but allow for the possibility of reciprocation, and it seems that *donation*, or *alienation*, in the sense of transferring something previously held highlights this asymmetry. (*Choice*, or *nomination*, is also paradigmatically asymmetric, but as it may not require an actual relationship, but only a relation, it is treated separately.) Finally, antisymmetry distinguishes the two interactants and forbids reciprocation or interchangeability: egalitarianism is neither present by definition, nor allowed by choice of the participants. It seems that *lordship*, or *domination*, (in the sense of Weber's *Herrschaft*) best high-

---

[25] See Lundberg (1939: 352) for a similar attempt to begin with "atoms" of relationships.

lights this inequality. Other relationships may also be worthy of attention, but these three will be pivotal for the ensuing discussion.

These contents give us some sense of what structures are likely to develop from the relationships in question. We may say that structures emerge when relationships concatenate in ways that are nonindependent and interpretable. For example, if one only makes a new relationship with someone else to whom one is not tied either directly or indirectly, a particular structure (a "spanning tree") results. In general, when the rules describing the nonindependence between relationships are strong and simple, the resulting structures also partake of structural clarity and simplicity.

When structures begin to form, they can begin to affect relationships: they may lead existing relationships to break, and new ones to form. In certain extremely interesting cases, they can lead to the production of new relationships that have structural principles that cut against their own structural principles. For example, patronage structures that consist of wholly vertical ties between nonequals unite several clients under a single patron, thereby establishing relations of structural equivalence between the clients, and possibly leading to new horizontal relationships of alliance between clients, relationships which challenge the logic of the patronage structure. Despite this frequent tendency for structures to undermine themselves, some are sufficiently stable to reoccur in a wide variety of situations when people need to spontaneously organize relationships of a certain type.

But of this relatively small set of stable, recurrent structural forms, fewer still are able to serve as the building blocks of larger structures. The problem lies in the principles that lead to structure in the first place. Every structural form must have some structural principles for it to be recognized *as* a form: the stronger these principles, the clearer the form. And yet this very strength, I shall argue, limits the ability of such structures to align while preserving their structural principles. In particular, one of the strongest principles we shall recurrently find is transitivity—the requirement that if person A has a relationship with B, and B with C, then A must have a relationship with C as well.[26]

Consider a case in which two smaller structures are concatenated perhaps by the addition of a new relationship. For example, imagine that person B, who previously had a relationship only with A, and was thus part of the same structure as A, adds a relationship with C, and thus joins C and the rest of the structure of which C is a part to A's structure. Transitivity means three things: first, new implied relationships must be formed—A must now have a relationship with C. Second, if B understands that the relationship in question is transitive, she can deduce relationships between the *other* two persons. Third, be-

---

[26] In contrast to many mathematical techniques in which transitivity is measured by the *absence* of *antitransitivity*, what is crucial here are those cases in which the *premise* of relationships between (on the one hand) A and B and (on the other) B and C holds.

cause transitivity allows certain structural principles to flow across sets of relationships, the resulting aggregate must possess the same structural properties as its components.

But transitivity is often "too strong"; it is too difficult to work out all the demanded relationships consistently, or too many possible relationships are implied, or people resist the imposition of relationships that have not been independently generated (cf. Park 1974: 22). Only one recurring structural form readily aggregates to make large structures, and this is the type of differentiated hierarchy that we will examine in chapter 6. This structure consists of vertical relationships that are concatenated according to a rule of " antitransitivity," whereby transitively implied relationships are *suppressed*. Such structures are locally weak, in that not much is demanded of the participants in terms of a consistent structural tendency, and for this reason they can be cascaded to span large numbers of people. These structures remain globally weak because of their intransitivity; as a consequence, there are recurrent attempts to introduce transitivity once aggregate structures have formed. We will find that the crucial structures underlying the nation-state—the structures that impressed Spencer and others as being akin to organs—tend to arise from such introduction of transitivity into previously antitransitive structures. But making this argument must await substantive investigation.

Thus we will see to what extent we can trace the development of large-scale but simple and spontaneous social structures. These may turn out to be relatively scarce in social life. The bulk of action seems coordinated not by these informal structures but by the categorical distinctions associated with institutions and the corresponding formal organization they make possible. Such formal structures can break the fragile crystalline structure of an emerging regular pattern of interaction; more generally, they will establish the boundaries of emergent structures. To borrow a lovely set of phrases from Eric Wolf (1977: 168), sometimes these spontaneous structures help complete the function of a formal one (his example, small group cohesion in the military), while in other cases they contravene it (informal work rules that decrease efficiency). In still other cases they cling to the formal structure "like barnacles to a rusty ship"—think, for example, the cliques that form within a lunchroom (but not in a classroom) because the social organization of the formal institution creates spaces for them. Thus spontaneous structures develop in the relatively interstitial realms that are sometimes ignored, and other times created, by institutions (see White 1992).

But these institutions themselves may well have derived from concatenation of smaller structures, and it is difficult to understand the larger ones without understanding their smaller components. Further, our analyses can, because of their very simplicity and purity, point to inherent tensions, limitations, and avenues of developments of certain large structures, even when the analytic account that derives these structures as concatenations of smaller structures is overly parsimonious from a rigorous historical perspective. In particular, chapters 7 and 8 present a schematic account of where armies and parties (respectively) come from, and while in few cases is such an account wholly satisfying as a historical argument, in most it still sheds light on the reasons for those regularities in regularity that we call social structure.

We can use words such as *army* or *party* because not only is there a regularity of interaction in a given army, such that we can speak of relationships, and a regularity of relationships so that we may speak of a structure, but there is also a regularity *across* structures so that the same sorts of regularities regularly recur. Although organizational mimesis is no doubt rampant, there is reason to imagine that this second-order regularity is related to the content of the most important relationships that compose the structure in question. If indeed there are a small set of structures that recur in social life, it should not be difficult to determine a priori the conditions under which they will arise. In fact, the most difficult thing is explaining why so few sociologists have tried to do so.[27]

The most important exception is the recent work of Charles Tilly (1998: especially 21, 47, 49, 51). Tilly also suggests that we examine "how transactions clump into social ties, [and] social ties concatenate into networks," and attempts to uncover fundamental units of structure, "a small set of network configurations that have reappeared millions of times at different scales, in different settings, throughout human history." (Tilly also comments that "no one has codified our knowledge of how they connect and operate.") Further, Tilly emphasizes the need to discover the developmental tendencies of each configuration, as well as the conditions for their successful concatenation, precisely the aim of the current work. The difference between Tilly's approach and that taken here is twofold. On the one hand, as the above quotation makes clear, Tilly is interested in scale-free configurations, while this book is only about local, interpersonal structures. Second, being interested in categorical inequality, Tilly incorporates organizations and categories, which here are considered institutional phenomena of a wholly different order. As a result, the local structures that Tilly uncovers (chain, hierarchy, and triad) are quite different from those that we will find fundamental, though he also finds the possibility of these small units combining to make larger ones.

It is also worth noting that the very different approach of Abbott (2001: 165, 167, note 8, 168), which stresses self-similarity in social structures, uncovers some closely related phenomena to those that prove to be central here, especially the resilience of patronage relationships and the importance of transitivity or the lack of same, especially when it comes to structural expansion via extension of hierarchy. But the emphasis on self-similarity leads to a focus on

---

[27] I thank Jerker Denrell for reminding me how Simon's (1962) work relates to this project; his arguments are considered in chapter 6.

particular structures across levels, not a range of structures at the particularly local level, as is the case here.[28]

Final Note on Sources

In what follows, I attempt to derive principles of social organization at this particular level of analytic abstraction by surveying types of social structures. While this survey cannot be systematic in terms of looking at "all" social organization, neither is it circularly selective, in dismissing examples of organization that cut against the claims being made as "bad examples." Instead, for each type of structure investigated, I study a wide variety of examples, explore commonalities and differences, and look for patterns (cf. Zerubavel 2007; Gould 2003: 12). I pay little attention to formal derivations that, given such and such conditions, some form of social organization *should* arise. It is far more interesting to determine what forms *do* arise, and then to see if these can be retroactively derived via heuristics. Consequently, in some cases careful attention must be paid to details that affect the interpretation; while the argument is generally robust in the face of omitted cases, it is not indifferent to the correctness of interpretations.

[28] Two other recent works are somewhat related to this endeavor and deserve mention. First of all, Hage and Harary (1983) provide a wonderful treatment of structural models in anthropology that is of relevance to sociology as well. This work is clear, focused, and accessible to the general reader. Indeed, because this work is so useful, I have forborne from giving technical recapitulations of the various structural models used, since they will be found in axiomatic form in this work. Hage and Harary (1983: 75, 178f) also unify their explication of these forms by concentrating on the axioms of (ir)reflexivity, (a)symmetry, (in)transitivity, and completion. While this in principle leads to $3 \times 3 \times 3 \times 2 = 54$ structures, they examine twelve. Their hierarchical organization of these relations, however, does not necessarily correspond to similarities at the level of lived experience; thus their most basic distinction has to do with reflexivity, which is frequently a matter of algebraic convenience. The next distinction introduced is symmetry, and as a consequence, there are no cases in which transitivity is important where symmetry or antisymmetry is not presupposed. Accordingly, they do not treat some structures considered here. More important, their book aims to discuss structural models and their applicability across levels of analysis; it is not (like the current work) an attempt to understand the structural principles inherent in the simplest relationships. In a later work, Hage and Harary (1991: 7) take a more Tillyan approach of specifying elemental structures, but they are considering the particular case of exchange structures, and therefore do not distinguish between asymmetric and antisymmetric relationships.

In contrast, Kontopoulos (1993: 3, 246, 252) also attempts to examine a limited number of mechanisms leading to social structure, but takes structure to mean any form of transindividual organization. Consequently, some of the relevant discussions are drawn afield from explication of structural principles, and while he also sees a duality between structures and "logics," Kontopoulos thus finds a logic for every institutional form. As this goes to press I discovered the wonderful work of Holzer (2006), which makes a number of points that appear here in the preface, chapter 1, and chapter 9 (see his pgs., 10, 14, 25, and 31).

2

From a Small Circle of Friends
to a Long Line of Rivals

Simplest Structures

This book is an attempt to derive the simplest structures of social interaction that develop spontaneously, and to do so by extrapolating the structural implications of the content of relationships. For the purposes of this initial study, I have argued that we may simply group contents into those that are symmetric, those that are asymmetric (but possibly reciprocated), and those that are antisymmetric. Of these three, symmetric relationships are simplest in their structural implications, for they do not imply any intrinsic differentiation of persons.[1] That is, a symmetric relationship does not establish one interactant as the giver, and the other as the receiver, one as the dominant, the other as the subordinate, or anything like that. Instead, the relationship is intrinsically an equal one. Perhaps the simplest such relationship is mere copresence—if I am with you at some time, you must be with me at this time. But the more interesting relationships tend to have a content that highlights the mutuality. The one that sociologists examine most frequently is often called "friendship." This notion of friendship (which is not the same thing as *wished-for* friendship) is fundamentally similar to the notion of *alliance*, which is the subject of much anthropological research. For both friendship and alliance, the relationship requires reciprocation if it is to be real. When taken extremely seriously, these relationships go beyond equality and establish a sort of equivalence—what you do to my ally or my friend you do to me.

We begin our examination of the tendency of certain relationships to take on structural forms by examining relationships of equivalence. We will also find that at least in some situations, thinking in terms of equivalence implies the opposite, antiequivalence. Depending on what they are trying to do, actors may focus on equivalence, on antiequivalence, or on both. It seems natural that such relationships should lead to clear structural forms. But as we shall see, this is rarely the case.

---

[1] For purposes of explication, we shall restrict attention to cases in which not only is the relationship mutual, but we are unable to distinguish between the people in any way relevant for the establishment of their relationship (thus we ignore cases in which one person chooses to interact with another who is not in turn free to decline).

Let us begin with the simple mutual relationships of friendship. Such relationships were the first sorts of interpersonal ties used by social scientists to derive structure, and they remain what most analysts assume when they imagine "ties" or other unspecified relations—they are the default for structural analysis. Since they impose no particular claims on the nature of persons (no role implications), we might imagine that they are the best material for composing building blocks that can be the basis for large structures. On the contrary, I shall argue, the structures that tend to arise from mutual relationships cannot be concatenated without some sort of fundamental transformation or weakening, and both transformation and weakening tend to undermine the relationships themselves. Thus we will begin with the nature of the relationship, derive structural forms, and then—just as Simmel would have appreciated—see how these forms cut against the nature of the relationship itself.

By the "nature" of the mutual relationship I mean the tendency to make connected persons equivalent. Such a tendency allows for clear structural forms to emerge—instead of many persons, each different from the other, a pattern emerges with a much smaller number of distinct positions. One such form of equivalence that social analysts continually rediscover for the case of mutual relationships is the clique. The clique, at least in the purest form, is generally considered to be a subset of persons, each of whom is tied to every other; here we will think in terms of sets of persons all of whom interact with one another. This interaction by definition does not distinguish between persons; indeed, in the clique, all members are "equivalent" in a technical sense. (If we denote "a has relationship R with b" by aRb, we say that a relationship R establishes equivalence classes if it is symmetric in that aRb implies bRa, reflexive in that aRa for all a, and transitive, in that aRb and bRc implies aRc.)

For example, below (figure 2.1) we see two cliques of five persons each. Within each clique, all possible interactions occur, while none occur between members of the different cliques. Because all members are equivalent, and all tied to one another, members are truly indistinguishable, and we may see the structure as only "horizontal."[2]

Where Do Cliques Come From?

The simplest ("pure") clique structure as illustrated below places every person in one and only one clique. Sociologists have often wondered why such structures would arise. One answer in purely structural terms is that the clique will

---

[2] This fundamental insight was later generalized to nonclique forms of equivalence, first the structural equivalence of White, Boorman, and Breiger (1976) and later the regular equivalence of Everett and Borgatti (1994). As our exploration progresses we shall see reasons why the latter more mathematically elegant understandings are probably less useful for social structures than is the original idea of structural equivalence.

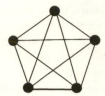 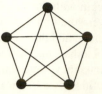

Figure 2.1. Two cliques

arise when people consider themselves equivalent. Such equivalence might be expressed as follows: "If you have a relationship with *A*, well then so will I. But if you do not have a relationship with *B*, I will not either." Such equivalence and resultant clique-formation might reasonably result when the relationship in question is that of *alliance*, since to be an ally means to say, "I will take an attack on you as an attack on me."

And indeed, there is intriguing evidence of clique formations appearing in alliance relations between groups. For example, K. E. Read (1954) studied political relations among the Highland New Guinea groups making up the larger unit of the Gahuku-Gama and provided a chart showing relations of alliance and enmity between the "subtribes." Although Read, unlike the later analyst Hage (1973; cf. Hage and Harary 1983: 59), did not notice this, inspection demonstrates that there are three cliques present.[3] Within any clique, all relations are positive relations of alliance. The relations between members of any two different cliques, however, are likely to be actively hostile, although in some cases they seem to be indifferent.

Similar clique-formation might reasonably occur between individuals when the relationship of "close friendship" is considered. For example, it may be extremely uncomfortable to befriend your close friend's enemy; an insult to your good friend must be an insult to you. Further, the existence of such cliques among schoolchildren is a well-known, or at least, well-believed-to-be-known, fact of American life.[4] Indeed, the recurrence of such cliques in schools is a reasonable supposition, but the reason for the structural tendency may be somewhat different from what is commonly assumed. Much of the interaction between children at school takes place in relatively short periods of time—the

[3] Hage (1973) actually concluded that there were two violations present, but I believe that this came from a poor drawing of the original graph by Read; one group (the Masilakidzuha) is placed at the intersection of a number of lines and appears to be the endpoint of two lines, while I am confident that this line connects two other groups (the Uheto and Nagamiza, who are in the same clique) that straddle the Masilakidzuha; the two errors as seen by Hage are a supposed positive relation from the Uheto to the Masilakidzuha and again from the Nagamiza to the Masilakidzuha.

[4] Schoolchildren most probably are organized in groups that tend to but fall short of pure cliques in that not all within-clique relations are present (or the density < 1), though between-clique relations are never or rarely present (density << 1).

group may be (partially) together during lunch or recess, but not throughout the day. If child *A* wishes to eat lunch with *B*, and *B* is going to eat lunch with *C*, *A* has no choice but to accept *C* along with *B*. Ties of "lunching together" with other children must be forsaken. It is then, the institutional structure—in this case and many others, the simple act of setting out separate lunch tables— that leads any regularity in interactions to take on a clique form (this point has also been made by Anderson 1979: 459).[5]

Structures produced by such institutional scaffolding cannot be said to have formed "spontaneously" and are thus poor material for us to use in understanding the emergence of structure from relationships. Still, this process whereby *A* and *C*, both of whom are friends with *B*, encounter one another more frequently and hence are more likely to establish a positive relationship, may be similar inside and outside such institutional forms. Most simply, as Homans (1950; 1974) has suggested, we should expect a positive feedback loop between the time people spend together and their degree of agreement across a host of measures. Those who find themselves in agreement will tend to like each other, and hence spend more time together. What is important is that such a process leads the relationship of friendship to become *transitive*: if *A* is friends with *B* and *B* with *C*, we can expect *A* and *C* to also become friends simply because of the increased likelihood of their spending time together.

Let us return to the definition of an equivalence relation *R* being (i) symmetric (*aRb* implies *bRa*), (ii) reflexive (*aRa* for all *a*), and (iii) transitive (*aRb* and *bRc* implies *aRc*). It will be seen that the first condition follows from the definition of mutual relations, and the second is trivial (all persons interact with themselves). The essence of the partitioning of some group up into cliques, then, turns on whether relations are transitive or intransitive, with transitive relations leading to equivalence relations and hence cliques. We shall investigate such transitivity below and find that despite the plausibility of Homans's idea, the evidence for the production of transitive friendship cliques is slight. But even should such a structural tendency exist, it is an inherently limited basis for the production of larger structures.

---

[5] Even further, institutions go beyond setting up structures that channel choices into cliques— they also imperatively require persons to interact with one another (e.g., members of a work team). While this cuts against the intuitive understanding of what we mean by "clique," from the perspective of structural constraints on interaction, we must admit that such situations of imperatively coordinated association are probably the most common form of cliquelike interaction. The children who whisper to one another about those whom they will exclude—often taken as the model for cliques—are interactionally less likely to form a clique than are a group of workers at the same position on the shop floor. These workers are likely to all interact with one another, and not with the other workers in the building who are simultaneously engaged in work-related interaction in a different area of the workplace. The paradox, then, is that while cliques have been assumed to result from the free choice of individuals who like to exclude, people rarely voluntarily form cliques. Instead, they more often are forced to.

Transitivity and Aggregation

To demonstrate this limitation, let us imagine that a number of cliques exist. Can these be the basis for the construction of some larger structure with clear formal principles? The answer is, not without fundamental disruption to the structural tendencies inherent in cliques.

If transitivity is to be preserved, the connection of two cliques requires *all* pairs of persons to establish relations. That is, using our example of the two five-person cliques above, if person *A1* in clique *A* establishes a relation between *B1* in clique *B*, then all other 24 (= $5 \times 5 - 1$) relationships must also be established. But it is probably the difficulty of sustaining so many relationships that has led to the small size of the various cliques in the first place.

We may call this the problem of "completion"—the very nature of the relationship (one that is egalitarian and transitive) puts too heavy a burden on interactants. We require all persons to have relationships with one another (thus the structure is "complete") if the structure is not to be degraded or transformed. Putting cliques together to make larger structures, then, is simply unworkable unless something is changed.

There are, then, two options for facilitating structure formation via the aggregation of cliques. The first is to introduce a second or perhaps also third type of relationship. Thus we may have a different type of interaction, "bridging," which is done by some but not all clique members. Such bridging is illustrated in the figure below (figure 2.2, top); the double line indicates a bridge, and the nodes connected to it can now be differentiated from the other nodes. In this case, we may say that within a clique relationships remain transitive, but we introduce a second type of relationship, the bridge, and therefore move to what I have called a complex structure, one that involves more than one type of relationship.

The second is to abandon the rigid transitivity requirement. Thus we allow some person(s) to be in more than one clique at a time. Once again, differentiation is introduced into what was an equivalence relation, as there are some nodes (we may call them "welds") at which transitivity stops. An example is given in figure 2.2, bottom, of our two cliques joined by one person. You will note the absence of transitivity, as (for example) *a5* and *b2* each have a relationship with the welding node, but not with one another.

Given this relaxation, it is possible for cliques to concatenate to form larger structures, although these structures lack the kind of absolute principles that might guide subjective action via clear heuristics. In particular, you cannot assume that your ally's ally will be *your* ally.

Let us concentrate on welds, which do not involve introducing a second relationship. (Most network analysts tend to assume the case of welds because they only have data on a single relationship.) Allowing for welds not only

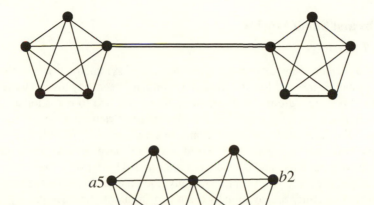

Figure 2.2. Bridge and weld

requires a sacrifice of strict transitivity, but of strict equality as well: we see the transformation of a wholly horizontal to a potentially vertical structure. The verticality comes in the fact that welds are qualitatively different, and where there is difference, there may be inequality. This point has been made most clearly by Burt (1992; 2004); looking at managers, he finds that welds get promoted faster, make more money, get better evaluations, and so on. In other cases, being a weld may be unfortunate—welds may have more work to do—but good or bad, they are different in a way that introduces inequality. The equivalence that was the essence of the relationship has been lost. Thus by solving the problem of completion (allowing some pairs of persons not to have relationships), we introduce the problem of inequality. Although the relationships are supposed to be equal, we introduce a vertical differentiation between the persons.

In this simple example of a single weld, this verticality can be expressed as a categorical distinction between welds and regular nodes. But as we attempt to build a larger structure, we are likely to find this clear distinction dissolving into a differentiation that is only a matter of degree, not of kind. At the same time, we find that the structural components (the two five-person cliques in this case) lose their clear identity. Instead of a clear structure, we have only some degree of *tendency* toward structure—some degree along a continuum stretching from total randomness at one end to separate cliques at the other. This tendency, however—one toward "clumpiness"—is still fundamentally related to that which we saw underlying the clique. We may term such sets of relationships "webs" and see to what extent their organization can reflect this structural tendency (also see, e.g., White and Harary 2001).

Webs and Small Worlds

Small Worlds

We may define webs in network terms as sets of symmetrical ties with low variance of degree and low density but a significant tendency toward transitivity or clustering—groups of three, all of whom are tied to one another. Two seemingly similar relationships that fit this bill are "friendship" and "acquaintance." For friendship, the low variance criterion means that although some people have only one really good friend, and some have close to one hundred, most have around ten, and no one has a thousand. The density criterion means that if you pick any two people randomly, the chances are low that they are friends. Acquaintance may initially seem very similar to friendship, only "less so"—it may be seen as an attenuated form of friendship. But acquaintance may have particular structural attributes. In particular, it may well be that a set of acquaintance relationships forms a "small world."

The "small world" is a set of relationships, envisioned as a network, in which the overall network is large and sparse, yet any two points are connected by a surprisingly small number of intermediaries (at least, surprising given the tendency toward transitivity and hence "clumpiness" of the web). This idea was introduced by Milgram (1967) with the finding that most Americans seemed to be connected by no more than "six degrees of separation"—six intermediaries could be found between A and H so that A knows B, B knows C, C knows D, D knows E, E knows F, F knows G, and G knows H.[6]

Such networks are important for communication (and hence for influence and social change), since they allow one to spread a message (or a disease) throughout a large population, and communication is not easily impeded by the removal of some relationships. While there actually is very little reliable evidence on the matter, for the sake of argument, I will assume that the web of acquaintance relationships does in fact have small-world properties. (It is worth emphasizing that acquaintance is not the same thing as friendship: for reasons we will uncover, it is unlikely that the small-world property holds for friendship relations.) Because most randomly generated networks of similar density and distribution of degree lack small-world properties (also see Strogatz 2001), we may ask what is it that might lead our social world to be a small one?

---

[6] So the source A and target H are here not considered the degrees of separation. Milgram found a mean length of 5, but some chains were never finished, suggesting 6 as a better median. Actually, as McCue (2002) emphasizes, these are *too many* links given the average person's numbers of acquaintances, if we assume that acquaintanceship is random. The "smallness" in question is best seen in terms of the size of a world with *random* connections that would have the same length connecting paths as does our far-from-random world. Technically, we can follow Watts (1999: 114) and define a small-world graph as one that has a characteristic path length that is similar to that of a random graph but is much more clustered than is a random graph.

One likely contender is movement. The following is sufficient to produce a small world. First, be born. Second, establish one hundred connections to the first people you see. Third, go to some new environment (this may or may not require geographical separation, but some such movements are necessary). Fourth, drop twenty old attachments (as long as the probability of retention is not too highly associated in a positive direction with age of the attachment), and form twenty new ones to people around you. Repeat steps three and four at intervals of approximately ten years until you are retired.[7] As long as a few people do this, they will bring the rest of us together in a relatively small world (compare the argument of Robins, Pattison, and Woolcock 2005: 921ff, and the discussion of chapter 5 in this book).

More technically, Watts (1999: 67, 241) has demonstrated that a small amount of random rewiring of a simple type of graph is sufficient to produce small-world graphs. In particular, consider the two separate cliques in figure 2.1 of this chapter—Watts considers this a "caveman" world in that people establish relationships with the few in their cave but have no relationships with those in other caves. Consider a process in which one tie is changed from a "within" cave to a "between" cave tie such that all caves are connected to those that are "near" them. This network is now connected, but does not necessarily possess small-world properties, and this is because the connection has happened according a spatial logic, and not a "relational" one.

A relational graph is one in which the probability of two nodes (e.g., persons) being tied is proportional only to the number (or proportion) of ties they have to nodes in common. Thus those with mutual friends are more likely to become friends. In a spatial graph, all the nodes are embedded in a space (whether a physical one or merely an analytic one), and the probability of a tie between two nodes is a (decreasing) function of their distance in this space.

This second type of graph would seem a natural model for social relations, since persons actually do occupy a position in a (nearly) two-dimensional space, and it is reasonable to expect that they are more likely to establish relations with those near them than with those far. Indeed, even within the local scale (that is, ignoring the attenuated probability of intercontinental friendships and so on), there is persuasive evidence that this is the case. In a wonderful study of relationships between adult graduate students in a student housing complex, Festinger, Schachter, and Back (1963) demonstrated that the probability of two persons or families being friends depended greatly not only on their general location, but the paths they would take on their daily entrances and exits from their apartments. Those who shared a staircase were more likely to become friends than those equally close but tending to use different stairwells.

---

[7] This also helps answer the mathematically more confusing question of how people can *know* the operating principles of their small world (see Kleinberg 2000).

As if there weren't sufficient reason to expect a spatial component to social networks, researchers have been in recent years greatly enamored of techniques (especially multidimensional scaling, but also correspondence analysis) that more or less create an analytic space to explain the pattern of relations. Thus a complex pattern of relationships among many persons is simplified by placing each person in a three- or four-dimensional analytic space (as opposed to a geographical space), and proposing that people form ties to those close to them in this space. The dimensions of this space might not have any intuitively accessible explanation, but they might also resolve to familiar social attributes such as education and income. Yet these efforts may be in the wrong direction if spatial analysis is false to the principles of social networks.

And false the spatial model must be (if the relationship in question is the small-world relationship of acquaintance): after the fact, the point that spatial graphs cannot be small-world graphs seems quite obvious, but I am not aware of anyone who saw its importance before Watts. The particular assumptions used by Watts may be problematic for direct application to certain social relationships, but the point should stand: a spatial organization leads the "big world" to stay a big world because by definition the areas of this space cannot come any closer together (see Watts 1999: 241). While random rewiring in a relational graph can produce a small world, any randomization added to a spatial model simply moves the graph more toward a random graph, without the clustering characteristic of small-world graphs.[8]

Yet given the well-known importance of spatial metaphors for understanding social life (such as the "social space" of Bourdieu [1984]), should we conclude that social networks are not spatial but are relational? The answer will depend on whether we are interested in strong ties like friendship or weak ties like acquaintance. I will argue shortly that strong ties probably follow a spatial logic. Weak ties do not, but it is not because this notion of social space is irrelevant; it is that it is not necessarily the case that all spaces are isotropic. It is this point, that weak ties are likely to defy the closure implicit in spatial logic, that was the important contribution of Granovetter's (1973, especially 1268) widely cited and widely misused article on the strength of weak ties.[9] Among other things Granovetter argued on theoretical and empirical grounds that it is only weak ties that should show evidence of a small world.

There may indeed be a social space in which we can position persons so that those near-by are more likely to form ties to one another than those far away. We do not need to specify in advance whether this space can be identified

---

[8] One may, however, produce a small world in a spatial graph by adding error that leads to tunneling through space, as in Wong, Pattison and Robins (2006). Spatial graphs may have strong tendencies toward clustering; in fact, a two-dimensional space can lead to the rigid clustering of the Davis-Leinhardt model discussed below (Davis 1979: 57, n5).

[9] Here also see Hammer (1979–80: 168).

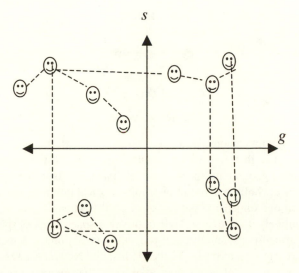

Figure 2.3. "OR" logic of acquaintance

with dimensions such as "capitals," or whether, after the fashion of Friedkin (1998) it should simply be considered a reparameterization of relational patterns. But in addition to this analytic space, plain old everyday geographic space also influences the probability of relationship formation and survival. As Watts (1999: 133) has argued, it seems highly likely that interpersonal relations will be affected by distance in two spaces, geographic space and social space. But precisely because two different spaces are involved, we cannot describe the formation of acquaintanceship by embedding all persons in a single analytic space and predicting that those close will form relationships.

For example, imagine a simpler two-dimensional space in which one dimension is "geographical" distance and the other is "social" distance (see figure 2.3). Denote the first distance g and the second s; the normal Cartesian distance between any two points i and j in this space would be

$$d_{ij} = \sqrt{(g_i - g_j)^2 + (s_i - s_j)^2}$$

There are, of course, other ways of calculating distance, but this is as good as any for illustrating the point that, according to normal spatial principles, you are basically only as close as you are far apart on the dimension *most* separating you. But it seems very likely that one will form at least a weak friendship with a next door neighbor who is not at all close in social space, and that similarly one may maintain a tie to one with whom one has a great deal in common even when that person is separated geographically (perhaps a school friend that one sees only at annual reunions or trade meetings). Hence we can imagine ties traversing this analytic space connecting persons who are very close on

Figure 2.4. Wheel

one but not both dimensions. Weak ties "tunnel" through the joint geographic-social space, since they operate on an OR logic: *A* is likely to know *B* if the two are close in geographic space *or* social space. (Thus in the figure above, the ties that are wholly horizontal or wholly vertical connect people who are very close on one dimension but far apart on the other, connections that are extremely unlikely if the overall logic in this two-space space is spatial.) Such a network probably has small-world properties (this point has recently been made in more rigorous terms by Watts, Dodds, and Newman 2002).[10] In other words, the overall set of acquaintances is such that everyone is reasonably close to everyone else.

Webs and Wheels

But people can also be reasonably close if some special persons have structural positions that facilitate the indirect connections of others. In the simplest such structure, there are as few ties as is compatible with a connected structure—all persons except the special person have ties only to this special person. This person (located at the center of figure 2.4) may be termed the "hub" of the structure, and the others may be called the "spokes."[11] A hub and its spokes may be called (what else) a "wheel."

We often see hub structures when a group has gelled around a particular charismatic individual. The group only exists so long as the hub person retains his or her charisma or activity. Of course, many charismatic leaders show a marked disinclination to have anything to do with one another, and hence their structures do not form the building blocks for larger structures. But in other cases, hubs establish relationships not only with their own spokes but also

[10] Indeed, Travers and Milgram (1969: 432f) found that the two ways people made connections to the target in their classic experiments was through geographical likeness or occupational likeness (that is, to reach a doctor in Boston, a mechanic in Nebraska might make a connection to a doctor in Nebraska or a mechanic in Boston). Also see Killworth and Bernard (1979: 480ff) for a detailed exposition.

[11] Technically, a spoke should be seen as the relationship itself, which connects the hub to the rim via a nipple, but hubs and nipples doesn't sound quite so theoretically impressive as hubs and spokes.

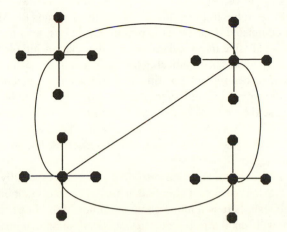

Figure 2.5. Multihub structure

with other hubs, thereby bringing their spokes into indirect connection, as shown in figure 2.5.

We shall explore such multihub structures in chapter 5 in terms of their properties for spreading information and influence. Here, we can imagine successively introducing "noise"—some random rewiring, allowing some spokes to have connections to other spokes, or some spokes to be attached to more than one hub—and moving from this structurally simple graph to one that would appear more or less indistinguishable from the small worlds we have seen above.

Indeed, a multihub structure might have small-world properties, in terms of having the characteristic path length of a random graph, but more clustering than a random graph (for a mathematical demonstration, see Yamaguchi 2002). And yet it would not be a small world as derived by Watts, for the reason that here there is, at least in principle, a qualitative distinction between two classes of persons. They may be considered hubs and spokes, central and peripheral, cosmopolitans and locals, but they are different and it should give us analytic purchase to describe the typical characteristics of each class.

Judith Kleinfeld (2002) has recently emphasized that merely on a priori grounds it is reasonable to imagine that much of the supposed small-world phenomenon is actually due to such a two-class structure. Some people (we can call them "locals") are embedded in cavelike cliques and have no ties outside their caves, while others (we can call them "cosmopolitans") have ties both to locals in their cave and to other cosmopolitans. Locals can only communicate outside of their cave by the good graces of the cosmopolitans. (She compares this to a bowl of oatmeal, with some parts lumpier than others.)

There must be some truth to this; it seems much easier for Milgram-type chains to be completed if the target is prominent.[12] I can get a message to our president with only five intermediaries under the relationship of "face-to-face acquaintance" (mayor, state political party chair, governor, senator, president), but my odds of successfully completing a transmission to someone less prominent are far lower.[13] Kleinfeld suggests that small-world studies have been skewed because they relied on a subset of unusually well-connected participants (almost all studies use volunteers), and completely skirt around the many ethnic enclaves that may be small worlds in themselves, but are not well tied to the rest of the world.

Certainly Kleinfeld's images are appealing—perhaps especially so to someone in a more remote area (Kleinfeld herself is a professor in Fairbanks, Alaska). Although there is nothing about a "lumpy" world that is necessarily incompatible with small-world properties, this derivation demonstrates something generally overlooked about acquaintanceship as a relation, and this is that it is *not* strictly symmetric. We are acquainted with those whom we remember, and we tend to remember more prominent people and forget the less prominent. People seem to remember their more successful distant kin and forget the unsuccessful (cf. Smith 1983: 67); I remember that I knew the mayor but she has probably forgotten all about me.

In sum, the set of "acquaintance" relationships may tend to have small-world properties, and this may indeed have something to do with the "random rewiring" that occurs when we pick up and move. It certainly has a great deal to do with the fact that we can be acquainted with those to whom we are close in *either* geographical *or* social space. But it also has to do with the fact that acquaintance turns out *not* to be an inherently symmetric relationship. There is both more and less equality in such relationships than we assume. There is less equality in that those whom we know do not necessarily know us. In some cases this has to do with a stratification of persons into more and less prominent, with the limiting case being a two-class world of cosmopolitans and locals. But it need not have to do with prominence: new students enter a college or a school with a largely empty set of acquaintances, and they busily begin adding to this set the moment they unpack. The upperclassmen and women they meet, on the other hand, have already largely filled their set of available

[12] This is discussed in terms of "contractions" by Watts (1999: 118, 146). Jane Jacobs (1989 [1961]: 134f) as a child invented the small world idea in playing a game "messages" with her sister, where they tried to think of the shortest way two "wildly dissimilar" persons could transmit information by word of mouth. The game was ruined once they thought of Eleanor Roosevelt, who might well know *anyone*.

[13] It is important to emphasize that there is as of yet no evidence that the *length* of completed chains increases when less prominent targets are chosen; it is that the probability of success decreases. I should also emphasize that I lived in a smallish town when I wrote this, and the mayor lived on the next street.

acquaintances and may well forget the new ones they meet simply because they have less room to store names.

Thus there is *more* equality than we might think. When we ask "whom do you know?" we may find great inequality—some prominent people are "known" over and over again. But there is less inequality in terms of the number of acquaintances that people *have*. Precisely because prominent people do not know all those who know them, they are more like the less-prominent in their number of acquaintances.

We shall return to the complications that arise when we allow for nominations to be unreciprocated at the conclusion of this chapter. But we set out to investigate specifically mutual relationships revolving around equivalence. Weak relationships of acquaintance turned out not to fit the bill; we now turn to stronger relationships of friendship.

Friendly Spaces

> Men are conjoined by a vast network of *acquaintanceship*. Brown
> knows Jones, Jones knows Robinson, etc.; and *by choosing your*
> *farther intermediaries rightly* you may carry a message from Jones
> to the Empress of China, or the Chief of the African Pigmies, or to
> anyone else in the world. . . . What may be called love-systems are
> grafted on the acquaintance-system. A loves (or hates) B; B loves (or
> hates) C, etc. But these systems are smaller than the great acquain-
> tance systems that they presuppose.
> —WILLIAM JAMES, *Pragmatism*

In this largely overlooked anticipation of the small-world problem, James posits that there are two networks spanning humanity, one of weak acquaintance ties, and the other of stronger ties. He also proposes that the latter is a proper subset of the former, which is eminently reasonable, since in order to love or hate someone, we must know them, but the reverse is not true. We have been concerned with the former type of relationship; let us now turn our attention to the latter. I propose that in contrast to acquaintanceship, close friendship satisfies the Cartesian AND formula in which *A* and *B* have to be close both in geographical space and in social space to become close friends. And this is why it is doubtful that sets of these relationships have small-world properties: they are probably a bit more like connected cavemen worlds, in which the caves are distributed in some space. (Somewhat loosely, two spaces that jointly affect relationship-formation via AND can produce a single space.)

Although Americans may be more likely to have friendship relationships that cross boundaries of social space than the French who formed Bourdieu's reference world (see Varenne 1977), it is still probably the case that the stronger the tie underlying the relationship, the greater the tendencies toward transitivity and hence closure. Louch (2000) points out that even if one has a will to retain ties with those in different sections of social space, it may be more difficult to do this with those from whom we differ considerably. I see my sociologist friends from California every year or so at a convention; my friends who were janitors or body therapists, never. It does not seem to be the case that truly close friendships weather separations that would break weaker ones—people are unlikely to retain close ties with those from whom they become geographically separated (Martin and Yeung 2006).

But for this very reason (i.e., spatialization), strong friendship relations are unlikely to rigorously follow rules of transitivity and lead to cliques, and it is worthwhile to consider why not. Winship (1977) generalized this transitivity criterion to be expressed in terms of social distance as follows: if the distance between persons X and Y is d_{xy}, and that between persons Y and Z is d_{yz}, then the distance between X and Z will be no more than the sum of d_{xy} and d_{yz}. This is called the "triangle" inequality because all triangles in a simple space satisfy the requirement. According to this light, it is entirely possible for people to be tied by *weaker-than-transitively-implied* ties. That is, if X and Y are "close" in this space (say, they are good friends), and Y and Z are also close (good friends), X and Z need not be good friends. But they are acquaintances on good terms. If X and W are also acquaintances on good terms, W and Z need not be friendly at all (see figure 2.6).

In sum, spatial models may be roughly appropriate to strong friendships; indeed, Watts's "connected caves" model may be roughly appropriate. One phenomenon supporting such a spatial model of connected small worlds is pluralistic ignorance (Allport 1924; O'Gorman 1986), or when everyone shares an incorrect belief, especially about what everyone believes. Such pluralistic ignorance easily arises when people only check the beliefs of those in their "cave" and conclude that "everyone" shares their beliefs. Thus pollsters report irate calls from members of the public demanding to know "who [the pollsters] were talking to" when the pollsters present results that seem obviously wrong to the callers (see, for example, Kagay 1999). Small worlds should be extremely good for spreading information robustly, yet the relationships that are used for political conversation—probably relatively close relationships—evidently do not communicate to around one-third of Americans that the other two-thirds still supported President Clinton around the time of his impeachment. A small world indeed![14]

---

[14] Further, Watts (1999: 211) shows that in small worlds, the local context increasingly mirrors the global context, which can make it hard for groups to create islands of prosocial cooperation. But such islands repeatedly form. Indeed, Kurzman (2004: 135) reports that in the preliminaries to the Iranian revolution, people deliberately tried to use the weakest possible ties they had to gauge the mood of the nation, understanding that to stay within their cave might lead them to get the sucker's payoff due to overestimating the general support for anti-Shah protest.

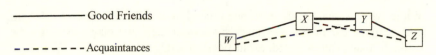

Figure 2.6. Spatial intransitivities

Conclusions on Mutual Relations

We began with the simple relationship of friendship as a starting point to witness the emergence of social structure. Making a distinction between friendship and acquaintance, we saw two different versions of a similar structural tendency—a tendency toward clumpiness. In both cases, this can be understood as a tendency toward transitivity. There are many ways in which this tendency can be understood, but the most intuitively reasonable one has to do with the exclusivity of copresence at any time: if C is often with B, it is difficult for A to be with B without sometimes being with C as well. This gives A more opportunity to form a relationship with C than with some otherwise equivalent D, and, if Homans (1950) is correct, probably goes further and actually encourages the formation of an attachment.

But we have found limitations to this tendency that forestall the emergence of clear structure—that is, sets with clear formal properties that are available on inspection both to analysts and to actors. In the case of mutual relationships it seemed that the expected structures would be pure cliques. For the case of the weak ties of acquaintanceship, clique formation is hindered by three things. First, there is the mobility of persons who retain some old ties and hence produce a small world. Second, since people make or retain weak ties when they are close in geographic or social space, there is a block to transitivity when we switch from closeness based on one space to closeness based on another.[15] Thus my neighbor knows my other neighbors, and my colleagues know my other colleagues, but my neighbors do not know my colleagues. Third, there is the fact that acquaintanceship is *not* strictly mutual.

For the case of stronger ties of friendship, the pressure toward transitivity is only strong enough to lead to clumpiness and not the development of clearcut cliques. And the reason seems to be that strong ties form according to distance in a compound social space, and so relationships lack strong transitivity—a web of close connections may span a large distance, and thus if a is close to b, b close to c, c close to d, d need not be close to a—a violation of transitivity. People may form clumps in webs that can be distributed across social space, but these clumps seem destined to fall short of clear structure.

[15] In a fascinating recent piece of research, Sorenson and Stuart (2001) find venture capitalist firms also having this dual-logic to tie formation—generally they are limited by geographical space, but network position that flows from a relational logic can be used to tunnel through spatial barriers.

While we can imagine these as one-time cliques that have been welded together, to the extent that they take on a spatial logic, we may expect it to be difficult to uncover bounded, exclusive structural units.

In sum, the heuristics that seem to lie behind the formation of acquaintance-ship and friendship do not seem to lead to structure. These heuristics may well be architectonic—that is, of the nature to lead to structural consequences—but they are not absolute. Most important, a mere *tendency* toward transitivity does not, in itself, lead to structure. "Likeness" is not the same thing as equivalence. But that does not mean that there may not be cases where actors take a relationship pertaining to equivalence and approach it with heuristics with clear structural import. Such a structural logic was proposed by balance theorists, who basically started the rigorous analysis of the emergence of structure from interpersonal relationships. These theorists began from an elegant and strong set of axioms about human reasoning that had testable structural implications. We can see that these axioms turned on the nature of the equivalence established by a mutual relation. But as theorists tried to apply the resulting claims to actual data, they were forced to successively relax the stringent structural assumptions made; tracing out this process takes us from the nature of equivalence to the nature of ranking.

In and Out of Balance

> Ch'u and Chin shall not go to war with each other. In their likings
> and dislikings they shall be the same. . . . if any would injure Ch'u,
> Chin shall attack them, and for Chin, Ch'u shall do the same.
>   —from Chinese alliance covenant, 576 BC, quoted in
>   Frank Kierman, "Phases and Modes of Combat in Early
>   China," in *Chinese Ways in Warfare*

Balance and Bifurcation

Above we considered the exemplars of a mutual relationship to be alliance or friendship, since they establish a kind of implicit equivalence between the parties in question. We examined friendship relationships to see whether they tended to take on structural forms that would allow actors to internalize simple and absolute heuristics; now we turn things around and see what the heuristics that might be applied to these relationships imply in structural terms. Perhaps alliance is a simpler case than friendship because it may be less multivalent and should be more rational. Those who make irrational alliances, we might guess, get selected out.

Alliances differ, but the strongest form is one that stresses the equivalence of the parties. Those making the alliance may swear that, as the old Anglo-

Saxon oath of commendation went, "Thy friends will be my friends, thy enemies, my enemies" (Bloch 1961 [1940]: 232). Let us return to this case but
make the additional simplifying assumption that those who are not allies or
friends are enemies. Alliance can be considered a positive relation (indeed,
given a value +1) and enmity considered a negative one (-1); for purposes of
brevity I shall call these "love" and "hate."

Taking this setup seriously, the psychologist Fritz Heider (1946; 1958: 212)
turned to Spinoza's arguments (1930 [1677]: 125–34) in propositions 22, 24,
and 31 of the third part of his *Ethics* regarding the relation between our own
loves and hates and those of others. "If we imagine that a person affects with
joy a thing which we love, we shall be affected with love towards him. If, on
the contrary, we imagine that he affects it with sorrow, we shall also be affected
with hatred towards him."[16] Taking these reasonable ideas and converting them
into all-or-nothing choices allows us to derive very strong predictions for the
class of possible structures (Harary 1955).

Indeed, from this Heider developed what is now known as "balance theory"
by noting that this implies that we want the signs of any chain of associations
or relations to make a positive when they multiply together (Heider 1946;
1958: 206). According to this reasonable model, even if two wrongs do not
make a right, two hates make a love, in that learning that someone hates someone you hate is enough to make you immediately like this person, or at least
choose him or her as an ally. All in all, four rules of action can be derived:
you will love anyone your friend loves, you will hate anyone your friend hates,
hate anyone your enemy loves, and love anyone your enemy hates (see Davis
1963: 450; Johnsen 1986: 278).

Quite simply, when applied to sets of relationships that can be either positive
or negative, balance theory implies that any social whole splits into two mutually hostile cliques or, even more improbably, one happy camp of universal
love (see Cartwright and Harary 1956: 286). Also, hopefully less improbably,
self-hatred was also ruled out, and so all relations had to be mutually hostile
or mutually friendly (otherwise they would contradict balance if *A* loved *B*
and *B* hated *A*, since *A* would have to hate herself to hate her friend's enemy).

Empirical adequacy aside for the moment, we see here a perfect example
of the duality of heuristic and structure—the empirical pattern can either be
described in formal terms (either in terms of an equivalence relation and an

---

[16] On the influence from Spinoza, see Heider (1983: 150). Spinoza (proposition 33) also posited
a tendency for reciprocity stemming from ego's attempt to win the favor of a favored alter, as well
(Axiom 1, fifth part). I have somewhat to my sorrow recently discovered not only that Ronald
Breiger anticipated me in drawing attention to Spinoza's relevance to balance theory but provided
a much more sophisticated treatment of these issues. (Of course, despite my sorrow, in accordance
with Spinoza's arguments, my appreciation of Breiger must increase to learn that he appreciates
what I appreciate.) See Breiger (2010).

antiequivalence relation or in terms of multiplication of sign) or in the subjective terms of the four rules discussed above.[17] To return now to the issue of empirical adequacy—there wasn't any. Cases of such clear bifurcation, or the presence of all four laws of action, were stunningly rare (see Abell 1968 for a discussion).[18] It does seem that in friendship many people will understand the force of the first heuristic, my friend's friend is my friend (Davis 1977: 58)—at least to notice violations as problematic. Thus Rousseau (1928 [1782]: 733) complained of the fact that while he gave all his friends to Friedrich Grimm, none of Grimm's friends became Rousseau's friends. There is even some evidence that people may be influenced by the rule that "an enemy of a friend is an enemy." But the other two heuristics do not seem to be recognized as structural laws in friendship (see Doreian and Krackhardt 2001: 60). Such laws *have* been followed in history, but they generally arise where two large opponents draw smaller allies among themselves (for some references to the use of balance theory for international relations, see Doreian 1971: 85).

A perfect example is the conflict between Sparta and Athens in the fifth century BC, in which almost all smaller cities had to ally with one in order to be protected from the other, though this alliance was also sure to bring down the wrath of the second (for a description of this taking of sides, see Thucydides VII: 57, p. 514). One way to choose sides was to use the rule "the enemy of my enemy is my friend." For one wonderful example, the Corcyraeans chose to ally themselves with Athens, even though they were Dorians and closely connected to the Peloponnesian party, because of their hatred of Corinth, which was allied with Sparta. Other examples occur in criminal gang conflict, where rival gangs will use the same principle to affiliate with two overarching alliance systems such as Bloods and Crips or People and Folks (for examples, see Venkatesh and Levitt 2000: 435; Hagedorn 1988: 67f).[19]

---

[17] Cartwright and Harary (1956: 291) reasonably pointed out that in addition to positive and negative relations, it was also possible for relations to simply be absent. When balance theorists began to allow for this possibility, it first seemed not to make very much of a difference—the set still seemed to have to split into two mutually hostile groups. Null relations were only possible *within* the relatively friendly group (Doreian 1971: 76f). But this was simply because the analysts were only looking at "graphs"—sets of relationships between persons that hung together—and the substantively reasonable case in which there were a set of groups that ignored each other was just out of the ballpark by definition, as it would lead to an unconnected set of graphs. More important for substantive purposes, it was still understood that balance involved the adherence to the four laws given above.

[18] Davis (1963) emphasized that these laws should not be considered as the rules of all social organization and reasonably suggested that they were akin to the rules of mechanical solidarity, in contrast to the structure of exchange theory a la Levi-Strauss, in which positive ties must unite groups, since the structure is held together by organic solidarity.

[19] Interestingly, the leaders of the official gangs in larger cities in may incorrectly assume that they have thus acquired authority over these affiliates, when the "joining" was not intended to imply any acceptance of central direction (Hagedorn 1988: 72) but merely to form alliances against local enemies. We will return to this when we examine party formation in chapter 8.

Now it is possible for the equivalent of the four laws (and consequently the bifurcation of the population) to arise in the absence of two major powers. In one interesting case, when traveling Polopa of Highland New Guinea (see Brown 1979: 727ff) come upon strangers, they immediately attempt to find either enemies in common or friends in common. Since they assume that there is no such thing as neutrality and hence "he who is not with me is against me," failure to establish alliance via one of these two rules (my enemy's enemy is my friend; my friend's friend is my friend) establishes a prejudice of enmity. Consequently, it seems that the alliance structure is "two colorable" (indeed, Brown actually referred to the alliance clusters as colors) in that there are two groups, with all intergroup relations negative and all intragroup relations positive (Hage and Harary 1983: 40).[20] But such cases of balance are the exception, not the rule, and in this case seems to be due to the exceptional vulnerability of the traveler.

Indeed, we shall see that even given only two states (love and hatred) and extremely rational participants, there must be rather strong institutional supports for the balanced structure to emerge, for the simple reason that the "laws" of balance assume a type of reactivity that is the opposite of what we would consider rational. Take the principle, "my enemy's friend is my enemy." It is a poor sort of enemy who allows himself to be guided by this maxim. Consider two enemies, A and B, the former of whom decides, balance theory be hanged, to attempt to make friends with B's friend C. If successful, B will have no choice (assuming he does not also abandon balance theory) but to turn C into an enemy. By assiduously courting all of B's friends, A should be able to leave B completely isolated.[21]

To conclude, there are cases in which the relationship of alliance—intrinsically a relationship of equivalence—leads to the production of perfectly balanced structures, which are bifurcations into two hostile groups. Yet such cases are an exception, even when we have a relation of alliance as opposed to hostility. This is not because the people in question are cognitively incapable of reaching the logical conclusions implied by balance theory, but because they are reasonable enough to avoid them.

---

[20] Even more interesting is Hage and Harary's (1983: 56) noting that there are other groups in the area in which the enemy of an enemy can be either friend or enemy; in this case, the structure that develops is a different one that we shall examine in the next section.

[21] For evidence that this does occur, see Doreian and Krackhardt (2001: 57). Leinhardt (1972: 204) noted that there could be good reasons for maintaining relations that defied the dictates of transitivity, though I do not know anyone before Doreian (2002: 106; also Doreian and Krackhardt 2001: 61) to point out that individual-level effects can destroy balance—if some person C is truly hateful, it is a bit much to criticize B for not liking C just because B dislikes A and A hates C. Finally, there is an important way in which the truest friendship *cannot* be bound to the dictates of balance theory (here see Silver 2002: 13).

Joking and Avoidance Relations

Further, it turns out not to be correct that the subjective possession of balancelike rules necessarily leads to bifurcations. As Levi-Strauss (1963: 161) emphasized, despite the duality of heuristic and structure, heuristics of bifurcation do not necessarily lead to bifurcated structures. Indeed, in the one case in which there is a repeated tendency toward the production of balanced bifurcations from the point of view of any particular actor, we see an inverse relationship between the existence of exhaustive subjective heuristics for allocating persons into two categories, and the existence of stable bifurcations in the population. That is, where we see actors struggling to systemize ideas of equivalence and antiequivalence, we see them reproduce the outlines of balance theory. Yet in these very cases in which people hold a set of subjective principles seemingly compatible with balance theory, we are *least* likely to see the stable division of persons into classes that balance theory predicts.

This case—one found in traditional societies from North America to Africa to Australia—involves the division of all possible kinsmen into "joking" partners or "avoidance" partners.[22] The former are treated with familiarity (the jokes frequently involve sexual innuendo and teasing), and the latter with deferential respect (sexual matters never raised or alluded to). Such a system seems to have generated independently in a wide variety of geographically disparate areas. Hage (1976; cf. Hage and Harary 1983: 47) takes the G/wi Khoisan of the Kalahari as an example (as originally discussed by Silberbauer 1961; 1972) and demonstrates the strong tendency toward balance. G/wi informants explicitly only discuss two of the four laws of balance: the joking partner of my joking partner is my joking partner, and the avoidance partner of my joking partner is my avoidance partner (Hage and Harary 1983: 47).

If the G/wi interpreted these rules as referring to triads, they would be sufficient to produce a balanced bifurcation of the society. That is, they might say to themselves, "that the avoidance partner of my joking partner is my avoidance partner implies that the avoidance partner of my avoidance partner is my joking partner too." But they do not—and note that the rules they emphasize are those that studies of American friendship have also found being used—my equivalent's equivalent is my equivalent and my equivalent's antiequivalent is my antiequivalent.

As a result of their selective interest (and contrary to Hage and Harary's reasonable attempt to emphasize this as a case of balance), the G/wi system does not lead to two supercliques of joking partners. First of all, contrary to implication, the G/wi do not find anything anomalous in three people all being

---

[22] Radcliffe-Brown (1940) was the first to emphasize the commonalities in joking/avoidance systems, though his theoretical explanation, influential as it may have been, is untenable and based on unsupported functionalist assumptions.

Figure 2.7. Bifurcations and two-colorings

mutual avoidance partners (Hage 1976: 41), which would imply a possibility of multiple cliques of joking partners. But this is also not what occurs—instead, the system is closer to a bifurcation, but one that is different for each person.

Perhaps a simpler way of deriving such a structure than Hage's (1976) emphasis on balance is to start with the fact that, as Hage and Harary (1983) mention, the resulting graph of a balanced structure is "two-colorable," meaning that any person can be assigned to one of two colors or cliques. Topology demonstrates that a map is two colorable if the boundaries of all regions are lines that do not stop within the area and the intersections of these lines occur at single points (as opposed to two lines overlapping for a while). The example in figure 2.7 is of a spherical area with a number of curves all of which reach to the perimeter of the area (left); the middle diagram shows that this is in fact two-colorable.

You will note that if a new line is drawn across the surface, the map will remain two-colorable: one only has to "flip" all colors on one side of the line. In the third panel, a new vertical line is added through the center—all the colors to the right are inverted, but the figure remains two-colorable. In a very close analogy, consider a set of distinctions that can be made between all persons. Between any two people who are alike in all other ways, being different on *one* distinction makes them antiequivalent. But adding a second distinction makes them *anti*-antiequivalent, which turns out to be the same as equivalent. Each distinction made is then like one of the lines in the above figure. The resulting set of social categories can then also be made two-colorable, so that whenever we cross one of these distinction-lines, we switch from one color to the other.

Joking/avoidance relationships seem to arise where there are such sets of distinctions, usually oriented around sex and parentage. These distinctions are put together to get at a more fundamental distinction, namely those who are equivalent to ego, and those who are antiequivalent (this corresponds to the distinction between black and white in the above diagrams).

It seems that in cultures that dichotomize all persons into joking and avoidance partners, the essential logic is closely related to the selection of possible marriage partners in a kinship system, which does *not* permit of division into exogamous moieties (the bifurcation underlying the restricted exchange examined in more detail in the next chapter). When there are moieties, people (taking ego as male) reason "I cannot marry *X*, because she is *like* me—a member of moiety *A*." In joking/avoidance systems, ego reasons, "I cannot marry *X*, because she is *unlike* me—an avoidance partner."[23] This logic is structured with distinctions that cut through all persons (as opposed to only being applicable to a subset of persons). These distinctions establish both equivalence and difference or, as I have called it here, antiequivalence. The term *antiequivalence* highlights the ways in which the transitive logic works—someone who is the opposite of someone who is opposite to me is the same as me. We can therefore simplify the sort of patchwork two-color graph above by constructing a two-portion graph with a single border—relations of antiequivalence imply a crossing of this border, while relations of equivalence do not.

Relations and Classes of Equivalence and Antiequivalence

For the G/wi, relations of equivalence are "marriage" and "same-sex sibling."[24] Relations of antiequivalence are "parent-child" and "opposite sex sibling." We can actually assimilate this system to the "two-colorable" graphs above by ignoring the equivalence relations and focusing on those of antiequivalence. So we may make two lines indicating "boundary crossings" to those who are antiequivalent. One is that of an alternate-sex sibling (the vertical line on the diagram in figure 2.8), and the other is that of an adjacent generation (the horizontal line). The fact that same-sex siblingship and marriage are equivalence relations need not appear—we only know that if we are traversing one of these relationships we do not move from whatever area we are in.

---

[23] At the same time, it is equally possible for these systems to be based on the fact that one *cannot* marry into lineages that are "like" one's own; as we shall see, the same cognitive heuristics can be used for this task.

[24] Similarly, Eggan (1970 [1955]: 70, 75) says that "the principle of the 'equivalence of siblings' is one of the basic principles for kinship systems of the Cheyenne and Arapaho type," two other societies with avoidance/joking relationships whereby one treats parents and opposite-sex siblings with avoidance/respect, grandparents and siblings-in-law with joking hilarity. Father's sisters and mother's brothers may be joked with, as can unspecified distant relatives. Where bilateral cross-cousin marriage is prescribed, this may lead one to joke with one's spouse's parents, because they are father's sister and mother's brother. Thus Chagnon (1968b: 70) reports a Makiritare informant explaining, "When you marry this way, you are. . . . good friends with [i.e. can play and joke with] your *wodöma* [father-in-law]. If you marry a different way, you must be careful around your *wodöma* and respect him." Thus we may hypothesize that despite the seeming similarity of the G/wi division of all persons into joking and avoidance partners to the dual organization compatible with cross-cousin marriage (see next chapter), the two systems cannot exist together (for if you joke with your father-in-law because he is your father's sister, you must avoid his daughter). In another case (the Nyakyusa of Tanganyika), the joking relationship is assimilated to cross-cousinship and also to rivalry (Wilson 1957); while cross-cousin marriage is generally forbidden, this still seems to be a way of designating potential affines.

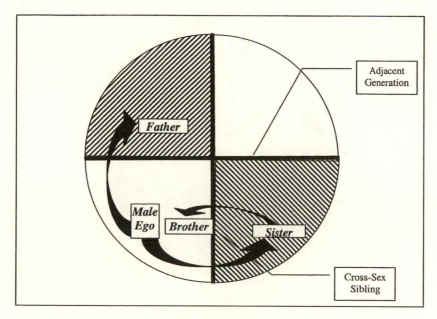

Figure 2.8. Equivalence and anti-equivalence

First, our male ego can empirically confirm that -1 x -1 = +1 for either of these relationships considered individually. If he crosses the vertical line (and hence thinks of his sister), and then "standing" there, crosses the line again to his *sister's* opposite-sex sibling, he ends up with his brother, an equivalence relationship. One can go back and forth over this line as many times as one wants, and multiplying negatives will not steer us in the wrong direction.

So too when it comes to the relationship of antiequivalence of adjacent generation (see figure 2.9). Ego must avoid his parents (and his children). But if he goes to his father and then to his father's father, he finds someone equivalent to himself. Both have to avoid ego's father. From this, one can imagine a chain of alternating generations—two-colorable—ascending upward and downward infinitely.

So for either of the single relations of avoidance, we find the balance theoretic approach works admirably. We can treat antiequivalence as a negative relation and allow relations to multiply. And we can then build on this for other cases. Relations of marriage equate the husband and wife, so that each must assume the avoidance and joking relations of the other, but since one should only marry a joking partner, confusions do not necessarily result (though there are exceptions discussed below). For this reason, one's father's brother's wife is an avoidance partner.

For the G/wi case, there are two complications. One is relatively minor and pertains to the way that cousins are treated—as in many cultures, parallel

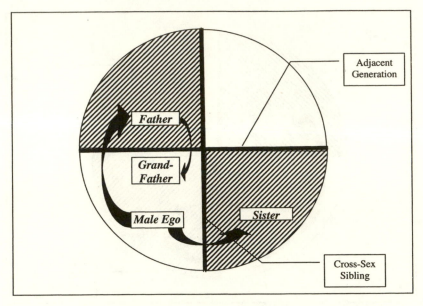

Figure 2.9. Equivalence of grandfather

and cross-cousins are differentiated and here treated opposite to how we might expect. This seeming violation is easily explained by the nature of cousin-marriage.[25]

But there is an even more glaring inconsistency, at least from the perspective of balance theory. Hage (1976) correctly points out that the G/wi system

[25] First, parallel cousins are given special treatment and considered siblings. Thus a male ego treats an opposite sex parallel cousin (say, father's brother's daughter) as his sister, and hence avoids her, as opposed to following the logic father = cross (to avoidance); brother = stay; daughter = cross (joking). Second, both mother's brother's son and mother's brother's daughter are treated as joking partners. Silberbauer (1961: 357) notes this "slight difficulty," but cannot explain it. This exception becomes explicable if there is a need to consider cross-cousin marriage as preferable over parallel cousin marriage; Hammel (1973) has demonstrated that such a preference is likely to occur in a polygamous society where men tend to be significantly older than the women they marry. Since the G/wi are indeed polygamous, it is reasonable to propose that the identification of cross-cousins as future marriage partners explains what seems to be a lapse of logic. The polarities of cross-cousins and parallel-cousins are reversed to facilitate marriages more in keeping with age differences between prospective spouses; cognitively, this is accomplished by seeing these cousins as cases in themselves. Thus just as a sister is a sister (and not a father's daughter), a male's cross-cousin is here not seen as "mother's brother's daughter" (which would be $-1 \times -1 \times -1 = -1$ = avoidance), but is seen (immediately) as "wife" (and hence joking).

In contrast, the Tikopia also have large classes of joking and avoidance partners (*tautau laui* and *tautau pariki*), with joking between grandparent-grandchild and between same-sex siblings and avoidance between parent-child and between opposite-sex siblings. Further, they stress the equivalence of spouses and same-sex siblings (hence a man jokes suggestively with his brother's wife). Yet the cousin polarity is reversed, as there is avoidance between cross cousins and not between parallel cousins. But in this case, cross-cousin marriage is seriously discouraged and is

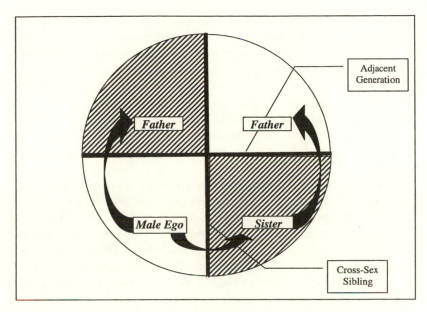

Figure 2.10. Contradiction of joking-avoidance system

gives rise to the intransitive triad of two joking and one avoidance relation
between a brother, sister, and their grandfather. That is, a male ego "correctly"
jokes with his grandfather (since the avoidance partner of his father, an avoidance partner, must be a joking partner); the same is true for a female ego.
The transitivity of joking should lead to the brother and sister joking, but of
course they do not. It is accurate to say both that this apparent inconsistency
only appears as an inconsistency because of a misunderstanding of the joking
system, and that this inconsistency reveals a more fundamental tension that
arises in all such systems, and leads all resolutions to possess some sort of
inconsistency.

Turning to the first response, note that the "problem" can more simply be
stated by pointing to the unbalanced triad containing a brother, a sister, and a
parent, all of whom will be avoidance partners (see figure 2.10). While the
logic of antiequivalence should make this impossible (as the avoidance partner

---

less common than parallel cousin marriage. Here the seeming anomaly is that a man jokes with
his mother's brother, but respects his father's sister and her offspring. Firth (1963 [1936]: 195,
199, 207f, 231, 285).

Despite the complexity of Hage's presentation of the G/wi case, he leaves out or misreports
crucial information reported by Silberbauer pertaining to the relation of a male ego to his father's
sister's children, and of ego to ego's nephews and nieces, both of which support my interpretation
here. Thus a male ego's brother's daughter is avoidance and his sister's daughter a joking partner.
This last is interesting because, since joking partners are potential wives, this implies the possibility of male-ego's marriage with sister's daughter. This type of marriage is compatible with a
polygamous society in which age of husband significantly exceeds age of wife.

of my avoidance partner should be my joking partner), it is worth remembering that G/wi informants themselves saw nothing anomalous in such a triad. Further, they simply do not consider their sisters (or brothers) their parent's daughters (sons); they are sisters or brothers. As Goody (1977) stressed, Western anthropologists tended to approach oral cultures with their own cultural tools such as "tables" and imposed these on a different form of reasoning. The table became a sort of cognitive procrustean bed, whereby those parts of practical logic that did not fit were simply lopped off. In this case, the "inconsistency" does not arise in actual practice because of the way in which people traverse their relational tasks.

Put another way, while these boundary crossings (from equivalence into nonequivalence) do indeed concatenate according to the antitransitive logic that should produce balanced relationships (in the way that $-1 \times -1 = 1$, and not -1), not all possible "walks" through the set of boundaries are reasonable. One's sister, after all, is one's sister, and not one's father's father's son's son's daughter, and one's father's father is one's father's father, and not one's father's sister's father. Recall that we found that in American friendships, people tend to follow the balance rules that the friend of a friend should be a friend and that the enemy of a friend should be an enemy, but not that the friend of an enemy should be an enemy or that the enemy of an enemy should be a friend. In both cases, people have an *order* whereby they traverse relationships. They *first* go to the equivalent, and *then* to the nonequivalent.

At the same time, the inconsistency is real and comes from a readily identifiable source, namely the prohibition on sibling marriage. The joking/avoidance system is essentially a way of adding two types of relationships, one having to do with opposite-sexness and the other having to do with adjacent generations. In general, the idea of two negatives making a positive works quite well, not only for generations, but for same-sex siblings (that is, the opposite-sex sibling of an opposite-sex sibling is a same-sex sibling). The problem is that these two cannot be wedded without some unmooring. This is not simply because one's opposite sex sibling's grandfather is one's own grandfather, but more fundamentally, because siblings are both similar (vis-à-vis common descent) and different (vis-à-vis prohibition on incestuous unions).

Put somewhat differently, in contrast to the simple incest taboo on all nuclear family relations, which may be seen as simply saying "all these people are too much like you," joking/avoidance systems attempt to use these taboos to determine a new sense of equivalence and hence a positive determination of marriage partners without recourse to marriage classes. Let us make the conventional distinction between "affines" (those related to one through marriage) and "cognates" (those related to one via common descent). The joking system thus introduces a notion of equivalence-as-affines that cuts across the notion of equivalence-as-cognate used in the kinship structure.[26] Indeed, in many systems it is clear that the important relationship is not so much equivalence with one's self as it is equivalence with one's *spouse* (e.g., see the Mossi case discussed by Hammond 1964: 262). In such cases, siblings of one's spouse are considered potential marriage partners (as second wives or replacement husbands), and sexual banter (in some cases sexual contact during carnival-like festivals) is appropriate (for example, the North Mexican Tarahumara [Kennedy 1970: 38]).

Similarly, in such groups we are also likely to see a subjective heuristic emphasizing the equivalence of same-sex siblings.[27] The wife's sister and the brother's wife are both seen as potential wives. The Cheyenne say, "The sister-in-law is like a wife" (Eggan 1970 [1955]: 57, 78f), and indeed may be taken as a second wife in a few cases, as a man may marry his brother's widow. Thus the chain of equivalences (spouse and same-sex sibling) point to potential spouses. You may also compete freely with these partners, leading to the playful—but often violent—joking behavior between brothers-in-law (see Kennedy 1970).[28]

The taboo on brother-sister incest, when coupled with the idea that marriage connects equivalents, makes it a natural conclusion that this relationship is one of antiequivalence. But the idea of alternating generations—that one jokes with grandparents and grandchildren but not parents, children, great-grandparents or great-grandchildren—is also reasonably widespread.[29] Thus it is not surprising that people repeatedly come up with the idea of antiequivalence: that is, the principle that two wrongs make a right, or that $-1 \times \times 1 = +1$.

[26] Viveiros de Castro (1998: 347, 360f) has emphasized the ambiguity of relationships to opposite-sex kin in systems that emphasize the affine/cognate bifurcation and has a beautiful discussion of different ways of conceiving of the logical relations between equivalence and antiequivalence.

[27] See note 24 on the equivalence of siblings in Cheyenne and Arapaho systems. In contrast, kinship systems that divide people into opposing categories but emphasize a connection between the cross-sex siblings, such as the Palauan studied by Smith (1983: 4f, 74f, 86, 312), do not lead to the joking system, even though there may be a principle of generational equivalence. In this case, the crucial concatenation of relationships happens by linking a cross-sex siblingship with a marriage (e.g., male ego, ego's sister, ego's sister's husband).

[28] In other societies which do not equate coaffines (those who have married into lineages into which one has married) and cognates, joking and avoidance relationships may simply map on to affines and cognates respectively. Thus among the Yanomamö, says Chagnon (1968b: 58f, 66), a man jokes with his brothers-in-law but treats cognates of his age with coolness, because the former are allies, while the latter are competitors (and indeed, the most enmity occurs between those who are classificatory cognates). This may be seen as one relaxation of the well-defined joking relationship of the G/wi (to emphasize the cognate/affine distinction); the other is to simply emphasize the generational classes, which is also common.

[29] A good example here is the Juang of central India, who divide all people into cognates (*kutumb*) and potential marriage partners (*bondhu*) (see Parkin 1993). Basically, all cognates are "avoidance" partners, though the degree of avoidance is not always very high. The principal of alternating generations then divides the *bondhu* into joking and avoidance partners, with the former potential spouses and the latter not.

The G/wi system is an unusually detailed version of a more widespread attempt to use logic to systematize relations of sameness and difference (for another example, see Marshall [1957] on the !Kung). In many kinship systems where we see a division into joking and avoidance partners we find that marriage, rather than being a relationship of equivalence, indicates antiequivalence. Here the logic is applied to the family or lineage, and not the individual. Others are divided up into "those I may marry" as opposed to "those I may not marry." One may not marry cognates, but one also may not marry those who have married those whom your family has married (coaffines).[30] An example here includes the Cheyenne, who also have institutionalized joking/avoidance relations. The same term is used for spouse's siblings and sibling's spouse (akin to our "brother/sister in law"), but the spouses of the spouses' siblings are treated as siblings (Eggan 1970 [1955]: 42ff).[31]

In sum, we have seen examples of people systematizing the relationships of equivalence and antiequivalence. In some cases such as the G/wi, this bifurcation is expressed in rules nearly akin to those of balance theory. Despite this, we do not see the structures that seem dual to these heuristics arising; the subjective understanding is not architectonic—compatible with structure.[32] I have stressed that this is because of the order in which heuristics are applied as people carry out their tasks at hand. Each ego can think from his or her own perspective without needing to see from the top down; each ego can compile a division of the population without these divisions needing to be compatible with one another.

Significantly, nearly all societies with exclusive divisions based on joking and avoidance relationships tend to have bilateral reckoning of descent—that is, they pay attention both to father's and mother's bloodlines.[33] As we shall see in chapter 5, while unilineal descent naturally leads people to conceive of

---

[30] Interestingly, Wikmunkan joking relationships seem to be based on the same structure—a division into kinsmen and affines—but reverse the polarity, as one jokes with those who do *not* give one wives and avoids those who do (Jackes 1969).

[31] This is a special case of the more general arrangement that Houseman and White (1998a, 1988b) call "sidedness." See their wonderful treatment for an exposition of such structures that are clear from the point of view of any ego but do not lead to classes. This sort of arrangement is also generally implied by Dravidian kinship systems that distinguish between parallel and cross relatives, identifying these with cognates and affines respectively (Ives 1998: 99).

[32] As Bo Anderson (1979) has argued, in the balance theoretic tradition there was too much attention to formal properties of graphs and not enough attention to human action (also see Opp 1984: 38; Doreian 2002; Hummon and Doreian 2003: 20). An exemplary attempt to disentangle different types of intransitivity, and predict which forms would be psychologically unpleasant and hence more unstable, was carried out by Hallinan and Hutchins (1980).

[33] Where there is unilineal descent, as among the Kiga of Rwanda studied by Freedman (1977), joking is likely to take place with the clan that gives one one's spouse, but not with all other clans, leading to selective joking but not the same bifurcated structure. Thus people here all agree as to the classes of equivalents (the clans), but do not make a bifurcation.

their relations in terms compatible with nested equivalence classes (for my cousin's cousin is my cousin), bilateral kinship does not. My cousin's cousin may be my second-cousin. Each person has a view of the social structure that is related to, but not reducible to, the views of all others. As a result, each person can use a logic that implies a division of all others into two classes without there being any two classes on which all can agree. Indeed, were this possible, there would be little reason for the subjective heuristics required by joking and avoidance relationships.

Thus we have seen two ways in which equivalence and antiequivalence may be systematized. There is the simple architectonic solution of cliques; within a clique all are equivalent, and across cliques there are no relations at all. If we assume hostility between all, we have the puzzle of whether to consider my enemy's friend my friend or my enemy, and the need for strategic thinking. But strategic thinking is famously incompatible with simple structures (Bourdieu 1977). The strategic actor cannot have her hands tied by "logic" or "rules," and the agonistically oriented strategist will often seek to frustrate those who attempt to predict her action by doing the opposite of what these others expect.

It is possible, however, for people to begin with relations of both equivalence and antiequivalence, as long as they use these relations not in an architectonic sense but in a "local" or ego-centered sense. Equivalence ripples through the population but does not lead to the emergence of stable cliques—that sort of rampant mechanical solidarity that some of the anthropologists imagined would destroy the larger society. There is another way to think about equivalence and antiequivalence without destroying society, and this is to moderate the transitivity; we close this section with an examination of the best known case.

The Transitivity of Contagion

Here we can consider the avoidance categories of the ancient Israelites codified in Leviticus 18 (ego, the recipient of the command, is assumed to be male). The transitive logic is explicit: "You shall not uncover the nakedness of your father, which is the nakedness of your mother; she is your mother, you shall not uncover her nakedness. You shall not uncover the nakedness of your father's wife; it is your father's nakedness. You shall not uncover the nakedness of your sister, the daughter of your father or the daughter of your mother, whether born at home or born abroad. You shall not uncover the nakedness of your son's daughter or of your daughter's daughter, for their nakedness is your own nakedness. You shall not uncover the nakedness of your father's wife's daughter, begotten by your father, since she is your sister. You shall not uncover the nakedness of your father's near kinswoman; she is your father's near kinswoman. You shall not uncover the nakedness of your mother's sister; she is your mother's near kinswoman. You shall not uncover the nakedness of your father's brother, that is, you shall not approach his wife; she is your aunt. You shall not uncover the nakedness of your daughter-in-law; she is your son's wife, you shall not uncover her nakedness. You shall not uncover the nakedness of your brother's wife; she is your brother's nakedness"[34] (further limitations on uncovering nakedness follow, but they are not about ego's kin but about the kin of the naked in question).

So we see here that starting with the essential taboo on uncovering the mother's nakedness, the father and other husbands of the mother are considered equivalent (as least for purposes of assessing nakedness-quality) with her and hence taboo. We can consider "mother" to be a many-to-one function of ego M(ego); because we always look from the perspective of some ego, we can more simply denote M(ego) $= M$. If we now denote spouse as a function $S()$, $S(M)$ denotes the spouse of the mother; according to Leviticus $S(M) \equiv M$ and hence S is an identity relation in that it does not change the avoidance status of a person. Consistently, we find $S(S(M)) = S(M) = M$ with the prohibition on the father's wife.

To continue, since the sister (or half-sister, as emphasized in the sentence after the next) is the daughter of either father or mother, she also falls into the avoidance category. (So if $C = M^{-1}$ denotes the relation child, $C(M) \equiv M$ and $C(S(M)) = C(M) = M$.) We know that there is a taboo on relationships with children, for it is the inverse of the taboo on relationships with parents. We also find the children's children taboo because of their relation to ego through their parents ($C(C(M)) = C(M) = M$ and $C(S(S(M))) = C(S(M)) = M$. From there, kinswomen of one's father are ruled out, and then mother's sister ($C(M(M)) = M(M) = M$), the relation "sister" establishing equivalence with the mother. Since the father is equivalent to his brother, the father's brother's wife is off limits (or if B=brother, $S(B(S(M))) = S(C(M((S(M))))) = S(C(M(M))) = S(C(M)) = S(M) = M$; similarly, since children are off limits, the son's wife is off limits ($S(C) = C$). Denoting males as triangles, females as circles, marriages as double horizontal lines, descent as a vertical line, and siblingship as a single horizontal line, and making ego the recognizable male, this translates to the following prohibitions, where a female "no" sign indicates one whose nakedness ego is forbidden to uncover (figure 2.11).

These prohibitions work on a transitive contagion logic—if you are to avoid uncovering your mother's nakedness, then also avoid uncovering her daughter's or her sister's nakedness.[35] If you avoid your daughter's nakedness, avoid your daughter's daughter's nakedness. But there is an inherent problem to the

[34] RSV Lev 18: 1–17.

[35] Now certain categories are not mentioned here, for example, the mother's brother's daughter's nakedness, but almost certainly because these are considered too far away to be worthy of discussion, not because of a preferential logic.

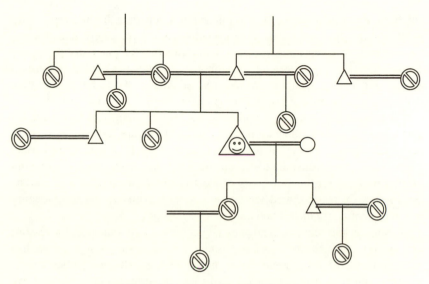

Figure 2.11. Contagion of equivalence

logic of these relationships, and this is that like all forms of logic, it tends to go too far. The problem of transitivity, then, is that the heuristic dual to some set of relationships may, if taken seriously, have perverse results whereby we must establish relationships with those with whom we would prefer not to, or with those who will refuse to establish relationships with us. In the case of Leviticus, where the relationship is "forbidden union," we might find ourselves successively eliminating one potential partner after another.

But actually, this system of prohibitions does not explode, since the taboos die out in practice as one gets a few relationships past ego. That is, while I called the relations implicit in the account of Leviticus "equivalence," it is understood that they do not concatenate forever without attenuation. Although one's mother's daughter is prohibited because there is a sense that the naked-ness of children is the same as the nakedness of their parents, this does not imply that one's mother's mother's daughter's daughter is necessarily prohib-ited, even though we could use similar substitution to derive this.[36] And this is because although your mother's sister's *nakedness* is your mother's nakedness, your mother's sister isn't your mother. We know this because you are not prohibited from your mother's sister's daughter's nakedness in the way that you are your mother's daughter's nakedness.

But if kinship is understood in terms of a set of qualitative classes with equivalences, so that all persons are in a fixed number of classes and any

---

[36] $C(C(M(M)))) = C(M(M))) = M(M) = M$.

person is equivalent to one of your near kin, even such limited transitivity would instantly make for a nation of bachelors. Not surprisingly, it is in societies in which such repeating kin classes are fundamental—and, just as significantly, often where possessing of a common name indicates not only a spiritual identity, but a fundamental *social* identity—avoidance has to be antitransitive to prevent all potential marriage partners from being avoidance partners.[37]

It is not that avoidance in Leviticus is transitive; rather, it is that while for the G/wi, avoidance is about *unlikeness* and two unlikenesses can make a likeness (while two likenesses also make a likeness), for Leviticus, there is only likeness, and one avoids the like. Thus here we start from ego and move out locally, allowing for the transitivity of identity to fade away eventually. In the G/wi system (as reconstituted here), however, there is no attenuation of identity and anti-identity, no matter how far from ego we go.

In sum, kinship relations tend to establish ideas of equivalence; for reasons that are still debated, there is a near-universal human tendency to establish relations of marriage preferentially to those who are different in at least some respects. But this does not always lead to a structure of classes (which we examine in the next chapter). When relations of equivalence are emphasized in the absence of classes, there is a fork in the road. One fork takes us down the road to Leviticus: one cannot marry the like; the relations of likeness are transitive but attenuate rather quickly and hence lead to strong local prohibitions but little overall structure. The other fork takes us to joking-avoidance structures: here one must marry the like; the relations of unlikeness concatenate eternally without any attenuation in strength, but they must be antitransitive so that there are some possible marriage partners uncontaminated with the sacred.

This antitransitivity seems, at first blush, to imply the formation of large-scale structure—a bifurcation along the lines of balance theory. But this is not at all what we have found; indeed, it is the *absence* of such a bifurcation, despite the general equation of cognates with coaffines, that seems to lead to the joking system itself. This case then casts light on the questions posed in the first chapter pertaining to the relationship between heuristics, small structures, and big structures. Without the benefit of close empirical examination, it would seem obvious on a priori grounds that persons holding certain heuristics will produce the analogous structures, and these structures will be indiffer-

[37] An example here is the !Kung, among whom a man may not marry a woman with the name of a prohibited female relative such as mother, sister, daughter, mother-in-law, etc. (see Lee 1972: 356f). Interestingly, among the Tikopia, siblings are distinguished not as male and female (as in our "brother" and "sister" but as "same sex as me" and "other sex," and these distinctions—with their implicit avoidances—transferred to their children, but not their grandchildren, leading Firth (1963 [1936]: 229) to comment that "there is thus a mechanism inherent in the kinship system for the continual conversion of certain restrained into free relationships."

ent to scale. Balance is balance. But instead we find that these heuristics are applied in a certain order to relatively local problems, and even here, do not produce a particular structure. Local structures do not seem to arise from subjective ways of putting together relationships; if anything, the reverse is true.

Triads and the Tribulations of Transitivity

We have seen that balance theory implied the bifurcation of interactants into two groups. Despite a fondness for bifurcations on the part of the species, and indeed a tendency for some societies to take a dual form (division into "moieties" or "phratries"), actual cases satisfying the original theory were few and far between. Clearly, there was something too stringent about balance theory. In part, it came from the assumption that those who are not allies are enemies— and those who *had* enemies were least likely to follow the ascribed heuristics. Perhaps the biggest breakthrough in balance theory came largely as a result of an indirect change due to computerization—more and more of mathematical psychology and sociology was conducted in matrix notation (as opposed to graph theory). While it takes a bit of cognitive flexibility to conceive of "a" graph that is not connected (or has two separate components), matrices are full of zeros and no one thinks twice about it. Thus people tended more and more to allow for indifference (relations that were neither positive nor negative) and for "unconnected" graphs. Researchers stopped thinking about their relations as (+1/-1), and thought of them as either present or absent (1/0).

This change in turn facilitated a focus on the transitivity of ties, as opposed to balance.[38] We saw that the clearest examples of relationships that highlight mutuality, friendship, and alliance imply some sort of equivalence between the parties involved. Equivalence is an inherently transitive thing: if $A = B$ and $B = C$, we know that $A = C$. (Recall that a relation R is transitive if whenever aRb and bRc, aRc). Balance may be understood as an extremely strong type of transitivity—so strong it is not realistic as a description of social formations. In Kurt Vonnegut's wacky novel *Cat's Cradle*, a scientist forms a variety of

---

[38] See for example Harary and Kommel's (1979) formulation of indices of the total degree of transitivity for −1, 0, 1 relational graphs. In addition to the mathematical elegance, there were good reasons to focus on transitivity coming from theories of cognitive development. Piaget privileged transitivity as a key element in deriving a mature and scientific understanding of the relationships inherent in the physical world. In an extremely important piece of research, Leinhardt (1972) analyzed children's groups across a number of grades to see whether (as Piagetians might expect) there was an increase in the tendency for choices to be transitive over time. There is, in fact, evidence of such an increase, although it is not necessarily continuous (he found jumps in transitivity at the kindergarten as opposed to prekindergarten level and at grade 5 as opposed to 4 for boys). But Leinhardt realized that some of this change might be due not to a more developed cognitive sense of transitive implications, but to the vertical differentiation of children—there would be a tendency toward transitivity simply arising from some children being more popular than others (Leinhardt 1972: 210).

ice that has a freezing point considerably above room temperature. It also has the property of transitivity: if it comes in contact with regular water, it transforms this substance into the liquid form of itself, and hence it freezes. Consequently, dropping a single piece of this ice into a stream leads, willy-nilly, to the stream freezing, the river into which it flows freezing, all other streams flowing into this river freezing, the ocean into which the river empties freezing, all oceans freezing, all rivers freezing, and then all naturally occurring water freezing. Strong transitivity in social relations is similar: were it to exist (and thank goodness, like Vonnegut's ice, it does not), it would instantly ripple through social networks and destroy society.

But could there be a weaker form of transitivity inherent in relationships such as friendship, one that might not lead to the complete bifurcation of balance theory, but still toward separate clusters? As we shall see, as researchers progressively tried to weaken the strong sense of transitivity inherent in balance theory, so as to better describe actual data, they found themselves abandoning the premise that the relationships they were learning about were horizontal relationships of equivalence. Instead—I suppose saying they were dragged kicking and screaming is an overstatement, but certainly this was not a planned result—they formulated models of an intrinsically hierarchical world. Every step toward more accurate description inexorably involved the introduction of more inequality.

Davis (1967) began by suggesting a relaxation that allowed for multiple cliques between which there were no relations (as opposed to hostile relations). These new type of cliques he called "clusters," which correspond somewhat better to the common-sense understanding of cliques. (These are identical to Watts's [1999: 43] "cavemen" graphs discussed above.) What is important is that thinking in terms of transitivity for binary relations (0/1) allowed for more than two clumps, since there were only friends, and no enemies.[39] Only one rule was maintained, namely, my friend's friend is my friend. If friendship is considered intrinsically symmetric, as is necessarily the case for clique formation, the individuals split into a set of cliques among whom there are wholly loving relations and between whom there is total indifference.

The researchers pursuing the nature of these clusters (especially Holland, Leinhardt, and Davis) realized that the structural implications could be studied on the triadic level: a classic balance structure (in which 0 could be treated as −1) would arise if for any three persons, either two were connected by

---

[39] It is eminently possible to derive clusters from signed graphs, as do Hage and Harary (1983) (in particular, see their interesting application to Young's data on food-giving friendships and enmities, 4). In this case, one can generalize to "colorings" of signed graphs, given the key theorem that absence of any cycle with one and only one negative line allows for the graph to be divided up into a number of clusters such that all intercolor ties are negative or null, and all intracolor ties are positive or null. I simply follow the historical progression here.

mutual ties and the third was not, or all three were connected by mutual ties. A cluster model (one that allowed more than two cliques) would also allow for triads in which no persons were connected by ties.

Both the cluster and the clique model rule out asymmetric relations, since if two people are in the same clique or cluster, each will choose the other. Yet respondents asked to name their friends often produced asymmetric data. That is, just because A "likes" or "chooses" B there is no reason to assume that B likes or chooses A. Now it must be emphasized that we are here talking about *relations* and not necessary *relationships*, that is, patterns of interaction. Yet the results reached by a study of these relations can inform the study of relationships. The cluster model simply was wrong for relations of choice, so how could the actual structure of these relations be portrayed?

To account for the asymmetric relations, researchers then proposed the "ranked clusters" model. In this model, there are still cliques or clusters, but it is possible for members of one cluster to try to form relations with those of a "higher" cluster (thus the clusters can be ranked). *Within* a cluster, all relations are mutual; *between* clusters relations are either not present (if the clusters are of equivalent rank), or are asymmetric (if one cluster is of higher rank than the other). The following diagram (figure 2.12, after Davis and Leinhardt 1972) indicates an example of the structure proposed: within a clique, all relations are mutual. Between cliques on the same level, there are no ties (hence no one from clique 2 chooses anyone from clique 3, or vice versa; this also holds for cliques 4 and 5). The double arrows indicate that this relation connects all members of one clique to all members of another clique. Members of cliques are still equivalent to one another. But their equality in large part comes from their *inequality* vis-à-vis the larger group. The population itself is fundamentally structured by inequality.

This understanding implied that the law of transitivity would hold for all relations. But because it was assumed that members of a "lower" cluster would always attempt to form relations with those of a higher cluster, one should not see triads with a single asymmetric relation and two null relations. That is, let the single asymmetric relation connect a to b. Since there is no relation between a and c, a and c must be in different cliques, neither of which is "better" than the other. The same logic must hold for b and c. But by equivalence, this would imply that a and b belong to cliques at the same "level," in which case there should be no asymmetric relation between the two.

Unfortunately for the model, triads with one and only one asymmetric relation are in fact very common—in certain environments (Holland and Leinhardt 1970). Most of the sociometric data available come from children choosing which other children they would like to interact with (sit next to, etc.). Where boys and girls are in the same classroom, and the data are pooled, these triads with a single choice tend to abound. This is because, as Leinhardt (1968) had earlier pointed out, there is a tendency for boys and girls to form indepen-

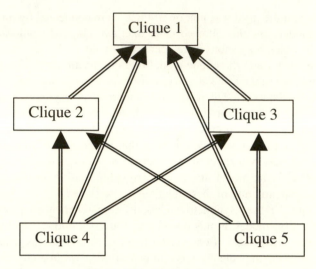

Figure 2.12. Ranked clusters

dent hierarchies (Davis 1979: 56). Permitting these triads still leads to a specification in which the relation in question is transitive: any triads compatible with transitivity are allowed. This resulting class of structures (which Holland and Leinhardt [1971] called "t-graphs") not only includes the ranked clusters model as a special case, but all the other models we have examined in this section.

It is worth remembering that we have followed analysts in examining *relations* that are not necessarily translated into relationships of actual interaction. If indeed it "takes two to tango," then it might well be that the asymmetric between-clique relations are unlikely to translate into patterns of interaction. All interaction will take place among within-clique subsets (and note that it is not necessarily the case that all members of the clique ever interact as part of a group).

Thus if we are interested in patterns of interaction, we may actually see symmetric (mutual) relations as being a wholly different type of beast from asymmetric relations—the former are an equivalence relation that partition the members into sets of possible interactants, while the latter express relations of longing that indicate the relative popularity of the cliques.[40] The "transitivity" of the graph, then, breaks down into two types of transitivity—the transitivity of a mutual relation that leads to clumping, and the transitivity of antisymmetric relations that leads to what we will call a "popularity tournament," namely

[40] Interestingly, early on Heider (1946; 1958: 183, 200–202) emphasized the important distinction between mutual relations of equivalence ("unit") and asymmetric relations of "liking."

the vertical differentiation of previously undifferentiated persons on the basis of the sociometric choice of other persons.[41]

The final relaxation to the t-graph model was made by Johnsen (1985), who started with the anomalous presence of forbidden triads with two mutual relations and one asymmetric. These triads had frustrated Davis (1979) because they violate the fundamental transitivity of equivalence. That is, we find that A seems equivalent to B (since they have a mutual relation), and B equivalent to C, but while A chooses C, C does not reciprocate. Johnsen showed that such triads arise because although there is a tendency toward cliquing in these structures, one cannot equate the equivalence relation leading to cliques with mutual choices. Although we can still define cliques in terms of their relations with one another, we must now allow for nonmutual relations within cliques.

To some extent, we have rediscovered something we already stumbled across when we first considered strong friendships. These friendships seem to have a spatial logic, which means that while there are necessarily *tendencies* toward transitivity, they will generally fall quite short of the *absolute* transitivity necessary to form clear structures. And this is because, although A is close to B and B close to C, A is not necessarily close to C. Then we were assuming that such relationships were mutual, at least in distinction to relationships of acquaintanceship. Now we find that relationships stronger than those of acquaintance also fall short of true mutuality, and again have more of a spatial logic than one of strict transitivity.

Let us imagine that people are to some degree rankable, that they know one another's rank, and that those of higher rank are more attractive as friends. Let us also assume that people will tend to reciprocate choices unless the person offering them the choice is too far below them in rank. In this case, we will see these anomalous triads. Imagine that in rank C is highest, then B and then A. A will choose B and C, and B will choose C. B will reciprocate A's choice, and C will reciprocate B's choice, but C will not reciprocate A's choice–A is too far below C to merit such attention. Thus the problematic triad emerges.[42]

In sum, we have traced the evolution of an understanding of structural tendencies that began looking at balance, a structural tendency assumed to flow

---

[41] Because of their paramount focus on individual-level transitivity, the simple model in which the cliques formed a single linear order (in which all cliques can be ranked on a single dimension such that given any two different cliques A and B, we may say A < B or A < B) was not originally considered. But Holland and Leinhardt (1971: 115) did note that if null relations are prohibited, then the graph must form a quasi series, in which the cliques are ordered (as opposed to partially ordered). This may also be seen as a popularity tournament in which people only reciprocate to (and probably only interact with) their exact equivalents; it may hence be seen as a linear ordering with a tendency toward equivalence. It is worth noting (as we will examine such structures in the next chapter) that there is no evidence of such a structure emerging in social data.

[42] Further exploration (e.g., Eder and Hallinan 1978: 242, 244f, though see Lubbers 2003) also suggests that girls have a stronger tendency to form isolated dyads than do boys, and this affects the evolution of the network as a whole.

from the nature of equivalence, and was progressively forced to make room for more and more asymmetry and ranking. This increased focus on asymmetry and ranking came, as is clear in retrospect, from the reliance on questionnaire data on "choices" of favored others (e.g., with whom would you like to sit?). The relation of the resulting data to interaction is not immediately clear. But if there is in some case at hand a hierarchical structure of persons in terms of their "attractiveness," it would be difficult to analyze interaction patterns without an understanding of this hierarchical structure. Indeed, this might be a good place to begin our investigation of intrinsically antisymmetric relationships. We will briefly look at the popularity tournament and in the next chapter continue examining the tensions between equality and inequality.

Popularity Tournament

As we have seen, simply asking "whom would you choose among the other group members to do X with?" can induce a vertical differentiation among otherwise undifferentiated persons, as some group members are more frequently chosen. The simplest measure of the vertical position of any person is the number of choices received, also known as the "in-degree" of the graph of the network in question (because it is the degree of arrows pointing "in" to that node). If we wanted to determine each person's overall attractiveness, we could standardize this by dividing by the total number of choices or something like that, but there is a complication due to patterns of nonreciprocation. We might imagine two people, each with an in-degree of four. The first reciprocates all four of her choices (and makes no other choices, having an "out-degree" of four), while the second only has an out-degree of one. If, as is generally the case, we interpret the process of choosing and being chosen as a latently agonistic one, in which one's status position is higher when one is chosen by others but does not choose them in return, we might see the vertical position of the second as higher than that of the first (also see the discussion of Coleman 1960: 86).

We shall not re-create the evolution of methods of disentangling the various aspects of such graphs, since the solution proposed by Holland and Leinhardt (1981) is so immediately interpretable and elegant. Since this model will be used to analyze data in the next chapter, we might as well introduce it here in a technically accurate form. The probability of person i choosing person j (as opposed to not choosing) can be seen as a function of three quantities: the "expansiveness" of person i (how likely person i is to choose others in general), the "attractiveness" of person j (how likely person j is to attract those choices which are made), and the tendency toward reciprocity in this group.[43] This

---

[43] If we denote a choice from i to j as $x_{ij} = 1$ with $x_{ij} = 0$ if the choice is not made, and we call the expansiveness of person i α_i, the attractiveness of person j β_j, and the tendency to mutuality ρ, we may write this model as follows:

$$\ln (\Pr[x_{ij} = 1] / \Pr [x_{ij} = 0]) = \alpha_i + \beta_j + \rho x_{ji}$$

"attractiveness" can be seen as akin to a location in a one-dimensional space that is oriented vertically.

Now if the value for each person's "attractiveness" references an intrinsic property of that person, the resulting structure is rather easy to explain, yet sociological analyses have almost never been able to defend such a simple interpretation. Instead, there is a recurrent sense that there is no attractiveness outside of the pattern of choices itself. The pattern of choosing generates the inequality as much as if not more than some inequality generates the pattern of choosing. Each person's attractiveness or, more generally, status in some hierarchy, must be considered an endogenous result of the tournament itself.

If so, there is a delicious instability to such processes, for they follow Merton's (1968) "Matthew Effect," namely, that to them who have more shall be given. Each additional choice person j garners increases his or her attractiveness, and thus increases the pressures on others to choose j. This logic was laid out for the case of heterosexual dating in college campuses by Willard Waller (1937: especially 730). Waller argued that for women, at least, the most important factor determining desirability as a date was popularity, "for the girl's prestige depends upon dating more than anything else; here as nowhere else nothing succeeds like success. Therefore the clever coed contrives to give the impression of being much sought after even if she is not." Thus if a woman successfully gave the impression of being sought-after as a date, this would jump-start the actual process of being asked on dates, and would then be (to take another of Merton's famous phrases), a self-fulfilling prophecy.

In other words, a popularity tournament in this substantively important sense is more than simply the variance in degree that arises when we relax the assumption that all choices must be reciprocated. It is a particular social dynamic that arises in situations where two important conditions hold. The first is that each person has some information about the popularity of others. This condition of publicity is not given sufficient attention: in many of the most familiar examples of the popularity tournament, such as generic (friendship) popularity among children, it is simply assumed, and not always for very good reason, that such perceptions of popularity are widespread and accurate on the part of the children. (For evidence supporting such social knowledge of rank among school children, see Ausubel, Schiff, and Gasser 1952). In other cases, there are specific institutional structures to distribute such knowledge. The sociology

---

In many cases the data gathering instrument is such that α_i is some constant c for all i (such as when people are asked to give three choices). If $\beta_j = \beta$ for all j, there is no vertical differentiation, and we have a simple web type structure. If $\rho = 0$, there is no tendency toward reciprocity, and this is a pure popularity tournament. If $\alpha_i = -\beta_j$ and $\rho=0$, we have a model for a ranking process that will be described in chapter 4. It will be noted that the ρ parameter captures some horizontal tendencies (tendencies toward mutualism and therefore equality), while the other parameters capture vertical differentiation.

of science quantifies the number of references made to any article as an indicator of that article's dominance in its field; in a wonderful bit of reflexivity, these procedures can now be used to deny tenure or promotion to sociologists for writing articles that are too dull to cite (perhaps including ones involving analyses of meticulous counts of citations to *other* scientists' papers).

The second condition for a popularity tournament to arise is that any additional choice received by a person increases that person's attractiveness. Popular children are more desirable as friends than nonpopular children (for whatever reason). If possible, a child will tend to drop a friendship with a nonpopular child and initiate one with a popular child.[44] One needs to cite frequently cited articles to avoid seeming ignorant (see Latour 1987 for a charming exposition of the logic of citation), although one can afford to ignore those that are ignored by others.[45]

Given these conditions, the popularity tournament tends to increase any preexisting differentiation. Further, there need be no preexisting differentiation at all for a final state to be reached with high differentiation, so long as each person revises his or her choices on the basis of the current popularity of each other person (i.e., A's estimate of B's "attractiveness" is a function of the choices currently received by B from all other persons: see Orléan 1988, 110; Gould 2002). In other words, if there is a good reason for actors to be oriented to one another's choices, then there is a strong probability of increasing vertical differentiation of the objects of their choices. Even if the initial choice received by B is a mistake, B is now more attractive and likely to get more choices.

We have seen the conditions that lead to a popularity tournament, but why on earth would people modify their preferences in such a fashion? We can understand why such modification might take place when people are choosing objects that they can later alienate (especially sell). This type of action is usually called "speculation," because people are not actually concerned with the popularity of this object when they buy it, but with its future popularity.[46] Unfortunately, they usually take current popularity as a good indicator of future popularity, and since people tend to have a limited ability to foresee anything

[44] Because there may be reasons for participants in the popularity tournament to have a certain number of relationships, they may not drop all relations with the unpopular.

[45] There certainly may be some persons who play popularity tournaments in a contrarian manner, choosing what is unpopular and dropping choices to items or persons that turn out to be popular. The presence of such contrarians leads to a tendency toward equalization, and such contrarianism is probably found in cultural fields in which certain aficionados are unable to enjoy anything that turns out to be popular (cf. Bourdieu 1984 [1979]). Interestingly, there are few good examples of such contrarianism for popularity tournaments in which it is other persons, and not objects chosen by other persons, that are being vertically differentiated. As Gould (2002: 1149f) suggests, the "contrary" choices that serve to put a brake on the feedback of popularity probably come from (1) the decreased availability of the popular and (2) the tendency toward reciprocity.

[46] More exactly, they are concerned with the change in the popularity of one thing relative to the change in the popularity of *other* things.

but steady increases or decreases in popularity over time, there is a tendency for purely speculative action to have feedback to a destabilizing extent, for example, in the famous tulip craze in Holland in the early seventeenth century (see the account of Mackay 1852).

But in other cases, it is possible for some of the popularity of the object to accrue to the possessor without the possessor alienating it. In such cases, the object is generally known as a "status symbol." (According to Veblen [1912: 128ff], it is necessary also that these objects be acquired only at considerable expense, but this is more or less the same as saying that they are in great demand.) Something similar can inspire persons to participate in a popularity tournament—their own status depends on their ability to establish ties with others. It is interesting that this understanding of the reason for enthusiastically taking part in the popularity tournament has been a consistent plank in the sociological understanding of heterosexual pairing, from the analyses of Waller (1937) discussed above to Rubin (1985). That is, for a male, "going with" a popular female increases the popularity of the male in question; for a female, "going with" a popular male increases the popularity of the female in question. For homosexual pairing, the idea is analogous but formally closer to the traditional (one-class) popularity tournament.

One may analyze this as a two-sided matching game (here see Roth and Sotomayor 1990): this is the sort of open-air choice situation in which persons try to get the "best" match they can in vertically ranked others, given that they are vertically rankable themselves. Such a situation is generally handled through trial and error—multiple iterations known as "dating" when it comes to heterosexual pairing—though there is a famous matching system of medical students and hospitals for residency that is accomplished through a single-iteration game. Such two-sided matching can lead to what is known as a Nash equilibrium—no one person has any good reason to change given that all others do not change (see Mortensen 1988). This does not mean that no one could be happier, nor that all matches are equal (one of the two parties may consistently get a better deal than the other, since equal rank does not imply equal value), but it is still a stable outcome. Emphasis on the stability of this outcome, however, can be misleading, for it leads us to assume that the choice process has solved the problem of inequality. Instead, as we have seen, it may generate it.

Logics of Mutual or Would-Be Mutual Relationships

Mutual relationships such as alliance or close friendship seem the perfect building blocks for large structure. The nature of the relationship is such as to clearly imply a set of subjective heuristics associated with equivalence—your friends are my friends, your enemies are my enemies. This implies a form of transitivity that leads to equivalence classes. And indeed, aggregating these classes should lead to larger and larger clumps. It would seem quite plausible that large-scale social structures would form through such an agglomerative process—different "tribes," say, forming alliances, and then alliances emerging between these first alliances, and so on.

But we have found inherent limits to such agglomeration. Transitivity cannot be maintained if only because we cannot keep track of thousands of close friends. Weakening transitivity leads to heuristics that are probabilistic or tendential, and not absolute. The correlative forms that sets of relationships take on are webs that lack the clarity of simple structures. Further, the vagaries of relationship formation in webs introduce differentiation and hence inequality between persons, splitting up equivalence classes into ranked orders.

Thus instead of seeing a clear path toward the formation of structure from mutual relationships, we have seen three different heuristics that can be used to guide tie formation. One (reciprocity) has to do with the level of the dyad: ego is likely to choose alter if alter chooses ego. This maintains the equality of the relationship but does not necessarily lead to larger structure. There are relationships which seem to be formed in accordance with such a heuristic. Most important, there is strong friendship, which is all about "closeness." The spatial component of the overall organization of these relationships leads to only a mild tendency toward transitivity. A second heuristic (preferential attachment) has to do with the individual level: ego is likely to choose those alters who are disproportionately chosen by others. The example here is the popularity tournament. While transitivity will arise, this is wholly a side-effect of the organization in terms of individual variability.[47] The third heuristic (transitivity) has to do with the level of the network or group. Technically we might argue that is has to do with the level of the triad, but substantively, this structural principle involves the linkage of dyads and the flow of characteristics of organization across the set of relationships. An example here is the set of acquaintances that might form a small world.

Consider the degree to which the subjective process of relationship formation can emphasize any of these heuristics—something that might run from "not at all" to "exclusive concern." We might then consider charting the analytic space in which relationships might be placed in terms of their mix of concern. Further, because there is a limit to the amount of concern one may have with the logic of relationships, if we restrict our attention to these three heuristics, we may treat them all as summing to the total degree of structural

---

[47] Boyd and Jonas (2001) demonstrate for the specific case of regular equivalence that allowing for such popularity effects does destroy the mathematical regularities of equivalence: unless there is a good reason why people stop adding relationships (their example of a relationship with a decreasing return to number of ties is the doctor-patient relation: past a certain number, doctors want no more patients), the logic of popularity—vertical differentiation—begins to replace the horizontal logic of equivalence.

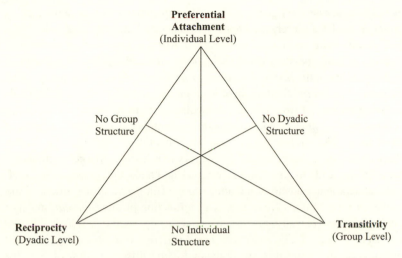

Figure 2.13. Heuristics for structure

imperative present. Consequently, we can chart the importance of these different levels of structure in figure 2.13 (here one may compare the very similar
diagram of Feld and Elmore 1982: 82). This sort of figure arises when we have
three different dimensions that cannot vary independently—maximizing the
value of any one involves minimizing the value on the others. We can imagine
lines parallel to any side and moving toward the opposing corner as indicating
values of the dimension that is "high" at that corner and "low" at the side.
Thus the side running between the points "dyadic level" and "individual level"
represents the lowest point for degree of group organization—if we were to
construct successive parallel lines moving toward the right and somewhat
downward, these would indicate higher and higher degrees of attention to transitive closure. Any position indicates a particular mix—say, $X\%$ emphasis on
reciprocity, $Y\%$ on preferential attachment and $Z\%$ on transitivity, where
$X + Y + Z = 100$.

It is worth emphasizing that in this case I do not mean in any technical sense
that increasing the tendencies toward reciprocity and/or preferential attachment would decrease the degree of measurable transitivity in any set of relationships. In fact, the reverse is true (Feld and Elmore 1982: 82). The poles of
the figure mean not "degree of" this structural principle in some group, but
"degree of concern with" this principle among a set of actors.

In part as a result of this limitation, the figure adds very little to a simple
verbal statement—to the degree that individual level structure is of paramount
importance, group level and dyadic level structure cannot be important, and so
on. This figure is placed here because similar figures will be of importance in
elucidating structure in further sections. Although there is only a rough degree

of parallelism across the figures, it is worth emphasizing that we may attach a substantive (and not merely a formal) significance to each of these poles.[48]

Let us anticipate somewhat and propose that the presence or absence of reciprocity is fundamentally about the *equality* of relationships. The degree of transitivity is about the *internal organization* of some set of relationships. And the degree of preferential attachment is about the degree to which individuals become *differentiated* from one another within the group.

It is tempting to imagine that we can draw a simple correspondence between each of these structural principles and some overall structure. For example, perhaps emphasizing equality and dyadic relations leads to markets, emphasizing transitivity leads to command hierarchies and trees, and emphasizing preferential attachment leads to dominance orders. But because the structural imperatives of relationships are in large part a function of their *content*, much of the difference between structures such as trees as opposed to orders is inherent in the nature of the relationship itself. These different principles, then, are best understood as moments that are relevant for the differentiation of possible structures *given* any particular relational content. Rather than find a direct mapping between these positions and naturally occurring social structures, we are likely to find a similarity of the trade-offs involved in concatenating different types of relationships into structures.

For an example, let us return once more to mutual relationships, which are those that by definition imply the same action profile for ego and for alter (as opposed to relationships that may or may not be reciprocated). If such mutuality is interpreted in terms of equivalence, then we conclude that your friends are my friends, and to say this is to make transitivity—particularly, triadic closure—a heuristic guiding the formation of relationships. The principle of triadic closure states that A is more likely to establish a relationship with B if B and A are both tied to some C. But this means that, all other things being *unequal*, as they always are, those alters with more ties are likely to garner further ties. (Thus if D has no friends, the law of transitive closure will not persuade A to form a tie with D no matter what.) Here the tendency toward inequality is not due to an actual tendency toward preferential attachment (all other things being equal). But the effect is, in some ways, the same—the *relationship* of equality has induced a new *relation* of inequality among persons.

What happens if they act on this new relation? It probably means that they try to establish relationships with those who already have many relationships, which pushes the structure toward a popularity tournament. Second, it proba-

---

[48] Interestingly, Bergman (1988) argues that the key algebraic forms tend to have three properties, one having to do with each element considered singularly (such as reflexivity), one having to do with pairs of elements (such as symmetry) and one having to do with triads (such as transitivity). The investigations here reach largely similar conclusions for the case of spontaneously formed social structures.

bly means that relationships are not mutual or symmetric. The popular have neither time nor inclination to befriend all of the hordes of the unpopular. The resulting set of relations will then be asymmetric or, at the extreme, antisymmetric. Thus there are different paths open for a reformulation of the fundamental structural principles guiding interaction.

One path involves an affirmation of the principle of hierarchy—a rejection of the equality implicit in mutual relationships. While analysts often mistake the existence of a mere popularity tournament for an order of domination—a "pecking order"—there is indeed an affinity between the two, since one way of dealing with the destabilization inherent in allowing the nonreciprocation of relations is to cement the vertical inequalities into a hierarchy. But not every vertical stratification requires an a repudiation of the principles of equality—indeed, it may be the grounds for the emergence of a new structural tendency toward equality.

Consider a hierarchy resulting from a popularity tournament in which the degree to which people want to interact with others is an increasing function of these others' position in this hierarchy. If everyone must interact with some number of people, we will find those close in rank tending to interact. (This is the result of the successful matching game discussed above.) The fact that those at the bottom wish to interact with those at the top has no observable effects. The resulting structure is easily compatible with a unidimensional "spatial" model of relations, in which position on the dimension indicates position in the hierarchy, and people choose those close to them in this space.[49] In other words, equivalence (or near-equivalence) is established in the structure of relationships, though the people remain starkly unequal.

Because of this, people may understand the inequality that arises when we allow for a nonreciprocation of relationships in terms of a "market" or at least in terms of "exchange." Of course, a matching game is not only not a market in the conventional sense, it is not even a barter market. As a result, none of the interesting properties of markets are relevant, and we gain nothing from assimilating the formation of structure to such a template. Thus if such structures are to handle the inherent inequality in the relationships, they must take a particular form. We go on to explore such "exchange" structures that *negate* this inequality, before going on and exploring those pecking orders that *enforce* inequality.

---

[49] This fact, that popularity tournaments coupled with a disinclination to interact with those far below one in status leads to matching of near equals for interaction, can easily be generalized to the case of two different groups and two different statuses. This fits the case of heterosexual pairing discussed by Waller (1937) and leads to the frequent confusion of such pairing structures with a price-making market (see Martin and George 2006). But the restrictive conditions necessary for a pure market need not be invoked when we simply see interaction follow a spatial logic induced by a popularity tournament.

3

The Preservation of Equality through Exchange Structures

Relations into Relationships

Equality and Inequality

The last chapter began with relationships of friendship and alliance that highlighted the equality, indeed equivalence, of pairs of persons. Such relationships imply a very simple structural form—the clique—and we followed analysts as they looked for this structure in everyday life. They found very, very few. In large part this had to do with *size*—the interactional demands of the clique grow exponentially with the size of the group, and hence cliques tend to be small. This in turn implies that we are unlikely to find cliques concatenating to form larger structures without some sort of change. But what sort?

We found the analysts needing to relax their expectation for cliques of mutual relationships and allow for asymmetric relations of "choices" of preferred interaction partner. Allowing for the nonreciprocation of choices tends to induce vertical differentiation among persons, as some receive more choices than others (the "popularity tournament") or do not reciprocate the choices they are given (one person *A* "chooses" another *B* as a friend while *B* does not "choose" *A* as a friend). Adding many more such dyadic relations, we find that "friendship" can no longer be understood simply as a relationship of equivalence uniting equals. Instead, it is a relationship that induces inequality—*B* is more popular than *A*.

This was our first encounter with the problem of equality—that is, the problem that certain relationships by definition require equality between the participants but may induce inequality. Yet it is also important to remember that just because there is a *relation* of inequality between *A* and *B* does not mean that there is any particular *relationship* between *A* and *B*—indeed, it may be that because *B* does not reciprocate *A*'s choice, the two never interact. Thus the existence of a popularity tournament does not itself determine what the social structure of interaction will be. But let us now assume that inequality does affect relationships and leads to asymmetry. That is, we consider relationships in which actions are performed by *A* to or for *B*, but not necessarily vice versa.

In some ways, this "solves" the problem of equality, by changing the nature of the relationship to one that is more in harmony with the relation of potential inequality between the participants. But in many cases allowing for such asymmetry also leads to a structural problem that I shall treat as the problem of *inequality.* In many cases, the natural effects of the popularity tournament—the "Matthew effect" by which "to them that have, more shall be given" (Merton 1973)—leads to an inherent instability. We wish to examine what local structures may arise that *contain* this problem. Once again, we start with the most fundamental form of an asymmetric relationship, and using empirical cases, deduce form from content.

Asymmetric Relationships

If the essential mutual relationship is alliance, the essential asymmetric one is probably donation or transfer, the action whereby A who possesses O relinquishes (alienates) this possession so that B may take charge of O. In many circumstances, this is considered a "gift" or, in the terminology of Mauss (1967 [1925]), a "prestation." Let us assume that it is understood that receiving a gift incurs an obligation to render the giver support when it is needed (Schwimmer 1973: 48). It is therefore reasonable for people to give gifts to the more powerful, as a form of social insurance.

Such conditions will lead to the same sort of positive feedback we saw in the case of popularity tournaments. The only problem is that some sorts of nonrenewable gifts will all flow eventually to the highest-ranking members of some society, and stay there to stagnate, unless there is some sort of redistribution. The increasing inequality may thus be disastrous. Further, aggregating smaller structures will only increase the problem, by increasing the intensity of the feedback effect. Consequently, or luckily, many societies have worked out ritually required forms of such redistribution, whereby the "big man" (say) gives these gifts back to people and thus increases or maintains his prestige. In other cases, rather than allowing all the goods first to accumulate and then to be redistributed (which we can consider the "two-stroke" motor of redistribution), there may be a structure that continuously keeps transfers moving in such a way that no one becomes bankrupted.

Following the anthropological tradition, I will call these "exchange" structures. The essence of such structures is that they temper the tendencies toward inequality inherent in asymmetric actions by ensuring that the difference between inflow and outflow to any person or group is relatively small over the long run. Such exchange structures, it must be emphasized, are quite different from the more familiar ones of contemporary Western market exchange, where fundamentally *different* goods are exchanged (A gives O to B and B gives Q to A). Where a specific Q is associated with some O (for example, A always votes for B and B always recommends members of A's family for jobs, and not vice versa) we do not have an asymmetric (but possibly reciprocated) relationship but an antisymmetric one; such structures will be examined in chapter 6.

The Arising of Exchange Structures

Now it is not always the case that donation relationships must be structured if inequality is not to prove ruinous. For an example, let us take the gifts given by thirty-seven Pokot herdsmen of Kenya in response to a drought as studied by Bollig (1998: data on 149). These gifts, usually a goat or sheep, were a form of help to afflicted households, and because each of the thirty-seven herdsmen was the head of a household, these transfers represent a substantively important part of life for considerably more than thirty-seven people.

In this case, the redistributive imperative is complicated by two other considerations. The first is the preexisting differentiation of the households by wealth, which affected giving practices.[1] The second is a general imperative of reciprocity that underlies much of the Pokot social structure. Put in terms of the schema introduced at the end of the previous chapter, we find that the tendency toward structure at the group level is pitted against the organization at the individual level (preexisting differentiation of persons) and organization at the dyadic level (reciprocity).

Both of these can be quantified using the model discussed in the previous chapter that breaks every asymmetric relationship between person A and person B into three parts, one having to do with characteristics of person A (in this case, does he tend to give a lot?), another having to do with characteristics of person B (does he tend to receive many gifts?), and a third having to do with the tendency of gifts to be reciprocated. (This is the Holland-Leinhardt [1981] p_1 model.) The first two sets of parameters capture individual-level structure, and the third dyadic structure. More important, the organization of individual-level parameters tells us a great deal about the likely results of the set of transfers. If a pure "charity" logic operated, the first two parts would tend to be negatively associated (as rich people would give but not get, and poor people would get but not give), and there would be no reciprocity effect. If balance was achieved by reciprocity and was indifferent to wealth, the reciprocity parameter would be positive and the others randomly distributed and nearly equal.

We can display this set of relationships as a network as in figure 3.1. Each person is placed on two dimensions, the vertical being the extent to which he was likely to give, and the horizontal being the extent to which he was likely to get. The axes are at the means of each dimension, which divides the space into four quadrants. Those who are above the mean in giving but below in getting are termed "givers"; those with reversed values are "getters"; those low on both are termed "peripheral"; while those high on both are termed

---

[1] The 27% comprising the richest group gave 44% of the gifts, while the 19% comprising the poorest gave proportionately little (9% of the gifts) and received proportionately more (28%). Yet as Bollig notes, the rich also received a fair amount of gifts (23% of all).

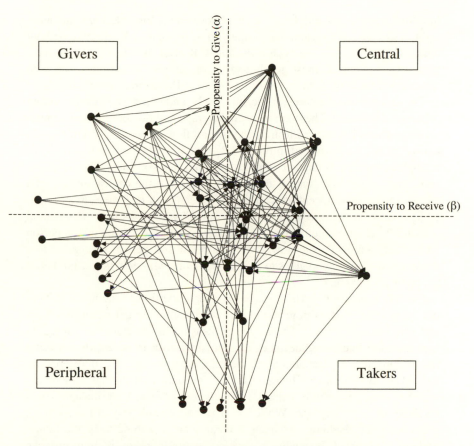

Figure 3.1. Donations among herdsmen

"central." There is a moderately large tendency toward reciprocity—the parameter is 1.15, indicating that the reciprocity observed is probably not an artifact of person qualities—which is easiest to see among the central, though it is worth emphasizing that the parameters used to determine centrality are estimated *controlling* for this tendency toward reciprocity.[2]

Interestingly, there is no correlation between the two types of person parameters.[3] If there was a negative correlation, we would have evidence of a deliberately redistributive system—there would be only givers and takers (those on the upper left and the lower right). If there was a positive correlation, we would

[2] That is, there are more reciprocations than expected simply because some people both gave and received a great many gifts.

[3] Because some people gave nothing and others received nothing, their parameter values are technically infinite. Depending on what was chosen to replace this infinite value, the overall correlation was affected, but outside of these cases, there was no relation.

have only central and peripheral players (those on the lower left and the upper right). Here we see a system that is likely to be de facto redistributive without being clearly organized in such a fashion. All must give (and the rich have more to give) but all must get as well. This allows the system to be both relatively redistributive in fact without violating the norm of reciprocity.[4]

The redistributive nature can be intuitively understood by reconstructing "chains" of transfers. These are paths in the graph that do not represent temporal connections but rather illustrate the overall flow of goats. Three randomly chosen chains are portrayed in figure 3.2.[5] One (the double-lined) consists of a single transfer, and another (the dashed line) has six links. The third (the solid line) begins with one of the more "giving" of the central actors, who gives to an even more central actor whom we can term B. B gives to a peripheral person who gives to a more central "taker" who gives to a more central person who gives to another central person who gives to a more taking person who gives back to B who now gives to a peripheral person who gives to a more central person who gives to a sink—someone who only takes, and hence the chain ends there.

Overall, we expect goods to move from the upper left to the lower right— but many others will both give and get, and presumably get when they need and give when they don't. The very vagueness of the structure can allow it to best meet the fluctuating needs of the herdsmen. But in cases where even a minor imbalance in accounts might be ruinous, there may be more pressure toward clarity of structure. Imagine, though it sounds foolish, that these herdsmen had the same level of capital, but herded elephants. Each lineage would be likely to have only one. While life may be tolerable if you have sixteen goats and your neighbor seventeen, it is quite another thing to be the family without an elephant. Inequality in such a situation is more likely to provoke extreme actions.

Still referring to figure 2.13 at the end of chapter 2, we may say that when the problem of inequality in donation arises—perhaps because the things being donated are nonsubstitutable goods—any movement toward structure can take us either toward the group-level organization (the lower right) or the dyadic (the lower left). Before treating such cases in depth, it helps to clarify what one means by exchange.

---

[4] Compare Hage and Harary's (1983: 36) analysis of a taro exchange system in Melanesia, which also finds relative egalitarianism combined with more central positions of village leaders. Schwimmer (1973: 119, 126) in the original analysis of this Taro exchange similarly found that there was little evidence of a concern with exact balance.

[5] Three edges (i,j) in the graph were chosen at random, with all edges getting equal weight. For each, starting with node j, an edge leaving j was chosen at random among all edges not already illustrated. The path stopped when that last j had no more new edges.

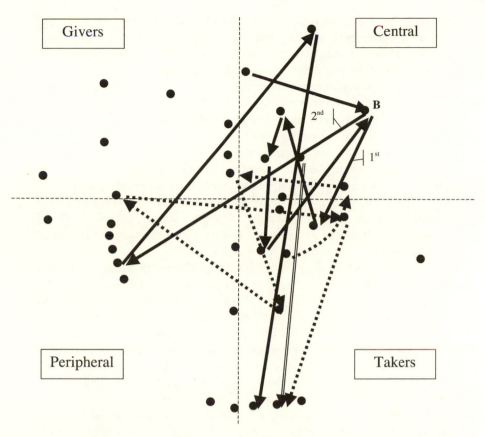

Figure 3.2. Possible chains

The Problem of Exchange

Are Exchanges Always Equal?

Let us for the moment consider the solution toward the lower left of figure 2.13, in which dyadic reciprocity is the basis for a structure. Our understanding of the structure of such dyadic exchange has been (somewhat ironically) seriously hampered by the obsessive interest with understanding social life in terms of exchange found in the social sciences. To make a long story short, there is something about capitalist society that leads many people to be easily convinced that exchange is the be all and end all of society. Consequently, there are recurrent waves of fanatical exchange theorizing, all foundering on the same ideological shoal. This is the dogma that all exchanges must be equal. To be fair, there is some analytic reason to wish for such an axiom: if it is true, it can be used to identify utilities not obvious at the start—plus, we can hope to always be able to talk our poorer neighbors out of killing us. Further, when social structures exist to *make* this true, social interaction is dramatically changed. However, the conviction that it is *always* true is perhaps the single least intelligent thing that can be said about exchange.[6]

The recurrent assumption that exchanges are always equal is particularly foolish since it does not even flow from the postulates of rational action (postulates that are indeed frequently useful, though the one thing we know about them is that they are not strictly true).[7] These postulates do not even allow us to derive the often assumed conclusion (e.g., Landé 1977a: xxvii) that for any freely made exchange, the costs cannot outweigh the benefits for either party. The costs of exchanges very frequently do outweigh the benefits to one party in a rational interaction; they simply are less than the costs entailed in *not* making an exchange. This is generally the case for exchanges between unequal parties in the absence of a true market, and we will see the importance of this in our analysis of patronage structures below.

For example, let us consider the ideal typical case in which a serf "exchanges" corvee labor for protection on the part of a lord. Of course, the "protection" supposedly provided by the lord may never actually materialize, and the serf would gladly inhabit a world with no lords at all (cf. Roemer's [1982] game theoretic analyses of different types of class relations). The "exchange" is only comprehensible when one understands that each serf must have *some* lord, and while we might imagine any serf trying to get the best lord he could "command"—itself a fanciful idea, though one that may have slight analytic value—this would simply be the best of a bad bargain.[8]

The fundamental inequality of such a relation is not a moral judgment but an important structural quality; the ability to identify such inequality is neces-

[6] It is both fascinating and deeply saddening to realize that these same mistakes were made by the supposed archenemies of the (individualist) exchange theorists, namely the (collectivist) functionalist theorists. As Gouldner (1960) has argued, they had the same incentive to find creative functions for every institution no matter how dreadful, and hence extortion structures could be similarly valorized, only the invented utility went to the group, not the victim. As a further consequence, they were led, as Gouldner emphasizes, "to neglect the *larger class of unequal exchanges*." Evidently, theoretical orientation is not as important as the desire to normalize when it comes to the direction of theorizing.

[7] See Stinchcombe (1990: 300). Generally conclusions regarding equality in exchange require additional assumptions that goods are infinitesimally divisible or that utilities are perfectly transferable across the trading partners *outside* this particular exchange. That is, if I trade a wagon for your air rifle, and your air rifle is better than my wagon, I will make it up to you in some way. Refraining from making this assumption leads to a class of noncooperative game-theoretic approaches that do not imply equality of exchange.

[8] For a pertinent example given the marriage exchanges we will explore below, Chagnon (1968a: 123) reports that weaker Yanomami groups that are forced to accept unequal exchange of women with some ally do have the option of "exit" but are reasonably afraid that their new neighbors will prove "even more exorbitant in their demands."

sarily lost when analysts attempt to demonstrate that this is still a "fair" exchange, by including the absence of the cost incurred were the exchange not made as one of the benefits of the exchange. According to this logic, the most valuable security services are "provided" by mobsters who "protect" one only against themselves.[9] There may be rational reasons to make an unequal exchange; this should not be assumed to make the exchange an equal one. One person may, for example, rationally give an object of greater value for one of lesser value if not doing so may have other consequences that may involve third parties (and not the exchange partner himself, as in the mobster scenario). For the case of marital exchange (either considered as exchange of women between groups or pairing on a mating "market"), not pairing may be equivalent to failure to reproduce; for the case of patronage relations or symbolic capital, not conducting financially ruinous exchanges may lead to a serious loss of prestige (we will see examples of this in chapter 6; also see Barth 1981: 50). To take all the situational reasons that would justify someone taking a bad bargain and to try to fold them in to the dyadic exchange itself is as ludicrous as formulating an optics of reflection that declared on axiomatic grounds that objects had to be "in the mirror."

Structure and Antistructure

We cannot, then, simply assume that if an exchange is made, we are free to declare that it must be equal. But there are ways in which exchange relationships can be patterned that tend to produce this equality as a result. One sort of equality is likely to arise if social structures are fractured into bits. Let us follow White (1992) in considering the "forum" to be a set of individuals accessible to costless mutual observation (copresence is generally sufficient but not necessary for this). An exchange that takes place in the forum is not necessarily different from one that takes place in private, unless there are other possible exchange partners with whom *A* can make the *same* exchange. Such knowledge of alternatives is widely assumed to increase the equality of exchanges, and this seems substantively reasonable even though it does not directly follow. But if we add a few more conditions—the presence of many different goods, that the goods negotiated be divisible, that participants be free to decline any and all exchanges, and that prices be attached to goods (see Stigler 1968: 5–12) —we have the sort of market that is assumed by conven-

---

[9] I have shown how this undermines Coleman's theory in Martin (2001a). Scott and Kerkvliet (1977: 449) are attentive to the problems that such extortion—quite common in actual social life—poses for equal exchange arguments. Furthermore, they point out that using the language of exchange fools nobody into thinking a protection racket is the same as hiring real protection. If an economic analysis cannot distinguish them, this speaks poorly of the analyst, not well of the racketeer.

tional economics, one that strongly tends to equate the marginal utilities of things exchanged for the exchangers. But even without these additional criteria, exchanges in a forum where there are alternative partners can induce regularities in the pattern of reciprocal action between *A* and *B* that can be said to be transdyadic in nature and indeed to constitute the benchmark of "fairness" (also see Barth 1981: 50, 55).

The market, or forum, is in some ways an "antistructure" in that the existence of obdurate social structures in the form of repeat transactions with the same parties is considered to be a sign of market imperfection or an indication that a true market has not yet emerged (see, e.g., McLean and Padgett 1997). But a contrary way of handling related interactions is to solidify the relationship between two interactants.[10]

In such a case, there is no reason to assume that any common metric emerges so that one may speak of mathematical equality in exchange, and no reason to think that where such a metric *does* emerge we find that exchanges are equal in these terms. Indeed, exchange may often magnify preexisting inequalities, for if the transfers always occur in one direction, they will tend to drain one party to the benefit of another, just as the larger of two twin stars may eventually suck up all the matter of the smaller, as each additional bit transferred only increases the gravitational field of the larger, as opposed to being "fair" and hence leading to equilibrium. One may, of course, consider this to be "fair" if gravity "should" be proportional to mass; indeed, Newton's laws force us to see a form of equality, but this should not distract us from the important fact that at the end, one star is there and the other is not. Given this drain, it is reasonable to call this an unequal relationship, and similarly unequal relationships that occur among persons lead to a similar drain. If we adopt a framework that in principle makes it impossible to identify unequal exchanges, we fail to notice those that are potentially ruinous for some participants. We then are unable to understand the principles of those structures that are best understood as determined efforts to control the emergence of hierarchy.

In sum, persons may try to organize relationships of donation in a reciprocal fashion—the problem of inequality arises when imbalances in donations cannot be tolerated past a certain point, and in which free interaction is not guaran-

---

[10] Much of recent work in economic sociology has attempted to deemphasize this distinction between the rational antistructure of pure markets on the one hand and the (economically) irrational structure of premarket society on the other, an attempt that increases the verisimilitude of studies of concrete economic relations in market societies but also downplays the very real differences between market and nonmarket societies. In particular, the important findings that force recognition that even "pure" markets have a social structure that has observable consequences (Swedberg 1994; Lie 1997; for a classic example see Baker 1984) can impede attention to the structural forms of exchange that arise in the absence of a market. In other words, to say that all markets have (some) social structure does not mean that all exchange structures are markets.

teed to equalize things. In these cases, rather than move toward the antistructure of a pure market, relationships may move toward an extremely clear social structure. Such structures have been explored most thoroughly in the anthropology of kinship understood as the exchange of women.

Restricted Exchange Structures

Who Really Exchanges Women?

We will begin with marriage as an example. In contemporary American society it is not surprising that marriage is often seen as an exchange. Yet such a statement as conventionally made has little analytic power for the investigation of structure, for once the "exchange" is made, the dyad leaves the forum and becomes a social structure of its own.[11] While it may at times be reasonable to treat the marriage decision in exchange terms, this is largely to miss the fact that the marriage itself is the construction of a relatively stable social structure that may (or may not) facilitate transfers that need to be reciprocated.

There are, however, other ways of understanding marriage as exchange, most importantly between lineages. This is relevant in societies in which lineage matters (ascriptive as opposed to achieved status, they used to say), which is to say nearly all of them, except for the modern and urbanized first world. Instead of focusing on the husband-wife dyad, many anthropologists focused on the ceremonial prestations—ritually fixed scripts of a series of gifts and countergifts—that occur between the man's family and woman's family.

But Levi-Strauss (1969 [1949]: 115, 36) argued that really what is exchanged is the women themselves, between groups, not between a man and a woman. (Thus in the matrimonial vocabulary of Great Russia, the groom is called "merchant" and bride "merchandise.") Any marriage is a net gain (+1 woman) for one lineage and a loss for the other (-1 woman). The trick in composing a stable social structure is to manage things so that no lineage runs out of women and becomes extinct. We must not, argued Levi-Strauss, be fooled by the universality of the incest taboo into thinking it is wholly unremarkable that lineages exchange women. It is structurally no different from two dogs exchanging bones (Adam Smith's example of a senseless exchange)—and indeed, groups that exchange women frequently have parallel structures for the exchange of other goods, immortalized in the Arapesh saying, "Other people's sisters . . . other people's yams . . . you may eat; your own

---

[11] Becker (1991: 130–34) famously uses a market approach to examine the joint utility of dyads, but this requires that utilities are perfectly transferable across persons, an assumption that is difficult to defend without generating paradox.

sister, . . . your own yams . . . you may not eat" (Mead 1940: 352; cf. Smith 1983: 75).[12]

This understanding of marriage as an exchange of women between patrilines (that is, patrilineal lineages) is indeed a good starting place not because it is the norm—rather, it is atypically simple and hence amenable to structural analysis. That is, many mid-twentieth-century anthropologists focused on marriage as an exchange of women, taking as paradigmatic the case in which some patriarchs made arrangements using women as chattel. This turned out to be problematic. In many applications, assuming the existence of such patriarchal logic and control was egregious and unnecessary to derive the marital patterns; in others some (male) informants may have used such heuristics to explain their philosophies of matrimony but there was considerable evidence that actual marriage was conducted differently. Patriarchal marriage exchange is the exception, in that in most cases, even those with nominally patrilineal descent, there is some degree of bilineality—for example, those descended from high-status women may well make sure that this is not forgotten (Sahlins 1968: 48). Further, contrary to the assumption that ego's wife is "lost" to her patriline, ties of obligation remain and her family generally has a stake in the reproductive consequences of her marriage (here see Singer 1973, especially 89; Lee 1972: 350; also Bourdieu 1977; Barth 1981: 142).[13]

Because the pure case of men exchanging women is an exception (though one that does occur),[14] the more anthropologists looked carefully at their cases, the more they found their results confounding the Levi-Straussian vision; as a result, there has been a tendency to ignore the results of this tradition, indeed to dismiss its outlook as patriarchal. This is probably both true and unhelpful, in that it leads to a paradox whereby identifying a patriarchal logic is itself patriarchal.[15] That is, it is a polar case in which there are three structural simpli-

---

[12] In a number of societies sharing is enforced by taboos against eating what you yourself have hunted; for the Guayaki of Paraguay, see Clastres (1972: 168ff).

[13] As Barth (1981: 66f, 72) emphasizes, bilineality of inheritance generally undercuts the capacity of lineages to cohere as corporate bodies, but so do other disruptions pertaining to unequal transmission of inheritance in land.

[14] An example might be the Tiwi of Australia, who made sure that all females (from birth if not before) are betrothed to some man; the details were in the hands of her mother's present husband (Hart and Pilling 1966: 14–20, 52), who used this asset to make alliances, repay debts, and invest in others. ("Tiwi men valued women as political capital available for investment in gaining the goodwill of other men more than they were interested in them as sexual partners.") Although widows escaped this control, and might have more say in their next marriages, they were also often under the thumbs of their brothers, or if older, those of their sons.

[15] In essence, this problem may be compared to one of dirty people looking at each other through binoculars. Dirty people are likely to have dirty binoculars, which means that when they look at others, they are convinced that these others are very dirty. However, we cannot from this argue that all persons are clean—surely if there are so many dirty binoculars there must be some dirty people.

fications that are compatible with patriarchy but also that imply clear heuristics of action. First, simply by assuming unilineal descent, we can treat any lineage as a bounded set of actors, each of whom has no complications of interest by virtue of belonging to multiple lineages. Second, by assuming patriarchal control, we simplify things further by identifying whose interests count—men who are assumed to want to reproduce their group. Finally, by assuming that men exchange women we have the key principle that an imbalance can be ruinous for the interests of the leaders of the lineage.[16]

This simplified perspective gives us one answer to the problem of inequality in asymmetric relationships, in part simply by assuming that one sex is fixed within the sib and the other is exchanged between lineages. The key is to remember that structurally, by "exchange" we really mean a directed, and possibly reciprocated, relationship, and not a "trade" or "purchase." We may imagine that some persons are indeed traded or shipped about, but even if they are not, simply seeing marriage as "female marries into some kin group" satisfies the definition of a directed and possibly reciprocated relationship between lineages.[17] Formally, it may seem to make no difference whether we imagine women exchanged or men exchanged,[18] but it is harder to handle polygynous cases from an "exchange of men" perspective, and there are considerably more polygynous cases than polyandrous.[19] Further, because of women's greater re-

[16] It is possible to develop a coherent structural approach to kinship as exchange starting from a bilineal system, as in the Leiden tradition. This approach is mathematically more general and leads in somewhat different directions. Most important, it blurs the distinction between generalized and restricted exchange. Thus a system of generalized exchange between four patrilines and four matrilines in which from one perspective, patrilines (or matrilines) exchange women (men) circularly, can also be seen as a system in which four groups are split into two sets of pairs taking part in restricted exchange, with children from any class being in a different class from their parents (e.g., Tjon Sie Fat 1990: 13, 21–22).

One important example forces a qualification of Levi-Strauss's dim view of the possibility of restricted exchange to produce unified societies. Tjon Sie Fat (1990: 198, 209–11) follows Turner and others in showing how marriage with father's father's sister's daughter's child in a four-class system can lead to restricted exchange at any generation, but the exchange partners alternate over three generations, leading to an indivisible society. A similar six-class system can alternate over two generations (thus children from matriline A marry opposite sex partners from matriline B in every odd numbered generation, but marry from matriline F in every even generation, so the structure cannot be split into two independent components).

[17] Adoption also has these structural characteristics, and it is significant that there are cases such as the Palauan in which adoption is used to tie lineages together, in that one family may request an infant from another family in order to create bonds of obligation. This may be a major source of social structure; more than half of the Palauan population studied by Smith (1983: 58, 184, 204f; also 207f, 223, 240, 244) had been adopted by another household.

[18] Levi-Strauss did not deny that there are cases in which men are in fact exchanged; on the duality between matrilineal and patrilineal analyses, see Levi-Strauss (1969 [1949]: 385, 409).

[19] Further, even in matrilineal cases it may actually be more accurate to understand action heuristics as men exchanging women. For example, among the Palauans, matrilineages are headed by men, who are in charge not only of the female descendents but other men who attach themselves

productive scarcity, the problem of inequality gains importance when we consider men as fixed. If a patriarch who cared only about the continued production of a line of male descendents had his druthers, he would likely be more concerned with the balance of women entering and exiting his lineage than would a matriarch concerned with the production of a line of female descendents, since (if we assume polygyny) only one man is needed to sire many offspring.[20]

Let us consider the possible responses to this problem of inequality in terms of heuristics of interaction. We can make a distinction between principles that are architectonic—compatible with the preservation of a structure of interaction—and those that are not. For an example of the latter, "take take take" is a possible response to a situation of necessity that is not necessarily compatible with structure. That is, if lineage A lacks women it may find some lineage B from whom they may be wrested by force or at least without the consent of the patriarch. For example, Yanomami with greater access to highly desired Western goods would accumulate women while giving up very few of their own (see Ferguson 1992: 215), imperiling the long-term survival of other groups.[21] Although there is no particular reason that lineage A should worry about the survival of lineage B, we still find that this heuristic is incompatible with that regularity of relations between particular persons that has here been termed social structure.

If we only consider architectonic heuristics that solve the problem of inequality, perhaps the most obvious would be the principle of reciprocity. Returning to figure 2.13 introduced at the end of chapter 2, such heuristics will lead to structures that emphasize dyadic level reciprocity (the left corner). But as we shall see, there are also structures corresponding to the right corner of the figure. We begin with the simpler dyadic case.

Reciprocity and Dual Organization

Let us, then, begin with the simplest case, namely the direct reciprocity that leads to what is called sister or daughter exchange: the males of lineage A exchange a nubile woman from their lineage for one of lineage B by having a male from A (A_M) marry a female from B (B_F) and some B_M marry A_F. If we

---

as clients. These heads attempts to increase the standing of his matrilineage in part by facilitating marriages of women in the matrilineage with men of other matrilineages. These ties are understood setting up conduits through which certain goods will pass (Smith 1983: 54, 78).

[20] Thus the exchange of women may indeed be central to patriarchy. Rubin's (1985) emphasis on this was reasonable, but she wrongly extended this to European societies with different marriage systems.

[21] Chagnon (1968a: 110) stressed the woman-stealing aspect of Yanomamö intervillage relations; recent evidence has cast doubts on Chagnon's emphasis on the nature of Yanomamö conflict, but his work on marriages is considered reliable and will be used below.

imagine, for a moment, these lineages to simply consist of one set of parents and their children, this is equivalent to "sister exchange" or "daughter exchange" (the two names come from seeing things from the point of view of the older or younger males). This means that a male offspring of a A_M–B_F union (say, Y) is related to a female offspring of a B_M–A_F union (say, X) in two ways: Y is X's father's sister's daughter (FZD), and X's mother's brother's daughter (MBD).

If we assume unilineal descent, then one of these children will end up attached to one lineage and the other to the second. One way to ensure that these lineages always exchange their women is to require that such cousins marry each other. Thus we might find a rule that men should marry either their MBD or their FZD. Such rules are found where there are classes that regularly marry with one another, which we shall follow Levi-Strauss in calling "restricted exchange."

Now consider a society neatly divided into two and only two exogamous marriage classes, called phratries or moieties, and with one's placement in a moiety being either patrilineal or matrilineal.[22] The difference between FZD marriage and MBD marriage is now academic, and indeed, in such societies there may not be a preference for one as opposed to the other. Although such organization is reasonably common (though see Levi-Strauss 1963, chapter 8) and ensures that a male ego's MBD (and FZD) are in the opposite moiety and hence marry-able, this does not necessarily solve the problem of equality. That is, if each moiety is itself composed of a number of distinct patrilineages, and it makes a good deal of difference to the members of some patrilineage whether they give up more women than they receive, the presence of exogamous moieties is not wholly comforting.

At the level of the individual lineage, it may prove hard to accomplish an actual daughter exchange simply because lineage A may have a daughter of marriageable age but lineage B does not. As a result, the parties may allow for a delayed repayment, which also makes sure that the various lineages stay together even when they cannot accomplish a tit-for-tat exchange (see, e.g., Gouldner 1960; Bourdieu 1990 [1980]).[23] It is possible that delayed reciprocity

---

[22] Thus a man in moiety A (A_M) must marry a woman in moiety B (B_F), while a man in moiety B (B_M) must marry a woman in moiety A (A_F). We can accordingly see four classes, A_M, B_F, B_M, and A_F, where classes are paired off and men circulate among classes in that the son of a man is in a different class from his father (Levi-Strauss 1969 [1949]: 146). There are other possible forms of dual organization in marriages that can arise but are not considered here, such as the "sidedness" discussed by Houseman and White (1998a: especially 79, 83f), which cannot be represented as a set of classes under unilineal descent. Sides are more complex entities that can develop in a set of bilaterally structured roles that have to do first and foremost with relations to land.

[23] It is important to note that this does not imply that the two lineages in question only have this relationship with each other—each may have a relationship of continuing exchange of women with a number of other lineages, just as businesspeople keep accounts with a number of others.

is handled by people remembering how many women any lineage is owed from any other, but this is not only a recipe for disagreement (for memories tend to differ in ways correlated with interest) but vulnerable to filibuster and threat. For example, stronger Yanomamö lineages may refuse an even exchange (see above), or they may also use delays to their advantage by exploiting the "float" that results in taking a nubile one and betrothing an immature woman in exchange.

A different way is to use individual heuristics for preferential marriage. Above we found that consistent daughter-exchange between two lineages might lead any ego to marry someone who was his FZD or his MBD. Now let us generalize to more than two patrilineal lineages exchanging women. Thinking from the perspective of a male from *A* about to be married, there is quite a difference between marrying a father's sister's daughter (FZD) as opposed to a mother's brother's daughter (MBD). The MBD is from the same lineage (*B*) that your mother is from—the same lineage that "gave" your patriline your mother. Your father's sister, however, has married into some other lineage, *C*. Thus marriage with MBD takes a *second* woman from *B* to *A*, while marriage with FZD cancels out a debt, by taking a woman from the lineage who took your father's sister.

Thus using the heuristic of "marry your FZD" is equivalent to a structure of reciprocity with a possible delay that does not require that people keep track of how many women have been transferred from one lineage to another (Levi-Strauss 1969 [1949]: 130f). Similarly, other heuristics are compatible with a longer delay in repayment. For example, consider the rule that male ego's spouse is in the same class as his father's father's sister's daughter's daughter (FFZDD)—the Maring, Manga, and Wogeo of Highland New Guinea speak of this particular rule as a return made for a woman given two generations earlier (Tjon Sie Fat 1990: 139). (That is, since one marries one's grandfather's sister's granddaughter, one has married a woman from a patrilineage to which one's own patrilineage gave a woman, the grandfather's sister.) Having several such rules can allow ego to choose a spouse from a lineage that is extremely likely to have given a woman to ego's lineage relatively recently, without tying ego to one particular generation of spouse (who may not exist).

Many of the classic elementary structures enforce delayed repayment by complicating restricted exchange. Moieties are divided into smaller marriage classes, and membership in classes alternates across generations (thus men of class *A* may need to marry women of class *B* and their children will end up in class *C* who must marry from class *D*, etc.). If the marriage class is neither too big nor too small, it may be able to decently coordinate exchange so that no patriline is likely to be bankrupted of women: from the position of a male ego in some class *A*, there are enough patrilines in class *B* so that there are nubile women to "take" but not so many that other ways of determining who shall marry whom must spring up to coordinate transfers of women.

But this is not the only way of ensuring that the A who gives O to B does not go without O. We have found that the difficulties turn on whether B actually has an O that B is willing to alienate. It need not be B who makes this dona-tion—it can be a third party, C. We go on to explore the resulting structures.

Generalized Exchange

Spreading Out

Such solutions to the problem of inequality—structures in which those who give get from someone other than those to whom they give—are usually called "generalized exchange," or "group-generalized exchange" or "net generalized exchange." I will reserve the term *generalized exchange* for the particular circular system as discussed by Levi-Strauss (sometimes called "chain-generalized" or "network-generalized" exchange), and term the broader case in which A will receive from *some X* (as opposed to particularly from a speci-fied C), simply "spreading out," since the essential thing is that either gains or losses (or both) are spread out among the group in some way—usually across persons and across time.[24] It is with such general cases (and not the specific case of elementary kinship structures) that we begin. I will speak of the transfer here as a "donation," since it is understood that it will not be reciprocated by the recipient, at least not immediately.

Of course, it is possible to have a structureless solution—that is, to have a norm in which someone gives when giving is likely to be needed (for example, blood donation)—but these fall outside the scope of the present work. When we consider structured solutions, we find two fundamentally different ways in which spreading out can be organized, one oriented around giving and one around getting. To discuss these, it is convenient to denote a donation from person A to person B as $A \rightarrow B$, meaning that A ends up with less than before and B with more.

One way in which spreading out can be accomplished is by following $B \rightarrow C$ with $A \rightarrow B$; this leads to A having less and C more than before the transfers took place. Person B has only suffered a temporary loss and has been recom-pensed by A. If we had a chain of four people, with their state at any time denoted as a vector, we might denote the first state as $[0,0,-,+]$—the third person has given up and the fourth person gained. The second state would look like this: $[0,-,0,+]$ and the third $[-,0,0,+]$. (Here see the analysis of Breiger and Roberts [1998: 247].) We can see the $-$ sign as a pulse moving backward as time goes forward (an example here are chains of *moka* exchange in New Guinea [see Hage and Harary 1991: 68]). It may be difficult to understand why

---

[24] On these two types of generalized exchange, see Yamagishi and Cook (1993); for a clearly defined spreading out marriage heuristic see Smith (1983: 92f).

three people would do this, as opposed to *A* directly giving to *C*. But there are two reasons why this often makes a good deal of sense. First, it spreads the loss out among a large number of people, and may thereby efficiently allocate resources or at least lessen the pain of donation. This can be observed at a busy working meeting involving somewhat absentminded persons. One person will suddenly attempt to get to work writing and find that she has no pen, at which point she will turn and request one from a neighbor. The neighbor may soon realize the need for a pen, and ask for one from a different party, as the first is still busily working. The nonpen thus circulates around without actually preventing anyone from writing who has a mind to write.

Second, it is possible that the person making the current transfer is always the one who has the greatest surplus. In this case, the system is de facto redistributive without taking anything away from anyone else (permanently)—a remarkable accomplishment possible only because the system lives off the "float" involved.

The second way in which spreading out can be thus accomplished is by following $A \to B$ with $B \to C$, etc. Using the same notation as before, we might see three states as [−,+,0,0], [−,0,+,0] and [−,0,0,+]. Here we can see the + sign as a temporary gain moving forward. Since *A*, however, ends up with a permanent loss, this is well suited for cases in which the cycle begins because of an unusual windfall for *A*. One important example of this system is discussed by Levi-Strauss (1969 [1949]: 466f, 471), namely the "marriage by purchase" found in parts of Africa. Far from being a system that individualizes the transactions (as would market purchase), the money given is not fungible and not consumed by the recipient—instead, it is immediately used to "buy" a wife (i.e., facilitate a marriage) for a brother or cousin. Thus the money circulates through the society accomplishing marriages like a Cupid.

Such a chain can be extremely efficient in redistributing surpluses in contexts in which people are separated and never get together in a forum for barter (e.g., the Tee exchange of New Guinea discussed further below; see Meggitt 1974: especially 181, 191, 195). Consider someone with a surplus of some good, which we call O_1. Required to donate something, he chooses O_1 to give to *B*. *B* similarly conducts an inventory and chooses the good of which he has the greatest surplus to donate. This good may or may not be O_1—if it is, we can imagine O_1 as a pulse that will travel until it reaches someone who lacks O_1, at which point some new O_2 takes off looking for someone in need of it (for an example, consider Smith 1983: 111, 117).[25]

---

[25] The Melanesian taro exchange studied by Schwimmer (1973: 130–36) demonstrates a similar principle of interaction with those geographically close, still linking an overall system together such that one object could in principle get from any one place to any other via intermediaries.

We have so far investigated simple line structures, but small variations on the line can lead to dramatic concentrations of wealth, at least temporarily. We are familiar with pernicious versions of such structures such as the "chain letter" pyramid or Ponzi scheme. The essence is simple: produce a pyramidal structure in which an ever widening base sends resources upward—the constriction increases the material density, so that those at the top profit greatly. This is a zero sum system, and the universe surprisingly quickly turns to have run out of willing participants, at which point those at the bottom lose everything.

But it is possible for concentration to be a net good. For example, in one version of what are known as "revolving credit associations," members all contribute some amount to a pot (say, $5.00 from 10 members) and each person gets the jackpot in turn. This makes sense even though the expected payoffs are exactly the same as the costs: imagine that all persons need $50 to purchase some piece of equipment. In the absence of the donation structure, all will need to wait 10 weeks (assuming all they can divert for savings is $5.00 a week) before making the purchase; with the lottery, only one of 10 must wait this long. There is a net benefit that would be lost, unless there are banks that pay interest for savings. Not surprisingly, revolving credit associations tend to arise where there are no such banks.

In between these two extremes are a variety of systems that involve temporary concentration and redistribution. Even a temporary concentration of wealth that is later wholly redistributed is a tremendous source of power, and it can frequently be harnessed by one person. The trick is to sit on top of the jackpot at a key point in the cycle; one need not even divert any of the flow to be elevated by it. We will explore some "big man" systems in chapter 6 that build on this logic; the Tee Exchange noted above also was used for this combination of redistribution and political entrepreneurship. The structure of relationships seems to have been a pyramidal spanning tree which was used to concentrate wealth, which would then be used to make matrimonial alliances which would in turn lead to material benefits, which could be used to repay those who had contributed. In essence, it allowed for the creation of giving relations between nonkin of a kind normally restricted to close kin.[26] Those at key positions could amass political power by building allies who in turn would be compensated by a "pulse" of donation going the other way (Meggitt 1974: especially 189; Wiessner and Tumu 1998).

In sum, depending on how the interactions are arranged, pulse chains can facilitate complex transactions that benefit everyone who participates, though

---

[26] Importantly, these pseudo-kin relations were not transitive, although kinship normally is (Wiessner and Tumu 1998: 300). If it were, it would threaten to have an "ice nine" effect (the example given in chapter 2) and make too many people kin.

some more than others.[27] While these structures can still be used to increase inequality—indeed, we shall examine this in another guise in chapter 6—they can also be used to prevent inequality. That is, a chain might pile up all the good things at one end, increasing inequality. The simplest structural solution that prevents inequality is to connect the chain into a circle. It is this solution that, following Levi-Strauss (1969 [1949]), we will term generalized exchange.

Circles and Uncles

In a generalized exchange structure, each participant must make a donation to a specific other participant, as shown in figure 3.3 below. The relation of transfer cannot be reciprocated if the circle is not to be disrupted; at the same time, no member can refuse to make required transfers. But members *can* refuse, especially if they are more powerful than others (hence the importance of inequality that we will explore below). Accordingly, generalized exchange always involves an element of trust (Levi-Strauss 1969 [1949]: 265), yet in contrast to less-organized systems of spreading out, this trust is a reasonable one. That is, since everyone can determine precisely who is supposed to give in some situation, compliance can be assessed and noncompliance sanctioned; even in the absence of sanctions, the concentration of responsibility seems to encourage participation (see the results of Yamagishi and Cook 1993: 244).

This structure is clearly a reasonable one given the imperative on maintaining equality, but how could it arise? It cannot be due to simple urges toward reciprocity, as might be the case in restricted exchange. Let us then derive it for kinship structures. It is clear that a focus on marriage with MBD (mother's brother's daughter) is compatible with generalized exchange,[28] for the men of lineage A all take women from the same lineage, but this is not in itself sufficient to produce a workable system. Is the system as a whole a consciously created architecture? If this were so, there should be evidence that participants are able to understand the overall construction, and hence have kinship terms to express the relevant relations (see Levi-Strauss [1969 (1949): 411, 419]). But recently, Bearman (1997) found a pattern of generalized exchange among Groote Eylandters who lacked descriptive labels for the implicit classes.

Clearly, in this case, the system could not have originated on the basis of conscious understanding of certain rules in terms of prescribed marriages between categories, even though the Groote Eylandters understood what was

---

[27] Even in the simple form of an endless cycle in which no exchanged goods are actually consumed, such as the archetypal *kula* ring of the Trobriand Islands, all individuals benefit simply from having their fifteen minutes of fame when they hold the ritual goods. See Hage and Harary (1991: 158, 167) for support for Malinowski's (1922) original interpretation.

[28] Tjon Sie Fat (1990: especially 128) shows that there are other preferential formulas compatible with generalized exchange.

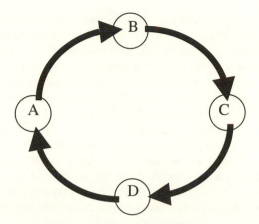

Figure 3.3. Generalized exchange

going on well enough to sanction those who violated these rules. Bearman (1997: 1411ff) points out that once the system was given a jump start, one would reasonably expect it to continue on the basis of the same rational principles that Yamagishi and Cook (1993) demonstrated would keep generalized exchange circuits going among people who did not understand the whole cycle.[29] The jump start might be the simple age difference between husbands and wives in a gerontocratic society. Following Hammel (1973), Bearman notes that the older husbands are than wives, the more likely they are to prefer marriage with MBD as opposed to FZD (father's sister's daughter). (This will be demonstrated shortly.)

We have already seen that marriage with MBD tends toward generalized exchange, as a patriline always takes women from the same lineage. Unless there are only two lineages, this either requires an infinite number of lineages or a circular system. Somehow people seem to have the foresight—at least in this case—to send the last lineage in the chain back to the first when it comes time to marry.[30]

---

[29] In particular, a quest to preserve balance in the sense that equivalence relations are consistent (e.g., the person whom the person you call brother calls mother is someone whom you can call mother) leads to reinforcement of the system.

[30] This example highlights the increasing conviction that classic models paid insufficient attention to age differences and their structural correlates, particularly the incompatibility of age bias and straight sister exchange or bilateral cross-cousin marriage (e.g., the simplest restricted exchange forms) (see Tjon Sie Fat 1990: 147f, 153ff, who formulates these as "spirals" in a cylindrical surface of generalized exchange that would lead to circles if there were no age bias). It is possible for the simplest heuristic of marriage with mother's brother's daughter to be compatible with an age spiral; if ego's father married a woman x years younger than herself, chances are that her brother's daughter will be around x years younger than her son. But other structures, based on marriage with sister's daughter, are also possible given a severe age spiral.

In sum, it seems reasonable that "spreading out" can lead to the strong structural form of circular generalized exchange; while participants need not be able to visualize the circular structure, they often do. It may seem strange that a lineage prefers to keep taking women from one group and giving to another, as opposed to coming to a square deal once and for all, but there is a heuristic that runs in the opposite direction of the heuristic of reciprocity. In Levi-Strauss's (1969 [1949]: 435) words: "One is the slave of one's alliance, since it is established at the price of transferring irreplaceable, or almost irreplaceable, goods, viz. sisters and daughters. From the moment that one is bound by it everything must be done to maintain and develop it. . . . the gaining of a sister puts one in a privileged position to obtain the daughter also."[31]

Thus generalized exchange is one structure that may arise to facilitate necessary asymmetric transfers while preventing a drain from one party to another. Such a situation occurs under lineages obeying some form of incest taboo. Generalized exchange is an answer based on the trust that comes from stability and equality, and a loss of either of these can shatter the system and lead to a reversion to restricted exchange, as people demand the security of immediate repayment (Levi-Strauss 1969 [1949]: 471).

Inequality and Generalized Exchange

The cheery scenario developed above suggests the robustness of generalized exchange—to make everything even, people tacitly agree to ties the ends of a chain together. Yet things are not always this simple. As Levi-Strauss (1969 [1949]: 266) says, confusion enters because "generalized exchange presupposed equality, and is a source of inequality." In contrast to restricted exchange, which conserves the relation and equality between the parties, in generalized exchange one interactant is a giver and one a taker, a potential source of inequality.

This danger of inequality was most clearly discussed by Levi-Strauss in his speculative reconstruction of Indian exogamous marriage.[32] If India began with

[31] This same logic can be seen in international capital flows, which often seem consciously intended and understood as "donations" intended to establish a lasting social relation and not as investment decisions determined on the basis of forecasted returns. While some debtors are "too big to fail," and hence it is in the interest of creditors to extend new loans if there is a possibility that they will contribute to solvency, the same pattern of "sending good money after bad" is found where debtors are small enough to fail. There is evidently an understanding that a relationship has been established that allows the donor (creditor) to have a fair amount of avuncular authority and gives the recipient (debtor) moral claims to further aid.

[32] Levi-Strauss (1969 [1949]: 419f) also suggests that in India a system of generalized exchange may have incorporated a group of external conquerors, but I will focus on the other possibility, namely the differentiation of statuses within an originally homogeneous society. Although the former may be historically closer to the truth, the latter may better express the tensions inherent in generalized exchange. Certainly many Indian subcultures combine patrilineal exogamy with hypergamy, in that the wife's family must be lower ranking than the husband's (e.g., the Rajput of Khalapur) (Tjon Sie Fat 1990: 280).

a system of generalized exchange, this would break down with the development of feudalism, as the upper classes would refuse to exchange their women with lower classes, and instead shift toward restricted exchange (Levi-Strauss 1969 [1949]: 416f, 420). These upper classes would orient to hypergamy, taking but not giving women, and breaking the cycle of generalized exchange.

Further—and here I follow Levi-Strauss (1969 [1949]: 474) more in admiration of the logical consistency of his approach, which can serve as an exemplar for the current work, than in conviction that this is a defensible claim—there is a second-order solution to the stoppage of generalized exchange due to inequality, and this is to promote a select section of the lower castes to the status of worthy-to-accept-higher-caste-daughters; the Indian term for this is *swayamvara* marriage. Levi-Strauss argued that European (Germanic) marriage is the residue of a disintegrated generalized exchange structure turned toward *swayamvara*, something that would certainly explain the ubiquity of "boy-of-humble-birth-marrying-princess" fairy tales.[33]

While the exchange of women is traditionally seen from the standpoint of patriarchs—male elders authoritatively determining the marriages of their children—the exchange of women (here we still treat women as having no input although this simplification is increasingly problematic the more we turn to individual decisions) may also be seen as a relationship established between a young man and an old man. The former is the groom and the latter the bride's father. Let us imagine that there are status differences between patrilines. If we assume men tend to increase in status as they age, then in a society in which "wife-taking" are generally superior to "wife-giving" patrilines,[34] it will be seen that marriage with a MBD (but not a FZD) establishes a relationship between men who are rough equals.

In the diagram shown in figure 3.4, marriage relations are transformed to diagonal double lines indicating status differences between patrilines, while vertical lines are lines of descent, and horizontal ones lines of sibship. Again, we start with a male ego. Otherwise the conventions are the same as those used in the previous chapter. Woman 1 is ego's MBD, and woman 2 is ego's FZD. It can be seen that marriage with woman 1 establishes a rough equivalence between ego and his future father-in-law, while marriage with woman 2 does not.

This seems to be a more common response to inequality among lineages than the dual one whereby wife-givers are seen as superior to wife-takers, which would be compatible with FZD marriage, though there are examples

[33] Unfortunately, there are also a number of "girl-of-humble-birth-marrying-prince" stories.
[34] It is not necessary that these status relations be transitive—it is possible for a circular generalized exchange system to exist with all participants considering themselves superior to those who give them wives for the very reason that the latter are wife-givers.

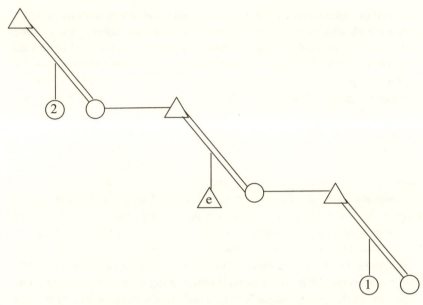

Figure 3.4. Gerontocracy and cross-cousin marriage

of this.[35] The rarity of female hypogamy may be partially explained by its poor fit with patriarchal principles. The former arrangement (wife-taking lineages are of higher status) is compatible with the "take take take" heuristic in which women are considered the objects—this is problematic only for the weaker lineages, and their extinction is not inherently worrisome to the more powerful.

For example, Padgett and Ansell (1993: 1294) argued that among the elite of renaissance Florence, it was understood that wife-giving families were of higher status than wife-accepting families (that is, that men married up).[36] In this case, rather than unite rough status equals, the marriage was often intended to secure a "political lieutenant" for the higher-status and older man. Thus what Levi-Strauss saw as akin to the *swayamvara* marriage—the exception that completes an otherwise broken cycle that follows the rule of female hypergamy—may in fact be not so much the exception as the contrary rule—a ten-

[35] Thus among the Tanimbar of Indonesia, others are divided into one's patrilineal descent group ("Men brothers"), wife-givers ("masters"), and wife-takers ("Sister's child") who are regarded as inferior (Tjon Sie Fat 1990: 224f, 266).

[36] Padgett and Ansell make the doubtful argument that this is linked to the general prestige that accrues to a donor—since this is not a usual pattern in the societies studied by the anthropologists to whom they refer, this is not convincing (also see Sahlins 1968: 57). It may perhaps be that in the European context in which land was scarcer than labor (in contrast especially to Africa), and hence bridegrooms generally "worth" more than brides (hence dowry as opposed to bride-price), a man from a low-ranking family was equivalent to a woman from a high-ranking one, and thus wife-givers would tend to be of higher status than their wife-takers.

dency toward female hypogamy or son-in-law elevation. With the introduction of fixed capital that requires management, heads of elite households need not only heirs but assistants who can be treated as inferiors; the bride's father looks for a worthy recipient of lesser status who will accept subordination and a bride as a package deal. Wife takers are thus of lower status than wife givers, and sons thus marry women of higher status than themselves.

What resulted, according to Padgett and Ansell, was a treelike structure down through which women trickled.[37] Of course, this is no solution to the problem of inequality with which we began—in contrast to a system of generalized exchange, a "trickle down" structure means that some groups become bereft of women and hence extinct. In hypergamous systems it is men of the lowest ranks who may be forced to remain unmarried; women of the highest ranks may have difficulty marrying, although this is not necessarily the case in polygamous societies. But given that Florentine sons had to marry up, those of the most distinguished lineages were hard pressed to marry—there was no one good enough for the sons of the elite to marry. In this case, there was no elegant structural solution, but rather a cheat: the elite, argue Padgett and Ansell, snuck away to other neighborhoods to find women as opposed to effectively announcing to their neighbors that there was a family of higher status than themselves.

In sum, the pulses of donations that lie at the heart of the cycle of generalized exchange can redistribute a surplus and deal with the inequality introduced by a windfall or a shortfall. In the simplest case (marriages arranged by an oligarchy of imperious patriarchs, equal in power to one another, who only care about maximizing their number of male descendents) we can assume a simple relationship between heuristic and structure. As we turn to progressively more complex environments, there is room for greater slippage between structure and subjectivity. I close this chapter by exploring how people may internalize the logic of these structures, and how these structures may fit into a wider class of mating systems.

Structure and Subjectivity

Heuristics of Exchange

Starting from the perspective that women are valuable yet cannot be kept within any specific lineage, we have seen the development of a number of structural problems. There are in turn a number of solutions that imply local structure, most important the "exchange of women." Because it is rarely the

---

[37] Padgett and Ansell (1993: 1295) called this a "hierarchical linear tree" or "pecking order," but actually drew nonlinear (that is, horizontally differentiated) trees. This form will be called a "triset" in chapter 5 and is a common social form of directed diffusion.

case that two lineages have women available for an actual exchange, this imperative can lead to rules of preferential marriage. These rules can be dually understood in terms of classes; such subjective comprehension in terms of classes—especially if they are given names—is frequently easier than thinking in terms of kinship preferences.[38]

But the existence of such classes is not necessary for the structural solutions. Most obviously, dual organization can be coordinated through cross-cousin marriage, without named moieties. For example, the Yanomamö prescribe bilateral cross-cousin marriage (that is, "wife" is placed in the same category as structurally equivalent with both father's sister's daughter and mother's brother's daughter). Not surprisingly, their villages tend to have two dominant lineages. "But while dual organization exists in a *de facto* sense, there is no overt ideology of dual organization. That is, the village does not have named halves, rules stipulating that half of the village should be the domain of one lineage and the other half the domain of the second, etc." (Chagnon 1968a: 141, 143). Instead, dual organization arises naturally from the limited trust that prevents generalized exchange—"males stand a better chance of obtaining a wife if they give their sisters consistently to the same group, for by giving women one can therefore demand them in return" (ibid.: 144). That is, rather than attempt to manage many exchanges, each of which may be insufficiently strong to provide a source of women, they prefer to put all their eggs in one basket.

Even further, more complex structures may lack any simple duality between categorical analysis and strategic analysis (that is, analysis in terms of heuristics). Thus Tjon Sie Fat (1990: 113) points out that there are distinct *structures*—that is, sets of classes of equivalents—that have the same marriage *rule* (for example, that male ego's spouse is in the same class as FFZDD). But the structure cannot be wholly derived from this heuristic alone; thus the heuristic is not correlative to a distinct structure.

Classically, it was assumed that complex structures involved the layering of multiple prescriptive systems (multiple elementary structures) or the progressive attenuation of their prescriptive force (cf. Levi-Strauss 1965: 20). But Tjon Sie Fat (1990: 226, 249) has questioned this, and instead proposes that, just as simple deterministic systems can lead to complex behavior when initial conditions are weighty, so much of complex behavior in kinship systems "may be the result of local interactions governed by simple rules." In other

---

[38] In the preface to the 2d edition of the *Elementary Structures of Kinship*, Levi-Strauss (1969 [1949]: xxxiv) seemed to move away from the emphasis on subjective understandings; in trying to clarify his position on the reality of the preferential rules that were related to each structure, he claimed that the test of a structure was precisely the degree to which spousal matches corresponded to categorical relations to ego; a "preference" in this understanding had nothing to do with ego's subjective inclinations, but had more to do with statistical overrepresentation. Yet Levi-Strauss (1965: 16) also argued that the role of deliberate, reflective systemization of marriage rules on the part of "so-called primitives" should not be underestimated.

words, both simple and complex structures may have subjective correlates that are simple heuristics—the difference lies in the initial conditions that actors face as they try to carry out these heuristics. Just as a generalized exchange structure might be understood as the combination of preferential MBD-marriage given a certain number of preexisting lineages as inexplicable initial conditions, so complex marriage structures may simply result from a different set of initial conditions.[39]

That is, if our question is "what structures arise given asymmetric relations?" we find that our answer has partly to do with the nature of the relationship and partly to do with other conditions. If we compare relationships to molecules and structures to crystals, we recognize that the initial conditions under which relationships begin to crystallize can make a great deal of difference to the resulting structure. Thus we cannot expect a general one-to-one mapping between relationship and structure, not even between heuristic and structure.

Evolution and Strategy

A second level of complication may arise when more than one heuristic is available to guide choice. The layering of multiple ways of understanding action can introduce exponential complexity into structure without introducing randomness. Boyd (1969) has suggested that the elaborate elementary structures found among Australians may arise as successive introductions of distinctions. Boyd examines the Arunta eight-class system, which can be seen as alternating four-class generalized exchange.[40] This confusing system may be derived algebraically as the successive addition of less complex heuristics, to wit (in temporal order) first a division into matrilineal moieties,[41] and then a

---

[39] Tjon Sie Fat (1990: 252, 254) pursues a number of interesting structures that correspond to plausible rules (e.g., male ego takes a spouse from the same line into which his mother's brother married in the previous generation by selecting MBWBD, which may be equivalent to FFZDD). He shows that given such rules, different initial conditions can lead to steady state or cyclical structures. Since there is generally more than one way of describing a potential spouse, which *subjective* system is used to understand existing structural arrangements may begin to turn an existing structure one way or another. When any ego can choose from more than one type of permitted spouse (and hence simple permutations that involve one-to-one mappings are inapplicable), the system may remain highly structured yet largely opaque to traditional methods of analysis. Further, there are many cases in which rules that have different structural implications (e.g., sister exchange and marriage by purchase) exist side by side (Tjon Sie Fat 1990: 257, 195).

[40] In this system one may marry a person of the opposite sex from one's father's mother's class, men are in the same class as their grandfather (which is implied by the former consideration), one's grandmother's grandmother is in one's own class, and one's father's great-grandmother is in the same class as one's mother's father.

[41] This establishes that one is in the same class as one's mother and one's grandfather, but not one's father. It is also possible to derive the system from patrilineal moieties that are then divided.

superimposition of patrilineal moieties.[42] If there is then a division within the restricted exchanging classes between "wife takers" and "wife givers," one has the eight-class system.

Whether this particular derivation is historically accurate is beyond our ability to judge. But this approach links the complicated structures with a number of heuristics that can be intuitively understood, as they spring from an attempt to make distinctions—distinctions between one's mother's people and one's father's people, and distinctions between givers and takers. In contrast to the joking-avoidance systems, in which such distinctions lead to only two classes that are paradigmatically different for all persons, here we have sets of stable equivalence classes, which might seem much more constraining on the action of the individuals involved.

In this case, the multiple prescriptions are mutually reinforcing; in other cases, they appear as alternatives that obscure structure. For example, the Iatmul of New Guinea had a number of prescriptive rules of exogamous marriage: marriage with FMBSD ("a woman should climb the same ladder that her father's father's sister climbed"), with FZD ("the daughter goes as payment for the mother") and with ZHZ ("women should be exchanged") (Bateson 1958:88–91). Multiple rules increases the flexibility with which one can act.[43] But even this flexibility was not always enough, and Bateson found some endogamous marriages. These "tabooed" unions were explained with a shrug: "She is a fine woman so they married her inside the clan lest some other clan take her."

How to explain this combination of rule-bound and rule-breaking action? It is correct, but not enough, to point out that for every law, there are conditions under which it makes sense to bend or break it (see Levi Strauss 1953: 538; Chagnon 1990: 96; Hart and Pilling 1966: 27, 57), and that this may lead to an inability to understand the resulting actions in purely structural terms (cf. Bourdieu 1990 [1980]). It is that the presence of alternative prescriptions makes it easier for these heuristics to be unmoored from particular structures. Structure has passed into institution—the frustration of many anthropological fieldworkers at the dissociation between actual marriage patterns and the norms expressed by informants is the result of the informants bringing these regularities to the same sort of conscious explication sought by the fieldworkers.

---

[42] This leads to a four-class system where one's father's father and one's mother's mother are from the same class as oneself; this is restricted marriage with alternating classes (that is, there are four classes, where class 1 marries class 2 and has children in class 3 if the father is from class 1, and children in class 4 if it is the mother who is from class 1; classes 3 and 4 similarly intermarry).

[43] Indeed, Sahlins (1968: 59) suggests that the reason bilateral cross-cousin marriage is more common than either prescriptive MBD or FZD marriage is simply that it allows elders more room for strategic considerations without violating prescriptions.

But pursuing this theme requires a more complete overview of the sets of structures that develop (and forms the core of the final chapter). Let us return to the question of what structures emerge for the relation of marriage between lineages. We find that the choices facing persons as they navigate the relationships—the trade-offs they face—are closely related to those explored in the previous chapter. Different heuristics can be employed depending on how one wants to handle any particular problem; sets of responses that use reinforcing principles cohere as systems (in this case, marriage systems). I close by considering these.

The Dispersion of Mating Structures

We have been examining well-studied structures that allow a system of transfers to avoid the production or exaggeration of inequality, despite the lack of mutuality of the fundamental relationship in question. The strength of such a system of generalized exchange is, however, its weaknesses—it claims too much in terms of the equality of participants. A lineage *B* gaining in importance can reasonably expect to receive women from *A* without giving any to *C*. It is probably not accidental that such systems thrive in conditions in which the threat of inequality is relatively low in two ways. First of all, material differences in wealth are less than in most other societies, and second, polygamy allows for what inequality there is to affect the number of connections made, not their nature.

We have followed this logic for the case of mating, but it is worth pointing out that this is not the only way to handle these tendencies toward inequality in this relationship. The first, which was raised at the end of the last chapter, is to go *toward* hierarchy; indeed, to embrace it in a principled fashion via a popularity tournament. This is the position marked "preferential attachment" in the figure at the end of chapter 2. A classic example for mating structures is the "rating and dating" system analyzed by Waller (1937). Here the problem of inequality arises in the form of a substantive contradiction between the mutuality established by the relationship (pairing) and the competitive ranking of persons in which every relationship begun or finished changes the balances that define equality. This problem is hard to solve simply through a determination to police the equality of the relationship. As Sprecher (1998) has found, emphasizing exact reciprocity in romantic relations—the paradigmatically rational action of refusing to accept transactions in which the costs outweigh the benefits—actually decreases subjective utility, since (given the human folly of overestimating one's own sacrifices and minimizing others') the closer the attention to reciprocity, the less likely that one will actually reciprocate.

The second polar position is to move toward mutuality and equality: vertical differentiation is suppressed by adopting a spatial model of likenesses (as in chapter 2), which I shall call homophily (one likes—or at least chooses—those like one). In this case, the closer one person is to another in social space, the more one loves the other, and since distance is inherently a symmetric quantity, the more that one is loved in return. This must beg the question—if there *is* a vertical ranking of persons in terms of some preexisting inequality, then homophily solves the problem of inequality by making it the solution. That is, imagine people ranked vertically, all looking upward and wishing they had someone closer to the top. The homophilous solution is more or less to knock this tower on its side and make sure that people now look for those who are close to them—in what was previously vertical position—without changing the overall ranking or disturbing the tendency for those of similar rank to pair.

Further, this solution leads to a tendency toward fragmentation that is a parallel to the dyadic withdrawal discussed by Slater (1963). This is what lies behind Levi-Strauss's reconstruction of Indian marriage, and the problem that faced some of the Florentine elite: if everyone insists on only marrying their equals, their society will cease to hold together as a solidary unit, but instead will shear off into separate layers. Marriage relations will not "spread out" and unify the group, which is accomplished by the generalized exchange structures that we have been discussing.

At the same time, the emphasis on likeness does solve the instability of preferential attachment. Because relationship formation is dependent on external considerations (as opposed to being wholly endogenous), we do not see the positive feedback of the popularity tournament. The logic of relationship formation may be unequal (all want to marry those from the richest family), but making a relationship does not increase the inequality (the wealthy do not get wealthier from marrying the poor).

These three possibilities may be schematized as follows (see figure 3.5 below). The parallel to the figure at the end of chapter 2 arises because there are similar trade-offs: between organizing relationships in terms of preferential attachment at the cost of true reciprocity or spreading out across the group, and so on. Classical anthropology has focused on cases in the bottom right, while analyses of American society based on college dating have generally focused on the upper corner. Analyses of marriage in the modern West have been more likely to accentuate the model given in the bottom left corner.

Of course, existing structures often involve a trade-off between these three imperatives, and it is possible to join an attempt to "spread out" with a spatial model of tie-formation. Thus in recent work, Bearman, Moody, and Stovel (2004) find dating structures in American high schools tend to form "spanning trees," simple graphs that can be understood as arising in a number of ways but have the notable properties that they efficiently connect as many nodes as possible with as few redundant ties as possible. (Technically, a spanning tree is a graph that has N-1 lines connecting N nodes.) Using the terminology from the previous chapter, we may envision this structure as the result of tie forma-

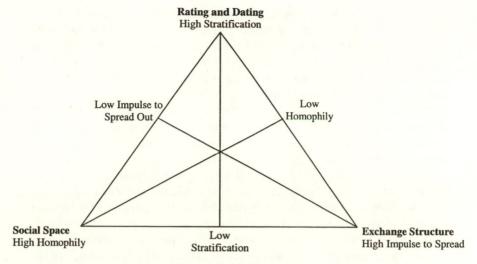

Figure 3.5. Mating systems

tion that follows a spatial but antirelational logic: one wants to pair with those like one, but not those to whom one is already indirectly tied.[44]

Although this scheme is then oriented around pure cases, it may be of use in organizing the actual dispersion of mating systems, because these dimensions are likely to vary in importance in accord with well-understood structural attributes. I have argued that classic exchange structures arise when lineages exist that could conceivably splinter off of a larger social group. In such a case, it is crucial that the structure connect persons, and to the extent that stratification impedes this, stratification is a threat.

Where such lineages do not exist, yet mating decisions involve substantial capital investments (capital in the broadest sense), it seems that the degree of homophily becomes the most important thing in leading to successful pairings. In such cases, it is understood that the decision of whom to marry is not an automous one—one that neither refers to which partner is most attractive (preferential attachment) nor to the involute rules of marriage classes. Rather, the relationship formation is structured because it is dependent on other factors, most important, the wealth or status of the family of the prospetive partner.

In the periods in which mating is divorced from such decisions (such as in "dating"), endogenous stratification may emerge as the organizing principle of

---

[44] Bearman, Moody, and Stovel (2004) suggest that the structures observed arise because of a tendency for the network to move away from cycles, as people follow the heuristic, "don't date your ex's ex's ex." But such structures are also produced if people are distributed in a space, and they try to establish ties to those of the other sex relatively near them. As they end relationships, they turn to others relatively near them. If they do not have too many partners, simulations demonstrate that spanning trees result.

mate selection. In other words, the mere fact of selection can generate a popularity tournament, but it takes something more to turn this into a viable social
structure. This "more" is the suppression of group interest. Both solutions at
the bottom of the triangle are compatible with the preservation of a lineage's
acquired capital—to the left, this capital is material and cultural, and to the
right, it is the women themselves.

"Group" interest, however, is an abstraction—we were able to use this idea
nonproblematically when (for purposes of derivation) we assumed patriarchy,
a particular combination of unilineal descent and despotic control. There are
other conditions in which group interest may be a reasonable simplification,
but in general, we should expect that as we move away from these conditions
associated with patriarchy we allow for mating structures to move away from
the bottom of the triangle, something that Collins (1971) discussed in terms of
the emergence of sexual "markets" in mating.[45]

It is worth briefly noting that these dimensions have some correspondence
to the three dimensions of organization discussed by Harrison White (1992),
namely differentiation, dependence and involution. When organization arises
because of the stratification of individuals, we may say that there is high *differentiation* of persons. When this organization relies on homophily, namely the
existence of distinctions external to the mating structure, we may say that we
see high *dependence*—that is, what takes place in this area is dependent on
valuations made elsewhere. Finally, when the organization involves an orientation toward the group as a whole and involves the linking of relationships in
a particular way, as in the "impluse to spread," we see a tendency toward
involution—that is, a particular form of nonindependence of relationships that
makes reference only to the pattern of *other* relationships. In the previous
chapter, we saw such organization as related to transitivity being itself a principle of organization. But just as there, here we see that this does not mean that
other ways of leading to organization do not lead to transitivity.

Let us consider the nature of transitivity of relationships for each of the
polar positions. In the "stratification" solution, attempted pairings are transitive
but uninterestingly so—the transitivity of choices is a by-product of the more
fundamental fact that individuals are rankable. There is no other pressure toward transitivity. Thus if the top ranked person A "mistakenly" chooses the
bottom ranked Z who also chooses the mid ranked M, there is no increased
tendency of A to choose M. In the "homophily" solution we see the limited
transitivity of the spatial logics we examined in chapter 2—because the probability of tie formation decreases with distance, the impulse of sociation dies out

---

[45] The reader will note that there is no place where "restricted exchange" is located in this
triangle, and this is because the fundamental idea is too vague. As Tjon Sie Fat (1990) emphasized,
some systems called "restricted" can unify an entire society; but this terminology is also compatible with a complete atomization of choices and destabilization of a group.

after a few links. In the generalized exchange structure, relations are actually necessarily *anti*transitive. If lineage *A* gives women to *B* and *B* does to *C*, *A* will not give women to *C*. And yet precisely because of this nontransitivity, the whole is engaged and no part can be removed. In all cases, then, a successful solution to the problem of inequality is incompatible with transitivity—either the group can be linked with antitransitive relationships, or the transitivity of relationships must be localized.

Let us conclude by returning to the problem of inequality. In the solution at the top of this figure, isolated individuals who need not preserve a lineage's balance vis-à-vis other lineages generate a hierachy via a popularity tournament. Because they are unconstrained by a structural imperative to preserve equality, they are free to develop a structure that maximizes inequality. And this, too, is a consistent way to handle the potential for inequality in asymmetric relationships—to systematize it, to make it clear and consistent.

In other words, instead of trying to ensure that transfers balance in general (as in generalized exchange), or by tying two transfers going in different directions (restricted exchange), or converting the relation to a mutual one (homophily), one may cast aside any attempt to preserve equality and convert the asymmetric relations to necessarily *anti*symmetric ones. One may turn, as Levi-Strauss (1953: 547) said, an intransitive and cyclical system into a transitive and acyclical one. The simplest arising structure is an order of statuses—it is akin to taking the results of a popularity tournament and elevating them to the status of social law. It is to such structures that we turn next.

4

The Institutionalization of Inequality:
Pecking Orders

> From the battles of cocks we can form no induction that will affect
> the human species.
> —ROUSSEAU, *Discourse on the Origin of Inequality*

The Question of Dominance Orders

What Are Dominance Orders?

As we have seen, once we allow for the possible nonreciprocation of interactions, inequality is likely to arise, at least in terms of some persons having
a greater number of relationships than others. While it is still possible for
relationships to crystallize in such a way as to lead to overall equality, the
resulting structures tend to be fragile. If inequality cannot be prevented from
emerging, it may not simply characterize *persons* (some more popular than
others), it may also characterize *relationships* themselves. The relationships
may become antisymmetric, in that the two parties are inherently unequal;
they have different "action profiles." If this occurs, as Levi-Strauss says, we
may see the development of a transitive, linear order, as opposed to some sort
of circle.

Levi-Strauss was thinking of the linear orders found among many animal
species including our chimpanzee cousins, structures called "dominance orders," or sometimes "pecking orders."[1] There is admittedly some general similarity between such dominance orders and the linearity induced by a popularity
tournament. As a result, it has been easy for casual analysis to maintain that
we are more or less chimps in clothes, driven by the same deep-seated instincts,
but dressing them up in more complicated guise—and covering them with
disingenuous rationalizations. But although the production of an order of antisymmetric relationships is indeed one way of stabilizing the problem of inequality—by making inequality no longer a problem but a solution—not all
inequality implies the particular structure of a dominance order.

Dominance as a relationship is special because it is intrinsically antisymmetric and hence *can* lead to an order (see Coleman 1960: 72). In an algebraic

---

[1] The term *pecking order* rightly applies only to poultry, but I will use the two terms interchangeably simply to break up the monotony.

sense, an order exists among a set of elements $\{a, b, c, \ldots\}$ when there is a binary relation between any two elements, which we can denote $>$, that has the following four properties: (1) it is antisymmetric (for any distinct a and b, if $a > b$ then not $b > a$); (2) it is reflexive ($a > a$; this is irrelevant for the substantive purposes at hand); (3) it is complete (for any distinct a and b, either $a > b$ or $b > a$); and (4) it is transitive (if $a > b$ and $b > c$, then $a > c$). Where the set of dominance relationships fits these criteria, we may say that a dominance order exists.

In cases where we find such a dominance order, we may also see other relationships that are "structured around" the dominance order in that they are influenced, though not wholly defined, by dominance relationships. For example, grooming among primates (an asymmetric relationship very close to donation) may be related to dominance, in that A may groom B rather frequently, and not vice versa, in large part because B dominates A. But it is not necessarily the case that B will *never* groom A (though B may never be dominated by A), nor is it necessarily the case that A will groom every other animal who dominates A (for an actual example, see Kaplan and Zucker 1980).

In other words, among animals, many forms of relationships may actually be structured by a simple linear dominance order, though these secondary relationships do not themselves take the form of an order. The same may be true for humans. Because the dominance order is a simple, and structurally elegant, social structure, and because it is a common feature of social life in some other primates, it is indeed reasonable to expect that we should see such orders spontaneously arising to cope with problems of inequality raised in chapter 2. And indeed, this is often assumed to be the case.

But writers making this claim generally confuse the inequality produced by popularity tournaments and that produced by dominance orders, leading to a tendency to see dominance orders among human beings where they probably are absent.[2] Because they assume that human inequalities are basically the same thing as dominance, such researchers have not looked closely at actual interactions to determine whether or not this simple and potentially powerful form of social structure does in fact tend to emerge among humans. In this chapter, I wish to examine the structural properties of dominance orders among animals and demonstrate that the loose understanding of dominance orders often applied to human social life does not even apply to animals. I then turn to humans and demonstrate that proper dominance structures only seem to arise among children and mid-adolescents.

---

[2] An important exception is the work of Roger Gould (2003: 22), who proposes a tendency for humans to form structures of dominance relationships similar to those of animals, though he stresses that such structures are likely to fall short of a completely transitive linear order. He also deliberately emphasizes the similarities between bureaucratic stratification and the dominance structures arising in honor cultures in which there are violent struggles for mastery.

How Do Dominance Orders Arise?

Dominance orders can arise in different ways. In one, a preexisting difference in some attribute or attributes leads to an inequality (e.g. *A* is "greater" than *B* in some respect); relations of inequality are then the scaffolding for interaction. So if all animals have some degree of individual characteristic ζ, animals *i* and *j* can compare themselves in terms of degree of ζ, with animal *i* submitting if $\zeta_i < \zeta_j$ and animal *j* submitting if $\zeta_j < \zeta_i$. For example, little animals may get out of the way when big animals approach. In this simplest case, the people or animals involved *observe* one another to determine the direction of inequality but do not need to *interact* to create their order.

It also may be the case that animals cannot observe the qualities that lead one to become dominant over the other without some sort of dyadic interaction. This dynamic is somewhat like the card game "war"—each animal has some stable individual quality, but this quality is unknown until a bout with another animal in which both turn over their cards at once. According to this conception, there actually is, from the get-go, an implicit ordering of the animals, although they themselves do not have immediate access to it. Instead, they must re-create this via agonistic interactions (or, more generally, some form of "paired comparison"). For example, school children attempting to create a height order seem unable simply to arrange themselves from tallest to shortest. Instead, they pair off (at least among rough equals) to determine which is tallest, and repeat this enough times until the order is re-created.

Until relatively recently, it was assumed by most researchers that this was how pecking orders formed; the underlying individual quality might be somewhat different in different species, but the idea was the same. Every animal has some "toughness," say; this toughness is a continuously variable quantity that is different in every animal, and so given any pair of animals, one will be tougher than the other. But closer observation of animal groups both in captivity and in the wild, and the experimental work of Ivan Chase that will be discussed below, has demonstrated that in a number of species, including some rather dim ones such as fish and chickens (e.g., Schjelderup-Ebbe 1935: 952), the formation of clear pecking orders seems to require awareness of the social pattern as a whole (see Sade and Dow 1994: 158), if only because the correlation of rank with observable characteristics (including observable "aggressiveness") is too low to produce the kind of consistency observed (Coleman 1960: 99; Chase 1974; Chase 1980; also see Dugatkin, Alfieri, and Moore 1994). Instead, Chase and others put forward a different understanding of the production of orders.[3]

---

[3] Schjelderup-Ebbe (1922), in the seminal article that initiated the work in dominance hierarchies, also reported this, although his work was misunderstood as supporting the idea of an order. In fact, Schjelderup-Ebbe (1922: 229, 231f, 234; 1935: 952f, 965) argued that the structures were almost never perfectly linear (especially if there were more than 10 hens), and that this demonstrated that physical strength could not fully explain position in the structure. (He even noted huge cycles, where the hen seemingly at the bottom of the order of 20 is able to dominate

In this conception, bouts are necessary not simply because they allow each animal to turn over her card but because the "qualities" that determine dominance are themselves created—or at least altered—in social interaction. This may be because each individual's latent state is changed by the results of the past bout; such a scenario is reasonable for many mammals based on what is known about the relationship between hormone levels, aggressiveness, and response to defeat. "Winner effects" refer to the increased confidence and aggression an animal experiences after besting an opponent, while "loser effects" refer to the opposite among those bested. Such effects could plausibly lead to an order in a set of animals that had originally been equal along all measures related to dominance (also see the more complex approach of van Doorn, Hengeveld, and Weissing 2003a, b).

But it is also possible that the formation of the structure is dependent on the sequence of interactions because animals observe the results of other interactions, and this affects their estimates of others' probability of submitting to them in an agonistic situation. That is, the interaction between A and B does not simply change the future interactions of A and B, but also those of some C who happens to observe them.[4] The linear order may be largely due to a combination of "winner effects," "loser effects," and "bystander effects" (in which those who see one hen beat another become less confident when encountering the victor and more confident when encountering the loser). From close observations of chickens, Chase actually finds that hierarchies tend to develop in the following way: two chickens have a showdown; the winner (call her A) then attacks and dominates the bystander (C). The previous loser (B) then can encounter (C), and no matter which ends up dominating the other, a transitive triad results.

This process is not the same as that witnessed among primates or among some other birds (see Chase and Rohwert 1987). There, a more complex heuristic may be used, but Chase (1982a) still suggests the possibility of the structure arising via the accumulation of local structures (including an increased probability of reversals in intransitive triads, which leads to a tendency toward transitivity).[5] While this process could also lead to the production of an order in

---

the hen at the top!) Indeed, the word he used was not the German for "order," but *Liste*, meaning list or register, perhaps because of its earlier meaning as the thin strip of land used in a jousting tournament, which has left us the phrase "to enter the lists." Instead of basing the order in simple physical attributes, Schjelderup-Ebbe reported that accidental conditions—momentary failure of courage, perhaps, or that the hen B appeared next to another C that the hen in question (A) already feared—can lead to hen A locking in a submissive relationship to B, though she might well beat B in a fight.

[4] Actually, this works for smaller groups, and other patterns are found in larger ones. See Chase (1985: 95).

[5] Evidence for this is seen in the fact that when three hens were put all together, the resulting set of three dominance relations were always transitive, but when they encountered each other as three isolated pairs, in 14% of the cases the resulting set of three relations was intransitive (Chase 1982b: 228).

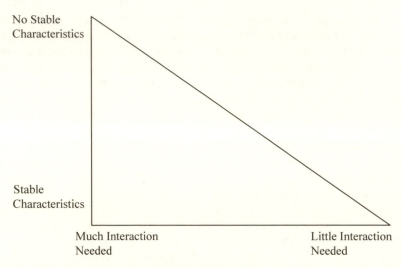

Figure 4.1. Space of pecking orders

the absence of preexisting differentiation, it might simply speed up the process whereby the "correct" order (that is, one congruent with preexisting differentiation) was established (also see Beacham 2003).

Now it may be that actually existing dominance orders fall somewhere between these scenarios—indeed, we can imagine these three conditions as poles in a space of possibilities formed by the two dimensions of the degree to which dominance is defined by comparison of stable individual qualities and the degree to which interaction is required (see figure 4.1). This space is triangular because if stable individual characteristics contribute nothing to the production of relationships of dominance, surely interaction will be required for the relation to be created. The early discussions of dominance in animals—and many contemporary ones of dominance among humans!—assumed that all cases fall in the corner on the right. Such an assumption is no longer tenable.[6]

This suggests that pecking orders generally require some degree of *visibility*—there must be some public sign that indicates to other animals that *A* is "higher" than *B*. The importance of visibility does not contradict the impor-

---

[6] Nor should it be assumed that there should be no cases found on the lower left—stable individual characteristics that require much interaction. An example here is found in the organization of pig litters. The emerging rank between siblings has a great deal to do with size, but size in turn has to do with "teat order" (which teat is commonly used by the pig). That social interaction has much to do with the resulting weight of the pig is seen in the fact that pigs reared individually have much less dispersion in weight than pigs raised together (Syme and Syme 1974: 35–38). Further, experimental work with Japanese macaques demonstrates that the highly hereditary nature of rank among females does not mean that specific interactional patterns are not necessary for the acquisition of rank (Chapais 1991; also see Berman and Kapsalis 1999).

tance of individual characteristics.[7] Both are generally involved, although the trade-off—and hence the exact position of any species in the triangular space above—depends on the species in question and perhaps the conditions (most important, captivity versus wild). There are no known cases in which dominance position is clearly totally divorced from individual attributes, but also no cases in which dominance position can be perfectly explained by measurable individual attributes.

Further, if we were to select one individual characteristic that is most commonly associated with triumph in an agonistic encounter it would be self-confidence (and not size, age, or strength per se) (see Schjelderup-Ebbe 1935: 955). Self-confidence in turn is associated with individual characteristics that—at least in the artificial situations usually studied involving the introduction of previously unacquainted animals—precede the formation of the dominance order (such as weight, age, strength). But it is also associated with position that comes *out* of the dominance order (e.g., mother's rank for the case of ranked matrilines) or out of the experience of interaction that itself constructs the dominance order (e.g., "winner effects" and "loser effects").

Self-confidence is crucial because the encounters that lead to submission rituals are generally ones that are themselves ritualized, and therefore involve restrained aggression. This does not mean that the encounter will never escalate to unrestrained aggression; on the contrary, this is indeed likely if both animals refuse to submit. This type of game—incidentally called "chicken" in the United States—is one that behooves both parties to make an accurate forecast of their own probability of triumph, since the cost of pursuing a "no-crack" strategy can be very high (on the psychology of choosing to submit, see Kummer [1982]). Animals apparently take their own sense of themselves into account (thus a maturing male will, perhaps through experimentation, sense that he is now strong enough to challenge another who has always dominated him), but also what they see around them.

We might understand the process whereby pecking orders form as follows, taking chickens as an example.[8] Each chicken not only has some degree of confidence, but some guess as to each other's confidence. Of course, they may under- or overestimate each others' confidence, but they change these estimates as a result of the interaction whereby if one hen estimates that a second is less confident than herself, she will attack. If the attacked is actually more

---

[7] Indeed, White (2002: 14, 31) draws our attention to the importance of visible comparability in the establishment of that sort of differentiation of quality that leads participants in a market to appear *as* individuals.

[8] Fararo and Skvoretz (1988) attempted a rigorous model of the formation of pecking orders based on expectation-states principles, and tested it with data. Their model revealed the importance of bystander effects, but underestimated the frequency of double-attacks, for reasons that I think are made clear by the model suggested in note 9.

confident than the attacker guessed, there will be a reciprocation. The first hen may repeat the attack, or she may lose some confidence and abandon the attempt. If so, other chickens will consider the unreciprocated attack important information to help refine their estimates of the birds involved.[9] Thus according to this simple model, there may be an individual-level quality that determines the outcomes of agonistic encounters, but it is one that is fundamentally tied to the ongoing social interaction.

In support of this interpretation, Ginsburg and Allee (1942) and Allee (1942: 124f) demonstrated that by "fixing" a series of bouts for mice (pairing them with others of a more or less aggressive species), one could—like Shaw's Professor Higgins who managed to train a Cockney flower girl to assume a place in Britain's upper class—condition a "bottom" mouse to have the confidence to move up in the hierarchy and eventually become a "top" mouse (or the other way around).

This space of possible processes that may lead to dominance structures is related to the space we saw in the previous chapter involving a trade-off between differentiation, dependence, and involution. The parallel is far from exact, for it is not the dimensions themselves that reoccur but the trade-offs. In this case, we find that the space of possibilities may be redrawn as in figure 4.2. That is, the differentiation characteristic of a pecking order must come from somewhere—either from some valuation *outside* the set of dominance relationships (and hence position in the dominance order is dependent), or from *inside*, due to the involution of relationships. This figure adds little to the previous for this particular case, but it illustrates a parallelism that will recur, namely that organization comes from somewhere, and from the perspective of any set of relationships, we may divide this into "from inside" and "from outside."[10] In this case, we are interested in a particularly *vertical* organization, one that militates against equality; in chapters 2 and 3 such equality or mutuality could itself be a focus of organization and introduce a set of related trade-offs; from here onward we will see equality of any two persons in terms of what is implied by the set of relationships as a whole.

---

[9] Formally, and using the same notation as above, if the confidence of the *i*th chicken is denoted ζ_i and this chicken's estimate of the confidence of some *other* chicken *j* denote $E_i[\zeta_j]$, we may imagine that initially $E_i[\zeta_j] =$ some constant c and ζ_i is initially randomly distributed. Chicken *i* pecks at *j* iff $\zeta_i > E_i[\zeta_j]$; if so, all chickens *k* (including *i* and *j*) update $E'_k[\zeta_i] = E'_k[\zeta_i] + \Delta_k$; $E'_k[\zeta_j] = E_k[\zeta_j] - \Delta_k$. If we assume $\Delta_k = \Delta$, $k \neq i, j$, $\Delta_i, \Delta_j > \Delta$, then we might understand the reason for double attacks. Finally, we might also expect that chicken *i*'s estimate of *j*'s confidence begins to wander randomly as time elapses from the last time *i* saw *j* interact with another chicken, at least up until the time in which *i* and *j* lock in a dominance relationship with one another.

[10] Further, to increase the parallelism with the preceding figure, this was constructed so that it implies that there can be both stable characteristics and high involution. We might better, however, define involution such that there is an intrinsic trade-off between the two. This would involve flipping the labels of all the poles, but leaving the fundamental logic intact.

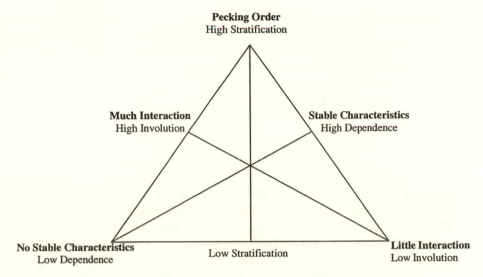

Figure 4.2. Recasting of figure 4.1

In sum, dominance orders arise when sets of agonistic contests are decided in a consistent way; consistency is rooted both in individual qualities (to some unknown degree) and to social processes of two types: first is the learning or biophysical effects that come from leaving a previous encounter a winner or loser, and second is the ability to witness outcomes of contests between other animals. This only sketches the boundaries of possibility of the dominance order; to learn about their structural characteristics, we must look more closely at well-studied cases.

Dominance Orders among Primates

From Poultry to Primates

Dominance orders were first discovered among poultry by Schelderup-Ebbe in the form of pecking orders (though see note 3; it is quite possible that this was known to agriculturalists previously). The pecks directed from one hen to another are clearly damaging—even the city-dweller first notices that certain hens (those at the bottom of the order) generally have a sorry, bedraggled look, due to pecks received at the top of the head. But then one realizes that as hens are generally of the same height, for the dominant hen to get in a good peck, the subordinate will actually have to lower her head slightly, or at least not raise it up. While hens lower their heads to feed, and are thus vulnerable at certain times, it turns out that they seem surprisingly willing to have their heads lowered when confronting dominant hens. This lowering of the body or just the head of the subordinate animal seems to be an extremely widespread symbol of submission in the animal kingdom. Among some of the more decent sorts of animals (e.g., cows [Syme and Syme 1979: 45f]), such a show of submission is sufficient to get one off the hook and escape punishment: among hens and similarly nasty creatures, however, this is not so, hence the bedraggled look of low-ranking chickens.

Similar structures (see Chase 1980 for a literature review) have been found in a number of other social animals, and what is crucial (I shall argue below) is that where such dominance orders are found, some similar symbolic demonstration of submission is also present. The list of animals with known dominance orders grows steadily and includes not only many herd animals (domesticated and wild) but even goes down to wasps and ants, which have a ritualized submission routine that involves lowering the head (Hölldobler and Wilson 1994). While orders can be *produced* in still other species by forcing competitive bouts (such as by restricting the food supply for caged animals), this does not necessarily imply that the dominance order exists as a naturally occurring form of social organization. Thus one can generate dominance orders in turtles, toads, and frogs (Boice, Boice Quanty, and Williams 1974), but no clear evidence of ritualized submission has been noted as of yet.

Because humans are generally classed as primates, dominance orders among primates have attracted the greatest attention by sociologists hoping to learn some lessons about human social organization (e.g., Tiger 1970). I shall argue against the presumed utility of this strategy below, but even if we accept the premise that examination of primates will give us a key to understand human dominance, it is hard to come up with a simple model of general primate dominance that can be applied to humans. As we shall see, research over the last few decades, while supporting the centrality of dominance hierarchies, has shattered any notion of a general linear form of dominance that is constant across species (see Yerkes and Yerkes 1935: 1019 for the classic statement). I will briefly review important results from primatology before going on to discuss what is known about humans. I will follow ethologists' convention and call the highest-ranking animal in some dominance order the "alpha" animal, the second ranking "beta," etc.

Differential Organizational Principles across Species

It is true that some form of hierarchy is common among the social primates, but it is not the case that the type of hierarchy is the same in all species. Among some, the order is clearer for males than for females, and in others the reverse is true. Among some, orders involve individuals, and in others families. For example, for gorillas and chimpanzees, the female order seems less fixed than the male order—indeed, in some cases for female gorillas there may be no consistent direction to their relationships—and females may be said both to have more quarrels but less serious aggression (cf. Schaller 1963: 260; Schaller 1964: 133; Walters and Seyfarth 1987: 312; Nishida and Hiraiwa-Hasegawa 1987: 168). But all species of macaques have a matrilineal hierarchy at the core of the society (de Waal 2001: 285). At least under some conditions, each mother has a position in the hierarchy, and immediately under her, all her daughters (with the younger generally ranking higher), all above the next matriline (Chepko-Sade, Reitz, and Sade 1989). Among patas monkeys, which (like gorillas) have large groups with one mature male each, the females tend to form a linear dominance order (Kaplan and Zucker 1980). In other species (such as the related Vervets and Sykes' monkeys), both sexes may form a single ranking, though sex difference is preserved in that the highest ranking male may perform some of the functions frequently attached to this "alpha" position even when he submits to an alpha female (see Rowell 1971: 634, 636 for examples).[11] Finally, in at least one species, the wooly spider monkey, close observation has found *no* evidence of a dominance order at all and an extremely low rate of agonistic interactions (Strier 1986: 244, 275).

The variability of dominance structure is related to differences in the normal social life of different species. Many primates (including most prosimians like bushbabies and tarsiers, but also the orangutan) are more or less solitary; some others form monogamous couples that forage together (examples here include certain new world monkeys and lemurs). Other groups range from large multimale groups (from the loose associations found in chimpanzees to the tighter ones found among most macaques and many baboons) to one-male groups (from the small ones of the famous hamadryas baboon to the large ones of the Drill and Mandrill baboons).[12] The hamadryas baboon is structured around "families" in which one adult male has ties to one or more females (ties that are generally respected by third parties), and adult males simply do not have ranks at all. Tension is resolved by both parties submitting, for even the victor risks loss of control over females during a prolonged conflict (Kummer 1995: 167ff).

Further, even within species, particular groups may vary greatly in their organizational principles (see Strayer and Cummins 1980: 94). Among small groups of chimpanzees, the males tend to have a clear hierarchy, while in larger ones this seems to be generalized to a few orders of more-or-less equivalents

---

[11] As a rule of thumb, species that exchange males tend to have a social structure revolving around ties between females, and species that exchange females tend to have a social structure revolving around ties between males (Smuts 1987b: 400).

[12] This information may be found in the table at the end of Smuts, Cheney, Seyfarth, Wrangham, and Struhsaker (1987) and Wrangham (1987: 287). Even among the great apes there is such diversity that one cannot speak of a general social form; the only thing they seem to share is a stronger tendency to female exchange where there are social groups, while most (but not all) monkeys exchange males, who enter a group with low rank and rise over time (see also Walters and Seyfarth 1987: 311, 313).

(e.g. high, middle, low) (Walters and Seyfarth 1987: 311). In other cases, differences between groups cannot be so directly linked to anything so simple and generalizable as group size but may depend on the particular mix of temperaments involved (see Capitanio 2004: 28; de Waal 1977: 243, 253).

Finally, while all dominance hierarchies have some sort of signal of accepted submission, the degree of violence associated with dominance varies dramatically. De Waal (1990: 157–66) points out that our conception of dominance hierarchies in monkeys comes largely from rhesus monkeys, the most studied species, which have strict rankings that are enforced with serious bitings (for an example of the perfect ordering of dominance relations among rhesus monkeys, see Sade 1972: 207). But the closely related stumptail macaque has a more relaxed rank system (e.g., subordinates will initiate contact with superordinates) and "punishments" by the superior animals tend to be painless rituals such as giving a mock bite on the wrist (and subordinates may defuse tense situations by offering a wrist for such a ritual bite). Thus even within closely related species of primates, there are many different forms of dominance orders, and if we attempt to extract implications for humans through simple analogy, the lesson we learn will appear quite different depending on the case we choose. However, there are also commonalities that shed light on those qualities of the relationship of dominance that have structural implications.

Dominance Is Relational

For one, it is clear that while size and aggressiveness are frequently useful in allowing one animal to assert dominance over another, dominance in general cannot be equated with a single individual attribute or even with a set of them (see Bauer 1980: 107). Thus de Waal (1998: 77f) discusses how to a naïve observer, it seems obvious that a particular chimpanzee is at the top of the dominance order because he is the biggest and strongest, but things really go the other way—the alpha puffs himself out and walks in an exaggerated way, while others, in submissive greeting rituals, make themselves look low and small.[13] While there is a general inverted-U shape curve relating dominance and age in many species (see, e.g., Nishida and Hiraiwa-Hasegawa 1987: 175), even age, size, and physical condition considered jointly do not wholly determine rank.

While individual attributes are important, an animal's position in this hierarchy generally expresses a balance of power in the group as a whole. In particular, among some species (most importantly chimpanzees), position in the dominance hierarchy is a function of alliances as well as individual qualities; further, position in this order does not unproblematically translate into agonistic tri-

---

[13] Similarly, among anoles (lizards that are able to change color), the dominant male is usually green, while the other males are brown (Evans 1936: 105).

umph in any particular encounter. In particular, alpha males often depend on female support (well-studied examples involve chimpanzees and different types of macaques [Smuts 1987b: 409f]).[14] If others can support, they can also undermine: De Waal (1998: 44; 2001: 282; also Goodall 1990: 46, 71) gives instances in which the whole group turns on the alpha male and sends him fleeing, in some cases permanently removing him from the position, indeed sending him from the top to the bottom (also see Kummer 1995: 301f).[15]

Structural Complications

Not only can dominance relations be due to systems of relationships (e.g., alliances) transcending a dyad, but these other relationships may themselves be structured. In other words, there are other forms of social organization that have (until recently) largely been overlooked (at least in the West [de Waal 1998: 137]). The best known is the male-female "friendship" studied among baboons by Smuts (1985), but horizontal relations connecting coreared infants may also cut across the lines established by a dominance order. There are also cases in which, at least among the more dominant members, there seems to be what de Waal (1998: 207; cf. 1987: 426) calls "a network of positions of influence" apart from the dominance hierarchy. Finally, Sade et al. (1988: 410), noting that monkeys have more than one status because they have positions in more than one network, put forward and examined a dimension of centrality that is partially independent of dominance status.

Further, there may be some degree of slippage between alpha position and leadership, which may (in the fashion famously proposed for small groups by Bales) be differentiated. De Waal (1998: 145f) describes a situation in which a young male became alpha with support from an older ex-alpha, but did not adopt the peacekeeping aspects of the alpha role, which seemed too difficult for a neophyte. Instead, the ex-alpha performed this role and was rewarded by being given preference in greeting by other group members, though he himself would defer to the new alpha. Kummer (1995: 53f) not only describes a similar divorce of dominance and leadership among baboons, but also the case in which the alpha position is taken over by a female (also see Stammbach 1987: 119).

Not only can there be a differentiation between dominance position and leadership, but positions in the dominance order are more labile than the term

[14] Speaking of rhesus monkeys, de Waal (2001: 301) argues that even in the wild "it is not always just a matter of which male is the strongest or fastest, because the collective support of the females may keep a male in the saddle well beyond his prime. They often prefer a familiar, predictable leader over a younger, aggressive upstart."

[15] At the same time, such alliances, while often necessary for achieving a dominant position are not by themselves sufficient—female support for the aging alpha studied by de Waal (1998: 88) may have lengthened the time it took him to be replaced, but in the end, replaced he was.

order suggests. The dominance relation between any two animals *A* and *B* may depend on the presence or absence of other animals. This is certainly the case for infants of many species—they have two ranks, one that is "their own" and another when their mothers are present that comes from the mother's rank. But this phenomenon often determines the relationships between adults as well: it is possible for some *A* to dominate *B* when *C* is present but not when *C* is absent. (Among Bonobos, the mother's rank influences the rank of males well into their adulthood; see Furuichi [1997].) We will return to this later when we examine how primates take the dominance order as a backdrop for action.

The dominance order, then, is not equivalent to the social structure of primate groups involved. Other relations (such as kinship and friendship, perhaps even coparenthood) also exist in at least some species, and the structure of any specific relationship (such as grooming) may make reference to these other relations and not simply the dominance order.[16] The pecking order is indeed a distinct structural form, but it is easy to overstate the conformity of existing groups to such an ideal typical order. With that caution in mind, we go on to explore the properties of dominance orders in animals and how they channel action.

Properties of Dominance Orders

The Centrality of Ritual

To summarize, we may say that a dominance or pecking order only arises where there are (a) frequent agonistic interactions that are (b) always resolved by an act of submission by one party (see Bernstein 1980: 80), and (c) the pattern of these submissions is mutually reinforcing. As we have seen, (c) entails that the relation in question be antisymmetric, transitive, and complete (cf. Hage and Harary 1983: 79).[17] These three conditions imply that the structure is an *order* in the algebraic sense.

Condition (a) pertains to the *content* of the relationships (agonistic interaction) and (c) to the nature of the *form* (an order); this seemingly complete specification makes it easy to ignore (b) as a crucial aspect of pecking orders (that is, the *process*). Yet it cannot be accidental that in all or almost all cases of known dominance orders, these confrontations involve *ritualized* submission (see de Waal 1987: 422–24), in which one animal signals defeat by unambiguously refusing to defend or attack, often presenting him- or herself in a

---

[16] For this reason, White's (1992) assumption that pecking orders would exist in predifferentiated human societies—an argument I shall use below—may not be wholly true, in that pecking orders themselves may involve a form of differentiation.

[17] Schjelderup-Ebbe (1922: 234, 237) emphasized this completeness: there are, he said, never any two hens that live together without the question of which dominates the other being settled.

physically vulnerable position, at which point the other animal ceases all physically dangerous aggression (for a general statement and analysis of the case of rhesus monkeys, see Bernstein and Gordon 1974: 306). It is easy to understate the importance of this, because we often assume that individual qualities (e.g., size) are all that is needed to produce a pecking order. But as this assumption has been shown to be false, we would do well to look closely at the relation of ritual to structure.

The idea of ritualized animal behavior sounds somewhat strange to modern ears, although it was taken for granted by early sociologists. In volume 2 of the *Principles of Sociology*, Spencer (1910 [1886]: 3, 34, 116, 220) began by analyzing ceremony and started with animals: for example, the dog crawls on its belly to indicate submission, and "a parallel mode of behavior occurs among human beings."[18]

Despite this bold beginning, there has been surprisingly little attention to ritual in animals among sociologists, perhaps because of an illogical belief that purely communicative action could not be reconciled with natural selection, since there is no advantage to evolving a symbolic display if others have not already evolved the ability to interpret it. But there is no contradiction, as Darwin himself understood—many ritual behaviors seem to be prolongations of intention movements, behaviors that precede an action. It is reasonable to expect that other animals will already have understood the "meaning" of such a functional gesture as opening the mouth to bite, for, as Mead (1934: 49) says, in uncharacteristically clear language, the meaning of a gesture is "what you [the observer] are going to do about it." Mead's example of a gesture that communicates meaning is the growl of an angry dog which "means" that the dog is aroused for possible attack. All the evolving animal need do to produce purely ritual behavior is to make use of the preexisting "meaning" of preparatory actions or intention movements by prolonging them and separating them from the action itself. The meaning need not be known to the animal making the gesture for it to be reinforced via selection. The dog who growls for some time before attacking may be the dog that does not need to attack; the crab

[18] Here Spencer seemed to echo Comte's conviction that these ritual forms of animal behavior are not fundamentally different in kind from human religion. Interestingly, Spencer (1910 [1886]: 24) then went on to develop a quite different analytic strategy for human rituals, tracing them from acts that once had a direct meaning now lost (thus we no longer need to show an absence of weapons, yet we still shake hands). But the need to make such evolutionary-vestigial derivations (so well criticized by Levi-Strauss 1969 [1949]) is cast into doubt by the case of the animals: the dog's action is symbolic *from the start*—rather than interpret the dog's crawling as dating from the time in which dogs did battle and the loser would grovel and imitate the expected death to mollify the rage of the superior and thus avoid being killed, Spencer postulates an inherent symbolic capacity of dogs. The same type of capacity should exist in humans. Interestingly, Darwin (1904 [1889]) used similar arguments as to the transition from once conscious and purposive action to reflex when discussing ritual behavior by animals.

that holds his claw open in front of his eyes for some time before pinching may be the one that never needs to pinch . . . and therefore is less likely to be flung against a rock (also see Wilson 1975: 224).

We are justified in calling the gesture that has been exaggerated, and is performed in the same way in the same circumstances because of its communicative value, a *ritualized* one. There are a number of different forms of such communicative ritual, but submission rituals are quite common in the animal kingdom. Many of these involve the submitting animal making itself physically lower than the other. These rituals are more likely to exist where animals live together in permanent or near-permanent fashion. Thus male rhinoceri and other ungulates that have a territorially based system of dominance (in which one male is dominant over a fixed area and other males either accept this dominance, stay off, or challenge) may have agonistic encounters, but these can end with the loser simply turning and running when it seems prudent to do so.[19] It is not necessary to publicly advertise this fact, since there is no "chorus" of bystanders who need to keep tabs on the relative positions of the two. Ritualized actions serve to make the outcome of a dyadic contest unambiguous and hence help avoid the necessity of its repetition.

Significantly, such ritual is not observed in animals that do not form dominance orders in the wild though they can be induced to by malicious experimenters who force them to compete for food. Thus box turtles will displace and bite each other, and occasionally hide in their shells, but do not necessarily submit (here see Boice 1970: 707). Retreat into the shell on the part of one turtle does not inhibit further aggression by another, and rightly so—that first turtle may reemerge and continue the fight. Further, even among primates with dominance orders, those that seem to lack a vocabulary of appeasement gestures have less rigid orders, and the combination of low general levels of aggression but serious damage when fights do take place that suggests an absence of inhibition on intragroup fighting (see Rowell 1971: 628–30).

It is not our place to speculate on the reason for the existence of such rituals here. But it is important that these rituals allow for a public signaling of the outcome of an agonistic contest, and it is these signals that determine the dominance order. Indeed, while it may go against the *realpolitik* assumptions of social scientists who pride themselves on their unsentimental perspective, the dominance order is better understood as the order of these ritualistic signals than as a matter of force and its results, since in many species (including chimpanzees), it is these rituals (and not necessarily the more physically important fights, displacements, or food-taking behavior) that take on the form

---

[19] Domesticated pigs retain some of this, requiring repeated losses before the loser accepts defeat gracefully (Syme and Syme 1974: 33). Kummer (1995: 281) shows the importance that the ritual sign be syntactically correct in that it appear in the proper place in an unfolding sequence of interactions.

of an order. Other interactions are only probabilistically related to position in the dominance order, and hence there may be "reversals" in terms of the outcome of fights, in that a low-ranking ape will best a high-ranking one (e.g. de Waal 1977: 233, 235).[20] But there are *no* reversals in greeting rituals. As de Waal (1998: 81) says, "Greeting reflects *frozen* dominance relationships. It is the only form of social behavior that is [perfectly antisymmetric among primates]."

Action and Orders

The essence of the pecking order, then, turns on the ritualized submission relations of the animals in question. The dog, as Spencer noted, crawls on its belly; submitting rats roll on their back and allow the dominant to rest its paws and head on the first's exposed belly (Baenninger 1970). These submissions are mutually reinforcing in that the animals can be more or less ranked in an order of dominance. But the order may be more than either an analysts' construct or a built-in genetic program that the animals are helpless not to recreate. It can be, and certainly is in the case of the higher primates, perceived as a "social fact" by animals who take the existence of structure into account and adapt their actions accordingly.

Now it is not clear how animals understand the pecking order; almost certainly, it varies by species. The pivotal question is whether each animal in a group of N remembers N-1 bits of information pertaining to each *relationship* it has with each other animal, or whether it remembers N *ranks* of individuals, or even *statuses* (that is, interval level as opposed to ordinal level distinctions). Given a perfect ordering, remembering ranks or statuses is superior in that at the simple cost of remembering one additional piece of information (although far more complicated information than the binary value of submit/dominate), the animal is able to re-create the relationships of all *other* pairs of animals, which allows for far more subtle interactions. As we shall see, it is impossible to explain the actions of animals of more intelligent and social species unless we posit that they have some sense not only of their own position vis-à-vis other animals, but of the order as a whole.

Such a sense of the social structure is seen, first of all, in the fact that in many primates and some birds the highest status animal is not merely able to dominate all others, but seems to fulfill some qualitatively different role. For example, among some old world monkeys, the alpha male—and not others— will respond to a stranger who presents a group threat (Bernstein 1964, 1966). Furthermore, the alpha may intervene in disputes on the side of the lower-ranking member or simply enforce the peace. Now to some extent, this may

---

[20] Especially regarding immature monkeys, the "order" that one would induce on the basis of observations depends greatly on which of a number of behaviors is taken to indicate dominance.

be a general feature of high rank (as opposed to a special position for the highest ranking), since in some species, higher-ranking animals are "loser supporters." Among poultry, the relation between any two birds is well predicted by their rank difference—the highest ranking hen will peck the lowest with the greatest intensity and savagery. But among more social (and intelligent) birds such as jackdaws, animosity is reserved for those who are actually potential rivals; the more dominant intervene in a struggle between two lower ranked birds consistently on the side of the lowest (Lorenz 1952: 148–50).[21]

But alphas do not merely support losers, they may suppress fighting, especially in multimale primate societies. Among chimpanzees, the alpha may keep order by breaking up fights according to the simple but effective principle, "hit anyone who hits." This generally means hitting the winning party who is less pleased with the premature end to the contest. (This is all the more notable because adult male chimpanzees tend to be winner supporters [Smuts 1987b: 404]). But even outside of such a melee, the alpha is likely to become a loser-supporter or protector (see de Waal 1977: 260, 263 for the case of Java monkeys [*Macaca fascicularis*]; de Waal 1987: 427; de Waal 1998: 117, 146). One need not see noblesse oblige in this action, nor any special altruism—while the alpha male may suppress conflict when he intervenes on the side of the loser, he can dramatically escalate it when he intervenes on the side of the winner (de Waal 1977: 265). The point about the alpha's intervention is not that it indicates that he occupies an altruistic role, but that there is a role at all.

The tendency for alphas in some species to be loser supporters suggests that the animals in question are able to cognize a sense of the ranks of others. We also see evidence of animals understanding each others' ranks in the fact that in some species, animals tend to fight more with those close in rank to themselves (see Bernstein 1969: 457; Bernstein and Gordon 1974: 308; Kummer 1995: 294), while in others, they seem to have more of their friends from these close rank positions (Rowell 1971: 637).

But this very strength of the pecking order—its ability to seem a socially objective "thing" in which all animals have fixed places—can undermine it. Once animals can in some way treat ranks as social givens, they can then orient their action strategically to this social structure. Instead of the social structure simply being the outcome of unreflective (if socially influenced) sets of interactions, the social structure can be part of the environment taken into account by animals as they act. Returning to the imagery of the dialectic of institutionalization with which we began, the dominance order emerges as a reified institution—"frozen" action, as de Waal interestingly called it above—

---

[21] There are some cases in which this has been observed for monkeys but others in which it has not (see de Waal 1977: 245f, who suggests that this adjacency phenomenon has only been observed in captive groups, and Rhine 1973 for some evidence of an adjacency effect for nonagonistic behavior).

that can confront spontaneous interaction (just as Simmel would have said) as an objective fact.

The most direct form of such second-order interaction is the alliance. In an alliance, one lower-ranking and one higher-ranking animal form what is in effect a mutual defense treaty. Now of course, this can be folded back into the dominance order in the form of raising the rank of the subordinate member. So if the sixth ranking forms an alliance with the second ranking, this may allow the sixth to move up to fifth rank. Indeed, early analyses tended to assume that all such alliances were folded back into the linear structure. In some cases this does occur: certainly lasting alliances among chimpanzee males can lead to changes in rank position.

But in other cases, alliances can lead to mutations of the dominance order. In what is known as "dependent rank," one animal may rank sixth when the second-ranked animal is not present and fourth when the second ranked is present. (In contrast, the ranking that arises from paired comparisons may be called the "basic rank" [Kawai 1958].) Far from being a minor complication, this more complex state is the one that determines behavior in most circumstances (at least in naturally occurring communities), may be prior in the life of each individual (because in many species infants originally take rank from their mother [Kawai 1958: 112; Bernstein 1969: 456]), and is often quite different from the basic rank (de Waal 1977: 226). While this dependency is often most clearly seen for the high-ranking females whose rank is tied to that of the high-ranking males (this is seen in a number of monkey species as well as Jackdaws [Lorenz 1961; de Waal 1977: 227]), or children of high ranking females (de Waal 1977: 242, 274; Sade 1967 on rhesus; McHugh 1958 on bison), it is also generally true for adult males, who, as Nishida and Hiraiwa-Hasegawa (1987: 175) point out, rarely interact without others present.[22]

As the preceding makes clear, formal ranks in a dominance order do not need to correspond to the actual ability to triumph in agonistic situations; this latter ability depends on situational factors including social alliances. While long-term changes in these factors can indeed lead to a change in position in the dominance order, it is not at all unusual for there to be a relatively long period in which the ritualized submission relations do not correspond to the outcomes of nonritualized contests (e.g., fights). This is true even with (perhaps especially with) the alpha position. Indeed, just because the alpha position is one that seems to be a "position"—a role divorceable from the individual who occupies it—there can be a difference between the power that would seem appropriate to the position and the power of the animal occupying it.[23]

---

[22] Chapais (1991: 263) goes so far as to say that "basic rank is nonexistent . . . in the context of the social group."

[23] De Waal (1998: 82) discusses cases in which an alpha male's position is clearly untenable; the other animals appear to know this (as does the alpha), but it takes a fair amount of time before a challenger is sufficiently emboldened to force the alpha to submit to him.

Further, in contrast to the facile assumptions made by some sociobiologists, intrasex dominance does not necessarily translate into reproductive fitness (Smuts 1987a: 389, 395f, 398; Smith 1994: 232; also see Qvarnström and Forsgren 1998; Takahata 1991: 133).[24] Where there are a number of mature males present, such as in chimpanzee groups, the alpha male does not "own" all females, who may prefer to mate with other, lower-ranking males (often those who are new or less aggressive to females, or those who are older and have ceded dominance to younger upstarts) (de Waal 1987: 429; de Waal 1998: 169; Streier 2000: 166).[25] Indeed, among some Lemurs, no correlation has been found between position in the intermale dominance hierarchy and reproductive success during breeding season; the same goes for female blue monkeys, which tend to have a very linear hierarchy. While individual female hamadryas baboons have transitive preferences when it comes to choosing males, they do not agree with one another in their preferences and these preferences are unrelated to rank orderings among males (Kummer 1995: 190; Cords 2002: 303).

Limits to Orders

We have seen that any view of dominance orders as rigid sets of rules for robotic animals is unlikely to account for the range of behavior displayed by the higher primates. The very importance of the order in structuring social life means that it can provide the backdrop for strategic manipulation. Those ritual signals that are the heart of the order can be feigned or suppressed.[26] Alliances cannot only affect position in the order, they can fracture it; instead of seeing this as a disturbance of an otherwise linear system, we can follow de Waal (1977: 271) and insist that dominance relations must be understood as intrinsically embedded in a more complex social context.

Accordingly, even if we accept the centrality of dominance and ritualized submission behaviors, we cannot conclude that the resulting structure of rela-

---

[24] Indeed, among hens, the opposite is the case (Syme and Syme 1979: 21), but most people tend to focus on male dominance and reproductive success.

[25] While the proportion of matings that are by the alpha chimpanzee male with any female tend to increase as the probable day of her ovulation grows closer (Streier 2000: 237), and alphas often have disproportionate numbers of offspring (Constable, Ashley, Goodall, and Pusey 2001), there is little evidence that other high ranking males have greater reproductive success than do lower ranking males. (Despite the popular image, for primates in multimale societies, chimpanzees are relatively tolerant of observing other males copulate [Nishida and Hiraiwa-Hasegawa 1987: 170, 175].) Interestingly, Smith's (1993: 475) data on rhesus monkeys suggest that future alpha males' reproductive success may rise *before* they achieve the alpha position; it may be that female choice is a cause, not an effect, of the male's position.

[26] An example here is found in the actions of the beleaguered chimpanzee alpha discussed above—de Waal (1986: 231, 233) reports that he not only feigned being in a good mood when being provoked by challengers (a tactic that was devastatingly effective in irritating his opponents), but also would hide his "fear grin" or even push his lips to a normal position with his hands to avoid signaling his lack of confidence.

tionships will be linear under all conditions (Deag 1977: 472). Indeed, there is evidence of horizontal differentiation. For example, among Java monkeys studied by de Waal (1977: 233), one-third of the possible relations of submission in one group, and 44 percent in the other, were simply not observed at all, despite the audio- and video-taping of seventy hours of interaction (both groups combined). Thus one of the most important parts of the definition of the order—namely that a relationship exist between all interactants—may not hold for medium- and large-sized groups (also see Sade et al. 1988: 410). Even in smaller groups, it sometimes appears that three levels of dominance arise, with little to differentiate between members of the top, middle, or bottom levels (see, e.g., for monkeys Rowell 1971: 638; for apes Bygott 1979: 415, 417). Other close examinations of primate social structure have found what appears to be a combination of wholly vertical orders and horizontally differentiated organization (sec, e.g., Nishida and Hiraiwa-Hasegawa 1987: 172).

Finally, and perhaps most disturbingly, there is increasing evidence that much of the dominance behavior first understood as inherent to various species may be specific to conditions that were deliberately created by humans in order to simplify the task of observation. Captivity is only the most obvious form of such altered context. The point is not that "naturally" some primate species is "nice" and only becomes "nasty" when jailed. It is that human observers tend to force a reorienting of social priorities. Ethologists make a distinction between the "contest" competition in which two animals face each other over a resource that only one can possess, and the "scramble" competition that results when animals compete only indirectly by attempting to independently gather as much of some resource as they can. The latter is common when some resource (e.g., food) is scattered about widely and commonly—it would be inefficient to waste time in an agonistic interaction with an opponent who possesses some resource as opposed to gathering it on one's own.[27]

Different species rely on different foodstuffs, but even members of a single species may at different times or places find their staples to be more or less clumped in space. And the greater the clumping, the more agonistic interactions are observed (see Wilson 1975: 244, 249; van Hoof 2001; Isbell and Young 2002). (There can also be scramble competition for mates, which is associated with lower interspecific conflict [Strier, Dib, and Figueira 2002].) Unfortunately, the breakthrough in observation of primates in the wild occurred when Jane Goodall began leaving piles of bananas outside her tent for the local chimpanzees. But Goodall eventually recognized that this affected the behavior of the apes—the availability of a high quality and tasty food source led the chimps to move in larger groups as opposed to dispersing, and the males became increasingly aggressive. Eventually interspecific conflict de-

[27] The social theorist may assimilate contest competition to Hobbes's view of the state of nature and scramble competition to Rousseau's.

veloped between chimpanzees and baboons, species which had previously largely ignored one another (Goodall 1988: 66, 140–43, 208). Further exploration has demonstrated that some observed behavioral patterns related to dominance, once thought to be innate to a species, were unique to or exaggerated among provisioned or captive populations (see Chapais 2004; Strier 2000: 22; Strier 2003: 6). Increased agonism is one of these (Rasmussen 1988: 324; Kummer and Kurt 1967).[28]

In sum, it appears that dominance orders among primates involve three things. The first is a symbolic capacity leading to widespread evolution of ritualized submission behaviors. The second is a set of agonistic conflicts that lead to antisymmetric dominance relationships. The third is a particular kind of caging that leads to the *completeness* of the relationship. Such orders are special cases of a more general class of partial orders of dominance (cf. Iverson and Sade 1990), the increased linearity and completeness emerging in small multimale groups of patrilocal primate societies, between matrilines in matrilocal primate societies, and when the degree of agonistic interaction is increased by contest competition, especially for concentrated, high-energy foodstuffs.[29]

Interestingly, this deviation from a pure ordering is what Schjelderup-Ebbe first found among hens, although his article is more often cited than read (though Koffka 1935: 669 notes the horizontality and sees its relevance for human organization). But while the set of relationships may not form a simple order, the dominance structure *is* of crucial importance in determining the nature of social interaction in these species. It is not surprising that many analysts expect a commensurate importance among humans (see, e.g., Tiger 1970: especially 297). I will go on to question this.

Dominance Orders among People: Why Are There So Few?

> No two people can be half an hour together, but one shall acquire an
> evident superiority over the other.
> —SAMUEL JOHNSON, ca. 1766.

The Absence of Dominance Orders

Chase (1980) began his pathbreaking discussion of dominance hierarchy by wondering why the same structure formed in both animals and persons. Given the results of the study of dominance in animals since then, however, the ques-

---

[28] Provisioning concentrates food sources and tends to force more "caged" behavior—the behavior of provisioned primates may be similar to their nonprovisioned kin who find themselves in environments with concentrated high-quality food sources (Rowell 1967: 228ff).

[29] Nonlinearity of dominance has been recognized for a number of nonprimates (for the case of rats, see Baenninger 1970).

tion might be asked another way: not why are there dominance hierarchies in humans, but why are there so few?

Of course, just because some behavior pattern is common to nonhuman primates, it does not logically follow that it must be suspected as innate to humans as well.[30] Certainly, the variation that we have seen across primates means that even if some of the requisites for the production of dominance hierarchies are present in humans, there is no one implied social structure. Further, it has become increasingly fashionable to argue that humans have some fundamental behavior patterns that come not from their common primate heritage (which would be very long ago, before the split between old world and new world monkeys) but from presumptions as to the nature of life in the early period of recognizably human existence (e.g., the Pleistocene).

But as Christopher Boehm (1997 and references therein) has recently argued, what is distinctive about those contemporary hunter-gatherers that most evolutionary psychologists assume are closest in social life to our neolithic ancestors is their *suppression* of dominance, and he postulates that among early humans, "the group as a whole kept its alpha-male types firmly under its thumb, instead of *vice versa*." The means of this suppression was moral sanctioning, which, though to some degree present in chimpanzees, is greatly facilitated by speech.

Boehm's re-creation is of course simply that; what is crucial is that his comparative perspective casts doubt on the crucial premise of facile equations of dominance in modern societies and dominance among apes that provokes researchers to extrapolate from the one to the other by simply drawing a straight line between the two points. Just as Hobbes created a state of nature based on his experience of anarchic seventeenth-century England, and this model was then (by others) imputed to our ancestors, so evolutionary psychologists tend to create a model based on their own society without sufficient comparative checks. If these are done, Boehm (1997: 347, 330) notes, one finds that foragers and most nonstate people are egalitarian: "Relations between males seem to be far more co-operative and cordial than competitive and agonistic." This is not because, thinks Boehm, humans do not have innate drives to dominate others, but because of the particular group structure that arises with foraging: if a faction develops but fails to take control it will split off, allowing the group to maintain moral consensus. Where people are more

---

[30] One reasonable response to the assumption of continuity between humans and other primates is to follow Engels's (1942 [1884]) line of argument regarding the naturalness of human monogamy and argue that it is precisely because we do *not* share a common primate feature such as dominance that we are distinct among the primates. Certainly, humans differ from all other primates in a number of features (e.g., permanent breast swellings among females, and the absence of the erectile hair that chimpanzees use to display dominance), and so there is no reason they could not differ by lacking a dominance orientation.

caged as Mann (1986) says, such consensus is weaker and hence control over potential dominants by the community weaker as well. Even if humans have an innate *drive* toward dominance, either as an end in itself or as a means to other desired ends, there is no reason to think that it leads to the particular structure of dominance *orders*.

Thus the prevalence of dominance structures among other primates need not make us assume their presence among humans—this is an empirical question. But answering this question is perhaps more difficult than it first appears. Consider Johnson's aphorism above, which expresses a conviction held by a number of social scientists. It is interesting and typical that Johnson did not specify whether the superiority would be evident to both parties, to only one, or to an outside observer (or some other combination). It is not very convincing if it turns out that the superiority is only evident to an observer such as (the committed antiegalitarian) Johnson himself. Nor is it convincing if the superiority is evident only to the superior party (as opposed to the subordinate, crucial to the ritual aspect of dominance orders among animals).

Thus some sort of consensus as to the result of these quality-tournaments is necessary. But I would confidently wager that after a half-hour with Voltaire, Johnson would believe himself superior (or at least convince himself he so believed),[31] while Voltaire (who once referred to Johnson as a "superstitious dog") would be convinced of his own superiority. And—this is most important—neither would ritually signal inferiority to members of the public.

Yet human beings do seem to have ritualized submission behaviors, many of which are probably found across most cultures; further, these ritualized submission behaviors are related to those seen in animals. (Examples are looking down and away from, raising shoulders, etc.) Other actions may also signal status difference (e.g., higher status people initiate touch with lower status people who accept this; higher status people in at least some circumstances interrupt lower status people;[32] lower status people may accommodate their vocal frequencies to those of higher status interlocutors [Gregory and Webster 1996]). Humans seem to be as good as fish at guessing the probable status ranks of others given their behavior (e.g., Ridgeway and Erickson 2000), and there is good reason to suspect that humans' endocrine systems would do well at producing a linear hierarchy, by contributing to "winner effects" (that is, the impulse to win a future agonistic encounter increases with each win) (Kemper 1990).

---

[31] The passage on the "evident superiority" is quoted by Boswell directly after a passage in which Johnson has a difficult time determining who was of the greater iniquity, Voltaire or Rousseau.

[32] The assumption that interruption and loquacity measure status is currently under reconsideration.

As a result, it is not completely far-fetched to imagine that an acute observer would be able to determine the presence of a dominance hierarchy among a set of individuals on the basis of behavioral patterns that the individuals themselves do not fully recognize. Unfortunately, sociology is not in a position to make a contribution here. There has been a serious resistance against any kind of observational analysis of human social behavior akin to what is found in studies of animals (though see McGrew 1972).[33] As a result, it is simply not known whether most interactions between adults produce a dominance order that could be ascertained by behaviors such as staring as opposed to looking away, touching, or interrupting. Thus the existence of such orders, though in no way demonstrated, cannot yet be unambiguously ruled out.

Of course, even if it were ascertained that there are such shadow dominance orders in social life, these would still probably be quite different from the dominance orders among other primates where the order is explicit and unambiguous. Consequently, I will proceed by assuming that we can safely count most adult groups as not having orders of the form we have examined above.

Orders versus Ranks

In opposition to this conclusion that dominance orders are quite rare in human life, some have argued that they are in fact ubiquitous. Such arguments, however, have generally referred to some form of *ranking*, which is not the same thing as a dominance order. People can frequently be ranked, but this does not necessarily have any clear implications for social interaction. Most important, the antisymmetric relation that is effectively induced via the popularity tournament is not the same as the relationship—the profiles of interaction—that actually structures the group. That is, we may say $P(A) > P(B)$ where $P(A)$ is the popularity of A, etc., but this does not mean that there is an actual relationship of dominance between A and B. A and B may never interact at all; the actual relation in question may be wholly mutual (perhaps either they play basketball together or they do not). It is possible for a relationship "gets along with on terms of absolute equality" to induce a very severe ranking of persons in some group, from those who "get along with" the most others "on the basis of absolute equality" to those who "get along with" the fewest.

---

[33] Professional sociologists are not given any sort of training in the basic facts about how humans interact, except, of course, to quite reasonably doubt that there are any such "basic facts." If any such facts *did* exist, they might be extremely illuminating; however, searching for them seems to be understood as "dehumanizing." The one school that is closest in intent to such a study, ethnomethodology, has been too involved with theoretical debates (despite the avowed intent not to) to accumulate much. Conversation analysts have made serious headway, but by restricting attention to one small part of interaction, have not told us much about social structures. Those who did such analyses (Erving Goffman, for one—see his [1971: x, xvii] call for a human ethology) were considered interesting but peripheral mavericks or "pop" sociologists.

It is also not the case that differences in power or wealth translate to pecking orders: as Collins (2000) has stressed, there can be a great difference between these inequalities and the "microsituational" inequalities that are relevant for dominance orders. For one, the presence of power relations does not imply a dominance order if relationships are not transitive (cf. Spencer 1910 [1896]: 480). Finally, even given transitivity, a dominance order may not arise if there is some sort of horizontal differentiation that allows some pairs of persons not to enter into the agonistic interactions that would lead them to assume a linear order (a case which we explore in the next chapter).

In sum, although one must leave open the possibility that humans give off subtle signals that could allow us to arrange them in a linear order, adult humans do not consistently organize themselves into dominance orders such that there are repeated displays of ritualized submission that form a transitive ranking system. Since people have the cognitive ability to understand transitivity, and the symbolic ability to signal ritualized submission, and (so far as we can tell) they are not entirely peace-loving and egalitarian by nature, one wonders, why not? I will begin by considering common answers, and then make a slightly different proposal.

The Question of Differentiation

A common answer has been that human society involves some sort of differentiation (see White 1992). Initially satisfying, this response runs into troubles. The simplest version of this argument is that humans can *get away*; dominance orders may be seen as requiring the absence of exit. But while too many initial observations were made of animals in captivity, dominance orders or at least partial orders have now been affirmed to be present in primates in the wild; really, as Mann (1986) has said, what is distinctive about civilization in the long-term perspective is that it "cages" *humans*. Exit is easier for adults in many of the primate societies that have the clearest dominance structures than it is for most adult humans, and indeed the form of social organization of such primates is often called "fission-fusion" bands, because of their tendency to temporarily compose larger aggregates out of smaller segments that can detach themselves and go their separate ways later.

A modified version of the differentiation hypothesis holds that at least with adulthood, persons interact in a number of different settings or fields that have different principles of stratification; to the extent that these are cross-cutting, it is impossible to have the kind of submission responses that require that the subordinate party debase him or herself (since this same submitting person may be dominant over the other in a different setting). This seems quite reasonable, but runs into three comparative problems. The first is that there is no historical or anthropological evidence of true dominance orders in nondifferentiated societies; though some of these societies are highly stratified by rank, the combination of agonistic encounter and ritual submission is apparently not an aspect of their social life. The second is that there is no reason to think that chimpanzees (say) do not have distinct skills. The third is that school-age children (as we shall see below) are somewhat likely to form dominance orders.

This last finding is often believed to be consistent with the differentiation hypothesis, as it is assumed that adult life is more differentiated and complex than that of children. While it may be true that students in the elementary grades in U.S. public schools see the same set of twenty to thirty children every weekday for ten months of the year, this does not seem very different from the normal work experience of an adult. By middle school or junior high school, students may be going to different classes with different teachers and different students, and experiencing a daily degree of social variety far surpassing that of the average adult.

There may indeed be something distinctive about children and adolescents that leads to the production of dominance orders. However, it seems unlikely that the nature of this crucial factor can be determined by simple armchair reflection. A more promising tactic would be an empirical exploration of those dominance orders that *do* arise among children. Fortunately, there is fair amount of detailed research into such orders, to which we now turn.[34] I will concentrate on one particularly rich study by Savin-Williams, which produced raw data that can be reanalyzed, though supplementing the conclusions with the findings from other studies.

Dominance Orders among Children and Adolescents

Nature of the Relationship

Many different interactions can be used to determine the direction of dominance relationships between children (such as who ends up with a disputed toy), but just as with animals, it seems that the key is the public signaling of submission through some sort of ritualized behavior. Thus in an examination of preschool children, Strayer and Strayer (1976: 984f) found around 25 percent of the total number of initiated agonistic interactions (here looking at physical attacks and threat gestures only) were in the "lower diagonal" of the arranged matrix—that is, were initiated by a lower-ranking child against a higher-ranking child. That is, there were too many attacks going "the wrong way" for us to conclude that a true dominance order was present.

---

[34] There are also investigations of preschool children that are not reviewed here which suggest that there is a relatively loose coupling between different relationships that might be expected to cohere in a true dominance structure, for example, victory in agonistic struggles over objects on the one hand, and attention paid on the other (see Vaughn and Waters 1980: 371; Abramovitch 1980).

But such data can be confusing due to differential aggressiveness which may be to some extent independent of differential dominance (if some children initiate agonistic dyadic interactions but do not triumph) (Strayer and Strayer 1980: 149, 154ff). Frequently a subordinate child would initiate an agonistic action as part of a sequence that would end in his or her submission, giving a misleadingly pessimistic quantitative impression of the degree of fixity of the order. We can better understand the linearity of the structure if we concentrate on dyadic interchanges that end in a submission response (even if it is only flinching). Then we find that for the above mentioned data, only 8 percent of the total agonistic encounters that ended with a submission display went against the grain.

Such data seem to suggest that true dominance orders or near-orders do form among children (also see Sluckin 1980: 164ff). This is probably especially true for smaller groups—in larger groups, linearity may decrease as one moves away from the top positions (see Barner-Barry 1980: 183). Yet other studies have not confirmed the centrality of dominance in similar settings.[35] Thus (perhaps as with the primates we reviewed above), we should simply say that dominance orders *can* arise among children. We want, then, to look closely at the environments where we do find evidence of such orders (understanding, of course, that not all environments have been subjected to the same attention), and also to examine the nature of existing dominance hierarchies. What actions actually characterize dominance relationships, and more simply, what personal attributes are associated with dominance rank? If, for example, dominance behavior generally takes the form of physical pressure, and stronger individuals are dominant over weaker, we will be led to one particular—and particularly simple—explanation of why and where dominance orders are likely to arise.

But just as with animals, it turns out that we must reject any facile equation of position in the dominance hierarchy and specific qualities possessed by children or young adolescents. It is true that dominant boys tend to be more athletic than are the nondominant—and this is also true for girls, at least in the camp studied by Savin-Williams. (Savin-Williams studied four groups of mid-adolescent boys, four groups of mid-adolescent girls, and then some older adolescent boys and girls. My discussion will focus on the more detailed evidence regarding middle adolescents.) But children often dominated others who

[35] For example, Lippitt, Polansky, and Rosen (1952: 44f) found in a study of boys' cabins of similar sizes that the "alpha" boy—the boy being named most often as the one who can "get the other [*sic*] to do what he wants them to do"—only got around 5.6 out of 8 possible choices in one camp, and 4.5 out of 8 in another. That is, opinions regarding who was the alpha boy fell quite short of consensus. Even if we add 1 to each of these to take into account the possibility of the alpha boy being too modest to name himself, this agreement is substantially less than one would expect in a comparable surveys of chimpanzees, should such a thing be possible.

were taller and heavier, even those who could beat them in a fight. In such cases, the subordinate child, though stronger, could not adequately defend him- or herself against more common means of asserting dominance such as ridicule (Savin-Williams 1987: 53ff, 76, 183f; cf. Adler and Adler 1998: 39; though compare Weisfeld, Omark, and Cronin 1980: 206 who find a strong correlation between dominance and "toughness").

Not only is there no unique basis for achieving a position of dominance, but (as with animals) there can be a dissociation between dominance position and "popularity" (although less so, it seems, for girls than for boys). Other boys may be more popular than the alpha precisely *because* they are nondominant and do not antagonize others or prevent them from having influence in group activities. Similarly, popularity may decrease as a boy's dominance rank increases over time and vice versa (for examples see Savin-Williams 1987: 111, 120, 64, 405; for a similar case among baboons see Kummer 1995: 49f).[36]

Action and Orders

We found evidence above that higher primates understand the relative positions of different animals within a dominance order; the same is true of children and young adolescents. Indeed, when we turn from apes to children, we are able to explicitly ask our subjects about their own and others' positions (Savin-Williams 1977: 403; Savin-Williams 1987: 193). For the young adolescents introduced above, explicit reports as to the ranks of others were collected, and they agree rather well with observers' reports (although there is somewhat of a tendency for the boys in the Savin-Williams study to overrank themselves).

More important, the children then take this "objective" circumstance into account when acting; that is, they cognize these positions and act accordingly. This may most easily be seen in the fact that (at least among boys), the highest-ranking child has a qualitatively unique position. For example, he may coordinate action or resolve quarrels between others (Savin-Williams 1987: 67, 180).

There are other indications that action took place within the established dominance order. Savin-Williams (1987: 66, 112) reports for one group he studied that children tended to interact more with others close in dominance, and that best friends were twice as likely to be adjacent in rank as expected by chance. But this is not a simple case of homophily (like liking like), for the children also had more agonistic contests with those closer in rank. Supporting conjectures made by Homans (1950), it seems that children tend to interact

---

[36] Further, especially among girls, there can be a tremendous difference between "popularity" and liking—"popular" cliques often link rivals in insecure and shallow friendships, while drawing the resentment and ire of the nonpopular girls. As a result, many popular girls need to condescend to the nonpopular if only as an insurance measure against a loss of popularity (Eder 1985: 162; Adler and Adler 1998: 59f, 64).

more with those close in status, and they tend to have more conflicts with those with whom they are in reasonable competition (also see Missakian 1980: 408). In other words, they approximate the jackdaw pattern, and not the poultry pattern.

To examine this, we can conceive of each child having a position on a single vertical dimension; application of the Bradley-Terry (1952) model for paired comparisons can be used to retrieve a latent status score for each person.[37] In this model, we assume that each child has some interval-level position on a single continuum of status, and the odds that A will triumph over B is proportional (in the logarithmic metric) to the difference between A's status and B's. Thus not all "adjacent" pairs of children are really the same distance apart— if A only wins 60% of the agonistic confrontations with B, he will be judged "closer" in status to B than if he won 90% of these contests, even if in both cases A and B are third and fourth in rank respectively.

Application of this model to Savin-Williams's data allows us to examine whether adolescents are more likely to have dominance interactions with those close in status to themselves; the answer appears to be yes. Since ego is then more likely to triumph in an agonistic encounter with alter the greater the status difference between ego and alter, but less likely to have the encounter in the first place, there is a curious relation between the distance in status between ego and alter and the number of "wins" of ego over alter, as can be seen in figure 4.3.

Here the dyads are ordered from those with the most negative status difference (that is, ego faces an alter of much higher status) on the left to those with the most positive status difference (ego faces an alter of much lower status) on the right. The vertical line indicates the midway point where ego and alter are of the same status. Only the relative ranking of the dyads is preserved, and not their interval-level difference, so that we may smooth the resulting data to produce a simpler picture. The shape filled in with squares indicates the total number of dominance conflicts between ego and alter ("bouts"). This shape is symmetric around the line of no status difference since every dyad is counted twice, once from ego's and once from alter's perspective. The lower shape filled with diagonal lines is the number of agonistic contests that ego won (the difference between this shape and the former is the number won by alter). As we can see, the *proportion* of bouts won by ego certainly increases with ego's status advantage, but the gross *number* levels out quickly. This is because the number of conflicts peaks when ego and alter are of moderate inequality.[38]

---

[37] If x_{ij} is the number of contests in which child i dominates child j, the Bradley-Terry model can be considered to be $\ln(x_{ij}/x_{ji}) = a_i - a_j$. See the related discussion in Coleman (1960:102f).

[38] It is worth noting that Savin-Williams (1987: 112; though compare Savin-Williams 1977: 403) did not find this to be the case, and this probably in part is due to his use of nonparametric ranks (as opposed to continuous statuses) to characterize position. The correlation between the absolute value of the status difference between ego and alter and the total number of domi-

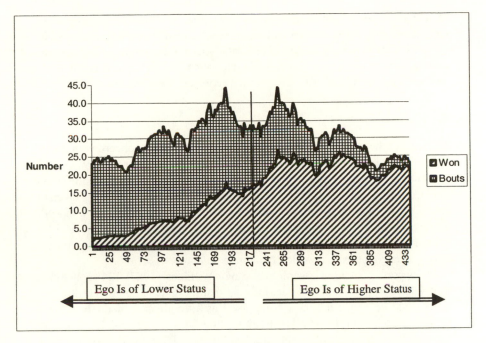

Figure 4.3. Agonistic interactions by status difference

This can be demonstrated more rigorously as follows: we can attempt to predict the number of bouts given the status difference (here making sure to count each dyad only once). Doing this leads to a relatively large negative coefficient, indicating that as ego's and alter's status difference goes up, the number of bouts goes down.[39] But this effect turns out to vary over the three measurement periods—it becomes increasingly negative over time. In other words, as the summer progressed, children became less likely to enter into conflictual relations with those far apart in status from themselves.

In sum, most examinations of the development of dominance orders in children have been exclusively concerned with the ordering of the children and the proportion of conflicts won and have ignored where the interaction takes place. The child of very high status may be almost sure to win all agonistic encounters with a child of very low status, but these agonistic encounters may not take place. Our interest in the patterns of repeated interaction leads us to examine the interactions that *do* take place, and not simply the odds that hypothetical interactions would follow a certain pattern *were* they to take place. Accordingly, we reach a conclusion that is easily overlooked by the favoring

nance encounters is highly significant and in the right direction ($r = -.172$, $p < .001$), but is substantively small.

[39] Because I go on to examine more refined models, I do not present these intermediate results.

of relations over relationships—status hierarchies need to spread people out so that there are sufficient spaces between each to reduce the sheer number of contests. This generally occurs in our data—over time, agonistic interactions zero in on the unresolved or reversible relations between those close in status and leave the larger differences as settled (compare Gould 2003).

Sex Differences

Critiques of the concept of dominance have suggested that concern with dominance is more characteristic of men than women (e.g., Haraway 1991); other evidence does suggest that men are more likely to differentiate vertically (Fennell, Carchas, Cohen, McMahon, and Hildebrand 1978). This might be taken to imply that boys but not girls will show evidence of dominance orders. Indeed, McGrew (1972: 122) could not even test the hypothesis of a dominance order for nursery school girls as he could for boys because he did not observe enough agonistic encounters with a clearly defined outcome.

In support of such an assumption, Savin-Williams (1987: 125) concluded that "although the quantified data indicate that the female adolescent interactions could be construed on a group level as a dominance hierarchy," there was no evidence of a linear hierarchy in three of the four female groups he studied. But results of fitting the Bradley-Terry model to the data do not confirm this. While we can quantify the degree of vertical hierarchy in any group with some conventional measure of fit such as the Cox pseudo-r-square (using this measure does not change our results), we can also measure the degree of verticality in terms of the spread of statuses. That is, the model retrieves latent (unobserved) statuses for all members—the further apart these are, the more vertical differentiation exists in the group (Martin 1998). I will use the standard deviation of these scores as a measure of this spread. Doing this, we find that of the half of the groups where the status hierarchy model fits best, half the groups are female and half are male.

Thus in contrast to popular impressions, it does not appear to be the case that American boys are more oriented towards chimplike dominance structures than are girls. Savin-Williams (1987: 109) himself found that because boys tended to contest dominance relations, the girls were in some cases more linear. Reanalysis using our parametric methods finds that while girls started out lower than boys in terms of the linearity of their dominance orders, they surpassed boys by the end of the summer (although this difference is not statistically significant).

This does not mean that girls do not differ from boys in their dominance behavior. Savin-Williams (1987: 105) found that boys tended to have more fights and verbal arguments, "but the most striking sex difference was in recognition of status behavior; giving compliments, asking favors, imitating, and soliciting advice occurred in every fourth encounter among female dyads, but only once in every sixteenth interaction among male dyads." In other words, while boys might participate in more of the dominance activities that would attract the attention of a casual observers (only 48 percent of girls' dominance related behavior was categorized as "overt," as opposed to 85 percent of the boys'), girls more than made up for this with ritualized demonstrations of subordination. Boys may engage in more of the activities that are associated with "dominance" in the popular use of the term, but *less* of the ritualized submission activities that are structurally crucial. The greater aggressiveness of boys actually *undermines* the clarity of the dominance order.

Even more interestingly, it turns out that boys' rankings seem to be constructed around the top ranking boy (the alpha boy), while girls' seem to be constructed around the bottom ranking girl (the omega girl). Just as Savin-Williams (1987: 109, 121) found, among boys, alphas keep their position over time, while among girls, omegas keep their position. It might be that boys are oriented to popularity, and girls to unpopularity.[40]

Further insight here can be gathered by close examination of the residuals from the Bradley-Terry model. That is, *given* that we position people on a continuum of status via this model, the residuals point to relationships that stand out. (Here we can use the traditional rule of thumb of examining standardized residuals greater than 2 or less than –2.) The results are quite surprising, and they give clear evidence of two types of departures from a simple status order, which I shall call "sender" and "receiver" effects. In a "sender" effect, one child tends to under- (or over-) dominate others compared with what is expected by the model. In three of the four girl groups, the omega girl was such an underdominator.[41] It is important to realize that this underdomination is *net* of her position at the bottom of the hierarchy. To illustrate, we could imagine that most girls initiated 12 acts of dominance against those one step below them in the hierarchy, and initiated 4 acts against those one step *above* them. But the omega girl, though receiving 12 acts from the girl above her, might return only one or none at all.[42] In other words, either omega girls quickly lose their ability to dominate, or those with a reticence to dominate are quickly assigned the position of omega (Martin 2009).

In the boy groups, however, there were fewer strong sender effects, and more "receiver" effects focused on the alpha and beta boy. That is, these boys had a special "force field" that led others to underdominate them, given the

---

[40] The boy model is in some ways similar to the crayfish, in which the alpha, and usually beta crayfish can be identified in four-animal groups, but it is difficult to determine the order between the third and fourth (see Bovbjerg 1953; though also see Ginsburg [1980: 355] on omega boys).

[41] In one case, the omega girl ceased underdominating by the second time period.

[42] Further, it is interesting that in the one group where there was no "sender effect" for the omega girl, the omega girl at the beginning was not the same as the omega girl at the end (this group following more of a boys' pattern).

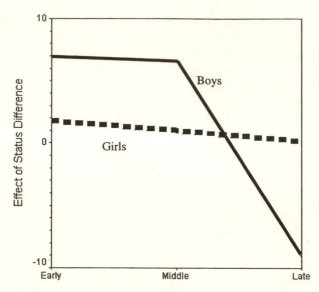

Figure 4.4. Change in effect of status difference on agonism

pattern of relations as a whole. For example, it might be that most boys initiated acts of aggression directed against those directly above them in the hierarchy, unless this was the alpha boy. This suggests that the concatenation of global structure may actually occur differently in boys and girls—extrapolating from these results, we would expect boys rankings to be more likely to develop through the equivalent of double-attacks ($A \rightarrow B$ followed by $A \rightarrow C$) as opposed to double-receives ($A \rightarrow B$ followed by $C \rightarrow B$).[43]

There is a further possible sex difference in the way in which the structure evolves over time. I noted before that one boy group had low vertical differentiation but very high levels of conflict. If we eliminate this one group, then an interesting sex difference emerges regarding whether people are likely to have more conflict with those close to them in status as opposed to those farther away. This is shown in figure 4.4, which displays regression coefficients indicating the degree to which status difference affects the number of bouts. We see that boys start out (unlike girls) with a strong *positive* effect of status— that is, initially the *greater* the status difference, the more conflict. But by the third period, this effect has turned strongly negative, indicating that conflict is happening among those closer in status. But there is no such effect for girls. Of course, this pattern comes from three of the boy groups—the fourth had quite the opposite pattern. Yet in a substantively important way, this exception

[43] In support of this speculation, McGrew's (1972: 125) analysis of nursery school boys found that 27% of the 41 agonistic encounters coded were triumphs of the alpha boy over the six next highest ranking boys (these six dyads being only 2% of the total).

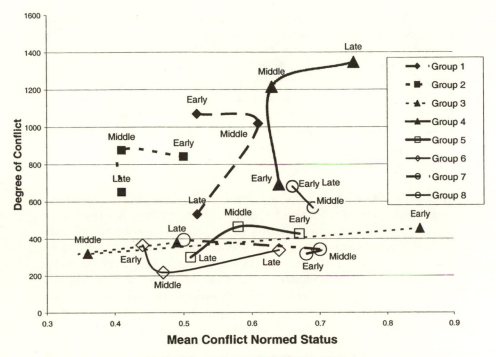

Figure 4.5. Evolution of dominance orders

does not militate against the interpretation here. This boy group did not fit either the girl pattern or the boy pattern, but rather stands shockingly out from the rest in terms of its remarkably high level of increasing agonism. This constitutes not so much an *exception* to the boy pattern, but a *failed* boy pattern; the members seemed to be aware of the lack of resolution of the dominance relations.

Figure 4.5 shows the progression of each group through a two-dimensional analytic space. The horizontal dimension is the "mean normed status difference"—it is the average difference in status between any two children who are having an agonistic interaction in some cabin at some period. The vertical dimension is the total *amount* of conflict. The girl groups are represented with circles and the boy groups with polygons. We see that (supporting the regression results graphed above) in most groups, boy groups especially, conflict is increasingly with those closer in status (the lines move toward the left). Further, as boys focus their conflict on those like them in status, the overall amount of hostility declines (the lines move downward). The exception is the failed boy pattern group, group 4—here the lower-ranking boys increasingly fight with those at the top of the structure, and the total amount of agonism increases as opposed to decreases.

Thus there seem to be sex differences in the ways in which children's dominance relations unfold. Girls orient quickly to outcast girls and tend to increase somewhat in the linearity of the hierarchies. Boys tend to orient quickly to leaders, and after these leaders have demonstrated the security of their status through a large number of interactions with those of lesser status, further conflict tends to be between those relatively close in status. But this need not happen—when some boys continue to contest the position of those above them in status, we may see an explosion of agonism.

Conclusions

Most of the data we have examined comes from children and young adolescents, although there is also evidence of similar hierarchies in older adolescents.[44] (It is important to stress that such dominance orders are not the same thing as results from popularity tournaments, which tend not to take on the same linear structure.)[45] These hierarchies also form in similar circumstances. What can we conclude about the nature of the conditions under which these dominance structures have formed? What do camp cabins and school life have in common—and perhaps in common with the provisioned primate bands reviewed earlier—that is structurally relevant?

It seems reasonable to propose that dominance orders arise in children when the children are caged but lack formal structures for conflict resolution. Hence the outcomes of agonistic interactions can be relatively weighty: children must live with the results of their decisions, and an unappeased opponent can escalate the conflict into verbal or physical attack. If individuals cannot avoid agonistic contests, then horizontal differentiation (of the type examined in the next chapter) is impossible. The only possibilities are a dominance order, intransitivity, or fission.

If dominance orders are to arise among adults, we would look for them in similar circumstances among adults. These circumstances are (1) that the individuals are relatively "caged" in that they have a great many interactions with one another and are not able to consistently avoid interactions with particular others; (2) that there are no formal structures for authority or conflict

---

[44] Savin-Williams (1980; 1987) repeated the basic study with two groups of older boys and one of girls in training to be junior counselors. Application of the stochastic model to the resulting data gives us no reason to believe that there is clearly a move away from linear structure as boys get older. Savin-Williams (1987: 150) suggests that girls may begin to form dyarchies, in which the top position is shared between an affective and an instrumental leader; there is some supporting evidence (e.g., Adler and Adler 1998: 77), but this needs to be explored in other settings.

[45] Perhaps among boys, but certainly among early- and mid-adolescent girls, the top few most popular girls can often be identified with a great deal of consistency, but there is no uniform ranking below them; indeed, many other children are considered roughly incomparable (Adler and Adler 1998: 85).

resolution. There are two reasonable contenders, namely criminal gangs and communes (prisons and nuclear families of course also cage adults, but break them up into smaller groups). We look at each in turn.

Dominance Orders in Small Adult Groups I: Gangs

Agonism and Its Limits

A popular image of gangs and gang members as both wild and disciplined— oriented to fighting and laws of force—leads many to expect that dominance orders will arise in such gangs (Gould 2003: 23). Since the seminal work of Thrasher (1963 [1927])—still considered a classic and taken quite seriously (Cummings and Monti 1993: 4; Jankowski 1991: 3)—it has, however, been recognized that there is wide diversity in gang social structure, and so there is no structural model (including the linear structure) that holds for all gangs.[46] But this does not mean that there may not be a tendency toward the production of dominance orders; certain features of gang life, most importantly the environment of agonistic conflict, make this at first blush a reasonable expectation.

Indeed, a number of observers have argued that to a great extent gang life turns on a quest for the establishment of status, which would seem to imply both the salience of status position and the interpersonal struggle that would produce a hierarchy. For example, Thrasher (1963 [1927]: 230f) argued that that "the gang may be viewed as a struggle for recognition" and "status" (see also Skolnick, Bluthenthal, and Correl 1993: 213 for an example) and develops a social structure in which individuals must be "more or less definitely subordinated and superordinated with reference to each other and the leader."[47]

This may be understood as reinforcing the anarchic view of gang life that expects that the bigger and meaner a member, the higher his rank in a status hierarchy. But this is not implied by the quest for status, for a number of reasons. First, just as we have seen with younger children, there is no one attribute or relationship that determines status—certainly, it is not fighting. Other skills, including verbal ability and general style, affect status and the winner of a fight does not necessarily rise in status (Horowitz 1983: 102; Short and Strodtbeck 1965: 192). But more important, even when fighting ability determines status, it does so in a way that is antithetical to the production of dominance orders.

---

[46] Because of this structural diversity, the generalizations made below can only characterize the dominant trends found in the gangs that have been the subject of sociological research; there may be other patterns.

[47] As a result, he adds, each person ended up with a definite position, dependent both on individual attributes and chance opportunity coming from interaction, mirroring the arguments regarding pecking orders above.

Fighting is indeed often a major aspect of agonistic encounters between gang members: Jankowski (1991: 24, 145) stresses the competitiveness of gang members, which leads them to continuously test their fighting ability by wrestling or hitting one another, usually playfully but sometimes to see if they are able to beat someone of roughly similar ability. (Schjelderup-Ebbe [1922: 248] argued that such probing of the strength of others was crucial for the evolution of dominance orders.) But as Horowitz (1983: 108, 190) reports, fights to prove one's honor must be conducted with equals. Verbal sparring matches are also common though they can lead to fighting if one party either feels that something said indicates a lack of respect, or if one lacks the verbal skills to respond adequately.

It is not the case that these intramural fights are conducted with such restraint that we would not expect the issue of signaling submission to even arise. Jankowski (1991: 148) writes that the gang members he studied "know how to fight in only one way—an all-out effort to destroy or immobilize the perceived enemy" and hence "they have no aversion to being as brutal as is necessary to win a fight with another member." Given the generally weak central control, it is indeed plausible that this would lead to dominance orders.

Yet dominance orders, as we recall, turn on ritually signaled submission, and this is the last thing that could be the basis for gang life. Jankowski (1991: 26, 29) argues that one thing gang members do tend to share is a "defiant air," which makes it nearly impossible to signal deference and maintain self-respect. Indeed, their defiant individualism makes it difficult for the gang to exist as a corporate body in the first place.

"Respect," he found, was a crucial structuring principle in interpersonal relations.[48] All members were required to build and then uphold their reputation, which involves directing aggression at anyone who does not respect them (or impugns their honor) (Jankowski 1991: 142, 79, 83, 145). Indeed, most gangs possessed codes forbidding one member to do anything "that could be construed as demeaning" to another. While Jankowski notes that members challenge each other to see who is the better fighter, he explicitly adds that it is "no disgrace to lose."

Similarly, Horowitz (1983: 22, 81, 89, 92, 101f) found among Hispanic gang members a concern with ensuring that one not be treated with anything approaching disrespect. Thus while one's honor means that one can "command deference," this deference cannot be such that another loses *his* honor. It is true that "the competition for honor among youths, unlike adults, results in a hierarchical ranking" and that position in this ranking is seen in competition

---

[48] In Chicano gangs "honor" was the key principle, which did not have to be earned by each member but was assumed to be one's birthright unless one allowed it to be compromised. Chicano youth gangs frequently are different from other gangs not only in their structure, but in members' deference to community standards of respectability (Moore 1978: 51f).

for deference. But Horowitz emphasizes that there is not a strict order *within* the group: "If the group were strongly and strictly hierarchical, no friendships would be formed because in any relationship one would be dominant and the other subordinate, an impossible state for any honorable man. For trust to develop, a relationship must be experienced as egalitarian, otherwise the dominant person would always be expecting the subordinate person to attempt to improve his position."

In sum, the quest for status, far from leading to an ordering of members and ritualized signals of subordination, instead leads members to *deemphasize* whatever status differences there are (also see Suttles 1968: 112, 191).[49] Instead of gang life involving constant struggles to improve one's position, common for maturing primates, challenges are instead directed toward nongroup members (also see Vigil 1988: 129). Instead of leaders gaining their position by cowing others into submission, "the overwhelming preponderance of their actions," thought Short and Strodtbeck (1965: 195) "is co-ordinating and nurturant." This incompatibility of ritualized submission with gang life probably explains why there is nothing approaching a dominance order. This does not mean that there are not vertical and linear structures in gangs. There are indeed, but they are basically matters of *organization* and not fundamental human responses to conflict.

Structural Variation

What structural forms *do* gangs take? As Thrasher found, if one looks hard enough, one will probably find a great number of different forms. More recently, Jankowski (1991: 64, 333 note 3, 74, 90, 66f; also cf. Sheley et al. 1995) examined gang organization based on extensive experience with a large number of different types of gangs from different cities and found three types of structure, which he called "vertical," "horizontal," and "influential." Vertical structures tended to be formal, having a president, vice president, warlord, and treasurer, the vice president often (as in the original plan for the United States) representing the forces of the minority in opposition, thus pacifying potential dissidents and uniting the gang. Nineteen of the thirty-seven gangs in his sample had such structures.

While horizontal gangs also had officers, these were not ordered in authority. These horizontal structures might result from challenges to a vertical structure which led to the formal structure being more of a federalist compromise. Such gangs tended to be the most democratic, if only because the leadership was relatively weak. Finally, the influential model refers to a more informal struc-

---

[49] Thus if status orders based on fighting ability emerge, it is likely to be among disorganized groups such as the "hoodlums" studied by Anderson (1976:158, 160, 162), who seemed to have a stable vertical ordering.

TABLE 4.1
Types of Gang Structure

	Informal	*Formal*
Weak	[Empty—not a gang]	Horizontal
Strong	Influential	Vertical

ture; while there is an understanding in such groups that some form of leadership was needed and would be supplied by certain persons, they have no formal titles nor formal rights or duties (p. 66f).[50] (These sorts of informal structures with little role differentiation are the ones emphasized by Hagedorn 1988: 92f; and Decker and van Winkle 1996: 96, 98, 275.)

We can arrange these three types in terms of the degree of strength and degree of formality of leadership as in a two-by-two table as follows in table 4.1. There is one logically possible cell that Jankowski did not observe, which makes perfect sense. A gang with weak, informal leadership would not appear a gang at all, as there would be little to hold it together.[51] While there are undoubtedly exceptions, in general, the greater the systematic and rational involvement with illegal activities for profit, the greater the formal structure (also see Venkatesh and Levitt 2000: 441f, 446; Fagan 1989: 655f).[52] Gangs that are more oriented toward community service (whether or not this service is appreciated by the community) as opposed to business enterprise tend to have looser structures, though many take the form of a number of similarly named but functionally independent gangs for different age sets (this is a common pattern of Chicano gangs: see Moore 1978: 35; Hagedorn 1988: 89; Vigil 1988: 92).[53] So while there is variation in gang structure, it is limited to a

---

[50] For evidence of similar variation, Skolnick, Bluthenthal, and Correl (1993: 195, 210f; also Decker and van Winkle [1996]: 97) report that while gangs in Southern California tend to be organized horizontally, those in the North tend to be organized vertically in that the more successful members are in illegal business, the higher their status. But the verticality of these gangs comes from business imperatives, not agonistic conflicts (though these occur, and are in fact encouraged by the vertical structure which leads to competition for a more important position). One person achieves prominence because he controls the supply of drugs, and in determining who can sell them and where, provides the outlines of a structure to the gang. Within this enveloping structure, there are different roles that are filled by people with different expertise and of different ages.

[51] As Jankowski (1991: 99) remarks, "If gangs fail to build and maintain a cohesive structure, they simply dissolve as organizations. The idea that gangs are generally loose associations, with little in the way of a cohesive leadership structure, is simply not accurate."

[52] Fagan doubts the centrality of drug sales in particular to formal organization, but this is because "party gangs"—gangs that have a high proportion who have sold drugs and whose members also *do* these drugs—tend not to have much formal organization. But it is quite possible that these drug sales are the low volume sales of users to support habits, not rational profiteering.

[53] Thus Moore (1988: 5, 15) stresses the absence of hierarchical relations between these sub-gangs in Los Angeles, not surprising given a general hostility to hierarchy in these cases that is not necessarily typical.

number of predominant models, and the choice of model is an understandable function of the gang's raison d'être and its relation to the wider community. It is not a generic result of the combination of an impulse to strive for status and an absence of formal structures of social control.

Conclusion on Gangs

In sum, vertical structures do appear in gangs, but they pertain to strong forms of formal organization—in other words, precisely the sort of organizational form whose presence negates the supposedly anarchic conditions that are often assumed to lead to dominance orders. And one gets a high position in a vertical gang not by winning in a series of interpersonal games of "chicken," but by political maneuvering not in principle different from that used by members of one-party states (see Janwoski 1991: 92).

Furthermore, this vertical structure may only apply to the top offices; below this, the social structure of the gang is likely to involve informal horizontal differentiation of a type we will examine in the next chapter. As Thrasher (1963 [1927]: 222) first pointed out, the gang is often an aggregate of cliques or clusters. These clusters may dissociate themselves from the gang if dissatisfied; while such clusters may have a central figure, the central figure of cluster 1 (except for the formal officers) cannot dominate the regular members of cluster 2 without leading the members of cluster 2 to feel a lack of respect and leave. Indeed, this suggests that gangs will either take on the differentiated hierarchy we will explore in chapter 5 or the multihub structure explored in chapter 2 and again in chapter 6 (here see especially Goddard 1992).[54] That is, in many cases, the "gang" is really an umbrella organization that has formed from an aggregation of smaller "sets" or "crews" that may retain substantial autonomy (for examples, see Venkatesh and Levitt 2000: 428, 438; Decker and van Winkle 1996: 115). So even in gangs, there is no evidence of dominance orders. Intentional communities are then our last possible venue.

Dominance Orders in Small Adult Groups II: Communes

Where Do Vertical Structures Arise?

Unfortunately, there is no systematic data on agonistic encounters in communes. There is, however, a great deal of data on perceived *power* relations among members of forty communes in 1974; these are a subset of the sixty

---

[54] There is actually some evidence of similar differentiation in children at camp: Hunt and Solomon (1942) studied 22 boys in four cabins and found that while there were three top boys— and a cycle of choices among these—almost all the other boys chose one of these three, or someone who chose one of these, and so on.

communes studied by Benjamin Zablocki and his associates. This remarkable study used a national sampling frame to get a great deal of information on interpersonal relations in a wide variety of groups. Using a stochastic model similar to the one used for the camp data above, Martin (1998) demonstrated that there was a tendency for power relations to form a vertical hierarchy—furthermore, there was no evidence of horizontal organization.[55] In other words, while power relations did not always seem to follow a vertical order, departures from a consistent vertical order did not appear to be *structured*.

Of course, absence of evidence is not the same thing as evidence of absence. Yet both "eye-balling" the data, and the participant observers' original reports (Zablocki 1980: 300) are in agreement with these negative results. There is no reason to think that there was any horizontal differentiation, whereby a high-status person would not have power over a lower-status person because they were in "different areas," in the way that a manager in sales might not be able to give orders to the office boy in parts. Thus the extent to which the vertical model fits is a rather good way of determining quantitatively the degree of vertical hierarchy in interpersonal power relations. Further, the degree of vertical hierarchy (measured in the same way as done earlier for the camp data) turns out to be related to other aspects of life in the group: more hierarchical groups tend to have more agreement in terms of beliefs but to dissolve faster than other groups (Martin 1998).[56]

Most important for our purposes, there is evidence that far from these orders arising where (as among children) we have caged persons without recourse to formal mechanisms of conflict resolution, there is evidence that the opposite is true. Figure 4.6 shows the mean degree of vertical hierarchy depending on the number of rules that the commune had. The difference, while only marginally statistically significant ($F = 2.73$ at 3 df; $p = .059$; eta $= .435$) is quite instructive: the more rules the group has, the *more* vertical stratification. The same result could be told using a host of other measures—far from this vertical ordering arising because of an absence of other structure, this ordering is stronger when other forms of vertical distinction are present, including strong and unitary leadership at the top.

---

[55] Since instead of a frequency of wins, we only have each person's self-report as to whether she has more, less, or the same amount of power in the relationship as alter, the model must be different in form from the Bradley-Terry model used above. Let $\Pr[x_{ij} = A]$ be the probability that person i claims to have power over person j; $\Pr[x_{ij} = B]$ be the probability that person i claims to be equal in power to person j; and $\Pr[x_{ij} = C]$ be the probability that person i claims to have less power than person j; let $\omega^A_{ij} = \Pr[x_{ij} = A]/\Pr[x_{ij} = B]$ and $\omega^C_{ij} = \Pr[x_{ij} = C]/\Pr[x_{ij} = B]$. Then this model can be written as two log-linear equations for the latent status parameters a and one additional constant b: $\ln(\omega^A_{ij}) = a_i - a_j - b$; $\ln(\omega^C_{ij}) = a_j - a_i - b$.

[56] Vertical hierarchy is measured as the standard deviation of the members' status parameters (here we take the logarithm of this standard deviation to be consistent with earlier work).

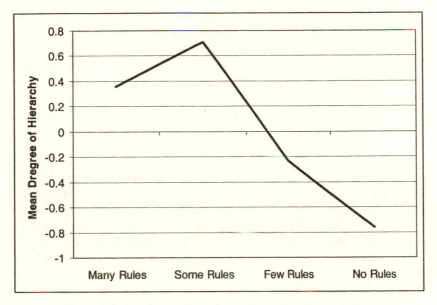

Figure 4.6. Dominance hierarchy and formality of organization

The implications of this are important—using data (self-reports on power) that is quite different from those used to study adolescents (outcomes of agonistic encounters) we find similar vertical structures emerging. But the conditions that foster the emergence of such a structure are quite different. While among children, these conditions seemed to be the absence of formal possibilities for conflict resolution, among adults, the opposite seems to be the case. As we found with gangs, more rigid and defined hierarchical social structures seem to provide or support the vertical differentiation of members in terms of status.

Gender and Power

When considering adolescents, we saw that there was reason to believe that boys and girls produced somewhat different power structures. Of course, in the communes, there are always men and women together, but one might still suspect gender differences. In particular, since the data are based on self-reports, there might be a tendency for men and women to answer in different ways. Martin and Fuller (2004) examined this and concluded that in many groups women were more likely to answer questions about interpersonal power with the response "we are equal." That is, a woman one unit of status above some man would be more likely to insist that the relationship was equal than would a man with the same status advantage. But this gender difference was basically a power difference—these groups tended to be those where women were, in general, of lower status; in the groups in which women tended to be of *higher* status, it was the men who seemed to be more prone to egalitarianism. There was, however, one exception to this gender symmetry. In general, groups with explicitly traditional gender ideologies tend to disempower women, and groups that have strict control over romantic relationships tend to empower women (Fuller and Martin 2004). But where the actual gender balance of power diverged from what we would expect given this pattern—whether or not women were advantaged by this divergence—women were more likely to label power relations as equal.

Thus we may see that in general, relations between men and women are symmetric in that both *see* power the same way (though women tend to have less of it), with one exception: where the power relation does not "fit" the structure, women tend to cover it up by blurring vertical distinctions. Dominance is not paradigmatically "male"—there was no evidence that women's relations with each other were less linear than men's relations with each other—but it is gendered nonetheless. This is because women seem to have the special role of normalizing power relations, which means covering them up if they are anomalous.

Conclusion: Why There Are No Dominance Orders

The Problem of Completion

We began with the question of why so few dominance orders seemed to exist in adult human groups. We are now in a position to answer that question: the answer is that a dominance order requires three things: unbridled physical agonism, absence of a change of venue, and caging.

If there is to be a dominance order, first there must be relationships of dominance. Although one might imagine that this implies that we first need things for people to strive for, there is no evidence that this is the case—status can itself be a desired good, and status in a dominance order therefore need not be related to other goods (though of course in many cases it is). What seems necessary for a relationship of *dominance* to form is that the result of conflict turns on an unambiguous display of ritualized submission. We have seen that there is a tendency for such relationships to become transitive, in part because of preexisting individual-level differentiation and also because of interaction effects: winner effects, loser effects, and bystander effects.

But in order for a single linear order to emerge, the set of relationships must be *complete*—people must be "caged" so that they cannot avoid one another nor avoid seeing each others' interactions. Adults frequently are "caged"— they see the same people for forty or so hours a week over and over again. But it is not necessary that one party signal submission for a hostile interaction to end. It is this that we can call "the problem of completion"—that actual set of relationships may fall short of a proper structure because there is no way to ensure that all pairs of actors establish a relationship.

This is because there are usually quite a few different formal mechanisms that can be invoked as an alternative to submission or escalation, which promptly defuses the production of dominance orders. That is, given a game of "chicken," in which neither A nor B submits to the other, A cannot simply raise the stakes—B has the option of shifting the venue in the sense of moving toward some institutionalized form of conflict resolution. Indeed, in most places, B has a responsibility to do so, for physical violence can invoke responses by external third parties (e.g., police). Thus B can respond to threatened violence with a threat to change the venue to a legal, communal, or authoritative, but in all cases nondyadic, context, and need not make a public submission. Of course, this only raises the question as to why violence is outlawed, and why laws against the use of violence are obeyed in some places and times and not in others. Children, despite the presence of supervising adults, seem to believe that such a change of venue ("tattling") is not a plausible strategy, perhaps because doing so invariably leads to a loss or rank, and hence live in a more Hobbesian world (see Adler and Adler 1998: 199).[57]

Of course, in gangs, such violence is not prohibited and may not even be contained. But if vertical structures arise, they come (as in communes) *because* of formal organization, not in spite of it. And this seems to be because members are insufficiently caged—the member who must ritually submit is a member deprived of respect and status, and one does not remain in a gang under such a cloud.

In sum, dominance orders do not arise simply because there is hostility and contest, nor even physical attack. They require hostility that will inexorably lead to an ever-increasingly dangerous physical struggle. Schjelderup-Ebbe (1922: 244) conducted experiments where he united two groups of hens in a single enclosure, but with a wire screen separating the groups. While they were able to peck each other through the screen—and indeed many did—it was possible for one hen to tire of the conflict and simply walk away. Since this hen never made a ritual submission out of fear, nothing had been settled. When the screen was taken away, all those hens that had fought inconclusive battles immediately picked up where they had left off, and only *then* was a dominance order established.

People tend to be in situations more akin to the wire-separated cage than the free-for-all; were chickens able to walk away or change venue, they, like

---

[57] As my nine-year-old said one day when questioned about a fight at school, "What happens on the playground, stays on the playground." It may be that similar dynamics are found among prisoners, but there is insufficient research.

humans, would not have pecking orders. Conversely, were we to have been
fortunate enough to study social environments where status was decided by
free-floating interactions before a small group of observers (e.g., Salon society), we might have been more likely to see dominance orders.

Strategies

I noted above that dominance orders seem to require the possibility of unconstrained escalation of physical conflict. It is not, of course, necessary that all
dominance contests be decided by violence—indeed, we have seen that sometimes ridicule by the self-confident is more effective—but where there are
boundaries placed on interactions, there can be a diversification of strategies
that undermines the transitivity of dominance relationships and produces circular patterns in which A dominates B, B dominates C, but C dominates A. For
some interesting evidence of this, we can consider the first systematic study
of dominance in young children. Here Hanfmann (1935) arranged children in
a paired-comparison experiment to see who was dominant and found a set of
interesting cycles at the top of the hierarchy (with simple linearity at the bottom). The reason for the cycle had to do with the strategies used by the different
children. The fourth ranked child (D) was concerned with keeping the social
interaction running smoothly; instead of responding to agonism with agonism,
he successfully defused conflicts with others with humor, with cheerful (and
often temporary) acceptance of alternative plans, or with gift offerings. This
allowed him to dominate six of the other eight children, but not the third ranked
child (C). This one had such forceful and clear ideas about what was to be
done that other children tended to go along with him, especially because he did
not attempt to enforce his ideas with violence but with reason and, if necessary,
withdrawal. His task-orientation led him to get his way over D, who was more
interested in preserving social harmony. C was in fact able to dominate seven
of the other eight children. The one child he could not dominate was the second
ranked child (B), whom Hanfmann calls "a little *gangster*."

B attempted to monopolize all the resources and direction, with no attention
to or respect for the putative rights of the other children. The grand schemes
of C and the winning charm of D counted for nothing with him. And indeed,
B was able to dominate seven of the other eight children. But as Hanfmann
says, "he is powerless against the child (A) who deliberately disrupts the situation of orderly play. The method of child A is destruction." This child A would
simply allow B to monopolize the blocks, do all the building, and would then
ruin whatever B had made. "As destroyer this child is invincible," yet he when
interaction was going smoothly, he would check these destructive impulses
and effectively be dominated by the lower-ranking children.

In other words, there is a "rock-scissors-paper" logic here, although there
are actually four different strategies. Affective leadership (D) works well, ex-

cept for a child who is so fixated on the task at hand that he would rather lose a friend than lose direction of the project. The affective leader, more interested in maintaining the social relationship, defers to the instrumental leader (C). But the instrumental leader cannot make headway in the face of determined and violent opposition on the part of the gangster (B) who refuses to cede control to the visionary. Yet all this gangster's primitive accumulation counts for nothing when paired with a destroyer (A) who doesn't care about whose tower it is, as long as it comes smashing down. But the destroyer in turn is easily captivated by children who can lead the interaction in a direction that is either socially or instrumentally productive and interesting. This cyclic pattern cuts at the transitivity that is the heart of the order—further, even when there is transitivity, the differentiation of strategies makes this property less useful in concatenating structures.

Heuristics and Concatenation

This sort of differentiation prohibits the applications of the simple heuristics such as bystander effects that facilitate the emergence of dominance orders. That is, B cannot assume that simply because A dominates him, and he dominates C, that A will also dominate C. But even where these heuristics are adequate, they are unlikely to help produce larger structures out of smaller units. The two fundamental structural principles of completeness (for any two persons, either $A > B$ or $B > A$) and transitivity (for any three persons, if $A > B$ and $B > C$ then $A > C$) imply that every such aggregation will lead to a fresh round of conflict. While transitivity can be used to fill in some of the possible relations after a few cross-group bouts have occurred, there will still need to be a fair number of contests in most cases. To illustrate, imagine the attempted fusion of two orders with four people each, the first where $A > B > C > D$ and the second where $E > F > G > H$. Let us say that our first agonistic interaction demonstrates that $A > E$. By transitivity, $A > F,G,H$; but the relation between F, G, H and B, C, D is undetermined. If $D > F$, all relations are determined, but other outcomes (except $H > B$) leave more contests necessary. One is not much worse off starting from scratch.

   Thus there are rather stringent conditions for the emergence of dominance orders, and even when such structures do arise, it is hard to fuse two of them so as to produce larger structures. Any hybridization whereby a dominance order is combined with another sort of structure allows for the possibility for a change of venue. Because such a change of venue deflates the pressure to follow through on all agonistic interactions until a ritualized show of submission is made, it destroys the clarity of the dominance order.

Toward Horizontality

Vertical relations are about comparability—the ability to take any two persons and say which is "higher" or "more" in some terms than the other. In some cases, there may be a preexisting dimension according to which the comparison can be made. In other cases, this dimension may emerge out of the pattern of asymmetric relations (the popularity tournament); if the development of such inequality is considered problematic an exchange structure may be able to prevent this. In still other cases, the dimension emerges from agonistic contests. Rousseau—who stressed the importance of interpersonal comparison for contemporary social life—dismissed the possibility that such contests would have effects analogous to those in poultry. We have found this to be largely correct. Dominance orders require not only that people be unable to decline agonistic contests but that these matter enough to force a choice between ritualized submission and escalation. In adult life, where the outcome of interpersonal interaction makes a difference, it seems that there is a possibility of avoiding agonistic interactions or of taking them in other paths.

This is, in effect, to return to the problem of completion that we first saw for the clique in chapter 2. We may find that a relationship has an implied heuristic that requires that *all* participants establish relationships with one another. Yet there are very good reasons why we expect them not to do this. This suggests an alternative type of structure. A pecking order, in which the relation is one of dominance, might be envisioned as a matrix with rows and columns ordered by rank, and a 1 in every cell in the upper triangle, and a zero below. (That is, the cell in the ith row and the jth column is 1 if i dominates j.) But it is one thing to say there can only be a 1 in the upper triangle (i.e., the lower triangle is all 0s) and saying that there *has* to be a 1 in the upper triangle in all places. Keeping the former rule but abandoning the latter leads to a form of organization corresponding to social structures where people are ranked, but have the opportunity to avoid agonistic contests; this introduces an element of horizontal differentiation. It is to these structures that we turn in the next chapter.

5

The Escape from Comparability and the Genesis of Influence Structures

Forms of Organization

Review

We have seen three pure forms of organization—three ways in which structure elegantly emerges from relationships. We found a tendency for certain types of relationships to move toward one of these forms, although there were always possibilities for alternate structures due to inherent ambiguities or polyvalences in the content of relationships. In chapter 2, considering the ever-popular relation of "choosing as a friend," we found that choices could be organized according to a "popularity tournament," in which those already disproportionately chosen are disproportionately likely to be chosen by others. Here the organization is subjectively understood in terms of the qualities of *individuals*—the social organization of relationships seems to disappear into the bodies of persons. Following Harrison White (1992) I will call this mode of organization "selection" (see figure 5.1).[1] Not all asymmetric relationships will be organized in such a fashion, but the range of environmental conditions under which the popularity tournament can emerge is rather broad, and hence it is both common and robust.

In contrast, wholly mutual relationships are more compatible with the development of isolated dyads. Again, following White, I will call this "commitment." Perhaps the best example of this is marriage, although we have seen

---

[1] A note on how I adopt this terminology without the underlying scheme: first, White calls the forms of organization "disciplines" and considers the dimensions of dependence, involution, and differentiation (briefly discussed in chapters 2, 3 and 4) to be something that, in some ways, appear "in between" the disciplines (thus if we were to put the disciplines as apexes in a triangular chart, these dimensions would appear as the sides). The exposition here loses this formal elegance and comes closer to lumping the two together (in effect, rotating the dimensions by nearly 120°). Thus the correspondence to White's terms falls quite short of a proper allegory, but much of the logic of trade-offs between different forms holds. Second, White considers selection characteristic of the "arena," the discipline in which (among other things) there is a tendency to transitive closure. I argue that all strong forms of organization are compatible with transitivity, but that the transitivity of selection is not a subjective heuristic but instead should be understood as a side effect of the stratification of persons.

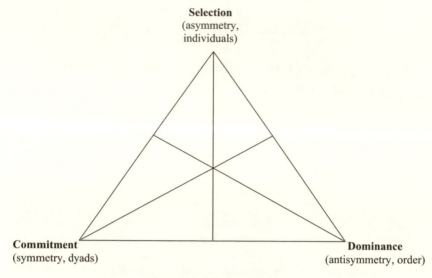

Figure 5.1. Three pure forms

that mating systems can vary along related dimensions as well.[2] Moving from the corner of the lower left point of figure 5.1 ("Commitment") upward we might find the rating and dating system (one that organizes by individual characteristics as if it were a choice process) about halfway between "Commitment" and "Selection." Equivalently, one could imagine moving from normal nominations of friendships toward this same structure by starting from pure "Selection" (the very top point of the figure) and moving downward and to the left by increasing the degree of commitment (e.g., "going out").[3]

Finally, inherently antisymmetric relationships are more compatible with the single "dominance" order (the lower right point of figure 5.1). This structure is in many ways isomorphic to the pure popularity tournament, but participants are likely to have a subjective conception of the transitivity requirement. It may be somewhat perplexing if someone who admires someone who admires me does not, himself, admire me. But it can be seriously troublesome if someone I dominate dominates someone who dominates me. We saw such a neces-

[2] White thinks more of producer markets than marriages here, which he subsumes under the discipline of the "interface," but he also highlights the importance of inequality and mutuality to the relationships.

[3] Thus one could perhaps redraw the figure below as three triangles (with an empty inverted triangle in the center), an upper one for asymmetric relationships like friendship choices (the base of which is a horizontal line midway between the apex and base of the larger triangle), a left and lower one for symmetric relationships such as marriage (the apex of which is midway on the left side of the larger triangle) and a right and lower one for antisymmetric relationships such as dominance (the apex of which is midway on the right side of the larger triangle).

sary focus on triadic relationships emerge with the antisymmetry of relationships when we began with the case of mating structures (down and to the left). This is the difference between restricted and generalized exchange—moving further right (toward "Dominance" from "Commitment") means renouncing some of the emphasis on dyadic exclusivity (and consequent symmetry) and moving toward antisymmetric relationships that spread out across the group.

Thus there *are* pure forms of organization, but human beings revel in impurity. We have seen some of the reasons for this in the previous chapter; let us review why, for one, dominance orders are so rare. We found that provisioned primates tended to form dominance orders because everyone wanted to be near the bananas. Absent the bananas and some would just walk away, leading to an inability to determine which animal "outranked" the other. It is not that human beings are never "caged" so that they have to encounter one another nor that they are never left to fight things out without a possible change of venue. But it is the case that these two rarely coincide. That is, the people who have the bananas also have procedures for conflict resolution other than potentially unbounded physical violence. Where there is no appeal other than through the fist, there usually aren't enough bananas to keep us in one place. As a result, when there are antisymmetric relationships of agonism, they are not *complete*—A and B need not interact and establish a relationship of dominance simply because there is some C to whom both are connected via a dominance relationship.

And this is why the resulting relationships are messy—they move away from the position on the lower right ("Dominance") of the above figure, introducing the voluntary selection characteristic of the popularity tournament. And this voluntary nature leads to the possibility of horizontal as well as vertical differentiation.

Enter Horizontality

In the previous chapter, we found little evidence that dominance orders were a prominent form of social organization among human beings. This was not because we found human relations to be uniformly egalitarian or mutual. On the contrary, we examined cases of hierarchical relations, but found them falling short of a pure order for two reasons. The first was that a dominance order requires displays of submission that are unlikely to be emitted if people have a good chance of having their conflicts resolved without ever-escalating physical violence. The second, and related, reason was that people are insufficiently caged—with an exit option, it is possible for two persons never to enter into the bout that would lead one to be victorious over the other.

Let us, then, relax our understanding of the antisymmetric relationship in question, and see if we find similarly relaxed structures appearing. That is, when A *can* dominate B and B cannot remove himself or somehow avoid A, A *will* dominate *B*. If *B* has the opportunity of exit in some sense (which may or may not involve physical removal), then even if *A can* dominate *B*, *A* may not end up having this relationship with *B*. There is now some element of *B*'s choice. In this case it seems that we are moving more toward something like "influence." When we say that *B* is influenced by *A*, we often mean an antisymmetric relationship that is based on *B*'s recognition of *A*'s superiority, but a recognition that must be freely given.

To anticipate, we can imagine bringing horizontality into our structure simply by beginning with a dominance order and then allowing some persons to politely decline to be dominated. The overall ordering of persons from low to high does not change, but there is a dramatic change in the social structure—that is, both in the form and in the content of the set of relationships. In terms of form, we move from a simple line to a more complex structure with both horizontal and vertical differentiation. In terms of content, we move from despotism to consent, from dominance to influence.

We will, as before, reach this conclusion inductively, by starting from relationships of influence and seeing how they tend to be structured. Here we shall use the term to denote only one person's changing her cognitions after encounter with those of another person, and not how one person gets another to do what the first wants. While influence will serve as the focal point for these analyses, it is worth emphasizing that the class of relationships that will take on similar structural forms is much larger and ill-defined—there is a degree of influence in many relationships that would be called friendship or acquaintance—and indeed these structures may be considered the default for many informal relationships. They are characterized by two environmental conditions—vertical differentiation and choice—that are much more widespread than those required for cliques, exchange structures, or pecking orders. And the resulting structures are, as we shall see, particularly weak in contrast to seemingly similar structures.

Relationships of Influence

Influence and Diffusion

Interpersonal influence has been a fundamental topic in sociology for so long that it is hard to imagine that there is anything new to say about it. When it seems that novelty is being introduced, it is often a result of the term *influence* being used differently, for the word can refer to a number of relationships that are substantively different, even if they shade into one another. On the one hand, we sometimes use the word *influence* to indicate implicit resistance. Thus if campaign donations allow corporation *X* to influence some politician, we assume that in the absence of this conduit of influence, the politician would not wish to act in a manner advantageous to *X*. At the opposite extreme we

TABLE 5.1
Types of influence

	Eager	*Reluctant*
Open	Contagion	Pressure
Selective	Diffusion	Authority

may imagine recipients of influence to require no incentive to overcome such implicit resistance. For example, we might consider much of peer influence to occur in circumstances in which it is of the greatest interest to some person to ascertain what others are doing or thinking and to act or to think accordingly.[4]

Second (and partially independently), in some cases we do not care from whom we get some information or opinion that can influence us. In other cases, however, we will only accept influence from someone who has a certain position, or who has a certain relation to us. This may be because others are not considered qualified, or it may be because certain positions bring with them some compulsive or persuasive power (e.g., priesthood), or because we simply do not trust some people.

If we dichotomize each of our dimensions (degree of resistance and degree of selectivity of source), we can imagine four types of influence (also see McGuire 1999: 79). Most ideal-typical categorization schemes are less than perfect; the types offered below are perhaps even less so than usual, and one can probably think of cases that are not illuminated by this scheme. Nevertheless, it can serve as a useful starting point for exploring the creation of differentiated structures. We thus divide relations of influence according to whether the recipient of influence is assumed to be implicitly resistant to adapting his or her behavior or beliefs ("reluctant") as opposed to being predisposed to adapt ("eager"); and according to whether the recipient is more likely to be influenced by some persons than others ("selective") or equally liable to be influenced by all classes of others ("open") as in table 5.1. Each resulting combination has been given an identifying name, though these distinctions do not correspond exactly to current social-scientific usage, in which these terms are used somewhat differently, and in many cases are considered interchangeable.

In the history of structural analysis the first relationships formalized were those pertaining to contagion, as these are the simplest. But this simplicity implied a lack of structure and so shed little light on the issue of what forms sets of influence relationships might take. Still, it was exciting to imagine taking principles first worked out in epidemiology and applying them to other cases in which persons are only distinguishable by their possessing or not

---

[4] Kant (1991 [1797]: 250) makes this distinction between a willful and free sharing in another's feelings on the one hand and an unfree sharing due to susceptibility that involves communicability.

possessing the transmissible unit in question (e.g., knowledge or fashion). Because of this background, I will refer to a person possessing whatever is to be transmitted the "carrier" or the "infected." (Here one may follow the treatment of Coleman [1964: 42ff], though he considers this a diffusion process and uses the word contagion differently. My notation is also somewhat different at first.)

Given any two people, A and B, the probability that A will transmit whatever is in question to B may be considered to be the product of (1) the probability that A and B will encounter one another; (2) the probability that A is a carrier; (3) the probability that B is not; (4) the probability of transmission from a carrier to an uninfected person in any contact. If we call the first of these p and the last q, we find that the most likely number of transmissions in any period is $pqx(N-x)$ where x is the number of carriers and N the total number of persons.[5] This leads to the familiar S-shaped logistic curve such as the one graphed in figure 5.2. Early sociological studies finding such a temporal pattern led to excitement that the contagion model would be able to explain many cases of interpersonal influence.

Utility of Contagion Models

But are all forms of interpersonal transmission of information contagious? One famous example of the use of this model—deliberately adopted from epidemiology—was Coleman, Katz, and Menzel's (1957; also see 1966: 71) study of the adoption of the use of a new drug (an antibiotic) by physicians. This model, as we recall, assumes no social structure—contacts are random. Although Coleman et al. (1957; 1966: 136) believed that there *was* some structure to the set of doctor-doctor relationships, they proposed that there were two classes: there were some who were connected, and others who were isolated. The contagion model seemed to fit the connected doctors (the isolated could be treated as having a constant propensity to adopt the innovation).

Coleman et al. (1957; 1966: 57) actually had a second, and partially contradictory model, namely, that physicians varied in some continuous degree of "centrality" and that those "in the center of things" tended to adopt the new drug sooner than the less popular. The more peripheral would be influenced

---

[5] If the number of carriers is x out of a total number of N persons, then the probability that j is not a carrier is $(N-x)/N$, and the probability that i is a carrier given that j is not one is $x/(N-1)$. We subtract the one because since we know that j is not a carrier, the probability that i is one of the x carriers increases somewhat. We multiply this product by p and q to find that the probability of successful transmission to be $pqx(N-x) / [N(N-1)]$. We then multiply this by the $N(N-1)$ possible dyads to figure out the probability that there is *some* transmission in a period. Calling pq k for short, this yields the familiar logistic expression of contagion in a fixed population: $dx/dt = kx(N-x)$. Assuming that $x = 1$ at $t = 0$, this leads to $x = Ne^{kt}/[N-1+e^{kt}]$ (here see Coleman 1964).

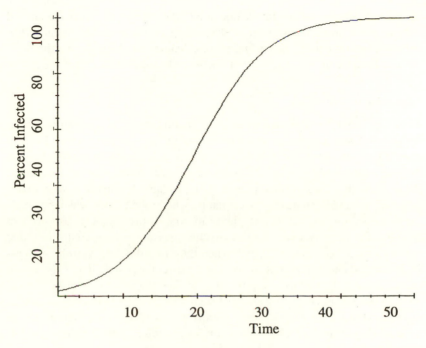

Figure 5.2. Simple contagion

by the central, leading to the hub and spoke model we saw in chapter 2 and to which we will return shortly.[6] But they liked the contagion model because they seemed to see evidence in the pattern of growth of adoptions over time.

Unfortunately, it turns out that many conceptually distinct processes are compatible with the basic logistic curve.[7] Indeed, the results are even compati-

[6] In support, Coleman et al. (1966: 114, 119, 123f) pointed to what seemed to be a greater tendency of those pairs who discussed matters with each other to adopt the drug at roughly the same time–at least in the first few months after release of the drug. This result, unfortunately, is probably spurious, due to the floor effect whereby no one could adopt the drug before it came out, and hence early adopters were more likely to adopt "close in time" to one another while late adopters were not. Coleman et al. made a second mistake: they equated being peripheral–receiving few choices from others as an influential person, a friend, a conversation partner–as equivalent to social isolation. But if influence flows as expected, it is not *being named* that means that Dr. X will convert to use of the new drug as a result of social influence, it is *naming others*–that is, being receptive to social influence.

[7] Other processes leading to a vaguely logistic form include normative pressure, competitive concern, and increasing returns to market share (for example, it makes sense to buy the operating system that more people have) (see Van den Bulte and Lilien 2001), all of which suggest an "overdispersion" logic according to which people are more likely to zero in on the same choices than would be predicted under a random diffusion model. As Granovetter (1978) has shown, it is basically impossible to use aggregate data to distinguish a diffusion process from one based on varying thresholds. Valente (1995: 81) suggests that in some cases one may be able to see the

ble with an absence of any interaction at all.[8] Anything that goes from around zero to some upper bound without decreasing is pretty much guaranteed to follow a similar curve.[9] The actual process leading to change—and the presence or absence of structure—is not visible in the aggregate data.[10]

Contagion and Pressure

Thus we cannot conclude that we have a structureless ("open") system merely because we see adoptions over time following an S-shaped curve. Further, even if we assume that the system is open, such data cannot help us distinguish between the cases in which recipients are eager (contagion) as opposed to those where they are reluctant (pressure). In this latter formulation, we propose that recipients have some resistance that may be broken down when they realize that everyone else *is* indeed "doing it" too. In the simplest case, we can imagine that there is some form of psychic pressure toward conformity that leads reluctant recipients to switch when they find themselves to be increasingly isolated and different. If so, we might expect the probability of successful transmission to be an increasing function of the number of persons who have already become infected. It seems that such a dynamic is frequently expected, at least in the United States, where parents assume that their children need to be explicitly instructed not to jump off the Empire State Building, even if everyone else does it.

---

difference between an "external" influence and a diffusion process by eyeballing the distribution, but there is little hope of demonstrating the reliability of such a procedure.

[8] Coleman, Katz, and Menzel (1966: 163) recognized and discussed the possibility that this curve results from simple heterogeneity in propensity to accept innovations–if this propensity is normally distributed, the cumulative density function is basically the same as the logistic (see Valente [1995: 64] for a more thorough treatment).

[9] Van den Bulte and Lilien (2001: 1410f, 1419, 1427) recently reanalyzed the setting of Coleman et al.'s study and found that the adoption of the innovation in question is better explained by advertising than by interpersonal influence, whether structured or unstructured. Coleman et al. (1966: 52, 53, 61) had reported that doctors themselves acknowledged the importance of commercial influences such as ads and pharmaceutical representatives ("the detail man") and indeed ranked such influences much more important than influence from other doctors, but Coleman et al. emphasized personal influence in their theoretical account.

[10] This despite the fact that Sorokin (1959 [1941]: 631f) had made precisely this point. Another example is Crane's (1972: 24f) argument that scientific growth is a form of what I am here calling contagion, and hence that the number of persons in some particular research field who accept some new idea should be proportional to the number who have already adopted. While Crane admitted that a number of cases she examined did not fit the model, she concluded that there was rather good evidence of science following this pattern. Yet close inspection of the curves suggests something else. Even if we discount the fact that for all research areas there was a big boom in the 1950s and 1960s, such that those that had previously seemed to be at their point of maximum "saturation" again began growing—due to the expansion of academia in the postwar era, and not with the internal dynamics of any field—and focus on the curves that seem to fit the contagion model, we cannot distinguish between any number of reasonable processes of monotonic increase.

It is easy to generalize the equations for the contagion model with the addition of one or two parameters that characterize the susceptibility to such pressure. For example, we can make the probability of one person adopting (given exposure to someone who has already adopted) a function of the number of other people who have already adopted.[11] We then get a class of curves, all of which look very much like the original S-curve, but with a change in the "inflection" point, that is, where maximum increase occurs. For the pure diffusion case it is when the proportion of people who are "carriers" is half the population, since this maximizes the number of uninfected people who meet infected people. Given a situation of "pressure," the inflection point is somewhat shifted to the right.[12] Contagion will take somewhat longer to get started, and then catch up quickly once a certain point is reached, but given the fuzziness of actual data—and this has perhaps not been appreciated—there is probably no way to distinguish a pure contagion process from a "pressure" process, even though the two make very different arguments about the fundamental nature of influence.[13]

The contagion model thus always appears to fit changes that go from low to high and stay there. Further, contagion models generally imply an end-state of total saturation, at least for the transmission of cultural elements such as beliefs,

[11] In the contagion model, we derived the probability of any person acquiring the innovation as $pq[x(N-x)]$. We might understand this pressure as generalizing the contagion model by allowing $q = (1 + b)x^a q_0$, where q_0 is some constant base rate; if $a = b = 0$ we have the classic contagion model. (This is a more general generalization than that following Coleman's [1964] contagious Poisson model. Thus it may be seen as the "overdispersed" equivalent of the normal diffusion process, just as the negative binomial is an overdispersed form of a Poisson process. This similarity is theoretically important and will be discussed below.) This leads to a new expression for the change as follows, namely $dx/dt = p(1 + b)x^a q_0 x(N - x)$. Calling $pq_0(1 + b)k^*$ for short, this is then $= k^* x^{a+1} (N - x)$.

[12] In the formulation given in the previous note, we find that the increase in infected is fastest when the proportion of the population that is already infected is $(a + 1)/(a + 2)$ (and note that this is .5 if $a = 0$). Since $dx/dt = k^* x^{a+1}(N - x)$, $d^2x/dt^2 = k^*[(N - x)(a + 1) x^a - x^{a+1}] = k^* x^a [N(a + 1) - (a + 2)x]$. Setting this equal to zero leads to one non-trivial root where $N(a + 1) = (a + 2)x$ or $x = N(a + 1)/(a + 2)$. The b parameter affects the total likelihood of spread, not where the curve is inflected.

[13] In some ways, this harks back to the failure of the first principled use of statistics in sociology, namely the application of Gaussian curves to demonstrate the existence of "social facts." Adolfe Quetelet and his followers in French sociology argued that the normal distribution of many individual measurements demonstrated the existence of social law–something must *constrain* individuals if their aggregate distribution conformed to this mathematical construct. This basic idea formed the heart of Durkheim's sociology and passed into Anglo-American sociology from there, but it is mathematically nonsensical. As William Lexis showed in 1879, the Gaussian is exactly what one would expect if there was *no* supraindividual constraint (Porter 1986: 249). Social constraint would be indicated by over- or underdispersion. Yet without an extremely strong theory of the precise nature of the process generating the data, it is well-nigh impossible to determine whether data show evidence of such constraint. So too with the contagion data.

tastes, or practices.[14] Yet this seems implausible, as there may well be something about many of these cultural elements that makes it unlikely that they will ever completely saturate a population. There may indeed be some people who prove completely resistant to some disease, but this is different from the *inherent* divisiveness of certain cultural elements; as Bourdieu (1984 [1979]) might point out, a cultural element that does not distinguish between persons is hardly a cultural element at all (also see Bearman and Brückner 2001).[15]

Further, in cases in which we might actually hold that a contagion process comes rather close to the mark in terms of explaining the process of adoption, the curve of prevalence over time may not look at all like a classic contagion curve, since there are forms of contagion that shift into reverse. Lieberson (2000) has given important examples of these—certain elements diffuse and become more and more popular but then "undiffuse" and become less and less popular over time.[16] That is, even where a simple contagion process takes place, people will find some way to throw it into reverse to make sure that there are always some who do, and some who don't. In these cases, persons are differentiated and maintain their differentiation. The weakness of these models, then, is that they ignore the differentiation of persons.

Differentiation of Persons

Two Types of Differentiation

Both the contagion and pressure models assume that all people are fundamentally indistinguishable—just as you can catch a cold from anyone who sneezes in your face, so the tension mounts for each additional adherent when you are not conforming to the group. The basic approaches can be generalized to take into account various forms of population heterogeneity (e.g., Morris 1993; Wiley and Herschkorn 1989), but most of these generalizations are open-ended methodological ways to encompass some sort of differentiation, should it exist. But what structural form is differentiation likely to take for influence relationships?

There are, we recall, two factors that determine the probability that A will transmit to B, the probability that they will interact (p) and the probability that there will be transmission given interaction (q). Thus we can divide selectivity according to whether the process is "p-differential" in that some dyads are

---

[14] When a disease is transmitted, the death of the infected and their replacement with younger uninfected can keep the equilibrium below saturation; when it comes to cultural transmission, transmission must be very spotty for normal turnover of population to prevent near saturation.

[15] This is not true of all cultural elements; there are some practices (for example, those that relate to new technologies) that may not contain any intrinsic limitation to their diffusion.

[16] For other studies of selective diffusion see Zachary (1977).

more likely to interact than others, as opposed to "q-differential" in that transmission is more likely between some pairs.

As a first approximation, we may propose that when people are eager for new information, p-differentiation is most important, and when they are reluctant to have their opinions or ideas changed, q-differentiation is more important. The logic here is that if you would be glad to get some piece of information, say, you will adopt it from the first carrier to come along, while if you are reluctant to change your ideas or adopt new ones, you will only do so when these are transmitted by certain people. You may encounter others, but you will not be persuaded.

I propose this only as a first approximation because it is not difficult to envision scenarios that do not fit this distinction neatly; indeed, since even reluctant people cannot have their minds changed by people they do not meet, p-differentiation will affect the actual spread of ideas or information where respondents are reluctant. But this distinction is sufficient to structure our investigation of the results of introducing differentiation to contagion models.

Diffusion

Let us thus consider the case of p-differentiation for eager listeners, which I have called cases of diffusion (in contrast to contagion). There are a number of coherent approaches for the general case of diffusion through social networks (including those that allow persons to have different degrees of stubbornness in terms of the number of their friends who must adopt some innovation before they go along [see especially Valente 1995: 73]). Such approaches treat the structure of relationships as given, and thus make reference to some *other* structured relationship (for example, friendship, organizational roles, family, etc.). But we may be able to say something about the forms that relationships established solely for the purpose of diffusing cultural elements might take.

First, because all recipients accept influence from those with whom they come into contact, there is no reason to expect that the relationship of transmission will be anything other than fully symmetric. The only formal issue is our ability to compile different pairs of persons' likelihood of interacting in such a way that we can see some structural principles emerging. As a result, pursuing this issue will lead us to replicate the logic of chapter 2, which examined mutual associations and ended up focusing on two sorts of web-structures, those with relational and those with spatial logics.

Spatial models are perhaps more appealing for the case at hand, for it is easier to adapt them to cases in which relationships are continuous as opposed to either present or absent. Thus we might expect people not only to be more likely to have had some interaction the "closer" they are, but to interact *more frequently* the closer they are. Most simply, geographical space directly affects diffusion; while it is not the only factor, a geographical model seems to account for the diffusion of certain cultural preferences (see Harton and Latané 1997 for some examples). Taking "social distance" into account may further increase the plausibility of a spatial representation for a diffusion process.[17]

Such spatial models may be used to account for diffusion, by maintaining that the contact that allows cultural elements to be transmitted is more likely to occur across short distances of social space. This is in itself not very interesting; what is more interesting is that this can lead to aggregate distributions that have certain structural properties; by throwing a wrench into the simple contagion model, these distributions may stop short of total consensus and display internal organization (see Abelson 1979; Harton and Latané 1997).[18] When we leave geographical space, and simply postulate a latent "social space" to parsimoniously explain patterns of adherence or transmission, it turns out to be quite easy to use a spatial model to account for diffusion when in fact no diffusion need be invoked to explain the spread at all. That is, we may assume that if A and B hold some competing versions of an idea or taste, say, and person C is "closer" in social space to A than to B, C will tend to receive A's version and not B's. But since the spatial logic is itself predicated on the likeness of A and C, A's influence may be redundant, as C may prefer the cultural innovation for the same reason that A does. Whatever it is that they have in common, and that leads them to be in the same area of this space, will lead to C's adoption without A's "influence." (This point underlies spatial analyses by market researchers; the key theoretical underpinnings of this are given by Spiegel 1961.)

Even apparent diffusion across *geographical* space may also simply be due to the slow movement of a source that independently spreads innovation like rats spreading the plague, or to likeness that happens to be geographically distributed, and not, in either case, interpersonal influence. One nice example is people all putting up their umbrellas at the same time, but there are less obvious cases. Consider the diffusion of home snowblowers.[19] The snowblower was first invented in 1925 by Arthur Sicard, (significantly) a Canadian farmer struggling to get his product to market; for many years it was a full-

---

[17] In chapter 2, we saw that the combination of these two types of space meant that weak ties of acquaintance were not likely to follow a spatial logic, since those close in *either* type of space are likely to be acquainted. But for stronger ties, the two distances may concatenate via an "AND" logic and hence lead to a spatial logic. For example, much (although not all) of the sexual interaction that can diffuse disease is likely to happen between people who are close both in geographical space and social space.

[18] It is also interesting that such models imply only weak transitivity, as pointed out by Erickson (1988).

[19] This example is hypothetical because longitudinal geographic data on snowblower use and/or sales is evidently so difficult to come by that the Nonroad Engine Emission Modeling Team of the EPA Office of Mobile Sources has created a computer program to estimate use based on climate data and housing stock. See their report NR-014, September 16, 1998. I am not making this up.

scale truck, not suitable for home use. (The first "walk behind" snowblower was then invented in 1951 by the Toro company.)

Unfortunately, we lack data on the adoption of this device, but it seems quite reasonable that if we were to examine aggregate sales by province and state, it might appear that spatial diffusion is responsible, since more would be sold in the northern latitudes at first, with sales in ever more southern latitudes increasing regularly. Thus one might assume from the data that Minnesotans learned of the innovation from Canadians, Wisconsinites and Iowans from Minnesotans, Missourians from Iowans, etc. But this could also result from the price being relatively high at first and the product only attractive to those with regular and heavy snowfall. As the price declined, we might expect the "threshold of snowfall" at which a snowblower became attractive to decline as well.

In such a case, the data have not been produced by a diffusion process. But a model that assumes that diffusion did occur, and was more likely the closer people were to one another in physical space, would fit the data quite well. Similarly, models that position people in a social space also often have a deceptive ability to "account" for diffusion.

Thus spatial-diffusion models have the problem that they seem to fit more cases than they should. A further drawback of a spatial model is that influence must be seen as inherently symmetric (see Erickson 1988:109–15). While the transmissible thing in question cannot go from an uninfected person to an infected person, but instead must go the other way, the contact itself is symmetric and the transmission only depends on who is infected and who not. Generalizing to the case in which more than one thing may diffuse, if one person is highly influential because she has many ties to others, she is also highly *susceptible* to influence. There is nothing in the distance between two persons that can lead us to determine that the relationship of influence should go one way and not another. The spatial position that is closest to overall influentiality is then "centrality"—being close to many other people.

Now it is possible to modify spatial analysis to introduce some asymmetry, as done by Friedkin (1998) in his study of scientific communities.[20] Friedkin allows some "central" persons to be more influential than others by giving people a differential "self-weight," that is, an innate resistance to influence (Friedkin 1998: 169, 195). Thus the various central players do not necessarily influence one another, despite their proximity.[21] But since one always is with

[20] This example is more complex than others, as the relational space constructed also takes into account structural similarities in addition to the mere presence of ties.

[21] While this might seem a bit arbitrary, one may reconceive space as a three-dimensional mountain range, where positions are not merely close to one another on the X and Y dimensions, but have different heights along the Z dimension, such that cultural elements will "roll" down from one person to another but not the other way around. Friedkin's technique may be understood as a version of such a model.

oneself, any differential self-weight must be seen as a q-differential phenomenon and does not get us further in understanding the nature of p-differential structures.

Finally, the spatial model may more fundamentally fail when the thing being diffused is information that others are eager to possess, for it assumes that the underlying probability of contact is a *cause* of information transmission, and not an effect. But if B is indeed eager to hear some type of information, possession of this information may allow A, normally "far" in space from B, to make contact. Suggestive evidence comes from the fascinating experiment conducted by Festinger, Schachter, and Back (1963 [1950]: 130), who planted rumors so as to trace the path of their diffusion. They found that transmission tended to follow lines of friendship, to stay close in social space. But the rumor also jumped across space, as people made contact with members of the governing council to whom they did not normally talk. As Ryan (2006: 230) emphasizes, "diffusion" generally misstates the process, which is one of deliberate *notification*.

Thus information transmission may move the opposite way from influence generally understood. Knowledge is power, at least to some degree. A person with knowledge certainly may, as Festinger et al. thought, cough it up the chain because it is "relevant" to the leader or simply because people are supposed to pass on all information upward. But even in the absence of such relevance, we might imagine that a person who possesses a piece of rare information experiences a temporary boost in status, such that she may initiate communication with someone who is of higher status in some setting, or is of equivalent status but not sufficiently well known to justify contact under most conditions (see, e.g., Blau 1955: 130; Erickson et al. 1978: 79). Even in a situation in which rank is formalized, the possession of information can itself alter one's position, and underlings with special information can command nominal superiors (Feld 1977: 79). Eager recipients may allow those possessing information to "tunnel" across what otherwise would be relatively great distances of social space, thereby defeating the utility of a spatial approach. Because spatial structures do not qualitatively distinguish vertical from horizontal separation, the changed distance that may arise when a person of low status possesses vital information cannot be adequately accounted for.

In sum, any vertical differentiation is likely to lead to a problem for a spatial model of diffusion of information, for two reasons. First, distance in a space is symmetric, which implies a fundamental horizontality between points. That is, it is as easy to get a piece of information located at point A to point B as it is to get a piece of information from point B to point A. In real life, however, we might reasonably expect that this is not always so. Second, the possession of information may itself change the social distance separating lower downs from higher ups.

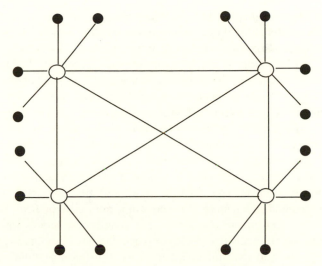

Figure 5.3. Hub-and-spoke structure

Center-Periphery Models

We may be able to capture some of what seems reasonable about the spatial metaphors, namely the idea that Coleman et al. had that some persons were more in the "center of things" than others, without adopting a strictly spatial logic. In the simplest form of this, we can use the reasoning of chapter 2 that saw one form of the web as leading to a differentiation of persons into hubs and spokes. Each spoke is attached to only one hub; hubs are attached to both spokes and to other hubs, but no hub is attached only to other hubs. (That is as much as to say that no hub is a "second-order hub," a "hub's hub.")[22]

In figure 5.3 the hubs are the larger blank circles, and the spokes the smaller, filled-in circles. This is basically the two-class model that has come to be assimilated to Merton's (1949) distinction between "cosmopolitans" and "locals" (cf. Fischer 1978). The cosmopolitans are mediators, those who are the first to learn of and synthesize new ideas, information, or opinions, and who then transmit these to the locals (we have seen this in Coleman et al.'s work; the best example is Katz and Lazarsfeld 1955; on evidence for such structures, see Lai and Wong 2002: 51).

The overall structure is clearly a sensible one, familiar to many of us from contemporary domestic airline travel, which is oriented toward a multihub system, though we see deviations from the pure case, as there are some spokes

---

[22] Because contact is symmetric we here assume that influence is symmetric; it is, however, possible to envision a structure in which hub-spoke relationships are antisymmetric.

that connect to more than one hub. Another example—and one that accentuates a particular combination of egalitarian communication between hubs, and authoritative direction within wheels—may be found in modern experimental science. Each laboratory is generally an extremely hierarchical form, though the number of levels and other particularities generally depend on the research setting (for example, firm versus university, large versus small, United States versus Europe). Communication, however, often occurs directly between hubs in a relatively informal way. This is true even though there are many institutional forms (for example, journals, meetings, societies) set up directly for the purposes of facilitating communication across work groups.[23]

Such structures arise in other realms (though often without the authoritarian relation between hub and spokes inside the wheel), because there is one thing they are very good at, which is robust communication.[24] Whether it is sending persons or signals from one place to another, multihub structures are excellent at getting things from any one particular place chosen at random to any other. This is in contrast to some other structures we will examine, which are good at getting an order from one particular place known in advance to every other place (command trees), or at diffusing news in general (webs or power grids), but not in terms of deliberate connection from any two places chosen at random. Given a trade-off between efficiency of communication and robustness in the face of damage, multihub systems are nearly ideal. They do involve redundancy (some people may get a message more than once if one is attempting to diffuse information throughout the network) and require somewhat more communicative work on the part of the hubs than is truly necessary, but these are generally small matters.[25]

To demonstrate this, imagine that we remove both diagonal lines connecting the hubs on the lower left and upper right in the picture above. This structure then has the same number of relationships as does the tree structure of figure 5.4. But in the ordered tree structure, it takes 4 "legs" (as flights from one node to another are sometimes called) to communicate from *any* one spoke to another spoke not attached to the same hub. If the apex is removed, the structure

[23] In a recent work, Karin Knorr-Cetina (1999: 180) suggests that in high-energy physics, a branch of science tied to extremely large experimental objects, the structure of work groups flattens considerably and leaders cease being apexes (those having an asymmetric relation to many others). Instead, they become mere hubs (those with symmetric relations to many others)–they are simply those "centrally located in the conversation conducted within the laboratory." Her parallel investigation of molecular biology, on the other hand, reveals the more traditional triangles.

[24] Some of the structures that we will investigate in the next chapter, such as the "big men" of certain Pacific Island societies, also tend to concatenate into multihub structures; it is therefore not surprising that Hage and Harary (1983: 38) report that the big men of Mount Hagen in New Guinea explicitly see themselves as "communication mediators."

[25] More intelligent systems that allow local structures to effectively contain knowledge of the structure as a whole can be more efficient than a multihub system, but these are difficult to establish without deliberate architecture.

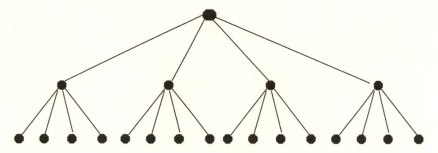

Figure 5.4. Tree structure

falls completely apart. But the nonordered multihub system can make most interwheel spoke-spoke communications in only three links, and the structure is relatively robust in the face of damage.[26]

Such structures are not only ideal to handle issues of dissemination of information when the source and recipient of that information are not easily specified in advance, but there is abundant anecdotal evidence that this is how people frequently create communication networks. For an example, the early use of the telephone in rural areas led to a hub-spoke system of between-town communication: a drug store in one town might be a communicative hub that linked to a drug store in another town (see Fischer 1992). Personal telegraph messages used a hub-spoke system, although the interaction connecting hub to hub (electric transmission through a wire) was different from that connecting hub to spoke (personal contact).[27]

Unlike airline routes, interpersonal communication structures are generally not planned, and it might seem unlikely that such a simple and efficient structural form would arise spontaneously. But it actually is extremely reasonable. First, assume that there are certain advantages to being connected. One has the ability to transmit and receive information. Further, assume that this advantage decreases with the characteristic path length of the network—the number of connections that will usually be necessary to reach someone. Given all this, it is quite reasonable that people will tend to operate according to the heuristic "connect to the 'hubiest' person you can." A "good hub" might be understood as one that gives one access to all other persons with fewer than some relatively

[26] It is worth noting that these structures must be understood as distinct from the more general small-world graphs we explored above; though multihub structures may in some cases have small-world properties, they need not (and probably do not when the degree of spoke-hub connections is high relative to the hub-hub connections). Though both are good at diffusing information, there is an essential difference in that small-world graphs come about *in spite* of tendencies toward social structure, while multihubs are themselves a form of structure.

[27] Hedström et al. (2000) have recently discussed the importance of such structures for diffusion but distinguish the pattern of connections between hubs as a "mesolevel" network distinct from the local networks revolving around each hub.

low number of connections. We might also expect that people may also find the maintenance of too many relations tiring, and hence some hubs will reject overtures.[28]

As a result, it is quite reasonable to expect that independent social processes will result in a rough equilibrium where there are just enough hubs to answer pressing communicative needs. Interestingly, then, we may see the multihub structure, which partitions people into two distinct classes of hubs and spokes, arising even when there is no preexisting categorical differentiation. While there may be some differentiation in people's subjective disinclination to be a party to many relationships, the multihub structure can arise even if all people are identically inclined.[29]

For example, imagine a structure formed by people coming together and wanting to make sure that they are in contact with others. While they do not particularly want to serve as hubs, they are unwilling to be too far removed from any other member (as would be the case if there were a large number of links required to send or receive a message from another). While they have an absolute limit to the number of people they are willing to be connected to, they would rather be connected to another hub (more likely to give them valuable information sooner, say) than to a spoke. Figure 5.5 below sketches the evolution of a multihub communication structure arising by the successive addition of persons who operate according to the following heuristics: (1) make sure you can reach every person with no more than two intermediaries; (2) consider connections to hubs (those with more than one connection) half as onerous as connections to spokes; (3) do not accept more than three spoke connections (or the equivalent, such as two spoke connections and two hub connections); (4) connect to the oldest member you can. Note that the dashed lines indicate a hub-hub connection—when person 3 becomes a hub at time 7, person 2 forms a new connection to her (since previously this would have brought 2's total connections to 3.5, over the maximum, but no longer does so, now that person 3 is a hub.)

Thus if people are to spontaneously form a structure for the purpose of diffusing information or other cultural patterns, it is quite plausible that multihub structures will emerge even when there is no variation in people's desires for communication frequency or timeliness.[30] However, in the cases in

[28] Although sociologists (e.g., Burt 1992), thinking of informal connections that cross-span formal organizations, have tended to stress the advantages that come from being able to broker information, there can be costs to being the person always expected to go to the source for some information, and then disseminate it to others. These costs may be expected to increase with the number of relationships actively maintained.

[29] Yamaguchi (2002: especially 175, 178) has recently formalized such a model of hub structures arising as an equilibrium from individual choices.

[30] For a different formalization leading to different results, see Jackson and Wolinksy (1996, especially 49f).

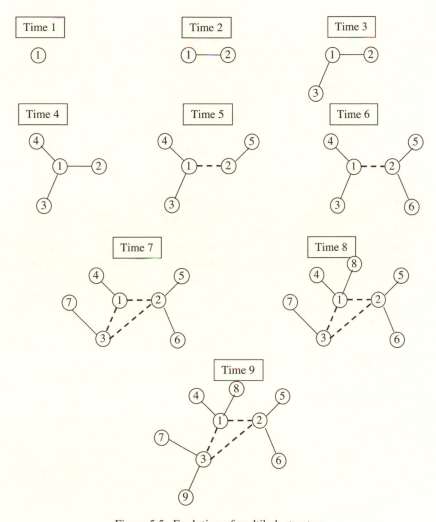

Figure 5.5. Evolution of multihub structure

which unanticipated information is diffused through general friendship connections, there is no reason to expect a multihub structure. Instead, it seems that communication follows a somewhat spatial logic, whereby the hubs are *least* likely to transmit information to those "far away" precisely *because* they are central—they are surrounded by similar people. While they have an advantage in communicating authoritatively to those around them, it is the more isolated, marginal persons who may utilize their weak ties and take information to other clusters (see Weimann 1982).

In sum, center-periphery or multihub structures may reasonably arise when people are deliberately oriented to the spread of something such as information, but are in general averse to having many ties. The structure serves to channel interaction in a more or less efficient way given that the respondents are basically eager to receive information. The resulting structures are very similar to the webs investigated in chapter 2. They have some of the characteristics of small-world graphs, though they tend toward more organization (in particular, a distinction between hubs and nodes and, most likely, a flatter degree distribution).[31] They are smaller than the set of acquaintance relationships, but unlike friendships, they may be actively constructed (that is, we seek out someone from whom to get information). Although hubs may transmit more to spokes than they receive, the relationship is, in principle, mutual, for no one would refuse a bit of information because they find the source unimpressive. For this reason, hubs have no special position over spokes—the structure cannot be turned to other uses, the way a set of influence relations based on power or authority might.

But what about when recipients are reluctant, such as when what is being transmitted is a belief that contradicts previously held beliefs? In such cases, mere exposure is not necessarily sufficient to ensure adoption. If differentiation is to enter, it is likely to enter in the form of some being more credible, authoritative, or persuasive than others. That is, in contrast to our hubs who differ from other people only in terms of their interactional pattern, we will expect to see people who differ in terms of how authoritative they are. We go on to examine such cases.

Influence Structures

Reluctant Recipients

In some cases people will tend to be reluctant to adopt new beliefs, if only because, as cognitive consistency theorists have emphasized (see Festinger 1957; Feldman 1966; and the essays collected in Abelson et al. 1968), changing one belief may require changing other beliefs, undertaking new actions, or

---

[31] There has been a great deal of hoopla in social networks research in recent years over the class of large graphs with very skewed degree distributions–examples are the World Wide Web, the Internet Movie Data Base, and so on. These graphs tend to have many people with low degree, exponentially fewer with medium degree, still fewer of high degree, and a very small number with a very high degree indeed. Breakthroughs in the mathematical treatment of such large and scale-free networks have been extremely important in network analysis but have led some casual observers to imagine that social networks must have a similar form (since there are also a lot of people). While there have been some innovative attempts to estimate the distribution of the number of people that we know (e.g,. Bernard et al. 1989; Bernard et al. 1990; and recently Zheng et al. 2006), no one has any idea what the actual distribution of degree of friendship or acquaintance is, if only because we are not sure what it means to be "acquainted." On social and cognitive grounds a scale-free distribution for either is implausible. (For acquaintance, a skewed normal distribution is most likely, and for friendship, an over-dispersed Poisson.)

revising one's sense of self. Whether they justify it on pragmatic (conditional) grounds—being influenced by C is going to be good for me—or on normative (unconditional) grounds—I should always be influenced by C on these matters—reluctant adopters, we may hazard, will tend to make a distinction between those from whom they should accept influence and those whom they can safely ignore.

The nature of this division between the influential and all others will likely depend on what types of beliefs are being transmitted. In some cases, C is considered a reliable guide to A's cognitions when it comes to interpretations and to adjudications between conflicting interpretations; it is only this "interpretation reliability" that I shall call "authoritativeness." In other cases, B is merely considered reliable when it comes to matters of observations; this "source reliability" I shall call "crediblity."

Now it may be impossible to make a theoretically perfect distinction between authoritativeness and credibility, as it is generally impossible to say where fact ends and opinion begins. Yet as actors we may be able to agree in practice as to where the division is, and it is this practical ability that will be related to structures of interaction. Even if there are intermediate cases along a continuum, we may distinguish cases in which person A considers person B credible but not authoritative from cases in which person A considers person B authoritative. The structures compatible with the first form of q-differentiation are not necessarily compatible with the second. We begin with credibility.

Credibility versus Authority

For person A to consider person B (but not necessarily person C) *credible* in some context or for some domain is for her to regard relevant statements from B as believable and, barring other credible information to the contrary, acceptable. For example, the American legal system is predicated on the assumption (correct or incorrect) that any adult without cognitive impairment is a credible witness. But such witnesses are (with exceptions generally pertaining to issues of character) not considered to have any particular *authority*. If a person claims that he saw a car go through a red light, this is considered credible unless contradicted by an equally credible witness, but despite his ability to make a potentially decisive contribution to an evaluation of guilt, he is not asked whether or not he believes the defendant to be guilty.

In contrast, expert witnesses are considered to have a different type of authority. They do not simply report that at 3:08 p.m. the Tuesday before that they saw a succession of bands on a computer printout—they state with authority that the two samples of DNA are from the same person or at least close family members. Similarly, a priest does not simply report that according to the Catholic Church (catechism #1857), a mortal sin must be done with full knowledge: like other experts, a priest hearing confession tells a parishoner when he is in mortal sin and what must be done to get out.

Structurally, the difference between authority and credibility is important, for it is reasonable to expect that it is easier for attributions of credibility to be mutual than for relations of authority to be mutual. Two citizens or two scientists can both expect the others' reports to be credible, but if a priest allows himself to be guided by a bishop's interpretation of some issue pertaining to church dogma, it seems unlikely that the bishop would also allow himself to be so guided by the priest.

Accordingly, there are cases in which q-differential credibility is organized in mutual fashion, most simply, in cliques. The earliest years of the Royal Society, as discussed by Shapin (1994), serve as an excellent example. No scientific discussion could take place unless a group could be assembled whose basic credibility was beyond reproach. One member could dispute an *interpretation* of an observation made by another member, but not (says Shapin) the observation itself. While it is possible to overstate this case, it seems plausible that the members drew on early notions of the qualitatively privileged position of honorable gentlemen to establish this clique as an equivalence relation (in the way in which the British used the equivalence relation "peer" in a distinctly exclusionary sense).

Although one would assume the credibility of other gentlemen, this was not a case of an open structure—there were others to whom such credibility was *not* extended. Thus common seamen might bring back many interesting observations but these would be treated differently from those returned by Royal Society members. It is certainly not the case, of course, that science as an institutional system continued to be reducible to cliques of saturated mutual relations of credibility.

This is because the very success of such a structure of equivalence, once set up, is its undoing. It is all very well to attribute blanket credibility to all clique members when one is dealing with matters of observation. But what happens once a set of equally believable persons are oriented toward the same observations? Sooner or later, we might imagine, there is a difference of interpretation regarding observations that all agree on. Since the issue cannot be settled simply by declaration on the part of the more authoritative, the community formed by this equivalence becomes oriented to the resolution of the difference. This resolution may be cooperative or it may be competitive, or both, but in any case, there are two results. The first is that statements of observation necessarily comprise a smaller and smaller portion of scientific interest. Discussion quickly zeros in on the work between observation and interpretation, and hence the base credibility of all participants becomes less and less important (also see Collins 1998: 533).

It follows (and this is the second result) that the process of community resolution, over time, leads some to be vindicated more often than others. The authoritativeness of the more-often-vindicated rises, in that would-be detractors without a record of vindication find themselves starting in any dispute with a handicap (if they did not start with one already). Even if there were no external forms of differentiation (e.g., political backing, personal magnetism, resources, and so on), we would probably find that a clique based on equivalent credibility would give rise to differential authority (see Latour and Woolgar 1979; Latour 1987). In sum, once again, we start from a clique and end up with a popularity tournament. We are hence drawn to examine q-differential structures that include some measure of vertical stratification of members into the more and less authoritative.

Hierarchical Models of Influence

Let us accept, then, that persons can be more or less authoritative. Because authoritativeness is (as Durkheim argued) an *attributed* quality, there may be disagreement about the authoritativeness of some person without this implying contradiction with our definition. Thus C may see B as more authoritative than A, while D believes A to be more authoritative than B. While we must briefly put this complication on hold, it is worth emphasizing that it does not necessarily undermine the project of looking for authority structures, for there can be a great deal of slippage between (on the one hand) the attributed authoritativeness of persons, and (on the other) an actual structure of relationships of authority—that is, not simply attributions of a characteristic, but a pattern of actual interaction.

Let us define such a relationship of authority to exist when A decides to treat B's pronouncements as valid guides for her own belief. We can begin by assuming A will only establish such a relationship if A thinks that B is more authoritative than she. We are now interested in whether *sets* of such relationships of authority can take on a structural form, and if so, what this form may be. We will use this to derive more general principles regarding the relation between subjective conceptions and structure that arise with the introduction of horizontal differentiation via incomparability.

By a "structure," we will mean a set of persons each of whom is tied to at least one other by a relation of authority such that the resulting graph is connected. If this structure is to be coherent, it seems reasonable that there is some sort of limit to the disagreement that persons may have about the distribution of authoritativeness. Let us call a set of (possibly disagreeing) views about the social distribution of persons that are compatible with the same structure of interaction "architectonic," since they do not contravene the establishment of a structural model.

Our question as to the architectonic principles of influence structures may be seen as a specific aspect of a more general question as to how horizontality can arise in a relationship that is inherently asymmetrical, such as "*A* is more authoritative than I am." We can begin to examine this more general question by considering simple conditions or heuristics that generate vertical structures, and then relaxing some assumptions.

The Introduction of Horizontality

We may take the simple case in which all persons are vertically ordered in terms of authoritativeness; all persons agree on the relative authoritativeness of one another, and a relationship of authority between *A* and *B* is established if and only if *B* is more authoritative than *A*. Since this is a general argument, we can consider "authoritativeness" one particular example of a personal attribute which we can denote ζ. Thus we may say $(B \rightarrow A)$ if and only if $\zeta_B > \zeta_A$. Such a case clearly implies the same transitive order that we examined in the previous chapter. Now let us consider how horizontal differentiation might be introduced into the order; as we allow for the relaxations that transmute dominance to influence, we will be able to derive a corresponding change in the structure of relationships.

We can begin with the simplest case, one in which all persons actually *are* vertically ordered but cannot correctly or reliably ascertain the difference in vertical position when they are rather close to one another. For example, we may imagine a group arrayed on a vertical dimension (figure 5.6, left), in which an antisymmetric relation is established whenever the distance between two persons exceeds some "just noticeable difference" (or JND, which we can imagine is some fixed quantity Δ). In other words, we now say that $(B \rightarrow A)$ if and only if $\zeta_B > [\zeta_A + \Delta]$; the corresponding heuristic might be "accept the dominance of *B* if *B* is *significantly* above you." The structure of this antisymmetric relation will not be a pecking order—instead, it will be what is known as a partial order, a set of elements and a relationship that is antisymmetric, reflexive, and transitive. The resulting partial order is displayed to the right of the order, toward the middle of the figure. This diagram is known as a Hasse diagram, as it does not include transitively implied relations: thus in the middle panel of the illustration below, from this we know that $(1) \rightarrow (5)$ since $(1) \rightarrow (3)$ and $(3) \rightarrow (5)$ and so this line is suppressed for the sake of clarity. As we can see, there has been an element of horizontality introduced by the de facto incomparability of adjacent persons. (This de facto incomparability is different from the *structural* incomparability we will examine shortly.)

If, however, the size of the JND is increased so that it is even harder to determine which of two persons is of greater authoritativeness (right panel), we decrease the number of "levels" in the structure while increasing the horizontal differentiation. As a first approximation, then, we might say that horizontality

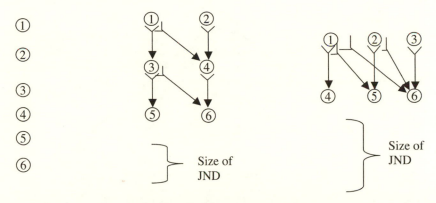

Figure 5.6. Horizontality and JND

can be increased by fuzzier distinctions between persons. Indeed, there are probably many good examples that could be found, and not all require that the JND be due to perceptual limitations. For one, if the antisymmetric relationship in question is one of ritualized submission behavior, it might be that the original ranking pertains to fighting ability, and person *B* is aware that his or her ability to give (a stronger) person *A* a rough time for his or her money is sufficient to exempt *B* from ritualized submission. For another, higher- status persons, when giving direction to lower-status ones, often initiate touch and physically displace others; this is most commonly seen when status arises on the basis of age difference. Given a ranking in terms of age, it might turn out that while a thirty-two-year-old feels that it is appropriate for her to give directives and perhaps physically guide to anyone younger than sixteen years old, and a twenty-five-year-old feels that it is appropriate to give directives to anyone under twelve years old, the thirty-two-year-old would not feel quite comfortable giving a directive to a twenty-five-year-old or initiating touch.

For these examples the resulting structure of interaction would form a partial order of the form seen above. Now in such a case, one can generally re-create the underlying order, simply by counting up the number of arrows leaving and entering any node (the out-degree and in-degree respectively).[32] Indeed, the participants themselves may be aware of the underlying order. But such awareness will not necessarily lead the structure of *interaction* to increasingly ap-

---

[32] In fact, this process leads to a special case of partial order where if we let the in-degree of person *i* be D_i (remembering to count the transitively implied relations that are suppressed in the Hasse diagrams printed above) and denote the relationship in question as $\rightarrow$, if $i \rightarrow j$, then $D_i < D_j$. If this condition holds or is approximated for some structure, this might be taken as suggestive evidence that there is an underlying ranking. That is, with proper discrimination we could say that if $D_i < D_j$, then we know that there exists some ζ as defined above such that $\zeta_i > \zeta_j$. Also see Landau (1953) for further explorations of such a score structure.

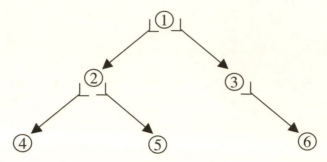

Figure 5.7. Architectonic interpretations

proximate an order—the hypothetical persons discussed above may very well know that age orders them without this reducing the size of the JND.

Slightly further away from verticality are those partial orders that do not allow us (or participants) to re-create an ordering even if such an underlying ordering exists and was in part responsible for the creation of the observed relations. Such a structure arises when the formation of an antisymmetric relationship between two people (which I shall refer to as a "choice," though forms of external assignment can also have this result) involves something other than the vertical positions of the two. For example, consider the partial order graphed in figure 5.7. If the antisymmetric relationship in question only forms from a higher to a lower person, there are a number of orderings that are compatible with this structure. It is possible that the ordering goes 1, 3, 6, 2, 4, 5 or that it goes 1, 2, 3, 4, 5, 6, etc. We know that 1 will be at the top and 4, 5, or 6 at the bottom, and we know that 2 will come before 4 and 5, and 3 will come before 6, but that is all. Even more importantly, we see that agreement among the members as to the underlying differentiation can be far from perfect without undermining the structural principles. Thus it might be that both persons 3 and 6 will hold that the true ordering is 1, 3, 6, 2, 4, 5, while person 4 holds that it is 1, 2, 4, 5, 3, 6. Thus person 6 justifies why she does not treat 2 as authoritative, and person 4 justifies why he does not treat person 3 as authoritative. These visions of the social world are contradictory in some ultimate sense, but as both are equally compatible with the structural ordering, they can be considered architectonic.

Structures such as the above, it will immediately be seen, will arise if persons are ordered (or orderable) and establish relations on the basis of this order, but at least one of the parties is free to decline the establishment of the relationship. More precisely, we may say $(B \to A)$ *only if* $\zeta_B > \zeta_A$ (but we do not say "if" or "if and only if" as we did in the pecking orders of chapter 4). This element of choice may come from the introduction of a new kind of "distance" (in addition to vertical distance)—the sort of distance that becomes possible when people are uncaged. For example, person (2) may simply have no interest in establishing a relationship of any sort with (6), and if this is permitted, (2) and (6) never compare their vertical positions. Such structures, or ones closely related, I will go on to argue, may reasonably be expected to arise in a number of situations in which the relationship in question is one of influence, especially influenced considered as a result of authority.

Uncaged Influence

Influence Trisets

The single best case of an influence structure that emerged in an informal group outside of any institutional constraints is still found in William Foote Whyte's (1981 [1943]) *Streetcorner Society*.[33] This case, in addition to its own merits, is of special interest because it inspired both theoretical (Homans 1950) and methodological work (Friedell 1967) on influence structures; unfortunately, as we shall soon see, the theoretical work inspired was in contradiction to the methodological work. An example of one of the diagrams that Whyte drew to communicate the structure of influence relations among men who formed a loose gang is reproduced in figure 5.8.

A number of things are immediately clear; the first is that there is a vertical organization—Whyte clearly assumes we will read this as flowing from top (Tony Cataldo) down to the bottom. Second, there is horizontal organization as well: there are two main cliques, so that few people in one clique influence anyone in another. But the horizontal organization goes further than that—it seems that Carlo is further "toward" the lunch room clique than Mike, since he influences Charlie who influences a lunch room boy. Gus seems to fall "in between" the two cliques, as Whyte deliberately drew him between the cliques despite the fact that he only influences Chris.

Even more, the overall organization seems somewhat reminiscent of an organizational hierarchy. Friedell (1967) was struck by this similarity, and argued that such influence structures were a special type of algebraic structure that we shall examine shortly, a "tree." A tree is a particular form of semilattice, which is in turn a particular form of partial order.[34] Basically, Friedell tried to assimi-

---

[33] There have been many network studies of influence over the past three decades, but most are influence relations within organizations, and thus do not fall under the class of the elementary structures considered here. However, even here, classic studies (e.g., Blau 1955: 129) find the same structural principles for influence relations. Other work on informal "ganglike" structures confirms the patterns described by Whyte (see, for example, Suttles 1968: 189f).

[34] The word *tree* is used in different ways; in some cases in graph theory it refers to any graph that has $N-1$ edges for N nodes. Here it will be used to denote the particular vertical structure in which any node has only one superordinate.

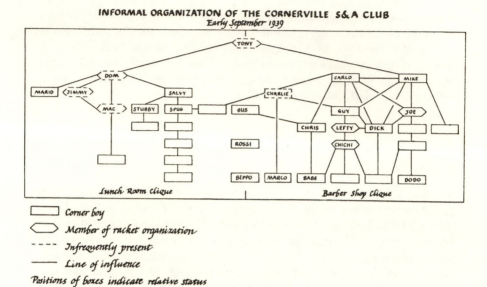

Figure 5.8. Informal influence in Cornerville.
Used by the kind permission of the University of Chicago Press.

late these structures to partial orders in which every two or more elements have a least upper bound—that is, a common superordinate—and hence all upper bounds of any subset are comparable to one another. To do this, Friedell had to drop certain relations of unclear direction. (His rendition is given in figure 5.9.) More important, since the binary relation defining a partial order is, as we recall, transitive by definition, Friedell made the strong claim that all transitive relations were present.[35]

Unfortunately, Whyte gave these diagrams without any explanation other than a cryptic legend, but in some cases transitively implied relations are explicitly drawn in, while in others they are absent (for a more detailed discussion see Martin 1998; Martin 2002). This suggests that Whyte did not believe that transitive relations were necessarily present. Homans (1950: 182ff) argued that such a lack of transitivity was quite reasonable given two seemingly contradictory forces at work. One the one hand, the leader tends to influence all others, but on the other hand, people tend to interact more frequently (and hence be influenced by) those closest in status to themselves. (We have seen support for this contention in our analysis of the camp dominance data in the previous chapter.) This implied that the leader's influence tends to be *mediated* by lieutenants.

[35] The ambiguity as to whether trees include all transitive relations is also found in the discussion of Hage and Harary (1983: 87).

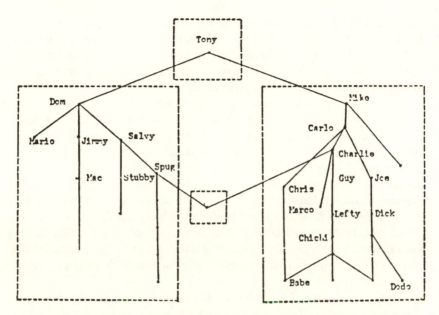

Figure 5.9. Friedell's interpretation of figure 5.8. Used by the kind permission of Morris Friedell and the American Sociological Association.

When the relation of "influence" that Whyte was describing is thus understood to mean *face-to-face* influence, and not "ultimate" influence, it is quite clear why transitivities are not implied—Carlo does not have a *relationship* of influence with Dodo because he would not take the time to talk to Dodo personally on a matter of controversy. But Joe would pass along Carlo's thoughts to Dodo. Even though the network is not a partial order *under the relationship of influence*, the members are partially orderable—Whyte is able to put them in a structure of top to bottom, with equality and separate lines of authority, including both incomparability and intransitivity.

While scholars of influence structures have tended to assume transitivity for reasons of mathematical elegance,[36] it is unlikely that influence structures really *are* transitive (here also see March 1957: 226). Yet they may still have mathematical properties. In particular, they may be arranged on paper so that all influence relations flow downward; written in matrix form, they can be permuted so that the lower triangular half of the matrix consists of only "zeroes" (no relationship), hence we can call them "trisets."[37] Returning to the

[36] An important exception is Harary (1959), who used the definition of tree that implied anti-transitivity and demonstrated that this allowed for a measure of status that was equivalent to a recursively defined set of partially ordered cardinals.

[37] Such structures turn out to have some interesting mathematical properties. In particular, if something diffuses through the influence relationships, the sets of possible states pertaining to

arguments regarding caging made at the beginning of this chapter, we may say that this is a structure that arises when we simply allow some people to reject relationships. It is like a dominance order with holes. Any relation that does exist is compatible with an ordering of all persons in terms of status, but not all relations compatible with this order *do* exist.

Such trisets may contain transitively implied relations, but they may not. It seems reasonable that if the transmission of information is costless and clean, it is economical to eliminate such transitively implied relations, just as Carlo would not bother to talk to Dodo when he could count on Joe to pass along his thoughts. If Carlo suspects that Joe does not reliably pass on Carlo's thoughts, however, he may have good reason to open up a direct channel of communication (cf. Evans 1975). But because of the lack of transitivity, the horizontality in such structures can be distinguished from that which we saw earlier, namely the horizontality that arises because of simple difficulties in discriminating who is higher in status than whom. In these cases, those on the top must directly influence more people than those below; this is not necessarily true in trisets.

For another example, Mary Sisock (2008) asked a community of persons who owned forest land whom they asked for advice about various matters pertaining to dealing with their land and trees and to whom they gave advice; she also asked the same questions of some of the forestry professionals who worked in the area to get a rather complete view of the network of influence. A portion of that network is graphed below in figure 5.10 (excluded are persons who were named by only one informant and were not in the data set, as well as some small unconnected components).[38] First, we can see that all persons can be arrayed so that no lines go upward—despite so many persons, there is not a single "cycle" whereby A advises B who gives advice to C who in turn gives advice to A.[39] Second, we can see that contrary to the JND model, those at the top do not necessarily influence more people than those lower down. Finally, we see that the structure is intransitive: just because A gives advices to B who in turn gives advice to C, it does not follow that A gives advice to C. In fact, in the entire network (bracketing the one mutual relationship), only three transitively implied relationships are present, two involving the same mediator (O5).

At the same time, it is not necessarily the case that we can determine someone's authoritativeness by their out-degree. Although DNR Forester 1 does have a special position of giving advice to many, O5 gives advice to far more

---

which people hold some thing at any time forms an algebraic structure (a lattice closed under union) from which the triset can be reproduced (Martin 2002).

[38] Persons in the data set are indicated by numbers; named professionals are given by their role. DNR stands for the Department of Natural Resources.

[39] There is one, and only one, mutual relation, that between persons O8 and O22.

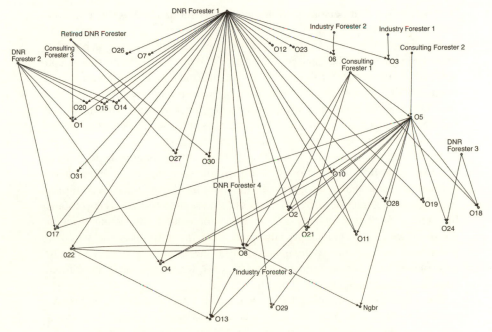

Figure 5.10. Influence relationships among forest landowners

people than do those from whom he gets advice. The structure, then, is a perfect example of a triset, implying that people can be perfectly ranked in terms of authoritativeness. We do not, however, know precisely what this rank is.

Trisets versus Trees

We have found that when people are ordered in terms of authoritativeness, influence trisets may emerge in which this order is only partially apparent. If we compare this structure to the pecking orders examined in the previous chapter, we see not only the introduction of horizontality but an implicit change in the correlative subjective heurisitics. A pecking order of influence relations would result if people followed the rule "always accept influence from those higher in status than you." A triset results if instead they follow the rule "never accept influence from those lower in status than you." Since pecking orders do not tend to arise for relationships of influence, we may conclude that while influence relations may be status-*conscious*, people insist on retaining some right of refusal (though we do not know whether it is higher-status or lower-status members who retain this right, or both). The additional rule, "do not directly influence someone who is influenced by someone you already influence" produces mediated trisets, but since actually existing trisets tend not to be *wholly* mediated (some transitively implied relations are present), it may be better to say that persons tend not to directly influence those who are too far "below them."

These heuristics allow for the sort of structure seen above, in which two or more lines go "into" the same person. Thus O13 near the bottom of the graph gets advice from another person in the data set, and industry fortester, and from a DNR forester. It seems that such an arrangement is quite consistent with informal influence structures. But consider what happens when influence "hardens" to the point in which the subordinate party *has* to accept the influence—when influence has passed over to command. Then one of ego's superordinates may contradict a command given by the other superordinate, putting ego in a rather difficult position. Not suprisingly, such multiple subordination is generally forbidden in what we will call "command structures," sets of relationships of command and control such as those seen in formal organizational hierarchies. Such relationships assume an environment of preexisting differentiation in which A is not simply attributed more "authoritativeness" by some B. Instead, there is some preexisting material inequality—A has access to or control over resources or outcomes that affect B. It is in *this* case that the tree structure Friedell discussed is likely to emerge.

The weakness of the influence triset for coordinating action goes beyond merely allowing for a person to receive contradictory orders. The triset's horizontal organization makes a poor basis for the organization of other relations. In contrast, the tree structure is such as to encourage the formation of heuristics for action that reinforce its own clarity. Indeed, as we shall see, it is a sufficiently useful structure for coordinating action that, when it does not exist, we are often forced to invent it.

Strength of Trees

To summarize, contrary to some earlier analysts, we have not found informal influence structures to take on the same form of the tree structure that is (as we shall see in chapters 7 and 8) a recurrent aspect of formal organizations that involve stratification and coordination of action. Yet these trees are exceedingly useful (at least to someone). They arrange antisymmetric relationships so as to maximize unambiguous direction and control while also facilitating other heuristics for action that are wholly horizontal. In fact, the unambiguousness of the verticality allows for the emergence of equivalence relations, returning us to the themes of equality first raised in chapter 2.

The relation between verticality and equivalence can best be seen in kinship relations—at least kinship as it is represented according to unilineal descent. If parenthood is antisymmetric (such that if I am your parent, you cannot be my parent), and each person has only one parent,[40] the tree structure below

---

[40] While it is possible to define a class of persons who all stand in the relation "mother" or "father" to some ego, it is also possible to make motherhood or fatherhood singular by definition.

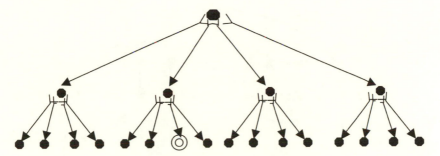

Figure 5.11. Tree structure

naturally arises. Of course, humans have more than one true parent, as their reproduction is not asexual, but if actors treat it as such, then relationships between men (or between women) can be cast as in figure 5.11.

What is so important about this structure is its implications for the organization of heuristics for action. In a technical sense, the vertical relationships of unilineal descent between generations induce a set of equivalence relations—and hence the possibility of a different social structure consisting of mutual relationships. Such structures can be formed by making "cut points" at some level; alternatively, they can be understood as sets of walks "upstream" and back "downstream." Thus if we let the relation R mean patrilineal parentage, so that iRj means that person i is the father of person j, then $C = R^T$ (the transpose of R) is the relation "is a son of." The compound relation CR defines the equivalence class of brothers (actually, "self and brothers"—all my father's sons); the relation $CCRR$ defines the class of male cousins (actually, "self, brothers, and cousins"—my father's father's sons' sons).

The tree structure of descent thus induces a different structure composed of nested sets of wholly horizontal relations or classes (also see Sahlins 1968: 15, 21). Such an induced structure is shown in figure 5.12. Each circle can be considered a horizon of relatedness. All those within the small circles consider themselves brothers, and all those within the larger one consider themselves cousins. The induced relationships of brotherhood are denoted with dashed lines and some—only the ones connecting the two groups of brothers on the left, to avoid drowning the diagram in lines—of the relations of cousinhood are denoted with light dotted lines. More generally, we can induce a new relation (T_k) whenever we go K steps back and then forward in time, with each relation T_k being C^kR^k; we can consider all those who are tied by a relation at level T_k to be T_k–equivalent. (Note that if two people are T_k–equivalent, they are also T_{k+n}–equivalent, where n is any positive integer.) These induced classes are indeed equivalence classes, which means that they are transitive—my brother's brother is my brother, and my cousin's cousin is my cousin (because your father's son is your brother, and your son's father is you, my father's

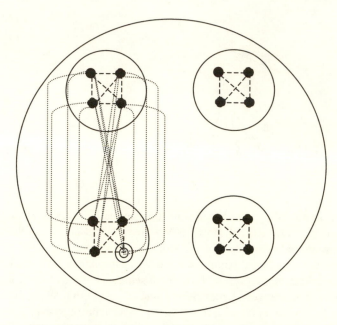

Figure 5.12. Equivalence relations induced by figure 5.11

father's son's son's father's father's son's son is necessarily my father's brother's son, or equivalently, my father's father's son's son, as am I myself).

It is really the existence of these induced equivalence classes, and the collective action they facilitate, that gives the unilineal family tree its importance. The tree itself rarely exists as much of a social structure, because a large number of the relevant nodes refer to dead people who do not interact (see Zerubavel 2003: 57–79). The tree is then less often an actual structure of interaction than it is a guide to the parsimonious construction of nested relations of equivalence, and hence the facilitation of certain interactions (also see Firth 1963 [1936]: 328).

Not surprisingly, where descent is unilineal (especially patrilineal), social organization often follows the implied structure of nested circles (though see Barth 1981: 149f for a qualification). Perhaps the best example here are a number of North African societies such as the Berbers.[41] Early Roman sources suggest that such tribes retained around five levels of organization: any person was a member of a family group (*domus*), in turn incorporated into extended family groups (*familae*), in turn incorporated into clans, in turn incorporated into subtribes, in turn incorporated into tribes, tribes which then formed con-

---

[41] A similar form of organization–families within clans, clans within bands, and bands within a troop–is also found in the extremely patrilineal organization of hamadryas baboons (see Kummer 1984; Kummer 1995: 144ff; Dunbar 1984: 16f).

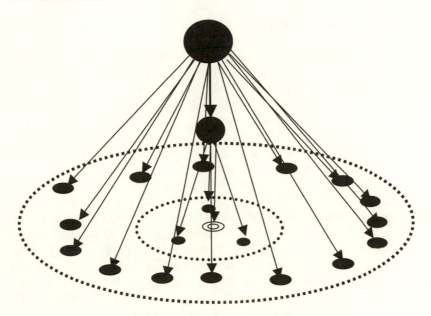

Figure 5.13. Nesting of equivalences

federations such as the Numidae (see Mattingly 1992: 36; Sahlins 1968: 24). In other cases, these classes may not be in continuous existence as corporate groups—they may be called into being to accomplish certain collective goals requiring coordination at a certain level, such as when the tribes of Israel were summoned to redress some collective outrage. Such groups can quickly assemble according to the simple heuristic "given an insult or injury coming from someone with degree of relation k to me, unite with all T_{k-1}-equivalents against him." (Among North and East Africans—it is attributed to a wide number of Bedouin and Sudanese groups—there is a saying: "I against my brother; I and my brother against our cousin; I, my brother and our cousin against the neighbors; All of us against the foreigner [Chatwin 2003: 201; cf. Sahlins 1968: 50f; Barth 1954: 166; Mair 1977: 37]).

In other words, from the perspective of any person—say, the double outlined circle in figure 5.11—the social order looks as arranged in figure 5.13. Inside the inner circle are ego's brothers, all under the same father (the somewhat larger circle above the double outlined one); inside the outer circle are ego's cousins, all under the same grandfather (the very large circle at the top), and so on, with successive circles of decreasing closeness. As Landé (1973: 106) writes, "Like the ripples from a stone dropped into a pool, the strength of kinship ties gradually declines as the genealogical and affective distance of kinsmen from ego." It is this pattern of ripples that is phenomenologically important to the actors. Even should the grandfather be removed, the relative distance of the different persons can be maintained and can be the basis for alliance.

What is of crucial import is the degree of consensus as to distance—because of the transitivity of equivalence, all "cousins" agree that they are all closer to each other than they are to anyone who is not at least a cousin. We might say that subjective representations of unilineal descent are architectonic in that they all speak to the same social structure of action (Fortes 1953: 29). But where descent is bilineal, while things may appear similarly to any one ego, the horizontal relations do not form equivalence classes, and so each person has a unique kin structure. For example, my cousin's cousin is not necessarily my cousin under bilineality: my mother's brother's daughter's mother's brother's daughter is probably not my cousin.[42] Such kinship then isolates each nuclear family, but also embeds it in a complex web of latent ties which may be activated.[43] As a consequence, there is no possibility of extended kin forming a bounded group (without the entry of much more complicated mechanisms involving regularities in marital exchange)—each person has two lineages, and those who share one do not necessarily share another. As Bloch (1961 [1940]: 138) notes, this leads the kin system to be poorly suited to form the backbone of the social structure as a whole—to channel all relations.

Consequently, we are not surprised to find a rough association between patrilineal organization and institutionalized feuding. This is not to say that there are not bilineal societies in which interfamily hostility and feuding are present; clearly there are many. But this is to say that bilineality tends to allow for dampening of the normal oscillations of the vendetta.[44] Unilineal trees, on the other hand, are more often associated with crippling series of violent exchanges, precisely because the tree is such a clear structure for forming alliances.

Such corporate organization recurs where strong states are lacking and descent unilineal. But it is not simply that an existing tree coming from a unilineal descent structure can facilitate alliances. It is also possible for persons to cognitively simplify their alliance relations by interpreting them as kinship relations,

---

[42] Note that since we must assume two sexes in bilineal descent, my mother's daughter is not necessarily myself (as I may be a man).

[43] In some cases, such as the !Kung Khoisan, one family or set of siblings can be the center of a politico-territorial unit, with concentric circles formed by the sibling's spouses, the siblings of these spouses, and spouses of these siblings, etc. (Lee 1972: 351; for the Pacific Northwest and a theoretical statement, see Ives 1998: especially 188ff; Sahlins 1968: 54f). The "ripples" that result from this initial structure then channel the possible corporate actors in ways that are heavily dependent on the precise nature of the founding.

[44] For example, while the Greek Sarakatsani shepherds consider all those as far as their second cousins (under bilineal descent) kin, it is the nuclear family that is a strong corporate group. Thus although the Sarakatsani tend to assume that the interests of families are mutually opposed and should and do lead to violence, such violence is contained by the fact that only one's immediate family have an obligation to take on revenge killings (Campbell 1964: 36, 42, 9, 41, 96, 55).

especially where kinship is already seen as unilineal (see Fortes 1953: 27). For one example, the tribal structure of ancient Israel, rather than a result of patrilineal descent of the "twelve children of Israel" (the man Jacob), was quite possibly a federation of tribes who then invented lineages justifying their mutual obligations. Thus a member of the tribe of Judah had greater responsibilities to come to the aid of a member his own tribe than a member of the tribe of Benjamin, and a greater responsibility to aid a member of the tribe of Benjamin than one descended from Jacob with a different mother, and even less interest in supporting a member of one of the neighboring tribes said to descend from Esau (as opposed to Jacob). Still more distant would be those descended from Ishmael. The Nuer similarly re-create lineages as they adopt new members to best make sense of the current alliances.[45] In a word, the tree structure is quite useful, and we have found that it cannot be derived from the structures that emerge from influence relationships.

In some sense, influence as a relationship is not hierarchical enough to establish equivalence. The choice element makes it impossible to use common influence to rationalize the horizontal social distance of allies, in what we can consider "social cladistics" (cladistics being the branch of evolutionary science that attempts to graph degrees of likeness through tree structures [cf. Zerubavel 2003]). But we cannot choose our fathers. In part because of this lack of choice, the tree structure can also be used to express certain ambiguities in vertical relations. In particular, the kinship tree can explain a relation of support from a higher-ranking person or family or clan to a lower-ranking one. Such relations are often called "patronage" relations, and it is significant that the word *patron* comes from the root "father." The patronage relationship allows unequals to assimilate their relationship to a well-understood familial one, thus justifying restraint from naked exploitation and resentment. Patronage relations can lead to actual adoption or merely the invention of more distant pseudo-familial connections (thus in the mid-twentieth century the Bobo tribesman who relocated to Mali generally became the client of a local protector and assumed the ethnic identity of this patron [Lemarchand 1972: 70]).[46]

---

[45] On the ancient Greeks creating a similar scheme of descent see Bury (1955 [1900]:79).

[46] The tendency of European colonists and well-armed explorers to be called "father" by those they overawed–often taken by the Europeans as a sign of the childlikeness of the natives and the legitimacy of European rule–was generally due to an assimilation of the Native-European relation to existing client-patron ties which were given familial terms (Jennings 1984: 7f, 40f, 161; for an example pertaining to the Algonquian, see Anderson [2000: 15]). These terms were taken quite seriously in that "son," "grandson," "nephew," or "brother" connoted different political relationships (and due to different child-rearing practices, to the Iroquois "father" did not connote the capacity to command), and disagreement as to which kin-term characterized the relationship could cause a serious breakdown in relations between Indian nations or between Indians and settlers. (On the attempt of Chinese rulers to identify feudal and familial terms during the Western Chou period, see Hsu [1965: 3, 7, 52]; on the flexibility of the Thai use of kinship terms to create, define, and express closer relations, see Kemp [1984: 60] and compare McLean [1996]).

The tree structure, then, facilitates collective action where other corporate groups are lacking. In some formal structures, they are deliberately constructed, but they may also emerge spontaneously. In many cases, such structures arise because of patterns of unilineal kinship. But in other cases, this same structure arises for other vertical, antisymmetric relationships. But this is not when the antisymmetric relationships express some sort of *endogenous* inequality—an inequality of choice, as in the popularity tournament or its vertical cousin, the influence triset. Instead, it is when the relationships are being formed against an exogenous backdrop of serious material inequality. Such an environment is an extremely common one, and it is therefore not surprising if such structures are either common or important or both. Indeed, we will find that the resulting social structures are generally the crucial building blocks for the largest political structures that first impressed Spencer and Comte. We go on in the next chapter to examine their emergence.

6

The Short Cut to Structure with Patronage Pyramids

IN THE PREVIOUS CHAPTER, we saw informal relationships of influence form structures that combined horizontal and vertical organization but were different from the "tree" structures common to formal hierarchies. These tree structures have a potential to facilitate collective action in the interests of a single person that influence structures do not. How could such structures arise? In this chapter, we examine relationships of patronage—relationships that are intrinsically antisymmetric and thrive in environments of inequality. We recall that the other structures that we investigated often foundered on problems related to inequality between persons—patronage relationships not only are immune to such problems, but they are likely to arise where other structures have generated inequality. Finally, we will find that such relationships naturally tend toward treelike structures; these spontaneous structures then can serve as the backbone for more deliberate governance structures, as will be explored in chapters 7 and 8.

Pyramids

From Hubs to Apexes

In chapter 5 we encountered "multihub" communication structures, in which the people in question can be divided into two types, hubs and spokes. Any spoke is only connected to a single hub, while hubs are connected both to spokes and to other hubs. Such structures, we found, reasonably arise when people must establish relationships for the purpose of spreading information. I previously treated communication as an intrinsically symmetric relationship. But some kinds of communication are inherently antisymmetric. An example might be religious-philosophical "schools" in the ancient sense: a charismatic teacher or prophet forms the center of a network of disciples. Such a structure is formally quite close to a hub structure, except composed of antisymmetric relationships.

Accordingly, we might recast the simple hub structure (reproduced in figure 6.1, left) in a way that accentuates the difference between the hub and spokes as in the figure on the right, which, following Scott (1972: 95; also see Clark 1973; Mayer 1966), I shall call a "triangle." To emphasize the difference be-

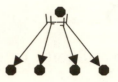

Figure 6.1. Wheel and triangle

tween triangles and wheels, I shall call the hub of a triangle the "apex," and the other members the "base."

The second figure clearly introduces a vertical dimension between the hub and the spokes, while the wheel representation does not, as the triangle spans a directed or vertical space (which is not necessarily true of the wheel).[1] It also uses the arrows that indicate an antisymmetric relationship. Thus while the overall arrangement of nodes and edges—people and their relationships— is the same in both figures, they differ according to the nature of the relationship. The bidirectional communication of acquaintances tends toward the former, and the unidirectional communication of master and disciple toward the latter.

This same type of triangular structure is found for other sorts of relationships, which while not primarily communicative in nature, still bear a familiar resemblance to the charismatic teacher. An important set of examples pertains to equally charismatic war chiefs. Tacitus describes the German barbarians as organized into such hubs led by charismatic warriors (*principes*—big men), who competed with one another to get a following, a personal retinue (a *comitatus*). As Tacitus (*Germany* 7, 12, 14, 11) says, the others listen to the leader "more because he has influence to persuade than because he has power to command. If his sentiments displease them, they reject them with murmurs; if they are satisfied, they brandish their spears."[2] This brings us to one of the characteristic features of these triangles, namely that the attachment of the "base" to the "apex" is conditional, even if fierce. (This is also generally true of leaders in hunter-gathering societies: for examples, see Helm [1972: 77] on the Dogrib; Hanser [1985: 61f] on New Guinea in general.) Members are always free to desert a teacher for a more charismatic one, or to switch to a more promising war leader. As Critchley (1978: 43, 32) says regarding the Germans, "If they did not get what they wanted they moved on."

---

[1] In a word, a hub structure is best seen as composed of symmetric relations if the space is understood as Cartesian, but if it is understood as polar (which would be natural if we were thinking of organization in terms of overall "centrality"), it is basically equivalent to a triangle.

[2] See also the description of a Yanomamö headman (Chagnon 1968b: 108) who cannot order followers, but just starts a task and hopes the others will eventually join in.

As a consequence, while the multitude of followers may tickle the apex's ego, she or he tends to be rather weak structurally. While such apexes appear outstanding, their charisma comes largely from their followers: says Tacitus, "It is the renown and glory of a chief to be distinguished for the number and valour of his followers." To keep the followers, the chief is forced to keep gifting them with feasts, and to do this, he must keep fighting victoriously, which in turn requires that he keep his followers. This holds for charismatic teachers as well as war chiefs: Jesus evidently was insufficiently attentive to the feelings of at least one member of his base leading to problems serious enough to lead to his temporal dethronement. As Zablocki (1980) argued, there is a serious sense in which the "big man" is not a man at all, but a node in a network. The very charisma that makes this person appear extraordinary may better be seen as a property of the pattern of *attributions* of charisma, reversing cause and effect. To understand the apex, then, we need to understand the formation of the triangle.

Formation of Triangles

In the previous chapter, we saw multihub communication networks evolving as all actors followed a single heuristic, namely "connect to the 'hubiest' person you can." While we imagined that there might be heterogeneity in willingness to be a hub, this was not actually necessary to produce a multihub structure. One could imagine such a structure arising among interchangeable persons. But with triangles, the antisymmetric nature of the relationship between the apex and base implies a categorical distinction between the two sorts of persons. Of course, in reality, the existence of this categorical distinction is far from obvious until the formation of the structure. While evidently some charismatic religious leaders know themselves to be apexes-in-training shortly after birth (if not before then), others pass through a less clear-cut developmental process. Many of these begin as base members and are appointed as apexes-to-be by the apex as successors. A few, like certain charismatic war leaders, become apexes by displacing (not always, but sometimes, killing) the former apex.

In many other cases, however, it appears that there is a relatively long process whereby one member distinguishes him- or herself from the others and rises to the position of apex. In the intermediate period, this person has ambiguous relations of near-equality to others, and hence the structure is relatively complex, until the rising member achieves a qualitative distinction and a clear triangle emerges. We only have good information on this process for relatively recent charismatic leaders, though there is good reason to think Jesus started as a spoke of John the Baptist (see Matt. 3:13–17, evidently trying to explain away the subordination of Jesus to John implied by his baptism reported more simply by Mark 1:9). Histories written after some person has attained an apex position tend to be silent on or even deny the existence of any preapex life, but for more recent cases we may witness an ascension process.

For one example, we can consider the case of Charles Dederich, the charismatic leader of the psychological/rehabilitation community Synanon. His ascension stretched out over many years, and during this time, it was largely relationships other than leader-follower that held the group together (such as informal friendships). Thus he could avoid relying on weak or incomplete charismatic leadership until his position was crystallized; at this point other relationships were abandoned and the triangular form solidified.[3] For another example, Mel Lyman, a now largely forgotten self-proclaimed avatar and God, began as an occasional harmonica player for Jim Kweskin's famous jug-band, and only became God after reducing Kweskin from hub to spoke (For Synanon, see Yablonsky 1965; Endore 1968; Ofshe et al. 1974; Mitchell, Mitchell, and Ofshe 1980; and Gerstel 1982; on Lyman see Felton 1972.)

Because in such cases the "group" is dominated by the structural imperative of the triangle, it is extremely fragile in response to the removal of the apex. More, we might say that society abhors a vacuum at the apex, and hence former spokes may suddenly find themselves becoming an apex when there is an unanticipated removal of the former apex. As may have been the case for early Christianity, the structure is reconstituted around new apexes who are sucked into the hole (in such cases, frequently rival apexes such as Peter and Paul).[4]

In these cases, the qualities of a particular person (real or imagined) lead him or her to become differentiated from other persons and so to establish a relation of inequality with others. In other cases, a preexisting material inequality is responsible. One historically important class of examples pertains to "households" in the patriarchal sense of a man's dependents, which would include not only children and grandchildren, often brothers and sisters and assorted in-laws, but also servants and anyone else who attaches him- or herself to the household. Indeed, as we shall see, this form often seems to be the template by which other homologous structures are given a cultural interpretation.

Hubs versus Triangles

Previously I emphasized the structural homology between a wheel and a triangle. While the quality of the relationship in question can distinguish them, their structural difference only becomes apparent when multiple structures are

---

[3] Interestingly, I found after writing this that Dederich described Synanon as a wheel with spokes and hub (Janzen 2001: 32).

[4] And probably the only reason people are so familiar with Christianity today is that Paul moved along frequently traveled channels between urban regions, setting up spatially distinct triangles in different city, along the lines recently discussed in formal terms by Hedström et al (2000). For Paul's work, see Meeks (1983).

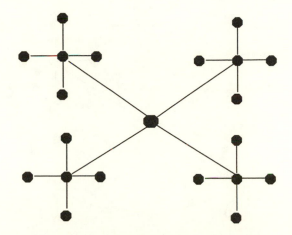

Figure 6.2. Wheels connected by hub's hub

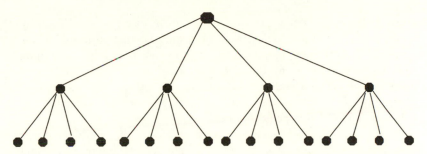

Figure 6.3. Figure 6.2 recast as tree structure

concatenated. Consider the unification of four wheels via the introduction of a "hub's hub"—a second-order hub that connects local hubs, as in figure 6.2. This structure, if properly pulled and stretched, reveals itself to be identical to the "tree" form that we saw characteristic of unilineal descent structures. (Imagine grabbing the central node, pulling upward, and viewing the structure from the side.) The structurally identical tree of the same relations is drawn in figure 6.3.

This sort of structure, which we can call a "pyramid" (defined below), involves only vertical ties between persons who may be seen as "higher" or "lower." In stark contrast is a structure that results from the concatenation of wheels via the establishment of *horizontal* ties between hubs, as in the following example from the previous chapter (see figure 6.4). Here, while there is some differentiation between hubs (two are connected to three other hubs, while the other two are connected only to two other hubs), there is not the same qualitatively different position of a "hub's hub."

The pyramid is, I propose, what true triangles are likely to form when aggregated. Accordingly, just as a molecular chemist can determine structure by

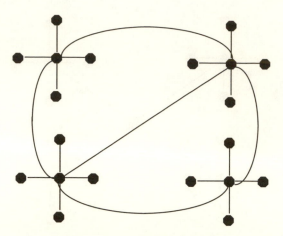

Figure 6.4. Multihub structure

growing crystals, we understand social structure by examining the larger structures that they tend to form. Now it is not the case that all triangles *can* be
aggregated: charismatic prophets, for example, are notoriously unwilling to
work together in any form. But if they do join forces, they will do so either
by subordination to a common superprophet, or by one acknowledging the
superiority of the other—they will not work together as equals (Benjamin
Zablocki, personal communication).

We have thus defined triangles as structural forms that are homologous to
wheels but involve antisymmetric relations and that concatenate as pyramids
(and not as multihub structures). But in previous chapters we have tried to
generate structure by looking at the nature of certain relationships. Let us return, then, to the relationships we have investigated in chapters 4 and 5. We
introduced horizontality into vertical relationships by allowing for some persons to decline to establish a relation with others. The resulting structures,
although combining horizontal and vertical differentiation, differed from trees
in that persons could have ties to more than one superior. This seemed to fit
the class of relationships understood as "influence," in which the underlying
inequality might be seen as inherently sociometric—even if people really *are*
rankable in terms of expertise, say, what is crucial for the emerging structure
is only the degree to which there is a an architectonic distribution of social
beliefs of authoritativeness.

To anticipate: when it comes to exogenous material inequality, however,
relationships may arise specifically to mitigate the inequality. The materially
advantaged can clearly offer the subaltern material support; the subaltern, however, can only offer their loyalty. Hence such relationships—generally called
"patron-client" relationships—tend to concatenate in structures that add an
additional heuristic to that of the triset (which was "do not accept influence

from someone lower than yourself"). This heuristic is, "do not accept a client who already has a patron." As in previous chapters, we now begin with the nature of this relationship and draw out its implicit structural potential.

Patronage Relationships

Conditions Conducive to Triangle Formation

This understanding of patronage is more or less the anthropologists' use of the word, as opposed to the political scientists' use (to follow the distinction of Weingrod 1968).[5] A patronage relation links a patron at the apex and a set of clients as the base of a triangle. The patron protects or advances the interests of the clients, and the clients rally to the support of the patron when he is challenged. These relationships, as political scientists and anthropologists have noted, tend to arise in settings in which either there is a strong anarchic component to social life, or where preexisting inequalities are severe and must be moderated for the purposes of interaction (Eisenstadt and Roniger 1980: 60; Bloch 1961 [1940]: 160).[6]

Taking the former point first, it has been noted that widespread patronage never coexists with strong states (Wolf 1977: 174; Weingrod 1968; Scott and Kerkvliet 1977: 443; Critchley 1978: 119).[7] Or perhaps it is more accurate to say that they exist only where strong states do not *reach*, which includes the contained anarchies of the interstitial realms of interaction within societies with strong states, such as illegal activities (for an example see, e.g., Cornelius 1977: 348). Further, as Bloch (1961 [1940]: 142, 148, 225, 443) suggests, patronage structures are more likely where kin groups are unable to fully protect people against violence, perhaps because of the decreased ability of bilineal structures to organize vendettas, as discussed in the last chapter. In violent

---

[5] Political scientists generally use the term to indicate the ways in which government officials may reward supporters. This does not always involve an abiding social relationship, which is what the anthropologists investigate.

[6] A further complication is that such relations also are favored where there is a shortage of currency; unable to rely on wages to exchange for services, employers or lords must either grant benefices or take underlings into their households (Bloch 1961 [1940]: 68, 163). (Such a shortage of money at the end of the Roman empire played a role in moving the patronage system to be fused with the system of dependency in access to land [Beeler 1971: 4, 11].) Since expansion of a monetary supply usually requires stable government due to the rareness of silver and gold and the ease of adulteration, anarchy also contributes to a disreliance on money, though this shortage may arise for other reasons.

[7] It may be to a nontrivial extent that both a reliance on the personalism of relationships and the small size of polities stem from nonexistence or scarcity of means of administration, most important literacy and other forms of communication (especially paper; van Creveld [1991: 38] points to the simultaneous arrival of paper and gunpowder from the east, both facilitating the expansion of Western governance structures).

circumstances, the alternative to organized vendettas may be anarchy. Such anarchy, as Landé (1977a: xxx) points out, leads to the weak being heavily dependent on the mighty for life and limb, but also leads the mighty to need to command followers in order to stand up to *other* mighties.

In sum, anarchy leads to a need for protection among the less powerful. For example, European feudalism was (as we shall see in more detail) largely a set of patronage relations, and one of the factors supporting the feudal system in the absence of a strong Frankish state was the anarchy resulting from feuds over land (in turn due in part to an absence of primogeniture among the landed).[8] Similarly, patronage systems were common in traditional east Africa where refugees would be provided for by patrons who would not technically adopt them but still refer to them as children (and be called "father" in return) (see Mair 1961: 316; Mair 1977: 95 for the case of the Gusii; and cf. Mair 1977: 97f, 141f). Where patronage becomes a normal part of coping with endemic anarchy (as in Europe after the fall of Rome), the very development of the patronage structure increases the need for the powerless to seek security, and the powerful to increase their number of clients (Ganshof 1964: 3, 23).[9] Conversely, when states are able to pacify their interiors, we see patronage relationships either weaken or reform into relationships of sponsorship that now focus on control of state bureaucratic careers (cf. Kettering 1986: 213f for seventeenth-century France).

Thus we see that the anarchy that promotes patronage systems is rooted in a more fundamental dynamic, namely a differentiation of persons in terms of power, and a symbiotic need for the more powerful and the less powerful to enter into relatively stable relationships (even if that "need" on the part of the less powerful is induced by threats on the part of the more powerful). Consequently, the precise form of the inequality in question may be crucial for the structural tendency. I begin by examining simple "two-class" systems, and then more continuous inequalities that may or may not be copresent with bifurcations.

Two-Class Systems

In many patronage systems, persons are divided up into two classes, potential patrons and potential clients, on the basis of some preexisting categorical distinction. Relations then may or may not be established that personalize and/or

---

[8] Indeed, even in the late Roman empire, the constant disruption led the rich to fortify their estates and made them look quite a bit like the noble lords that were to come (Anderson 1974: 94; Contamine 1998 [1980]: 16); it is at this time that the word *patron* becomes standardized for such protectors (Beeler 1971: 2).

[9] The negative character of early vassalage (Ganshof 1964: 84)–a promise not to injure the lord–is a good indicator of the relation between the institution and the anarchy of the time. It must be admitted, however, that such anarchic conditions and a resulting need for protection do not seem fundamental to Indian feudalism (see Sharma 1965: 33).

mitigate the inequality associated with this bifurcation. Most obviously, if land ownership is the basis of the division, there may be a clear tendency toward a neat bifurcation: either one owns land or one does not (see Mintz and Wolf 1950; we deal with complications later).

In certain cases, this division is established by colonization: for example, in Peru (as in many other parts of Latin America), the native Quechuan population was divided up (frequently along preexisting lines of community) and "given" to an individual Spaniard, who then became their lord (Guasti 1977: 424; Critchley 1978: 134f). Similarly, Turnbull (1962: 151–54, 203f) describes how Bantu families "owned" the local pygmies (Mbuti). It is worth reemphasizing that the essential point is not the division into two classes, but the establishment of "many-to-one" interpersonal relations between them.

In a few other cases, a similar bifurcation can arise on other bases, such as the division of a number of East African kingdoms into (presumed "original") ruling and (presumed immigrant) subject classes (Mair 1977: 114, 141), or the division of Rome into plebeians and patricians. The Roman "patron" was paradigmatically a man who had freed a slave but retained rights and obligations with respect to him (Kenny 1960: 14): seeing Rome as divided into patricians and losers, the Romans concluded it was the duty of the former to fatherly guide the latter (Critchley 1978: 101). According to the (historically doubtful) account of Dionysius of Halicarnassus, the Roman system of patronage stems from a decree of Romulus, who allowed "every plebian to choose for his patron any patrician whom he himself wished" (Wallace-Hadrill 1989: 66; Taylor 1968: 41; Drummond 1989: 91f). This case nicely encapsulates the voluntary nature of the patronage relation: the choice of patron is in most cases formally voluntary (though the relationship is also often hereditary), but cannot (at least in a two-class system) be understood without recognizing that there is at least a healthy dollop of compulsion mixed in.[10] Thus in the two-class system of Rwanda, every Hutu "chose" to be the client of some Tutsi; those who did not were defenseless against the predation of other Tutsis. But "even if it is true that no Hutu could afford to be without a lord, he could still choose between different lords" (Mair 1961: 315; 1977: 143, 154).

Systems based on land are easily made near universal (as in the famous edict of Charles the Bald of 847: "We also wish that every free man in our kingdom may choose as his lord whomsoever he will" [Ganshof 1964: 30]). Since everyone needs somewhere to stand, declaring that one must be a client of he who holds this land is a rather good way to extend the structure of patronage relationships to encompass more persons and their various interactions. Indeed, this principle of "nulle terre sans seigneur" (no lordless land) was taken in France (though not Germany) by the thirteenth century to imply that there could be no privately held ("allodial") property whatsoever (Ganshof

---

[10] The *Domesday Book* further suggests that at that time in England it was acknowledged that clients always had the right "to betake themselves to another lord" (Bloch 1961 [1940]: 185).

1964: 130, 155; Beeler 1971: 151, 214, 217; though Anderson 1974: 148 points out the limits to enforcing this principle). Various changes in economic conditions or taxation policies can force small freeholders into seeking protective alliance of greater lords, in something akin to the proletarianization of the petit bourgeois (this seems to have occurred in France at the turn of the millennium [Fourquin 1976: 51]).

While a basis in ownership of land can lead a patronage system to be quite simple and inclusive, this depends on the specifics of property relations. Multiple rights in land, as seen in feudal Europe, or practices akin to subletting, can lead a property-based structure to be rather complex.[11] In such cases, we are more likely to see continuous patronage structures, to which we turn next.

Continuous and Complex Structures

We have seen patronage structures arising when there are two discrete classes. But it is also possible for patronage relations to arise where there are more than two classes. For example, we are likely to see "sponsorship" forms of patronage where there are stratified systems of ranking such as those associated with institutions such as the military or the priesthood that are highly encompassing of their members' lives and organize these lives into careers that may progress upward in organizational terms. But here there is a preexisting interaction structure that makes this a less central case for the current investigation, though I return to such cases briefly below. Other than such formal structures, then, it seems that the major alternative to the "two-class" basis for patronage relations is when the inequality arises on the basis of some continuous ranking of persons in terms of some resource we will denote as ζ. Then, given any two persons, A and B, if we use the notation from the last chapter, we can say that if a relationship arises between A and B such that A is the patron and B the client, we know that $\zeta_A > \zeta_B$. (Fourquin 1976: 124 has an informal version of this derivation for the case of feudalism, where ζ is termed "power.")

Most frequently, patronage relationships grounded in such continuous inequality exist within a stratum that is, if not elite, at least not totally subjugated—for example, European feudalism (see, e.g., Bloch 1961 [1940]:444).[12]

[11] In Italy, the Roman emphasis on a distinction between alienation rights and use rights limited the flexibility with which such multiple ownership could be systematized. In Germany, where the issue was the enjoyment of a property, multiple "enjoyment" was quite easy to comprehend, and, says Critchley (1978: 19f), "in England, the common lawyers lived in a world of their own." For the tie between grants of land and pseudo-kinship relations among Palauans, see Smith (1983: 40).

[12] As will be discussed in more detail below, there is some vagueness in what the word *feudalism* denotes; a narrow definition sees it as the prevailing structure of interelite relationships in Western Europe in the 10th to 12th centuries, especially in the center of the Carolingian area (Ganshof 1964: xv, xvii; Bloch 1961 [1940]: 448), perhaps calling the earlier system "vassalage" (e.g., Fourquin 1976: 45, 66), while a wider one sees it encompassing practically all European governmental systems between the fall of the western Roman empire and the Protestant reforma-

While serfs might not necessarily have patron-client relationships with their lords, such relations did at times exist; more important, the lords were then arranged in patronage pyramids as in the simplified diagram of figure 6.5 (note the imperfections of the elite structure and the incomplete absorption of the nonelites into the structure).[13] Thai feudalism was basically similar, in the

---

tion (also compare the discussion and typology of Andreski 1968: 143). Here it will be used to describe the connection between (on the one hand) granting of benefices, which involved rights of land utilization and dispensation of justice, and (on the other) vows of fealty, which involved obligations of military or financial support. The mere presence of powerful magnates with armed retainers who usurp governance functions does not deserve the term if there is no linkage of vassalage and benefice (e.g., early Byzantium and Byzantine Egypt, Merovingian Europe; see Bachrach 1967; Andreski 1968: 56; also see Anderson 1974: 98).

On the other hand, even in European feudalism, an important component was often the presence of such retainers (the lord's "men"). Indeed, for the case of 14th-century England (after the devolution of the strict form arising from the Norman conquest), Bean (1989; cf. Bloch 1961 [1940]: 167–71, 236) has argued that while the relations between the king and his vassals fits this classic model, the most important relationships between most lords and their own underlings was an extension of the household relationship. That is, the lord attempted to treat more and more persons as if they were his personal staff and owed him the same obedience as a dependent who resided wholly within his house. This is different from the construction of a feudal pyramid on the basis of agreements of fealty. Bean argues that such householdlike relations both predated and postdated feudal relations properly understood. For one, an important part of compensation packages was often special wages for the time the retainer appeared in the lord's household, implying that such presence was a regular part of being a client. This emphasis on the household does not seem to be as important in the 15th century, but in the 16th century we see not only an explosion of livery but arrangements whereby retainers were provided with fees and sponsorship in the court and in suits instead of benefices (Bellamy 1989: 79f, 82f, 91ff, 96).

Accordingly, feudalism was often "purest" in relatively earlier periods where it was less widespread, though early vassalage often was not closely tied to transfer of rights in land (e.g., the well studied case of Burgundy). Certainly "feudalism" here has nothing to do with the mode of production associated with the Middle Ages, namely serfdom (see Fourquin 1976: 13, 43, 46); though the two are often confused they are to a fair degree historically separable (while true feudalism does not coexist with free labor, there are many forms of serfdom that do not involve patronage pyramids within the elite). There are, of course, wide geographical differences: in England feudalism came from the invasion of 1066 in a top-down fashion, in Germany there was less feudal consolidation and the land aspect was emphasized over the bond of vassalage, while in the Carolingian areas (especially in Northern to Eastern France [Fourquin 1976: 71, 73f, 76]) feudalism was a result of the disintegration of a hasty empire built on Roman administrative ruins. In general, Bloch (1961 [1940]: 188) suggests that places where feudalism was imported exhibited a higher degree of structural simplicity and regularity than where it spontaneously developed.

[13] Some might distinguish patron-vassal relations from patron-client relations, reserving the former for cases in which the subordinate party is still a member of an elite, and the latter for when the subordinate party is not, but I do not think this is a structurally crucial distinction. Indeed, medieval treatises on law used the word *client* to refer to vassals (especially subvassals); Tacitus describes a warrior retinue as clients (Critchley 1978: 102f), and Asian and Indian high kings referred to kings who had submitted to them as "slaves" (and in medieval India, such subkings might have to fan the emperor as a humiliating service [Sharma 1965: 26; Hanson 2001: 34]). The issue was not the terminology but the obvious status of the participants–"homage" was at times used to describe both the relation between lords and serfs and higher lords and noble vassals

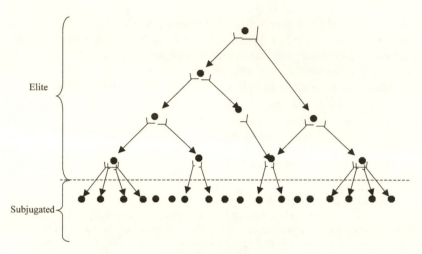

Figure 6.5. Patronage pyramid

bottom level of the pyramid being the subjugated, with less categorical distinctions between higher-level patrons. A third example is Rome in the imperial age—the relationship between patrons and *liberti* (the freed slaves who took their ex-masters as patrons) was different than that between the patrons and their other clients. The former relationship was fixed by law, the latter only by interest and custom. While there was only one level of *liberti*, the patron of one client might himself be the client of another (Wallace-Hadrill 1989: 76f; Drummond 1989: 100f).

When both discrete and continuous inequalities serve as the basis for patronage relationships, there is a fundamental division in the population, usually based on ownership of land or membership in a governing elite. Every member of the nonelite may be assigned to the domain of one elite. Within the elite, there is a more or less continuous gradation (although many persons are roughly "equivalent"), and elites lower down appeal to those higher up for sponsorship and promise service and support in return. (This is a common Mediterranean pattern we shall examine below.)[14] Thus it is possible for a patron to be the client of a second-order patron; following Scott, we will call the highest-order patron, her clients, and her clients' clients a "pyramid."[15] For

---

(Bloch 1961 [1940]: 161, 261; though see Duby 1991: 73), though no one would confuse the relationships (for one thing, only the latter had to be renewed each generation).

[14] It is possible that there were patron-client relationships within the subjugated stratum, but if so, these have gone undocumented, and probably quickly shaded off into forms of criminality.

[15] There are also cases of other pyramids in which the top layers are not necessarily "noble," such as the magnates' courts of 17th-century Poland as discussed by Pośpiech and Tygielski (1981: 77), consisting of the magnate (a major lord) as the apex of a pyramid of personally connected clerks organized hierarchically (from chamberlain, secretary, equerry, treasurer) on top of serving men on top of valets and liverymen.

example, in addition to the fundamental division between Hutu clients and Tutsi patrons, poorer Tutsi could also be clients of richer Tutsi, leading to a pyramid that connected all adult men and ended with the king as the patron of the greatest patrons (Mair 1961: 322; Mair 1977: 143f). Similar relationships develop between heads of state when one is conquered by the other but left in power as a client (for examples from the Indian subcontinent, see Gunawardana 1992; for the Aztec case see Hassig 1988: 19, 26, 125, 177, 256f).

In sum, patronage structures arise from preexisting inequality, when there is a conscious attempt to ameliorate this inequality by the introduction of diffuse personal relationships (Eisenstadt and Roniger 1980: 49f; Kettering 1986: 38; Bourne 1986: 57, 190). Given our investigations in the previous chapter, we might expect structures of such relationships to form trisets similar to those we uncovered for influence relations. But instead, patronage relations tend to form *trees*. Why is this?

We will soon explore the structural imperatives that lead to the production of trees, but we can begin by pointing to their cultural correlative, namely a subjective understanding of the relationship as akin to parent-child relations. Thus it is natural for the patronage structure to be assimilated to the unilineal trees seen in the last chapter. How can one be inferior to someone yet have a positive relationship? One answer is, "if the inequality is similar to that between a father (as it turns out) and a child." The word *patron* comes from father, the words *vassal* and *thegn* from young boy or servant (the former from the Celtic) (Ganshof 1964: 5; Critchley 1978: 104; Bloch 1961 [1940]: 155f, 182); both *signeur* and *Herr* come from the "seniority" of the patron (Fourquin 1976: 115; Bloch 1961 [1940]: 145). In Japan since the Tokugawa period patron-client relations (ubiquitous in many fields) are called *oyabun-kobun* relationships: parent-status / son-status (Critchley 1978: 105).

The connection between patronage structures and patrilineal descent trees is more than a vague affinity: patronage structures differ dramatically according to whether or not an actual patrilineal familial structure underlies social relations—where it does, patronage structures are simply absorbed into lineages.[16] It is generally only where patrilineal divisions are not major structural principles for social action (other than inheritance) that classic patronage structures exist (cf. Anderson 1974: 232). Perhaps for this reason, patronage structures are frequently found in bilineal cultures (notably those around the northern shore of the Mediterranean). Indeed, the classic patronage relationship is often that of the "godfather" relation in which a nonkin of generally

---

[16] In some cases, such kin relations cannot be the framework for a patronage structure because changes (usually associated with colonization and consequent modernization) have disempowered the elders. An example here is found in the "clans" of postcolonial Senegal that are really the political entourages of a single patron and have no real kin basis but fill the power vacuum left by the weakening of previous intercaste patronage relationships (see Foltz 1977: 245).

higher social standing becomes, at christening, a special protector and sponsor of a child, a role that in a patrilineal society might be reserved for an agnate (e.g., Campbell 1964: 222f; compare Duby 1991: 63).

In sum, patronage structures arise as independent social structures to deal with inequality when there is not a preexisting patrilineal structure that is linked to the inequality. Because the amelioration of inequality is so crucial for understanding the structural nature of the relationship, we go on to examine this aspect in some detail.

The Nature of the Relationship

Amelioration

Given preexisting inequality, patronage systems are understood to reduce the potential arbitrariness of the domination of the superior party by establishing affective quasi-familial ties that imply limits to exploitation (see, e.g, Guasti 1977: 424; Powell 1970: 412). While the inequality may be quite formal (e.g., the case of bifurcations) and/or specific (e.g., the case of landlordism), the relationship of patronage may be quite informal, generalized, or diffuse (Landé 1977a: xxi). What is essential is that the relation of patronage implies a paternalistic bond whereby the patron deigns to take the interests of the client to heart. This bond may merely "soften the terms of an unequal exchange" (Graziano 1977: 363 for the case of Sicily; also see Campbell 1964: 261, cf. 218) and hence refer only to the interaction between the patron and client, or it may involve actions that the patron takes with others on behalf of the client (the client thus being the indirect, not the direct, object of the patron's actions). Just as the mitigation of the unequal exchange may still be seen as in the ultimate interests of the patron, so such sponsorship can also be seen as a self-interested act whereby a patron pits his client against some other patron's client so that the former's success redounds to his own glory.

Since the existence of paternalistic protection is often one of the legitimating arguments claimed by those persons eager to support existing systems of inequality, there has been a tendency for social scientists to discount its very existence, thereby simplifying their implicit or explicit critique of such inequality. But this is a dangerous game of ignoring precisely that aspect of inequality that is its greatest strength, namely its (conditional) weakness. Whether these limitations are enforced or only voluntary, they affect the structural tendencies associated with relationships between unequals. The existence of the bond in no way contradicts the vast inequality between parties; on the contrary, it presupposes it. Similarly, there is nothing particularly warm and wonderful about the fact that the relationship is indeed personalistic—this very quality can be the ground of new forms of power over clients as patrons become free to interfere in their clients' personal affairs (see, e.g., Pośpiech and

Tygielski 1981: 95). Similarly, the pervasive nature of the inequality between patrons and clients should not lead to skepticism about the protection offered by the patron; it is for this very reason that this protection is necessary.

Voluntary and Spontaneous

The first feature of the patron-client relationship, then, is that it exists to ameliorate preexisting inequality. Accordingly, the discussion here will not touch hub systems that *generate* inequality (if there be any); whether these can aggregate into the pyramidal structures that prove characteristic of patronage relations is a separate question that will be dealt with later. The second feature of these relationships is that they are voluntary, by which I mean that at least one of the parties (and not necessarily both) has the option of refusing the relationship. In the Thai case, clients were free to choose other patrons and patrons to reject clients (Englehart 2001: 22). Now given a case in which one portion of a population is expropriated and left at the mercy of the other, we might be hesitant to describe as "voluntary" any relationship in which the former attached themselves to the latter for protection from the most outrageous abuses.

But it may make a great deal of difference for the resulting structure whether or not all members of the expropriated class are linked to a patron, and if so, whether they have any choice in which particular member of the expropriating class is their patron. If the answers to these questions are "yes" and "no" respectively, and hence a specific relationship is imposed on each client, the resulting structures may be quite different from other cases in which a personalistic relationship ameliorates inequality. Thus the case of colonial conquest and privatized government over groups of conquered natives as in Spanish South America that was mentioned above may not constitute a true patron-client system. On the other hand, patronage relations in similar areas between outright slaves and their owners (as in Brazil as described by Hall 1974; also see Downing 1992: 39), may have been good examples of patron-client systems, for the simple reason that not all slaves had relations of clientage with their owners. Thus the "voluntary" nature of the relationship—in that the owner did not necessarily take all slaves as clients—is likely to be related to other aspects of the relationship, both in terms of its content (what actions were involved) and its structural potential. In particular, relationships in which the clients lack any choice as to patron are likely to be relatively flat, as the patrons need less from second-order patrons in order to maintain their clientele.

This spontaneous or voluntary nature of patronage relationships probably has a great deal to do with their durability once constructed: the severing of one relationship may not change the structure, since it is quickly replaced with a similar one. Indeed, it is the very durability of patronage relationships that has led to their neglect by American social scientists: as the heirs of upper-middle-class reformers dedicated to quash any arisings of such "irrational" relationships in urban machine politics (see, e.g., Hofstadter 1955), for quite some time social scientists evidently thought that the best thing that could be done with patronage relationships was to ignore them and hope (indeed theorize) that they would go away. This meant ignoring a type of relationship that (at least until extremely recently) was of fundamental importance perhaps in most of the world's societies, including most European democracies, especially those with large agrarian populations.[17]

One justification for such marginalization was that in the developed world an emphasis on patronage across fields or domains of action seemed related to the particular religious orientations of certain Mediterranean societies, and hence was a cultural aberration as opposed to an inherent aspect of social structure. Certainly in many Mediterranean cultures there is an understanding of religion as patronage, where saints (or minor gods) are treated as simply the higher-level patrons (Whyte 1981; Foster 1977 [1961]: 16; Weingrod 1968: 390; cf. Eisenstadt and Roniger 1980: 68, who add some unfounded assertions), with God perhaps as the ultimate patron, the only one who needs no favors from anyone (Kenny 1960: 15, 22f on Spain).[18] Many other theologies also begin with the assumption that people are basically powerless and must petition some divine spirit for favors. But what leads to a patronage structure in the divine realm is two additional features. The first is that the divine insists on service and loyalty in exchange for favors. The second is that there is no clear break between relations between saints or gods and relations between persons.[19]

It thus not an absurd thought that certain religious traditions are in part responsible for the ubiquity of patronage relations across southern Europe (Hall 1974). But while there may be a cultural predisposition for patronage structures to arise in certain areas, they are too widespread to be understood as simply a specific Catholic, Orthodox, or Mediterranean cultural feature. Instead, this cultural predisposition may be better explained by structural arrangements discussed above: inequality in the absence of either strong states

[17] Indeed, residues of feudal property rights (though not obligations for military service) persisted into the 19th century in Sicily and the German states, and into the 20th in Scotland (Graziano 1977: 362; Critchley 1978: 22f), and even after abolition, fundamentally feudal patterns of interaction–tied to the fundamental fact of land ownership–frequently remained for generations afterward (see, e.g., Bell 1994).

[18] And since, as we shall see, these patronage structures are the core of factions, it is possible for patron saints to be the "leaders" of factions, as in the case of the Maltese studied by Boissevain (1964).

[19] A counterexample might be ancient Greece, where it was also assumed that the gods were the masters of men, and that men were dependent on gods as a client on a patron, and that this dependence could never be fully paid off. Yet the "free" Greek citizen was not similarly beholden to some mortal (Vernant 1995: 7f), and thus an integrated structure did not develop in the same way as in later Catholic countries.

or relevant patrilineal structures. But assuming that we understand where patronage relationships arise, we do not yet understand how they work. To answer this, we must examine the content of the relationship.

Reciprocation of Duties

The essence of the patronage relationship can be parsimoniously summarized as one that "imposes reciprocal obligations of a different kind on each of the parties" (Silverman 1965: 176; Eisenstadt and Roniger 1980: 49f; Bloch 1961 [1940]: 451; Bourne 1986: 5). Given the mutual contributions, it is tempting for theorists to understand the relationship as one of exchange; exchange, moreover, that (like all exchanges) is assumed to be equal by definition.[20]

This, however, is a serious misunderstanding. First of all, there is no reason to believe that the "exchange" (assuming it is useful to consider there to be one) is equal (see chapter 3). Indeed, as Landé (1977a: xxvii) has pointed out, frequently the premise of the exchange is that it is vastly unequal, with the client being unable to ever repay the great debt he owes the patron (see Powell 1970: 413; Wolf 1977: 174; Duby 1991: 38f; Campbell 1964: 230; Guasti 1977: 423; Englehart 2001: 22; Kettering 1986: 27; Mair 1977: 143; Scott and Kerkvliet 1977: 445 for other limitations to the idea of equal exchange). The client is generally dependent on the patron, and not vice versa (Barth 1977 [1965]: 218; see Fourquin 1976: 49 for the case of feudal relations between lords and lesser vassals). Further, in most cases the client is easily replaceable, so that even if the clients' contributions in aggregate are substantial, no one client does much for the patron.

The precise nature of the obligations depends on the substantive context (see Lemarchand 1972: 73), but certain generalizations are easily made, such as that the patron's main obligation is in the form of intercession or mitigation, and the client's main obligation is a display of loyalty. In many cases, the services of the client are almost purely symbolic, such as holding the stirrup of the lord as he mounts his horse (Ganshof 1964: 82; Fourquin 1976: 121).[21]

---

[20] Funnily enough, even though clearly mutual relations such as spending time together obviously satisfy the frequent demand that exchanges be equal, theorists have not attempted to analyze *these* relations in terms of exchange, probably because of the very incorrect assumption that there is no reason to exchange one thing for an identical one, or perhaps to avoid the paradox that this generates (for how could two unequal people exchange the same amount of time with one another?). Instead, they have attempted to analyze obviously unequal relations as involving equal exchange.

[21] Holding a stirrup does make it easier to get on a horse, especially if one has on armor, and it can be embarrassing to be unable to mount elegantly. That this aid was symbolic of the servile and supportive nature of the vassal, however, is indicated by the fact that this role is found outside of the case of armored knights: see the example of a Mexican "big man" whose apprentice had this job in Friedrich (1977: 269).

Both the client and the patron are, paradigmatically, giving a form of *support* to the other. The patron usually gives material support or uses influence, while the client gives what little he or she can. In settled democracies or oligarchies, this may mean electoral support. (As Cicero said, "Men of slender means have only one way of earning favors from our order or of paying us back and that is by helping us and following us about in our campaigns for office" [Taylor 1968: 42; cf. Wallace-Hadrill 1989: 65].)

When conditions are more anarchic, and violence as opposed to votes determines elite dominance, the chief obligation of the patron is to protect the vassal, and the chief obligation of the client is to support the patron through armed service when fighting breaks out (Fourquin 1976: 125, 107, 122). During the classical age of feudalism, military service was undoubtedly the most important thing brought by the vassal to the relationship, though "counsel" was also often included (Ganshof 1964: 87; Farris 1995: 118, 282f, 297; and Critchley 1978: 35 for the case of Japan; Mair 1977: 141, 143 for the Ankole and Hutu-Tutsi systems; Sharma 1965: 99f, 199, 264, 271 for medieval India; Ikegami 1995: 81 for Japan). Such military service has been a fundamental structure linked to grants of land-use across the globe and throughout history (for examples, see Mair 1977: 98 on East Africa; Guasti 1977: 425 on colonial Peru; and Pośpiech and Tygielski 1981: 83 on early modern Poland).[22] The most complete and structurally elegant form of military-based European feudalism came in the Norman conquest, which both imported a complete feudal system and highlighted military service at the same time. Those who conquered England were basically volunteers doing it "on speculation" and their pay could only be the lands they had helped conquer; these in turn would only be granted if the military relationship was solidified. Unlike the previous thegns who had other duties tied to their possession of land pertaining to community service (especially bridge and wall repair), the new lords cared little for their conquered underlings and hence emphasized military service (Bloch 1961 [1940]: 270, 383; Powicke 1996 [1962]: 17f, 26).

In most cases, even where military service is the paradigmatic form of client obligation, other services (in feudal England, known as "sergeanty" service, a distinction we shall explore in the next chapter) could also be exchanged for a benefice of land. Such service was usually minor or degrading or both: in return for the manor of Hemingstone, the tenant was required to "leap, whistle and fart for the king's amusement" every Christmas day (Prestwich 1996: 67).[23]

Despite this emphasis on reciprocity (cf. Powell 1970: 412), there is no advantage gained by conceiving of the relationship as one of exchange, for the

---

[22] Indeed, this link was so strong that in a number of cases it led to ladies taking up arms: if they held the land, it was natural that they should fight (Contamine 1998 [1980]: 241).

[23] As discussed in chapter 7, administrative service was often part of the obligations of a vassal in medieval India (Sharma 1965: 100).

patronage relationship differs from an exchange relationship in two ways. First, the obligations of each party, while frequently negotiable in degree, are generally fixed in kind and the subject of relatively broad consensus (see, e.g. Critchley 1978: 103f for feudalism). Second, in contrast to other exchanges, the responsibilities are diffuse and protracted (Scott and Kerkvliet 1977: 443; Weissman 1987), and often involve face-to-face interaction.

In a nutshell, just as we do not say that a pie is an exchange of crust for filling, in relation of patronage, the patron does not "trade" protection for subservience; that is what patronage *is*. While an exchange can be decomposed into two transfers that are in principle separable (and hence forms of generalized exchange may arise), in patronage the two are uniquely fused. In the absence of one half, one either has aggression or toadying, and these are readily recognized as such. When the two action profiles become separable, in that either has a stable existence without the other, then indeed one may find some offering to trade toadying for diminished aggression, but this is seen in different terms from true patronage relationships—in particular, third parties are less likely to imagine that either party is particularly loyal to the other.[24]

Finally, if the patronage relationship was simply an equal exchange we would expect sets of relationships to take on structures we have seen arising for mutual ties (chapter 2) or reciprocated donations (chapter 3). But there are important structural implications to the difference between patronage relationships and exchange: most important, it is possible for a "rational" patron to commit to relationships in which the clients gain more from the interaction than he does. Indeed, there are good reasons why a patron would want to initiate or cement such a relationship that leads to a net loss. The accumulation of clients may be necessary for prestige (see, e.g., Kettering 1986: 28), or it may be a wise investment in the case of future situations in which favors will be needed, or it may be necessary to be a patron in order to take some other form of action which is restricted to patrons (e.g., a matrimonial alliance); finally, there is no need to deny in principle the possibility of altruism (for the example of Rome, see Taylor 1968: 42f).

Because the avenue of transfer from the clients (as a group) to the patrons (as a group) is not wholly contained within the patronage relationship itself, the patron can give more to the client than is received from these particular clients without the structure being destabilized (as he may get from other subalterns whom he does not treat as clients) (see, for example, Ikegami 1995: 178).

---

[24] Thus historically, feudalism as an institution developed in accordance with the fusion of two different institutions, that of vassalage in which a vassal transferred his self-direction to a lord, and the granting of benefices, in which a lord granted the use rights to certain property to someone below cost (Ganshof 1964: 15). When they became separated again later, allowing for the de facto sale of benefices, the relationship became one of exchange and the pure structural qualities we are about to examine dissolved.

We shall later see that the seemingly similar relationship of the "big man" and followers is not so robust in the face of unequal transfers.

In sum, the patronage relationship connects nonequals, and though each has obligations to support the other, it is not expected that these contributions be equal. Indeed, such an insistence would be to deny the patronage of the patron, which is the free gift of ameliorating the (already) disadvantaged position of the client. Now that we understand the nature of the relationship, what does this tell us about the larger structure that sets of relationships form? I go on to argue that these aspects of the relationship answer the question raised above, namely why patronage relationships form trees instead of trisets.

Structural Properties of Patronage Triangles

The Concatenation of Structure

In chapter 2, we first examined the puzzles that confront us when we consider the aggregation of existing structural units. There is frequently more than one way in which units may be joined and which way is chosen may—as Simmel would appreciate—change the content of the relationship in question. In the case of cliques as examined in chapter 2, it turned out to be extremely difficult for cliques to join without such change. What are the options for patronage structures? Is it possible for units to be aggregated in such a way that the essential content of the relationships is preserved?

It might first of all be expected that just as we saw "wheels" aggregating into multihub communication structures in chapter 5, we shall see the same structures arise for the homologous patronage triangles. But there we examined a symmetric relationship of communication; patronage, however, is an inherently antisymmetric relationship because it is based on a preexisting inequality. Hence if relationships were to join patrons, either they would not be patronage relationships (taking us out of the realm of simple structures), or the resulting aggregate would lack the horizontality of the multihub structure. As we shall see, it is the latter that seems to be a recurring structural feature of patronage relationships—they concatenate into large "pyramids" in which any two patrons are connected only by a set of vertical ties, just as any two persons in the unilineal family tree can be so connected.

In our exploration of the formation of patronage structures, we may take for our example feudalism—the relationship in which grants of benefices are tied to vows of fealty. In most cases feudal systems involve the granting of use-rights (in land or in the form of tax farming or both) to those who promise military service; such systems have arisen independently in many societies (see a review in Critchley1978: especially 23, 28; Beeler 1971: 154, 169f; see Fourquin 1976: 134 for examples of nonland based benefices), not only medieval Europe and Japan, but ancient Greece, Babylonia, and the Maya (Adams

1991: 192f). (While specialists frequently like to emphasize the distinctiveness of any particular system, for our purposes, the commonalities are far more interesting than the differences.)

We, however, are not interested in such feudalism as a governmental or military scheme, or even a way of organizing property rights, but in terms of interaction. Only to the extent that it implies a patron-client relationship—that is, a *diffuse* relationship of reciprocated support between lord and vassal, not a *specific* exchange of rights—will feudalism be of concern to us; for this reason, medieval Europe is probably the most central example. Japan, which is sometimes seen as more feudal than Europe, in that lordship was unambiguously related to military command (Farris 1995: 372, 374f; Critchley 1978: 64, 30), is in our sense a less paradigmatic example of patron-client relations for that very reason.[25]

Pursuing the example of feudal relationships, then, we hope to investigate the structural properties of patronage relationships by examining the larger structures that are formed when patron-client triangles are aggregated. Doing so reveals two principles of the aggregation of patronage relationships: the suppression of horizontal relationships, and a tendency toward mediation. We investigate each in turn.

The Suppression of Horizontal Relations

The general question, then, is how a set of triangles may be joined: given two triangles, one with apex (patron) A and clients $A1$, $A2$, . . . etc., and a second with apex (patron) B and clients $B1$, $B2$, . . . , how is one unified structure formed? Is a horizontal relation between A and B created, leading to multihub structures we examined above? In classic patronage systems, the answer is no: the connection occurs by the addition of vertical relationships. Either A can become a client of B (or vice versa), or we may introduce some C who will be a patron's patron to both A and B—in any of these cases, the triangles have fused into a multilevel "pyramid" (see Lemarchand 1972: 76).

This form of concatenation, then, logically implies the suppression of horizontal relations, and it is gratifying to the analyst that patrons frequently agree and attempt to prevent such relations from arising (at least between their clients), even though this may decrease the communicative efficiency of the structure. For extraordinarily clear-cut example, when telephones were introduced to Swat, the ruler (Aladdin) had all connections pass through his own capital, so that there could be no horizontal communications between provin-

---

[25] Relations between samurai were stronger and more militaristic than the patronage relations of the court. While the lord-vassal relation was assimilated to father-son relations in the ideal, the reality was generally that relations were tenuous and self-interested (see Farris 1995: 312; Varley 1999: 55f; Ikegami 1995: 78).

cial lords without his knowledge (Critchley 1978: 88). While self-interest often leads empires that have conquered other states to allow horizontal trading relations between their client states, they generally attempt to suppress other political relations and will also suppress trade relations if these are believed to be political conduits (see, e.g., Hassig 1992: 91f; Randall 1993: 185). Such self-interest, however, can become a general matter of principle: Bloch (1961 [1940]: 354ff, 445; also Anderson 1974: 194; see Duby 1991: xv on other horizontal challenges to medieval verticalism) remarks that the reason the new political form of the commune (the association of burgers) was seen by feudal contemporaries with such loathing was that as a group tied by horizontal bonds of equality, it made hash of a social system predicated on relationships only connecting superiors to inferiors. In other cases, this suppression seems a matter of course: students of traditional Thai society remark that it was taken for granted that no two people confronted each other as equals (Kemp 1984: 59; Englehart 2001: 20).[26]

This thought experiment does not mean that all patronage structures arise because of the concatenation of preexisting triangles. However, it is important that there be a sociologically consistent answer to the question of how two small structures could be joined if larger structures are to be coherent. In this case, we are able to see how an extension of the principles underlying the smaller structures naturally leads to an aggregate that has a formal homology to the unilineal kinship structures seen in the previous section. As we will see in the following chapter, this solution was in many empirical cases (for example, European feudalism) always an incompletely realized tendency overwritten with other imperatives, yet these other imperatives (for example, horizontal ties or inconsistent rankings) were understood by the participants as troubling—comprehending and navigating the structure leads to an appeal to subjective heuristics compatible with tree structures.

The Principle of Mediation

But what does the treelike nature of the resulting structure imply about interaction between clients and "second-order" patrons? We saw in the previous chapter that there has been a tendency in the mathematical analysis of informal social structures to see forms such as patronage pyramids as trees in the algebraic sense of semilattices where all upper bounds are comparable (Friedell 1967); semilattices are a particular type of partial order, and one of the charac-

---

[26] A partial exception is the importance of samurai organizations of equals (*ikki*) and other horizontal associations of nonsamurai that gained importance in the late medieval period. Still, comments Ikegami (1995: 128f, also 122, 337), "Japanese history in the 16th century is the record of a process of violent suppression of horizontal forms of social organization by a strictly hierarchical system of samurai vassalage."

teristics of a relation in a partial order is that it is *transitive*: denoting the relation $\rightarrow$, transitivity, we recall, means if $A \rightarrow B$ and $B \rightarrow C$, then $A \rightarrow C$.

Such transitivity seems natural for patronage structures given their foundation in some system of inequality. That is, patronage relations are antisymmetric (if $A \rightarrow B$, then B not $\rightarrow A$) because they correspond to some ranking of persons on some attribute (if $A \rightarrow B$, there must be some ζ such that $\zeta_A > \zeta_B$). By extrapolation, this might be understood to imply transitivity, since if $A \rightarrow B$ and $B \rightarrow C$, there must be some ζ such that $\zeta A > \zeta_B > \zeta_C$, and hence we might expect that $A \rightarrow C$. But this is rarely the case. Instead, the opposite (antitransitivity) is generally true: if $A \rightarrow B$ and $B \rightarrow C$, the one thing we know is that A not $\rightarrow C$.

This rule was explicitly formulated for the case of feudalism in fourteenth-century century France: "queritur utrum homo hominis mei sit meus homo. Et dicendum est quod non": my vassal's vassal is not my vassal (Ganshof 1964: 97; also see Duby 1991: 28; for Japan, see Ikegami 1995: 82, 235, 237).[27] The tendency toward antitransitivity was made clear by Gould (1996) in his analysis of the patronage relations underlying the American Whiskey Rebellion, and he stressed that the reason for this was that it makes no sense for a patron to support a client who can already be supported by one of his other clients. This principle of mediation helps us understand the tendency of patronage structures to form pyramids. If (a) persons are ranked, and (b) very high-rank people do not interact with very low-rank people, and (c) patronage is a fundamentally personalistic relationship with more clients than patrons, the patronage structure *must* form a multileveled pyramid (Landé 1977b: 508).

Brokerage

The antitransitivity of patron-client ties may lead us to assimilate these relationships to the general case of brokerage. This relationship, discussed by Simmel (1950 [1908]:154ff) as an important case of *tertius gaudens*, the third who profits by standing in between two others, has inspired much network theory (especially Burt 1992; Gould and Fernandez 1989) because of its richness

---

[27] At the same time, there was an understanding that the transitively implied relationship has *some* content (Montgomery 2007): thus my lord's lord, while not my lord, is my "lord suzerain," though this probably only appeared as the structure of vassalage was breaking down in the 14th century (and transitively implied relationships became common in the 17th [Kettering 1986: 21]). Further, there were some exceptions to the suppression of relationships with the lord's lord. One was that when a lord died without an heir, his vassals would temporarily be regarded as vassals of the lord's lord until an heir was chosen. A second was when a tie of vassalage was broken due to the improper conduct of the lord, the lord's lord could assume the relationship with the client, to avoid the latter being left unprotected (Bloch 1961 [1940]: 228f, 146). Third, kings were at times able to make sure that those swearing fealty to one of their vassals maintained primary allegiance to the crown (Duby 1991: 214).

in explaining organizational power in managerial hierarchies and exchange networks. Furthermore, patronage relations studied by political scientists often involve a great deal of brokerage: most important, the patron brokers relationships between his clients and more cosmopolitan powers such as regional or national governments. In such a setting, the patron is the one who can tell a client how to navigate these unfamiliar waters, who can gather clients together to make a forceful demand of a central power (and take a cut from any resulting grant), or who can smooth the client's path with a word to someone in power. The assimilation of patronage relations to brokerage relations is doubly plausible because this would explain the tendency toward antitransitivity as a result of broker-entrepreneurs who insert themselves between two previously unconnected parties.

Despite all this, there is reason to suspect that brokerage is not fundamental to the case of mediated patronage triangles. Most important, an emphasis on brokering (or occupying "structural holes") assumes the existence of a desire among two unconnected echelons to interact. But this very desire is foreign to the nature of mediated hierarchy. In the next chapter, we shall explore what happens when this desire arises (usually by virtue of military need), but it should not be assumed as given.

It is true that there are many examples of patrons brokering between local communities and the state, helping locals navigate bureaucratic intricacies or smoothing their way over hurdles set in place by unsympathetic officers. But such a relationship necessarily preassumes the existence of such a bureaucratic state. Patronage relations, however, are likely to have arisen before this type of state.

As a result, it is easy to reach mistaken conclusions regarding the intrinsic structural tendencies of patronage relationships on the basis of an examination of the roles of brokers. Prior to the massive state penetration of the past two centuries, such functions were not crucial to patronage systems (this point has also been made by Lemarchand and Legg 1972: 154, 158; Parish and Michelson 1996: 1045).[28] This emphasis on brokerage, where it has occurred, involves a modification of traditional dyadic patronage relationships to emphasize mediation and brokerage as opposed to reciprocity between unequals (see Kaufman 1977: 114, 118; also Dietz 1977: 441; and Mouzelis 1985: 343 on Latin America). For one, the new ability of patrons to serve also as brokers may have increased their power vis-à-vis their clients (see Scott and Kerkvliet

[28] Thus Weingrod (1968: 382) equates patronage with brokerage, emphasizing as a condition for the development of patronage the existence of "gaps" in the structure of society due to primitive transportation systems or markets, linguistic diversity, laws against migration, etc., also. But his examples (the classic Chinese state, for one, and his own study of Sardinia in response to increasing national integration) demonstrate that these pertain to situations in which a state already exists. For another study of such patronage, see Stokes (1995: 16) on Peru.

1977: 453f).[29] More important from a structural perspective, a switch to an emphasis on brokerage instead of amelioration leads patronage relationships to become more like the "big man" relationships we shall explore below, and hence to concatenate in multihub structures, in that there are more horizontal connections between big men than in a patronage system, in which all relations are ideally vertical. A classic example here is the "amigocracy" described by Kenny (1960) in Spain—the big man or patron is one with a horizontal connection to a "friend" in the right place. These patron-patron ties, explicitly noted by Kenny (1960: 23; cf. Guasti 1977: 423; Schwartz 1990: 153), are foreign to the purest form of a patronage pyramid, if only because the purer forms are based on land-ownership, and there is little that a peasant needs from a *different* landowner that he cannot get from his own.[30]

To illustrate, we can take the rather well studied case of Italy. Because Italy was formed by consolidation of previously separate regions, there were quite understandably many "structural holes"—gaps in the structure of relationships making it difficult for some persons to reach others—that would frustrate the ability of locals to navigate the nebulous national power structure. As a result, "the most valuable patron was neither the wealthiest nor the most generous, but the one with the best connections." In consequence of the focus on "connections," the patronage structure found in central Italy tended to be more like a multihub structure than a pyramid—patrons were distinctive in having ties to other patrons outside the community. But Silverman (1965: 179, 180, 182) comments, "Yet this aspect of the patron's role was elaborated only in the late nineteenth and early twentieth centuries."[31]

Brokerage, then, is not intrinsic to patronage (also see Mayer 1966: 113f for a clear distinction between the two). The introduction of cosmopolitan state structures has in many cases led local patrons—in some cases, the local government as a whole—to function as brokers between the community and the national or regional government (e.g., Mair 1977: 228). In such cases, the seeming "broker" may really be simply a first-order patron only having ties to second-order patrons (that is, the broker lacks horizontal ties to brokers of

[29] In other cases, the increased emphasis on brokerage can disempower those who previously held semiformal positions of leadership; see, e.g., Helm (1972: 78) on chiefs of the Dogrib Indians now expected to be brokers: "My people come to me for help," says one, "and I have nothing to give them but my fingernails."

[30] Or rather, little he was likely to get. This is a simplification of actual peasant life, but as life approaches this point of simplicity, patronage relations become more purely vertical.

[31] Similarly, the process of state-building in 17th-century France involved the state transforming local patrons into brokers who could be used to extend central control into the provinces; indeed, the state *intendants* were arranged in some places to form an alternative pyramid through which patronage could flow, starving the great nobles and transforming patrons into brokers (Kettering 1986: 91, 159, 234ff); we return to this case in chapter 9.

equivalent status).[32] Where the introduction of these cosmopolitan political structures allows patrons to become true brokers (who have ties to *other* brokers, or to other locals independent of ties to second-order patrons), they tend to produce different structures associated with the "big men" discussed above, or with the more exploitative "boss" relation (someone with all the rights and few of the duties of a patron) (see, e.g., Graziano 1977: 363).

Subjective Heuristics

We have seen that patronage relationships tend to take on a particular treelike structure. That informal relationships should spontaneously take on such a restricted formal structure seemed quite surprising to some analysts (e.g., Friedell 1967). But it can easily be shown that this structure will occur whenever people follow two simple heuristics.

We have already seen the first: it has to do with the preexisting inequality that is the basis for the relationship. Since the relationship of patronage arises to ameliorate this inequality it stands to reason that A will only take as a patron some B with more of whatever it is (previously denoted ζ, with the amount of this resource possessed by A denoted ζ_A) than A has. As stressed in the previous chapter, if we assume that ζ is continuously distributed with no perfect ties, a linear order will emerge if people follow the simple rule $B \to A$ if and only if $\zeta_B > \zeta_A$. That is, there is an antisymmetric relationship between A and B if and only if there is a relation of "greater than" between the two.

Assuming no ties, such a structure would lead to $N(N-1)/2$ directed relations, since a relationship of inequality will exist for every dyad, whereas a tree structure will involve only $N-1$ relations, as every person except the apex is a client of someone, and these are the only relations present. With the exception of a single long line, a tree structure will also include horizontal, as well as vertical, differentiation. We saw in chapter 5 that a horizontal structure will arise if there is some minimum "just noticeable difference" (JND) Δ between any two people before a relationship will be established. (That is, they follow the rule $A \to B$ if and only if $\zeta_A > \zeta_B + \Delta$.) But the "JND" rule does not produce mediated trees; instead, as we have seen, it produces structures where those higher up have relationships with all those at the bottom, and we have not found this to be characteristic of patronage structures.

In other words, while some difference in resource is *necessary* for the establishment of a patronage relationship, it is not *sufficient*: that is, the rule must really be closer to "$A \to B$ only if $\zeta(A) > \zeta(B) + \Delta$." But even more important, there seems to be a rule (for the classic structures we are explicating) to the

---

[32] For the case of Peru, which seems to have such vertical relations, as opposed to an "amigocracy," see Stokes (1995: 55).

effect that "every client can have only one patron" (Wolf 1977: 174). Such a rule of exclusivity is not found, as Landé (1977a: xx) points out, in structures organized around "stars" or "hubs," and hence patronage structures are qualitatively different from networks that simply have high variance of degree (number of ties per node). There are exceptions to the "one patron rule" which I shall discuss below, but the rule itself comes out of a fundamental aspect of the relation in question, in which the client gives loyalty above all else. While it is possible to promise loyalty to more than one patron, it seems likely that such loyalty is a bit different from the loyalty promised to one and only one.

This "one patron rule" is reinforced when patronage is tied to ownership of or control over land: tenancy can be the basis for an inherently exclusive relationship of clientship where tenure is defined so that only one person can "own" the land occupied by the client, and where clients only occupy and work a single plot (cf. Hall 1974; also Duby 1991: 139). In such cases, while patronage relations may be an important part of the societal fabric in general, it is possible for these particular relationships to be relatively disconnected from one another: each landlord is patron to his tenants, and is not necessarily the client of anyone else.[33] Landlords need not compete with one another for clients.

Things are not necessarily this simple, of course: in some cases, there may be multiple forms of ownership of land.[34] In other cases, even though land ownership is the basis for patronage relationships, tenants may supplement the patronage received from the landlord by adopting other patrons and may even play these against the landlord (Barth 1977 [1965]: 215). And there are resources other than land that may be stable bases for patronage relations (e.g. Guasti 1977: 429); what is essential is that they can be wholly monopolized, so that there is no chance for enterprising ex-clients to strike out on their own and few opportunities for advancement in a wholly different line of endeavor (Hall 1974).[35]

In sum, in patronage pyramids, there is a strong tendency for any person to be the client of one and only one patron. But it is not the case that the patron can have only one client; indeed, the opposite is generally true. Since what the

---

[33] To take the case of the Polish magnates of the 17th century, there was clearly a well understood relationship between rights to land and clientship. Thus the lord Tomasz Zamoyski assumed he had the right to terminate the lease of a man who had taken a different patron: "For whoever takes a lease from me becomes my serving man, and . . . as he was serving another man, he could not lease property from me" (Pośpiech and Tygielski 1981: 84; cf. 87).

[34] When there is a distinction between use rights and alienation rights over the land, patronage is likely to flow from the former as opposed to the latter (see Silverman [1965: 176f] and Weingrod [1968:391] on the *mezzadria* [sharecropping] relation in Italy).

[35] Even a land-based system can be unstable if there is unclaimed arable land (Scott and Kerkvliet 1977: 448).

client has to offer is of much less value than what the patron has, a number of clients must be assembled before their support is of much use.

These simple rules (accept as a patron only someone of higher ζ than you; have only one patron) lead to the production of the treelike structures that are so familiar to comparative political scientists. The nature of the relationship, then, has clear structural implications that have been noted by analysts in settings widely varying in location and time. These structural implications are clarified by a comparison to those involving somewhat different relationships, such as "big men" and their retinues.

Comparison of Different Structures

Big Man Structures

The term *big man* comes from anthropological investigations of Pacific Island societies in which those of great prestige have neither power over others (as would kings with a permanent staff) nor monopolize any resources (Sahlins 1968: 22, 26f; Hanser 1985: 61, 104, 331). Instead, these "big men" are big precisely because they *give away* what they have.[36] Their prestige can then be used for purposes of garnering resources (others will court the big man's favor through gifts so as to have a prestigious ally; the big man can then redistribute these gifts to increase his prestige). "Little men" (if they can so be called) tend to attach themselves to a particular big man, forming the wheel structure we previously investigated. Thus the "big man-little man" relationship is like a patronage relationship in that it connects unequals through mutual support, but, as we shall see, it tends to concatenate into different structures.

What is most important about the classic big-man structure in terms of its structural potential is that it does not build on preexisting inequality, but is itself the generation of that inequality. While patrons may be able to choke off the access of others to resources (see Wallace-Hadrill 1989: 73 for the case of Rome), the big man has no special access (though some are born with "better" kin than others). A big man is one who has many followers who will make donations to him; these donations in turn allow him to provide feasts for followers and demonstrate that he is in fact a big man. The bigness of a big man, at least in its purest form, comes wholly from the allegiance of his followers.

Since big men do not arise on the basis of preexisting inequality, they require a jump-start,[37] and given the conditional allegiance of their followers, generally

[36] Outside of this context, "big men" may not necessarily be men, but I retain the gendered term for consistency with earlier accounts.

[37] As one big man recalled, it was once he had some valuables that "I could start doing things in feasts, and making a name for myself" (Keesing 1983: 67)

face constant competition from other big men for clients (Sahlins 1963: 291; cf. Kenny 1960: 22). The nature of the jump start is various, but fortunately for the analyst, the beginning is not as important as what happens next: the big man becomes the hub of a wheel supported by (potentially unequal) transfers. Indeed, we may derive the hub structure from what we have learned about the interaction-profiles associated with exchange. If the relationship of exchange is to be the basis for obdurate social structure, it must involve not only reciprocity but delay in repayment (otherwise there is no unifying function of the debt) (see Silverman 1965: 176 for the case of patronage relations in Italy; Bourdieu 1977 for a general statement). Given this, it is possible for relational entrepreneurs to quickly amass social capital simply by borrowing from some and giving to others. The "big man" system is basically redistributive, and someone becomes a hub merely by the sleight of hand that makes it appear that the bread you eat today is not the bread you gave to the big man yesterday, but that it is in fact "his" bread (see Keesing 1983: 7; Meggitt 1974: 190, 195). As a consequence, such hub structures are riddled with paradoxes or circularities that can turn vicious.[38] Just as we saw in chapter 2 popularity tournaments containing positive feedback that could spin out of control, so big man systems contain an aspect of mimetic speculation (Orléan 1988) whereby all wish to be clients of the important patrons—that is, those with many clients (compare Wallace-Hadrill 1989: 83; we explored such "go with the winner" games in chapter 2 in the form of the popularity tournament).

In particular, "big man" systems are very sensitive to dislocation of the delicate balance between spoke-hub and hub-spoke transfers. Since spokes in such systems are generally free to drop and pick up hubs on the basis of their power and largesse (such as among the Melanesians discussed by Sahlins 1963: 292; or the Mandari of Eastern Africa discussed by Mair 1977: 98; cf. 64), hubs may not be free to desist from ruinous relationships (see Park 1974: 271 for the case of the Anuak headman). What is crucial is not that where the

---

[38] It must be conceded that it is possible for a patronage structure to arise without clear claim to the resource in question if a similar sleight of hand can be used to grant what is not yours to grant. In a word, if *A* has *X* but is not strong enough to keep it, while *B* is not strong enough to take it unilaterally, *C* may benefit from "giving" *X* to *B*. Since *B* will naturally then defend the legitimacy of *C*'s right to allocate *X* and other resources, *C*'s act is something akin to a self-fulfilling prophecy. A tolerable approximation of this process may in part underlie the development of feudalism in Western Europe (alternatives are discussed below). Having previously expropriated church property to give to supporters in the constant civil wars of the 7th-8th centuries (Bachrach 1972: 98), the Frankish monarchs needed to pacify relations with the church and to retrieve some of the power that had devolved downward. The solution was to claim de jure ownership over the property held de facto by the lords, and thus to allow these powerful military leaders to continue to hold that which they were unlikely to give up, while asserting an ultimate right to control that over which they had no real control . . . at the time (Ganshof 1964: 16f). The efficacy of this move, however, presupposed the other factors we have already examined.

clients have more choice they have a better bargain (though this is in fact the case): it is that where the redistribution is wholly contained *within* the patronage structure (as opposed to extraction being outside the structure), any intensification of the redistributive schedule can destroy a big man. A wonderful example is given by Barth (1977 [1965]: 218f; 1981: 68) concerning the Swat Pathans. When a patron begins to lose influence and becomes poorer, he must *increase* his hospitality, even if this means liquidating his capital. One informant made it clear that his relationship with his clients was not an equal exchange but still the lesser of the evils confronting him. While entertaining guests required selling off land, "on the other hand, if people stop sitting in my men's house, I shall lose the land even faster; only this constant show of force keeps the vultures at bay."

More generally, as a "big man" gets bigger and has more obligations, there is more pressure on him to squeeze more resources from his entourage (most simply, by increasing the time between when he gets something from them and when he gives it back, but also by increasing his cut from the redistributive process) or even better, if he is able, to squeeze resources from nonfollowers (see Mair 1977: 136f). As he becomes more powerful, this seems a plausible tactic. But if clients then become dissatisfied and leave, his very power is his weaknesses. As Sahlins (1963: 293) says, "Paradoxically[,] the ultimate defense of the [big man's] position is some slackening of his drive to enlarge the funds of power. The alternative is much worse."

As a result, hubs may indeed be sociometrically privileged without being materially privileged. The apexes of the Senegalese "clans" that dominated postindependence politics were required to share their profits with their followers to the extent that they frequently were no wealthier than their retinue (Foltz 1977: 245). Similarly, Bashi (1997) finds that hubs who help West Indian immigrants relocate to the United States gain little besides prestige from their efforts. The requirement to redistribute collected surpluses may be the most important factor leading to the preservation of horizontality in hub-spoke systems that follow big-men lines. The big man system generates and destroys inequality at the same time.

True patronage relationships, however, can exist in a stable vertical form as long as there is an exogenous generator or regenerator of inequality. At the same time, patronage relations lack the same endogeneity of the popularity tournament that the big man system possesses. That is, there is no particular limitation to the number of clients that a big man can get—indeed, each additional client only increases the probability that another person will attach himself to the big man. But a patron may only have so much land to give out (cf. Major 1964: 637). Thus despite their formal homology (a central person with clients), big man and patronage relationships produce different larger structures, as we go on to find.

Structural Implications

In general, big man structures concatenate into the multihub structure charted above, as opposed to the pyramids of patronage relationships. Put another way, while some big men are bigger than others, there are no "big men's big men" who have entourages consisting only of (smaller) big men. A perfect opposition between big men and their entourages (on the one hand) and patrons and their clients (on the others) comes from Sahlins's classic comparison of the multilayered pyramids of Polynesian patronage structures to smaller, unstable, and segmental entourages of Melanesian big men (Sahlins 1963: 287, 292ff).

There are, of course, intermediate cases. In particular, we found that the introduction of cosmopolitan state structures to localities previously organized along patronage lines leads the patrons to assume a new role of brokers or gatekeepers (see Kenny 1960) who can put a client in touch with other patrons. As a result, the relationship tends to be more of one of "communication" than one of amelioration, and consequently there is a tendency toward horizontal connections between patrons and an approximation of the multihub structures that arise in communication networks. Similar are cases where patronage degenerates into mere "sponsorship," a condition associated with relaxations of the "one-patron" rule examined below.[39]

But in such cases, we may find that the relationship itself has changed and may be better described as a "boss" relationship. "Boss" (or *cacique* in Latin America) is a term frequently used in political anthropology to denote someone who has the power of a patron but without the legitimacy (see Scott and Kerkvliet 1977: 443 on differences between patron and boss). Like the big man, the "boss" relation does not build on preexisting inequality; rather, the "boss" is an upstart who creates the inequality of the relationship. In contrast to big men, who have little power except the respect they garner, the boss is generally considered to be important but self-oriented and hence has few followers who have more than a pragmatic loyalty (see, e.g., Cornelius 1977, especially 339, 341).

---

[39] For example, in 17th-century France, Kettering (1986: 56, 59, 85, 99, 140ff) argues, most clients tried to secure ties to more than one patron, and brokers (both those who had resources of their own and those who were mere go-betweens) were crucial in mediating ties between patrons. But already this is a form of patronage that is heavily connected to an emerging national state, with parallel clienteles based in the nobility and in the administration; further, these brokers played a role in pushing forward the national political integration of a still poorly coordinated state. They managed to cement the provincial nobility to the crown by centralizing the source of all patronage, but at a cost: to the extent that patronage was given with no strings attached, the patrons allowed their clients to build up an independent power source; to the extent that the center retained control, patronage was politicized. In chapter 8 we shall see how this tends to provoke civil war.

Further, bosses tend to be brokers: the *cacique*'s real or pretended ties to central elites are an important reason for his getting support. (Thus in the Caribbean plantations on the coast of South America, Amerindian *caciques* stood in between plantation owners and African slaves [Whitehead 1992: 141].) More generally, the "boss" may be said to differ from a patron in that there are no clear obligations that the boss has toward his clients, and thus although he may favor them with a great deal of what is commonly considered "patronage," these seem spontaneous acts of grace.[40]

Three Pure Types

Each of the three relationships has something in common with the other two; these commonalities and differences can again be clarified by means of a diagram (figure 6.6). We will find a similarity in the nature of the trade-offs between these dimensions and trade-offs we have investigated in the previous chapters. The first dimension has to do with whether there is a preexisting ranking of persons on some dimension that is ameliorated by the relationship. This is true for patronage structures, but not the other two where the relationship in question must generate the differentiation between the persons. Without payoffs, the boss ceases to be a boss; without esteem, the big man is no longer big, but the noble without fealty is still a landowner.[41]

The second opposition has to do with the nature of transfers made in the relationship. Both the patronage structure and the big man structure are fundamentally redistributive (though not necessarily to the long-term disadvantage of the superior party): the patron gives some of what he naturally gathers as a superior person back to the lowly (though they may pay a high "price" for this through military service); the big man receives gifts and gives them back as "his" feast. In contrast, the boss takes, and takes more than he receives. There is generally a direct relation between this dimension of redistributivity and perceived legitimacy by clients.[42]

The third opposition, which distinguishes the big man from the other two, is that the responsibilities of the small man versus the big man are not enforce-

---

[40] For an example of irregular patronage in a "boss" system of patronage in New York, see Johnston (1979: 395); this irregularity of obligation–and indeed ambiguity of the clients' own obligations–is also pointed to in the case of the Sicilian capitalist broker-patrons by Graziano (1977: 363).

[41] This corresponds to the dimension of *dependence* on some external scaffolding for establishing a preexisting vertical ordering of persons.

[42] To the extent that the system of relationships is redistributive, this lessens the *differentiation* of persons though there may be other relationships that increase this differentiation, if this structure is *dependent* on another structure. We recall that this parallels an emphasis on equality as opposed to inequality; while all these relationships are vertical, it is the boss relationship that heightens the perception of inequality in its negative sense.

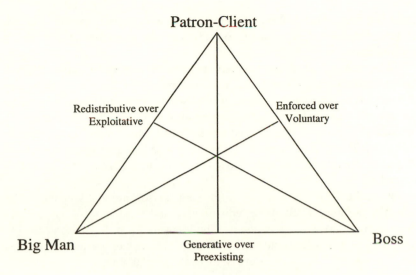

Figure 6.6. Three polar relationships

able via sanction, as are those of the boss and patronage relationships. Perhaps because of this absence of enforcement, more emphasis is placed on impressing upon followers the charisma of the big man, or the accumulation of "symbolic capital," as Bourdieu (1977) calls it. What leads to charisma of the big man, as Zablocki (1980) has argued, is largely nothing other than the fact that he is seen as charismatic by *others*.[43]

All empirical examples fall somewhere on this space; they are mixtures, but they are not random mixtures. Thus many bosses do *some* redistribution, which pushes them out of the "boss" corner a bit; many patrons do *some* exploitation and even feudal kings required some personal charisma to maintain their followers (Reuter 1999: 27). Lords often followed the paradoxical recipe of the "big man" that he who has the most is he who gives all away. An eleventh-century Norman lord, Richard of Aversa, was said by a contemporary to have "carried off everything he could and gave it away, keeping little . . . in this way the land about was plundered and the number of his knights multiplied" (Gillingham 1999: 64; cf. Adams 2005: 146f; Englehart 2001: 25).

Thus the reasonableness of the foregoing scheme depends not on the purity of empirical cases, but on there being an empirical trade-off between movement on any two dimensions and the third: as with our previous conclusions, we find that there are limitations to the number of principles that can simultaneously structure relationships. Taking the first opposition pertaining to preexistence of inequality, it does seem quite reasonable that to the extent that

---

[43] This may correspond (albeit quite roughly) to the *involution* of relationships–their spontaneous organization and feedback.

there is a preexisting ranking of inequality, it is both easier for the structure to be enforceable with regard to outside sanction and more of a need for redistribution.

Taking the second opposition pertaining to the degree of exploitation, it seems reasonable that exploitative relationships will be more likely to require the support of external sanctions. It also seems reasonable that it is easier for unequal relationships to avoid exploitation if they build on a preexisting inequality. That is, there is no need for this particular relationship to generate inequality. That does not mean that it is impossible for a patron-client relationship to be exploitative, but it does mean that, in contrast to a boss relationship, it need not be.

Taking the third opposition, it again seems reasonable that voluntary relationships are more likely to be redistributive and to spontaneously generate the inequality involved as opposed to building on them, for reasons already alluded to. Hence we conclude that this scheme has virtues that are not obvious yet not obscure. The next step is to draw similar conclusions regarding structure.

We have seen that, building on preexisting inequalities, patronage relationships are more stable (less conditional) than big-man relationships. Further, it is easier for them to aggregate into a multitiered pyramid. However, if there is not a single apex to this pyramid, it is still possible for patron-patron conflict to spill over into arenas that require the mobilization of clients. If clients can abandon weak patrons and go to stronger (as among that Pathans discussed above [see Barth 1977 [1965]: 214]), clients become relatively empowered and the system tends to veer off in the direction of a big-man structure. In contrast, "boss" structures may approach simple pyramids due to the tendency of the boss to be an intermediary.

As a result, the type of relationship in question tells us a great deal about the likely structural patterns formed in concatenation of dyadic relationships, but the specifics of the relationship—the degree of underlying inequality, the presence or absence of conflict between higher-ups, etc.—also tell us a great deal about the structural pattern. In fact, we may derive a similar (though not homologous) space of three related structures, namely the web, the pyramid, and the multihub structure, with three similarly related dimensions (see figure 6.7). It is important to note that the corners on the two triangles do not match exactly: while patronage does tend to be associated with pyramids, big manism may form either webs or multihub structures—indeed, in some cases, no concatenation happens at all, since there seems to be a general disinclination on the part of big-man wheels to aggregate to form large structures. Yet the nature of the oppositions and trade-offs between these structures is similar to those we saw for the relationships.

A multihub system, we emphasized before, differs from a pyramid mainly in only having two levels—there are no "hubs' hubs." Webs of antisymmetric

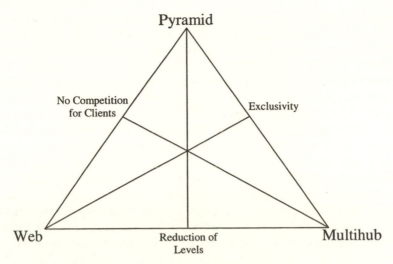

Figure 6.7. Three polar structures

ties, understood as more general structures, also lack the clear gradation of a pyramid: while there may be a continuous variation in quantity of attachments of any node, this undermines any attempt to make a distinction of kind. But in contrast to multihub structures (and patronage structures), webs lack the exclusive connection of any spoke to a hub. Finally, both a patronage system that builds on preexisting inequality and a web that lacks exclusivity defuse the potentially ruinous nature of competition between hubs for spokes.

The difference between the two analytic spaces allows us to understand how two patronage systems may have different structural shapes. For example, all other things being equal, a patronage structure that is based on land will be more likely to fall toward the top of the figure, while one based on less exclusive and more competitive principles may tend more toward a web or multihub structure. Further, we can see that either a multihub or web structure may be pushed toward a pyramid by enforcing exclusivity of patronage and weakening the ability of clients to force patrons to compete. And indeed, this is exactly what we see in cases of feudal organization: in Thailand, just as in feudal Europe, it was declared that all had to have only one patron, and while the lowest ranking clients (*phrai*) did frequently desert one patron (*nai*) for a better one, and hence spur the patrons to compete with each other, this was outlawed (Englehart 2001: 43; cf. Ikegami 1995: 130, 334).

But why would anyone wish to do so—to push the structure further toward a pyramid? As we shall see, patronage structures are special in that they can bring a number of persons together in a single structure under a wide range of conditions. We have, we recall, been searching for simple structures that can form the building blocks of larger structures. We have found some structures cannot be concatenated at all—for example, two exclusive dyadic relationships must involve four participants, not three. Other structures make unrealistic interactional demands when aggregated—participants must establish huge numbers of consistent relationships (e.g., the clique, the pecking order). Still other structures may be able to aggregate, but these aggregates may only survive in a relatively narrow range of environments. Thus generalized exchange requires equality among persons or units but tends to generate inequality and hence undermine itself. Like an environmentally sensitive organism that pollutes its surroundings, it necessarily leads a precarious existence.

But with patronage structures, inequality in the environment poses no problem, since it is the fundamental premise of association in the first place. And the antitransitivity means that two structures can be joined at a single place, without examining whether all the implied dyadic relations work out. That is, if two groups with N_1 and N_2 members each, each group organized into a pecking order, decide to aggregate, then even if the bottom person in the first group successfully dominates the top person in the second, we still have N_1N_2 − 1 relationships that may possibly go awry and force a reorganization. But if a patron takes on another patron as a client, the "sub" patron's clients need not acknowledge the sovereignty of their patron's patron (compare Simon 1962: 476). Accordingly, when there is widespread social disorganization, patronage structures are often the first social organization to move in; the formation of a richer institutional life often depends on the transformation of these patronage structures, or, seen another way, their breakdown. We go on to examine the conditions of such breakdown.

Rise and Fall of Patronage Structures

Concatenation in the Service of the Production of Governance Structures

Concatenation of distinct and nontransitive patron-client relations can lead to a sprawling structure which, if weak in many respects, is still able to move support and sometimes money upward and (some) control and protection downward; consequently, patronage pyramids are relatively frequent governance structures that can link the humble local peasant to the central power. Once established, they are surprisingly resilient, for reasons to be explored below. For an elegant example of governance through a patronage structure, we may take the Thai political system of the late Ayudhya period until 1873 (Landé 1973: 111).

At the bottom were *phrai* (commoners) who belonged to some *nai* (noble)—while their relationship was personalistic as opposed to being fixed by law or contract, the *nai* was basically in charge of mobilizing the labor of his *phrai* for higher ups. An edict of 1356 required that all people were required to register under some patron who in turn would be treated as an official: for quite some time, all *phrai* had to have the name of their *nai* tattooed on their body (Terwiel 1984; Englehart 2001: 23, 36–39, 42).[44]

These *nai* were then clients of higher patrons, "etcetera etcetera," progressing steadily upward toward the king. The state was thus the aggregation of these triangles, with almost all governance indirect through clients of clients (Englehart 2001: 55).[45] Most important, this joining was based on the principle of mediation, or intransitivity. As Hanks (1977 [1966]: 164) says regarding the Thai structure, "Ordinarily a lowly person must reach the high through one or more intermediaries, and then it would seem ridiculous that anything a woodcutter might need could not be handled as well by a less elevated personage. So the extremes rarely meet, and more effective connections lie a few short steps up or down the hierarchy."

The story of European state formation is, in broadest outlines, the story of the creation and transformation of such patronage pyramids.[46] In ideal-typical form, we may state that the first step is the evolution of hub structures into patronage triangles, as when charismatic warrior bands are the basis of well-developed feudalism. This has been suggested as the origin of European feudalism: two institutions were combined, the first the personal retinue of the war leader's band, and then second the Roman "precarium," a form of sharecropping that had become tied to military service (in place of rent) in the fifth and sixth centuries (Beeler 1971: 4; Critchley 1978: 102; Mallett 1999: 211; cf. Anderson 1974: 94, 98, 115, 130). Then the patronage structure is transformed into a command structure. We shall examine this aspect of the creation of governance structures in the next chapter.

The use of patronage pyramids as governance structures is not limited to the political realm, but can easily be found in economic governance. In postwar Japan, many industries were organized according to patron-client principles (*oyabunkobun*, as said above), an interesting contrast to the accounts of the

---

[44] While Englehart (2001: 20, 27) emphasizes that in the Siamese context, it was labor, and not land, that was in short supply and was to be mobilized through the pyramid, and that "land was not a source of power because it was abundant and because anyone could hold it," his own work suggests that this is an oversimplification. While it is true that even villages (*meuang*) were defined as assemblages of rights over persons, as opposed to rights over land, there was clearly some relation of patronage to land: there was an attempt to designate rank in the patronage pyramid in terms of *sakdina* (or *sagdinaa*), which means "power of the [rice] fields" and was originally measured in land area (Terwiel 1984: 22; Englehart 2001: 26, 59).

[45] Kemp (1984) stresses the simplicity of this view of the Thai structure, which emphasizes the most formal forms of patronage at the expense of more affectual, ambiguous, and flexible relations often described using kinship terminology.

[46] This is also true of Japan, as argued by Ikegami (1995: 37f), who stresses that the early modern Japanese state was created via the destruction of horizontal relationships and the consolidation of a particular structure of vertical relationships of vassalage. Ikegami also notes the duality between the cultural understanding of the nature of the relationship in question and the structural form evolving.

development of multidivision firms we will examine in the next chapter. Lower level labor bosses controlled workers in a fashion similar to contractors (they were paid and paid their workers in turn); in turn, these *oyabun* were the *kobun* of higher *oyabun*, etc. (Nakane 1970).

In sum, it is now possible to specify why patronage structures are so frequently seen. They are one of the few simple structures that thrive in conditions of inequality and which can be concatenated without necessarily undermining their structural cohesion. That does not mean that there are not structural tensions. I go on to explore these as a way to understanding the reasons why patronage structures may transform into other forms.

Breakdown of Patronage

Patronage structures tend to be extremely stable. Just as we saw many higher primates able to "fold in" to a pecking order all relationships (e.g., alliance) that might be understood as undermining this order, so people are able to fold in potentially contentious relations into a patronage order. Many of the tendencies toward change that patronage structures do have are ones that actually *strengthen* the structural tendencies. Most important, there is a tendency toward the "spillover" to new forms of service (that is, patrons take on a new form of patronage and/or clients a new form of clientage [see Lemarchand 1972: 76]).

Political scientists have repeatedly noted—often to their dismay—the resilience of patronage structures which often only release their hold over interactions when an expanded (national or imperial) state deliberately weeds them out. Even in such cases, states frequently prefer to exploit and hence reinforce these existing relations (Lemarchand 1972: 79). Yet any simple opposition between stable patronage structures and the states that destroy them is misleading, for, as I have suggested, the structures associated with the modern state have in large part derived from patronage structures.[47] This change was predicated on the few structural instabilities inherent in patronage structures.

Patronage structures, we recall, may be understood as resulting from three rules, the first of which stems from the presence of inequality (form a tie from A to B only if there is some ζ such that $\zeta_A > \zeta_B + \Delta$ where Δ indicates a just noticeable difference). The unsaid correlate to this is that all relationships are vertical, and no relationships exist for any A and B where $|\zeta_A - \zeta_B| < \Delta$, which

---

[47] Much of the early work on patronage was motivated by the modernization theories of comparative political science, which took universalism in political systems as some sort of timeless benchmark according to which other systems would be understood, and hence it was usually concluded that patron-client structures were vestigial at best or deliberately obstructionist at worst. The actual breakdown in patronage systems that might arise with economic development or world system political integration was therefore misunderstood as successful evolution; such interpretations are not reviewed here.

we might consider to be a "horizontal" relationship. The second rule was that any client could only have one patron. The third rule was antitransitivity. Abrogation of any one of these principles weakens the patronage structure, and we consider each in turn. In every case, the patronage structure, durable as it is, does tend to arouse the very forces that would destabilize it.

HORIZONTAL RELATIONS AND STRUCTURAL EQUIVALENCE

The patronage pyramid is premised on the inability of clients, especially bottom-level clients, to form relationships among themselves that would allow them to bargain collectively with the patron. Yet the patronage triangle establishes a *relation* between clients of structural equivalence that can serve as the basis for a *relationship* of active collusion that may undermine the patronage structure. It may appear that the clients need only perceive that their latent categorical identity can be the basis of actual relationships of solidarity—to go from being a category *in* themselves to a category *for* themselves—for the structure to collapse.

Interestingly, this scenario seems to occur only quite rarely, and not only because of the general powerlessness of clients (and the lack of accountability of patrons). It is that it is not enough for clients to collude—to declare their *wish* to bargain as a corporate group with the patron—they must somehow *organize* and put forward a representative to bargain with the patron. But this representative of the clients now has a qualitatively different position from the others, and indeed has an antisymmetric relationship with them (they pass up grievances, he passes down information). Accordingly, their relationship can easily slide into one of patronage (Powell 1970: 424; cf. Stokes 1995: 70, 112), and so the challenge to the system is easily absorbed simply by incorporating one new patron. Patronage structures, then, tend not to break down due to the destruction of the position of the patron by uprising clients. Instead, breakdown is more likely occur from what seems to be an enthusiastic endorsement of the principles of patronage than it is from a spirited rejection. If it is so good to have a patron, why not have more than one?

MULTIPLE PATRONS

There are a fair number of cases in which clients attempt to better their position by having more than one patron, though these tend to be cases in which the relationship is "weak" in that the obligations on the parties are neither onerous nor inescapable.[48] Wolf (1977: 175; cf. Kettering 1986: 75) suggests that such weak patronage is likely to occur where the society's institutional structure is

---

[48] One strange exception is the Hutu-Tutsi case, where clients supposedly could have more than one patron by assigning different sons to perform the required duties (Mair 1977: 144).

"far flung and solidly entrenched"—where no coherent patronage structures can exist independent of the formal structure of the society, but neither can that formal structure be totally aligned with the structure of patronage (as can unilineal descent groups, as we recall). In such cases, patronage degenerates to "sponsorship," for what the patron provides is access to important nodes in the formal structure of the society.[49]

A good example of this is the Roman republic: the structure of patronage relationships was of vital importance, but there were too many contrasting and overlapping arenas for it to be rationalized. Accordingly, it was possible for clients to have more than one patron, though the ideal was exclusivity (Saller 1989: 53; Taylor 1968: 42; this was also on occasion true in Greece; see Kagan 1987: 299;[50] also see the sophisticated discussion of Johnson and Dandeker 1989: 231). This form of patronage as sponsorship was also crucial to the Italian city-states from the Renaissance to the early modern period (on renaissance Florence see McLean 1998). Frequently the "patronage" that is spoken of by political scientists, although an umbrella term for almost all deviations from the universalistic prescriptions of democratic theory, refers to cases of such sponsorship when it does not simply indicate a spoils system.

Such examples of sponsorship may be analytically considered a "degeneration" of the pure form of patronage, but this is not necessarily historically true.[51] However, a real breakdown of the one patron rule is seen in our chief example of European feudalism. When feudalism first developed in Europe, it was clear that no vassal could serve more than one lord—"a thing which is not pleasing to God," in the words of one twelfth-century writer. Yet by the turn of the tenth century, at least in the west of Francia, this had already become possible (Bloch 1961 [1940]: 211; Ganshof 1964: 31, 49; Fourquin 1976: 128),[52] and by the twelfth century was common throughout Europe. This was inherently problematic, as any tendency toward factionalization could leave

---

[49] The shift from patronage to sponsorship is associated with an increased ambiguity in the nature of the relationship and, dually, a decreased structural clarity (see Silver [2002]). There is also decreased clarity when there are two semi-independent hierarchies, as in the case of France discussed in note 39, or in medieval Japan in which there were both ties of vassalage and a second set of relationships pertaining to landholding (the *shoen* system) and tied to the imperial court (Ikegami 1995: 80, 121f)

[50] While the citizens of the democratic city-states such as Athens in the classical age generally did not have formal patrons, they often had sponsors, and in Athens, the metics–free noncitizens, often immigrants from other Greek cities or freed slaves–were required to have a citizen as a *prostates*, who would mediate between them and political institutions (Millett 1989: 34).

[51] For example, in Japan the samurai at first had multiple samurai patrons, a relation of vassalage separate from the relation some had as clients of the aristocracy (Ikegami 1995: 78f, also 123).

[52] Of course, as Fourquin (1976: 116) points out, serf-master relations by nature remained "one patron."

the vassal with divided loyalties. As Fourquin (1976: 128) says, "To be the vassal of several was really to be the vassal of none."

Some considered resolutions were to simply prohibit a fief-holder from inheriting an additional fief, to favor the patron from whom one received the largest benefice or to have all relationships save the first explicitly undertaken with a proviso that they could not upset earlier pledges (Critchley 1978: 23; Ganshof 1964: 102f).[53] But the most successful resolution—and that which became the dominant form of feudalism in France, England, and Italy—was "liegancy": one lord, the "liege lord," had priority over the others. From the others, one could accept benefices and give conditional support, but never unconditional support that might lead to conflict with the interests of the liege lord. This resolution more or less simply re-created the patron-client relation under a new name, and since the conditions remained unchanged, it is not surprising that before too long, there were cases in which vassals took more than one liege lord (Bloch 1961 [1940]: 217; Ganshof 1964: 103f; Fourquin 1976: 129); the same attempts to resolve contradictions began again.[54]

This change probably came from a slow transformation from the basic structural unit being a warlord and his direct dependents in an anarchic situation to being a privileged person in a protostate.[55] While one can only serve one master in battle, one can have more than one sponsor. This shift to sponsorship, as we see in the next chapter, is often associated with the monetarization of relations, as in what is often called "bastard feudalism" in England (here also see the discussion of Kettering [1986: 207–10]).

Even where clients may not hold multiple patrons at the same time, it has been suggested that they can play off one patron against another if there is the possibility of exchanging one for another. This may be true (for example, see Fourquin 1976: 132; and Kettering 1986: 21, 28), although it is easy to mistak-

---

[53] Such careful agreements were found where a lord pledged support of a prince with reservations so that this agreement did not contradict previously existing vassalage. Thus when Robert II, count of Flanders, made a treaty with Henry I of England in 1101, he agreed to support Henry except against the king of France (Philip), to whom he had pledged fealty. He would attempt to dissuade Philip from attacking England, but only by "supplication" and not by undue influence or bad council (Contamine 1998 [1980]: 49).

[54] Similarly, the particular relationships underlying feudalism (the linkage of the granting of a benefice to the vow of fealty) also broke down when vassals were able to alienate fiefs that in some sense were not theirs to alienate, most profitably by subenfoeffment but also by sale (Fourquin 1976: 157). While such acts were outlawed in England in 1290, the new law simply led to more complex ways of allowing multiple claims on the product of certain property (Critchley 1978: 20). The underlying tendency, probably a result of the increasing power of vassals due to the continuous appropriation of benefices, could not be suppressed by legislation.

[55] For example, Bean (1989: 236) argues that in late medieval England we can see a shift from "lordship" to "patronage," meaning a shift from what the lord offers the client is his own wealth to one in which it is his ability to sponsor.

enly assume that the mere existence of patron-patron conflict will empower clients (e.g., Wolf 1977: 174). Patrons can compete *using* clients without necessarily competing *for* clients, and even when clients have the ability to reject one patron in order to take up another, this does not necessarily increase their bargaining power. This increased power of clients arises only if the supply of clients is limited and their support necessary.

Consequently, patrons facing competition for clients can respond by attempting to recruit new members to the system as a whole. There is some reason to believe that the extension of Roman citizenship was spurred by the desire of patrons to enlarge their retinues. If all those in some area granted citizenship can be expected to swear fealty to the patron in charge, this patron will benefit dramatically from their political inclusion, and this might explain the "democratic" leanings of many popular military leaders (see Taylor 1968: 22, 46f; Wallace-Hadrill 1989: 78f).[56] In sum, allowing for multiple patrons will push a pyramid toward a web structure; empowering the clients so that an effective competition takes place will probably push a pyramid toward a multihub structure, though the mere fact of competition between patrons does not itself produce the establishment of horizontal patron-patron ties of alliance (which we examine in chapter 8).

TRANSFORMATION INTO COMMAND STRUCTURE

The final way that patronage structures can be obliterated is somewhat different, for the structure seems on the surface to be unchanged, and this is by the elimination of the principle of mediation, and its replacement with transitivity. Mediation means that those at the top often have the de facto responsibility for supporting those a few rungs down, but have no control over them. The great strength of patronage structures is this very weakness—because of the lack of transitivity, relationships can be concatenated to make large structures in a way that the other relationships we have examined cannot. But members of large and weak structures have received little in the way of a guarantee that the structural principles involved will not be changed.

In particular, and not surprisingly, a change from mediation to transitivity is often pushed for on the part of those at the top of the structure, and is resisted by those in the middle. If accomplished, the patronage triangle has become what I will call a *command tree*. This process is historically of the greatest importance, for it may be that what we call government originates in patronage relationships (cf. Mair 1977: 141), but involves the substitution of transitive command relations for antitransitive patronage relations.

---

[56] For example, Caesar enfranchised the Transpadane region, inflating the number of citizens by as much as 50%, "and making the new citizens his personal clients" (Taylor 1968: 173).

Large modern states do many things—they deliver mail, inspect meat, hand out passports, manage forests, and so on. But as sets of social structures they vary from other forms of government most notably in the ways in which we find large numbers of commoners mobilized, namely the army and the party. We go on to examine how these structures emerge via the imposition of transitivity into previously intransitive patronage pyramids.

7

The Institution of Transitivity and the Production of Command Structures

Why Hierarchy?

Structures for Command

We began by noting the admiration that early sociologists had for the vast social structures that were able to coordinate large numbers of persons in the service of what appeared to be social level functions. Some of these—for example, the ability to pursue large-scale warfare on land—were clearly related to the rise of the modern state (see Arrow 1974: 69). Our task was to determine to what extent we could shed light on where these structures came from. In chapter 5, we examined tree structures and found that they possessed a number of properties making them useful for coordinating such actions. In chapter 6, we saw that such structures tended to emerge in environments of inequality. Or, rather, we saw the emergence of structures that were *nearly* the same as those investigated in chapter 5. The patronage pyramid takes on much of the same structural form as the tree more commonly understood, but it lacks the transitivity that is required of a command tree.

Such command trees—or at least ones that approximate this form—are indeed used to pass down commands in organizations across a number of domains. In particular, trees are found both in management and in military structures (cf. Fukuyama and Shulsky 1997: 1), two arenas that are easily seen as meeting important social functions (making and taking stuff respectively). While it is easy to exaggerate the similarity between the two (especially given the penchant for capitalists to understand their competition in martial terms), there is indeed a common problem that the tree structure solves in both cases, and this is control (also see Simmel 1950 [1908]: 206f; Van Fleet and Yukl 1986: 18).

Control is facilitated by the structural principles of the tree: that subordinates have only one superordinate, and superordinates may have more than one subordinate. First, this ensures clarity of control by avoiding multiple subordination. Second, it allows superordinates to maximize the "span of control" (the number of persons who can be kept under control by the top). Third, it allows superordinates to increase their control by concentrating information that is sent upward (Feld 1959: 19). The importance of the tree structure for the project of control can be seen by simply imagining the likely results of an inverted tree structure for some management hierarchy (a vision Henry [1954: 141] calls "horrifying to specialists in industrial organization"). Even if the relationships involved were unchanged, the structure would tend to devolve control to the lower ranks as opposed to concentrating it in the highest.[1]

Tree structures are thus useful for those at the top of some hierarchy, but as we shall see, there is no justification for the fervent belief in their overall efficiency, a belief often used to explain their existence. Control is not the same thing as efficiency in reaching some instrumental goal. But in any case, fitness explains survival, not origin: where do these tree structures come from? Focusing on the development of military organization, I will argue that command trees can best be analytically understood as the result of a three-stage process. In the first, patronage triangles form. In the second, a pyramidal structure is formed by the concatenation of these triangles. In the third, some form of transitivity is imposed on the previously intransitive pyramid. While this is by no means a universally valid story explaining every case, it is relatively close to the historical account for the development of many important armed forces, and more important, it may still correctly point to the structural tendencies and tensions of a command hierarchy.

Multidivision Firms

It would certainly be simpler if rather than trace the historical development of command trees, we could demonstrate their efficiency, and then propose that we tend to see such structures since other, less efficient, structures will be selected out. This argument was made most famously by Oliver Williamson for the case of firms. The archetypal large company has a social structure that has two characteristics. First, it has a treelike structure of supervision and authority. Second, it has a multidivisional structure, with the subunits having at least on paper a certain degree of independence. The question then is: Why do firms take on the particular structure that they do? We will briefly consider the second feature and then turn to the first.

Why would a firm have several semi-independent branches—why would each branch not be a firm of its own? Building on classic work by Coase, Williamson (1981a; 1981b; 1985; also see Arrow 1974: 33) has attempted to understand the nature of the firm in terms of market failure: where transaction costs are likely to be so high that a transaction beneficial to both parties will not be conducted via market exchange, there is incentive to restructure the firm so that the exchanging units are part of the same organization.[2] Exchanges that

---

[1] In the 1980s there was a fad called "matrix management" whereby people would have two or more supervisors. The near-total abandonment of this anomalous approach is consonant with the claims made here.

[2] Williamson (1981a: 553) defines these as the costs of moving goods or services across a technologically separable interface.

would not clear a market will successfully occur within the firm. While as Douglass North (1981: 41) has pointed out, this idea of hierarchy entering to solve problems of market failure is historically backward (since hierarchies preexisted markets), it may still be an analytically useful scheme.

This approach has, however, come for a lot of hard treatment for its circular nature: one can always find *something* that seems to explain why a firm is rational in some circumstance (see Davis 1986: 149). Since the conditions that lead to such market failures include bounded rationality (which is what we have by definition of being human) and opportunism (which is what economists assume by postulate), and evaluating the contribution of these two factors to any particular case rather subjective, it is hard to imagine that such an approach will give us much leverage in saying why in some cases we see markets and in other cases firms. A second criticism, more common among sociological circles, is that the claims are simply historically false. While Williamson (1985: 280) relies on Chandler's (1977) history of the multidivision (or "M") form, this history demonstrates that the crucial organizational issues revolved not around efficiency but around control (Fligstein 1990).

The development of the distributional infrastructure of the United States (most simply the rail and road system, but also the wholesale and retail structure) allowed for many commodities to be produced for a national market. To produce on such a scale, firms would have to increase in size. This led to an organizational dilemma: treating a large firm like a small one with upper-level managers attempting to control everything led to too much information overloading a few persons, while treating it as a looser holding company meant a loss of control (see Chandler 1966: 382f, 154). The resolution of this dilemma—that of control, not of efficiency—was the development of a diversified managerial structure.

Indeed, Freeland's (2001) reanalysis of the development of the hierarchy in General Motors leads to drastically different conclusions. He argues that the actual management structure of GM was changed continually in response to a constant struggle between owners and top-level managers. In contrast to the ideal put forward by Chandler as the efficient solution, the key innovations by Alfred P. Sloan (who became president in 1923) involved violations of the distinction between overall strategy managed by the center and tactics devolved to divisions—instead, he worked to bring division heads into the decision-making process and "sell" them on strategic decisions. If divisions could not be convinced, Sloan would attempt compromise; if compromise failed he was often inclined to let them have their way, apparently reasoning that an enthusiastic effort at a second-rate plan was better than a sullen effort at a first-rate one. When, after Sloan's retirement, GM did move to an M-form division between strategic and tactical planning in 1958, just as Sloan feared, this destroyed the good will of the divisions and led to a cycle of increasingly dictatorial control from the general office and increasing resistance from the divisions. Freeland (2001: 295, 297) thus finds the M-form not to be the natural equilibrium reached when competition forces large firms to be efficient, but a form that maximizes owner control, whether or not it is efficient.

Now Williamson (1985: 288, 273, 392f, 236) did not deny the importance of control, nor even that the new form of organization required, as Fligstein (1990) emphasized, a new cultural conception of control.[3] Further, he admits that other factors such as "the quest for monopoly gains" and "the imperatives of technology" contribute to "vertical integration," or the unification with one's suppliers and/or distributors into a single firm. He simply maintains—on faith, it seems—that these are secondary and that "mistaken" vertical integration will rarely be sustained and should be replaced by a more efficient form. But as Oberschall and Leifer (1986: 246) pointed out, socialized property in the Soviet Union did not get institutionalized because it was the best way to decrease transaction costs—it was institutionalized on the basis of political power. One may reply that the Soviet Union was not a market-based economy where less efficient forms can be expected to be weeded out. But if the applicability of Williamson's argument to any case depends on factors in the economic environment (the larger economy in the case of the individual firm, the international economy in the case of the Soviet Union), then the focus on transaction costs is incomplete. Transaction costs are not determined by the simple factors that Williamson discusses, but the texture of the organizational environment.

The comparison of the multidivision firm to state socialism made by Oberschall and Leifer is particularly apt. What is so interesting about the structure of control within a multidivision firm, in which the central decisions regarding relations between subparts must be carried out in terms of costs, not profits, is that it well describes interfirm transactions in Russian-style state socialism. (As Lindblom [1977] stressed, it was interfirm transactions, rather than consumer or even labor markets that state socialism attempted to replace with authoritative direction from the center). Lenin (1932 [1917]: 84) had argued that in socialism, the whole society would be an enormous factory. While this was not quite accurate, it might not have been wrong to say that it was an enormous corporation. Similar conditions—the paradox of (on the one hand) unified ownership (which forbids pricing of transfers to be set by an antagonistic market process) and (on the other) the need for coordinated production (which militates against a mere conglomerate)—led to similar structures both in Russia and in large corporations involving the replacement of market transactions with authoritative direction. This replacement came about not because of technical problems but because of political power.[4]

[3] "The conglomerate form of organization," wrote Williamson, "whereby the corporation consciously took on a diversified character and nurtured its various parts, evidently required a conceptual break in the mind-set of Sloan and other pre-war leaders."

[4] Interestingly, Williamson (1981a: 567) was happy to recognize the important part played by power and to admit that it can cut against "efficiency"–but only when it was the power of workers. According to his logic, unions should only appear where the "asset specificity" of workers is high,

In sum, we have a hard time understanding the reasons for the multidivisional structure of modern firms by treating it as the most efficient way of organizing units making exchanges (more efficient than them being in separate firms, that is). But really, the units within firms do not necessarily exchange anything at all. We have seen in chapter 3 the tendency of theorists to confuse transfers with exchange; along these lines, Williamson failed to see that the distinctive nature of the M-form is not in facilitating exchange, but in ordering transfers. Thus a shop might make machined stainless steel discs whether or not it is a member of a multidivision firm. But it is the multidivision firm that forces this shop to give these discs to another shop, without anything coming from that second shop in return.[5] In other words, the firm may be seen as involving the fundamental relation of transfer, yet the structure comes from a different relation, namely *authority* (cf. Arrow 1974: 64). This brings us to the first characteristic of firm structure, namely the arrangement of persons in hierarchies.

The Wheel of Fortune

We have seen that the contours of firms were drawn not to maximize efficiency, but to maximize control. What about the more fundamental issue of the presence of hierarchy? Can this be explained by efficiency considerations?

In unashamed and heated dialogue with Marxists who claimed that production should be organized cooperatively, Williamson (1975: 46) had earlier argued that truly cooperative decision making among workers would require an "all channel" network (a clique in the terms used here) in which each person was connected to every other (figure 7.1, left).

Since the number of "channels" grows as the square of the number of persons, Williamson was sure that "reorganizing from the all-channel to wheel network [figure 7.1, right] and assigning responsibility to specific access rules [i.e. what goes on] to whichever member occupies the position in the center avoids the need for full group discussion with little or no sacrifice in the quality of the decision." Williamson regretfully adds that it is unlikely that all could

meaning that workers tend not to be easily replaceable. But indeed unions are frequently found where one would expect more of a "spot" labor market. Williamson argues that "these outcomes are driven more by power than by efficiency considerations. Employers in these circumstances will thus be more inclined to resist unionization; successful efforts to achieve unionization will often require the assistance of the political process; and, since power rather than efficiency is at stake, the resulting governance structure will be relatively primitive." It is far from obvious why workers can successfully pull down the power of the state to lead to outcomes that deviate from efficiency in their interests, but owners and managers cannot.

[5] While M-forms frequently attempt to create internal prices to introduce a semblance of exchange, these are largely fictional since the central authority still determines the exchange rates. It is only when prices are fixed to match those of external suppliers of comparable products that one might be able to analyze the transactions in terms of exchange.

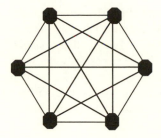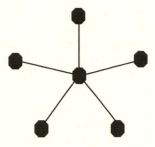

Figure 7.1. Clique versus wheel

take turns being the center, since the important skills required are probably not to be had by all. Thus hierarchy (somewhat disguised by the bird's eye view of the "wheel") is derived from simple issues of communicative efficiency (also see Arrow 1974: 68f).

Yet as Williamson should have known, the structure on the left has been demonstrated to have certain advantages for decision making, including the speed with which complex decisions can be made (here see Shaw 1964, especially 117, 119). Centralized structures turn out to be good for some tasks, especially simple ones, but poor for others (and they seem to discourage collective learning). Any general assumptions about the inferiority of cliques to wheels are certainly false.[6] What is the relation between structure and efficiency of decision making, then? It is surprising, but almost all of our supposed knowledge on this matter comes from highly artificial experiments; very few people have examined actual decision-making groups and determined what their structure was and how it was related to their success or failure.

While it is beyond the bounds of this work to provide results along these lines, as an example, I take what I believe to be the single best example of a decision that was an unimpeachable success and is well documented; this is the decision regarding how the United States should respond to the discovery that the Soviet Union was deploying nuclear missiles in Cuba. That the decision was a stunning success cannot be doubted; the range of possible outcomes to be avoided went from thermonuclear war to a serious decrease in the collective security of the United States to a loss of domestic power to "hawks." While not all will agree as to the relative weights placed by the Kennedy administration on these goals, these are the backdrop for our evaluation. In an extremely tense environment, the decision made achieved all of the desired goals. How was the group that made this decision organized?

It was a deliberately nonhierarchical and nonstructured group, lacking even a chair to "facilitate" discussion (Kennedy 1969: 24; Allison and Zelikow

---

[6] For a formalization of certain conditions in which the star network is the only equilibrium, see Goyal and Vega-Redondo (2005). For a different formalization, see Dodds, Watts, and Sabel (2003).

1999: 347).[7] It was, in other words, the exact opposite of the structure William-son declared to be most "efficient" for making decisions. There is not one most efficient structure: the structure that is best suited to making a single, momentous decision (given time for deliberation) is not necessarily the same as that which is best for making innumerable relatively trivial ones, nor is it necessarily the same as the one best suited for making decisions in less than a minute (Wilensky 1967: 75ff).[8] A generic defense of hierarchy as efficient is wholly foolish.

What *is* known about hierarchy from the simple laboratory experiments is not that it is invariably efficient but that the person in the center enjoys his or her role very much, and the people at the spokes do not like their job at all (Leavitt 1951; Glanzer and Glaser 1961: 5, 13). In fact, it seems quite plausible that if some person had the choice of either participating in a more efficient egalitarian structure that gave him an enjoyment of 65.6 (to use a real number from a psychological study, though one with no particular meaning), or to participate in a less efficient one that gave him an enjoyment of 97 and every-one else an enjoyment of 31.2, he would "rationally" choose the latter. If he had resources to force this choice on others, it would be rational for him, though it would lead to a collective decrease in utility.

Analyzing the rise of hierarchy in the factory system in British textiles, Mar-glin (1974; 1975) emphasized that analysts and apologists had confused the undeniable increase in output of the factory system with its *efficiency*. By no stretch of the mind could it be demonstrated that intensive factory production was efficient in any standard economic sense. For this to be true, it would require that workers who had other options would find that they, too, could maximize their overall utilities by switching from nonfactory work to factory work. But we know that in most cases, when they had other options, no matter how poorly remunerated, they would decline factory labor. Indeed, the first factories were "manned" not by men with other options, but by women and pauper children— virtual slaves—whose labor was rented to others for the benefit of third parties (this point is stressed by Landes [1986: 594] in his rebuttal to Marglin). Far from being analyzable in terms of internal exchange, hierarchy arose precisely *because* relying on market relations was disadvantageous to elites.

In other words, hierarchies are effective, often brutally so, and *effective* is not the same as *efficient*. Hierarchies can arise where markets are efficient and some people are unhappy with their efficiency because it costs them too much;

---

[7] John F. Kennedy, and, when the president was not in attendance, Robert F. Kennedy, had a special role in guiding the meetings, though neither used this role to silence others' opinions. More important, the president did not attend regularly, allowing participants to speak without trying to second-guess what he would like to hear and allowing them change their opinions or criticize others without fearing a loss of face (Kennedy 1969: 9, 11, 23).

[8] In particular, Cerulo (2006: 193, 218–21, 225, 230) argues that treelike control structures are more likely to have "positive asymmetries" in their decisions–that is, to assume best-case scenar-ios and ignore the worst–while web-type "service structures" tend toward negative asymmetry.

further, it is the effective, and not the efficient, organization that will tend to survive.[9] Markets, especially labor markets, require vast institutional supports whereby elites are prevented from muscling workers into doing what they want (Fligstein 2001). The wolfonomics that confuses profit with efficiency works by drawing the boundary of the system so that workers' utilities are ignored and comes to conclusions as silly as any other partial view (e.g., the economics that considers thievery the most efficient production because the profit is so high). And this partiality is important because it is the theoretical counterpart to the structure of hierarchy. As Fukuyama and Shulsky (1997: 7) have emphasized, the hierarchical enterprise of the classic vertical organization was predicated on the assumption that individual workers could not and should not be assumed to possess internal motivation to do well, but since "it was assumed that they were motivated by relatively simple economic incentives," they could be controlled and channeled into doing what was wanted. In other words, hierarchy is an effective logic of control when one assumes—and perhaps enforces—a division of mental and manual labor, of command and obedience, just what Williamson tried to derive.

Now Williamson's context was a discussion of peer group organization of labor as opposed to hierarchy—he was not (explicitly, at any rate) attempting an apology for capitalism, inequality, or anything else academics in 1971 were likely to treat with suspicion. Yet because he, like most other economic theorists, assumed for heuristic purposes that we begin with equal persons competing in markets, he missed the actual reasons for hierarchical organization of labor, some of which we have seen in the last chapter. Real command structures begin with unequal persons, of whom those with more power attempt to control those with less. Only from this starting point can we derive structure.

Hierarchy and Control

It is, in other words, somewhat simple-minded to insist that hierarchy arises when it is efficient, since hierarchy is about control. But why does the project of control imply multilayered tree structures? The answer usually is that there

[9] Because rampant Panglossianism is often confused with economics, a thought experiment helps. Imagine a pure labor market which is completely efficient; some firm has exchange relations with N independent workers of some form who together add x total value to some existing capital expenditure and are compensated y; the schedule of x and y arises on the basis of the demand for this type of labor, the disutility and opportunity costs of the work, and the number of workers. Brought into a hierarchy (e.g., slavery) and compelled to work harder for less *cannot* be efficient (we know the efficiency price of their labor from the pure market is different), but the organization that has values $x^* > x$ and $y^* < y$ will tend to be selected for. One may assimilate this to the wide class of cases in which firms profit from externalities leading to a divergence of profit maximization from collective utility maximization. Note that this structure may be technically inefficient as well as economically inefficient: it may produce less per input energy because it externalizes the cost of producing some of its inputs. Thus an inefficient technology can replace a more efficient one if the producers are not required to replenish all inputs at their cost prices.

are two conflicting tendencies that attenuate the strength of control in a social structure.

To derive these, consider "control" an antisymmetric dyadic relationship: if A controls B, B cannot control A. Control involves three things: direction, surveillance, and sanction. That is, A must be able to give B some set of pre-scriptions or proscriptions regarding B's action. But A must also be able to tell what B is actually doing. Finally, A must be able to exert some control over B's future such that B has a proximate interest in complying with A's directives.

It is reasonable to expect that the project of control requires a certain amount of time and effort. While this time and effort per person may decrease as the number of persons controlled increases (and so it is not necessarily five times as difficult for A to control ten people as it is to control two), still, the relation between change in number of persons controlled and change in amount of effort required can be assumed always to be positive. If there is some minimum amount of control required by any underling, then past some point, each addi-tional subordinate decreases the ability of A to control her underlings (compare the discussion of Hechter 2000: 41). While the efficiency of control is therefore a continuous quality of (past some point) diminishing returns to each additional subordinate, we often consider A's "span of control" to be the number of subor-dinates she can control without obviously losing control.

It might be expected that because of the costs of the span of control, people will form structures with small triangles. But if we are trying to link up T total people in a command structure, the smaller the span of control, the more levels the structure will involve. And each level requires an additional transmission of a directive from the top. That is, A must transmit his directive to B, who transmits it to C, etc. Each one of these links allows for the possibility of a loss of control. A good control structure, then, is one that works out a reason-able trade-off between the span of control and the number of levels. But there are three complications that prevent those interested in control from simply determining the perfect structure using some formula (Williamson [1967] pro-posed an elegant approach to determining such formulae).

The first is the influence of the environment. In a nutshell, some environ-ments are less predictable than others, and the less predictable the environment, the more freedom of movement subordinates generally need (van Creveld 1985: 269). In fact, it may make sense for the "controller" to refrain from giving directives at all (since she or he may not know enough about the local conditions faced by a subordinate), but instead simply offer an incentive struc-ture to reward successful performance (the simplest being that failure leads to being fired or executed).[10] One will note that this is basically the exact contrary

---

[10] This was the general approach of the Qing dynasty in China–because the empire was too big to manage from the center given the surveillance and communications technologies of the day, the emperor instead concentrated on ascertaining who had succeeded and who had failed and apportioning rewards and punishments accordingly (Yeung 2006).

of Williamson's scenario: here, bounded rationality provokes moving *away* from hierarchy and *toward* markets.

The second complication comes from the need for relationships other than control. Supervisors do not only need to control and watch subordinates, they also need information. Should they try to construct a completely independent structure for gathering information, or should they attempt to weld this function onto the command structure? There are certainly efficiencies in attempting to have the same social structure do more than one thing, but the best structure for *implementing* decisions is generally not the best structure for *making* decisions. In particular, one can often trust one's closest associates to comprehend and carry out one's instructions but, because of this very closeness, they are likely to be poor at bringing to light information or possibilities that one has not thought of (see especially Wilensky 1967). Further, the relationships used for surveillance cannot unproblematically be used for sanction: If we ask someone to "get me a stick to beat you with," we are likely to get a very slender branch indeed.[11]

The third complication comes from the genesis of structures. It is all very well on paper to derive the perfect structure. But as we have seen, large structures are generally composed of preexisting smaller elements. These elements may do exactly as expected when aggregated, or they may not. To understand the production of command structures, we would do well to consider how they are produced from such smaller units, and how they adapt to the problems of combining other functions with command in environments that may vary unpredictably. The best example of a structure of interpersonal command relationships faced with uncontrollable features of the environment is probably the command structure of armed forces. Thus we can understand the development of command hierarchies by studying the development of armies; at the same time, since command armies were a key social structure of the modern state, we can start to answer the questions with which we began.

Armed Force and Command Hierarchy

The Need for Obedience

> For there is nothing *in War* which is of *greater importance*
> *than obedience*.
> —von CLAUSEWITZ, *On War*

Not all collective violence is perpetrated by armies. Armies are large, long-lasting, social structures that aim to coordinate persons so as to increase their potential to harm others. In many times and places, collective violence is either

---

[11] This point was made by Bill Cosby.

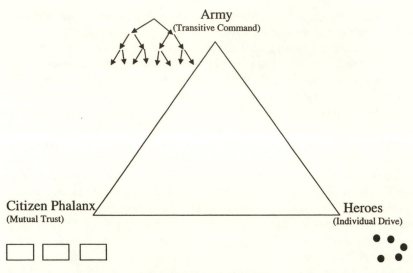

Figure 7.2. Ways of fighting

not coordinated at all, or takes place through the simple coordination of clumping. In the warfare of the Homeric times, perhaps few individuals were heroes, but all heroes were individuals—that is, fighting was conducted by persons usually fighting side by side, but as individuals (for other examples, see Parker 1996: 130; Hanson 2001: 315f). In other cases, citizens of a small city-state armed themselves for defense and tended to form tightly assembled groups— often dense squares—and relied on their preexisting social solidarity to wage a stubborn resistance to often superior forces. Classic examples are the Greek hoplites (Adcock 1967; Garlan 1995) or their analogues in twelfth- and thirteenth-century Northern Europe (McKinley 1934).

These possibilities parallel those we uncovered in chapter 2 regarding simple emphases of organization (see figure 7.2). In heroic warfare, it is the individual that organizes action, and hence there is little organization beyond the *differentiation* of individuals into more or less heroic. In the citizen phalanx, relationships of mutual trust produce the same sort of clique structure that we found to be the objective correlative to mutual relationships. But these relationships are *dependent* on preexisting relationships of co-membership in other groups. The army, in contrast, by emphasizing transitivity, requires an organization that binds triads together into a treelike form.[12] In particular, the army, at least in its fully developed state, is distinguished by the layers of officers who do not themselves fight, analogous to managers who do not work, but command.

---

[12] Thus the emphasis on transitivity parallels some of the organizational principles that have been associated with *involution*, although this is only a limited parallel.

In the previous chapter, we saw the emergence of patronage pyramid structures that had the ability to span social inequalities and bring many different persons into a single connected set of relationships. Since the relationship in question revolved around reciprocal (though distinct and not necessarily complimentary) obligations, such structures are rather workable ways of passing surplus up or down a vertical divide. But this does not mean that they necessarily are good at passing down commands. First of all, clients may have obligations to support patrons, but they generally do not have obligations to obey whatever command the patron might happen to make. But even if they did, the structure's intransitivity makes it a poor vehicle for commands. To bring the whole pyramid into play, one must command one's clients "come out with all your clients to support me, and command your clients to bring their clients, and command your clients to command their clients to bring their clients, and command your clients to command their clients to command their clients to bring their clients," etc.[13]

There is something clearly awkward about such a scheme. A command structure cannot rely on such mediated relationships if it is to be used to coordinate actions. And such coordination is implied if social aggression is carried out through armies as opposed to citizen phalanxes or heroic warriors. The idea-typical tree structure derived above, while generally not realized to completion in actually existing armies, is far from an arbitrary construction of the theorist, for there is a powerful selective mechanism favoring those structures that implement its principles (see Weber [1978] on organizational selection; Andreski [1968: 38, 92] for the case of war).

Most forms of weaponry (especially those that involve projectiles such as arrows or bullets), and nearly all forms of defensive armaments, are more effective if coordinated, and soldiers who run off to loot are easier to defeat than those who remain alert in formation. Consequently, effective armies generally require that soldiers obey first and foremost (for cases in the Middle Ages, see Contamine 1998 [1980]: 236; Downing 1992: 60; Prestwich 1996: 137, 179f). Soldiers, however, may not particularly wish to risk life and limb

---

[13] This exaggerated scenario was often approximated to some extent in feudal practice, since a summons of the king to a lord was often to come out himself and to bring at least some of those men who owed him fealty. For example, the Norman lords had obligations of military service that included the number of men at arms they would bring. To meet this quota, they might use their own household knights or fief-holders—in other words, the pyramid of which they were the apex. The Domesday book makes clear that at least in some places in England, the king called those lords not vassals of others, these (who had no intermediate between the king and themselves) would forfeit all their lands if they did not come. But those who were vassals of some other lord would only be fined forty shillings. It was obviously assumed that their mobilization was in the hands of their own lord, pointing to some degree of assumed transitivity. But this sort of rigor and control owed much to the particularities of the Norman conquest, which left a clear set of nested obligations leading up to the king (Beeler [1966] 1995: 265f; Fourquin 1976: 122; Contamine 1998 [1980]: 53; Powicke 1996 [1962]: 214; Prestwich 1996: 58–60; Mann 1986: 422).

in a cause that is rarely their own (see the nice discussion of O'Connell 1995: 113f). As a result, a social structure that can effectively transmit commands and ensure their being carried out increases the probability of military success. Or as the soon-to-be Roman emperor Otho explained to his soldiers in the civil wars after Nero's death, "It is by obeying, not by questioning the orders of commanders, that military power is kept together. And that army is the most courageous in the moment of peril, which is most orderly before the peril comes" (Tacitus, *History*, I: 84). While there are a number of reasons why less-efficient organizational forms can persist,[14] in general and over the long term, there is still a strong pressure pushing armies toward a structural form that maximizes the effectiveness of command (Lang 1972: 58; cf. Hanson 2005: 139). I go on to describe that structure, emphasizing its contribution to tactical success.[15]

Command Pyramid Structure

The U.S. Army is divided into three "teams" oriented around combat, combat support (which includes artillery and aviation), and service support (logistics and supply) (here I rely on Kaufman 1996: 35–38). Soldiers are assigned to twenty-one branches divided among these three. The principal unit is the division, which may be infantry, armored, or airborne (with a few variations on some of these types); two or more divisions are combined in a corps commanded by a lieutenant general. A division (commanded by a major general) normally consists of three brigades (each commanded by a colonel), each of which consists of up to three battalions (commanded by a lieutenant colonel). An infantry battalion normally consists of five companies, each commanded by a captain; each company generally consists of three or four platoons, each commanded by a lieutenant. Finally, a platoon consists of three or four squads, consisting of four to nine men, each commanded by a staff sergeant. The actual structure is somewhat more elaborated, as there may be fourteen ranks between a private and a general (Keegan 1988: 335).

This is a decent example of the current type of structure found in the portion of an army devoted to combat (though there are many complications, as

---

[14] Some inefficient organizational forms persist even in competitive environments because all competitors have them; this can be the case when the different competitors draw on the same experts or virtuosos to construct their organizations (cf. DiMaggio and Powell 1983). In the case at hand, common reliance on mercenaries can produce organizational isomorphism–convergence on a single organizational scheme (see Black 1991: 10)–whether or not this is a good form of organization. Further, armies with poor organization can still triumph as long as the country fielding the army is large enough to replace casualties with fresh troops and has the economic capacity to supply and deploy them.

[15] Tactics refers to winning the battle, and strategy to winning a war. The command structure is most notable for its contribution to the former.

well as other structures that have various degrees of connection with the combat structure). This structure can be seen, as a first approximation, as a tree in which higher levels pass down commands to multiple units at a lower level so as to coordinate their action. This is only a first approximation; we shall see some of the reasons why the actual social structures of preparation for conflict and for carrying out conflict differ from this plan. What is most striking, however, is not that there are deviations from this simple ideal structure, but that the same principles for the organization of armies recur persistently throughout history. These principles are as follows: first of all, the mass of soldiers fight because they are ordered to (as opposed to being inspired to prove their valor or win booty). Second, these soldiers are organized in some sort of hierarchy that can also be seen as nested subsets (the way three squads compose a platoon, four platoons a company, etc.). Third, the army is organized into semi-independent divisions. Fourth, major units (those at relatively high levels) are headed by specialized commanders who give orders, as opposed to leading by example. Fifth, at the highest levels a general staff coordinates the whole. Sixth, this staff combines the functions of information gathering with command.

Not all armies have had all of these features. Indeed, it may be said that they appear roughly cumulative in history, in that it seems harder to have the features later in the list without the earlier ones. Actual cases consequently appear to form a Guttman scale, in that there are many examples of armies (say) with the first four features but not the last two, while there are none with the last two but not the first four. Because the presence of all is necessary for the development of a modern command structure, and there are selective pressures that make such a structure a reasonable telos for the armies, we should pay attention to all when examining the construction of command structures.

OBEDIENCE

Weber (1978: 1149f) has stressed the difference between heroic warfare and modern rationalized warfare. While there are some serious problems with using his dichotomy to understand the rationalization of war in European history,[16] at the crudest level, the point is a reasonable one. The most fundamental division between groups of (almost always) men bent on hurting others is between those in which some have to obey and those in which obedience is not paramount. While I am treating most of the structural features as present or absent, the emphasis on obedience is the sine qua non for permanent armies, and hence will be found more or less everywhere. But it is not found everywhere to the same degree—the armed forces that we would consider the strong-

---

[16] I make this point in Martin (2005).

est have generally stressed this obedience more than did others, and these are
the same armies that have more of the other features of a command structure.
Thus the Roman recruit's oath was not simply to fight courageously or die
nobly or some such, it was to obey superiors and to carry out their orders
(Dodge 1995 [1891]: 49, 82f; Delbrück 1990 [1920]: 289). While other European armies had also generally considered it good that soldiers obey, the Romans enforced this with punishments that were "immediate and severe." In-
stant death was earned not only by treasonous behavior or desertion, but failure
to keep proper order in battle, leaving a post without permission, or simply
being out of the call of the trumpet.

HIERARCHICAL ORGANIZATION

The second major feature is the presence of some sort of hierarchical organization of command, with those at any level commanding more persons at a lower
level. As we have seen in chapter 5, the tree structure unites two ways of
speaking about hierarchy—hierarchy as vertical organization, and hierarchy
as nested sets of inclusion. Beyond a certain size, armies that are based on
obedience tend to be organized around such a structural principle. To continue
with the case of Rome, the army was organized in nested levels of ten. The
earliest armies were composed of 1000 men from each of the three tribes of
Rome, each tribe's men divided into ten centuries; cavalry was organized identically except the numbers reduced by a factor of 10 (Dodge 1995 [1891]: 36f;
Goldsworthy 1996: 13f, 34f; 2006: 193). Later, there were at least six distinct
levels ranging from the consul or praetor in charge of the army (there was
generally more than one) to the decurions (those in charge of 10 men).

As might be expected, the Roman army was rather more organized than
most premodern armies. But the basic structural principle is nearly universal
(though, as I shall emphasize below, it is not always clear how central this
structural principle was for organizing battle) (Simmel 1950 [1908]: 172f).
This "decimal organization" whereby the army is organized as a set of nested
groups of ten groups of ten organized into a hundred, ten hundreds organized
into a thousand, etc., is found in Genghis Kahn's army, which overran most of
Europe and Asia (Fletcher 1986: 29f; Keegan 1994: 204) and the earlier Kitan
army (McNeill 1982: 58f), the ancient Indian army (Srivastava 1985: 13, 97),[17]
very possibly Chinese armies in the "Warring States" period (decimal organization is discussed by Wei Liao-Tzu [Sawyer 1993: 245; Sawyer 2007: 244])

---

[17] Ten men were under a sergeant, 10 of these units under an *anusatîka*, and 10 of these (1000
men) under a *sahaoerika*, and 10 of these (10,000 men) under an *âyâtika*, in turn under orders of
the chief of infantry, the *mahâbalâdhyaksa*.

and the Japanese army of the seventh century (Farris 1995: 50),[18] the medieval Byzantine army[19] (*Praecepta Militaria*, I.1 McGeer 1995: 13, 203), the ancient Incan (de la Vega 1961 [c. 1609]: 18f), and quite possibly the medieval English army.[20] It is not the "ten-ness" of the structure that is important for us—rather, it is the adoption of a tree form that can be used to facilitate the coordination of multiple actions.

DIVISIONS

Past a certain size, however, armies become too big to carry out any unified actions no matter how well coordinated they are. As a result, there is a tendency for large armies to break up into semi-independent divisions (see Weigley [1967: 335, 386] and Demchak [1991: 72] on two cases of the introduction of divisions in the U.S. Army). As might be expected, the Roman system of largely independent legions provides the best example of such divisions among premodern armies (see Hanson 2001: 116), although it is possible that the ancient Assyrian army had similar subunits (see Mann 1986: 233).

In many senses the Roman structure survived the fall of the empire in that successor states used similar titles and organization schemes; indeed, actual legions might survive with little alteration in terms of their organization, uniforms, and weaponry for generations after their loss of all contact with Rome (Bachrach 1972: 41, 128). But the general devolvement of the scale of armies moved away from structures with real divisional independence. It was only in the late eighteenth to early nineteenth century that European armies again organized themselves around divisions (Wilson 1999: 200; Ward 1957: 162f; Fuller 1955: 414; Parker 1996: 150; Lynn 1984: 252).

Thus far, we have seen armies that consist of multiple semi-independent divisions that take the form of hierarchies that pass down commands. These structures are not only hierarchical in the sense of being vertical, they are hierarchical in the set-theoretic sense of being nested relations of proper inclusion—in other words, no person has more than one commander at any level. Such a hierarchical structure makes true command *possible*, but not all hierarchies have what we should call true commanders.

---

[18] Ten men formed a squad (*ka*), five squads formed a platoon (*tai*), and two platoons a company (*ryo*).

[19] *Dekarchs* were placed over 10 men, *pentekontarchs* over 50, and *hekatontarchs* over 100, all part of a larger unit of 1,000 soldiers known as a taxiarchy or chiliarchy.

[20] Most medieval armies moved away from geometrically organized command structures, if only because the important part of the army had no one to command, being composed of gentlemen knights. The English army, however, had more organization: it might be divided into three or four large chunks or "battles," each consisting of three or four ranks, and infantry were organized into units of twenties (led by a vintenar) and hundreds (led by a mounted constable) (Contamine 1998 [1980]: 229f; Prestwich 1996: 48f, 60f, 127f, 160).

COMMAND AS OPPOSED TO LEADERSHIP

This point may at first seem strange to the modern reader. But throughout most of history, armies have generally been directed by *leaders* as opposed to *commanders* (cf. Keegan 1988: 61). A leader is someone who models behavior for followers; he is first in battle, directing others by example. This is famously seen in the Homerian heroes, as Weber (1978) noted, though later Greeks also considered it right that a general should fight with his men: a Greek leader in hoplite days was little more than a hoplite on the right wing with the dubious privilege of being the first to meet the enemy (Keegan 1988: 18; Hanson 2000 [1989]: 108–10). Even larger ancient armies were generally headed by leaders as opposed to commanders. As Keegan (1988: 81, 90) remarks of Alexander the Great, once he entered the fray, he lost any ability to command, and became one soldier among many (also see Delbrück 1990 [1920]: 232; Anderson 1970: 71; Hanson 2003: 235, 2005: 242; Adcock 1967: 6; Van Creveld 1985: 41).

A commander, in contrast, should be situated apart from the front lines, somewhere where he can survey the course of the battle and make adjustments by issuing orders. While a leader is often criticized for cowardice when he does not personally appear where the need is greatest (e.g., Varro at Cannae [Dodge 1995 (1891): 379]), commanders are criticized for doing just this, and jeopardizing success of the whole for their individual glory (e.g., Ney at the battle of Waterloo, whose actually picking up a musket and fighting was understood, says van Creveld [1985: 53], as "a clear sign of mental derangement"). In either case, the death of the chief can be catastrophic for the army, but in the case of the leader, his nonappearance at the front is itself deeply demoralizing (for examples, see Beeler [1995 (1966): 20]; Bury [1955 (1900): 625]).

Two factors tend to encourage the replacement of leaders with commanders.[21] The first is a reliance on surprise tactics. Where war revolved around quick forward and backward moves and encirclements by skilled horsemen, as in most central Asian, Turkish, and Arab armies, chiefs tended to command from the flanks or the rear, where they were more likely to see weaknesses in the enemy (Keegan 1988: 117). The second is a reliance on commoners, itself usually a result of an expansion of the size of armies. Conversely, as army sizes decline, leadership generally reemerges and the distinctiveness of the command function attenuates.

For example, with the devolution of the Roman Empire to medieval armies, there was a decrease in the development of the command structure. Indeed, only the absolute head was a true commander, since all others above the lowest

---

[21] This shift is seen in the West as early as the 4th century BC, where Xenophon stressed the importance of a commander ensuring his physical safety; someone had to be alive to send in the reserves (Hanson 2000 [1989]: 111; Keegan 1988: 120, cf. 331; also see *Praecepta Militaria* I.6, IV.17; McGeer 1995: 27, 49; and Goldsworthy 1996: 154f, 169).

ranks were knights who were obligated by codes of honor to fight (van Creveld 1985: 49f). And though there are cases in which kings held themselves apart from the battle,[22] this was not general practice (e.g., Beeler [1966] 1995: 274). More typical was the commander in chief leading the last of three major divisions (though see Contamine [1998 (1980): 236] for a caution against overstatement). With the larger early modern armies that, like the Romans, involved commoners bound by no honor code to fight of their own accord, leadership again receded and command rose to the fore of the chief's role (van Creveld 1985: 53; Feld 1977: 75; Keegan 1988: 122f).

With the great armies of the early nineteenth century, this change was largely complete. The best example of this is the Napoleonic wars, conducted as vast, wasteful conflicts of commoners directed by commanders standing on hills, looking downward at the battlefield as if it were a large game of chess. Commanders would still frequently appear at the front, whether to gather information about conditions, take charge of operations that were in disarray, or to inspire confidence; being a commander was far from a recipe for safety (Keegan 1988: 97, 99, 103, 116, 156, 303f; for an example, see Anderson 2000: 362f). But the large, hierarchical armies that require command to coordinate them also require commanders able to give these commands, and this gave rise to a new sense of duty—an obligation to shirk engagement with the enemy, which in turn decreased the possibility of exercising leadership (van Creveld 1991: 174). Thus the Duke of Marlborough wrote home in 1758, "I must do my duty as a general, keep clear of the smoke and consequently out of shot to see what is going on in order to give proper orders" (Black 1991: 40).

GENERAL STAFF

The hierarchical tree structure of nested tenths seems quite logical, and yet there is a potential conflict of interest for most commanders. On the one hand, looking upward, they are to allow themselves to be put at the disposal of the coordinating higher officers—they are to pass down orders, interpreting them in light of the current situation. But looking downward, they are the heads of units for which they have responsibility, and these units make claims on their leaders that interfere with the impartial orientation to the whole expected by the top layers. And, there are all the foibles of human nature: the desire to justify one's actions as opposed to giving evidence of mistakes, even if such evidence contains valuable information; the jealousy of others countermanding or questioning one's judgment; and the temptation to appropriate one's authorized power. For all these reasons, commanders-in-chief may move to develop

---

[22] In contrast to usual patterns of leadership in medieval Britain, Edward III set up headquarters at Crécy, Napoleon-style, in a windmill–a high point that allowed him to survey the battle (Prestwich 1996: 159, 181f). What he could do if he did not like what he saw, however, is unclear.

what is known as a general staff—a small command structure that mirrors the overall hierarchy but does not consist of people attached to specific units.

We get the term *general* for such higher-ups precisely because they were general: a major-general was equivalent to a major, but instead of being attached to a particular regiment, he served only the central command structure (though see Strachan 1984: 146). This simple issue of independence from attachment to a unit was a sufficiently important breakthrough that in Britain it was quite some time before there was any effort to *train* future members of this staff in any serious sense, though the Prussian general staff always emphasized some education in military history (Ward 1957: 25f, 31, 35; van Creveld 1985: 110f, 114). Despite the half-hearted nature of these starts—nineteenth century general staffs were tiny in comparison to those of today's armies—as well as the widely recognized powerlessness of the central command over much of what an army actually did, the general staff turned out to be an irreversible innovation. The reason lies largely in the integration of information and command it makes possible.

Those who have some idea of what they are talking about are likely to give better commands than those who do not. Hence it is quite reasonable that information should be sent to commanders. And as a rule, this is taken for granted: the same structure that is used to pass commands down is used to pass information up. As Feld (1977: 78; cf. Davis 1963: 46 for management) says, "To state it simply: the flow of commands is from superior to subordinate, the flow of information from subordinate to superior." But for this very reason, command structures tend to be problematic for the effective transmission of information. If information goes from subordinate to superior, lateral transmission is unlikely, for the person making the gift of information is as good as announcing his subordination. And relying on those whom one commands for information as to the extent to which they have carried out commands is rather like asking persons to write their own letters of recommendation.

As a result, there is a very good reason for the commander in chief to try to develop a specialized staff that can gather information on the state of subordinate units with some degree of independence from these units themselves (see, e.g., Weigley 1967: 322f). Once set up, this staff may be reintegrated with the command structure but retain independence from local units. Thus one has the ideal-typical command structure: from the top to the bottom, an efficient, hierarchically organized social structure that has a succession of commanders passing down directives to obedient soldiers. While not all armies move toward this polar position—as we have shall see, there are good reasons why many stop well before this point—those that do not develop a command structure are generally at a serious disadvantage compared to those that do, and hence heightened military competition can lead toward the evolution of command structures.

Evidence of Selective Pressures: The Case of the Spanish Anarchists

If this is contested, we need simply look at the remarkably unsuccessful careers of those armed forces that dispensed with control. Perhaps the best case is that of the republican armies in the Spanish Civil War, originally largely composed of anarchist (antiauthoritarian) workers' forces.[23] As might be imagined, there was a potential contradiction here: as one anarchist journal declared, "Discipline is obedience to authority; Anarchism recognizes no authority" (Bolloten 1979: 302). While other armies in revolutionary situations (for example, the Continental Army during the American War of Independence, or the French Army during the revolution) produced relatively undisciplined units with weak officers (often elected) and strong enlistees (see Martin 2005), this was taken to an extreme in the Spanish case—one telling estimate is that around 70 percent of the naval officers were killed by their subordinates (Bolloten 1979: 54).

Yet the anarchist workers valiantly enlisted and formed "columns"—a good name, since each was beholden only to its own political faction, leading to a parallel (and stubby) columnar structure as opposed to a tree. Each column was led by an elected committee with no special privileges and was broken down into smaller groups with elected delegates akin to sergeants. Instead of receiving orders, units would be cajoled, and they might take hours to democratically deliberate the wisdom of an action that would need to be carried out immediately. Irrationalities and inefficiencies were great even according to normal wartime standards for armed forces, since there was no viable central command able to bring information together and determine the most important directions for further effort. Most political parties or unions had their own independent command headquarters that proceeded without considering the overall armed position; indeed, different units considered each other competitors as much as allies. While there was a war ministry that attempted to coordinate these militias by assigning them missions, "whether these missions were carried out," said the then president Manuel Azaña later, "depended on the mood of the men, the whims of the subordinate officers, or the directives of the political organizations. . . . [What professional officers there were] had to convince their subordinates that orders should be obeyed. . . . If the men retreated in disorder, if they disobeyed, or fulfilled an order badly, the commander could not deal harshly with them." No real coordination could be assumed, since some group was sure to fail to do its part—and indeed, every party was pleased with the chance of blaming the others for failure (Bolloten 1979: 246f, 307; Bolloten 1991: 250–61).

---

[23] The case of the decentralized armies of the Renaissance Italian city states is dealt with briefly in chapter 9.

Eventually, even these principled anarchists soon admitted the functionality of discipline, and there were attempts to gain control over, and institute strict discipline for, all the Nationalist forces, which in some important cases led to armed uprisings. By that time, however, the tiny communist party had come to dominate the loyalist forces because it had from the first organized itself in a hierarchical and disciplined fashion (Bolloten 1979: 127f, 306–9; Bolloten 1991: 262, 326–38, 422, 128, 268). The anarchists had not lacked any will to fight (and such élan is far from irrelevant to military success): it should not seem necessary that they have someone over them, able and willing to give them orders and punish them for noncompliance. And yet that is what they were missing.[24]

Punishment and Command

The command tree, then, is not simply a social structure for transmitting *ideas*—information upward and direction downward. It is a structure of control, and control requires, in the last analysis, the capacity for punishment. Generally control with some measure of consent is more effective and efficient, and good controllers frequently attempt to gain such consent (as Freeland [2001] found for GM). As a result, it is tempting for analysts to try to model even control relations in terms of freely chosen adaptations of both parties (for example, by considering hierarchy in terms of principal-agent problems; recently, see Adams [1996]; Kiser and Schneider [1994]).

But no modern army relies on material rewards alone to motivate its soldiers—instead, they institute *control*, up to and including the threat of death. This is not to say that rational pursuit of self-interest is never involved in the creation of command structures—indeed it often is. Armies may make use of self-interest by allowing soldiers to win booty (see, e.g., Stacey 1994: 34f; also Maenchen-Helfen 1973: 139). Far from this leading to stronger, more efficient structures, however, there are many humorous stories about troops failing to vigorously prosecute the defeat of the enemy because they were too busy lining their purses.[25] Thus reliance on self-interest, while a possible tactic to ensure

---

[24] There have been cases of democratically organized regiments that proved to be formidable fighting forces, such as some of the volunteer groups in the American Revolutionary War (see Fischer 2004: 26–30, 146). While such groups might elect their own officers and refuse corporal punishment, they did recognize the right of the continental general (Washington) to direct their actions. The initial pillarization whereby each colony fielded its own independent army–often larger than Washington's continental forces–was recognized to be untenable and more centralization was eventually introduced.

[25] For examples of the use of booty as an incentive, see Prestwich (1996: 102f, 108), Mallett and Hale (1984: 186), Peckham (1979: 118). Regarding the lack of discipline due to motives for material gain: the Hamdanid emir once escaped certain capture by pursuing Byzantines by ordering his gold and silver to be scattered along the trail, which substantially slowed the pursuers (McGeer 1995: 323).

compliance, is a weak one that tends to promote disorganization. It also promotes desertion; a rational soldier would loot when the going is good, and flee otherwise. And indeed, desertion rates have generally been extremely high, and probably higher where command structures were weaker (for example, feudal armies).[26] While oversees campaigns saw less desertion than those closer to home, there was always the chance that soldiers would prefer to set up a new home where they were than hope to make it back to their old one. Until the development of uniforms, the side an infantryman was on was usually indicated only by a simple token like a scarf which could be changed at will depending on how the battle unfolded (Roberts 1967: 198).

In sum, real command structures are not contracts between mutually interested parties: it is weak command structures that have approximated this model. While armies are tree forms like management hierarchies, they are qualitatively different in that they routinely put followers in situations where normal contractual behavior breaks down (since one party gives up basically all rights, at least in certain conditions). The fundamental distinction between the structures of armed forces and other structures is easily seen in the distinction made between soldiers and civilians in modern armies. Many contemporary commands actually involve far more civilians than soldiers: for example, 92 percent of the 126,000 employees of the Army Material Command in the 1980s, the portion of the army in charge of designing and supplying weapons and supplies, were civilians (Demchak 1991: 64). These employees could *not* be shot for disobeying an instruction from a supervisor, even in wartime; similarly, a supplier determined to have failed to meet contractual obligations need fear no worse than mild public scandal and perhaps a loss of future contracts.

It is thus not surprising that to the extent that they were strong, large armies have generally emphasized command structures not simply to pass down information and coordinate motions, but to sanction disobedience. A Chinese military strategist, Wei Liao-tzu (fourth century BCE) described the secret of success in creating trained troops marching to drum beats in time: "If the drummer misses a beat, he is executed. Those that set up a clamor are executed. Those that do not obey the gongs, drums, bells and flags, but move by themselves, are executed" (McNeill 1994: 110; for other examples, see Sawyer 1993: 133, 152).[27]

---

[26] Black (1991: 38) says that desertion was "a major, generally the major, source of troop loss" in early modern Europe; Parker (1996: 55–57) comments that "in certain places and at certain times, almost an entire army would vanish into thin air." In medieval England, Prestwich (1996: 128, 141) writes, desertion "began the moment levies left their county muster points."

[27] Even in ancient Greece, where the hoplites' status as wealthy citizens precluded the harsh preemptory discipline of most ancient armies (Garlan 1995: 67; Hanson 2001: 52), commanders could be exiled for failure to carry out an assignment (for one case, see Thucydides, IV:104–7; V, 26, 72, p. 393). Thucydides himself seems to have received this treatment, but remained a firm advocate of obedience. He (II:11, 130; VI:72, 455) has the Spartan king Archidamus remind his troops to "follow your leaders, paying the strictest attention to discipline and to security, giving

To conclude, command structures are seen in their starkest form in armies; these structures, at their most developed, organize soldiers hierarchically in semi-independent divisions headed by specialized commanders, coordinated by a general staff that gathers information and issues commands, which are ultimately enforceable on pain of death. This is indeed a recipe for a strong social structure. Yet such a fully developed structure has historically been the exception, not the rule.

Limitations to Command

The Rarity of Command

We have seen that there are clear selective pressures that point toward a rationalized command structure as the most "fit" response to environmental pressures. And yet there are many reasons why existing structures for collective violence have usually fallen considerably short of this pure type. In perhaps most societies, such violence involves the assemblage of relatively ad hoc alliance patterns, frequently based on the nested set of concentric circles of relatedness-to-ego of each of the disputants as described in chapter 5 (cf. Gould 1999). In other cases, violence is ritualized and may take the form of men from two sides pairing off into dyadic fights that occur side by side but are otherwise independent (Landé 1973: 110; for examples, see Wiessner and Tumu 1998: 292; Hart and Pilling 1966 [1960]: 84f; also see Whitehead 1990: 152). Thus there can be collective violence without any real leadership.

It is quite possible that rudimentary command structures developed first among raiders and pirates, as the classic predatorial strategy—a well-organized small group against a larger but less-organized set of victims—calls out for some sort of coordination, especially when this also involves piloting a ship. When the led are free warriors who choose a chieftain (for example, the Vikings or the warriors of early feudalism [see Ganshof 1964: 4; Clarke 1999: 42 for these cases]), the leader probably could not punish those who disobeyed and deserted, but even where leaders had this sanctioning ability, there was not necessarily a hierarchical structure of intermediaries. Given the difficulty of passing down commands in battle (more on this below), when such intermediaries were present, they might often be instructed in the overall wished-for plan, and then have de facto autonomy during battle. This may have been true

---

prompt obedience to the orders which you receive. The best and safest thing of all is when a large force is so well disciplined that it seems to be acting like one man," and proposed that "as for choosing the generals, they should be few in number and they should have unrestricted power; the people should swear an oath to them guaranteeing that [the generals] would be allowed to carry out their responsibilities exactly as they thought fit. This would . . . allow the whole defense programme to be carried through smoothly without the need for giving continual explanations for what was being done."

for classic Greek warfare (Adcock 1967: 8, 92), with the exception of Sparta
and perhaps Thebes (Mann 1986: 203; Hanson 2005: 138).[28]

Given the intense, stubborn, and weighty nature of conflict between Greek
city-states, one may question whether command hierarchies are really so useful
as I have made them out—if so, why didn't they quickly develop in these
cases? It turns out there are a number of circumstances which inhibit the development of command structures, and that these circumstances are extremely
common.

Limits to Intelligence and Communication

In order to give useful commands, a commander must be able to assess the
current state of his own troops vis-à-vis the enemy and communicate directions
to them in a speedy fashion. Both of these have been extremely difficult
throughout most of history.

Since soldiers generally had short lines of sight, and many matters in their
visual field demanding attention, communication of instructions often involved
sound, such as trumpets, drums, or gongs (for China see the *Ssu-Ma* translated
in Sawyer 1993: 140, cf. 270; for the Aztecs see Hassig 1988: 95f, 111; for
Carthaginians see Dodge 1995 [1891]: 65, 71, 482). Such media have a limited
ability to transmit complex information; while a trumpet might be used to
coordinate a relatively complex plan like a feint and then main attack, it could
only be used to indicate that all should progress to the next stage in a preor-
dained sequence (for examples, see Prestwich 1996: 178; Anderson 1970: 80;
Kagan 1987: 231; and Thucydides II: 84, 90; IV: 10).

But audio communication can be almost completely blocked simply by putting on a metal helmet (for Greek examples, see Hanson 2000 [1989]: 71;
Hanson 2003: 182; Hanson 2005: 144; Thucydides VI:44; IV: 34). Medieval
knights could of course raise the visor to hear better, but at the risk of a spear
in the eye. Perhaps in recognition of this problem, it seems that some persons
were given the task of transmitting order by shouting (Prestwich 1996: 325,
336). Since noise often made such auditory signals nearly useless after battle
had been joined, the visible signal of the position and movement of the standard (a banner) was probably the most important coordinating signal, though

---

[28] In Sparta, there were five layers of hierarchy, the smallest consisting of a half-dozen men
(Keegan 1988: 125). That this was not common practice can be seen in the fact that Thucydides
(V:66; p. 390) assumed that he had to explain the Spartan system to his readers: the Spartan king,
he wrote, "gives the word to the divisional commanders and it is passed on from them to the
regimental commanders, from them to the company commanders, from them to the platoon commanders, and from them to the platoons. So, too, if an order has to be passed along the line, it is
done in the same way and quickly becomes effective, as nearly the whole Spartan army, except
for a small part, consists of officers serving under other officers, and the responsibility for seeing
that an order is carried out falls on a great many people."

an extremely simple one. Occasionally flags or smoke would be used, though the latter could be disrupted by the enemy simply filling the air with smoke (for China see Sawyer 1993: 270; for the Aztecs see Hassig 1988: 95f, 111; for the Carthaginians see Dodge 1995 [1891]: 181, 242; for disruption see Thucydides III: 2, 205; for flag signaling see Keegan 2003: 27, 99; Palmer 2005: 132, 144, 174).[29]

While these are examples from ancient and medieval armies, similar limitations to the communication of commands persisted well into the nineteenth century: the speed of the transmission of orders during the Napoleonic wars was around 5.5 miles an hour, "a speed that had hardly changed for millennia" (van Creveld 1985: 87). The signals used were still primitive in substance—thus Wellington ordered his main forces to attack Napoleon's at Waterloo by waving his hat three times in the forward direction (Keegan 1988: 101; Fuller 1955: 538). Even by the start of the First World War, when telephones were few and even buried lines quickly broken with shelling, communication fell back on visual signals: armies had no communicative means adequate to coordinate the tasks they planned (Keegan 2000: 22, 162f; Keegan 2003: 100).

Given these limitations to communication during the middle of battle, explicit orders (command) were unlikely to be more influential than example (leadership) in changing the course of battle, and when the two conflicted, soldiers were likely to do what they saw, not what they heard (for an example, see Prestwich 1996: 178f). Since generals were unable to do much to affect the course of battle once it was underway (here see Mason 1974: 47), they typically attempted to arrange their troops according to anticipations of the likely developments of the battle; responses to foreseen events were built into the synchronic structure of the army. This emphasis on organizing troops before battle instead of coordinating them in battle is nearly universal, though it is seen in perhaps most elaborated forms in prescriptions for warfare in ancient India, which codified all possible orientations and actions (Srivastava 1985: 76; cf. Garlan 1995: 65f on ancient Greek warfare).[30] Given the serious limita-

---

[29] Indeed, Palmer (2005: 5, 13, also cf. 28, 46, 53) suggests that Nelson's success as an admiral came largely because he could explain the outlines of his ideas to subordinate commanders and dispense with the conventional rigid signals altogether.

[30] The Roman army is in many ways the exception that proves the rule. While the Romans faced the same problems with communicating complex commands that we have discussed above, they made a number of innovations, such as using the standard as a traffic signal which, by posting the current order, could pass relatively complex instructions. This emphasis on real-time coordination also required an increase in real-time sanctioning; the Romans thus instituted a special corps of military police (lectors). As each infantryman's name and century number was painted on his shield, it was possible to note misbehavior during the heat of battle and punish afterward; if on the spot discipline was required, the officers would respond to breakdowns in command with a combination of example, entreaty, threat, and execution (van Creveld 1985: 45; Dodge 1995 [1891]: 43, 46, 66, 74, 77, 82, 665; see Delbrück 1990 [1920]: 275 for skepticism that infantrymen would actually turn to look at the standard during battle).

tions to real-time communication, it was more sensible to attempt to forecast the evolution of battle and set up the board accordingly than to attempt to develop a full-fledged command structure for responding to contingencies.

Limitations to Formality of Structure

We have seen limitations in the nature of communicative technology that often prevent the emergence of a command structure. But even where a rudimentary command structure may arise, there are forces that tend to check its formal elaboration. To some extent, it is simply less likely for any sort of formal structure to emerge where there are a small number of persons involved. It may be a sociological truism that as the number of participants decreases, the influence of the particularities of individual personalities increases: the structures that would work for one group of three may not work for another group of three. As a result, there are smaller returns to formal organization in smaller groups. Certainly, one would expect fewer levels of command where there are fewer people *to* command, and in many cases, such size differences account for a great deal of the variance in command structures. The uncharacteristically large armies that sometimes appeared in premodern cases were frequently temporary assemblages that did not exist long enough to justify the creation of a command structure (for examples from Carolingian and medieval armies, see Reuter 1999: 28; Powicke 1996 [1962]: 3f, 8f for pre-Norman England; Prestwich 1996: 118, 127f for post-Conquest period; see also Anderson 1974: 142).

Further, even where a formal hierarchical structure developed, it was likely to arise to deal with problems of logistics (e.g., supply) or information gathering, as opposed to command. For example, the *Six Secret Teachings of T'ai Kung*, dating from China's Warring States period but suspected to contain earlier traditions, has an ideal description of the numbers of various general officers for an army. While there is no reason to suspect that this corresponds to practice, the relative balance indicates a plausible division of attention in ancient Chinese war. Three officers are dedicated to the task of "secret signals," namely using pennants and drums for signaling (including disinformation),[31] and seven officers dedicated to matters of intelligence (the "ears and eyes"). These seven officers are "responsible for going about everywhere, listening to what people are saying." Only three officers are responsible for "authority," namely the coordination and implementation of unusual and probably novel plans (Sawyer 1993: 61). Intelligence gathering was thus clearly considered of greater significance than ensuring the dissemination of commands.

---

[31] There are another two "officers of techniques" responsible for spreading slander and eight roving officers for spying on the enemy.

Finally, even where a formal command structure developed, it could rarely provide the only, or even the dominant, organizational principle guiding action. This distinction between the official structures of organizations (those that appear on paper) and the actual informal social interactions of the members is well known in the sociology of organizations but has assumed particular importance in the sociology of war, in part due to studies of small-group cohesion. Such studies found what Lang (1972: 73) calls the "cardinal rule" that the closer a unit is to the actual fighting, "the more the formal organizational control becomes diluted." But it is not the mere existence of informality that is important, it is that the informal structure inherent in small-group cohesion is a *horizontal* one, not a vertical one, and indeed cuts against the sorts of distinctions inherent in the organizational plan of a command structure.[32]

The elaboration of a formal command structure is thus limited by the small size of many armies, by the presence of informal structures, and by the presence of other formal structures (for most large armies, like other large organizations, are amalgams of different systems with often clashing organizational principles [Lang 1972: 86]). Such limitations to formal organization do not necessarily limit the efficiency of war-making; indeed, they can substantially contribute to it. Like a canine mutt, mongrel structures are often more robust than their purebred cousins. In this case, there is an inherent tension between two goals of military action. On the one hand, the need for coordinated action, especially involving *planned* surprise, calls for a centralization of control. On the other hand, the need for flexibility in dealing *with* surprises or unanticipated conditions more generally calls for decentralization (this point was recently made by Fukuyama and Shulsky [1997: x] and is elegantly put in terms of decoupling by White [1992: 182] for the case of firms). Indeed, in some such cases, horizontal communication between low-level groups may be the only way to avoid disintegration (for examples, see Travers 2005 [1992]: 71, 78). Thus to the extent that the environment remains uncontrollably uncertain, informality has its advantages.

Political Limitations

Disorganization often has, then, advantages for the military itself. It even more frequently has advantages for the nonmilitary elites. Hence even where a formal structure might develop in a rational direction toward a clear command tree, political forces may oppose this development out of a justified fear of an integrated military structure free from political oversight. Political leaders might deliberately compose their army as a hodge-podge of distinct nationalities to avoid this threat. Indeed, most medieval armies had such a patchwork

---

[32] In addition to such cohesion, pseudoformal differentiations may spring up that ignore the formal structure and create their own division of labor (see, e.g., Demchak 1991: 120f).

quality based on mixing recruits from different nations.[33] Even bracketing the many problems caused by fights breaking out between these nationalities,[34] the sheer multiplicity of languages was a problem for a transitive command structure.

As armies turned to more national recruitment patterns, other ways had to be found of preventing the emergence of a politically strong, unified army. Ancient Greeks usually chose leaders for specific expeditions, as opposed to allowing the same people to occupy permanent positions of command (Bury 1955 [1900]: 261); other Greeks and the Romans had consuls alternate command day by day (Andreski 1968: 93; Delbrück 1990 [1920]: 76, 336, cf. 287). Where continual command was necessary, this solution was infeasible, and political leaders might simply choose to inject political control at various points in the command structure, even though that broke the transitivity of command. For example, while fifteenth-century Venetians understood the advantages that would come were they to institute a true commander in chief, they feared giving too much power to a potential Caesar. Instead of constructing a rational command structure, they put together a confusing system of contradictory responsibilities including civilian advisors ("proveditors") who joined companies to "make suggestions" and report intelligence, leading to recurrent tensions and disagreements (Mallett and Hale 1984: 122, 176f, 179, 267f; Downing 1992: 236f).

At least an army composed of mercenaries could be dismissed when no longer needed. A standing army of nationals, generally considered to be the great support for a political regime, could also be its undoing: without a war to keep them busy, soldiers might turn their eyes to the government as the ultimate prize. In cases in which political control was not already in military hands the specter of soldiers unified under a strong command structure was frequently terrifying. With the increasing appropriation of governing power by a bureaucratic state apparatus (instead of a nobility or oligarchy), whether or not this apparatus was under the control of a monarch, there was a renewed struggle to lessen the potential autonomy of the newly strengthened army. An example is nineteenth-century Britain: while the army was generally admitted

[33] McKinley (1934: 205) says of the Middle Ages, "A French or German army looked like a ragged League of Nations." Marino Sanuto of Venice spoke of the "Noah's Ark" quality of the Italian armies (Mallett and Hale 1984: 317, 486; for examples, see Fuller 1955: 131; Anderson 2000: 189; Parker 1996: 60). Such armies were generally recognized to be weaker than their opponents (for examples, see Thucydides I:141; 1974: 120; Mallett and Hale 1984: 315; Beeler 1971: 75; cf. Mann 1986: 439f).

[34] A simple dispute over a cask of wine between Norman regulars and Flemish mercenaries forced Stephen to abandon his invasion of Anjou (Prestwich 1996: 179; also see McGeer 1995: 236); a wrestling match between a Roman legionnaire and a Gallic ally supposedly led to the destruction of at least two cohorts during the civil wars after Nero's death (Tacitus, *History* II:68).

to be fractured to the point of administrative chaos, unifying it would increase the threat of its political power and interference (Strachan 1984: 8, 246).[35]

This attempt to retain as much peacetime control as possible leads to a common system whereby there are basically two parallel structures, one pertaining to supply and logistics and the other to battle command. It is hard to make a clean separation between command and support functions, and in the case of the British system, there was a charmingly pathological duplication in which the standard military command (the "commander in chief" associated with the "horse guards" of the king or queen) was in charge of most troops, but the "master general of the ordnance," an administrative agency dating back to the fifteenth century and independently subordinate to the crown, had not only the responsibility for supplying all the troops, but set up its own hospitals, bought its own stores, and controlled its own forces. Even the ordnance department, however, had a rival, in the Commissariat of the treasury, a wholly civilian entity "neither subject to military discipline nor in any way under the commander in chief" (Ward 1957: 40f, 75; Sweetman 1984: 59ff, 78, 42).

The British situation is somewhat extreme, stemming from the unbroken heritage of much of the government from medieval times. Thus in addition to the commander in chief and the master general of the ordnance, there was the secretary of state "for" war and the secretary "at" war (originally the king's secretary when the king served as commander in chief himself) (Brewer 1988: 44; Ward 1957: 6; Sweetman 1984: 87, 96, 106; cf. Strachan 1984: 230).[36] But other armies had similar splits; indeed, this separation is still characteristic of modern armies, including the United States, in which the actual relations between the (civilian) secretary of defense and the military (the Joint Chiefs of Staff and Departments of Army, Navy and Air Force) change in every administration and for every conflict (for examples see Craig 1956: 125; Williams 1996: 67f, 70; Mowbray 1996: 87; Fukuyama and Shulsky 1997: 55; Demchak 1991: 66).

Thus while in an ideal world, one might expect the emergence of a unified and structurally simple tree of command, political leaders have often had very good reasons for preventing this from emerging. It is often said that war is too important to be left to the generals. That may be, but most rulers have feared giving them peace even more; if an incoherent structure was the price to be paid for this, that was an acceptable price.

---

[35] As one British officer later put it, "There's no such thing as *the* British Army. . . . That's why there could never be a coup in this country" (Fischer 2004: 34).

[36] After the Crimean war this structure was considerably reformed, though it still remained comparatively disorganized (Sweetman 1984: 37, 50f, 125, 129, 131). To some extent the structural complications came from a rational adaptation to the division in tasks confronting an army that had to be prepared for home defense against European enemies while pursuing colonial wars of a very different sort (Strachan 1984: 229–31).

Class Limitations

We have found a number of times that the internal organization of a structure can be limited if the relationships that compose it cannot be sheltered from other forms of differentiation between persons.[37] This has been quite consequential for the evolution of command structures, for it is not simply those elites running the state who have opposed the development of a rational command structure. In many cases, military participation was monopolized by upper status men. These were likely to refuse to take orders from commoners, if they allowed commoners on the battlefield at all.[38] In some cases, the brotherly ethic of the elite forbade multiple levels of hierarchy: As van Creveld (1985: 50) says regarding medieval armies (though with some exaggeration), "For the exercise of command to be possible there must be somebody to obey orders; medieval armies, however, were made up purely of officers."

Participation in armed forces was limited to the elite in two important general cases. The first was where battle was conducted largely by mounted warriors. Since it was a considerable expense to purchase and maintain the warhorse (in the Middle Ages a horse cost around as much as forty to one hundred sheep), war was basically restricted to the nobility, though commoners might be forced to stand with often ludicrously inefficient weapons, like bowling pins waiting to be knocked down (see Hanson 2005: 224; Prestwich 1996: 30–37; cf. Contamine 1998 [1980]: 58, 96; Parker 1996: 70; also see Farris 1995: 15; Ikegami 1995: 97f for Japan).[39]

The second case of upper-class monopoly involved infantry, but infantry who were heavily armored and, as invariably was the case, paid for their armor themselves (for the example of the Greek hoplites see Greenhalgh [1973: 151]; though see Hanson [1996: 294] on the possible incorporation of the landless into the Athenian army and [2005: 226] on the later importance of cavalry). Among the Greeks, there might be some hierarchy approximating a command tree, but position was still largely a function of general social status, and not

---

[37] In other words, *dependence* on upstream or downstream valuations (White 1992) can limit involution.

[38] Thus Queen Elizabeth chose Lord Howard of Effingham instead of Sir Francis Drake to be commander in chief during the campaign against Spain in 1588 though Drake was the better sailor and soldier because only someone of high rank could actually get others to obey him. When Robert Knollys was given a command of 4,000 in 1370 despite his modest ancestry, the captains under him were required to given written oaths in advance that they would not sabotage the mission, which they did anyway (Fuller 1955: 16; Palmer 2005: 54; Prestwich 1996: 161, 164, 166).

[39] This has led to the almost universal hierarchical relationship between cavalry and infantry, easily assimilated to that between patron and client (on this classic association, see Roberts 1967: 209; Hanson 2001: 136). Indeed, the word *infantry*, as Keegan (1994: 357) points out, comes from the same root as "infant."

experience or ability to lead (Garlan 1995: 62; Keegan 1994: 249).[40] In either case, when the upper classes monopolized warrior positions, they generally opposed any progression toward a command army, even if this would increase the effectiveness of their forces (for the case of Poland, see Downing 1992: 148).

To summarize, we have seen a number of reasons why selective pressure may not encourage the development of full-fledged command structures. If these conditions are strong (for example, reliance on mounted warriors, limited communication mechanisms, and a reasonable fear of uncontrollable political ambitions of soldiers), a structure put together on the basis of patronage relations might prove preferable for coordinating armed force. But when these conditions change, this inherent pressure toward a true command structure is likely to lead to a radical change in structural principles. I begin by discussing how patronage structures serve as skeletons for armed forces, and then how such scaffolds are transformed to produce true command structures.

From Patronage Structure to Command Structure

Patronage Pyramids and Armies

Patron-client pyramids have, throughout history, formed the skeletons on which command armies emerged.[41] There are two fundamental layers to the patronage army, and there is a rough temporal sequence whereby armies are put together by adding the second to the first. The first layer is a core consisting

---

[40] Once again, Rome stands out in its approximation of a pure command army–only Rome had a stratum of low-level officers in charge of command functions drawn from the common soldiery (Delbrück 1990 [1920]: 429–31; van Creveld 1991: 139; although see Goldsworthy 1996: 165).

[41] It is worth noting that similar relationships can produce patronage pyramids where the units are not persons, but states; this often occurs in the construction of what have been called "hegemonic" empires through conquest (Hassig 1992: 84). One king conquers others, but lacks any governance structure capable of enforcing rule on the territory that is now "his," and hence allows the conquered king to maintain his position as long as tribute is sent and the sovereignty of the high king acknowledged (see, e.g., Critchley 1978: 83, 92). The Aztec political structure (see Hassig 1988: 28–30, 177—257; Adams 1974: 381, 383f, 386f) seems to have been such a set of cascaded triangles united as a tribute-extraction scheme. In schematic terms, the Aztec structure is delightfully treelike, descending from the top kings (*tlahtoani*) who ruled provinces or towns, as well as client *tlahtoani* (*teuctlahtohqueh*) who were largely supported by tribute. Under these nobles were lords (*teteucin*), then *pipiltin* (sons of the higher nobles, divided in rank according to the parents' status), and then the *cuauhpipiltin* (elevated commoners), then the ward headmen (*calpolehqueh*) and then the commoners (*macehualtin*) and finally the slaves (*tlatlacohtin*). But this was not a command tree–connections to the center were generally defined simply in terms of allegiance and tribute. Other empires combined both direct governance of conquered territory and hegemony (for example, the Roman Empire in its treatment of its western and eastern domains respectively) (Anderson 1974: 64). Finally, we should note that such patronage relations between cities can be combined with patronage relations between persons, as in the relationship between Florence and other Italian cities during the renaissance (see Fabbri 2000: 231; Black 2000: 297).

of the personal retainers of the king or chief lord. These can vary from close friends and relatives (who rightly or wrongly are frequently more trusted than others) to professionals who are personally dependent on the lord. These loyal followers of the leaders are given special privileges and more or less put in the position of protecting the leader should the mass of the army default, if not also given the job of executing the defaulters. Historical examples are the "Sacred Band" that formed the core of the ancient Carthaginian army, the bodyguard of Spartan kings, the "companions" of the early Greek Macedonian kings, the *celeres* that were the bodyguard for the first Roman leaders; and finally, the famous Praetorian guard. The Merovingian armies were largely composed of powerful dukes who brought their own armed retainers with them, and their Carolingian successors also formed around a core of Charlemagne's personal vassals. Even England, which progressed furthest toward a professional army, had at its center from the eleventh to the mid-fourteenth century the royal household (a band of dependents that might consist of five to eight dozen knights); indeed the core of William the Conqueror's army consisted of his own tenants. (For references, see Beeler [1966] 1995: 11; Beeler 1971: 219; Dodge 1995 [1891]: 14, 37; Bury 1955: 55; Anderson 1970: 245; Adcock 1967: 26; Keegan 1988: 34; cf. Anderson 1974: 50; Bachrach 1972: 51f, 99; Anderson 1974: 139; Prestwich 1996: 38; Mallett 1999: 211; Housley 1999: 123; Powicke 1996 [1962]: 64; Bean 1989: 128, 139; Ikegami 1995: 93.)

Of course, few kings had personal retinues sufficient to comprise a decent army (though see Contamine 1998 [1980]: 166). But because in a patronage-based governance system, the king is really a glorified patron's patron, he could attempt to assemble an army by calling on his vassals to call out their vassals in turn. An army was thus formed by a succession of mobilizations of vassals: the king or prince would call out his vassals; each of these similarly had a core retinue of household knights as well as a number of vassals that could be mobilized. At the higher levels, the clients being called in were vassals who generally had been given a benefice in land; the larger the benefice, the more knights one could command (an important vassal of a prince in medieval Europe might command around a dozen bannerets, each of whom would bring a dozen knights). At the lower end of the pyramids, the clients being called in were frequently tenants (Beeler 1971: 34f; van Creveld 1985: 49; for the case of England, see Prestwich 1996: 41, 44; and Bean 1989: 180, 182; on the relation between clientage and tenancy in ancient Roman armies, see Brunt 1962: 71; for the structurally identical process whereby Japanese magnates mobilized not only their own household but those farming their land, see Farris 1995: 67, 75 and cf. 163f, 180–90).[42] Thus land ownership, which we have

---

[42] In England it was frequently the case that military obligations were extended to all those of property, whether or not they held some specific benefice that had military service attached. These extensions, however, aroused resistance and were not very successful (Prestwich 1996: 77, 81).

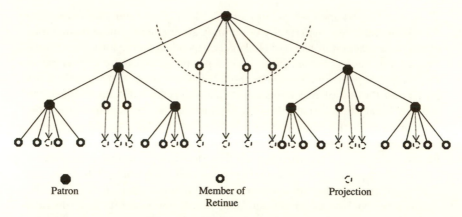

Patron   Member of   Projection
                Retinue

Figure 7.3. Feudal army

seen frequently forming the basis of patronage relationships, would also be the basis of officer-soldier relationships.[43]

Simplified, the tree then looked more like a bush (see figure 7.3). At every level, a higher-level patron mobilized both his own retinue (who brought no underlings), and his vassals, who in turn had a retinue and, in some cases, vassals of their own. The dashed curve separates the inner layer of the leader's own retinue from the outer layer of those mobilized through direct and indirect ties of clientage. Further, in contrast to the perfect command tree, in the ideal version of this structure all persons entered as combatants (hence in the above diagram, higher-level persons appear twice, once as patrons mobilizing their clients, and again as fighters (the "projection" linked to their position in the hierarchy by a dashed arrow).

Since armies were assembled by recruiting clients, the organization of armed forces was more or less a residue of patronage relations. But most large armies supplemented this mobilization of clients and clients' clients with other troops.[44] Some came from general levies of commoners, as in the ancient Mesopotamian army (Mann 1986: 101; cf. 244), or on local levies whereby communities had obligations to provide a certain number of soldiers (also see Bloch 1961 [1940]: 151f; Wilson 1999: 199; Beeler [1966] 1995: 126 for examples). While such local levies were a significant force in several medieval armies (on the Merovingian military, see Bachrach 1972: 65, 69, 71), many militias were more trouble than they were worth (see Mallett and Hale 1984:

---

[43] Even in 18th-century Germany, Junker captains were allowed to recruit their own peasants, "releasing them for farm work for most of the year," linking the army more closely to the relationship between landowner and his peasants (Ertman 1997: 254f).

[44] In some cases, horizontal relations of alliance would be employed (for the case of Japan see Farris 1995: 150), but this only pushes the question of mobilization to a different lord.

75 on communal militias in Venice).[45] In other cases, it was mercenaries or other "irregular" forces who supplemented the patronage pyramid (see Mallett 1999: 225; Mallett and Hale 1984: 485). As a result, even in feudal Europe, it was not necessarily the case that the *bulk* of any army was there because of patronage relations (though see Porter 1994: 49); but aside from the foreigners recruited by strong and suspicious kings for their own defense, it was the troops attached to the patronage pyramid that were most reliable (Beeler [1966] 1995: 317; Prestwich 1996: 67; Contamine 1998 [1980]: 100).

Weakness of Antitransitive Patronage Structures

But reliability is not the same thing as strength—patronage relationship were relatively weak conduits for giving commands. As Keen (1999a: 7) points out, it was hard for such a ruler to do anything but "present himself as the companion and generous patron of his martial, aristocratic subjects, to heed their sensibilities and maintain their privileges." Certainly it was difficult to reduce them to underlings who would merely receive and pass on orders. Consequently, to take a wonderful phrase from Christiansen (2000: 42) (speaking of the Hundred Years War), "The chain of command was usually more like a disintegrating net."

Thus even though the armies formed on the basis of patronage pyramids look somewhat like trees, they lack the transitivity that would allow them to be used for sending threats and punishments down, and surveillance and information up. As Scott and Kerkvliet (1977: 442) put it, "If the patron could simply issue commands, he would have no reason to cultivate a clientele in the first place" (cf. Anderson 1964: 151).[46] When the interests of clients and apexes converged, the system could work rather well.[47] But when these interests diverged, clients' clients could not be compelled to obey the apex. For example, Charlemagne found his subjects refusing to serve on the grounds that as their particular lords had not summoned them, they were unable to comply

[45] Of course, when it was in their own interests, local levies–especially of the larger towns with their own military organizations–could bring out strong forces. But such forces were generally limited to defense of their locality. Further, there was a constant, and often petty, struggle between rulers and locals over the precise obligations entailed; not surprisingly, armies that relied heavily on local levies tended to be selected out (see Powicke 1996 [1962]: 10f, 17f, 50, 59f, 188; Anderson 1974: 160; Beeler 1971: 224; Contamine 1998 [1980]: 49, 84ff; for the 12th-century Assize of Arms in Britain see Beeler [1966] 1995: 190ff, 314; for China, Hsu 1965: 71).

[46] Similar structural tensions have arisen in the modern world between nations that have a relationship of military patronage, usually initiated by a patron nation that plans to enlist the client in fighting its own battles. But as Mott (1999) has shown, the material dependence of the client does not translate into effective control, and hence the probability of the patron's success is low.

[47] A successful example of such a decentralized military structure is found in the way most Persian empires up to and including the Ottoman generally allowed their local leaders a great deal of independence in starting and stopping wars (Murphey 1999: 2f).

(Ganshof 1964: 56). When the divergence in interests became sharp, important patrons could bring their clients with them when they rebelled (for the case of Ancient China see Critchley 1978: 118; for medieval England see Bean 1989: 200; and for France see Major 1964: 640).

These weaknesses are tolerable in the relatively small, noble-based armies of high feudalism, but this loss of control can become fatal when there is an attempt to enlarge armies by mobilizing commoners. Many rulers have proposed arming the poor to vanquish an enemy—a mistake they might only have the opportunity to make once. Thucydides describes such a mobilization of commoners in response to a serious external threat: "But as soon as the [common] people found themselves properly armed, they refused any longer to obey the government" (Thucydides III: 27, 208; also see Downing 1992: 61; Garlan 1995; Keegan 1988: 34; Keegan 1994: 233; Hanson 2005: 92f; Mann 1993: 243; Contamine 1998 [1980]: 88, 156).

It is beyond the bounds of this chapter to fully discuss the historical factors impelling the mobilization of commoners. Obviously political competition can lead to such mobilization, but so can the introduction of new weaponry requiring relatively little skill, such as the crossbow and the musket (on the lack of skill required for such arms, see Hall 1997: 20, 148; Hanson 2001: 20, 224, 248, 250f; Roberts 1967: 197; Parker 1996: 17; McNeill 1982: 68; Keegan 1988: 169). These new weapons, though originally not as effective as a longbow, could more easily be used by the untrained.[48] Since such untrained men were more likely to accept command, more likely to need it if they were not to overthrow their rulers, and much more effective with it, there would be an increased incentive for heads of pyramids to attempt to institute transitivity and hence form command structures.

From Patronage Pyramids to Command Hierarchies and Back Again

Such institution of transitivity can, in broadest outline, be seen as a crucial component of the creation of states out of feudal relationships. While theorists such as Weber (1978) have stressed the importance of the ruler gaining control over the top stratum of officials—an estate in the case of German feudalism—merely controlling one's clients does not guarantee that one can control one's client's clients. One may attempt to strengthen the control that one's clients have over *their* clients, but then find that this has in turn weakened one's own control.

---

[48] It took between 100 and 175 lbs of force to pull back a longbow, but someone who could handle one could let loose an arrow every three seconds (Prestwich 1996: 133)–probably two orders of magnitude higher than a musket at that time, which even in the hands of the best trained infantry in the early 19th century could only manage to be fired every twenty seconds at best, and a crossbow took even longer (Hall 1997: 18–20; Keegan 1988: 115). (If twenty seconds sounds quick, count to yourself and imagine someone with a sword running at you.)

Something along these lines happened to Charlemagne in 810, when he ordered that "every *dominus* [i.e. landowning lord/patron] [should] exercise pressure on his *juniors* [dependents] so that they become more and more obedient and accept the imperial orders and prescripts" (see Fourquin 1976: 40, 51f), thus trying to "utiliz[e] for the purposes of government the firmly established network of protective [feudal] relationships" (Bloch 1961 [1940]: 157–59).[49] To do this, Charlemagne attempted to strengthen the bond of vassalage by making the lord responsible for his vassal's behavior (and hence institute some form of indirect control), and by decreasing the ability of vassals to change lords and get a better bargain. But instead of this strengthening the king's control over his client's clients, the middle strata (e.g., the counts) became effective independent powers because of their command over soldiers. What Charlemagne's system lacked, as we have seen, was transitivity.[50]

Rulers attentive to this possibility will therefore deliberately forgo some potential armed support by weakening the power of lords over their own underlings. This happened in late-fourteenth-century England as the crown sought to rein in the magnates' reach (e.g., no longer to allowing them to treat dependents outside their household, including public officials, as "their" men). While this itself did little to strengthen the state, it put the crown in a stronger position for other actions, such as when in the fifteenth century Henry V refused to dispense patronage to those retained by lords, forcing clients to make a choice between allying with the super-patron of the king or a second-rate patron in the nobility (Bean 1989: 202f, 210). Once the independence of noble patronage was undercut, it was easier to transform underlings into officials.

The introduction of transitivity into feudal pyramids is only one part of the story of the rise of the modern state, in part because few feudal principalities rested solely on relations of vassalage, and in part because such an abstraction does not speak to the material factors involved in state building. Further, the story is not a unidirectional one. Indeed, that is part of the point of the structural analysis: while I have emphasized the transition from pyramid to command structure, due to the particular structures that first caught the attention of sociologists, in nearly as many cases command structures have devolved into patronage pyramids, as I go on to discuss.[51]

---

[49] In addition, the Carolingians attempted to bolster their control over officials by coercing these to become vassals as well (also see Beeler 1971: 12). This worked for the Tokugawa shogun in Japan because he could rely on his own landholding for economic support and required nothing of his major vassals but their dependence (Ikegami 1995: 157–60).

[50] Of course, it can be even riskier for a ruler to set up a governance system with intermediates if he does *not* tie the underlings to him through something akin to vassalage. An example here is King Stephen of Hungary's (ruled 1001–38) reliance on counts to govern his territory. This was a wonderful way to jump start a flourishing government, but the counts were able to block any later attempts at centralization (Ertman 1997: 270f).

[51] There is, as of yet, no case of a complete devolution of a modern state into real feudalism, although the breakup of various colonial and noncolonial empires–Britain and France in the early

From Command Structures to Pyramids

If indeed modern state armies can be understood as the introduction of transitivity into feudal patronage pyramids, these feudal patronage pyramids (at least those in the Mediterranean and in Europe) can themselves be understood as a result of the loss of transitivity in Roman command structures. In the later Roman Empire, armed force was of necessity dispersed across regions; not only were most troops beyond the immediate control of Rome, but they were to find themselves beyond its remunerative capacities as well. Forced to provide for themselves (at first simply for land grants or pensions after service, later for regular wages), the soldiers looked on their generals as patrons, and these patrons in turn appropriated their offices (Brunt 1962: 76; Taylor 1968: 17–21, 47; Anderson 1974: 68; also see Mann 1986: 259, 292).

Rome—like other weak centers, which is what it had become—was torn between attempting to suppress these generals-turned-magnates in pursuit of its monopoly on the legitimate use of force, and encouraging them, since it was they who really supported the empire and its laws. The military structure of Merovingian Europe was largely a residue from the dissolution of the Roman military structure into semi-independent groups. While the Carolingian empire imposed minimal unity on some of these pieces, its demise in 987 marked the devolution of power to local lords. It is this undoing of the transitivity of empire that we call feudalism, which finally led to the independent power of the castellans—basically anyone who for whatever reason had a big house of stone to hide in (Bachrach 1972: 16, 24; Fourquin 1976: 24f, 68f, 87–94).[52]

At the beginning of the chapter we saw that command structures are ideally independent of preexisting relationships (in contrast, most notably, to citizen militias). But this independence only pushes off the issue of dependence: the project of control, like that of empire, is expensive and often requires subsidy. Precisely because the command tree is detached from surplus extraction (in contrast to the feudal "bush" structure), its viability is always an open question. The patronage pyramid is shockingly wasteful but it does pump surplus upward and is in a sense self-funding. In contrast, we take for granted that no modern army is responsible for paying its own way. It is thus dependent on infusions of support from *other* social structures, and is therefore vulnerable to changing

---

and Russia in the late 20th century are good examples–led to a partial feudalism in the sense of magnate rule (and not relationships of vassalage) in some of the freed areas.

[52] This does not quite hold for Germany nor, of course, for England, which at this time was instituting feudalism from above. While in France, the castles were eventually taken over by the monarchy, and thus their independent power used *against* the middle stratum of the counts, in Germany the territorial princes and counts were able to retain control over castles, and hence this source of power weakened kings in favor of princes. Italy was quite different in that in many areas, urban regions maintained control over the countryside (Beeler 1971: 194–202, 217).

allocations of surplus. As a result, a seemingly invincible command structure can rapidly bankrupt itself and revert to a patronage pyramid.

A somewhat similar devolution of power to feudal lords is seen in the case of medieval India (here I rely on Sharma [1965]; for purposes of brevity I ignore differences between regions and kingdoms). Starting somewhere around the turn of the first millennium AD, the Maurya state began to give up its control over previously centralized taxation, economic regulation, social order, and defense functions as a result of benefices that were granted to Brahmins. A prince might make such a grant to accumulate merit, or to be rid of a bothersome chore (or to encourage certain forms of economic activity)—one cannot be sure what motivated any particular transfer. In any case, the process started by donating the rights to tax some area, but this led rulers to progressively give up other administrative and social control functions: why conduct a census if there is no one to tax? How can one enforce the laws without tax revenue? By the thirteenth century, such "religious" grants could be made to non Brahmins in exchange for their service, military or otherwise, leaving India a checkerboard of small principalities with independent governance structures of all sorts, in which the kings depended wholly on their vassals for military support.

Thus patronage pyramids can develop from the degeneration of command structures, and accordingly, those wielding command structures may attempt to thwart the development of patronage ties.[53] In other circumstances, however, they may foster them. While this seems like a deliberate weakening of the position of the apex, a more sympathetic reconstruction often finds the attempt to introduce patronage relationships within a command structure a reasonable one—the ruler fears that without cementing the relationship between ruler and staff in personalistic terms of vassalage, he will be unable to control his underlings. This evidently explains the Carolingian monarchs' attempt to make their officials vassals (see note 49 above; Ganshof 1964: 22, 51, 161, 163). This is a devil's bargain, as it is likely to encourage the appropriation of offices by underlings, and hence disempowers the ruler in the long run.[54]

---

[53] An example here is found in the Ottoman Empire. The empire forbade state actors to hold their benefices (in this case, the *timar*, akin to a prebend) indefinitely or to pass them down to descendents and thus establish themselves as regional patrons. At the same time, it inserted particular officials such as tax collectors between peasants and the *timar*-holders, preventing the latter from acting as reliable patrons to the former. While there was an independent judicial hierarchy, the judges here also could not assume the role of local patrons because they too were rotated. Thus functions that might solidify a patronage triangle in other agricultural societies were divided among a number of short-term exploiters, undermining any possible power structure other than the central state (see Barkey 1994: 65, 89, 91f, 100, 103, 107, 140, 240).

[54] Further, in times of dramatic state building or contest, strains on organizational capacity tend to lead to a devolution of central power to local leaders and hence the potential regrowth of patronage pyramids (for examples, see Farris 1995: 121f, 139, 251; Barkey 1994: 36; Yeung 2006; and Parrott 2001: 14, 277ff, 284).

In sum, the structural tensions and tendencies present in, say, a largely feudal government structure with a king able to call out a general muster of the population, are largely independent of whether we are catching a transition from feudal warlordism to a centralized state, or the other way around. The crucial issue is the degree of transitivity: how much control overlings have over their underlings' underlings and where there are likely breaks in the continuity of command. Although we see that transitivity sometimes increases and sometimes decreases, because it offers a selective advantage in military conflict, all other things being equal, there are pushes away from patronage pyramids and toward transitive command structures. I go on to examine more closely the nature of these structural pushes.

The Introduction of Transitivity in Armed Forces

The Uses of Transitivity

It might be thought that a "chain" of command might work rather well even were it not strictly transitive: that is, a lieutenant can give an order to a sergeant, who can give the order to a private, even if the lieutenant cannot give the order directly to the private. Indeed, why have a chain at all, if intermediaries can be bypassed (which is presumably demoralizing to the bypassed intermediaries)? If a command structure successfully links self-contained units that can be trusted to carry out their assignments without constant management, we might expect that transitivity is of little importance in command structures.

But there are four limitations to this reliance on mediated relations. The first is that battle is an excellent site of what Herbert Simon called "bounded rationality"—not all happenings can be prepared for in advance, and a commander may reasonably feel that coordination must be continually asserted from a central point if different sections of the army are not to slowly diverge in their understanding of the proper (and hence coordinated) response to unforeseen changes. As a result, a number of commanders have found themselves scurrying around battlefields to transmit commands and gather information. This need for personal coordination was so strong that after being wounded at Poltava in 1709, King Charles of Sweden had to be carried from place to place on a litter (Keegan 1988: 198, 220f; Fuller 1955: 178). In sum, while it is easy for commanders' "micromanagement" to cause more problems than it solves, it is frequently important for commanders to be able to directly deal with lower units in order to keep them in coordination given changing circumstances (see Snyder 1993: 33).

The second limitation to a reliance on mediated relationships comes when "links" are lost in battle: as we have seen, in an antitransitive patronage structure, the clients of this link may reasonably conclude that their obligation to participate has ceased along with the life of their patron. Thus after Tiberius

Sempronius Gracchus was killed in an ambush in the second Punic war, his soldiers simply left, claiming that (as freed slaves) they had been bound only to him (Dodge 1995 [1891]: 464; for another example see Parrott 2001: 294). A command structure, if it is to be resilient, must have a principle for the reestablishment of relationships in such a situation (see Janowitz 1958: 481). This principle is transitivity, and it is such transitivity that allows a commanding officer (at times) to maintain control over the somewhat disorganized forces that are to be expected in battle or retreat (see, e.g., Keegan 1988: 224; van Creveld 1985: 91). A wonderful example of the uses of transitivity comes from the disaster that overtook the 106th Division of the U.S. Army in 1944; surprised and retreating, they clogged the roads and kept reinforcements from arriving while they themselves could not leave either. Movement was only made possible by a crossing guard who stood at a key intersection and directed traffic—he was a brigadier general whom everyone had to obey (Demchak 1991: 133; see Whiting 1981: 58).

The third reason for instituting transitivity lies in the fact that command structures are invariably used to pass information upward as well as downward (though there may be other structures for information as well). Sociologists and organizational theorists have long pointed to the pathologies that come with mediated information in a hierarchy in which lower levels may be sanctioned on the basis of information they send upward (see Fukuyama and Shulsky 1997: 10, 49); as van Creveld (1985: 75) argues, there is a tendency for information to become vaguer (if not sugar-coated) as it goes upward. Even if the problems of deliberate distortion or suppression can be eliminated, the time lost in mediated transmission is frequently a severe problem for military action. Mediated communication leads orders to disappear before they reach their ultimate destination, or to be seriously misinterpreted at great cost (two famous cases of supposed disobedience in the British Army, Nolan's insistence that sent the Light Brigade to their deaths in the Crimean war and Sackville's non-appearance at Minden, seem due to simple confusion following ambiguous mediated orders [see Mackesy 1979: 93, 230, 102; Moyse-Bartlett 1971; also Hanson 2003: 123f for another example]).

The fourth reason is that war, like all other state functions, is not an outcome of a unitary actor, but an organization of interdependent actors with different beliefs and goals. To a surprising extent, the actual prosecution of any aspect of a military campaign generally is only partially directed at the purported enemy—to a varying degree, it is part of a incessant internecine battle within the organization. The colonel does not simply want to defeat an enemy—he wants to become a general, often at the expense of another colonel. It is difficult for an immediate superior to contain the dysfunctional consequences of a rivalry between his subordinates. Transitivity increases the control that the highest levels have over the otherwise centrifugal tendencies of ambitious and contentious subordinates.[55]

For all these reasons, higher-ups may need to be able to short-circuit the mediating levels (Julius Caesar supposedly instituted this in the Roman army; Napoleon was renowned for doing just this). At the same time, mediation is still required, especially with regard to the transmission of information upward. While a commander needs the ability to jump over intermediaries and have direct communication with lower levels, the reverse is not true for simple numerical reasons—one commander will be deluged with information if mediation is wholly removed (Janowitz 1970: 102; van Creveld 1985: 71, 75, 77; cf. Feld 1959: 17; Strachan 1984: 149f; Kennedy 1969: 94; Keegan 2003: 9).

Thus transitivity allows for superordinates to directly gather information from those at the bottom of the hierarchy. There is, of course, a cost—as Simmel (1950) and Henry (1954: 145) have noted, this transitivity can lead to the "blanketing" of subordinates with commands. Just as the hen at the bottom of the pecking orders is in such sorry shape because anyone can peck her, so the poor private is overwhelmed because anyone can give him or her a command. But all in all, the transitive system has clear advantages for the deployment of armed force against an opponent.

The Need for Structure

We have seen that governmental systems can be constructed by cascading patronage triangles into pyramids, but that the resulting structures tend to be weak militarily. They can tap wide geographical regions for taxes, but generally deliver to the apex a relatively low proportion of the total extracted—too low to support a strong war effort for long. While patronage pyramids can assemble many persons for war, they cannot coordinate them so that a large proportion of those mobilized actually engage the enemy in a helpful fashion (which is to say a maximally destructive one).

Introducing transitivity into the social relationships that underlie governance is a simple, but crucial, part of the story whereby strong states can be created. While it is only part of the story—and it is a not a simple story of a unidirectional progress from patronage pyramids to states—it may be that transitivity, especially in the armed forces, was a crucial aspect of the creation of state

---

[55] Often the most difficulties in terms of the institution of transitivity come at the interface between civilian leaders and the second-highest military authorities; military leaders often resist the implication that, e.g., the secretary of war can override an order from a top general. In the United States (Weigley 1967: 137f, 192f, 249) conflict over this issue began in Monroe's administration and was not completely resolved until the 20th century. In between, the nation survived without the role of the commanding general being specified in constitutional law, sometimes with a complete lack of communication between the Department of War and the army's high command.

structures.[56] Gorski (1993; 2003) has recently argued that state building was strongest in Protestant countries with a Puritan or perfectionist tradition because this supplied leaders with disciplined material for bureaucratic taxation and military structures. But as Gorski also (2003: 76) stressed, existence of disciplined personality, necessary though it may have been, could not in itself be sufficient: the commandable needed to be placed in a coherent structure for their potential to be actualized.

As a counterexample, we may consider the military orders that grew up as a by-product of the first crusade in the early twelfth century in what is now Israel, beginning with the famous "Order of the Temple," also known as the Knights Templar. Here we see a rationalized military mentality emerging from monasteries closely paralleling the rationalized economic mentality that was later to come from similar organizations. The members of such orders, while generally laymen, were as disciplined as monks (probably a great deal more so than the average monk); they took the same vows of obedience, poverty, and chastity, and their rules were generally closely based on existing rules of other orders (Forey 1992: 1f, 188f; Edbury 1999: 95, 96).

John Keegan (1994: 295), one of the foremost authorities on the history of war, has argued that it may be that "the dissolution of the monastic orders in Protestant lands during the reformation carried into the state armies—through warrior-monks who secularized themselves to become lay soldiers—the system of hierarchy, of commanders and their subordinate units, that had made the orders the first autonomous and disciplined fighting-bodies Europe had known since the disappearance of the Roman legions."[57]

Indeed, the discipline and consequent effectiveness of these warriors were well known, and hence members of orders were frequently put at the front or rear of a formation when mixed with other troops. But we should not overstate their degree of organization: their internal divisions were crude and based on

[56] This story clearly leaves out a great deal of the development of modern states, especially the role of nationalism as an ideology, but I find it quite interesting that Mann (1993: 230) describes the role of ideology in nation building in terms of its "transitivity" especially in contrast to "particularistic patronage" structures. Ideology could transcend such local structures through general moral imperatives, increasing general discursive literacy, and providing common reference points that could be used to relativize social practices. Hechter (2000: 37, 42f, 45) also emphasizes the development of the modern state via a two-stage process in which there is first the spontaneous development of units and their concatenation into larger assemblages that, due to limitations in the technology of surveillance and control, must rely on indirect rule. Second, there is the replacement of this indirect rule with central control.

[57] To support this clearly Weberian scenario, here are the words of Guibert of Nogent: "In our time God has instituted holy wars, so that the equestrian order and erring people . . . might find a new way of meriting salvation. They are no longer obliged, as used to be the case, to leave the world and to choose the monastic life and a religious rule; they can gain God's grace to no mean extent by pursuing their own profession, unconfined and in secular garb" (Forey 1992: 13). Here is Luther's innovation, only centuries earlier and packing a harder punch.

normal feudal considerations of the difference between knights of noble descent and nonknights of common descent. The ability of the officials in charge of such orders to supervise their subordinates was seriously limited by their geographical dispersion. Perhaps more important, there was no coordination between different orders. While the members of such orders may have taken a vow of obedience, this did not mean that they were deployable units in a coordinated enterprise (Forey 1992: 83f, 195f, 88, 174f, 166, 208).

In sum, even after the technological innovations that gave a decided advantage to whatever army could increase its coordination, there was no reason to expect that transitivity would immediately follow. Instead, most armies were locked into a reliance on semi-independent contractors that put a relatively low upper limit on the amount of possible transitivity that could be instituted. Sir Francis Drake, during the historic battle with the Armada in 1588, was set to lead the fleet in a night chase after a vulnerable Spanish enemy, but in the middle of the action, the light in his stern, there to guide the other British ships, suddenly disappeared and the plan ground to a halt. In the morning it turned out that Drake had heard that Don Pedro de Valdez's ship, which contained much booty, was helpless for the taking, and so he extinguished the light and turned about, so as to take the prize for himself. His companions-in-arms were disgusted by this blatant elevation of personal gain over sound military tactics—unless he was to share the treasure (Fuller 1955: 25).

What was missing in nearly all armed forces up until the modern period was a coherent tree structure of command and punishment. Such a structure could not come merely from the willingness of people to be commanded, nor could it come through blind mutation and selection. Instead, such structures generally came from aspects of military life other than command, namely the recruitment, supply, and punishment of soldiers.

Origins of Organization

We have seen that patronage pyramids formed the skeleton for armed forces primarily by attaching obligations to benefices of various sizes, for example.[58] Thus medieval armies were frequently composed of sections that had more to do with how the fighters were *recruited* and not how they fought in battle. These same structures, however, could be used for other purposes once the soldiers were mustered—supplying them and paying them above all else (Contamine 1998 [1980]: 229; Prestwich 1996: 41, 62, 64f; cf. Powicke 1996 [1962]: 21).

Thus the social structure implicit in the patronage relationships could be used for both recruitment and administration; rationalization of this structure

---

[58] Similarly, the decimal organization of ancient Indian armies may have derived from patterns of feudal control over villages (Srivastava 1985: 13, 97).

was likely to be provoked by needs of administration or logistics (the supplying and movement of troops), as opposed to command (cf. Fukuyama and Shulsky 1997: 55). While these administrative matters might only lead to a rudimentary form of structure, if a prolonged war impelled administrative reform, this could end up rationalizing the command structure (for an early modern example, see Mallett and Hale 1984: 23, 101, 103, 381; on the British see Strachan 1984: 160f). One crucial way in which structural reform could take place that could help institute transitivity was to replace as many patronage-based transactions as possible with monetary ones. This involved the splitting of a largely unitary structure into two structures—one of command and one of surplus extraction (taxation) (also see Eisenstadt 1963: 24–29). This allowed for the purification of the military structure as one of command, but also increased its dependence on this parallel structure.

The Monetarization of Obligations

The institution of transitivity in command was inseparable from the monetarization of military obligations. While a replacement of personalistic feudal obligations with monetary ones did not always produce a transitive command structure, it was a necessary first step, and in general, kings have preferred to convert feudal obligations into cash flows when feasible (see Mason 1974: 51). An elegant illustration is found in Thailand, used in the last chapter as an illustration of the pure case of governance through patronage pyramids. In the Third Reign of the Bangkok period (1824–51), the pyramidal form was strengthened through tax farming and an extension of the practice of tattooing patrons' names on clients' bodies, but at the same time, in-kind obligations were monetarized (converted into monetary obligations). The patrons then had less personalistic relations with their clients, functioning more as simple tax collectors. But this threatened to increase the power of middlemen over the king, and such monetarization was deeply problematic because of a lack of general state capacity—collectors either could not get taxes or refused to transmit them to the central state (see Terwiel 1984: 30f). Englehart (2001: 83f, 88, 92–96, 100) argues that the "Weberian" model of a centralized state was consciously used by the Thai ruler Chulalongkorn (reigned 1868–1910, though he only came of age in 1873) to assert central control. He did this by attempting to bureaucratize tax collection with an audit office and a professional civil service composed of administrative officials lacking any personal discretion. He thus transformed an almost pure patronage structure into a nearly pure command tree.

Turning to the European continent, roughly in the thirteenth century one sees a general move away from feudal institutions for armed service and toward monetarization, though in areas with a serious shortage of manpower, personal service might remain a more attractive option than competing with high wages.[59] These monetary relations still might be masked as feudal ones—in France in the early fourteenth century warriors recruited for their skill were given "fiefs" that turned out to be cash, not land. Not only might more obligations be defined in monetary terms, but those with feudal obligations could be allowed—indeed encouraged—to buy these off with money (called "scutage" in England). This aided the monarch as the money taken in lieu of service was sufficient to provide for a larger number of professional soldiers, whose skill (and loyalty) were generally more reliable than that of a vassal, especially when the king left something to be desired in the realm of popularity. While some such professionals (for example, the Renaissance *condottieri*) might be given land similar to a benefice, in general, part of the attraction of professionals was their dissociation from existing patronage relationships and the directness of their relationship with the central power (Beeler 1971: 42, 100; Contamine 1998 [1980]: 89f, 163, 79, 100; Downing 1992: 59; Duby 1991: 166, 169; Edbury 1999: 93; Housley 1999: 124f; Ganshof 1964: 90f; Prestwich 1996: 14f, 63, 151; Powicke 1996 [1962]: 49; Wilson 1999: 189f; Fourquin 1976: 123; Mann 1986: 423; McGeer 1995: 200f; on the earlier introduction in Britain see Beeler [1966] 1995: 186, 280f, 289).[60]

The classic example is Prussia: Frederick William (the Great Elector) basically sold the Junkers back their feudal obligations in 1653: they gave him a grant of 530,000 talers, with which he could raise a modern army, and in return allowed them to own their estates outright—and tax their peasants without turning over a cut to him—as opposed to holding them as feudal grants of land in return for military service. While he thus did create a strong nobility more independent of his wishes, with the cash he could begin setting up a small, but nonfeudal, state and military.[61]

Now historians who have had their fill of unidirectional changes from one thing to another—changes that seem posited more because if they *had* oc-

---

[59] To some extent, this shift toward monetarization and contractual arrangements was driven by the need of lords to compensate new forms of nonmilitary (serjeanty) service by proto-professionals who did not need land (Waugh 1986: 817).

[60] Academics will be familiar with the structurally similar process by which faculty with grants can buy off their course obligations and be replaced with dedicated lecturers. The similarity goes further, in that what seemingly is in the interest of the party able to exempt themselves from onerous service turns out to be their downfall, as they find the social structure re-created without needing them. Finally, it should be noted that monetarization only increases central control when the center is able to forbid *others* to hire mercenaries (McKinley 1934: 204). Even so, a reliance on mercenaries could in some cases *support* the power of feudal lords in cases where they retained political control, as in England and the Italian city states (here see Powicke 1996 [1962]: 166, 213, 235; Contamine 1998 [1980]: 160–63; Mallet and Hale 1984: 14, 18, 33, 65–89, 101, 187–89, 292; also Adams 2005: 7).

[61] Gorski (2003: 83f, 88f) has argued against the importance of this transaction, but his critique has more to do with associated claims that this led to some sort of alliance between the nobles and the crown. The later centralization of administration by Frederick William would not have been possible if raising funds for military exploits had further entrenched the powers of the estates.

curred, they would nicely explain something else—have grown accustomed to dismiss the analytic importance of any one explanatory factor such as the "monetarization of obligations." But while it is indeed impossible to find a unidirectional change from completely "in kind" obligations to completely monetarized ones—especially within a delimited period of a particular historian's expertise—it does not follow that this change is not of great analytical importance.

Thus one must not deny that many historically important cases involved amalgams of different forms of remuneration and obligation, and these are likely to be misunderstood if forced into a framework of a simple transition, especially because the language used can be ambiguous (see, e.g., Beeler [1966] 1995: 307).[62] Similarly, in most medieval contexts (and perhaps especially in England), armies were always mixtures of different types of forces, some serving on the basis of feudal obligations, some on the basis of cash incentives, and many with a bit of both (cf. Bloch 1961 [1940]: 329; Downing 1992: 158). A different mixture occurred in Japan in the Warring States period: the warlord would hire soldiers but have his vassal command them, thus using the existing patronage structure as the scaffolding for a command structure but instituting disciplined transitivity and lessened dependence on middle rungs for mobilization (Ikegami 1995: 140ff).[63]

Yet over the long term, there was without doubt a tendency to replace feudal obligations with blanket legal ones (e.g., conscription) or with monetary incentives. Indeed, some of the confusion over the *historical* replacement of feudal obligations with monetary taxes comes precisely because the "feudal" obligations that seemed to be pursued by monarchs with such vigor were only insisted on precisely *because* all parties expected them to be replaced on an *individual* basis with a payment. Such monetarization, however, while it generally strengthened the central power, did not automatically lead toward a command structure; indeed, monetarization can also facilitate farming out the actual organization and/or deployment of troops to others. In many cases, monetarization led to the introduction of intermediaries into what were previously more centralized structures (Prestwich 1996: 113; Contamine 1998 [1980]: 92, 98, 162f; Adams 1974: 130, 145; Parker 1996: 64; Hall 1997: 225). In particular, mercenaries under independent contractors are generally the core of the army in relatively rich city-states (e.g. Greece, Carthage, renaissance Italy; see Garlan 1995: 79; Dodge 1995 [1891]: 11f; Mallett 1999: 216, 222, 228; Keegan 1994: 231); in such cases, monetarization tends to foster indirect rule.

[62] For example, in 14th-century England lords generally gave their retainers regular cash payments but these were called "rents" (Bean 1989: 42).

[63] The Japanese path toward transitivity was somewhat different, but the structural tensions were identical (Ikegami 1995: 235–37).

But systems based on subcontracting are rarely the first choice when it comes to an empire or large nation that attempts to dominate peripheral regions. Princes find it quite expensive to pay mercenaries year-round, but if released at the end of hostilities, they tend to ravage the countryside. If paid to leave, they still need to traverse the Prince's land and are now without any effective control. Even during war, mercenaries are difficult to control: they are prone to leave without ceremony when they fail to receive their pay, and it is difficult to punish them for desertion (Barkey 1994: 174; Keegan 1988: 173; Mallett 1999: 223, 214; Mallett and Hale 1984: 21, 24; Prestwich 1996: 152; Powicke 1996 [1962]: 246).

A reliance on mercenaries was not, then, in the long run, as effective as a true command structure. That does not mean that there were simple, unidirectional pressures toward the evolution of a structurally purified command structure. In part, this was because even a nation that could assemble a centralized, standing army with a true command structure for one task (land war at or near home) might find other—more extensive—military tasks beyond the reach of this social structure and would revert to patronage-pyramid tactics. For example, early modern states that had moved toward a command army might use patronage pyramids to assemble navies (composed largely of privately owned ships).[64] Similarly, just as contemporary first world nations may rely on patronage-pyramids when attempting warfare in third world battlefields (this is often known as "military assistance," but there is a difference between military assistance to a de facto sovereign state and client warfare), so early modern armies often reverted to feudal levies when forced into sprawling colonial wars.[65]

But the monetarization of obligations was the sine qua non of the development of a transitive command structure. Such a development then made possible the changes that a number of scholars (especially Michael Roberts [1967]; also see Parker [1996: 24]) have termed the "military revolution" of the seventeenth century.[66] (The exemplar of this change is the Swedish king and military leader Gustavus Adolphus who forever changed armed forces from raggedy feudal ensembles to efficiently administered and disciplined troops who could

---

[64] Naval warfare generally involved greater barriers to communication and hence a throwback to forms of coordination requiring less control (Palmer 2005: 37); also see Hillman and Gathman (2007).

[65] Thus in the Seven Years War, Britain allowed the feudal practice of granting commissions to gentlemen who raised their own battalions from their clients (Anderson 2000: 488). When officers had responsibility for raising the troops they commanded from their clientele they might then be allowed to appoint their subordinate officers, potentially undermining central control (Black 1991: 79). For other examples, see Porter (1994: 87), Goldsworthy (2006:23). This is one of the many ways in which war imperatives can lead to a decreased strength of central government (cf. Brewer 1988: 138).

[66] Of course, once the idea of a revolution became of interest, historians found it in different countries (Roberts originally proposed it for Sweden) and, as Prestwich (1996: 334f) points out, during the period in which they specialized.

truly be commanded [Fuller 1955: 52, 60ff].)[67] While the existence of the military revolution itself as a continentwide, demarcated period is doubtful, European armies became larger, better trained, used the bow and arrow or musket as opposed to the pike or lance, were more strategically oriented, and made greater claims on the state in terms of taxes. These new forms of battle required coordination and drill, and hence transitive command structures. Further, these command structures were better integrated with administrative structures. Although great progress towards the rationalization and bureaucratization of command occurred in the eighteenth and early nineteenth centuries, such innovations built on firmly instituted transitivity (Prestwich 1996: 336; van Creveld 1985: 52, 38f; Roberts 1967: 197f, 205; Contamine 1998 [1980]: 165–72; Porter 1994: 90; Hall 1997: 207).[68]

This transitive command structure eventually made its way even to those forms of colonial, naval, and imperialist war often farmed out to subcontractors. To some degree, this involved a change in the practicability of centralized control due to the easing of the technical limitations discussed above. Yet there has not been an ever-increasing approximation to a pure structure. Just as we saw above for the case of management hierarchies, so even in armed forces there is, past a certain point, a declining return to command strength.

Advantages of Disorganization

Thus far, I have emphasized the advantages of clarity of structural imperatives. Yet there are, at the same time, often advantages to structural incoherence that stem not from external conditions (e.g., communication technology) but the nature of the military task (though these may also be felt in the command hierarchies of business enterprise). Coordination of efforts (paradigmatically when different actions must converge on the same goal) points to the virtues of centralized control, while the ability to respond quickly to changes in the environment points to the virtues of delegation of control to lower levels. Armies are in the unfortunate position of constantly having to do both types of

---

[67] After the cessation of hostilities ended the self-funding nature of its army, Sweden was to shift to a *more* feudal basis for its military. But as Downing (1992: 203–5) has emphasized, the Swedish state could afford a more decentralized system because it was not propped up by as many irritated peasants as were the other major powers.

[68] In chapter 9 we examine 17th-century France, where state formation occurred largely through the crown siphoning patronage from pyramids headed by great nobles and redirecting it to new clients who formed an independent governance structure (see, e.g., Kettering 1986: 208, 221f, 225f; Major 1964: 635, 644). In this way, the monetarization of obligations increases transitivity by decoupling military service and surplus-transmission. That is, professional soldiers require money, which requires a professional administrative apparatus, and this can be used to break the power of nobles–the administrators, unlike the nobles, must work for a salary and find it harder to appropriate their own offices (Weber 1968).

tasks simultaneously (Fukuyama and Shulsky 1997: 21), two imperatives that jointly prohibit a consistent organizational form of a simple type. We can readily imagine that transitivity can strengthen a command structure's capacity for coordination. Interestingly, transitivity can also allow for needed *disorganization*. Normally mediated command relationships can be short-circuited and extra attention brought to bear on goings-on that would otherwise be far removed from central planning.

If transitivity is accompanied by overcentralization and micromanagement—the top echelons insist that they receive all information and make all decisions—there are likely to be overloads on processing capacity.[69] But allowing subordinates to process information and translate general instructions into specific plans can leave the upper level a mere figurehead. As a result, command hierarchies often have a hybrid nature, with routine affairs being mediated by middle-level officers or managers, with special "tunnels" that allow the top levels to make direct contact with the bottom. Indeed, in the situations in which limited war aims may still have weighty political repercussions, we may see the direct commanding of minor units on the part of the absolute apex of the command structure (van Creveld 1985: 98; Fukuyama and Shulsky 1997: xiii, 30, 61; Ward 1957: 156f, 164, 167–69, 230; Fuller 1955: 494; Strachan 1984: 147; see Keegan 2000: 194 for an example).

Not only are there reasons to avoid a textbook tree structure for sending information up, but there are reasons to avoid it in terms of sending commands down, since subordinate units generally require some degree of flexibility and initiative. This leads to an attempt to make some distinction between tactical and strategic decision making—the former is generally left for the lower-level commanders who are more "in touch" with what is happening "on the ground." For military structures, the degree of flexibility required has changed over time, increasing in the past century, so that effective modern armies often have *less* control over the lower layers than their less-effective opponents. This devolution of decision making in modern armies was first seen in the Prussian/ German Army in the war of 1866 and in the First World War. But it became the rule as opposed to the exception in the twentieth century. With increased firepower and a reliance on gasoline-powered vehicles, war involved dispersed units with increased needs for independent decision making and hence a deemphasizing of the command hierarchy, something reflected in the U.S. "doctrine" of AirLand Battle. At the same time, in part because of an increase in the number of specialists with technical training, the command pyramid began

---

[69] For example, while in general an efficient commander, Wellington rarely delegated any substantial decision making to subordinates. Since the most important intelligence communications therefore went directly to him–and in raw form, as opposed to the digested and summarized briefs of today–the simple act of losing the keys to his file boxes actually halted the processing of information for a week.

to bulge in the middle: fewer "GI Joes" and more middle-level personnel (van Creveld 1985: 120, 131, 140, 145–47, 168–71; Kaufman 1996: 47, 52; Janowitz 1970: 35; Keegan 1988: 246; Martin 1981: 98, 101ff, 113; Mowbray 1996: 86; Travers 2005 [1996]: 108). There are further technological imperatives that cut against the two cardinal principles of the tree structure (the absence of horizontal communication and the uniqueness of supervision), but it is as of yet unclear whether command structures will change appreciably as a result.[70]

We have seen that the patronage pyramids that are regular products of anarchic situations with material inequality can be transformed into command structures through the institution of transitivity. This is by no means an inevitable transition, nor an unproblematic one. Yet it is a transition that allowed for the creation of modern command structures, seen most importantly in armies. For most of the world's history, the various barriers to the development of a true command hierarchy for military endeavor were insurmountable, but the development of nations coincided with changed conditions making possible the institution of transitivity into structures that were originally conglomerations of patronage relationships (compare Andreski 1968: 144; Wilson 1999: 202). Thus armies may be "seen" in functional terms, as Spencer and Durkheim might have liked, as sets of persons who carry out a relationship to the whole of defense against external enemies. This is not completely wrong. But it is far more accurate to say that they generally arose from the transformation of earlier structures and allowed an extension of state power against both external and internal enemies.

The commandable army was perhaps the most important of the hierarchical structures that comprise the organized interactions of the nation state. A second is the "bureaucracy," the combined administrative functions that until relatively recently were focused on the extraction of taxes, and the various subsidiary tasks necessary to facilitate this (for example, censuses and regulation of trade). We saw that the development of the command army required its separa-

---

[70] It is indeed possible that, as Janowitz (1970: 37) suggests, horizontal communication is needed to establish a secure environment for specialists in different vertical lines of authority to coordinate their efforts. Horizontal information provision has generally been anathema to officers (since it is understood that to give information is to acknowledge oneself the subordinate [Feld 1959: 18f; 1977:77f; Goetzinger and Valentine 1963])–and their superiors may also discourage it. (During World War II, Douglas MacArthur forbade his subordinates to communicate directly, leading their radio operators to spy on one another to stay informed [Palmer 2005: 270f].) Despite this, such horizontal communication is likely to be built into future weaponry. Both the Abrams tank and Bradley fighting vehicle feature an Inter-Vehicular Information System that coordinates information for commanders who can see the battlefield from the positions of all the vehicles (Kaufman 1996: 58). Similarly, increased possibilities for detailed coordination and interservice cooperation threaten to produce the situation in which one person obeys more than one superordinate (Williams 1996: 69f).

tion from functions of surplus extraction and concentration—these jobs were organized in a different social structure. Although we briefly return to this structure in chapter 9, the further evolution of state bureaucracy is less central for the current project: the taxation system is basically a structure for moving money around. There are admittedly myriad interpersonal interactions involved, but these are a means to an end, not an end in themselves. In contrast, the military command structure is an attempt to mobilize persons, predominantly against external enemies, by organizing their interactions in a particular structure. In this way, it is very much like the party, which is mobilized for internal, as opposed to external, conflict or action. And the mass political party is above all else the other social structure that can be said to be distinctive to the modern state. We go on to examine the development of parties from patronage pyramids.

8

From Pyramid to Party

What Is a Party?

Parties and Mobilization

In the previous chapter we saw that command structures, in particular the army that is the backbone of the modern state, could be constructed out of the building blocks of patronage triangles. First the patronage triangles were arranged into pyramids that could span vertical distances of social space, and then transitivity was introduced. This command army is one key large-scale social structure of the modern state; a second is the modern party.

In this chapter, I will conduct a somewhat parallel examination of the structural origin of political parties. We are hampered here in that while there is little ambiguity as to what constitutes an army, there have been a number of different definitions of party that take us in very different directions. Out of conceptual inertia, sociologists frequently start with Weber's (1978 I: 284–88; II: 938f) definition of parties as associations seeking to influence the distribution of power within some organization.[1] In so doing, Weber was certainly being true to the colloquial usage of "party," according to which factions are one sort of party. But even at the time he was writing, it should have been obvious that this definition was a poor one.

The clearest evidence of this is the widespread existence of single-party states. Such states are common among nations that achieved independence or underwent major revolutions in the twentieth century. They are characterized by the presence of a party in which membership is voluntary, and where the party's actual influence on the government, while frequently formally recognized to some degree in law, exceeds all formal descriptions. Most notably, other parties are forbidden de jure or de facto. In such states, then, the party is not intended to struggle for power—indeed, any such struggle would delegitimate the party and the state's claim to represent the general interest. Instead, it is clear that the party's function is to *mobilize* citizens just as the army mobilizes soldiers (cf. Porter 1994: 199; Wilentz 2005: 516).

---

[1] Weber further distinguished "patronage parties" that attempt to accrue control over material advantages for their members from "ideological parties" that represent either broader groups or constellations of ideal interests. We will see later that this distinction, while inexact, gets at a crucial structural bifurcation.

It seems that it is this mobilization that is crucial for parties, and for this reason, from a structural point of view, it is not immediately clear that we should divide organizations into "parties" and "social movements" (or "pressure groups"). Both involve the mobilization of persons to accomplish political ends (cf. Key 1964: 9, 11, 154). While it is tempting to distinguish the two by arguing that parties are "inside" the system and social movements "outside," this may exaggerate the actual differences. For one thing, groups are often contesting precisely what is inside as opposed to outside, indeed, whether there *can* be a legitimate contest or not. Furthermore, many nonparties seen as social movements are composed of insiders to the governing elite while there are parties composed wholly of outsiders (compare Scientists against Nuclear Exchange to the Communist Party USA).

We also cannot support our distinction by reference to the particular goals being sought by the organizations. The social movement organization MoveOn works to support the election of particular candidates, while the Green Party seeks wide ranging social and environmental change. Finally, we cannot distinguish between parties and social movements on the basis of their degree of social organization: the single term *social movement* hides the radical difference between inchoate (and potentially illusory) trends and fashions (such as New Age spirituality) on the one hand and formally elaborated organizations such as the National Organization of Women on the other.

Is there, then, any difference between a social movement and a political party? There is one, and it is simply that party membership is almost invariably understood as exclusive. Whether or not the Communist Party in Russia had succeeded in outlawing all others, members could belong to no other party. The same is generally true of other parties. This exclusivity leads to an increased analytic clarity—just as the patronage pyramid is so clear because people can only have one patron, and the military structure clear because soldiers can have only one immediate commanding officer, so the party structure is clear because people belong to only one party. Like the military, this structure can be used to mobilize and coordinate large numbers of people.

Thus we see the fundamental parallel between the modern party and the modern army. The army is a social structure that seeks to mobilize a significant portion of the general population so that they can effectively carry out elites' wishes against others usually (though not invariably) in different nations. The party is a social structure that seeks to mobilize a significant portion of the general citizenry so that they can effectively carry out elites' wishes against others in *the same* nation.[2] (We are free to expect that in many cases the wishes

---

[2] Although the Communist Party in the Soviet Union did not compete with other parties, it was organized to combat internal enemies. Also, it is worth emphasizing that by "elites" I do not mean to imply that these must be social elites–they may be political elites who lack other positions of distinction.

of the elites are greatly constrained by the actions or opinions of nonelites, but the definition works as stated.)

Given this clear parallel, there are reasons to expect that parties will tend to have the same structural principles as armies (forming transitive tree structures) and may even arise similarly. And, to anticipate, there is indeed evidence that antitransitive patronage structures form the core of early parties. But the particular form of mobilization required in competitive national-level party systems means that such vertical structural principles must be supplemented with horizontal relationships.

Where Do Parties Come From?

It is, unfortunately, difficult to assess the idea that we can analytically derive parties from the aggregation of vertical patronage-type relationships. For if we look at any party to determine where it came from, in almost every case the answer is, "other parties." This is because most party systems have a relatively old lineage; even where the governmental system has changed dramatically, we are able to trace out relations of descent connecting later parties to organizations that played a role in an earlier constellation of the political field. There are, of course, exceptions: the late-nineteenth-century People's Party in the United States (here see Goodwyn 1978; Hicks 1931; Pollack 1967; Woodward 1938, 1951) was built not out of elements of another party, but out of very different types of organizations such as the Farmer's Alliance. Still, the evolution of such parties is highly constrained by the structure of the existing organizational environment (in the fashion discussed by DiMaggio and Powell 1983; Meyer and Rowan 1977).[3]

We rarely witness the cataclysmic change of a party system that leads to the formation of a set of parties almost, if not entirely, from scratch. One such case is seen in the countries coming out of the breakup of the Soviet Union, particularly Russia. Within a matter of years, a one-party system in Russia transformed into a completely different multiparty system. Here there were two preexisting sources from which parties could be built, corresponding roughly to the "traditional/personalistic" and "modernist" theories of state formation, namely patronage relationships (on the one hand) and voluntary associations (on the other).

Regarding the former, the Soviet system of bureaucratic careerism had revolved around a particular form of patronage relationship in which the up-

---

[3] However, where the party system is weak, the reliance on such external structural forms can be determinative of the nature of the party system. Both Italian and Spanish fascism were built on preexisting structures, the former on local agrarian organizations that provided collective goods and the latter on the army. As a result, the former could be used for radical mobilization and transformation, while the latter simply allowed typical *caciques* to boss others around (Riley 2005: 300–305).

wardly mobile required a patron among the higher-ups (see Willerton 1992: 6, 9, 11, 64, 76, 85, 115, 117, 224, 238; also Eyal, Szelényi, and Townsley 1998: 7). Once ascendant, the occupant would work to form a wheel around himself, which would not only make him locally secure, but be the inner ring in a widening coalition involving both vertical and horizontal ties. Further, most clients seem to have had only one patron, and hence the structure tended toward a pyramid or a set of pyramids of different sizes. These pyramids not only consolidated the support of a leader, but says Willerton (1992: 73, 233), "helped bridge the political distance between Moscow and the periphery."

The latter form of preexisting structure was the organization. Most important was the Communist Party itself, but this could not unproblematically be the source of postcommunist parties. Second, there were what the Soviets generally called "unofficial" or "informal" organizations. This term included pretty much any form of voluntary organization one could think of—everything from teenagers' rock bands to sports teams to artistic groups to nascent political organizations. Such organizations had been somewhat tolerated before Perestroika, as long as their activities were circumscribed, but with the loosening of the Gorbachev era, their number increased dramatically, to around thirty thousand by 1988 and perhaps twice that by 1989. These organizations were free to turn their attention to political reform, and many did—representatives of a number of such groups gathered in Moscow to create the Democratic Union as an opposition organization, while others served as the basis for new parties. Well before Yeltsin abolished the CPSU's status as the only legal party in 1990, it was clear that a de facto multiparty system had developed (Luchterhandt 1992: 1044; Tolz 1990: 10f, 37ff, 56, 84; McFaul and Markov 1993: 2).

At the same time that protoparties were developing from the bottom up, they were developing from the top down, as the Communist Party began to split. Informal groupings of reformers solidified, as did some antireform groups, and both eventually spawned parties (Tolz 1990: 65, 68, 72–78; Luchterhandt 1992: 1039f, 1043). Given the zeal with which new parties were formed—up to one party a month in 1990 (McFaul and Markov 1993: 12)—and the seemingly insatiable demand for new forms of political mobilization and expression, one might be surprised to find that these new parties had very little effect on the emerging party system (almost none were present a decade later). As Fish (1995: 55–57, 109, 114, 137, 197, 204) emphasized, these new parties were unable to establish either vertical or horizontal transitivity. Taking the first, their "hyperdemocratic" organization meant that there were many leaders and few followers. This might seem a wonderful thing, but it meant in practice that there was no discipline and no coordination.[4] Taking the second, the party system did not interface with any division of the population into groups with conflicting interests. Indeed, it is notable that membership and

---

[4] The exception seems to have been the Democratic Party of Russia, headed by Nikolai Travkin (see his interview in McFaul and Markov 1993: 67, 73f).

even leadership was not considered an exclusive relation. Thus there was little connection between what any particular group of leaders advocated and what a particular group of citizens wanted. The party was unable to organize, aggregate, and represent interests.

Rather than these new party organizations, it was the wheel system that seemed to be the most important institutional form for effective party formation. As the CPSU began to dissolve, members attempted to preserve pieces or make new factions out of the resulting debris (Luchterhandt 1992: 1043); in many cases these efforts to carry existing patronage structures out of the bureaucracy were almost as successful as similar attempts to carry money or heavy equipment out of state-run plants. In the words of Perkins (1996: 363), "The communist party had considerable organizational assets and, while the ideology may have been discredited, [these assets] were still available for co-optation by enterprising politicians."

While a simple transplantation was not often possible (except for some of the highest-level leaders), the basic structural form was preserved—apexes transplanted their existing triangles as best they could and used the advantages of their position to build new relationships. For example, a survey of 1992–93 found that most of the new parties were headed by former Communist Party leaders and were factions that had previously existed within the Communist Party but now became parties of their own (McAllister and White 1995: 50f). (A description of the party field circa 1990 can be found in Lentini 1992.) In other cases, a "party" was simply those willing to support a particular politician—indeed, in the regional elections of 1994, most candidates did not even have a party affiliation (Kropp 1999: 295, 300f, 303).

In sum, while the preexisting informal organizations did contribute to the creation of a new party system, it was the existing patronage triangles disembedded from the old party system that were the dominant seeds of future crystallization (and we may say that the further east the republic, the less disjuncture there was between the old patronage pyramids and the new; see Tolz 1990: 44f). Thus we should not assume that when parties are allowed to form and compete for offices in elections they will arise in a textbook fashion: those who share common interests will band together and push forward a representative. Instead, it seems that people are likely to scramble to knit together whatever strong relationships are at hand, most important, patronage relationships.[5]

Of course, not all parties will form in a context in which patronage relationships are already so entrenched. Yet it may be that if we examine the nature of party formation more closely, we will find analogous structural developments at the core. That is, when we look at the case of a set of parties forming

---

[5] Similarly, during the Second World War Japanese parties were dissolved as the country moved to military rule, but the informal personal connections between politicians that were retained then formed the nucleus of the parties emerging in the newly democratized postwar political field (Ike 1972: 77).

from scratch, we find that they are built out of particular *relationships* of persons and not out of formal organizations. We will begin with a purely analytic explication, which produces a useful typology of protoparties, and then determine to what extent this can be the basis for a historical derivation.

From Patronage to Faction

People and Machines

We are all familiar with one way in which parties are based on patronage relationships, namely the urban "political machine" of the late nineteenth century. Studying the classic case of Tammany Hall, Shefter (1976: 34, 41) argued that "the machine in its earlier stages more closely resembles a feudal hierarchy: the regime's officials, the ward leaders, are given control over its resources—they are given patronage to distribute to their subordinates—in return for supporting the regime, but the distribution of benefits increases the bargaining power of these officials against the central regime because it enhances their influence within their petty domains. In order to overcome this paradoxical consequence of the distribution of patronage, Tammany's leaders cultivated a series of alliances and engineered a number of changes in party organization, recruitment, and finance, that are akin to those fostered by patrimonial rulers in their efforts to centralize feudal regimes."

Even were this generalizable, however, it would not demonstrate that political parties are based on patronage relationships, for three reasons. The first is simply that the sort of urban patronage system discussed by Shefter is a historical *consequent* of the development of a party, not its antecedent. The second is that the presence of feudal-like retinues supported by patronage does not necessarily imply the concatenation of vertical patronage relationships that, as we saw in chapter 7, proved so important in the construction of armies. The third, and most important reason, is that in an important sense the urban machines are generally seen, and rightly so, as antithetical to the nature of the modern party. Their "corruption" was intrinsically related to the way in which they mobilized people not so much to compete against other parties, but instead to *avoid* competition.

As the "sage of Tammany Hall," the wonderfully named George Washington Plunkitt explained, the machine was founded "on the main proposition that when a man works in politics, he should get something out of it" (Riordon 1982 [1905]: 3, 38, 91). The politician accumulates various good things that could be dispensed at will to constituents, assuring their support. With their support, he could establish his fiefdom more securely, and hence the process was a reinforcing one. In the ideal world (at least for Plunkitt), all politics would be amiable in that the politician would never have to worry about someone from a challenging party.

Factions, Parties, and Patronage Systems

When things are running smoothly, the machine politician's position is relatively secure. In unsettled times, however, he may confront a set of dedicated and hostile rivals. We can follow general usage and call such contending groups within a party "factions." The terms *party* and *faction* have often been used interchangeably. In English there was no clear distinction between the two words until the nineteenth century, although "faction" generally had a more pejorative sense (Hofstadter 1970: 10; for example, see Madison in *Federalist* #10; Cooke 1961: 57). But as parties became accepted as fundamental aspects of a democratic system, "party" lost its sense of illegitimacy while "faction" retained it. More important, "party" has come to connote a formal organization, while faction generally connotes an informal one. From a structural standpoint, however, a more important distinction is that we have no trouble understanding that there can be factions within parties, but we would have a harder time accepting the idea that there are parties within factions.

Indeed, considering the case of factions within parties can help us determine what we mean by factions. Such factions are likely to be noticeable where party competition is relatively low. Another good example is Japanese politics in the postwar period. The parties were generally considered conglomerates of "factions" ("*ha*") that formed around a patron possessing seniority, skill, and resources with which he could provide positions and funds to his followers (Scalapino and Masumi 1964: 15, 18f, 54, 79, 32; Ike 1972: 25f, 81ff).

There are three crucial things to note about the factions in this case. First, they are defined by vertical connections, not necessarily horizontal alliances (contra Scott 1972). Second, they generally partake of the same exclusivity as do patronage triangles, in that one can be a member of only one faction (Wolf 1977: 174f and references therein). Horizontal relationships usually only exist between factions in the form of loose alliances (which will be discussed below). The third important thing to note is that the factions involve only elites, or active participants. Thus a faction may be seen as a set of led elites who struggle to increase their degree of control over some relatively small group (also see Landé 1977a: xxxii; Boissevain 1964).

The organization of the faction around dominant personalities has led to interest in its connection to patronage structures, leading to the reasonable hypothesis that a faction is a patronage structure embedded within a group (paradigmatically a party) (see Nathan 1977 [1973]: 383f). But we have seen in the machine that patronage structures may be embedded in a group without leading to factionalism: the bureaucrat who appropriates his or her office and uses it as the basis for personalistic amassing of power becomes a patron, but does not form a faction. Only when the patron uses his or her clientele to best another patron do we speak of a faction. Following Weber (1946 [1918]), we may consider "politics" the struggle to influence the distribution of power.

Thus we may provisionally propose that factions are *politicized* patronage structures and inquire as to what conditions lead to such a transformation.

Division and Indivisibility

Why would we see such a politicization of a patronage structure (for an example, see Nicholas 1977)? In some cases, the patronage structure exists within a larger corporate body (for example, a state). Politicization is likely to arise when there are areas of this corporate body that are considered to be available for domination by a patronage pyramid. Such "fallow areas" appear when a corporate body is created for the first time via the amalgamation of existing patronage triangles, when an existing corporate body makes a relatively sudden extension of its jurisdiction, or when for exogenous reasons the structure previously controlling this area is rendered substantially less effective. In either case, the unsettling of previous relations and the promise of new good things is likely to provoke an increase in conflict. But why would not the various patrons divide up the spoils according to their relative strength?

The answer is that in some cases the good things that the group can produce or deliver to members turn out to be relatively nondivisible. Many patrons can exist within a government bureaucracy and dispense jobs to their clients without needing to come into conflict with other patrons. Even if one patron consolidates a position at the head of the organization, she may allow others moderate amounts of various resources as consolation prizes. This, however, assumes that the goods that the patrons have access to are divisible. But other goods are "winner-take-all"—those who are not members of the victorious faction get nothing.[6] This is, speaking roughly, generally the case in stronger organizations—the power of the organization can be considered fungible and hence is itself a compelling prize, as opposed to the relatively minor matters of material rewards *within* the organization. Every patron must attempt to mobilize his or her clients so as to be victorious, and every client will try his or her best to make sure that he or she ends up on the winning side. Put somewhat differently, while there may be some preexisting inequality that allows patrons to transfer good things to followers, the faction exists to the extent that the good thing that attracts the followers depends on the faction prevailing, and success in turn (at least to some extent) depends on the adherence of followers.[7]

In chapter 6 we noted that the patron-client relationship differed from "boss" and "big man" relationships in that it assumes a dependence on preexisting

---

[6] The importance of this distinction for analyzing systems of political patronage has been emphasized by Clark (1975: 328) and especially (1973b).

[7] At the same time, a sudden shortage of patronage may force machine-type patrons to mobilize their followers for more violent action, not so much because the good has become winner-take-all but because there is a good chance of loser-take-none (see Auyero and Moran 2007:1356f).

inequality (as opposed to generating the inequality). Because of this dependence, the patron is generally limited in terms of the number of clients he can
support—past some point, he runs out of surplus to return to them. A shift to
winner-take-all goods lessens the dependence of the relationships on preexisting inequality and hence removes such inherent limits. Like the "sponsor,"
the faction leader who has a large number of followers can support all the
more (see Major 1964: 637; though see Ike 1972: 82). Thus the faction system
is formally similar to the endogenous popularity tournament in necessarily
being based on self-fulfilling prophecies.

As a result, faction systems share some of the instabilities of popularity
tournaments. While each follower can generally be part of only one faction,
followers frequently cast sidelong glances at other factions to determine
whether now is the time to bolt to a stronger group. It is for this reason that in
"factional" politics actions and statements are continuously examined for their
signification—every act or decision is pregnant with implications for the only
thing that matters, namely, winning or losing.

The politicization of factional struggle has important structural correlates.
First, there is a necessity of horizontal (or somewhat horizontal) alliances between faction leaders (barring the interesting cases in which there are only two
faction leaders to begin with). The reason for this is clear to see: generally
only one faction or alliance can control the group. A leader can give her followers nothing if she is not among the winners, yet she cannot generally triumph
over all others alone. As a result, alliances are necessary, and the general outlines of the process of alliance formation can be understood along the lines
discussed in chapter 2. When faction leaders can unproblematically deliver the
support of their followers, the structural dynamics of the faction system can
be analyzed in terms of the horizontal leader-leader ties of alliance and not the
leader-follower ties.

When political scientists have done this, they have repeatedly noted a tendency for two major segments to develop in factional systems (Nathan 1977
[1973]). In the Japanese case discussed above, processes identical to those we
investigated in chapter 2 invariably led to two alliance systems of factions;
the leading alliance (whichever it happened to be at the time) was known by
the sensible name "the Main Current" and the other the "anti-Main Current"
(Scalapino and Masumi 1964: 59). Similarly, in local politics, it is common
that where a mayor or governor has widespread appointment powers two factions form, roughly the "ins" and the "outs" (for the example of Greek villages
in the mid twentieth century see Campbell 1964: 224). Historians of early
American politics struggled for generations with an attempt to define the
"court" and "country" politics in terms of the expected relationship to class
distinctions, only to realize that the only thing that "court" meant was "in,"
and "country" was everyone else.

Why this tendency toward bifurcation? We have seen in chapter 2 one elegant explanation, namely balance theory. If people operate according to these logical rules, they will have no choice but to sort themselves into one or two cliques. But we also saw that no political actor worth his or her salt would follow such crippling rules as a general heuristic. Some situations, however, can force action to be objectively consonant with balance theory even though participants have no subjective heuristic that is correlative to the balanced situation (Barth 1981:22). Imagine that there are a number of different factions, each with size N_i and that they can make alliances; victory depends only on the size of the alliance. Thus the largest faction (call it 1) will gain control over all the goods produced or gathered by the group . . . unless faction 2 can make an alliance with some other faction 3 (if we assume that $N_2 + N_3 > N_1$). At this point, faction 1 attempts to gain the support of faction 4 (or, perhaps thinking ahead, faction 5 as well), and the process repeats. When all factions are incorporated into one of two groups, the larger will take control. While the losers would presumably like to join the winning alliance, the winners will have little incentive to thereby dilute the amassed goods. Hence a one-alliance system is unlikely, as is a three-alliance system. Any third group is likely to be swallowed back into the binary opposition, though perhaps changing the losing faction to a winning one. If one faction's victory is so complete as to completely obliterate the other, the same forces that led to factions in the first place generally lead to a split in the victorious faction.

It is worth emphasizing that this logic requires that the goods involved be winner take all. Thus it makes perfect sense that in a political system such as that of the United States, in which any congressional district elects one person (and where the chief executive is chosen almost directly by the voters at large), that this logic will generally lead to two parties (Duverger 1963 [1954]; cf. Key 1964: 208f, 274).[8] Not all political systems are winner-take-all, and hence it is not at all surprising that parliamentary systems with proportional representation tend to have many parties.

Two Directions of Party Formation

We have seen two different ways in which we can imagine a change in a situation in which a small number of elites monopolize some set of good things associated with governance. Both begin with triangles of "patronage," but in-

---

[8] Of course, in the United States there are dozens of other parties, everything from the American Fascist Party to the World Socialist Party to the American Beer Drinker's Party. These have not, as a rule, been consequential over any long period of time. The exceptions, such as the Green, People's, and the Farmer-Labor parties, prove the rule, in that they only worked at the state level where they could capture a governorship, and make a brief splash at the national level for a single election. Such parties generally only survived where a national party was, for its own reasons, willing to funnel them patronage (Key 1964: 274f).

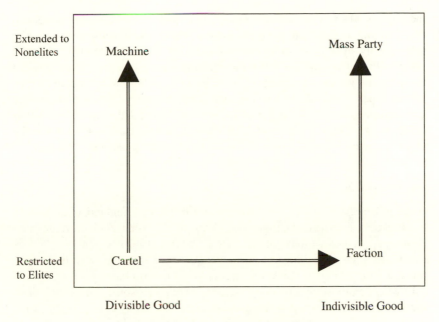

Figure 8.1. From patronage to party?

volve different forms of elaboration (see figure 8.1). In the first (the machine), relations of patronage are extended outside the elite, but the nature of the goods involved remains divisible. Because anyone holding some resource can break off a chunk of it, there is always some to go around (even if people rarely feel that they have enough). Consequently, the overall level of competition is muted, even though a larger proportion of the population may be involved. In the second (the faction), elites are forced to make exclusive commitments to one patron because control over the organization is requisite for the delivery of any good thing to oneself or to one's allies. While fewer nonelites participate than in the machine, there is greater competition between patrons.

Despite these differences, these formations have one thing in common, and that is that they tend to be restricted in scope. The machine is a local phenomenon, and factions tend to either to be local, or to be possible when a very small elite is able to monopolize all positions of power (for example, the inner circle of the Chinese Communist Party). Both fall short of the mass party of the modern nation state.[9]

Analytically, we might expect that either the machine or the faction might be the basis for the development of the mass party—the highly mobilized party that operates at a national, not merely local, level. We will go on to explore

[9] These three types of party (faction, machine, and mass) are also adumbrated by Perkins (1996) in similar terms.

the process whereby factions are first formed, and then extended to nonelites, thus forming a party. Can the party evolve first by the development of a machine (or its equivalent) for divisible goods, and then a switch to indivisible goods? Historically, we know that the machine is not a precursor to the modern party but rather the outgrowth of it. Indeed, by definition a machine exists within a party; outside of a party such a social structure would simply be a patronage pyramid. Such pyramids may indeed find themselves suddenly confronting an indivisible good. This route, however, does not always strike us as "party formation"—instead, we are more likely to term it "civil war."

Elizabethan England

As an instructive example, we can consider Elizabethan England, often loosely considered a hotbed of factionalism, given the constant court intrigues and shifting appeals to various patrons. Yet as Adams (1982) emphasizes, "a faction was not the same thing as a clientage; nor was it the exercise of patronage; nor was it the taking of sides on a major political issue: a faction was a personal following employed in direct opposition to another personal following." Such factional politics were quite rare; Adams identifies only two periods in the sixteenth century, the first relatively brief.[10] The second (during the 1590s) was a result of one influential lord (Essex) attempting to monopolize all patronage. This in effect made a previously divisible good winner-take-all. Since even minor acts of patronage came to symbolize one's connection to the winning side, all government acts became increasingly politicized. In the interim, Queen Elizabeth was skilled at making sure that different patronage pyramids had roughly equal fortunes, and thus that goods were in some sense divisible (see MacCaffrey 1961: 98ff; Neale 1958: 70f; Somerset 2003: 338f—43, 476, 500–503).[11]

But this new concentration destabilized the relation between pyramids. In a brilliant analysis, Bearman (1993) examined these changes in patronage structures by examining the appointment of rectors to local parishes.[12] The increased dominance of the court—in part due to the weakened ability of the church and local magnates to act independently of the crown—forced local elites to align their strategies with those of the center, the ultimate source of all good things. Thus patronage transfers became aligned into long chains, somewhat like the

[10] This (1548–52) was during the period after Henry VIII's death in which the new king was ten years old and rebellion broke out, a situation in which a number of contenders might reasonably hope to dramatically influence the character of the new government.

[11] Indeed, one key problem was that Essex followed the rule of balance–my enemy's friend is my enemy–and thus increasingly isolated himself. He was actually to rise in rebellion when his difficult nature led to him being refused a key patronage appointment (see, e.g., Lacey 1971: 214).

[12] Analyzing Scotland in the next century, Sunter (1986: 68f) argued that such appointments were "the most hazardous of all forms of patronage" in terms of the controversy they evoked.

lengthy cycle of the *tē* exchange discussed in chapter 3. Interestingly, we also see a change whereby rectors stopped being appointed for nonreligious reasons and were instead appointed on the basis of their religious convictions and history. These changes were not independent—it was the new chains of patronage that became the organizational frame for gentry Puritanism, the force that was to oppose the king in a civil war (Bearman 1993: 95–101, 132f). In a pattern that will reappear, stark, principled religious differences became a useful way for theorizing the bifurcation between competing patronage pyramids.

Thus the success of the late-Elizabethan program was a delicate one—by amassing all patronage in the center, it depended on the continual adjustments on the part of the crown to keep all contenders satisfied with what they had. But if the crown were to stop enforcing a division of patronage, it would provoke patrons to ally into factions to capture the center.[13]

And such an identification with a single faction was precisely what characterized the approach of James I, and which led to a breakdown of the political system and, in part, to the Civil War (Neale 1958: 84). This breakdown corresponded to an increased politicization of patronage politics. On the one hand, there was fiercer competition between pyramids, and on the other, this competition was linked to an extension of the electorate and hence an increase in political mobilization (Pocock 1980: 9).[14]

Put more generally, we may say that one route to party formation is likely to be bloody, and this is when patrons with already mobilized followers confront a shift, from divisible to indivisible, in the nature of goods for which they compete. As the nature of the game shifts to zero-sum, there is no balance of power or equilibrium to ensure that this is accepted by all. As Hobbes (1909 [1651]: 95) wrote in his explanation of the English Civil War, "If any two men desire the same thing, which nevertheless they cannot both enjoy, they become enemies; and in the way to their end, endeavour to destroy, or subdue one an other." If one does not have nonelite followers, one must make alliances between other elites and try to establish a faction. But if you actually have a pyramid—a set of patronage relations in which the lower down offer support

---

[13] The alert reader will notice that the main point of this chapter is a generalization of the arguments made here by Bearman.

[14] Something quite similar happened in 17th-century France. The use of patronage as a governance strategy had led to a constant drain from the crown in favor of the great provincial nobles. In the late 16th century the fiscal weakness of the center led to a dramatic reduction of this trickle-down of patronage. (At the same time, the general replacement of military with administrative obligations discussed in the previous chapter led to a politicization of clientship.) The key state-building ministers (Richelieu in particular) worked not simply to stem the outflow but to create their own, largely parallel, clienteles in the provinces. Just as in England, this focused discontent on the center and led to the noble uprising known as the Fronde (which was to a large but not complete degree an alignment of feuding noble clienteles), though in the long run it increased the central state's power by furthering the replacement of indirect with direct rule (Kettering 1986: 144, 176, 182f, 190f, 209, 235; Ranum 1993: 121, 183f, 272, 344f).

for agonistic activities—why turn your pyramid into a party? Why not turn it into an army?[15]

When, on the other hand, there is a switch to an indivisible good *before* substantial mobilization, the process of extension can happen in a regulated fashion. As we will see, there are clear reasons to expect that mobilization happens via a set of expanding (and sometimes contracting) circles of inclusions, and that these extensions will happen in a reasonably controlled or balanced fashion.[16] It is this process that is more commonly understood as the process of party formation. To trace it out, we must return to factions.

From Faction to Party

Parties from Scratch

We begin to trace out analytically the process whereby parties can form out of other social structures. Although I will draw on several cases, I focus on perhaps the best documented example of party formation on the national level, that of the United States of America. By 1800 no one doubted that national parties existed in the United States. But in no sense did this party system exist a mere twelve years previous. While most new party systems—indeed, even the Russian one discussed briefly above—drew at least in part on previously existing parties, this was impossible in the new United States of the 1789 constitution.

It is not that national-level politics had not previously existed. Even before the Declaration of Independence, the colonies assembled a Continental Congress, and there were predictable divisions in votes pertaining to (at first) how to respond to parliamentary policies, then later how to prosecute the war, and finally, how to negotiate with other nations and set national and international policies.[17] But because the American revolutionary movement had involved a few corresponding conspirators and a wider set of local elites stumbling into revolution—and not a dedicated political party (Chambers 1963b: 17; Hender-

---

[15] Put somewhat differently, to say that goods are divisible is as much to say that a strong state does not exist, allowing for the development of semi-independent patronage triangles to mobilize nonelites, as we saw in chapter 6. Also see Ranum (1993: 12).

[16] There does, however, seem to be a "ratchet" effect whereby it is harder to contract than to expand. For example, in 1790 in Poland there was an attempt to contract the electorate to landholding nobles only–the result was that four hundred commoners were ennobled in a matter of weeks (McLean 2005b: 22).

[17] Initially debate at the national level seemed to be between the "radicals" and "conservatives," but as a genuine commitment to an ideological program is an aid to political maneuvering in very few cases, moderates assumed central roles and the main axis of division became that between the North and the South (Henderson 1974; Jillson and Wilson 1994: 114, 62, 173; Risjord 1978: 268, 377, 394; Chambers 1963b: 85, 116; Cunningham 1957: 93).

son 1974: 19)—political organization at the federal level was relatively rudimentary at the birth of the new nation. To the extent that there was organized
political dissent, it was largely geographic: elites who shared interests on the
basis of a shared economic fate might be expected to vote together. But there
was little way to change others' minds and hence no reason to form party
structures.

Whence, then, came these national level parties? Substantively, as we shall
see, they came from a combination of (on the one hand) divisions between
regions and (on the other) alliances of elites *across* these regions, most important, alliances between Virginians and New Yorkers. Analytically, we may
say that parties came from a fusion of two structural principles, a vertical one
in which relationships were used to coordinate and command and a horizontal
one involving the alignment of local oppositions. Above we derived the possibility of faction—politicized vertical relationships of patronage—arising to
coordinate small-scale political contestation. But it is also possible for politics
to occur mainly through horizontal relationships of alliance and sameness. We
begin by examining the political structures of New York and Virginia before
independence to illustrate these two types, and then follow the construction of
a national-level party structure.

To anticipate, my argument will be that (1) the building blocks of parties
are of two types, horizontal relationships of alliance and vertical relationships
more akin to patronage; (2) either of these may be sufficient to coordinate local
or relatively nonmobilized politics, and indeed we see reasonable approxima-
tions to these polar cases in certain colony party systems; (3) establishing a
national level party requires melding these relationships, although the process
may depend on the preexisting degree of national unification. I begin by considering how factions can serve as the basis for local parties.

The Mobilization of Factions

We know that, although there might be factions within parties, we did not find
parties within factions. This is because the party, unlike a faction, involves the
mobilization of nonelites, and hence often has an abiding presence as a formal
organization. Not only will mobilization spur a tendency to extend the faction
further downward toward nonelites, it also leads elites to convert existing (antitransitive) patronage relations into something more closely approaching a command structure (for the development of parties out of patronage relationships
in Rome, see Taylor [1968: 7–11, 23, 63]). The extent to which control is also
bottom-up as opposed to only top-down is of great interest to political scientists
concerned with democratization, but this may turn out to be secondary from a
structural point of view.

Such an extension of mobilization may have a number of precedents. Commonly proposed ones include competition between factions (which we shall

discuss in greater detail later) and the pursuit of long-term as opposed to short-term interests (here see Goodman 1964). However, neither of these is necessary for party formation: all that matters is that elites believe that the mobilization of commoners will accomplish something that cannot be accomplished without a party, and they are willing to risk losing some control to accomplish these ends.

There are relatively simple cases in which mobilization takes place wholly through the extension of vertical patronage structures—political participation seeps downward like water down an icicle, progressively extending its reach. In such cases, social scientists holding to various favored theories of democracy are likely to be confused at the apparent dislocation between parties and the interest-groups assumed to compose the society. A well-documented example is Toulouse, France, in the nineteenth century (Aminzade 1977; also see Mayer 1966). It might first seem inexplicable that the royalist party was largely composed of workers. This seeming incongruity was due to the patronage relations connecting workers to the elites—relations which, as in the archetypical ones seen in chapter 6, involved commitments of the superordinates to support the subordinates, especially in times of economic downturn, and for the latter to offer what support they could, including military support. In more peaceful times, this support was electoral and hence the patronage relationships formed the skeleton of a party.

The formation of parties in New York also approximates this pattern. Unlike many other states such as Virginia, New York politics were not based on region.[18] While there were conflicts of interests between those more attached to land and those more attached to trade, this sort of division cut across geographical regions (Bonomi 1971; Varga 1960: 253f; also Egnal 1988: 53). Since the various divisions overlapped only imperfectly, New York politics was characterized by a morass of constantly shifting alliances between factions. Such shifts in alliances were encouraged by the sensitivity of fortunes to political processes: land was often subject to multiple claimants, governors were in the position to grant large tracts to their favorites, and trade was also sensitive to legal judgments.[19] New York was not the only colony where such internal disputes were important, but this sensitivity to local politics was coupled with the absence of a stable division between the elites, leading to a particularly contentious political environment (see Katz 1968: 57, 145).

The political elite of New York was a relatively stable set of families—in the mid eighteenth century they were the van Rensselaer, Livingston, van

[18] Although New York, unusually, possessed two vital cities, Albany and New York City, this was not the basis for a bifurcation in politics. (Many of the upstate landowners actually made most of their money from trade in New York City, where they dwelt most of the time.)

[19] While Virginian land speculation involved land to the west of the established colonies, and hence first royal and later national policies, in New York land claims were for coastal land and turned on colony-/state-level decisions.

Cortlandt, Schuyler, Beekman, Philipse, Morris, and DeLancey families, all tied by multiple marriages and occasionally business partnerships.[20] While most of these possessed considerable landholdings, the Morrises and the Livingstons were more fundamentally tied to land than the Philipses or van Cortlandts (Becker 1909: 9f, 13; Leder 1961: 21, 24, 79, 121; Bonomi 1971: 60–69, 143–46; see Shorto 2004: 57, 132, 139 on van Rensselaer).[21] Families, we recall, approximate the nested sets that imply hierarchy, though there are here the complications due to bilineality—since degrees of common closeness are ambiguous, they are responsive to willful decisions and hence encourage sophisticated maneuvering in which some allies are dropped and past enemies befriended.

Throughout the late seventeenth and eighteenth centuries, politics was a succession of shifts in which one allied set of families would come into power, and the others would be purged from their positions. It was this position of being "in favor" with the governor that structured politics—what was called the "popular" party was often just a residual category of whoever was not "in" at the time. Because of this wonderful personalism, even an analytic overview must follow particular persons and families (Becker 1909: 8; Egnal 1980: 46f; Egnal 1988: 51; Leder 1961; Bonomi 1971: 76–79, 82, 86).[22]

While New York's political history was a succession of reversals whereby outs became ins, there was an overall direction to its evolution in terms of increased mobilization. Indeed, the very back and forth nature of politics spurred this development. An enterprising "out" could paint himself as an antielitist and mobilize nonelites against the "ins."[23] Such popular mobilization

---

[20] The passion for intermarriage between these families is shown in the fact that in the 1970s, influential in Albany and New York politics was Brigadier General Cortlandt van Rensselaer Schuyler (Shorto 2004: 4). It is difficult to describe the high degree of consistency and in-breeding of this large clique; suffice to say that while working in the Livingston College of Rutgers University, I would be more likely to see the names Livingston and Rutgers in the documents examined here than in departmental mail. I have also profited from the genealogical compilations made public by Marshall Davies Lloyd, as well as from consultation with my friend and dean of the Rutgers Honors Program, Muffin Livingston Lord.

[21] Despite having a stable set of elite families, New York politics were relatively egalitarian, at least in that it was possible for young men of low birth or little funds to affiliate with these families and assume central political roles.

[22] Of course, there were real divisions in economic interests between families that led to splits on crucial issues, especially to what extent the French should be mollycoddled so as not to upset the fur trade.

[23] The most important example of this is seen in the mid 18th century in which a new governor (Cosby) arrived and, not atypically, sided with the outs (the Philipse and DeLancey faction) and made them ins. But Cosby also began a vendetta against the chief justice of New York, Lewis Morris, replacing him with a DeLancey. Morris responded with a full-fledged political assault, galvanizing a party behind him. He (opportunistically) broadened the issue to a fundamental one of populist philosophy and embarked on new forms of mobilization such as founding a political newspaper and organizing a petition campaign. This appeal to the populace was apparently a successful tactic as he and his allies gained seats in the next election while Philipse and DeLancey

had unplanned-for results, including a general drift of the parties "leftward." This slow drift received a sudden push with the general radicalization of politics coming in the wake of the Stamp Act riots of 1765 and the organization of the extremist "Sons of Liberty." Associated with this group was Captain James DeLancey. The DeLanceys—more rooted in trade than in landownership—had been hit hard by the depression of the 1760s and were responsive to the idea of an economic protest aimed at Britain. The Livingstons, on the other hand, were affected less by the mounting debts to British shippers and more by a tenant uprising in 1766. Suddenly the idea of stirring up the people seemed a decidedly unpleasant prospect to such landowners (Champagne 1963: 62; Egnal 1988: 173–76).

Thus the Livingstons, previously considered to be the more "popular" party, were now seen as conservative in contrast to the DeLanceys. Captain DeLancey gained street credentials by refusing a seat on the appointed council (claiming he preferred the approval of the people to that of the governor) and was clearly poised to bring his family into the center of patriotic politics. When the 1768 elections gave the DeLanceys control of the assembly, however, they simply kicked out the Livingstons and the Morrises (Bonomi 1971: 235f—63; Becker 1909: 18f, 42, 46, 5, 59f).

Thus the DeLancey faction became the "in" group, while the Livingston group were the outs, forced to appeal to the citizenry with popular policies. It was a poor time to be an "in"—as the revolution drew nearer, the DeLanceys, the previous darlings of the Sons of Liberty, became the loyalists, and the Livingstons the patriots, if only because to justify their opposition to the governor they needed to appeal to more and more provocative principles (Champagne 1963: 77ff; Egnal 1980: 56; Egnal 1988: 281; Bonomi 1971: 265f , 276f; Becker 1909: 86; Randall 1993: 265). Only the Livingstons' alliance would survive to have an impact on New York's later politics.

It was thus largely an accident of timing that the Livingston-Schuyler-Morris faction survived the War as "Patriots" as opposed to the DeLanceys and Philipses.[24] And it was this vertical organization that was available for New Yorkers who sought to form national-level parties in the new nation, and one of the reasons why New Yorkers played such a pivotal role.

We must stress the importance of this preexisting structure and not the mere cycle of mobilization via "outs" becoming "ins." Pennsylvanian politics also involved an alternation between ins and outs that mobilized the electorate in

---

lost theirs (Bonomi 1971: 74f, 87–90, 105, 107f, 110, 133, 149; Leder 1961: 249–53, 284; Varga 1960: 265). Morris had earlier responded similarly in a number of occasions, first by escalating a conflict with the new governor of New Jersey via a full-scale politicization against the proprietary regime which he had till then supported, and then again by opposing an *antiproprietary* governor by suddenly becoming a populist and switching his power base from council to assembly (Sheridan 1981: 23ff, 70).

[24] In a nice illustration of some of the themes emphasized here, when Livingston joined the patriot side, his more radical tenants were pushed into loyalism (Nash 2005: 246f; also see 241).

a particularly ideological fashion (see Egnal 1980: 44f; Nash 1968; 2005: 29; Wendel 1968: 290–304; Dargo 1980: 102f; Argersinger 1992: 36). This very ideological development, however, came at the expense of structural elaboration. New York's political elite was, from a relatively early date, predominantly composed of lawyers. But in Pennsylvania, elites were much less likely to be lawyers, and more likely to be merchants, doctors, and (increasingly) printers.[25]

While printing is perhaps the ideological occupation par excellence,[26] making a career in law generally required the support of a lawyer patron (the word might be explicitly used by an applicant),[27] since in a world without law schools and with only sporadic examinations, the only way to become a lawyer was to clerk for one and get his endorsement (Hamlin 1939: 6, 12, 36, 41, 96f, 120ff; Stahr 2005: 15, 19). It was frequently the case that aspiring Federalists had studied law with a more established Federalist (e.g., Hamilton's lieutenant Robert Troup studying with John Jay or Monroe with Jefferson [Fischer 1965: 310, 419; also see Kirschke 2005: 15]).[28] Thus the New York political system was in the hands of professionals who tended to be concentrated in a tiny portion of the state, and who lacked any organic relation to class or sectional interests, as did the Virginia planters, or to the fraternity of elite schools, as did the Massachusetts clergy, or to religion, as did the Pennsylvania Quakers and Anglicans. They were primed to organize themselves in hierarchical factions, as opposed to blocs of those sharing a common regional interest.[29]

[25] Here I principally rely on Fischer's (1965) exhaustive biographies of the leading Federalists, both the old generation of revolutionary war veterans and the new generation that entered into real competition with the Republicans. I omit the most prominent to emphasize the "average" elite: including the prominent would only increase the direction of the trends reported here. I also count as "lawyer" only those who at least in part practiced (Fischer 1965: 207, 209). In New York, even in the older generation two-thirds of the Federalists were lawyers, and in the newer generation all of 89% were. In Pennsylvania, only around half the Federalists were lawyers. (Were we to look at Republicans, the patterns across states would probably be the same; once George Clinton brought a set of "new men" into prominence in New York, however, this changed somewhat). These patterns are also seen in the make-up of states' delegations to the House in the first three Congresses. While New York had no doctors or ministers, doctors and ministers held on average 7% and 16% of Pennsylvania's seats respectively. I thank Adam Slez for making these data available to me.

[26] Although the clergy also may be seen as an ideological occupation in that it was indeed a bully pulpit for many ministers, the effective range of persuasion was usually limited to the local.

[27] See the letter from William Laight to Alexander Hamilton, March 14, 1797, reprinted in Hamilton (1910: 162f). Doctors, as Banner (1970: 188) stresses for Massachusetts, lacked the hierarchical organizational backbone to their practice; further, because medicine was itself an avenue for upward mobility, doctors were less likely to have clientage or affinal connections to high-status men who would support their political careers.

[28] Such patronage did not assure loyalty–many of the antifederalists in New York had been sponsored by those in the Livingston or Schuyler families but later turned against them (for examples, see Young 1967: 43ff).

[29] Somewhat similarly, in early modern France it was the Parlementarians who formed a closely knit group of persons concentrated in a small area who had the greatest capacity to organize as a contending faction (also see Ranum 1993: 16).

With the DeLanceys out of the picture, the Livingston-Schuylers faction seemed to have hegemony and indeed were in a good position to benefit from the increased centralization of the national government (and hence were "federalists").[30] Any challenger would need a new type of power base. It was George Clinton, who became governor in 1777, who did this by becoming the apex of a political party not on the basis of his landholding (as did the great families) but his potential political patronage (Hendrickson 1985: 234f; Bernstein 1970: 66f, 250).[31] With this he could break up the monopoly whereby (in his words) "all the great opulent families were united in one confederacy" (Young 1967: 4f, 122, 169, 172, 575). Clinton's attack on the established families implied an attack on their centralizing policies (and hence he must become an "antifederalist"), and it was this set of oppositions that New York brought to the new nation of 1788.

Growing Pains

Thus New York's political evolution has much in common with the analytically elegant case whereby patronage structures turn into parties. Such a process is, however, restricted to the local context and is perhaps relatively unusual even there. After all, unlike those forming an army from patronage relationships, a party leader cannot generally shoot rank-and-file members for failure to do as they are told. Generally there will be an appeal to other interests. Those attempting to form a party at the national level (with a few exceptions such as the great Roman generals like Caesar) cannot rely on the distribution of patronage because it is simply too expensive. Hence as the electorate increases, there is a tendency for the rewards going to clients to shift from divisible patronage to indivisible goods. The increase in the number of supporters is, in turn, generally due either to an extension of the effective franchise or a switch to mobilization at the national level—in other words, due to a previous shift toward less divisible goods (see Bourne 1986: 139ff, 160 on nineteenth-century England).

We first derived the party on the basis of insiders finding that the struggle over the distribution of "good things" had transformed into a winner-take-all game. We saw that there would be a tendency for factions to establish horizontal alliances, as there was little profit to remaining aloof and independent. Something very similar happens in the context of party formation regarding alliances between local elites, often heads of local patronage pyramids. But

---

[30] For purposes of clarity, "federalism" will indicate the attempt to strengthen the union in contrast to "antifederalism," and "Federalism" the party of Washington and Hamilton in contrast to "Republicanism."

[31] Although Clinton's electoral success owed a great deal to his military reputation, he had studied law with William Smith, one of the leaders of the Livingston faction (Kaminski 1993: 13).

party formation goes beyond the simple self-fulfilling dynamics of the "go with the winner" game. The payoff is winner-take-all and involves redirecting organizational resources to satisfy preexisting interests. Thus mobilizing nonelites requires the ability to craft policy, a plan to jointly satisfy different interests. We can refer to the ability to mobilize different groups of non-elites through such a proposed direction of organizational resources as an "alignment" of interests. Interests are not homogenized nor necessarily compromised; rather, their collective fulfillment is conceived of as a distinct possibility.

As interests are aligned, so are previously independent struggles or sets of oppositions. Through horizontal relationships of affiliation (e.g., side A is to side C as side B is to side D), these oppositions become oriented in the same direction, potentially *before* any vertical social relationships exist to coordinate action. Such alignment may be facilitated by a common identity that establishes a presumption of future concord instead of the opposite, but such an identity is never an explanation of party behavior, but rather an outcome to be explained.

In the case at hand, New York's factional system, by dividing into federalists and antifederalists, was clearly poised to align with similar divisions in other states. But how to join the vertical structure of a faction-based party to another one? There was no easy way to make such an organizational innovation. It proved easier for a more rudimentary party system to be the basis for such alliances if it could foster horizontal connections.

Virginia and the Politics of Horizontality

Let us return to the "null case" of a set of elites monopolizing all goods (the cartel). The simplest evolutionary step from here is, as Spencer and Durkheim would have said, simply to multiply the number of units but not their relationships. That is, instead of a set of elites "here" monopolizing all good things (wherever "here" is), we have elites in *this* area monopolizing *their* resources, and elites in *that* area monopolizing *theirs* (this is a "segmentary" form of organization). This is a common occurrence where politics is in the hands of large landowners. By definition, each landowner will dominate a particular area. Virginia well approximates this pattern.

As a plantation society Virginia, despite its large population, had a relatively small and involuted elite. While marrying was often strategic, prominent Virginians like Washington and Jefferson were unlikely to be true outsiders joining a prominent family for the first time (as might be the case in New York), but instead were well-connected members of the elite simply looking to cement their positions or replenish their purses. This elite, even more importantly, was spread out so that there was relatively little contestation in any area. As a result, politics were traditionally in the hands of local notables, and elections were, in Ammon's (1963: 162, 165) words, "popularity contests in which issues had been distinctly secondary." While it is possible to overstate the claim—aristocrats had to campaign for office and, like George Washington in 1755, could lose elections—this elitist character tended to lead to a low level of competition (for example, simply setting out drinks on election day might constitute a fine campaign) (Randall 1993: 2–6, 92, 119, 494; Cunningham 1957: 250; Wills 2002: 12; Fischer 2004: 12; Ellis 2004: 35).

At the same time, there were occasionally conflicts between personalistic factions. For an example that may have turned out to be quite weighty for the later evolution of national politics, Patrick Henry was allied with John Tyler (father of the future president). As a result, a local rival of Tyler's, Edmund Randolph (patron to the Jeffersons) allied with the Washington circle including Madison and Monroe (Risjord 1978: 81–86, 357).

But when there were serious conflicts they generally mapped onto regional differences. Geography is one of the most common bases for political contest, especially between elites, because geography is generally a stand-in for interests. (When nonelites are not excluded from politics, the elite/nonelite division may cut across geography.) There are debates as to precisely where one should draw the lines, but one can make a general distinction between the northern area, which was dominated by a few large landowners who rented to tenants with no voting rights, and the southern areas, which had more small landowners. Since the main political problem was a shortage of money (and widespread debt), one key political issue for the new state of Virginia was whether to redeem or even simply pay interest on the outstanding state and federal securities that had been bought, at depreciated values, by the rich of the northern regions. Thus the two main parties were one representing the debtors (led by Patrick Henry) and the other the creditors (led in part by James Madison) (Egnal 1988: 92; Main 1955: 97f, 109ff; Risjord 1978; Hendrickson 1985: 166).

In sum, politics thus approximated a fusion of the electioneering techniques of the machine and the noncompetitive regional block voting that characterized early national-level voting in the Continental Congress. The most important relationships characterizing a party were largely horizontal relationships between fellow elites who shared sectional interests; as all those in a region had similar interests, their relationships tended to take on the simple form of a clique. Now let us see how these protoparties—debtor and creditor—became aligned with those in other states. The debate over the ratification of the federal constitution in 1787 led to a simplification of politics (one is either for or against) as well as new names for the sides ("federalist" and "antifederalist"), which allowed for a further increase in the level of political organization and mobilization. Leading the federalists in Virginia was James Madison, and leading the antifederalists was Patrick Henry. Although many of the issues were new, the regional divisions remained relatively constant (Ammon 1953:

287; Risjord 1978). And it was this set of oppositions that Virginia brought to the board.

What was key was not that region structured Virginian politics but that the elite were spread out—this not only increased the horizontality of politics but (as we shall see) made Virginia a better springboard for building national-level structures. This extreme horizontality can best be highlighted by making a comparison to Massachusetts, which was also hierarchically organized with little competition for political positions. As in Virginia, politics in Massachusetts were structured by regional divisions, but politics had long been monopolized by well-educated Bostonians—indeed, other representatives often had a difficult time attending sessions of the legislature (Alexander 2002:12f; Zemsky 1971; Dallinger 1897: 10; Egnal 1980: 48, 57; Patterson 1973: 24–27, 42–45, 117, 144f, 187f, 247; Goodman 1964: 74; Banner 1970: 7; Sharp 1993: 59; Fischer 1965: 13).

As a result, while Virginian politics involved shifting alliances between rough equivalents scattered across the state, each a king in his own domain, in Massachusetts it was difficult to maintain autonomy and yet strike bargains. Indeed, both leading figures coming out of Massachusetts were remarkable for their relations: John Hancock was friends with everyone (at the minor cost of principles), and John Adams friends with no one. Virginia led to more common success stories of clearly locatable party leaders such as Madison and Jefferson. Indeed, it was these who were to successfully create new alignments and the first true political party in the nation.

The Creation of National-Level Party Systems

Local Alignments

We have seen that local-level party systems can arise through the politicization and extension of patronage pyramids; in environments with significantly less elite conflict, we may instead see regional division into relatively stable "blocks." But national-level party systems involve the coordination of such local systems and, indeed, their fusion into a single structure that involves both vertical coordination and horizontal alignment of interests (on the similar case of Canada, see Chhibber and Kollman 2004: 92, 184f).

We have, as we recall, been investigating combinations of horizontality and verticality since chapter 5. But this sort of horizontal alliance is something substantively quite different from the horizontality that arises merely as an *absence* of vertical relationships. When deriving command structures, we could do rather well by treating all relationships as fundamentally vertical. Although the more complex command structures did involve horizontal relationships between subsections, this was a minor analytic complication, because the key organizational principle—the transitivity—was fundamentally a vertical one.

In this case, however, we are finding that the organizational glue can come from a secondary set of relationships, namely alliances *between* subsections (and thus we begin to leave the class of simple structures behind). In many cases, such alliances do not lead to anything remotely like a superparty, spanning and organizing the local parties. Rather, sets of horizontal relations connect elites who remain rough equals and produce the multihub structure we examined in chapter 2. There is, we recall, no reason to imagine that the connections in such a structure are transitive, and good reasons to think that they are not. (Strategic actors will tend to befriend their enemy's friends, for one.) But transitivity can, as Mann (1986; see chapter 6) pointed out, be introduced via ideology.

We can pursue the example of the development of the English civil war. Bearman found that the key structural changes that presaged the split in the English elite were in place a full half-century before the outbreak of violence, yet what was missing was "a mechanism for concatenating local factions into the national arena." "This mechanism was provided by religious heterodoxy" (Bearman 1993: 177). Religious dispute is indeed an obvious contender for a coordinating mechanism—that is, a heuristic for action that would allow for de facto coordination in the absence of explicit central control. While in general alliances do not imply any transitivity beyond what is advantageous to participants at the time, the heuristic of ideology will tend to impose stark divisions— the sorts of things that may be of great interest to structural entrepreneurs— with rapidity.

Let us return to the balance theory as discussed in chapter 2 to flesh out this point. Political scientists have discovered that one way that vaguely informed persons can act politically in a relatively sophisticated manner is to use what has euphemistically been called a "likeability heuristic," but might be properly called a "hate their guts" heuristic (see Sniderman, Brody, and Tetlock 1991). If we hate the same person or persons, and do whatever we imagine will really make their lives miserable, we are likely to find ourselves acting in reasonable concert. Anything that helps divide all contenders into two camps can be used to provide for coordination of local disputes. In chapter 2, we saw that local groups might seize on the oppositions of outsiders as a way to express and coordinate their own patterns of hostility (in the ways that local gangs might seem to affiliate with the Bloods or the Crips, but only to show whom they were *against* [Decker and van Winkle 1996: 87]). Religious controversy is well suited to a stark bifurcation that can be used to coordinate local competitions.

But so can other forms of abstract ideology. For example, charting the political career of a famous radical in the French revolution, M. G. A. Vadier, Lyons (1977: 80–82, 89) demonstrates that his choice of political side in a rapidly bifurcating field was grounded in a battle between his family and another (the

Darmaing) for control over his locale—"a long-standing family rivalry, on which political labels like Jacobinism and federalism were now superimposed." As the Darmaings became the latter, Vadier became the former. Vadier's success was marked by his rise to a position of authority sufficient to allow him to execute as "counterrevolutionaries" the Darmaings and others who had snubbed his family before the revolution.

Thus parties can develop through such alignment of local oppositions. This alignment is generally far from complete—even in well-developed and competitive party systems, there can be substantial slippage between what a party represents in one locality and what it represents in another (Schwartz 1990: 10, 280). That is, the transitivity involved may encompass only a small portion of the "programs"—the plans and interests—of the members of a "party." However, both the horizontal transitivity of ideological agreement and, for us perhaps more important, the vertical transitivity of the command structure, tend to increase (at least initially) with the level of competition between parties.

Competition

In the most important theoretical statement on party formation in recent years, Martin Shefter (1994: 6, 30) starts from the empirically supported assumption that elites "will construct a strong, broadly based party organization only if it is necessary for them to do so in order to gain, retain, or exercise power." Being nobody's fools, elites realize that mobilization of nonelites will threaten their own positions, and so if possible, they would prefer to collude with other elites (even enemies) rather than begin a cycle of escalating mobilization.[32]

But when competition heats up, it will be very tempting for elites to try to increase the breadth and depth of mobilization. For example, in close electoral races elites will have a reason to extend the franchise in directions they believe will disproportionately increase their support (for post-Independence Virginia see Pole [1966]). This was, says Shefter, historically especially true for countries that had a meritocratic civil service, because the only goods that could be linked to support for one faction were necessarily of the form of "winner-take-all" goods, thereby spurring the development of a competitive structure. In contrast, where there was no true civil service, goods were more divisible (i.e. "corruption" could flourish in its manifold guises), and hence party formation was rudimentary (Shefter 1994: 11, 14, 21, 30–35). Thus the switch to indivisi-

---

[32] I here consider only what Shefter would call "internal mobilization" and leave to the side the case of "external mobilization" that is provoked by challenges by outsiders who are generally unable to use patronage. For example (returning to the case of 19th-century France), Aminzade (1987) argues that the republican party, unable to grant patronage as could the royalists, was forced to promise collective goods delivered to structural equivalents and hence push toward a modern party system.

ble goods tends to increase mobilization as elites compete, and mobilization tends to decrease the reliance on divisible goods because it is too expensive to pay off each supporter individually. Such mobilization can involve concatenation both in horizontal and in vertical directions.[33]

And indeed, it was competition, specifically competition for the presidency, that led toward the emergence of national-level parties in the United States. These parties gratifyingly involved not only the fusion of vertical relationships (as seen in the politics of New York) and horizontal relationships (as seen in the politics of Virginia), but indeed the fusion of these two structures. Further, the key organizational innovation involved melding two forms of transitivity. On the one hand we see the vertical transitivity that would result were elites able to cascade patronage triangles into a pyramid and then enforce transitivity of relationships. On the other hand we see the horizontal transitivity that would arise when horizontal relations of alliance are systematized either on the basis of ideology or on the basis of commonality of interest (or both). We can begin by sketching the state of national politics before the new government.

From Federalism to Federalists

The acceptance of the new constitution of 1787 led to the triumph of the federalists—those who wanted to increase the power of the national government. The insiders of the Washington and Adams administrations retained the name *Federalist*, even though they now had no organized opposition. But merely strengthening the power of the center did not eliminate regional differences in interest; in fact, it highlighted them and in large part reversed them. For the new Federalists found their support in states that had previously led the antifederalist side (such as Rhode Island and other small states like Connecticut, New Hampshire, and Delaware, as well as their larger compatriot Massachusetts), while it was the South (excluding South Carolina)[34] that tended toward the opposition (see the data compiled by Charles 1956: 95; also Buel 1972: 72; Fischer 1965: 222; Hoadley 1980; Slez and Martin 2007). This was in part because the large southern states that had wanted a stronger union did not necessarily want to pay off the debts of the profligate ones such as Massachusetts and South Carolina.[35]

But this plan (termed the "assumption" of debts) was promoted as key to the survival of the union by the new secretary of the treasury under Washington, Alexander Hamilton. More than any single person, Hamilton pushed forward

[33] In a brilliant analysis, Chhibber and Kollman (1998: 336, 338; 2004) show that in polities with single-member districts there is a strong tendency for a more national party system to emerge as the national-level government takes charge of a greater proportion of societal surplus.

[34] As Kipling would say, and you must not forget South Carolina, best beloved.

[35] And now you see why you must not forget South Carolina.

party formation on the national level. Although a bastard in the technical sense, Hamilton made his way into elite New York society in part through letters of introduction to the Livingstons. The Livingston in question was William (whose grandmother was a Schuyler), whose daughter Sarah was to marry John Jay.[36] Thus Hamilton was introduced into the relatively tightly knit dominant faction which, as we recall, had taken the patriot side. Through their assistance Hamilton got an appointment as captain in the Army; from there he became Washington's aide. It was in this capacity that he met and married Elizabeth Schuyler, daughter of General Philip Schuyler (Schuyler's wife was a van Rensselaer, herself the daughter of a Livingston; see Flexner 1978: 55; Hendrickson 1985: 33f, 63, 255f).

As he moved to a position of political centrality, Hamilton was able to join the hierarchical nature of many family ties with political collaboration (as opposed to the latter being the free correspondence of equals). His "creatures" (as they were sometimes disapprovingly termed) might be those working under him in the Treasury or those who owed him in some other way, as well as those allied with the Schuylers. Indeed, Hamilton's very choice of the Treasury as his power base (which may seem to modern readers a relatively minor position in contrast to the presidency) came from his sense that true control would flow downward with the money (Lodge 1898: 136; Risjord 1978: 407, 413; Buel 1972: 103; Flexner 1978: 443).

There were many elites who favored Hamilton's proposals for reasons of interest or conviction, but Hamilton believed he (and the country) would need more organization to coordinate the opposition to his opposition. Hamilton's rudimentary party organization, however, was based on the relationships discussed above—a personalistic set of those whom he could convince, who owed him something, or who had already thrown in their lot with him—and was sporadic, arising only when there was a particular contest to be won. He was unable to delegate grunt-work (for example, supervising poll watching) to others and might end up doing it himself (Cunningham 1957: 164; Charles 1956: 23; Risjord 1978: 362; Reichley 1992: 85; Chambers 1963a; 1963b: 29, 40; 1972: 41f; Young 1967: 137; Kaminski 1993: 252). But still, this sort of organization could push the party system beyond simple geographic bloc voting.

The Counter

Hamilton's contribution to party formation, however, came less in whom he mobilized than in whom he provoked. For it was the interests threatened by Hamilton's program that led to the counterorganization that was to be the Republican Party (though see Aldrich and Grant 1993). The opposition initially

---

[36] Jay was already related to the Philipses, and had previously proposed to two of DeLancey's daughters (Bernstein 1970: 23).

had its coherence only through regional bloc voting, the southern states tending to oppose the Federalist administration. The first organization of the opposition party was, as a result, a coalition of loosely associated notables with a name (the Republican Party) but no real social structure. This core made alliances with others, especially the Clintonians of New York, who opposed the Federalist administration for largely independent reasons (Risjord 1978: 406f, 412; Chambers 1963b: 57, 66; Hendrickson 1985: 15, 202; Cunningham 1957; Ammon 1953: 297; Charles 1956: 80ff, 88, 95; Reichley 1992: 45; Fischer 1965: 202; Young 1967: 578; Ketcham 1990: 326; Chibber and Kollman 2004: 81).

Let us return to New York's local politics. While the Schuylers and Livingstons had been united against the DeLanceys, once the DeLanceys were out of the picture, relations between the first two families became tenser. Although first protected by the Livingstons, once married into the Schuylers Hamilton threw all his weight on their side in a number of patronage battles. This provoked the leader of the Livingstons, Robert R., to take control of the charge against Hamilton's policies. Hamilton's disregard of the Livingstons opened an opportunity for Aaron Burr, Hamilton's doppelganger and nemesis. Burr made an alliance with Livingston and the two met with Madison and Jefferson in their 1791 tour across New York, apparently laying the groundwork for the opposition that was to become the Republican Party (Lodge 1898: 80f; Risjord 1978: 415; Hendrickson 1985; Cunningham 1957: 81, 91; Young 1967: 160f, 571; Ketcham 1990:287; also see Randall 1993: 525).

Burr became the most industrious Republican leader in New York during the 1796 election, and Burr and Hamilton then faced each other in New York elections as leaders of their respective state parties—indeed, their hatred of one another spiraled to the point at which Burr later manipulated Hamilton into a duel and killed him.[37] But for the time being, there were clashing factions in New York based on preexisting cleavages between elite families contending for control over patronage (Hendrickson 1985: 535, 574, 218, 325, 4; Randall 1993: 570; Cunningham 1957: 107, 117, 177, 245; 1963: 53, 149ff, 206, 213).

It was this consolidation of local rivalries that allowed Republicanism to gain a foothold in New York. In contrast to some other states, here the Republi-

---

[37] Similarly, Burr pioneered methods of mobilizing and it was his organizational importance that led to his being offered the vice presidency. Because the 1800 election turned on the electors from New York who would be chosen by the legislature, which would depend on the vote from New York City, everything turned on this local election. Burr formed a committee with a militarylike structure–a retinue of dedicated followers and then nested circles of inclusion–that reached into the electorate in an unparalleled way. Burr actually had drawn up a list of every voter in the city with information as to his political leanings and past behavior and personally scoured the streets drumming up voters, which a Federalist newspaper found extremely degrading . . . until a Republican paper noted that Hamilton was doing the same (Lomask 1979: 238ff., 244; Sharp 1993: 233).

cans drew heavily on the previous antifederalist ranks;[38] while these antifederalists opposed the Hamiltonian scheme for assumption of state debts, it was not because this was against the interests of their state or because they were opposed to rewarding speculators (Young 1967: 169, 172, 174, 194ff; Kaminski 1993: 197). Instead, as we have seen, they were pushed to be Republicans because they were not Federalists. Indeed, the overriding need to maintain local oppositions led to quite interesting changes—the leading Virginian antifederalist and opponent of Madison, Patrick Henry, found himself becoming a Federalist as the leading Virginia federalist, James Madison, became a Republican. In a very real sense, their party affiliations were unchanged in anything other than name.

The first noticeable national-level organization, then, involved the alignment of largely disconnected political oppositions in different localities. Even though there was no "apex" coordinating (say) Burr's actions in New York and Madison's in Virginia, or even any formal organizational presence,[39] the two could trust that their acts were mutually supporting because they had agreed that they had common enemies.

On the federal level, then, the Republicans developed as a largely horizontal network of elite politicians (especially in the legislature) with its core in Virginia. That is, it began from the network of rough equals that was the backbone of Virginian politics, as opposed to the hierarchy characteristic of New York. Hamilton was not averse to directly contacting people he wanted to influence— he was known to corner people in halls and make impassioned arguments for his favored policies. But he did not do what the Virginians Madison and Jefferson did—namely journey to a different state to talk to equivalents and determine whether they could work in some reasonable concert. Hamilton might beg Washington to call Patrick Henry out of retirement to turn his fearsome rhetoric against the Madisonians in the Virginia assembly, but he did not attempt to discover who the most formidable rising elites were and strike a bargain with them. It was such bargains that allowed for truly national parties to emerge.

[38] Indeed, the word *Republican* was clearly used to characterize the antifederalist (Clintonian) side in New York as early as 1787 (for example, the New York City Federal Republican Committee), far earlier than Jefferson's usage of the 1790s, which is often taken to indicate the birth of the party (see Kaminski 1993: 125, 147, 152, 170, 187, 225, 229).

[39] As early as 1788 antifederalists had employed "committees of correspondence" to spread information and opinion from area to area. But these societies–like the more radical "democratic societies" that also were briefly popular in imitation of French circles–were oriented to mobilizing public opinion, not winning specific elections. The Jeffersonians also used the social club of the "Sons of St. Tammany" in New York and similar societies (such as the Federalists' Washington Benevolent Societies) spread to other states, but it was quite some time before even the New York society was actually used for coordination (Fischer 1965: 111f, 114; Young 1967: 202f, 398f).

Further Development

Political Philosophies

We have seen the emergence of political parties as horizontal alliances of existing elite oppositions, some of which were already tied to well-developed factional structures. On the local level the elaboration of party structure unfolded differently. First, it was generally not that people affiliated with the opposition to Federalism because of their opposition to Hamilton's programs. In states with large frontier areas, this whole controversy seemed relatively distant from divisive concerns. But wherever local elites were affiliated with Federalism—which seems to have been more often than not—there was a natural incentive for their enemies to identify as Republicans, just as we saw with the spread of the Bloods and the Crips as national gangs. A good example here is Vermont, in which a regional division (between those wanting to form an independent state and those wanting to remain part of New York) was mapped on to the Federalist/Republican controversy, even though there was little in the Republican ideology relevant to the debate. Conversely, where elites identified with Republicanism for sectional reasons, their enemies might need to embrace federalism (Goodman 1975: 85; Risjord 1978: 473; Cunningham 1957: 72, 4; Buel 1972: 73, 86; Hillman 2003: 11f, 16–18, 30; Fischer 1965: 203, 206f; Ketcham 1990: 234; Nash 2005: 241).

We saw in the case of early modern England that religious ideology could be an enzyme for such an alignment. Just as effective in establishing a coordination of local oppositions was the French Revolution, not because it was a model that anyone wanted to emulate, but because it served as a mascot that could be used to simplify and express party divisions. The serious political issue of whether the United States should ally itself with England, or with France, or with neither, could be used as an ideological litmus test to bifurcate the populace (Ammon 1963: 159; Appleby 2003: 21; Hendrickson 1985: 234; Buel 1972: 52, 97f, 102f, 236; Risjord 1978: 431; Lodge 1898: 135; Chambers 1963b: 39f, 43, 49, 63, 105, 109; Cunningham 1957: 64f; Bell 1973: 139).

While ideology might be used to *describe* the emerging coalitions, there was little reason to believe the ideology *motivated* these. The Republicans, drawing their strength from the South, might rail against monarchic oppressions of the rights of man and glorify the French commitment to liberty, equality, and brotherhood, while it was the Federalists who (having less to lose) favored the cause of abolition (Appleby 2003: 29; Wilentz 2005: 163). Similarly, the Alien and Sedition laws of 1798 were a blatant attempt by the Federalists to use the powers of government against their political opponents and represented a serious blow to the Republicans. The Republicans retreated to their strongholds of southern state governments and became firm advocates of the rights of the state governments in contrast to the federal (Cunningham

1957: 126f, 137).[40] When the Republicans came into power, the Federalists did the same and now became the ideological advocates of states' rights (Banner 1970). What ideology was good for, then, was to align local conflicts that only imperfectly overlapped with each other.

Further, ideology was a way for actors to break through the constraints of regional bloc voting. We saw above that regional alignments were paramount before the new constitution and dominated the logic of parties immediately afterward. Protagonists might variously refer to the opposition as "democrats," "republicans," "Whigs," or, significantly, "the Southern party." But the new constitution of 1787–88, with its strong executive, increased the "winner-take-all" nature of political action at the federal level. Accordingly, it behooved all factions to court disgruntled fractions of other factions and to organize so as best to triumph in the key political battle, the contest for the presidency. This meant that the majority within one state would court the minority in another; neither local vertical ties of patronage nor horizontal ones of region could express this political logic. "Principle" was all that was left.

Competition and Mobilization: What If They Had a Mass Party and Nobody Came?

> They are drilled and disciplined with the regularity of an army, and
> their plans can be counteracted only by equal organization.
> —Federalist pamphlet of 1805 commenting on Republicans

Competition between the Federalists and Republicans, especially competition for the presidency, led to them to approach in form to what we would now understand as a "party"—a national-level social structure to mobilize and coordinate the actions of non-elites so as to win elections.[41] Only the presidential election required the alignment of local conflicts, as the important state elections were generally those for the state assembly (which in most cases would then elect a governor), and these elections were on the district level, not statewide. Even where elites in different localities were internally divided (which would break the regional alignments), something else was needed if these conflicts were to be aligned in any stable way.

The Republicans, originally an opposition out of power, led the way in moving toward party organization. They made up for their lack of numbers in local meetings by coordinating their actions beforehand; their candidates might

---

[40] Patrick Henry, the antifederalist who had strenuously opposed the new powers of the federal government, argued "ideologically" against this increase in local autonomy that might benefit his opponents.

[41] The epigraph at the beginning of this section comes from Cunningham (1963: 141); also see Banner (1970: 245).

explicitly campaign, a practice still on the border of respectability. The Federalists, reasonably complacent in their monopoly of power, initially did much less in the way of organizing (see Goodman 1975: 58; Chambers 1963b: 32; Risjord 1978: 498, 512; Cunningham 1957: 114, 148, 205, 207, 250f, 258).

But Federalists were eventually forced to copy Republican organizational innovations, prompting the Republicans in turn to increase *their* attempts at mobilization and organization, for example, by moving toward a more formal committee system and a more democratic structure.[42] Even more important, a subtle shift was taking place in the eyes of many actors by which parties ceased to be merely a means to get elected (and then follow one's conscience) and instead became the end in themselves, requiring the subordination of personal preferences (Fischer 1965: 33, 52f; Cunningham 1957: 114, 159f; Cunningham 1963: 131, 141, 156, 161, 174, 283, 301f).

Competition also increased electoral participation, which was in effect an extension of the franchise: the previously apathetic gained interest, and the competitors were more willing to interpret voting qualifications loosely if it might help them. And organized parties could then as now transport the wavering or the disabled to the polls (Goodman 1964: 136f; Banner 1970). This increased mobilization in turn forced an increase in competitiveness in most areas.

Although competition spurred party efforts, and thus from an outsider's perspective we may see it as "friendly" to the growth of parties, from the perspective of parties it was competition that was the true enemy, and much of their effort went not into competing but into attempting to neutralize competition through, for example, the disenfranchisement of likely opponents (as in New York in the 1780s). Most important, the rules for the selection of representatives to the electoral college were set by the states, and so the party in control of the state legislature could rewrite laws to favor itself. In 1800, anticipating the election, Virginia made its procedure for choosing electors "winner-take-all" to ensure that no pockets of Federalist support could contribute to Adams's candidacy. Massachusetts transferred the selection of electors to the state legislature, though in this case, it was to maximize the *Federalist* vote. In Pennsylvania and New York such machinations were avoided only because each party had sufficient strength to block any innovation (Young 1967: 67; Cunningham 1957: 144–47, 150f, 184, 195; 1963: 192; Goodman 1964: 141f; also Formisano 1981: 54 for New Jersey).[43] But competition could not be contained, and it drove the evolution of parties in structural terms.

---

[42] As Hamilton wrote to his friend Bayard, "We must consider whether it be possible for us to succeed, without, in some degree employing the weapons which have been employed against us, and whether the actual state and future prospects of things be not such as to justify the reciprocal use of them" (Hamilton 1910: 335).

[43] Interestingly, these tactics may have actually increased mobilization–by switching to a winner-take-all system the parties needed to mount statewide campaigns, which required an elabo-

The structure that both parties were gravitating to was a hybrid, a set of command hierarchies joined at the top through more horizontal ties. At the state level, there was generally a set of hierarchically nested committees that were used to channel nominations upward and coordinate actions (generally geared to getting out the vote) downward: state committee over district committees, district committee over county committees, and county committee over town committees, to use the example of the Federalist Party of New York. At the national level, parties were used not to win election but to coordinate the activities of elected officials and to control the nomination process, usually via an informal caucus. Thus the overall structure was paradigmatically a set of organized pyramids coordinated by a less formal oligarchy at the top (Fischer 1965: 60–63, 72–76, 83; Cunningham 1957: 151–61; Cunningham 1963: 180, 99–102, 125–29, 167, 174, 177, 201, 301f; Banner 1970: 248–51).

The rapid mobilization was not without costs—the Republicans implicitly promised more than they could deliver as the price of gaining popular support: as one Federalist maliciously predicted, "When the gentry find that there are more PIGS than TEATS, what a squealing there will be in the hog pen." Indeed, serious splits arose in the key middle states of New York, Pennsylvania, and Delaware over patronage. As the Federalist Party crumbled and a new party system developed, both the hierarchical discipline of party and the extent of mobilization were increased. This led to a decrease in the importance of region, with parties competing seriously in nearly every state (Fischer 1965: 25; Dallinger 1897: 44; McCormick 1975: 111f; Reichley 1992: 50, 59; Hofstadter 1970: 209f; Chambers 1963b: 191, 197, 200; Cunningham 1963: 183, 203, 215, 221, 283; Ketcham 1990: 466; also see Goodman 1964: 147, 153).

In sum, competition was sufficient if not necessary to lead elites to feel pressure to mobilize commoners, which led to the extension of party forms. Because the issues of contention at the national level were in part regional ones, party formation was somewhat stunted in states in which there was near unanimity of interests. Such places could be extremely powerful bases of support from which one might intervene in federal level politics—there is no better basis for democratic action than an antidemocratic district. But if dissent between elites could be found in a number of regions, there was always the possibility of aligning these so as to strengthen the emerging party system. The precise nature of the party system (two national-level parties) of course has much to do with the particular institutional forms that were the backdrop for action, but we may draw general lessons about the elaboration of parties as social structures.

---

ration of their formal structure and greater centralization, and which made them more formidable competitors (for Massachusetts, see Banner 1970: 237).

Parties as Structure

Routes to Party

We have seen that modern parties combine three structural features. First of all, they are forms for mobilizing large numbers of persons. Second, they involve hierarchical organization—hierarchical at least in the sense of inclusive levels, whereby cities are within counties (say), counties within states, and states within the nation. Third, they rely on some external interest constellations (that is, interests that existed prior to members joining the party). Not all forms of political organization have these features, and indeed, parties tend to evolve from other forms that are different. In particular, "blocs" exist when there are stable interest constellations but not well-developed coordinative structures. Such blocs tend to approach the clique structure that we investigated in chapter 2, as they arise from the simplest forms of equivalence. Because commonalities of interest are generally based on stark social divisions (such as region or landholding status) there is relatively little middle ground and hence relatively little competition. No one can be swung either way.

In such cases, then, there is little reason for political mobilization to be high—representatives may be entrusted with all political action, as their interests can be counted on to resemble those of the represented. We saw this approximated in Virginia. But political mobilization can also be low where, rather than representing interest constellations, political organizations involve the hierarchical relations of a narrow elite. Here, members of a faction may have no common interests prior to their joining the faction; the commonality of interest comes only in the winner-take-all nature of the goods for which they struggle. In such cases, there is far more structural elaboration than in bloc voting, as factionlike maneuvering can lead to multilevel hierarchies, but political actors need not act as representatives of others. We saw this approximated in New York.

Figure 8.2 schematizes this using a tripolar scheme similar to that used in chapter 6, for once again there are somewhat incompatible structural forms. Each vertex is labeled according to a rough symbolization of structural principles. The bloc form differs from factions and parties in its lack of elaborated organization; the faction in terms of the insulation of the political actors from the lay polity. The party is distinguished by its degree of mobilization—its hierarchical reach down to local-level actors who can be inspired and coordinated. (This figure differs from that presented earlier in the chapter, which pertained only to the relationship between elite and nonelite, as opposed to being a template for the dispersion of possible structures.)[44]

[44] Once again, there is a rough correspondence of our three dimensions to differentiation, involution, and dependence, though in this case (as in chapter 4) we deal with a dispersion of structures in which there is no possible source of differentiation other than involution or dependence (as there would be were "individuals" available for heuristics guiding relationship formation). In contrast to chapter 4, however, here we find differentiation to increase only where there is *both* involution and dependence. The faction lacks the dependence on preexisting structure characteris-

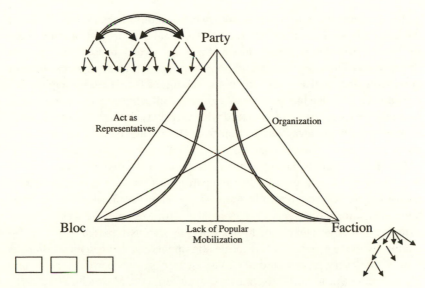

Figure 8.2. Three structures

It is the fusion of the features of the bloc and the faction that leads to a real party—a combination of organizational elaboration and a linkage between elite and mass interests. This latter is labeled "act as representatives" in the figure as this is the paradigmatic form of linkage in contemporary parties. But in patronage parties—and to a large extent this holds true for single party states— the connection between elite and mass interests comes because of the party's ability to grant access to various materially advantageous opportunities in re- turn for loyal support, as opposed to a share in the overall direction of policy.

The arrows indicating trajectories of party formation are impressionistic, but suggest that in most cases of national party formation the first movement from a faction will be toward the incorporation of the horizontal ties character- istic of a bloc system, while the first movement from a bloc will be toward the incorporation of the vertical ties characteristic of a factional system. We saw an example of the latter in the U.S. case, which is one of federal integration of previously established local polities, and an example of the former in the Russian case, which is one of disintegration of a strong nationalized system. But the logic does not seem to be restricted to these cases.[45]

---

tic of both blocs and parties; the bloc lacks the involution and emphasis on vertical triadic relation- ships and their transitivity characteristic of both the faction and the party. Because of the low degree of mobilization of commoners present in either faction or bloc, they have less differentia- tion than the true party.

[45] Thus in postwar Japan, parties in rural areas followed the Virginian pattern of horizontal organization of local notables, while urban areas were based on transitive extension of personal machines—one's friends and relatives "plus *their* friends and relatives" (Ike 1972: 99f).

The diagram above is, however, somewhat deceptive because it implies that the true party structure at the apex leaves factional and bloc systems necessarily behind. But this is not so. Just as there are virtues to loosening control in army structures, so there are reasons why party formation stops short of eliminating factional and bloc structures. Taking the latter first, we might wonder why it is possible that certain subregions are effectively single-party states. One might expect competition to lead whatever party is currently out of power to attempt to break away one section from the ruling coalition by offering a more tempting package of policies.

But there are limits, however broad, to the capacity for such maneuvering at the state or local level given that the party must ensure a certain pattern of horizontal ties or—equivalently—represent certain sectional interests. Thus the compositional differences across locales—for example, the fact that there simply are a large number of farmers in one area as opposed to another—coupled with the pattern of cross-locale alignments can dampen local competition. While every party would like to be all things to all persons, one cannot always both be profarmer in Nebraska and antifarmer in Massachusetts if there are federal-level decisions on farm policy that need to be made.

Thus the party is necessarily in-between two extremes. One extreme would be completely independent lower-level configurations, and the other would be a monolithic structure the contours of which are independent of locale. This in-betweenness is a necessary consequence of the fact that the integration of local structures happens not only by imposition of a common superordinate (e.g., a national committee) but through alliance, coalition, and compromise. As Key (1964: 334) says, "If politics did not make strange bedfellows, there could be no national party."[46]

Thus we do not see a single transition from a patronage faction to a modern party via increasing mobilization, perhaps due to competition. Rather, the party develops as a melding of preexisting blocs, generally based on region (or related divisions such as ethnicity and religion that are key to constellations of interests), and factions, generally based on preexisting vertical relations. Even more important, it is difficult to simply fuse the two forms of bloc and faction. For one, movement toward increasing organization due to competition tends to undermine the bloc form, as the attempt to make advantageous alliances leads to new interest constellations that cut across the preexisting blocs. Yet when secure, factions may attempt to move *toward* a bloc system as a way of decreasing competition. Thus while blocs are defined as the basis of common interests, they are compatible with a noncompetitive political system that does little for the populace.

---

[46] Even better, as Allan Silver has said, "politics *is* strange bedfellows" (see Kopelowitz and Matthew 1998).

On the other hand, blocs tend to blunt factional politics, in that any increase in the relevance of shared interests among political actors for decisions takes the wind out of complicated maneuvering. Indeed, it may well be that the insulation of a political elite can play a crucial role in the development of parties by allowing for the complex organization of faction that would be unlikely where representatives simply vote the interest of their bloc. It is this organization that can then allow for the mobilization of the populace on a large scale once transitivity is introduced.

Transitivity and Large-Scale Structures

Such transitivity is introduced into parties in two forms. The first is a simple one of command processes—the arranging of sets of vertical relations so that subordinates do not have an independence that allows them to undermine the directives of superordinates. The weakness of command in contemporary American parties is still noted by observers, but it has vastly increased since the first party system (for an example of the development of transitivity of command in the early parties, see Banner 1970: 254f).

Thus it is not simply the structure of command, but the specifically transitive nature of the relationships, that allows for imperative coordination. Further, the transitivity is not just one that implies disciplined cadres (although this is a nontrivial aspect of the party). It also allows for the flow of information upward that can be vital for the coordination of efforts across localities. But as Key (1964: 316) emphasized, while the party is, in structural terms, a hierarchy of nested inclusion such as the tree we derived from unilineal kinship, the higher levels cannot coordinate the lower ones simply "by the exercise of command," but instead require "a sense of common cause."[47]

And this brings us to the second form of transitivity, namely that coming from ideology (see Mann 1986 as discussed in chapter 6). Here the transitivity between relationships is established indirectly; more exactly, we may say that it is mediated by a cultural abstraction. Rather than struggle to force c to accept a relationship with a because a has the relationship with b and b with c (that is, aRb and bRc implies aRc) we simply let a, b, and c define their relationships with one another on the basis of their common ideology i (aHi, bHi, cHi, where H is a new relation of "holding").[48] In line with the arguments made in chapter 1, this is a form of cultural pattern that is dual to the social divisions. This

---

[47] Indeed, Key (1964: 328f) explicitly argued that the party, while formally treelike, is quite different from a military hierarchy because "the linkage is from the bottom up rather than from the top down." "Party organization constitutes no disciplined army. It consists rather of many state and local points of power, each with its own local following and each comparatively independent of external control." This is, however, generalizable to many armies as well.

[48] More technically, we may follow Breiger (1974) in considering relations between participants R expressed as a matrix to be equal to HH^T, where the superscript T indicates the transpose.

sort of transitivity is not that of the command hierarchy—it is that of the clique. Such wholly horizontal relationships thus enter political structures either (in the case of relatively rudimentary mobilization) through bloc voting, or (in the case of greater mobilization) ideology. In both cases, preexisting commonalities of interest are necessary for such horizontal transitivity to develop quickly.[49]

These two forms of transitivity have something in common, something that we also found in military structures, and that is that they must be limited in order for the organization to maintain flexibility (also see Key 1964: 283, 341). If parties are driven to attempt to split all blocs, to enter into every locality and compete there, they must, first of all, allow for local independence of movement, just as must armies. And for the very same reason, they must also allow for ideological disconnection—to be passionately committed to one's own justice and coolly indifferent to that of others. The first form of flexibility must distress the partisan, and the second the philosopher, but it is hard to imagine that things could be otherwise.

---

[49] It is also important that these forms of horizontal transitivity allow for a generalization to continuous degrees of overlap, as opposed to all-or-nothing equivalence. Finally, a parliamentary system can allow for the emergence of national parties less tied to local alignments and hence with somewhat crisper ideologies.

9

From Structures to Institutions

WE BEGAN with extremely simple structures for simple relationships, namely cliques of friendships, and worked our way toward large-scale structures that were fundamental to the nature of the modern nation state. Despite an attempt to restrict attention to simple structures (those that involved only a single type of relationship), the final structure investigated—namely, the mass party—required that we consider a somewhat more complex situation. The party necessarily moved toward a unification of vertical and horizontal relationships and thus two different forms of organization. Rather than this being a source of instability, this heterogeneity seemed to nullify some of the inherent tendencies of simple structures toward their own dissolution.

This final chapter does three things: first, it completes the abbreviated sketch of the structural evolution of the state; second, it draws together some general results across the investigations; and third, it further considers the limitations to simple structures and how they break down or transform.

Big Structures and Little Stories

The Dependence of Civil Functionaries on Military Structures

In the previous two chapters, we examined the creation of two of the most distinctive social structures that comprise the modern state, namely, the command army and the political party. The third obvious structure would be the civil service. We may, however, conclude this project without sustained attention to this social structure because in most cases the development of the civil service is completely bound up with the development of the command army. This is not to say that state growth is a simple product of war or that civil service functions were never important before the rise of the modern state. They were, but nonmilitary functions (other than taxation) were usually local and not united as part of a single social structure. For a classic example, in medieval England each locality might be responsible for its own bridges, an eminently nonmilitary governmental function, but one that did not occur at the level of the nation.[1] We tend to read modern state forms into our understanding

---

[1] There are some particular variations on this pattern, but a large civil service is in almost all cases quite recent. For example, despite a tenfold increase in civilian employment at the federal level in the 19th-century United States, the numbers were still quite small and almost all in the postal service (Porter 1994: 257).

of other polities and assume a much higher level of the development of civilian government than is warranted. Even in the Roman Empire, the nonmilitary employment of the state would have numbered in the hundreds—as Mann (1986: 274) says, "The state was largely an army."[2]

With only moderate exaggeration we can say that the nation-state too was originally little else than a life support system for an army. The first nonmilitary functions to be elaborated at the national level were with only few exceptions those pertaining to the gathering of taxes to support the army (Kiser and Kane 2001: 184; for England, see Brewer 1988: 40). As a result, the construction and extension of tax systems was closely intertwined with the development of the command army explored in chapter 7. It was generally the creation of the military structure that called for the development of a bureaucracy, as military competition requires states to mobilize a much greater proportion of their resources and hence to develop a more sophisticated and more efficient tax gathering system (Tilly 1990).[3] In almost all cases, this leads to a growth of central power at the expense of local powers; it also often led to the development of the transportation and communication infrastructure that further facilitated

---

[2] Early empires may have had well-developed bureaucracies, but they should not be seen as "prestate" forms that could be building blocks of states; rather, they are advanced forms of governance that themselves emerged from earlier structures. It is hard to gather data on their building blocks; for the structural basis of empire building, the classic work is still Eisenstadt (1963). Still, even the empires with bureaucracies seem to have had a very small fraction of the population in the civil service. The most important case is ancient China (here one may consult Hucker 1985). From the Chou dynasty (1122 BCE—256 BCE) on, there were bureaucrats with some responsibility for nonmilitary functions. By the Eastern Han dynasty (25–220 CE) well-functioning civilian bureaucracies dealt with economic and educational functions. However, it is not at all clear how many subordinates such high-ranking ministers actually had, nor how far outside the capital city their reach extended. In most cases such nontax, nonmilitary functions were really restricted to the emperor's enlarged household (which could include much of the capital as a whole). The outlying territories were, of necessity, linked to the center though feudal relationships that were, interestingly, assimilated to those of unilineal kinship. The weakness and indeed antitransitivity of these relationships—that is, their deviation from the relationship of command—is shown in the fact that at this time, even a *ruler* would find it repugnant if a minor elite would disobey his "father" (his own lord) to support his "father's father" if the former were to rebel against the latter (Creel 1964: 164–69). Further, there were, not only in the Han dynasty but in the later T'ang (618–907 CE), serious problems regarding the connection between the central and local governments; in both cases, efforts to solve these through the introduction of intermediaries led to the dissolution of the empire. That is, although there were some nonmilitary functions, they were largely epiphenomenal to the underlying problems of introducing transitivity into military hierarchies, and it was the latter that were key for structural growth.

[3] This does not imply a perfect temporal correspondence. As Parrott (2001: 549f, 552) in particular has emphasized, 17th-century European armies were first likely to grow via a devolution of control to subcontractors and not increases in the bureaucracy of the central government. Correspondingly, the financial pressures of war generally led to a set-back for any attempt to rationalize the tax structure (Brewer 1988: 20f). But the associated weakening of the nobility coming from the monetarization of obligations laid a platform for further centralization.

central control (for a discussion of the Warring States era in China, see Kiser and Cai [2003: 516f, 521]).[4] Not all states developed stronger taxation system, but those that did tended to win the wars and impose their structural innovations on others (Hechter 2000: 57f, 60f).

But for our purposes, what is key is that in most cases the civil service sprang from the same social structure as did the army (a set of cascaded patronage triangles) and developed into a largely parallel structure, namely a command hierarchy (see, e.g., Gorski 2003: 99).[5] Regarding the origin, although we derived the intransitive patronage pyramid as a set of relationships ameliorating preexisting inequality, once created, this structure can be used for surplus extraction, and this is what happens as obligations are initially monetarized. Each individual patron allows his clients to collect tribute from their own dependents on the condition that these clients pass on a share (for the case of the Nkole see Mair [1977: 142]).[6] The essential thing is that the structure was truly a "pyramid scheme" in that it concentrated resources upward by virtue of decreasing numbers of occupants at higher levels. How the actual collection that occurred at the very bottom level took place was often up to the discretion of the least important, not the most important, members.[7]

In chapter 7 we noted that part of the creation of the command army involved splitting this social structure from revenue collection. The latter activities were, however, also eventually organized into a system in which control

---

[4] One exception is the 16th-century Netherlands or United Provinces. Although the formation of an army *was* crucial to the *unification* of the provinces, it did not inherently lead to *centralization*. This was in part because of the reliance on mercenaries, but even more so, because of the local basis to taxation. Increased demand for taxes thus boosted local, not central power (Porter 1994: 95–97; Gorski 2003: 46ff).

[5] It is not clear if this is true for the large empires. Zhao (2004: 604) argues that the state of Chu in "Spring-Autumn period" (722–476 BCE) managed to develop bureaucratic control over outlying areas independent of a feudal structure (though see Kiser and Cai 2004). Similarly, there is evidence that the Aztecs also had a reasonably well-developed bureaucracy despite not needing to support a paid army. There is evidence of hierarchically organized and differentiated departments dealing with revenue, military, trade, justice, and religious matters (Adams 1991: 389, 391). The Incas, too, seem to have had a number of well-developed civilian functions, such as a postal service of runners who transmitted oral messages and accountants (*quipucamayus*) who were skilled in the use of the knotted strings that functioned as calculating and mnemonic devices. The *quipucamayus* also served as local historians; others kept track of births and deaths to aid in the allocation of various forms of forced labor. Most of these functions were in the hands of locals, but there were also *tucuy-ricoc* (the all-seeing) who supervised these on behalf of the center and were themselves hierarchically organized (de la Vega 1961 [c. 1609]: 157, 159f, 22 also 25, 87).

[6] The fundamental structure was generally the same whether it spanned relationships between *individuals*, or relationships between *polities*, in the way that the Incan empire was a pyramid of tribute extraction (Mann 1986: 122).

[7] Even attempts to strengthen the state by instituting stronger tax policies could (as in renaissance Florence) increase the strength of patron-client relationships, as citizens turned to their patrons for tax relief (McLean 2005).

is transitive and centralized. This transformation accordingly involved a loss of personalistic relationships in exchange for impersonalized ones. The influence of a Polanyian economic sociology has led us to appreciate the importance of trust in economic relations, and we are, as a result, liable to overestimate the advantages that come from making use of preexisting personal relationships. But as Flache and Macy (1997) have argued, there is a "weakness of strong ties," especially when it comes to command, because it is hard to sanction those to whom we are emotionally close. For example, the rulers of ancient China originally saw their bureaucratic underlings as family. That might sound very comforting, but was deeply problematic: one cannot fire sons for poor performance (Hsu 1965: 96, 140).[8] Put another way, patrimonialism (having your subordinates have personal ties of dependence to you) sounds wonderful, but it often means that one's subordinates' subordinates have personal ties to one's subordinates (and not to one's self), impeding transitivity; introducing transitivity generally requires breaking these personal ties (see, e.g., Gorski 2003: 101).

Thus there is a selectionist argument to explain the transition toward the more bureaucratic structures, though this in no way implies that there is no point at which the returns to further impersonalization are negative. We may divide the process whereby this more effective structure was produced into two portions, centralization and bureaucratization. Regarding the first, tax gathering in almost all nonmodern states was in the hands of notables or officials largely under local control (e.g., "tax farming"). This localization might be attacked before there was any attempt at bureaucratizing the overall structure. For example, in many cases (such as France in the eighteenth century), the state was more concerned with centralizing an existing tax farming system than in moving away from tax farming. Indeed, because of the incentive structure of tax farming, it was often easier to allow for a private development of techniques of taxation before taking it over (Kiser 1994: 299; Kiser and Linton 2001: 421f; also see Kiser and Kane 2001: 192, 208; Brewer 1988: 93).

Still, sooner or later states attempt to shift away from tax farming to a bureaucratic structure, as seen in England in the seventeenth century.[9] This is generally easier with indirect taxes such as import duties, specific sales taxes, or use taxes (the original "patents") than with direct taxes such as property

---

[8] Further, in a personalistic system bosses are responsible their subordinates' well-being—even in the late 17th-century English bureaucrats generally paid their staff from their personal monies. Decreasing the bonds of clientage may have decreased patrons' control but it also decreased their costs (Brewer 1988: 83f).

[9] This generally involved breaking possible personal relationships; for example, as centralization of direct taxes trickled downward in England, a crucial innovation was to move assessors from one locale to another (Ward 1952: 539; Jones 1978: 69; Brewer 1988: 110), a pattern familiar to students of Chinese imperial history.

taxes, given the difficulty of collecting accurate data on wealth or ownership (Baxter 1957: 83–86; Brewer 1988: 65f, 68, 92, 100ff; Ertman 1997: 204; Kiser 1994; Kiser and Kane 2001: 187, 192; Kiser and Linton 2001: 422). So a common pattern involves a state moving toward centralizing an inefficient process of collection or revenue from the productive masses (e.g., agriculturalists), and then adding more bureaucratic taxes on trade. Since such taxes tend to disproportionately burden urban and coastal elites (those who buy and sell a great deal), there is an effective demand for "fairer" taxes—that is, an increasing bureaucratization of the taxes on the masses.

Bureaucratic Models and Taming Clients

It is not always the case that the taxation system begins from the same patronage pyramid that is used to carry out collective violence. In some cases, elites may deliberately construct a patronage pyramid parallel to that involving nobles if these latter are too recalcitrant to be tamed. This seems to have been the case in seventeenth century France where the great ministers created a new kind of clientele at the same time as they extended the central bureaucracy. This bureaucratic clientele both allowed the royal officials to have reasonably trustworthy underlings in various locales and served to broker central patronage to the provinces. This parallel structure thus served as a scaffolding that allowed for a dismantling of the preexisting patronage structure that was in the hands of problematic nobles (Major 1964; Kettering 1986: 91, 181, 184–86, 214, 220–23).[10]

Finally, there are a few interesting cases in which at least the core of the bureaucracy appears not to have been developed out of a patronage pyramid— I noted above that ancient China may be such a case.[11] It is, not surprisingly, quite difficult to determine what historical estimates of numbers of officials are believable, to separate civilian from military positions and, perhaps most important, to determine what proportion of these positions were the equivalent of "no-show" jobs designed to buy off a middle elite (similar to the state bureaucracies in many postcolonial nations, especially those with oil revenues). But it is clear that there was a sufficient independence to the bureaucratic structure for political thinkers to attempt to develop heuristics for action as opposed to simply relying on preexisting structures of relationships.

One of these political thinkers was Shen Pu-hai in fourth-century BCE China, a chancellor whose thoughts were collected in a book that seems to have remained influential into the Ming dynasty. Grappling with the recurrent

---

[10] And during the revolt against royal authority of the Fronde, the Parliament moved quickly to destroy this structure of *intendants* (Ranum 1993: 122).

[11] I am especially indebted to Scott Boorman for references in this section.

imperial problem of preventing ministers from usurping their prerogatives and growing over-mighty, Shen Pu-Hai wrote that the ruler must bind the ministers together "like the spokes of a wheel" (Creel 1964: 161). In other words, he proposed a structure homologous to that which resulted from the concatenation of patronage relationships.

This is not, as Amar (1996) has stressed, the only structural model that might be used to describe the apex of a bureaucracy. The British model involved the ruler's advice-givers working *jointly* (the Privy council). The U.S. constitution, in contrast, seems to have been close to Shen Pu-Hai's vision (hence Amar [1996: 661, 667] calls it a hub-and-spoke model). The framers clearly understood the different implications of the two models and emphasized not only the individualization of responsibility that would arise in the hub-spoke model but also a check on transitivity—an expectation that normally the president will not go "under the feet" of a cabinet secretary and have direct dealings with subordinates.

In sum, in most documented cases, the formation of a nonmilitary governmental structure on the national level largely paralleled the formation of the military structure. Sometimes (such as in Tokugawa Japan) there was a deliberate and conscious attempt on the part of elites to construct their state by rationalizing patron-client ties (see Ikegami 1995: 68, 162f, 166, 270). More generally, what state-builders had at hand to work with were patronage pyramids. From these, the military and nonmilitary structures were separated out once obligations were monetarized; this in turn facilitated the consequent introduction of transitivity (for an example, see Brewer 1988: 102). The two structures then gradually diverged, but had the same source. In other cases, a parallel clientalistic structure was first constructed before the intransitive patronage structure was dispensed with. Finally, in still other cases, rulers may have constructed a civilian structure independently of the military and consciously adopted the same basic tree (or wheel) structure. But overall, the most important structural story in terms of the creation of government bureaucracy has to do with the imposition of transitivity and the creation of the command army.

The party also initially relied on the presence of antitransitive patronage type structures that could cascade into those spanning trees that can efficiently join many persons. But the party cannot come from the same social structure that the tax bureaucracy and the army do, namely preexisting pyramids that connect persons at the level of the nation-state. This is because when parties do mobilize such spanning social structures, the resulting competition leads to civil war. Instead, parties form by connecting smaller pyramids via horizontal alliances or by factions slowly extending downward to mobilize nonelites. This is, of course, an incredibly simplified story. But if we are to see whether structural analysis can make a contribution to a general sociology, even simple initial accounts are encouraging. We may indeed be able to find regularities in structure that help explain both comparative and historical variation.

Let us therefore leave the lives of retainers and bureaucrats, party bosses and deserting soldiers, with all their messiness and confusion, and return to the questions of simple structures. What have we learned about the processes whereby relationships spontaneously aggregate to form structure?

Structural Problems and Solutions

Wherefrom Structure

We began with the idea of social structure as developed by early social theorists. These theorists started with the general analogy of society to an organism. Just as organisms had parts, or structures, that met certain functions, so might society as a whole. Thus social patterns could be explained with reference to this overall pseudo-organism and its needs.

In one sense such analyses were, and still are, relatively powerful—with few additional claims, one is able to explain a fair amount of the "why" for any social pattern. But the amount that could be explained is generally pretty much the same as the amount that is available on inspection. That is, from "the job of the police is to maintain law and order" to "the *function* of the police is to maintain the social order" is so short a distance that we are unlikely to be continually impressed with the explanatory power of such an account.

When the immediate gratification of a quick functional answer to every question dies away, we may become interested in the more difficult issues pertaining to the actual formation of these structures. That is, if we are not merely interested in what the *justification* of a structure might be, we turn our attention to what it is in structural terms and how it may have thusly arisen. Now the story of the formation of any particular structure may be too idiosyncratic for us to use as a building block for a general theoretical account. And certainly, we cannot hope to analyze the origin of any state from scratch— from a set of relationships. As Haas (1982: 5) has emphasized, political archeologists have yet to find a clear case of a state arising wholly independently of other existing states.[12] Yet if we can identify common pressures that facilitate

---

[12] The possible areas of "pristine" state development are Mesoamerica, Andean South America, Mesopotamia, China, India, and Egypt, though the last of these is more doubtful. It is worth noting that the analyses that *have* been conducted are compatible with the account given here—there is evidence of high inequality (e.g., differences in housing, differences in nutrition and growth evident in bone fragments from burial grounds of different classes) and indeed often internal conflict (e.g., class warfare, as seen by defensive fortifications protecting large houses *within* unfortified communities) preceding the development of state forms. Thus if states arise with increasing trade, warfare, or irrigation, it seems less related to any *coordinating* functions than a response to the increasing stratification resulting from these activities (see, e.g., Haviland 1967: 320; Adams 1991: 55, 82, 193, 205; Haas 1982: 88, 95f, 102, 107ff, 136, 209).

or impede the construction of regular aggregations of relationships, we may be able to move toward an account that is both historical and structural.

This has been the approach of the current work. Along the way, we have uncovered patterning to the variations in related structures. At a number of points it proved useful to construct tripolar, two-dimensional figures, which arise when there is a necessary trade-off among triplets of attributes. For example, in chapter 3 we found three polar mating structures, the rating and dating system, class marriage, and generalized exchange, which implied three dimensions: endogamy, homophily, and stratification. In a number of cases, I noted that the three dimensions bore some resemblance to three dimensions discussed by Harrison White (1992), namely involution, dependence, and differentiation. For example, homophily arises when the structure of mating is dependent on orderings outside the mating system; stratification pertains to the total degree of differentiation, and this tendency to for statuses to spread out vertically is closely related to involuteness—the nonindependence of different relationships in the structure. Although there was not a one-to-one parallelism between these figures, exploration of their commonalities helps us establish a reasonable vocabulary with which to frame some very general conclusions before turning to specifics.

What are these general conclusions? We have been looking at structure in the sense of formal regularities across sets of relationships. At the crudest level, we may say that this structure can emerge from within the set of relationships or from without. When this structuring is sensitive to *other* relations established between actors (from what we might call upstream or downstream valuations depending on the circumstance), then the overall structure may be said to be *dependent* on characteristics of the environment. When we are examining relationships that tend to mutuality or that are embedded in a space of likeness, such dependence tends to lead to either isolated dyads (as in chapters 2 and 3) or cliques (as in chapter 7). When we are examining intrinsically directed relationships, this dependence tends to lead to an order (as in chapter 4) or a tree (as in chapter 6).

In many cases, such dependence limits the degree to which structure can emerge from wholly self-referential processes. Such processes, if allowed to unfold unhindered, will make the set of relationships more *involute*. Because it becomes impossible to consider any relationship in isolation from all others, involution tends to imply specific constraints on possible triads and in most cases an emphasis on the transitivity of relationships.

Thus in the simplest cases the trade-off between dependence and involuteness comes merely because structural principles coming from the "outside" compete with structural principles coming from the inside. However, the relationship between involution and dependence varies according to whether "individuals" exist as a structuring principle exogenous (in the eyes of actors) to the set of relationships.[13] "Individuality" can be a third source of differentiation; where it is unavailable, differentiation must find its source either in dependence or in involuteness or both.

For example, when we investigated mutual relationships, we found that "preferential attachment" was a heuristic that treated individuals as "there" (that is, having exogenous attributes) for the purpose of making relationships. In this case, we found that existing structures involved a trade-off between (on the one hand) allowing the "qualities" of these individuals to organize relationship formation and (on the other hand) emphasizing equality within a dyad or (on the third hand) transitive patterns across triads.[14] Where there is no realm of differentiated individuality distinct from involuted or dependent differentiation (as in the pecking orders investigated in chapter 4), then we may find that the differentiation of persons—their elaboration into a hierarchy—can come either from the internal arrangement of relationships (e.g., bystander effects) or from things properly seen as external to the set of relationships (such as the rank of the matrilines of the animals involved).[15]

The similarity in the trade-offs that we have seen comes from the nature of the heuristics correlative to certain structures—one cannot always follow two rules at once. But even more, one cannot always follow one rule at once. That is, a set of actors cannot all orient themselves in a way consistent with this heuristic. The very nature of the relationship's action implications poses a structural problem. We found evidence of three recurrent structural problems, which I called the "problem of equality," the "problem of transitivity," and the "the problem of completeness" respectively. I treat each of these in turn.

The Problem of Equality

The problem of equality is, at heart, that certain structures require equality among participants. Anything that interferes with this equality can impede the formation of a coherent structure. There are then two subtypes of this problem. The first has to do with the dependence of these relationships on other valuations (especially those "upstream"). It is hard to shelter one arena of action from all others, and it is rarely the case that all actors are equal in all respects.[16]

---

[13] That is, we may well argue that the qualities that actors attribute to individuals are themselves endogenous products of the arrangement of relationships, in the way that the "attractiveness" of the popular in the "rating and dating" system explored in chapter 3 is a product of the set of choices thus far established. But actors presumably believe this attractiveness to be inherent in individuals as individuals, and this may guide their subjective heuristics.

[14] A similar possibility of organization by individuals appeared with the "rating and dating" complex in chapter 3 and with "heroic" warfare in chapter 7.

[15] Similarly, we found in chapter 8 that the differentiated organization of the party can draw both on dependence on downstream interest constellations and on factional involution.

[16] Recall that in chapter 7 we briefly noted that substantial portions of a modern state are devoted to partially sheltering labor markets from such exogenous power differences.

For a trivial example, children's friendship cliques can have structural problems if friendship choices go to the more affluent. We may expect a tendency for cliques to be among rough equals, but especially at the higher end of the distribution, it is difficult to assemble a large group of children whose parents are exactly equivalent in status. Even though the formal principle of the "leading clique" may be "rich kids stick together," the mutuality may break down given inequalities within this clique.

But the problem of equality is not restricted to issues of external dependence—in some cases the problem comes from *within* the structure. This occurs when there are divergent implications of relationship (on the one hand) and structure (on the other) regarding the equality of any two persons. For example, consider symmetric relationships. The symmetric relationship implies equality if not interchangeability between the two persons involved. However, the web-type structures investigated in chapter 2 have no inherent predisposition toward equality. Thus while persons A and B may be tied by a symmetric relationship (say, mutual friendship), there is no reason why A cannot have twenty friends and B only three. In that case, there will be strains placed on the egalitarianism of the relationship between A and B, as B finds himself comparatively less valued. Thus the equal relationship is belied by a structure that gives the participants unequal positions.

For another example, consider the asymmetric relations of unilateral transfers examined in chapter 3—one person gives a gift to another, the daughter of one lineage marries a son from another, and so on. In such cases differential popularity can be ruinous—if I give to five persons but receive from only one, it is only a matter of time before I am bankrupt. People may develop exchange structures (most important, generalized exchange) to cope with the threat of a continual drain from one node to another. In this case, instead of an inegalitarian structure composed of equal relationships (as in the friendship web discussed above), we have an egalitarian structure composed of unequal relationships. But in both cases the structural form in some ways fights against the content, and so structures in both cases are potentially fragile.

We also found that these problems could not be solved merely by throwing out the demand that relationships be equal, for there was a problem of *inequality* that was just as destabilizing. When inequality is endogenously generated (as in the popularity tournament), inequality generates more inequality, so much so that the structure may shatter completely—the unpopular are so unpopular that no one will have a relationship with them. In chapter 3, we found that dependence on external considerations could dampen these feedback effects—mating according to social homophily did not lead all people to be equal, but it prevented a cycle of social speculation from spinning out of control. Thus dependence seems to prevent the instabilities of endogeneity that interfere with both equal and unequal relationships.

While this falls short of a general proof, it seems reasonable that the inherent problem of equality becomes harder and harder to solve as the structure gets bigger. With four groups we might imagine that mutual observation and/or affective ties might be enough to allow a system of generalized exchange to proceed without an opportunistic break; with twelve groups we might imagine things somewhat more tenuous but still plausible, but with six thousand impossible. Thus the problem of equality may put constraints on the capacity of structures to grow.

In sum, even if it is good, equality poses a problem. There are, however, structures that do not require equality but the opposite. The most elegant forms, however, imply transitivity—unless we rely on preexisting "individuals" as the heuristic for relation formation, the differentiation comes because of the involution of the set of relationships. This puts serious limits on the capacity of the structure to grow—each person is tied not just to every other person but to every other *relationship*. And this is the second problem, the problem of transitivity.

The Problems of Transitivity and Completion

We set out to examine whether and how simple social structures might spontaneously emerge according to the *content* of the relationships in question. In most cases we found that such structural emergence was made possible because the content of the relationship implied transitivity—in the way that saying "you are equivalent to me" implies saying "your friends are my friends." It is this transitivity that allows structural imperatives to flow across and connect relationships. But this also makes it difficult for large structures to arise—if smaller structures are put together, too many new relationships must be forged for the structural principles to remain unchanged. Put somewhat differently, it seems that there is a scale constraint to the simpler forms of involuteness. Moving toward a larger aggregation requires some relaxation of the structural constraint of transitivity. But such a change in the structural principles can lead to a loss of coherence and a submergence of the formal properties. In subjective terms, a loss of transitivity means that no actor can be quite sure as to whether or not to expect a relationship between any two other persons with whom she may have a relationship.

For some structures, we could not distinguish this problem of transitivity from the problem of completion—the unrealistic imperative for all persons to have relationships with all others. In the clique, for example, transitivity implies completeness. But when we examined pecking orders, we found that the two tended to separate, and there even seemed to be evidence that where structures were complete (as in chickens) they were not transitive and where they were transitive (as in certain monkeys) they were not complete. This had strong implications for human relationships: our dominance relations avoid a pure order because even if they are relatively caged, people need not resolve their conflicts through the agonistic interaction that leads to the establishment of dominance. Just as (balance theory be hanged) no one can force us to be friends with all our friends' friends, so too no one can force two unwilling participants into a dominance bout.

The analysis of these structural problems—those of equality and inequality, of transitivity, and of completeness—not only shed light on the development and evolution of local social structures, they account for our finding as to which structures can become big, namely patronage structures.

Patronage Structures and Structural Problems

First, patronage structures do not suffer from the problem of equality. This is, of course, because they assume inequality between participants. But even more, there is no dislocation between the content of the relationship and the structure—the more powerful have more relationships—and so if participants induce a heuristic for action it only reinforces the structural potential of the relationship. At the same time, these structures do not have the problem of destabilizing inequality. Because patrons support clients on the basis of surplus extracted from nonclients (as well as, perhaps, from clients), patronage relationships are highly dependent on preexisting inequality. As a result, they do not have the "boom-and-bust" positive feedback that we found in structures in which inequality was endogenously generated, such as the popularity tournament, the faction, or even the big-man structure. Patronage structures are (cases of civil war aside) inherently self-limiting as each patron can only support so many clients.

Second, patronage structures do not suffer from the problem of completion. Indeed, not only is there no requirement that all pairs of persons establish a relationship with one another, but the opposite is in fact the case—any client who has a relationship is not allowed to have a second. As a result, the pure form of the patronage triangle has the absolute minimum number of relationships necessary to create a single structure (it is a "spanning tree").

Third, patronage structures do not suffer from the problem of transitivity. Again, the logic of the relationship is precisely the opposite—one should not take on as a client one of one's own clients' clients. As a result, patronage structures are relatively weak. Although in formal terms they look like the trees that can be used by an apex to coordinate action, the apex of a patronage structure is likely to be continually frustrated. The antitransitivity allows every act of disobedience, willful incomprehension, foot-dragging, or outright rebellion to cause the structure to fragment. Hence those in the position of apex will try to institute transitivity into an already-existing patronage structure that spans many persons. But the structure can only grow large when it is weak. The result is that a great deal of the story of the formation of large-scale social structures involves patronage triangles being concatenated into pyramids, and transitivity then being introduced (at least in limited degree). Other structures are, by and large, doomed from the start to stay small.

Even where simple social structures do not get large, however, they may be important. Further, it may be possible to build on the analyses here to move beyond the case of simple structures—those in which persons are connected only by a single type of relationship. In a moment, I will comment briefly on a few avenues of possible *methodological* extension. But in other cases, even when we set out to look for a simple structure, such as that of marriage relationships, we find the interactants *themselves* transcending these scope limitations. For example, they may graft other relationships onto the marriage relationship (as in the son-in-law elevation discussed in chapter 3). Or they may consciously attempt to de-structure the set of relationships to allow for greater freedom of movement. In such cases the conclusions we have reached above may point the way toward a *theoretical* extension. After discussing methodological extensions, I return to the issues with which the book began and assess the contribution of a structural analysis.

Across the Limits of Simple Structures

I began by proposing that certain relationships had inherent "structural tendencies"—that they were more likely to reach toward one sort of arrangement than another. We may therefore say that the content of a certain type of relationship has an implicit duality with a particular structural form. As persons try to arrange relationships in a way consistent with their understanding of meaning of this relationship, this form tends to emerge. Although restricted to the simplest structures consonant with such tendencies, the investigations here point the way to future extensions.

First, we found that the grossest aspects of the structural tendencies inherent in the content of different relationships can be expressed in simple terms pertaining to symmetry, transitivity, and the like—attributes of subsets that are well understood in terms of set theory and graph theory. This suggests the possibility of a methodological integration whereby the process of structuring is conceived of as a set of possible algebraic transformations (the classic example is Boyd 1969). Dually, thinking in terms of heuristics might allow for a parallel formalization but made in terms of social actors, perhaps conceived of as a dynamic model using differential equations but more likely in terms of discrete game theory.[17] Of course, the social sciences have strong impulses toward premature formalization. If we attempt to model a process

[17] Some specific (as opposed to general) approaches along these lines were briefly referred to in chapter 7.

without a serious substantive comprehension, we abandon the possibility of insight in exchange for a shallow monism. That said, any substantive generalizations uncovered in these pages may be a suitable platform for future formal synthesis.

Second, we have also seen that certain structures have a tendency to undermine themselves, especially when they grow. For example, the clique structure implies that every outsider who forms a relationships to someone in the clique then forms a relationship with everyone else. Either the entire world is eventually divided into a smaller number of gigantic camps of close friendship or the structural clarity of the clique must degrade. But it is possible for some of the structural tendencies inherent in the clique to reappear at a larger level not as tendencies shaping the relationships between persons, but as tendencies shaping the relationships between *sets* of persons. For example, we noted that balance theory well predicted not friendships but alliances between states when there were two major antagonists. Thus we might attempt to generalize toward what we may call a "second-order" integration involving not relationships between individuals, but relations between *sets* of individuals, or between institutions, or perhaps even between relations.

Indeed, in chapter 2 we saw sociologists formulating a social structure that was a dominance hierarchy in which the units were *cliques*, not persons. In other words, the structure is a structure of a *compound* of relationships—we have dominance relationships being applied to sets of friendship relationships. As a rule, we might expect that such compounds achieve greater structural clarity when we replace individuals with sets of persons organized by symmetric relationships, paradigmatically the clique. The nature of the equivalence established by such mutual relationships makes it relatively unproblematic to have a pecking order composed of cliques, while it is harder to conceive of a clique of pecking orders. (These sorts of problems are investigated in algebraic theory; see, for example, Ganter and Wille [1999].) At the same time, when vertical structures are transitive and take on a tree form, the potential for unified decision making allows them to function in a compound structure as if each was an individual. Thus we can have exchange structures where the units are lineages, or firms. Indeed, there have been reasonably successful attempts to set up exchange structures between trees composed of cliques, where the cliques are producers' organizations such as local groups of farmers united into a state-wide cooperative.

Thus it is not at all implausible to imagine an extension of the approach here to cover compound structures. Such an investigation—an attempt to develop a pure science of organization—seems possible, and White (1992; also 2002: 206f) has already made substantial inroads. But that which social scientists can unproblematically "black box" as a single unit for analysis (for example, "Corcyra" has "a" relationship of alliance with "Athens") can always be taken apart by actors. Hence a second-order analysis is unlikely to be strictly parallel to the first-order analyses developed here.

Third, we also saw that some relationships seemed to have (at least in some environments) inherent structural tendencies away from simplicity in that actors could not arrange one set of relationships in a coherent manner without invoking a second set. In some cases, this may involve the "overlaying" of two relationships between the same persons—for example, elites may overlay the relationships "son-in-law" and "junior partner." Thus two persons are connected by two relationships, even though some other persons are connected by only one of the relationships (and thus the two relationships have not fused in the way that the relationships of benefice and vassalage were fused in feudalism).

In other cases, the second relationship connects persons unconnected by the first. Thus instead of having two different types of relationships between two persons, we have three persons connected by two different types of relationships, but in a structurally coherent way. For example, vertical factional relationships in an environment conducive to competition reach for supplementary horizontal relationships of alliance. The analysis of the resulting party structures in chapter 8, however, remained relatively rudimentary in that it only was able to grasp this complexity as the combination of two sets of largely independent structural principles that were identical to the principles of structures involving these relationships alone. But it may be that compound or overlaid relationships have distinct structural principles amenable to inductive analysis.

Finally, we have seen that some structural tendencies are potentially self-negating. It is important to distinguish such intrinsic degradation from mere de-structuring. De-structuring may happen simply because whatever process of crystallization that led to the emergence of structure is reversed. We go from a coherent structure with imperatives that span relationships to a set of disconnected relationships. Examples are the collapse of an alliance, the breakdown of a system of generalized exchange, or the dissolution of a routed army. More complexly, we may find a single relationship splitting and leading either to a loss of structural clarity or to different structures. We saw this occurring with patronage pyramids; in feudalism, the classic example would be the separation (or reseparation) of the giving of benefices from the vow of fealty.

But in other cases the set of relationships loses structural clarity but gains in another form of clarity (White 1992). Here it is the very fact of the structural tendency that becomes problematic, at least once the actors develop a subjective version of this tendency. Such transformations can best be understood as "institutionalization," not in the sense of "becoming reliably entrenched" but in the sense of "passing into institution." And it may be that structural analysis can actually shed a great deal of light on this process—the process that explains the absence of structure as defined here.

Institutionalization

From Relationships to Relations

In the first chapter, I made a distinction between *relations*, by which I meant
attributes of some dyad, and *relationships*, which were interpreted as conduits
for actual social action. Yet in several cases we saw one kind of structure
emerging among relationships, but a different—often simpler—structure
emerging in terms of relations. For example, a structure of the relationship
"spending time with" can induce an order in terms of an attribute "popularity,"
which then implies a relation "more popular than" for any two persons, even
those who do not interact. What Simmel would have appreciated is that this
virtual structure—an ordering of persons that does not directly correspond to
actual social interaction—may be subjectively noticed by the participants and
may be treated as an "objective" phenomenon, one that is in fact more important than the actual structure of social interaction that gave rise to it. If
this relation is itself turned into a relationship, there are then two conflicting
principles trying to organize the same type of interaction.

As a result, structures can undermine their own clarity. The structure of
relationships induces sets of relations; these relations then have implications
for interaction that cut against the heuristics that are dual to the prior structure
of relationships. For example, a strong patronage structure composed solely
of antisymmetric client-patron relations induces a relation of structural equivalence between the clients. Patrons, usually aware of this, may expend a great
deal of effort trying to keep this relation from turning into a relationship, by
isolating clients from one another, attempting to broker all relations clients
have with others or even forbidding horizontal relations outright. But if this
effort fails and the implicit equivalence becomes a set of actual relationships,
patronage may pass into corporatist bargaining between the patron (on the one
hand) and the organized set of ex-clients (on the other).

In this case, the relations induced lead to a new, and still relatively simple,
structure of interaction. We now have two relationships, one of alliance between ex-clients, and one of antagonistic bargaining between the clients as an
organized group and the patron. But in other cases, the relation of structural
equivalence induced by the clarity of the structure of relationships is not the
basis for a new simple structure. Instead, the structural equivalence allows for
a generalization of the principles of action inherent in the structure. If indeed
we may describe any structure as the result of a subjective heuristic, it is possible for actors to internalize this heuristic, and then transpose it across contexts
(see especially Clemens 1997: 49). This can actually lead to an undermining
of formal coherence, as the principles are applied to form relationships that do
not necessarily concatenate to a simple structural form. The structure has
passed into institution.

Simmel on the Dialectic of Institutionalization

We began with what I called the dialectic of institutionalization, formulated most elegantly by Georg Simmel. If interactions are repeated, and participants have a subjective understanding of the boundaries and contents of this interaction, something new becomes created whether or not the participants intended this—the "relationship" or tie seems a thing in itself. People can then orient to the relationship, as opposed to one another.

In a similar fashion, if people become aware of the subjective heuristic that is the dual counterpart to some simple structure, they can seize on this and make their understanding of the content of the relationship separable from a particular structure. Most obviously, once some sort of equivalence relations arise via structure and are intuited by the participants, these actors are free to dislodge themselves from their immediate interaction-partners without losing their ability to act. What has happened is that the individual has been able to understand the structural principles in terms of *prescribed relational contents*: it is not that I interact with *A* and not *B* or *C* that is important, only that I find, say, *some* employer—*any* one will do. To the extent that individuals are able to reduce structural patterns to subjectively comprehensible interpretations of actions, they may set up shop wheresoever they please.[18]

This analytic reconstruction is assuredly not a general historical account detailing a sequence of necessary steps always traversed from beginning to end. In most cases, we form relationships according to existing institutional templates. Yet the analytic account can, as I go on to show, shed considerable light on actual historical developments.

The Case of Patronage Relationships

Let us take the case of patronage relationships, which we found to be crucial for the construction of large structures. The patronage relationship is an anti-symmetric one in which two persons provide one another with different types of support in an unequal environment. In this case, as said above, the nature of the relationship (unequal) is mirrored in the nature of the structure—the more powerful party is permitted to be the more "popular." This is because what the subordinates can offer is support, but by virtue of their lesser power, several of the lesser powerful must be combined to form a decent retinue. Thus arises the treelike form discussed in chapter 6.

---

[18] Thus Harrison White (1992: 116) says that institutions are "robust articulations of networks populations, articulations which draw primarily on structural equivalence. Institutions invoke story-sets across disparate discipline species." They form "when disciplines from distinct network populations crisscross according to stories of regular patterns."

But how to subjectively comprehend this tree form? One could think of the heuristics in their bare bones fashion—"every person should find one and only one other occupying the next highest stratum and form a relationship with this person," though this is somewhat awkward. Or one could assimilate this relationship to another well-known relationship that has the identical structural form. As we saw at the end of chapter 5, unilineal descent is such a relationship and people will tend to identify the patronage relationship with that between a father and son as a way to negotiate their behavior. Thus actors may, in good faith, explain the character of some unequal relationship by appealing to the inherent obligations of a paternal-filial relationship; one *feels* this way about the other. But once actors come up with such a rich sense of the meaning of relationships, they may further manipulate the ties by making extensions and elaborations at the level of this cultural understanding, for example, by "feeling" filial to more than one person (see Kettering [1986: 207f]).

A wonderful and well-documented example of this is the case of fourteenth-century Florence, though it is quite possible that earlier Italian (even Roman) urban patronage and sponsorship relations were, to some extent, similar. (Here I rely on the work of McLean [1996: 89, 113, 159, 325, 327; 2007: 4f, 136–44].) In an environment of intense localism yet dispersed and decentralized power, venturing out of one's immediate neighborhood to initiate relationships, whether business or family, was precarious, and hence one would benefit from a protector and broker. While one had only one father to serve in such a role, one could create new pseudofathers, such as godfathers (a patronlike role). More generally, when requesting aid or support from an equal in status, Florentines might address that person as a brother; when addressing someone of greater status, as a father (though age differences also affected choice of term).

Despite the common use of the term *patronage* to describe this relationship, it is quite different from the simple patronage of a feudal-type system or the one that we have seen in Thailand in chapter 6. Instead of each person being "under" a specific and single patron, all "players" attempted to weave a web of supportive relationships around themselves; the cultural template of father-hood was one way of accomplishing this (McLean 1996: 385). "Carissime tanquam pater"—"dearest like a father" is the opening salutation of letters attempting to create or maintain such relationships. The multiplicity of patrons that signals the breakdown in the structural imperatives examined in chapter 6 coincides with an emphasis on creating relationships according to *culture*—an intersubjectively valid understanding of what a relationship means and what it entails. Thus the cultural understanding of the relationship of patronage could be detached from any particular structure and deployed creatively—indeed, in the interests of freeing oneself from rigid structural constraints.[19]

---

[19] And it is in this period that McLean (1996: 699) finds a shift "from a role-based interdependent conception of the self to a more situational, fluid, constructionist conception of the self as interdependent, coincident with the rise of civic humanism."

Even further, this cultural orientation can be transposed to a different relationship leading to structural innovation, because from now on, organization happens not on the basis of particular ties but on the basis of intersubjectively valid scripts for action.[20] We can no longer make sense of the formation and dissolution of relationships in terms of structure; instead, what we have before us is an *institution*.

What Are Institutions?

I began by considering the nature of institutions, starting with the classic work of Linton on roles. From the Lintonian perspective, roles are fundamentally about matters of intersubjective consensus regarding legitimate expectations, an eminently reasonable point of view. This led Parsons to bring everything back to the ultimate values—shared conceptions of the generally good—that he believed oriented action. Institutions, in this light, "are still normative patterns, but on a less general level; they are differentiated relative to the situational exigencies and structural subdivisions of the system" (Parsons 1960: 171). Thus if we were put in the unhappy position of the psychology laboratory rat in a maze, we might value the cheese, but whether we went left or right would be dependent on our position in the maze. Put another way, from values we can derive norms, and from norms, institutions.

Such a conception conforms to our prejudices about how we act (we are always basically doing the right thing, though we often must adapt to "circumstances") and not to what is known about human action. While certain "values" are relatively stable (and so probably very, very few people would be willing to tolerate turning human infants into goat food, even if this were economically rational), the everyday world of hustle and bustle—the world consisting of institutions properly so called—far from being derived from values if anything *induces* those values. As Milgram (1974) famously demonstrated, institutional patterns seem far more stable than the values that supposedly inspire them. But that we cannot derive institutions from values does not mean that the two are unconnected.

Then how to make sense of this connection? We have seen above that people can internalize the structural heuristics that are dual to concrete structures and then unmoor these heuristics. It is these free-floating heuristics that we call institutions. An institution tells us "what to do" because we know what *types* of people we are interacting with (as opposed to focusing on the particularity of well-known others). Further, the "what to do"-ness of institutions is not generally understood only in instrumental terms (or "hypothetical," in Kant's

[20] Padgett and McLean (2006: 1468, 1471) argue that Florentine bankers took the subjective conceptions they had of the relationship of "dowry" that united their families through marriages and applied them to the emerging relationship of "business partner."

terminology)—that is, as *conditional* on what we are trying to accomplish. The sense of aptness associated with institutions has if not always a moral character at least a categorical one, in that it does not require an appeal to something *beyond* an institution. If the institution contains within it directives that actors may unpack into a subjective sense of aptness—and hence a valuation of some end-states as better than others—we may say that it is the institution which provokes the valuing.

This may resonate with the earlier investigation of the relation between structures and heuristics, for in a number of ways we must understand institution as a generalization and abstraction of structure. With an institution, instead of defining the situation in terms of our relationships with particular people, we define it in terms of relations with *types*. But, further, we may say that the duality of heuristic and structure becomes generalized to the duality of value and position.

Social structure is about a regularity that can be subjectively internalized: we may call this subjective internalization "position." In all cases, it is accurate to say that position is defined vis-à-vis the position of other persons in a circle that is no more vicious than social life itself. But in the case of what I have here called "structure," that definition takes place with regard to the existence or nonexistence of *relationships*—recurrent patterns of interaction—between particular others. As a consequence, structures are intrinsically discrete or qualitative, and formal analysis takes us toward graph theory and the algebra of sets.

The requirement that structure be considered in such specificity is relaxed once cultural templates for action arise with institutionalization. With these transposable subjective rules we move to a correlatively continuous sense of position in which we may be above or below, near to or far from, to the right of or to the left of, others with whom we do not interact. To be "in elementary school" is an institutional position that has a similar meaning for millions of children who do not interact with one another. It means to be the pupil of "a" teacher (which one is immaterial), and the classmate of other fellow elementary schoolchildren. If there is something that elementary schoolchildren generally know they are to do—some aptness that is inseparable from this position—it is not that they deduce the necessity of this imperative from the combination of an abstract value and their particular situational exigencies. On the contrary, the value seems to be the result of whatever all elementary-school-nesses have in common. Thus the child moving from one school to another is able to orient more or less successfully because the institutional position has not changed.

The transposability of the heuristic for action necessarily is mirrored in a transposable (and hence abstract) sense of value. And yet values may change predictably with position, just as people's sense of what is "appropriate" to them varies with their stage of life and social position. In that case, we may argue that the set of institutions that actors traverse is organized as an institutional field whereby the question for actors of "what am I to do" changes from the prohibitively complex "how do I fulfill abstract and ultimate values given my particular situational exigencies?" to "what is my position in this field?" Just as heuristics simplify the task of navigating the concrete complexity of a structure of relationships, so position helps simplify the task of navigating the abstract complexity of a set of institutions.

Thus the examination of social structures carried out here, despite its restricted scope, has implications for the more common case of social organization via institutions. We have seen unusually simple structural forms and correspondingly simple senses of "what to do," and this may help us approach the more complex cases in which we cannot rely on a clear structural analysis to ground our understanding of actors' orientations. Most important, we have seen that actors can undo structure precisely *because* they can form subjective representations that are adequate to these structural forms. Structural analysis can be a powerful tool for understanding how actors navigate strong and simple social forms, but it cannot keep them from leaving these structures.

References

Abbott, Andrew. 2001. *Chaos of Disciplines*. Chicago: University of Chicago Press.

Abell, Peter. 1968. "Structural Balance in Dynamic Structures." *Sociology* 2: 333–52.

Abelson, Robert P. 1979. "Social Clusters and Opinion Clusters." Pp. 239–56 in *Perspectives on Social Network Research*, edited by Paul W. Holland and Samuel Leinhardt. New York: Academic Press.

Abelson, R. P., E. Aronson, W. J. McGuire, T. M. Newcomb, M. J. Rosenberg, and P. H. Tannenbaum. 1968. *Theories of Cognitive Consistency*. Chicago: Rand McNally.

Abramovitch, Rona. 1980. "Attention Structures in Hierarchically Organized Groups." Pp. 381–96 in *Dominance Relations: An Ethological View of Human Conflict and Social Interaction*, edited by Donald R. Omark, F. F. Strayer, and Daniel G. Freedman. New York: Garland.

Adams, Julia. 1996. "Principals and Agents, Colonialists and Company Men: The Decay of Colonial Control in the Dutch East Indies." *American Sociological Review* 61: 12–28.

———. 2005. *The Familial State: Ruling Families and Merchant Capitalism in Early Modern Europe*. Ithaca, NY: Cornell University Press.

Adams, Richard E. W. 1991. *Prehistoric Mesoamerica*. Rev. ed. Norman: University of Oklahoma Press.

Adams, S. L. 1974. "The Gentry of North Wales and the Earl of Leicester's Expedition to the Netherlands, 1585–86." *Welsh History Review* 7: 129–47.

Adams, Simon. 1982. "Faction, Clientage, and Party: English Politics, 1550–1603." *History Today* 32: 33–39.

Adcock, F. E. 1967. *The Greek and Macedonian Art of War*. Berkeley: University of California.

Adler, Patricia A., and Peter Adler. 1998. *Peer Power: Preadolescent Culture and Identity*. New Brunswick, NJ: Rutgers University Press.

Aldrich, John H., and Ruth W. Grant. 1993. "The Antifederalists, the First Congress, and the First Parties." *Journal of Politics* 55: 295–326.

Alexander, John K. 2002. *Samuel Adams: America's Revolutionary Politician*. Lanham, MD: Rowland and Littlefield.

Allee, W. C. 1942. "Social Dominance and Subordination among Vertebrates." *Biological Symposia* 8: 139–62.

Allison, Graham, and Philip Zelikow. 1999. *Essence of Decision: Explaining the Cuban Missile Crisis*. 2d ed. New York: Longman.

Allport, Floyd. 1924. *Social Psychology*. Boston: Houghton Mifflin.

Amar, Akhil Reed. 1996. "Some Opinions on the Opinion Clause." *Virginia Law Review* 82: 647–75.

Aminzade, Ronald. 1977. "Breaking the Chains of Dependency: From Patronage to Class Politics, Toulouse, France, 1830–1872." *Journal of Urban History* 3: 485–506.

———. 1987. "Party Formation, Social Class, and Suffrage Reform: A Comparative Study of Urban Politics in Nineteenth-Century France." *Political Power and Social Theory* 6: 1–25.

Ammon, Harry. 1953. "The Formation of the Republican Party in Virginia, 1789–1796." *Journal of Southern History* 19: 282–310.

———. 1963. "The Jeffersonian Republicans in Virginia: An Interpretation." *Virginia Magazine of History and Biography* 71: 153–67.

Anderson, Bo. 1979. "Cognitive Balance Theory and Social Network Analysis: Remarks on Some Fundamental Theoretical Matters." Pp. 453–69 in *Perspectives on Social Network Research*, edited by Paul W. Holland and Samuel Leinhardt. New York: Academic Press.

Anderson, Elijah. 1976. *A Place on the Corner*. Chicago: University of Chicago Press.

Anderson, Fred. 2000. *Crucible of War: The Seven Years' War and the Fate of Empire in British North America, 1754–1766*. New York: Knopf.

Anderson, J. K. 1970. *Military Theory and Practice in the Age of Xenophon*. Berkeley: University of California Press.

Anderson, Perry. 1974. *Passages from Antiquity to Feudalism*. London: New Left Books.

Andreski, Stanislav. 1968. *Military Organization and Society*. Berkeley: University of California Press.

Appleby, Joyce. 2003. *Thomas Jefferson*. New York: Henry Holt.

Argersinger, Peter H. 1992. *Structure, Process, and Party*. Armonk, NY: M. E. Sharpe.

Arrow, Kenneth J. 1974. *The Limits of Organization*. New York: Norton.

Ausubel, David P., Herbert M. Schiff, and Edward B. Gasser. 1952. "A Preliminary Study of Developmental Trends in Socioempathy: Accuracy of Perception of Own and Others' Sociometric Status." *Child Development* 23: 110–28.

Auyero, Javier, and Timothy Patrick Moran. 2007. "The Dynamics of Collective Violence: Dissecting Food Riots in Contemporary Argentina." *Social Forces* 85: 1341–67.

Ayton, Andrew. 1999. "Arms, Armour, and Horses." Pp. 186–208 in *Medieval Warfare: A History*, edited by Maurice Keen. Oxford: Oxford University Press.

Bachrach, Bernard. 1967. "Was There Feudalism in Byzantine Egypt?" *Journal of the American Research Center in Egypt* 6: 163–66.

———. 1972. *Merovingian Military Organization, 481–751*. Minneapolis: University of Minnesota Press.

Baenninger, Louise. 1970. "Social Dominance Orders in the Rat: 'Spontaneous' Food, and Water Competition." *Journal of Comparative and Physiological Psychology* 71: 202–9.

Baker, Wayne E. 1984. "The Social Structure of a National Securities Market." *American Journal of Sociology* 89: 775–811.

Banner, James M., Jr. 1970. *To The Hartford Convention: The Federalists and the Origins of Party Politics in Massachusetts, 1789–1815*. New York: Alfred A. Knopf

Barkey, Karen. 1994. *Bandits and Bureaucrats: The Ottoman Route to State Centralization*. Ithaca, NY: Cornell University Press.

Barner-Barry, Carol. 1980. "The Structure of Young Children's Authority Relationships." Pp. 177–89 in *Dominance Relations: An Ethological View of Human Conflict and Social Interaction*, edited by Donald R. Omark, F. F. Strayer, and Daniel G. Freedman. New York: Garland.

Barth, Fredrik. 1954. "Father's Brother's Daughter Marriage in Kurdistan." *Southwestern Journal of Anthropology* 10: 164–71.

————. 1977 [1965]. "Political Leadership among Swat Pathans." Pp. 207–19 in *Friends, Followers, and Factions: A Reader in Political Clientalism*, edited by Steffen W. Schmidt, James C. Scott, Carl Landé, and Laura Guasti. Berkeley: University of California.

————. 1981. *Process and Form in Social Life: Selected Essays of Frederik Barth.* Vol. 1. London: Routledge and Kegan Paul.

Bashi, Vilna. 1997. "Survival of the Knitted: The Social Networks of West Indian Immigrants." Ph.D. diss., University of Wisconsin-Madison.

Bateson, Gregory. 1958. *Naven.* 2d ed. Stanford, CA: Stanford University Press.

Bauer, Harold R. 1980. "Chimpanzee Society and Social Dominance in Evolutionary Perspective." Pp. 97–119 in *Dominance Relations: An Ethological View of Human Conflict and Social Interaction*, edited by Donald R. Omark, F. F. Strayer, and Daniel G. Freedman. New York: Garland.

Baxter, Stephen B. 1957. *The Development of the Treasury, 1660–1702.* Cambridge, MA: Harvard University Press.

Beacham, Jeffery. 2003. "Models of Dominance Hierarchy Formation: Effects of Prior Experience and Intrinsic Traits." *Behaviour* 140: 1275–1303.

Bean, J. M. W. 1989. *From Lord to Patron: Lordship in Late Medieval England.* Manchester: Manchester University Press.

Bearman, Peter S. 1993. *Relations into Rhetorics: Local Elite Social Structure in Norfolk, England, 1540–1640.* New Brunswick, NJ: Rutgers University Press, ASA Rose Monograph Series.

————. 1997. "Generalized Exchange." *American Journal of Sociology* 102: 1383–1415.

Bearman, Peter S., and Hannah Brückner. 2001. "Promising the Future: Virginity Pledges and the Transition to First Intercourse." *American Journal of Sociology* 106: 859–912.

Bearman, Peter S., James Moody, and Katherine Stovel. 2004. "Chains of Affection: The Structure of Adolescent Romantic and Sexual Networks." *American Journal of Sociology* 110: 44–91.

Becker, Carl Lotus. 1909. *The History of Political Parties in the Province of New York, 1760–1776.* Madison, WI: Bulletin of the University of Wisconsin No. 286.

Becker, Gary S. 1991. *A Treatise on the Family.* Enlarged ed. Cambridge, MA: Harvard University Press.

Beeler, John. 1995 [1966]. *Warfare in England 1066–1189.* New York: Barnes and Noble Books.

————. 1971. *Warfare in Feudal Europe 730–1200.* Ithaca, NY: Cornell University Press.

Bell, Michael Mayerfeld. 1994. *Childerley.* Chicago: University of Chicago Press.

Bell, Rudolph M. 1973. *Party and Faction in American Politics: The House of Representatives 1789–1801.* Westport, CT: Greenwood Press.

Bellamy, J. G. 1989. *Bastard Feudalism and the Law.* Portland, OR: Areopagitica Press.

Bergman, George M. 1998. *An Invitation To General Algebra And Universal Constructions.* Berkeley: Henry Helson.

Berman, Carol M., and Ellen Kapsalis. 1999. "Development of Kin Bias among Rhesus Monkeys: Maternal Transmission or Individual Learning?" *Animal Behaviour* 58: 883–94.

Bernard, H. Russell, Eugene C. Johnsen, Peter D. Killworth, Christopher McCarty, Scott Robinson, and Gene A. Shelley. 1990. "Comparing Four Different Methods for Measuring Personal Social Networks." *Social Networks* 12: 179–215.

Bernard, H. Russell, Eugene. C. Johnsen, Peter D. Killworth, and Scott Robinson. 1989. "Estimating the Size of an Average Personal Network and of an Event Population." Pp. 159–175 in *The Small World*, edited by Manfred Kochen. Norwood, NJ: Ablex.

Bernstein, Irwin S. 1964. "Role of the Dominant Male Rhesus Monkey in Response to External Challenges to the Group." *Journal of Comparative and Physiological Psychology* 57: 404–6.

———. 1966. "Analysis of a Key Role in a Capuchin (*Cebus albifrons*) Group." *Tulane Studies in Zoology* 13: 49–54.

———. 1969. "Stability of the Status Hierarchy in a Pigtail Monkey Group (*Macaca nemestrina*)." *Animal Behavior* 17: 452–59.

———. 1980. "Dominance: A Theoretical Perspective for Ethologists." Pp. 71–84 in *Dominance Relations: An Ethological View of Human Conflict and Social Interaction*, edited by Donald R. Omark, F. F. Strayer, and Daniel G. Freedman. New York: Garland.

Bernstein, Irwin S., and Thomas P. Gordon. 1974. "The Function of Aggression in Primate Societies." *American Scientist* 62: 304–11.

Bernstein, Leonard H. 1970. "Alexander Hamilton and Political Factions in New York to 1787." Ph.D. diss., New York University.

Black, Jeremy. 1991. *A Military Revolution? Military Change and European Society, 1550–1800*. Atlantic Highlands, NJ: Humanities Press International.

Black, Robert. 2000. "Arezzo, the Medici, and the Florentine Regime." Pp. 293–311 in *Florentine Tuscany: Structures and Practices of Power*, edited by William J. Connell and Andrea Zorzi. Cambridge: Cambridge University Press.

Blau, Peter M. 1955. *The Dynamics of Bureaucracy*. Chicago: University of Chicago Press.

Bloch, Marc. 1961 [1940]. *Feudal Society*. Translated by L. A. Manyon. Chicago: University of Chicago Press.

Boehm, Christopher. 1997. "Egalitarian Behaviour and the Evolution of Political Intelligence." Pp. 341–64 in *Machiavellian Intelligence II*, edited by Richard W. Byrne and Andrew Whiten. Cambridge: Cambridge University Press.

Boice, Robert. 1970. "Captive Feeding Behaviours in Captive *Terrapene C. Carolina*." *Animal Behaviour* 18: 703–10.

Boice, Robert, Carol Boice Quanty, and Richard C. Williams. 1974. "Competition and Possible Dominance in Turtles, Toads, and Frogs." *Journal of Comparative and Physiological Psychology* 86: 1116–31.

Boissevain, Jeremy. 1964. "Factions, Parties, and Politics in a Maltese Village." *American Anthropologist* 66: 1275–87.

Bollig, Michael. 1998. "Moral Exchange and Self-Interest: Kinship, Friendship, and Exchange among the Pokot (N.W. Kenya)." Pp. 137–57 in *Kinship, Networks, and Exchange*, edited by Thomas Schweizer and Douglas R. White. Cambridge: Cambridge University Press.

Bolloten, Burnett. 1979. *The Spanish Revolution*. Chapel Hill: University of North Carolina Press.

————. 1991. *The Spanish Civil War: Revolution and Counterrevolution*. Chapel Hill: University of North Carolina Press.

Bonomi, Patricia U. 1971. *A Factious People: Politics and Society in Colonial New York*. New York: Columbia University Press.

Boorman, Scott A., and Harrison C. White. 1976. "Social Structure from Multiple Networks. II. Role Structures." *American Journal of Sociology* 81: 1384–1446.

Bourdieu, Pierre. 1977. *Outline of a Theory of Practice*. Translated by Richard Nice. Cambridge: Cambridge University Press.

————. 1984 [1979]. *Distinction: A Social Critique of the Judgment of Taste*. Translated by Richard Nice. Cambridge, MA: Harvard University Press.

————. 1990 [1980]. *The Logic of Practice*. Stanford, CA: Stanford University Press.

Bourne, J. M. 1986. *Patronage and Society in Nineteenth-Century England*. London: Edward Arnold.

Bovbjerg, Richard V. 1953. "Dominance Order in the Crayfish *Orconectes virilis* (Hagen)." *Physiological Zoölogy* 26: 173–78.

Boyd, John Paul. 1969. "The Algebra of Group Kinship." *Journal of Mathematical Psychology* 6: 139–67.

————. 2002. "Finding and Testing Regular Equivalence." *Social Networks* 24: 315–31.

Boyd, John Paul, and Kai J. Jonas. 2001. "Are Social Equivalences Ever Regular? Permutation and Exact Tests." *Social Networks* 23: 87–123.

Bradley, R. A., and M. B. Terry. 1952. "Rank Analysis of Incomplete Block Designs, I: The Method of Paired Comparisons." *Biometrika* 39: 324–45.

Breer, Paul E., and Edwin A. Locke. 1965. *Task Experience as a Source of Attitudes*. Homewood, IL: Dorsey Press.

Breiger, Ronald L. 1974. "The Duality of Persons and Groups." *Social Forces* 53: 181–90.

————. 2000. "A Tool Kit for Practice Theory." *Poetics* 27: 91–115.

————. 2010. "Spinoza: The Problem of Order." In *Sociological Insights of Great Thinkers: From Aristotle to Zola*, edited by Christofer Edling and Jens Rydgren.

Breiger, Ronald L., and Phillipa E. Pattison. 1986. "Cumulated Social Roles: The Duality of Persons and their Algebras." *Social Networks* 8: 215–56.

Breiger, Ronald L., and John M. Roberts. 1998. "Solidarity and Social Networks." Pp. 239–62 in *The Problem of Solidarity: Theory and Models*, edited by Patrick Doreian and Thomas Fararo. Amsterdam: Gordon and Breach.

Brewer, John. 1988. *The Sinews of Power: War, Money, and the English State, 1688–1783*. Cambridge, MA: Harvard University Press.

Brown, D.J.J. 1979. "The Structuring of Polopa Feasting and Warfare." *Man* 14: 712–33.

Brunt, P. A. 1962. "The Army and Land in the Roman Revolution." *Journal of Roman Studies* 51: 69–86.

Buel, Richard Jr. 1972. *Securing the Revolution: Ideology in American Politics, 1789–1815*. Ithaca, NY: Cornell University Press.

van den Bulte, Christophe, and Gary L. Lilien. 2001. "Medical Innovation Revisited: Social Contagion versus Marketing Effort." *American Journal of Sociology* 106: 1409–35.

Burnham, Walter Dean. 1970. *Critical Elections and the Mainsprings of American Politics*. New York: Norton.

Burt, Ronald S. 1992. *Structural Holes: The Social Structure of Competition*. Cambridge, MA: Harvard University Press.

―――. 2004. "Structural Holes and Good Ideas." *American Journal of Sociology* 110: 349–99.

Bury, J. B. 1955 [1900]. *A History of Greece to the Death of Alexander the Great*. London: Macmillan.

Bygott, J. David. 1979. "Agonistic Behavior, Dominance, and Social Structure in Wild Chimpanzees of the Gombe National Park." Pp. 405–27 in *The Great Apes*, edited by David A. Hamburg and Elizabeth R. McCown. Menlo Park: Benjamin/Cummings.

Campbell, J. K. 1964. *Honour, Family, and Patronage: A Study of Institutions and Moral Values in a Greek Mountain Community*. Oxford: Clarendon Press.

Capitanio, John P. 2004. "Personality Factors between and within Species." Pp. 13–33 in *Macaque Societies: A Model for the Study of Social Organization*, edited by Bernard Thierry, Mewa Singh, and Werner Kaumanns. Cambridge: Cambridge University Press.

Carneiro, Robert L. 1990. "Chiefdom-Level Warfare as Exemplified in Fiji and the Cauca Valley." Pp. 190–211 in *The Anthropology of War*, edited by Jonathan Haas. Cambridge: Cambridge University Press.

Cartwright, Dorwin, and Frank Harary. 1956. "Structural Balance: A Generalization of Heider's Theory." *Psychological Review* 63: 277–93.

Cerulo, Karen. 2006. *Never Saw It Coming*. Chicago: University of Chicago Press.

Chagnon, Napoleon A. 1968a. "Yanomamö Social Organization and Warfare." Pp. 109–59 in *War: The Anthropology of Armed Conflict and Aggression*, edited by Morton Fried, Marvin Harris, and Robert Murphy. Garden City, NY: Natural History Press.

―――. 1968b. *Yanomamö: The Fierce People*. New York: Holt, Rinehart and Winston.

―――. 1990. "Reproductive and Somatic Conflicts of Interest in the Genesis of Violence and Warfare among Tribesmen." Pp. 77–104 in *The Anthropology of War*, edited by Jonathan Haas. Cambridge: Cambridge University Press.

Chambers, William Nisbet. 1963a. "Party Development and Party Action: The American Origins." *History and Theory* 3: 95–106.

―――. 1963b. *Political Parties in a New Nation: The American Experience, 1776–1809*. Oxford: Oxford University Press.

―――. 1972. *The First Party System: Federalists and Republicans*. New York: John Wiley.

Champagne, Roger. 1963. "Family Politics versus Constitutional Principles: The New York Assembly Elections of 1768 and 1769." *The William and Mary Quarterly*, 3d Ser., 20: 57–79.

Chandler, Alfred D., Jr. 1977. *The Visible Hand*. Cambridge, MA: The Belknap Press.

Chapais, Bernard. 1991. "Matrilineal Dominance in Japanese Macaques: The Contribution of an Experimental Approach." Pp. 251–73 in *The Monkeys of Arashiyama*, edited by Linda Marie Fedigan and Pamela J. Asquith. Albany: State University of New York Press.

―――. 2004. "How Kinship Generates Dominance Structures: A Comparative Perspective." Pp. 186–203 in *Macaque Societies: A Model for the Study of Social Orga-*

nization, edited by Bernard Thierry, Mewa Singh, and Werner Kaumanns. Cambridge: Cambridge University Press.

Charles, Joseph. 1956. *The Origins of the American Party System*. New York: Harper and Brothers.

Chase, Ivan D. 1974. "Models of Hierarchy Formation in Animal Societies." *Behavioral Science* 19: 374–82.

———. 1980. "Social Processes and Hierarchy Formation in Small Groups: A Comparative Perspective." *American Sociological Review* 45: 905–24.

———. 1982a. "Behavioral Sequences during Dominance Hierarchy Formation in Chickens." *Science* 23: 439–40.

———. 1982b. "Dynamics of Hierarchy Formation: The Sequential Development of Dominance Relations." *Behaviour* 80: 218–40.

———. 1985. "The Sequential Analysis of Aggressive Acts during Hierarchy Formation: An Application of the 'Jigsaw Puzzle' Approach." *Animal Behaviour* 33: 86–100.

Chase, Ivan D., and Sievert Rohwer. 1987. "Two Methods for Quantifying the Development of Dominance Hierarchies in Large Groups with Application to Harris' Sparrows." *Animal Behavior* 35: 1113–28.

Chatwin, Bruce. 2003. *The Songlines*. London: Vintage.

Chepko-Sade, B. Diane, Karl P. Reitz, and Donald Stone Sade. 1989. "Sociometrics of *Macaca mulatta*, IV: Network Analysis of Social Structure of a Pre-Fission Group." *Social Networks* 11: 293–314.

Chhibber, Pradeep, and Ken Kollman. 1998. "Party Aggregation and the Number of Parties in India and the United States." *American Political Science Review* 92: 329–42.

———. 2004. *The Formation of National Party Systems*. Princeton: Princeton University Press.

Christiansen, Eric. 2000. "A Fine Life." *New York Review of Books*. November 30.

Clark, Terry Nichols. 1973. *Prophets and Patrons: The French University and the Emergence of the Social Sciences*. Cambridge, MA: Harvard University Press.

———. 1973b. "Centralization Encourages Public Goods, But Decentralization Generates Separable Goods." Research paper #39 of the Comparative Study of Community Decision-Making."

———. 1975. "The Irish Ethic and the Spirit of Patronage." *Ethnicity* 2: 305–59.

Clarke, H. B. 1999. "The Vikings." Pp. 36–58 in *Medieval Warfare: A History*, edited by Maruice Keen. Oxford: Oxford University Press.

Clastres, Pierre. 1972. "The Guayaki." Pp. 138–74 in *Hunters and Gatherers Today*, edited by M. G. Bicchieri. New York: Holt, Rinehart and Winston.

von Clausewitz, Karl. 1968 [1832]. *On War*. Harmondsworth, UK: Penguin.

Clemens, Elisabeth S. 1997. *The People's Lobby*. Chicago: University of Chicago Press.

Coleman, James S. 1960. "The Mathematical Study of Small Groups." Pp. 7–149 in *Mathematical Thinking in the Measurement of Behavior*, edited by Herbert Solomon. Glencoe, IL: Free Press.

———. 1964. *Introduction to Mathematical Sociology*. New York: Free Press.

Coleman, James, Elihu Katz, and Herbert Menzel. 1957. "The Diffusion of an Innovation among Physicians." *Sociometry* 20: 253–70.

———. 1966. *Medical Innovation: A Diffusion Study*. Indianapolis: Bobbs-Merrill.

Collins, H. M. 1974. "The TEA Set: Tacit Knowledge and Scientific Networks." *Science Studies* 4: 165–86.

Collins, Randall. 1971. "A Conflict Theory of Sexual Stratification." *Social Problems* 19: 3–21.

———. 1998. *The Sociology of Philosophies*. Cambridge, MA: Belknap Press.

———. 2000. "Situational Stratification: A Micro-Macro Theory of Inequality." *Sociological Theory* 18: 17–43.

Constable, Julie L., Mary V. Ashley, Jane Goodall, and Anne E. Pusey. 2001. "Noninvasive Paternity Assignment in Gombe Chimpanzees." *Molecular Ecology* 10: 1279–1300.

Contamine, Philippe. 1998 [1980]. *War in the Middle Ages*, translated by Michael Jones. New York: Barnes and Noble.

Cooke, Jacob E., ed. 1961. *The Federalist*. Middletown, CT: Wesleyan University Press.

Cords, Marina. 2002. "Friendship among Adult Female Blue Monkeys (*Cercopithecus mitis*)." *Behaviour* 139: 291–314.

Cornelius, Wayne A. 1977. "Leaders, Followers, and Official Patrons in Urban Mexico." Pp. 337–53 in *Friends, Followers, and Factions: A Reader in Political Clientalism*, edited by Steffen W. Schmidt, James C. Scott, Carl Landé, and Laura Guasti. Berkeley: University of California.

Craig, Gordon A. 1956. *The Politics of the Prussian Army, 1640–1945*. Oxford: Oxford University Press.

Crane, Diana. 1972. *Invisible Colleges*. Chicago: University of Chicago Press.

Creel, H. G. 1964. "The Beginnings of Bureaucracy in China: The Origin of the Hsien." *The Journal of Asian Studies* 23: 155–84.

van Creveld, Martin. 1985. *Command in War*. Cambridge, MA: Harvard University Press.

———. 1991. *Technology and War: From 2000 B.C. to the Present*. Cambridge, MA: Harvard University Press.

Critchley, J. S. 1978. *Feudalism*. London: George Allen and Unwin.

Cummings, Scott, and Daniel J. Monti, eds. 1993. *Gangs: The Origins and Impact of Contemporary Youth Gangs in the United States*. Albany: State University of New York Press.

Cunningham, Noble E., Jr. 1957. *The Jeffersonian Republicans: The Formation of Party Organization, 1789–1801*. Chapel Hill: University of North Carolina Press.

———. 1963. *The Jeffersonian Republicans in Power: Party Operations, 1801–1809*. Chapel Hill: University of North Carolina Press.

Daggett, David. 1799. *Sun-Beams May Be Extracted from Cucumbers but the Process is Tedious*. New-Haven: Thomas Green and Son.

Dallinger, Frederick. 1897. *Nominations for Elective Office in the United States*. New York: Longmans, Green.

Dargo, George. 1980. "Parties and the Transformation of the Constitutional Idea in Revolutionary Pennsylvania." Pp. 98–114 in *Party and Political Opposition in Revolutionary America*, edited by Patricia U. Bonomi. Tarrytown, NY: Sleepy Hollow Press.

Darwin, Charles. 1904 [1889]. *The Expression of the Emotions in Man and Animals*. London: John Murray.

Davis, James A. 1963. "Structural Balance, Mechanical Solidarity, and Interpersonal Relations." *American Journal of Sociology* 68: 444–62.

———. 1967. "Clustering and Structural Balance in Graphs." *Human Relations* 20: 181–88.

———. 1977. "Triads as Multi-Variate Systems." *Journal of Mathematical Sociology* 5: 41–59.

———. 1979. "The Davis/Holland/Leinhardt Studies: An Overview." Pp. 51–62 in *Perspectives on Social Network Research*, edited by Paul W. Holland and Samuel Leinhardt. New York: Academic Press.

Davis, James A., and Samuel Leinhardt. 1972. "The Structure of Positive Interpersonal Relations in Small Groups." Pp. 218–51 in *Sociological Theories in Progress*, edited by Joseph Berger, Morris Zelditch, Jr., and Bo Anderson. Boston: Houghton Mifflin.

Davis, Keith. 1953. "Management Communication and the Grapevine." *Harvard Business Review* 4: 43–49.

Davis, Lance E. 1986. "Comment on Wallis and North." Pp.149–61 in *Long-Term Factors in American Economic Growth*, edited by Stanley L. Engerman and Robert E. Gallman. Chicago: University of Chicago Press.

Davis, Shelby Cullom. 1937. *The French War Machine*. London: George Allen and Unwin.

Deag, John M. 1977. "Aggression and Submission in Monkey Societies." *Animal Behaviour* 25: 465–74.

Decker, Scott H., and Barrik van Winkle. 1996. *Life in the Gang*. Cambridge: Cambridge University Press.

Delbrück, Hans. 1990 [1920]. *Warfare in Antiquity*. Vol. 1. *History of the Art of War*. Translated from the 3d ed. by Walter J. Renfroe, Jr. Lincoln: University of Nebraska Press.

Demchak, Chris C. 1991. *Military Organizations, Complex Machines*. Ithaca, NY: Cornell University Press.

DenBoer, Gordon, ed. 1984. *The Documentary History of the First Federal Elections 1788–1790*. Vol. 2. Madison: University of Wisconsin Press.

Dietz, Henry A. 1977. "Bureaucratic Demand-Making and Clientelistic Participation in Peru." Pp. 413–58 in *Authoritarianism and Corporatism in Latin America*, edited by James M. Malloy. Pittsburgh: University of Pittsburgh Press.

DiMaggio, Paul J., and Walter W. Powell. 1983. "The Iron Cage Revisited: Institutional Isomorpohism and Collective Rationality in Organizational Fields." *American Sociological Review* 48: 147–60.

Dodds, Peter Sheridan, Duncan J. Watts, and Charles F. Sabel. 2003. "Information Exchange and the Robustness of Organizational Networks." *Proceedings of the National Academy of Sciences* 100: 12516–21.

Dodge, Theodore Ayrault. 1995 [1891]. *Hannibal: A History of the Art of War among the Carthaginians and Romans down to the Battle of Pydna, 168 B.C., with a Detailed Account of the Second Punic War*. Cambridge, MA: Da Capo Press.

van Doorn, G. Sander, Geerten M. Hengeveld, and Franz J. Weissing. 2003a. "The Evolution of Social Dominance, I: Two-Player Models." *Behaviour* 140: 1305–32.

———. 2003b. "The Evolution of Social Dominance, II: Multi-Player Models." *Behaviour* 140: 1333–58.

Doreian, Patrick. 1971. *Mathematics and the Study of Social Relations*. New York: Schocken Books.

———. 2002. "Event Sequences as Generators of Social Network Evolution." *Social Networks* 24: 93–119.

Doreian, Patrick, and David Krackhardt. 2001. "Pre-Transitive Balance Mechanisms for Signed Networks." *Journal of Mathematical Sociology* 25: 43–67.

Downing, Brian M. 1992. *The Military Revolution and Political Change*. Princeton, NJ: Princeton University Press.

Drummond, Andrew. 1989. "Early Roman *clientes*." Pp. 89–115 in *Patronage in Ancient Society*, edited by Andrew Wallace-Hadrill. London: Routledge.

Duby, Georges. 1991 [1987]. *France in the Middle Ages, 987–1460*. Translated by Juliet Vale. Oxford: Blackwell.

Dugatkin, Lee Alan, Michael S. Alfieri, and Allen J. Moore. 1994. "Can Dominance Hierarchies Be Replicated? Form- re-form Experiments using the Cockroach (*Nauphoeta cinerea*)." *Ethology* 97: 94–102.

Dunbar, R.I.M. 1984. *Reproductive Decisions: An Economic Analysis of Gelada Baboon Social Strategies*. Princeton: Princeton University Press.

Durkheim, Emile. 1933 [1893]. *The Division of Labor in Society*, translated by George Simpson. Glencoe, IL: Free Press.

———. 1938 [1895]. *The Rules of Sociological Method*. Translated by Sarah A. Solovay and John H. Mueller. Glencoe, IL: Free Press.

Duverger, Maurice. 1963 [1954]. *Political Parties: Their Organization and Activity in the Modern State*. New York: John Wiley.

Edbury, Peter. 1999. "Warfare in the Latin East." Pp. 89–112 in *Medieval Warfare: A History*, edited by Maurice Keen. Oxford: Oxford University Press.

Eder, Donna. 1985. "The Cycle of Popularity: Interpersonal Relations among Female Adolescents." *Sociology of Education* 58: 154–65.

Eder, Donna, and Maureen T. Hallinan. 1978. "Sex Differences in Children's Friendships." *American Sociological Review* 43: 237–50.

Eggan, Fred. 1970 [1955]. "The Cheyenne and Arapaho Kinship System." Pp. 33–95 in *Social Anthropology of North American Tribes*, edited by Fred Eggan. Chicago: University of Chicago Press.

Egnal, Marc. 1980. "The Pattern of Factional Development in Pennsylvania, New York, and Massachusetts." Pp. 43–60 in *Party and Political Opposition in Revolutionary America*, edited by Patricia U. Bonomi. Tarrytown, New York: Sleepy Hollow Press.

———. 1988. *A Mighty Empire: The Origins of the American Revolution*. Ithaca, NY: Cornell University Press.

Eisenstadt, S. N. 1963. *The Political Systems of Empires*. Glencoe, IL: Free Press.

Eisenstadt, S. N., and Louis Roniger. 1980. "Patron-Client Relations as a Model of Structuring Social Exchange." *Comparative Studies in Society and History* 22: 42–77.

Ellis, Joseph J. 2004. *His Excellency: George Washington*. New York: Alfred A. Knopf.

Endore, Guy. 1968. *Synanon*. Garden City: Doubleday.

Engels, Frederick. 1942 [1884]. *The Origin of the Family, Private Property, and the State*. New York: International Publishers.

Englehart, Neil A. 2001. *Culture and Power in Traditional Siamese Government*. Ithaca, NY: Cornell University Press.

Erickson, Bonnie. 1988. "The Relation Basis of Attitudes." Pp. 99–121 in *Social Structures: A Network Approach*, edited by Barry Wellman and S. D. Berkowitz. Cambridge: Cambridge University Press.

Erickson, Bonnie H., Liviana Mostacci, T. A. Nosanchuk, and Christina Ford Dalrymple. 1978. "The Flow of Crisis Information as a Probe of Work Relations." *Canadian Journal of Sociology* 3: 71–87.

Ertman, Thomas. 1997. *Birth of the Leviathan: Building States and Regimes in Medieval and Early Modern Europe*. Cambridge: Cambridge University Press.

Evans, Llewellyn Thomas. 1936. "A Study of Social Hierarchy in the Lizard, *Anolis carolinensis*." *Journal of Genetic Psychology* 48: 88–110.

Evans, Peter B. 1975. "Multiple Hierarchies and Organizational Control." *Administrative Science Quarterly* 20: 250–59.

Evans-Pritchard, E. E. 1940. *The Nuer*. Oxford: Clarendon Press.

Everett, Martin G., and Stephen P. Borgatti. 1994. "Regular Equivalence: General Theory." *Journal of Mathematical Sociology* 19: 29–52.

Eyal, Gil, Iván Szelényi, and Eleanor Townsley. 1998. *Making Capitalism without Capitalists: Class Formation and Elite Struggles in Post-Communist Central Europe*. London: Verso.

Fabbri, Lorenzo. 2000. "Patronage and its Role in Government: The Florentine Patriciate and Volterra." Pp. 225–41 in *Florentine Tuscany: Structures and Practices of Power*, edited by William J. Connell and Andrea Zorzi. Cambridge: Cambridge University Press.

Fagan, Jeffrey. 1989. "The Social Organization of Drug Use and Drug Dealing among Urban Gangs." *Criminology* 27: 633–69.

Fararo, Thomas J., and John Skvoretz. 1988. "Dynamics of the Formation of Stable Dominance Structures." Pp. 327–50 in *Status Generalization: New Theory and Research*, edited by Murray Webster, Jr. and Martha Foschi. Stanford, CA: Stanford University Press.

Farris, William Wayne. 1995. *Heavenly Warriors: The Evolution of Japan's Military, 500–1300*. Cambridge, MA: Harvard University Press.

Faust, Katherine. 1988. "Comparison of Methods for Positional Analysis: Structural and General Equivalence." *Social Networks* 10: 313–41.

Feld, Maury D. 1959. "Information and Authority: The Structure of Military Organization." *American Sociological Review* 24: 15–22.

———. 1977. *The Structure of Violence: Armed Forces as Social Systems*. Beverly Hills, CA: Sage.

Feld, Scott L., and Richard Elmore. 1982. "Patterns of Sociometric Choices: Transitivity Reconsidered." *Social Psychology Quarterly* 45: 77–85.

Feldman, Shel. 1966. *Cognitive Consistency*. New York: Academic Press.

Felton, David. 1972. "The Lyman Family's Holy Siege of America." In *Mindfuckers: A Source Book on the Rise of Acid Fascism in America Including Material on Charles Manson, Mel Lyman, Victor Baranco, and Their Followers*, edited by David Felton. San Francisco: Straight Arrow Books.

Fennell, Mary L., Patricia R. Barchas, Elizabeth G. Cohen, Anne M. McMahon, and Polly Hildebrand. 1978. "An Alternative Perspective on Sex Differences in Organizational Settings: The Process of Legitimation." *Sex Roles* 4: 589–604.

Ferguson, R. Brian. 1992. "A Savage Encounter: Western Contact and the Yanomami War Complex." Pp. 199–227 in *War in the Tribal Zone*, edited by R. Brian Ferguson and Neil L. Whitehead. Santa Fe, NM: School of American Research Press.

Festinger, Leon. 1957. *A Theory of Cognitive Dissonance*. Stanford, CA: Stanford University Press.

Festinger, Leon, Stanley Schachter, and Kurt Back. 1963 [1950]. *Social Pressures in Informal Groups*. Stanford, CA: Stanford University Press.

Feuerbach, Ludwig. 1983 [1843]. "Provisional Theses for the Reformation of Philosophy." Pp. 156–71 in *The Young Hegelians: An Anthology*, edited by Lawrence S. Stepelvich. Cambridge: Cambridge University Press.

Firth, Raymond. 1963 [1936]. *We, The Tikopia*. Boston: Beacon Press.

Fischer, Claude S. 1978. "Urban-to-Rural Diffusion of Opinions in Contemporary America." *American Journal of Sociology* 84: 151–59.

———. 1992. *America Calling*. Berkeley: University of California Press.

Fischer, David Hackett. 1965. *The Revolution of American Conservatism: The Federalist Party in the Era of Jeffersonian Democracy*. New York: Harper and Row.

———. 2004. *Washington's Crossing*. Oxford: Oxford University Press.

Fish, M. Steven. 1995. *Democracy from Scratch*. Princeton: Princeton University Press.

Flache, Andreas, and Michael W. Macy. 1997. "The Weakness of Strong Ties: Collective Action Failure in a Highly Cohesive Group." Pp. 19–44 in *Evolution of Social Networks*, edited by P. Doreian and F. N. Stokman. Amsterdam: Gordon and Breach.

Fletcher, Joseph. 1986. "The Mongols: Ecological and Social Perspectives." *Harvard Journal of Asiatic Studies* 46: 11–50.

Flexner, James Thomas. 1978. *The Young Hamilton*. Boston: Little, Brown.

Fligstein, Neil. 1990. *The Transformation of Corporate Control*. Cambridge, MA: Harvard University Press.

———. 2001. *The Architecture of Markets*. Princeton, NJ: Princeton University Press.

Foltz, William J. 1977. "Social Structure and Political Behavior of Senegalese Elites." Pp. 242–50 in *Friends, Followers, and Factions: A Reader in Political Clientalism*, edited by Steffen W. Schmidt, James C. Scott, Carl Landé, and Laura Guasti. Berkeley: University of California.

Forey, Alan. 1992. *The Military Orders from the Twelfth to the Early Fourteenth Centuries*. Toronto: University of Toronto Press.

Formisano, Ronald P. 1981. "Federalists and Republicans: Parties, Yes—System, No." Pp. 33–76 in *The Evolution of American Electoral Systems* by Paul Kleppner, Walter Dean Burnham, Roland P. Formisano, Samuel P. Hays, Richard Jensen, and William G. Shade. Westport, CT: Greenwood Press.

Fortes, Meyer. 1953. "The Structure of Unilineal Descent Groups." *American Anthropologist*, n.s. 55: 17–41.

Foster, George M. 1977 [1961]. "The Dyadic Contract: A Model for the Social Structure of a Mexican Peasant Village." Pp. 15–28 in *Friends, Followers, and Factions: A Reader in Political Clientalism*, edited by Steffen W. Schmidt, James C. Scott, Carl Landé, and Laura Guasti. Berkeley: University of California.

Fourquin, Guy. 1976. *Lordship and Feudalism in the Middle Ages*, translated by Iris and A. L. Lytton Sells. New York: Pica Press.

Freedman, Jim. 1977. "Joking, Affinity, and the Exchange of Ritual Services among the Kiga of Northern Rwanda: An Essay on Joking Relationship Theory." *Man*, n.s. 12: 154–65.

Freeland, Robert F. 2001. *The Struggle for Control of the Modern Corporation: Organizational Change at General Motors, 1924–1970*. New York: Cambridge University Press.

Freeman, Linton C. 1992. "The Sociological Concept of 'Group': An Empirical Test of Two Models." *American Journal of Sociology* 98: 152–66.

Friedell, Morris F. 1967. "Organizations as Semilattices." *American Sociological Review* 32: 46–54.

Friedkin, Noah E. 1998. *A Structural Theory of Social Influence*. Cambridge: Cambridge University Press.

Friedrich, Paul. 1977. "The Legitimacy of a Cacique." Pp. 264–79 in *Friends, Followers, and Factions: A Reader in Political Clientalism*, edited by Steffen W. Schmidt, James C. Scott, Carl Landé, and Laura Guasti. Berkeley: University of California.

Fukuyama, Francis, and Abram N. Shulsky. 1997. *The "Virtual Corporation" and Army Organization*. Santa Monica, California: RAND.

Fuller, J.F.C. 1955. *A Military History of the Western World*. Vol. 2. *From the Defeat of the Spanish Armada to the Battle of Waterloo*. New York: Da Capo Press.

Fuller, Sylvia, and John Levi Martin. 2003. "Women's Status in Eastern NRMs." *Review of Religious Research* 44: 354–69. Furuichi, Takeshi. 1997. "Agonistic Interactions and Matrifocal Dominance Rank of Wild Bonobos (*Pan paniscus*) at Wamba." *International Journal of Primatology* 18: 855–75.

Ganshof, F. L. 1964 [1952]. *Feudalism*. New York: Harper and Row.

Ganter, Bernhard, and Rudolf Wille. 1999. *Formal Concept Analysis: Mathematical Foundations*. Berlin: Springer Verlag.

Garlan, Yvon. 1995. "War and Peace." Pp. 53–85 in *The Greeks*, edited by Jeane-Pierre Vernant. Translated by Charles Lambert and Teresa Lavender Fagan. Chicago: University of Chicago Press.

Gerstel, David U. 1982. *Paradise Incorporated: Synanon*. Novato, CA: Presidio Press.

Giddens, Anthony. 1984. *The Constitution of Society*. Berkeley: University of California Press.

Gigerenzer, Gerd, Peter M. Todd, and the ABC Research Group. 1999. *Simple Heuristics that Make Us Smart*. Oxford: Oxford University Press.

Gillingham, John. 1999. Pp.59–88 in *Medieval Warfare: A History*, edited by Maurice Keen. Oxford: Oxford University Press.

Ginsburg, Benson, and W. C. Allee. 1942. "Some Effects of Conditioning on Social Dominance and Subordination in Inbred Strains of Mice." *Physiological Zoölogy* 15: 485–506.

Ginsburg, Harvey J. 1980. "Playground as Laboratory: Naturalistic Studies of Appeasement, Altruism, and the Omega Child." Pp. 341–57 in *Dominance Relations: An Ethological View of Human Conflict and Social Interaction*, edited by Donald R. Omark, F. F. Strayer, and Daniel G. Freedman. New York: Garland.

Glanzer, Murray, and Robert Glaser. 1961. "Techniques for the Study of Group Structure and Behavior, II: Empirical Studies of the Effects of Structure in Small Groups." *Psychological Bulletin* 58: 1–27.

Goddard, Michael. 1992. "Big-Man, Thief: The Social Organization of Gangs in Port Moresby." *Canberra Anthropology* 15: 20–34.

———. 1995. "The Rascal Road: Crime, Prestige, and Development in Papua New Guinea." *Contemporary Pacific* 7: 55–80.

Godelier, Maurice. 1998. "Afterword." Pp. 386–413 in *Transformations of Kinship*, edited by Maurice Godelier, Thomas R. Trautmann, and Franklin E. Tjon Sie Fat. Washington: Smithsonian Institution Press.

Godelier, Maurice, Thomas R. Trautmann, and Franklin E. Tjon Sie Fat, eds. 1998. *Transformations of Kinship*. Washington: Smithsonian Institution Press.

von Goethe, Johann Wolfgang. 1963 [1809]. *Die Wahlverwandschaften*. Munchen: Deutscher Taschenbuch Verlag.

Goetzinger, Charles, and Milton Valentine. 1963. "Communication Patterns, Interactions, and Attitudes of Top-Level Personnel in the Air Defense Command." *Journal of Communication* 13: 54–57.

Goffman, Erving. 1971. *Relations in Public*. New York: Basic Books.

Goldsworthy, Adrian. 1996. *The Roman Army at War, 100 BC–AD 200*. Oxford: Clarendon Press.

———. 2006. *Caeser*. New Haven: Yale University Press.

Goodall, Jane. 1988. *In the Shadow of Man*. Rev. ed. Boston: Houghton-Mifflin.

———. 1990. *Through a Window: My Thirty Years with the Chimpanzees of Gombe*. Boston: Houghton-Mifflin.

Goodman, Paul. 1964. *The Democratic-Republicans of Massachusetts: Politics in a Young Republic*. Cambridge, MA: Harvard University Press.

———. 1975. "The First American Party System." Pp. 56–89 in *The American Party Systems*, 2d ed., edited by William Nisbet Chambers and Walter Dean Burnham. New York: Oxford University Press.

Goodwyn, Lawrence. 1978. *The Populist Moment: A Short History of the Agrarian Revolt in America*. New York: Oxford University Press.

Goody, Jack. 1977. *The Domestication of the Savage Mind*. Cambridge: Cambridge University Press.

Gorski, Philip S. 1993. "The Protestant Ethic Revisited: Disciplinary Revolution in Holland and Prussia." *American Journal of Sociology* 99: 265–316.

———. 2003. *The Disciplinary Revolution: Calvinism and the Rise of the State in Early Modern Europe*. Chicago: University of Chicago Press.

Gould, Roger V. 1996. "Patron-Client Ties, State Centralization, and the Whiskey Rebellion." *American Journal of Sociology* 102: 400–429.

———. 1999. "Collective Violence and Group Solidarity in Corsica." *American Sociological Review* 64: 356–80.

———. 2002. "The Origins of Status Hierarchies." *American Journal of Sociology* 107: 1143–78.

———. 2003. *Collision of Wills: How Ambiguity about Social Rank Breeds Conflict*. Chicago: University of Chicago Press.

Gould, Roger V., and Roberto Fernandez. 1989. "Structures of Mediation: A Formal Approach to Brokerage in Transaction Networks." *Sociological Methodology* 19: 89–126.

Gouldner, Alvin. 1960. "The Norm of Reciprocity: A Preliminary Statement." *American Sociological Review* 25: 161–78.

Goyal, Sanjeev, and Fernando Vega-Rodondo. 2005. "Structural Holes in Social Networks." Unpublished MS, University of Essex.

Granovetter, Mark. 1973. "The Strength of Weak Ties." *American Journal of Sociology* 78: 1360–80.

———. 1978. "Threshold Models of Collective Behavior." *American Journal of Sociology* 83: 1420–43.

———. 1985. "Economic Action and Social Structure: The Problem of Embeddedness." *American Journal of Sociology* 91: 481–510.

Graziano, Luigi. 1977. "Patron-Client Relationships in Southern Italy." Pp. 360–81 in *Friends, Followers, and Factions: A Reader in Political Clientalism*, edited by Steffen W. Schmidt, James C. Scott, Carl Landé, and Laura Guasti. Berkeley: University of California.

Greenhalgh, P.A.L. 1973. *Early Greek Warfare: Horsemen and Chariots in the Homeric and Archaic Ages*. Cambridge: Cambridge University Press.

Gregory, Stanford W., and Stephen Webster. 1996. "A Nonverbal Signal in Voices of Interview Partners Effectively Predicts Communication Accommodation and Social Status Perceptions." *Journal of Personality and Social Psychology* 70: 1231–40.

Guasti, Laura. 1977. "Peru: Clientalism and Internal Control." Pp. 422–38 in *Friends, Followers, and Factions: A Reader in Political Clientalism*, edited by Steffen W. Schmidt, James C. Scott, Carl Landé, and Laura Guasti. Berkeley: University of California.

Gunawardana, R.A.L.H. 1992. "Conquest and Resistance: Pre-State and State Expansion in Early Sri Lankan History." Pp. 61–82 in *War in the Tribal Zone*, edited by R. Brian Ferguson and Neil L. Whitehead. Santa Fe, NM: School of American Research Press.

Haas, Jonathan. 1982. *The Evolution of the Prehistoric State*. New York: Columbia University Press.

Hage, Per. 1973. "A Graph Theoretic Approach to the Analysis of Alliance Structure and Local Grouping in Highland New Guinea." *Anthropological Forum* 3: 280–94.

———. 1976. "Structural Balance and Clustering in Bushmen Kinship Relations." *Behavioral Science* 21: 36–47.

Hage, Per, and Frank Harary. 1983. *Structural Models in Anthropology*. Cambridge: Cambridge University Press.

———. 1991. *Exchange in Oceania: A Graph Theoretic Analysis*. Oxford: Clarendon Press.

Hagedorn, John, with Perry Macon. 1988. *People and Folks: Gangs, Crime, and the Underclass in a Rustbelt City*. Chicago: Lake View Press.

Hall, Anthony. 1974. "Patron-Client Relations: Concepts and Terms." *Journal of Peasant Studies* 1: 506–9.

Hall, Bert S. 1997. *Weapons and Warfare in Renaissance Europe*. Baltimore: Johns Hopkins University Press.

Hallinan, Maureen T., and Edwin E. Hutchins. 1980. "Structural Effects on Dyadic Change." *Social Forces* 59: 225–45.

Hamilton, Allan McLane. 1910. *The Intimate Life of Alexander Hamilton, Based Chiefly upon Original Family Letters and Other Documents, Many of which Have Never Been Published*. New York: Charles Scribner's Sons.

Hamilton, Charles V. 1979. "The Patron-Recipient Relationship and Minority Politics in New York City." *Political Science Quarterly* 94: 211–27.

Hamlin, Paul M. 1939. *Legal Education in Colonial New York*. New York: New York University Law Quarterly Review.

Hammel, Eugene A. 1973. "The Matrilateral Implications of Structural Cross-Cousin Marriage." Pp. 145–68 in *Demographic Anthropology: Quantitative Approaches*, edited by Ezra B. Zubrow. Albuquerque: University of New Mexico Press.

Hammer, Muriel. 1979–80. "Predictability of Social Connections over Time." *Social Networks* 2: 165–80.

Hammond, Peter B. 1964. "Mossi Joking." *Ethnology* 3: 259–67.

Hanfmann, Eugenia. 1935. "Social Structure of a Group of Kindergarten Children." *American Journal of Orthopsychiatry* 5: 407–10.

Hanks, L. M. 1977 [1966]. "The Corporation and the Entourage: A Comparison of Thai and American Social Organization." Pp. 161–67 in *Friends, Followers, and Factions: A Reader in Political Clientalism*, edited by Steffen W. Schmidt, James C. Scott, Carl Landé, and Laura Guasti. Berkeley: University of California.

Hanley, Eric, Lawrence King, and István Tóth János. 2002. "The State, International Agencies, and Property Transformation in Postcommunist Hungary." *American Journal of Sociology* 108: 129–67.

Hanser, Peter. 1985. *Krieg und Recht: Wesen und Ursachen kollktiver Gewaltanwendung in den Stammesgesellschaften Neuguineas*. Berlin: Dietrich Reimer Verlag.

Hanson, Victor Davis. 1996. "Hoplites into Democrats: The Changing Ideology of Athenian Infantry." Pp. 289–312 in *Dçmokratia*, edited by Josiah Ober and Charles Hendrick. Princeton: Princeton University Press.

———. 1998. *Warfare and Agriculture in Classical Greece*. Rev. ed. Berkeley: University of California Press.

———. 2000 [1989]. *The Western Way of War: Infantry Battle in Classical Greece*. Berkeley: University of California Press.

———. 2001. *Carnage and Culture*. New York: Doubleday.

———. 2003. *Ripples of Battle*. New York: Doubleday.

———. 2005. *A War like No Other*. New York: Random House.

Harary, Frank. 1959. "Status and Contrastatus." *Sociometry* 22: 23–43.

Harary, Frank, and Helene J. Kommel. 1979. "Matrix Measures for Transitivity and Balance." *Journal of Mathematical Sociology* 6: 199–210.

Haraway, Donna J. 1991. *Simians, Cyborgs, and Women*. New York: Routledge.

Hart, C.W.M., and Arnold R. Pilling. 1966 [1960]. *The Tiwi of North Australia*. New York: Holt, Rinehart and Winston.

Harton, H. C., and B. Latané. 1997. "The Social Self-Organization of Culture." Pp. 355–66 in *Self-Organization of Complex Structures*, edited by Frank Schweitzer. Cambridge: Gordon and Breach Science.

Hassig, Ross. 1988. *Aztec Warfare*. Norman: University of Oklahoma Press.

———. 1992. "Aztec and Spanish Conquest in Mesoamerica." Pp. 83–102 in *War in the Tribal Zone*, edited by R. Brian Ferguson and Neil L. Whitehead. Santa Fe, NM: School of American Research Press.

Hauser, Marc D. 1988. "Invention and Social Transmission: New Data from Wild Vervet Monkeys." Pp. 327–43 in *Machiavellian Intelligence*, edited by Richard W. Byrne and Andrew Whiten. Oxford: Clarendon Press.

Haviland, William A. 1967. "Stature at Tikal, Guatemala: Implications for Ancient Maya Demography and Social Organization." *American Antiquity* 32: 316–25.

Hayano, David M. 1974. "Marriage, Alliance, and Warfare: A View from the New Guinea Highlands." *American Ethnologist* 1:281–93.

Hechter, Michael. 2000. *Containing Nationalism*. Oxford: Oxford University Press.

Hedström, Peter, Rickard Sandell, and Charlotta Stern. 2000. "Mesolevel Networks and the Diffusion of Social Movements: The Case of the Swedish Social Democratic Party." *American Journal of Sociology* 106: 145–72.

Hegel, Georg W. F. 1949 [1803]. *The Phenomenology of Mind*, translated by J. B. Baillie. London: George Allen and Unwin.

Heider, Fritz. 1946. "Attitudes and Cognitive Orientation." *Journal of Psychology* 21: 107–12.

———. 1958. *The Psychology of Interpersonal Relations*. New York: John Wiley and Sons.

———. 1983. *The Life of a Psychologist*. Lawrence: University of Kansas Press.

Helm, June. 1972. "The Dogrib Indians." Pp. 51–89 in *Hunters and Gatherers Today*, edited by M. G. Bicchieri. New York: Holt, Rinehart and Winston.

Henderson, H. James. 1974. *Party Politics in the Continental Congress*. New York: McGraw-Hill.

Hendrickson, Robert A. 1985. *The Rise and Fall of Alexander Hamilton*. New York: Dodd, Mead.

Henry, Jules. 1954. "The Formal Structure of a Psychiatric Hospital." *Psychiatry* 17: 139–51.

Hewlett, Barry S., and L. L. Cavalli-Sforza. 1986. "Cultural Transmission among Aka Pygmies." *American Anthropologist* 88: 922–34.

Hicks, Frederic. 1979. "'Flowery War' in Aztec History." *American Ethnologist* 6: 87–92.

Hicks, John D. 1931. *The Populist Revolt: A History of the Farmers' Alliance and the People's Party*. Minneapolis: University of Minnesota Press.

Hillman, Henning. 2003. "Factional Politics and Credit Networks in Revolutionary Vermont." ISERP Working Paper 03–02.

Hillman, Henning, and Christina Gathman. 2007. "From Privateering to Navy: How Sea Power Became a Public Good." Unpublished MS, Stanford University.

Hinde, R. A. 1979. "The Nature of Social Structure." Pp. 295–315 in *The Great Apes*, edited by David A. Hamburg and Elizabeth R. McCown. Menlo Park: Benjamin/Cummings.

Hoadley, John F. 1980. "The Emergence of Political Parties in Congress, 1789–1803." *American Political Science Review* 757–79.

Hobbes, Thomas. 1909 [1651]. *Leviathan*. Oxford: Clarendon Press.

Hofstadter, Richard. 1955. *The Age of Reform*. New York: Vintage Books.

———. 1970. *The Idea of a Party System*. Berkeley: University of California Press.

Holland, Paul W., and Samuel Leinhardt. 1970. "A Method for Detecting Structure in Sociometric Data." *American Journal of Sociology* 76: 492–513.

———. 1971. "Transitivity in Structural Models of Small Groups." *Comparative Group Studies* 2: 107–24.

———. 1981. "An Exponential Family of Probability Distributions for Directed Graphs." *Journal of the American Statistical Association* 76: 33–50.

Hölldobler, Bert, and Edward O. Wilson. 1994. *Journey to the Ants*. Cambridge, MA: Harvard University Press.

Holzer, Boris. 2006. *Netzwerke*. Bielefeld: Transcipt Verlag.

Homans, George C. 1950. *The Human Group*. New York: Harcourt, Brace.

van Hoof, Jan A.R.A.M. 2001. "Conflict, Reconciliation, and Negotiation in Non-Human Primates: The Value of Long-Term Relationships." Pp. 67–90 in *Economics in Nature*, edited by Ronald Noë, Jan A.R.A.M. van Hoof, and Peter Hammerstein. Cambridge: Cambridge University Press.

Horowitz, Ruth. 1983. *Honor and the American Dream*. New Brunswick, NJ: Rutgers University Press.

Houseman, Michael, and Douglas R. White. 1998a. "Taking Sides: Marriage Networks and Dravidian Kinship in Lowland South America." Pp. 214–43 in *Transformations of Kinship*, edited by Maurice Godelier, Thomas R. Trautmann, and Franklin E. Tjon Sie Fat. Washington: Smithsonian Institution Press.

———. 1998b. "Network Mediation of Exchange Structures: Ambilateral Sidedness and Property Flows in Pul Eliya (Sri Lanka)." Pp. 59–89 in *Kinship, Networks, and Exchange*, edited by Thomas Schweizer and Douglas R. White. Cambridge: Cambridge University Press.

Housley, Norman. 1999. "European Warfare *c.*1200–1320." Pp. 113–35 in *Medieval Warfare: A History*, edited by Maruice Keen. Oxford: Oxford University Press.

Hsu, Cho-yun. 1965. *Ancient China in Transition*. Stanford, CA: Stanford University Press.

Hucker, Charles O. 1985. *A Dictionary of Official Titles in Imperial China*. Stanford, CA: Stanford University Press.

Hummon, Norman P., and Patrick Doreian. 2003. "Some Dynamics of Social Balance Processes: Bringing Heider Back into Balance Theory." *Social Networks* 25: 17–49.

Hunt, J. McV., and R. L. Solomon. 1942. "The Stability and Some Correlates of Group-Status in a Summer-Camp Group of Young Boys." *The American Journal of Psychology* 55: 33–45.

Ike, Nobutaka. 1972. *Japanese Politics: Patron-Client Democracy*. 2d ed. New York: Alfred A. Knopf.

Ikegami, Eiko. 1995. *The Taming of the Samurai*. Cambridge, MA: Harvard University Press.

Isbell, Lynne A., and Truman P. Young. 2002. "Ecological Models of Female Social Relationships in Primates: Similarities, Disparities, and Some Directions for Future Clarity." *Behaviour* 139: 177–202.

Iverson, Geoffrey J., and Donald Stone Sade. 1990. "Statistical Issues in the Analysis of Dominance Hierarchies in Animal Societies." *Journal of Quantitative Anthropology* 2: 61–83.

Ives, John W. 1998. "Developmental Processes in the Pre-Contact History of Athapaskan, Algonquian, and Numic Kin Systems." Pp. 94–139 in *Transformations of Kinship*, edited by Maurice Godelier, Thomas R. Trautmann, and Franklin E. Tjon Sie Fat. Washington: Smithsonian Institution Press.

Jackes, Mary. 1969. "Wikmunkan Joking Relations." *Mankind* 7: 128–31.

Jackson, Matthew O., and Asher Wolinsky. 1996. "A Strategic Model of Social and Economic Networks." *Journal of Economic Theory* 71: 44–74.

Jacobs, Jane. 1992 [1961]. *The Death and Life of Great American Cities*. New York: Vintage Books .

Jankowski, Martín Sánchez. 1991. *Islands in the Street: Gangs and American Urban Society*. Berkeley: University of California Press.

Janowitz, Morris. 1957. "Military Elites and the Study of War." *Conflict Resolution* 1: 9–18.

———. 1958. "Changing Patterns of Organizational Authority." *Administrative Science Quarterly* 3: 473–93.

———. 1970. *Sociology and the Military Establishment*. Rev. ed. New York: Russell Sage Foundation.

———. 1975. *Military Conflict*. Beverly Hills, CA: Sage.

Janowitz, Morris, and Edward A. Shils. 1948. "Cohesion and Disintegration in the *Wehrmacht* in World War II." *Public Opinion Quarterly* 12: 280–315.

Janzen, Ted. 2001. *The Rise and Fall of Synanon, A California Utopia*. Baltimore: Johns Hopkins University Press.

Jennings, Francis. 1984. *The Ambiguous Iroquois Empire*. New York: Norton.

Jillson, Calvin, and Rick K. Wilson. 1994. *Congressional Dynamics: Structure, Coordination, and Choice in the First American Congress, 1774–1789*. Stanford, CA: Stanford University Press.

Johnsen, Eugene. 1985. "Network Macrostructure Models for the Davis-Leinhardt Set of Empirical Sociomatrices." *Social Networks* 7: 203–24.

———. 1986. "Structure and Process: Agreement Models for Friendship Formation." *Social Networks* 8: 257–306.

Johnson, Terry, and Christopher Dandeker. 1989. "Patronage: Relation and System." Pp. 219–42 in *Patronage in Ancient Society*, edited by Andrew Wallace-Hadrill. London: Routledge.

Johnston, Michael. 1979. "Patrons and Clients, Jobs and Machines: A Case Study of the Uses of Patronage." *American Political Science Review* 73: 385–98.

Jones, J. R. 1978. *Country and Court, England, 1658–1714*. Cambridge, MA: Harvard University Press.

Kagan, Donald. 1987. *The Fall of the Athenian Empire*. Ithaca, NY: Cornell University Press.

Kagay, Michael R. 1999. "Public Opinion and Polling during Presidential Scandal and Impeachment." *Public Opinion Quarterly* 63: 449–63.

Kaminski, John P. 1993. *George Clinton: Yeoman Politician of the New Republic*. Madison: University of Wisconsin Press.

Kant, Immanuel. 1991 [1797]. *The Metaphysic of Morals*. Translated by Mary Gregor. Cambridge: Cambridge University Press.

Kaplan, J. R., and E. Zucker. 1980. "Social Organization in a Group of Free-Ranging Patas Monkeys." *Folia Primatologica* 34: 196–213.

Kasakoff, Alice. 1974. "Levi-Strauss' Idea of the Social Unconscious: The Problem of Elementary and Complex Structures in Gitksan Marriage Choice." Pp. 143–69 in *The Unconscious in Culture: The Structuralism of Claude Levi-Strauss in Perspective*, edited by Ino Rossi. New York: E. P. Dutton.

Katz, Elihu, and Paul F. Lazarsfeld. 1955. *Personal Influence*. Glencoe, IL: Free Press.

Katz, Stanley Nider. 1968. *Newcastle's New York: Anglo-American Politics, 1732–1753*. Cambridge, MA: Belknap Press.

Kaufman, Daniel J. 1996. "The Army." Pp. 33–62 in *America's Armed Forces*, edited by Sam C. Sarkesian and Robert E. Connor, Jr. Westport, CT: Greenwood Press.

Kaufman, Robert R. 1977. "Corporatism, Clientelism, and Partisan Conflict: A Study of Seven Latin American Countries." Pp. 109–48 in *Authoritarianism and Corporatism in Latin America*, edited by James M. Malloy. Pittsburgh: University of Pittsburgh Press.

Kawai, Masao. 1958. "On the Rank System in a Natural Group of Japanese Monkey [*sic*]." *Primates* 2: 111–12.

Keegan, John. 1988. *The Mask of Command*. New York: Penguin.

———. 1994. *A History of Warfare*. New York: Vintage.

———. 2000. *The First World War*. New York: Vintage.

———. 2003. *Intelligence in War*. New York: Alfred A. Knopf.

Keen, Maurice. 1999a. *Medieval Warfare: A History*. Oxford: Oxford University Press.

———. 1999b. "The Changing Scene: Guns, Gunpowder, and Permanent Armies." Pp. 273–91 in *Medieval Warfare: A History*, edited by Maruice Keen. Oxford: Oxford University Press.

Keesing, Roger M. 1983. *Elota's Story: The Life and Times of a Solomon Islands Big Man*. Fort Worth: Holt, Rinehart and Winston.

Keister, Lisa A. 2001. "Exchange Structures in Transition: Lending and Trade Relations in Chinese Business Groups." *American Sociological Review* 66: 336–60.

Kemp, Jeremy H. 1984. "The Manipulation of Personal Relations: From Kinship to Patron-Clientage." Pp.55–69 in *Strategies and Structures in Thai Society*, edited by Han ten Brummelhuis and Jeremy H. Kemp. Amsterdam: Antropologisch-Sociologisch Centrum, Universiteit van Amsterdam.

Kemper, Theodore D. 1990. *Social Structure and Testosterone*. 1990. New Brunswick, NJ: Rutgers University Press.

Kennedy, John G. 1970. "Bonds of Laughter among the Tarahumara Indians." Pp. 36–68 in *The Social Anthropology of Latin America: Essays in Honor of Ralph Leon Beals*, edited by Walter Goldschmidt and Harry Hoijer. Los Angeles: University of California Press.

Kennedy, Robert F. 1969. *Thirteen Days: A Memoir of the Cuban Missile Crisis*. New York: W.W. Norton.

Kenny, Michael. 1960. "Patterns of Patronage in Spain." *Anthropological Quarterly* 33: 14–23.

Ketcham, Ralph. 1990. *James Madison: A Biography*. Charlottesville: University of Virginia Press.

Kettering, Sharon. 1986. *Patrons, Brokers, and Clients in Seventeenth-Century France*. Oxford: Oxford University Press.

Key, V. O. 1964. *Politics, Parties, and Pressure Groups*. 5th ed. New York: Crowell.

Kierman, Frank A. Jr. 1974. "Phases and Modes of Combat in Early China." Pp. 27–66 in *Chinese Ways in Warfare*, edited by Frank A. Kierman, Jr. and John K. Fairbank. Cambridge, MA: Harvard University Press.

Killworth, Peter D., and H. Russell Bernard. 1979. "A Pseudomodel of the Small World Problem." *Social Forces* 58: 477–505.

Kirschke, James J. 2005. *Gouverneur Morris: Author, Statesman, and Man of the World*. New York: St. Martin's Press.

Kiser, Edgar. 1994. "Markets and Hierarchies in Early Modern Tax Systems: A Principal-Agent Analysis." *Politics and Society* 22: 284–315.

Kiser, Edgar, and Yong Cai. 2003. "War and Bureaucratization in China: Exploring an Anomalous Case." *American Sociological Review* 68: 511–39.

———. 2004. "Early Chinese Bureaucratization in Comparative Perspective: Reply to Zhao." *American Sociological Review* 69: 608–12.

Kiser, Edgar, and Joshua Kane. 2001. "Revolution and State Structure: The Bureaucratization of Tax Administration in Early Modern England and France." *American Journal of Sociology* 107: 183–223.

Kiser, Edgar, and April Linton. 2001. "Determinants of the Growth of the State: War and Taxation in Early Modern France and England." *Social Forces* 80: 411–48.

Kiser, Edgar, and Joachim Schneider. 1994. "Bureaucracy and Efficiency: An Analysis of Early Modern Prussia." *American Sociological Review* 59: 187–204.

Kleinberg, Jon M. 2000. "Navigation in a Small World." *Nature* 406: 845.

Kleinfeld, Judith. 2002. "The Small World Problem." *Society* 39: 61–66.

Knorr-Cetina, Karin. 1999. *Epistemic Cultures*. Cambridge, MA: Harvard University Press.

Knox, Kerry L., and Donald Stone Sade. 1991. "Social Behavior of the Emperor Tamarin in Captivity: Components of Agonistic Display and the Agonistic Network." *International Journal of Primatology* 12: 439–80.

Koffka, K. 1935. *Principles of Gestalt Psychology*. New York: Harcourt, Brace.

Kontopoulos, Kyriakos M. 1993. *The Logics of Social Structure*. Cambridge: Cambridge University Press.

Kopelowitz, Ezra, and Matthew Diamond. 1998. "Religion that Strengthens Democracy: An Analysis of Religious Political Strategies in Israel." *Theory and Society* 27: 671–708.

Kuhn, Thomas S. 1962. *The Structure of Scientific Revolutions*. Chicago: University of Chicago Press.

Krentz, Peter. 1985. "The Nature of Hoplite Battle." *Classical Antiquity* 4: 50–61.

Kropp, Sabine. 1999. "From Communist Predominance to Multiparty System." Pp. 283–309 in *Local Parties in Political and Organizational Perspective*, edited by Martin Saiz and Hans Geser. Boulder, CO: Westview Press.

Kummer, H. 1982. "Social Knowledge in Free-ranging Primates." Pp. 113–30 in *Animal Mind—Human Mind*, edited by D. R. Griffin. Berlin: Springer-Verlag.

———. 1984. "From Laboratory to Desert and Back: A Social System of Hamadryas Baboons." *Animal Behaviour* 32: 965–71.

———. 1995. *In Quest of the Sacred Baboon*, translated by M. Ann Bierderman-Thorson. Princeton: Princeton University Press.

Kummer, H., and F. Kurt. 1967. "A Comparison of Social Behavior in Captive and Wild Hamadryas Baboons." Pp. 65–80 in *The Baboon in Medical Research*, edited by Harold Vagtborg. Austin: University of Texas Press.

Kurzman, Charles. 2004. *The Unthinkable Revolution in Iran*. Cambridge, MA: Harvard University Press.

Lacey, Robert. 1971. *Robert, Early of Essex*. London: Phoenix Press.

Lai, Gina, and Odalia Wong. 2002. "The Tie Effect on Information Dissemination: The Spread of a Commercial Rumor in Hong Kong." *Social Networks* 24: 49–75.

Laitin, David D. 1986. *Hegemony and Culture: Politics and Religious Change among the Yoruba*. Chicago: University of Chicago Press.

Landau, H. G. 1953. "On Dominance Relations and the Structure of Animal Societies, III: The Condition for a Score Structure." *Bulletin of Mathematical Biophysics* 15: 143–48.

Landé, Carl H. 1973. "Networks and Groups in Southeast Asia: Some Observations on the Group Theory of Politics." *American Political Science Review* 67: 103–27.

———. 1977a. "The Dyadic Basis of Clientelism." Pp. xiii-xxxvii in *Friends, Followers, and Factions: A Reader in Political Clientalism*, edited by Steffen W. Schmidt, James C. Scott, Carl Landé, and Laura Guasti. Berkeley: University of California.

———. 1977b. "Group Politics and Dyadic Politics." Pp. 506–10 in *Friends, Followers, and Factions: A Reader in Political Clientalism*, edited by Steffen W. Schmidt, James C. Scott, Carl Landé, and Laura Guasti. Berkeley: University of California.

Landes, David S. 1986. "What Do Bosses Really Do?" *Journal of Economic History* 46: 585–623.

Lang, Kurt. 1972. *Military Institutions and the Sociology of War*. Beverly Hills, CA: Sage.

Latour, Bruno. 1987. *Science in Action: How to Follow Scientists and Engineers through Society*. Cambridge, MA: Harvard University Press.

Latour, Bruno, and Steve Woolgar. 1979. *Laboratory Life: The Social Construction of Scientific Facts*. Beverly Hills, CA: Sage.

Lawler, Edward J., Cecilia Ridgeway, and Barry Markovsky. 1993. "Structural Social Psychology and the Micro-Macro Problem." *Sociological Theory* 11: 268–90.

Leavitt, Harold J. 1951. "Some Effects of Certain Communication Patterns on Group Performance." *Journal of Abnormal and Social Psychology* 46: 38–50.

Leder, Lawrence H. 1961. *Robert Livingston (1654–1728) and the Politics of Colonial New York*. Chapel Hill: University of North Carolina Press.

Lee, Richard Borshay. 1972. "The !Kung Bushmen of Botswana." Pp. 327–68 in *Hunters and Gatherers Today*, edited by M. G. Bicchieri. New York: Holt, Rinehart and Winston.

Leinhardt, Samuel. 1972. "Developmental Change in the Sentiment Structure of Children's Groups." *American Sociological Review* 37: 202–12.

Lemarchand, René. 1972. "Political Clientalism and Ethnicity in Tropical Africa: Competing Solidarities in Nation-Building." *American Political Science Review* 66: 68–90.

Lemarchand, René, and Keith Legg. 1972. "Political Clientelism and Development." *Comparative Politics* 4: 148–65.

Lenin, V. I. 1932 [1917]. *State and Revolution*. New York: International Publishers.

Levine, Donald N. 1985. *The Flight from Ambiguity*. Chicago: University of Chicago Press.

———. 1991a. "Simmel as Educator: On Individuality and Modern Culture." *Theory, Culture, and Society* 8: 99–117.

———. 1991b. "Simmel and Parsons Reconsidered." *American Journal of Sociology* 96: 1097–1116.

Levi-Strauss, Claude. 1953. "Social Structure." Pp. 524–53 in *Anthropology Today: An Encyclopedic Inventory*, edited by A. L. Kroeber. Chicago: University of Chicago Press.

————. 1963. *Structural Anthropology*, translated by Chaire Jacobson and Brooke Grundfest Schoepf. New York: Basic Books.

————. 1965. "The Future of Kinship Studies." *Proceedings of the Royal Anthropological Institute of Great Britain and Ireland* 13: 22.

————. 1966 [1962]. *The Savage Mind*. London: Weidenfeld and Nicolson.

————. 1969 [1949]. *The Elementary Structures of Kinship*. Translated by James Harle Bell and edited by John Richard von Sturmer and Rodney Needham. Boston: Beacon Press.

Lie, John. 1997. "Sociology of Markets." *Annual Review of Sociology* 23: 341–60.

Lieberson, Stanley. 2000. *A Matter of Taste*. New Haven: Yale University Press.

Lindblom, Charles E. 1977. *Politics and Markets*. New York: Basic Books.

Linton, Ralph. 1936. *The Study of Man*. New York: Appleton-Century-Crofts.

Lippitt, Ronald, Norman Polansky, and Sidney Rosen. 1952. "The Dynamics of Power: A Field Study of Social Influence in Groups of Children." *Human Relations* 5: 37–64.

Llamazares, Iván. 2005. "Patterns in Contingencies: The Interlocking of Formal and Informal Political Institutions in Contemporary Argentina." *Social Forces* 83: 1671–96.

Lodge, Henry Cabot. 1898. *Alexander Hamilton*. Boston: Houghton Mifflin.

Lomask, Milton. 1979. *Aaron Burr: The Years from Princeton to Vice President, 1756–1805*. New York: Farrar. Straus, Giroux.

————. 1982. *Aaron Burr: The Conspiracy and Years of Exile, 1805–1836*. New York: Farrar. Straus, Giroux.

Lorenz, Konrad Z. 1961. *King Solomon's Ring*. New York: Thomas Y. Cromwell.

Lorrain, François, and Harrison White. 1971. "Structural Equivalence of Individuals in Social Networks." *Journal of Mathematical Sociology* 1971: 49–80.

Louch, Hugh. 2000. "Personal Network Integration: Transitivity and Homophily in Strong-Tie Relations." *Social Networks* 22: 45–64.

Lubbers, Miranda J. 2003. "Group Composition and Network Structure in School Classes: A Multilevel Application of the *p** Model." *Social Networks* 25: 309–32.

Luchterhandt, Galina. 1992. "Die rußländische Parteienlandschaft: kommunistische und sozialistische Parteien und Bewegungen." *Osteuropa* 42: 1037–49.

Luhmann, Niklas. 1995 [1984]. *Social Systems*, translated by John Bednarz Jr., with Dirk Baecker. Stanford, CA: Stanford University Press.

Lundberg, George A. 1939. *Foundations of Sociology*. New York: Macmillan.

Lynn, John A. 1984. *Bayonets of the Republic*. Urbana: University of Illinois Press.

Lyons, Martyn. 1977. "M.-G.-A.- Vadier (1736–1828): The Formation of the Jacobin Mentality." *French Historical Studies* 10: 74–100.

MacArthur, Robert H. 1972. *Geographical Ecology: Patterns in the Distribution of Species*. New York: Harper and Row.

MacCaffrey, Wallace T. 1961. "Place and Patronage in Elizabethan Politics." Pp. 95–126 in *Elizabethan Government and Society*, edited by S. T. Bindoff, J. Hurstfield, and C. H. Williams. London: Athalone Press.

Mackay, Charles. 1852. *Extraordinary Popular Delusions and the Madness of Crowds*. New York: Farrar, Straus and Giroux.

Mackesy, Piers. 1979. *The Coward of Minden: The Affair of Lord George Sackville*. London: Allen Lane.

Maenchen-Helfen, Otto J. 1973. *The World of the Huns*. Edited by Max Knight. Berkeley: University of California Press.

Main, Jackson T. 1955. "Sections and Politics in Virginia, 1781–1787." *William and Mary Quarterly*, 3d ser, 12: 96–112.

Mair, Lucy. 1961. "Clientship in East Africa." *Cahiers d'études Africaines* 2: 315–26.

Mair, Lucy. 1977. *Primitive Government*. London: Scolar Press.

Major, J. Russell. 1964. "The Crown and the Aristocracy in Renaissance France." *American Historical Review* 69: 631–45.

Malinowski, Bronislaw. 1922. *Argonauts of the Western Pacific: An Account of Native Enterprise and Adventure in the Archipelagoes of Melanesian New Guinea*. London: Routledge and Kegan Paul.

Mallett, Michael. 1999. "Mercenaries." Pp. 209–29 in *Medieval Warfare: A History*, edited by Maurice Keen. Oxford: Oxford University Press.

Mallett, Michael E., and J. R. Hale. 1984. *The Military Organization of a Renaissance State: Venice c. 1400 to 1617*. Cambridge: Cambridge University Press.

Mann, Michael. 1986. *The Sources of Social Power*. Vol. 1. *A History of Power from the Beginning to A.D. 1760*. Cambridge: Cambridge University Press.

———. 1993. *The Sources of Social Power*. Vol. 2. *Rise of Classes and Nation States, 1760–1914*. Cambridge: Cambridge University Press.

March, James G. 1957. "Measurement Concepts in the Theory of Influence." *Journal of Politics* 19: 202–26.

Marglin, Stephen A. 1974. "What Do Bosses Do? The Origins and Functions of Hierarchy in Capitalist Production." *Review of Radical Political Economics* 6: 60–112.

———. 1975. "What Do Bosses Do? Part II." *Review of Radical Political Economics* 6: 60–112.

Marshall, Lorna. 1957. "The Kin Terminology of the !Kung Bushmen." *Africa* 27: 1–25.

Marshall, S. L. A. 1978. *Men against Fire: The Problem of Battle Command in Future War*. Gloucester, MA: Peter Smith.

Martin, John Levi. 1998. "Structures of Power in Naturally Occurring Communities." *Social Networks* 20: 197–225.

———. 2001. "On the Limits of Sociological Theory." *Philosophy of the Social Sciences* 31: 187–223.

———. 2002. "Some Algebraic Structures for Diffusion in Social Networks." *Journal of Mathematical Sociology* 26: 123–46.

———. 2005. "The Objective and Subjective Rationalization of War." *Theory and Society* 34: 229–75.

———. 2009. "Formation and Stabilization of Vertical Hierarchies among Adolescents: Towards a Quantitative Ethology of Dominance among Humans." *Social Psychology Quarterly* (forthcoming).

Martin, John Levi, and Sylvia Fuller. 2004. "Gendered Power Dynamics in Intentional Communities." *Social Psychology Quarterly* 67: 369–84.

Martin, John Levi, and Matt George. 2006. "Theories of Sexual Stratification: Toward a Theory of Sexual Capital and an Analytics of the Sexual Field." *Sociological Theory* 24: 107–32.

Martin, John Levi, and King-To Yeung. 2006. "Persistence of Close Personal Ties over a Twelve Year Period." *Social Networks* 28: 331–62.

Martin, Michel L. 1981. *Warriors to Managers: The French Military Establishment since 1945*. Chapel Hill: University of North Carolina Press.

Marx, Karl. 1906 [1867]. *Capital*. Vol. 1. Edited by Frederick Engels. Translated from the 3d German edition by Samuel Moore and Edward Aveling. Chicago: Charles H. Kerr.

Marx, Karl, and Frederick Engels. 1976 [1845–46]. *The German Ideology*. Vol. 5. *Collected Works*. New York: International Publishers.

Mason, Philip. 1974. *A Matter of Honour*. New York: Holt, Rinehart and Winston.

Mattingly, D. J. 1992. "War and Peace in Roman North Africa." Pp. 31–60 in *War in the Tribal Zone*, edited by R. Brian Ferguson and Neil L. Whitehead. Santa Fe, NM: School of American Research Press.

Mauss, Marcel. 1967 [1925]. *The Gift*. Translated by Ian Cunnison. New York: W. W. Norton.

Mayer, Adrian C. 1966. "The Significance of Quasi-Groups in the Study of Complex Societies." Pp. 97–122 in *The Social Anthropology of Complex Societies*, edited by Michael Banton. New York: Praeger.

McAllister, Ian, and Stephen White. 1995. "Democracy, Political Parties, and Party Formation in Postcommunist Russia." *Party Politics* 1: 49–72.

McCormick, Richard P. 1966. *The Second American Party System: Party Formation in the Jacksonian Era*. Chapel Hill: University of North Carolina Press.

———. 1975. "Political Development and the Second Party System." Pp. 90–116 in *The American Party Systems*, edited by William Nisbet Chambers and Walter Dean Burnham. New York: Oxford University Press.

McCue, Brian. 2002. "Another View of the 'Small World'." *Social Networks* 24: 121–33.

McFaul, Michael, and Sergei Markov. 1993. *The Troubled Birth of Russian Democracy: Parties, Personalities, and Programs*. Stanford, CA: Hoover Institution Press.

McGeer, Eric. 1995. *Sowing the Dragon's Teeth: Byzantine Warfare in the Tenth Century*. Washington, DC: Dumbarton Oaks Research Library and Collection.

McGrew, W. C. 1972. *An Ethological Study of Children's Behavior*. New York: Academic Press.

McGuire, William J. 1999. *Constructing Social Psychology*. Cambridge: Cambridge University Press.

McHugh, Tom. 1958. "Social Behavior of the American Buffalo (*Bison bison bison*)." *Zoologica* 43: 17–23.

McKinley, Silas Bent. 1934. *Democracy and Military Power*. New York: Vanguard Press.

McLean, Paul. 1996. "Patronage and Political Culture: Frames, Networks, and Strategies of Self-Presentation Renaissance Florence." Ph.D. diss., University of Chicago.

———. 1998. "A Frame Analysis of Favor Seeking in the Renaissance: Agency, Networks, and Political Culture." *American Journal of Sociology* 104: 51–91.

———. 2005a. "Patronage, Citizenship, and the Stalled Emergence of the Modern State in Renaissance Florence." *Comparative Studies in Society and History* 47: 638–64.

———. 2005b. "Faction into Party: Elite Networks and Constitutionalism in Late Eighteenth Century Poland." Paper presented at the Annual Meeting of the American Sociological Association, Philadelphia.

McLean, Paul. 2007. *The Art of the Network: Strategic Interaction and Patronage in Renaissance Florence*. Durham, NC: Duke University Press.

———. Forthcoming. "Networks, Culture, and Political Mobilization in Eighteenth-Century Poland." Unpublished Ms.

McLean, Paul, and John F. Padgett. 1997. "Was Florence a Perfectly Competitive Market? Transactional Evidence from the Renaissance." *Theory and Society* 26: 209–44.

McNeill, William H. 1982. *The Pursuit of Power*. Chicago: University of Chicago Press.

———. 1994. *Keeping Together in Time: Dance and Drill in Human History*. Cambridge, MA: Harvard University Press.

Mead, George H. 1934. *Mind, Self, and Society: From the Standpoint of a Social Behaviorist*, edited by Charles W. Morris. Chicago: University of Chicago Press.

Mead, Margaret. 1940. "The Mountain Arapesh, II: Supernaturalism." *Anthropological Papers of the American Museum of Natural History* 37: 317–451.

Meeks, Wayne A. 1983. *The First Urban Christians*. New Haven: Yale University Press.

Meggitt, M. J. 1974. "'Pigs Are Our Hearts!' The Te Exchange Cycle among the Mae Enga of New Guinea." *Oceania* 44: 165–203.

Merton, Robert K. 1949. "Patterns of Influence: A Study of Interpersonal Influence and of Communications Behavior in a Local Community." Pp. 180–219 in P. F. Lazarsfeld and F. Stanton, eds., *Communications Research, 1948–1949*. New York: Harper.

———. 1968. *Social Theory and Social Structure*. New York: Free Press.

———. 1973. *The Sociology of Science: Theoretical and Empirical Investigations*. Chicago: University of Chicago Press.

Meyer, John W., and Brian Rowan. 1977. "Institutionalized Organizations: Formal Structure as Myth and Ceremony." *American Journal of Sociology* 83: 340–63.

Milgram, Stanley. 1967. "The Small World Problem." *Psychology Today* 2: 60–67.

———. 1974. *Obedience to Authority*. New York: Harper and Row.

Milicic, Bojka. 1998. "The Grapevine Forest: Kinship, Status, and Wealth in a Mediterranean Community (Selo, Croatia)." Pp. 15–35 in *Kinship, Networks, and Exchange*, edited by Thomas Schweizer and Douglas R. White. Cambridge: Cambridge University Press.

Millett, Paul. 1989. "Patronage and Its Avoidance in Classical Athens." Pp. 15–47 in *Patronage in Ancient Society*, edited by Andrew Wallace-Hadrill. London: Routledge.

Mintz, Sidney W., and Eric R. Wolf. 1950. "An Analysis of Ritual Co-Parenthood (Compadrazgo)." *Southwestern Journal of Anthropology* 6: 341–68.

Missakian, Elizabeth A. 1980. "Gender Differences in Agonistic Behavior and Dominance Relations of Synanon Communally Reared Children." Pp. 397–413 in *Dominance Relations: An Ethological View of Human Conflict and Social Interaction*, edited by Donald R. Omark, F. F. Strayer, and Daniel G. Freedman. New York: Garland.

Mitchell, Dave, Cathy Mitchell, and Richard Ofshe. 1980. *The Light on Synanon*. New York: Seaview Press.

Montgomery, James. 2007. "The Structure of Norms and Relations in Patronage Systems." *Social Networks* 29: 565–84.

Moody, James. 2002. "The Importance of Relationship Timing for Diffusion." *Social Forces* 81: 25–56.

Moore, Joan. 1978. *Homeboys: Gangs, Drugs, and Prison in the Barrios of Los Angeles*. Philadelphia: Temple University Press.

———. 1988. "Introduction" to John Hagedorn, with Perry Macon, *People and Folks: Gangs, Crime and the Underclass in a Rustbelt City*. Chicago: Lake View Press.

Morris, Martina. 1993. "Epidemiology and Social Networks: Modeling Structured Diffusion." *Sociological Methods and Research* 22: 99–126.

Mortensen, Dale T. 1988. "Matching: Finding a Pattern for Life or Otherwise." *American Journal of Sociology* 94: S215–S240.

Mott, William H. 1999. *Military Assistance: An Operational Perspective*. Westport, CT: Greenwood Press.

Mouzelis, Nicos. 1985. "On the Concept of Populism." *Politics and Society*: 329–49.

Mowbray, James A. 1996. "The Air Force." Pp. 83–111 in *America's Armed Forces*, edited by Sam C. Sarkesian and Robert E. Connor, Jr. Westport, CT: Greenwood Press.

Moyse-Bartlett. 1971. *Louis Edward Nolan and His Influence on the British Cavalry*. London: Leo Cooper.

Murphey, Rhoads. 1999. *Ottoman Warfare, 1500–1700*. New Brunswick, NJ: Rutgers University Press.

Nadel, S. F. 1957. *The Theory of Social Structure*. Glencoe, IL: Free Press.

Nakane, Chie. 1970. *Japanese Society*. Berkeley: University of California Press.

Nash, Gary B. 1968. *Quakers and Politics: Pennsylvania 1681–1726*. Princeton: Princeton University Press.

———. 2005. *The Unknown American Revolution*. New York: Viking.

Nathan, Andrew J. 1977 [1973]. "A Factionalism Model for CCP Politics." Pp. 55–73 in *Friends, Followers, and Factions: A Reader in Political Clientalism*, edited by Steffen W. Schmidt, James C. Scott, Carl Landé, and Laura Guasti. Berkeley: University of California.

Neale, J. E. 1958. *Essays in Elizabethan History*. New York: St. Martin's Press.

Nicholas, Ralph. W. 1977. "Factions: A Comparative Analysis." Pp. 55–73 in *Friends, Followers, and Factions: A Reader in Political Clientalism*, edited by Steffen W. Schmidt, James C. Scott, Carl Landé, and Laura Guasti. Berkeley: University of California.

Nishida, Toshisada, and Mariko Hiraiwa-Hasegawa. 1987. "Chimpanzees and Bonobos: Cooperative Relationships Among Males." Pp. 165–77 in *Primate Societies*, edited by Barbara B. Smuts, Dorothy L. Cheney, Robert M. Seyfarth, Richard W. Wrangham, and Thomas T. Struhsaker. Chicago: University of Chicago Press.

Nolan, L. E. 1860. *Cavalry: Its History and Tactics*. 3d ed. London: Bosworth and Harrison.

North, Douglass C. 1981. *Structure and Change in Economic History*. New York: W. W. Norton.

Ober, Josiah. 1994. "Classical Greek Times." Pp. 12–26 in *The Laws of War: Constraints on Warfare in the Western World*, edited by Michael Howard, George J. Andreopoulos, and Mark R. Shulman. New Haven: Yale University Press.

Oberschall, Anthony, and Eric M. Leifer. 1986. "Efficiency and Social Institutions: Uses and Misuses of Economic Reasoning in Sociology." *Annual Review of Sociology* 12: 233–53.

O'Connell, Robert L. 1995. *Ride of the Second Horseman: The Birth and Death of War.* New York: Oxford University Press.

Ofshe, Richard, Nancy Eisenberg Berg, Richard Coughlin, Gregory Dolinajec, Kathleen Gerson, and Avery Johnson. 1974. "Social Structure and Social Control in Synanon." *Journal of Voluntary Action Research* 3: 67–77.

O'Gorman, Hubert J. 1986. "The Discovery of Pluralistic Ignorance: An Ironic Lesson." *Journal of the History of the Behavioral Sciences* 22: 333–47.

Olson, Alison Gilbert. 1980. "Empire and Faction: A Comment." Pp. 61–69 in *Party and Political Opposition in Revolutionary America*, edited by Patricia U. Bonomi. Tarrytown, New York: Sleepy Hollow Press.

Opp, Karl-Dieter. 1984. "Balance Theory: Progress and Stagnation of a Social Psychological Theory." *Philosophy of the Social Sciences* 1984: 27–49.

Orléan, André. 1988. "Money and Mimetic Speculation." Pp. 101–12 in *Violence and Truth*, edited by Paul Dumouchel and translated by Mark R. Anspach. London: Athlone Press.

Padgett, John, and Christopher Ansell. 1993. "Robust Action and the Rise of the Medici, 1400–1434." *American Journal of Sociology* 98: 1259–1319.

Padgett, John F., and Paul D. McLean. 2006. "Organizational Invention and Elite Transformation: The Birth of Partnership Systems in Renaissance Florence." *American Journal of Sociology* 111: 1463–1568.

Palmer, Michael A. 2005. *Command at Sea: Naval Command and Control since the Sixteenth Century.* Cambridge, MA: Harvard University Press.

Parish, William L., and Ethan Michelson. 1996. "Politics and Markets: Dual Transformations." *American Journal of Sociology* 101:1042–59.

Park, George. 1974. *The Idea of Social Structure.* Garden City, NY: Anchor Books.

Parker, Geoffrey. 1996. *The Military Revolution: Military Innovation and the Rise of the West, 1500–1800.* Cambridge: Cambridge University Press.

Parkin, Robert. 1993. "The Joking Relationship and Kinship: Charting a Theoretical Dependency." *Journal of the Anthropological Society at Oxford* 24: 251–63.

Parrott, David. 2001. *Richelieu's Army: War, Government, and Society in France, 1624–1642.* Cambridge: Cambridge University Press.

Parsons, Talcott. 1960. *Structure and Process in Modern Societies.* New York: Free Press.

———. 1968. *The Structure of Social Action.* 2 vols. New York: Free Press.

Parsons, Talcott, and Edward A. Shils. 1956. *Toward a General Theory of Action.* Cambridge, MA: Harvard University Press.

Patterson, Stephen E. 1973. *Political Parties in Revolutionary Massachusetts.* Madison: University of Wisconsin Press.

Pattison, Philippa. 1994. "Social Cognition in Context: Some Applications of Social Network Analysis." Pp. 79–109 in *Advances in Social Network Analysis*, edited by Stanley Wasserman and Joseph Galaskiewicz. Beverly Hills, CA: Sage.

Peckham, Howard H. 1979 [1958]. *The War for Independence: A Military History.* Chicago: University of Chicago Press.

Pempel, T. J., and Keiichi Tsunekawa. 1979. "Corporatism without Labor? The Japanese Anomaly." Pp. 231–70 in *Trends toward Corporatist Intermediation*, edited by P.C. Schmitter and G. Lehmbruch. Newbury Park: Sage.

Perkins, Doug. 1996. "Structure and Choice: The Role of Organizations, Patronage, and the Media in Party Formation." *Party Politics* 2: 355–75.

Pocock, J.G.A. 1980. "Civil Wars, Revolutions, and Political Parties." Pp. 1–12 in *Party and Political Opposition in Revolutionary America*, edited by Patricia U. Bonomi. Tarrytown, NY: Sleepy Hollow Press.

Pole, J. R. 1966. *Political Representation in England and the Origins of the American Republic*. London: Macmillan.

Pollack, Norman, ed. 1967. *The Populist Mind*. Indianapolis, IN: Bobbs-Merrill.

Porter, Bruce D. 1994. *War and the Rise of the State: The Military Foundations of Modern Politics*. New York: Free Press.

Porter, Theordore M. 1986. *The Rise of Statistical Thinking, 1820–1900*. Princeton, Princeton University Press.

Pośpiech, Andrzej, and Wojciech Tygielski. 1981. "The Social Role of Magnates' Courts in Poland." *Acta Poloniae Historica* 43: 75–100.

Powell, John Duncan. 1970. "Peasant Society and Clientalistic Politics." *American Political Science Review* 64: 411–25.

Powicke, Michael. 1996 [1962]. *Military Obligation in Medieval England*. Oxford: Clarendon Press.

Prestwich, Michael. 1996. *Armies and Warfare in the Middle Ages: The English Experience*. New Haven: Yale University Press.

Prince, Carl E. 1970. "The Passing of the Aristocracy: Jefferson's Removal of The Federalists, 1801–1805." *Journal of American History* 57: 563–75.

Purvis, Thomas L. 1986. *Proprietors, Patronage, and Paper Money: Legislative Politics in New Jersey, 1703–1776*. New Brunswick, NJ: Rutgers University Press.

Qvarnström, Anna, and Elisabet Forsgren. 1998. "Should Females Prefer Dominant Males?" *Trends in Ecology and Evolution* 13: 498–501.

Radcliffe-Brown, A. R. 1940. "On Joking Relationships." *Africa* 13: 195–210.

Ramon J. 1973. "Variation and Consistency in the Social Behavior of Two Groups of Stumptail Macaques (*Macaca arctoides*)." *Primates* 14: 21–35.

Randall, Willard Sterne. 1993. *Thomas Jefferson: A Life*. New York: Henry Holt.

Ranum, Orest. 1993. *The Fronde*. New York: W. W. Norton.

Rasmussen, Dennis R. 1988. "Studies of Food-Enhanced Primate Groups: Current and Potential Areas of Contribution to Primate Social Ecology." Pp. 313–46 in *Ecology and Behavior of Food-Enhanced Primate Groups*, edited by John E. Fa and Charles H. Southwick. New York: Alan R. Liss.

Read, K. E. 1954. "Cultures of the Central Highlands, New Guinea." *Southwestern Journal of Anthropology* 10:1–43.

Reich, Wendelin. 2000. "Heuristics as Plausible Models of Rationality?" *Acta Sociological* 43: 251–58.

Reichley, A. James. 1992. *The Life of the Parties*. New York: Free Press.

Reinhardt, Viktor and Annie Reinhardt. 1981. "Cohesive Relationships in a Cattle Herd (*Bos indicus*)." *Behaviour* 76: 121–51.

Reuter, Timothy. 1999. "Carolingian and Ottonian Warfare." Pp. 13–35 in *Medieval Warfare: A History*, edited by Maurice Keen. Oxford: Oxford University Press.

Rhine, Ramon J. 1973. "Variation and Consistency in the Social Behavior of Two Groups of Stumptail Macaques (*Macaca arctoides*)." *Primates* 14: 21–35.

Ridgeway, Cecilia L. Ridgeway, and Kristan Glasgow Erickson. 2000. "Creating and Spreading Status Beliefs." *American Journal of Sociology* 106: 579–615.

Riley, Dylan. 2005. "Civic Associations and Authoritarian Regimes in Interwar Europe: Italy and Spain in Comparative Perspective." *American Sociological Review* 70: 288–310.

Riordon, William L. 1982 [1905]. *Plunkitt of Tammany Hall*. Mattituck, NY: Amereon House.

Risjord, Norman K. 1978. *Chesapeake Politics, 1781–1800*. New York: Columbia University Press.

Roberts, Michael. 1967. "The Military Revolution, 1560–1660." Pp. 195–225 in *Essays in Swedish History*. Minneapolis: University of Minnesota Press.

Robins, Garry, Philippa Pattison, and Jodie Woolcock. 2005. "Small and Other Worlds: Global Network Structures from Local Processes." *American Journal of Sociology* 110: 894–936.

Roemer, John. 1982. *A General Theory of Exploitation and Class*. Cambridge, MA: Harvard University Press.

Rogers, Clifford J. 1999. "The Age of the Hundred Years War." Pp. 136–60 in *Medieval Warfare: A History*, edited by Maurice Keen. Oxford: Oxford University Press.

Rossi, Ino. 1974. "Structuralism as Scientific Method." Pp. 60–106 in *The Unconscious in Culture: The Structuralism of Claude Levi-Strauss in Perspective*, edited by Ino Rossi. New York: E. P. Dutton.

Roth, Alvin E., and Marilda A. Oliveira Sotomayor. 1990. *Two-Sided Matching: A Study in Game-Theoretic Modeling and Analysis*. Cambridge: Cambridge University Press.

Rothenberg, Winifred Barr. 1992. *From Market-Places to a Market Economy*. Chicago: University of Chicago Press.

Rousseau, Jean-Jacques. 1928 [1782]. *The Confessions of Jean-Jacques Rousseau*, translated by W. Conygham Mallory. New York: Albert and Charles Boni.

———. 1967 [1755]. *Discourse on the Origin of Inequality*. Edited by Lester G. Crocker. New York: Washington Square Press.

Rowell, T. E. 1967. "Variability in the Social Organization of Primates." Pp. 219–35 in *Primate Ethology*, edited by Desmond Morris. London: Weidenfeld and Nicolson.

———. 1971. "Organization of Caged Groups of Cercopithecus Monkeys." *Animal Behavior* 19: 625–45.

Rubin, Gayle. 1985. "The Traffic in Women: Notes on the 'Political Economy' of Sex." Pp. 157–210 in *Toward and Anthropology of Women*, edited by Reyna Reiter. New York: Monthly Review Press.

Ryan, Dan. 2006. Getting the Word Out: Notes on the Social Organization of Notification." *Sociological Theory* 24: 228–54.

Sade, Donald Stone. 1967. "Determinants of Dominance in a Group of Free-Ranging Rhesus Monkeys." Pp. 99–114 in *Social Communication among Primates*, edited by S.A. Altmann. Chicago: University of Chicago Press.

———. 1972. "Sociometrics of *Macaca mulatta*, I: Linkages and Cliques in Grooming Matrices." *Folia Primatologica* 18: 196–223.

Sade, Donald Stone, Michael Altmann, James Loy, Glenn Hausfater, and Judith A. Breuggeman. 1988. "Sociometrics of *Macaca mulatta* II: Decoupling Centrality and Dominance in Rhesus Monkey Social Networks." *American Journal of Physical Anthropology* 77: 409–25.

Sade, Donald Stone, and Malcolm W. Dow. 1994. "Primate Social Networks." Pp. 152–66 in *Advances in Social Network Analysis*, edited by Stanley Wasserman and Joseph Galaskiewicz. Beverly Hills, CA: Sage.

Sahlins, Marshall D. 1963. "Poor Man, Rich Man, Big-Man, Chief: Political Types in Melanesia and Polynesia." *Comparative Studies in Society and History* 5: 285–303.

———. 1968. *Tribesmen*. Englewood Cliffs, NJ: Prentice Hall.

Saller, Richard. 1989. "Patronage and Friendship in Early Imperial Rome: Drawing the Distinction." Pp. 49–62 in *Patronage in Ancient Society*, edited by Andrew Wallace-Hadrill. London: Routledge.

Savage-Rumbaugh, Sue, and Kelly McDonald. 1988. "Deception and Social Manipulation in Symbol-Using Apes." Pp. 224–37 in *Machiavellian Intelligence II*, edited by Richard W. Byrne and Andrew Whiten. Cambridge: Cambridge University Press.

Savin-Williams, Ritch C. 1977. "Dominance in a Human Adolescent Group." *Animal Behavior* 25: 400–406.

———. 1980. "Dominance Hierarchies Groups of Middle to Late Adolescent Males." *Journal of Youth and Adolescence* 9: 75–85.

———. 1987. *Adolescence: An Ethological Perspective*. New York: Springer-Verlag.

Sawyer, Ralph D. 1993. *The Seven Military Classics of Ancient China*. Boulder, CO: Westview Press.

———. 2007. *The Tao of Deception: Unorthodox Warfare in Historic and Modern China*. New York: Basic Books.

Scalapino, Robert A., and Junnosuke Masumi. 1964. *Parties and Politics in Contemporary Japan*. Berkeley: University of California.

Schaller, George B. 1963. *The Mountain Gorilla: Ecology and Behavior*. Chicago: University of Chicago Press.

———. 1964. *The Year of the Gorilla*. Chicago: University of Chicago Press.

Schjelderup-Ebbe, Thorleif. 1922. "Beiträge zur Sozialpsychologie des Haushuhns." *Zeitschrift für Psychologie* 88: 225–52.

———. 1935. "Social Behavior in Birds." Pp. 947–72 in *The Handbook of Social Psychology*, edited by Carl Murchison. Worcester: Clark University Press.

Schwartz, Mildred A. 1990. *The Party Network: The Robust Organization of Illinois Republicans*. Madison: University of Wisconsin Press.

Schwimmer, Erik. 1973. *Exchange in the Social Structure of the Orokaiva*. London: C. Hurst.

Scott, James C. 1972. "Patron-Client Politics and Political Change in Southeast Asia." *American Political Science Review* 66: 91–113.

Scott, James C., and Benedict J. Kerkvliet. 1977. "How Traditional Rural Patrons Lose Legitimacy: A Theory with Special Reference to Southeast Asia." Pp. 439–58 in *Friends, Followers, and Factions: A Reader in Political Clientalism*, edited by Steffen W. Schmidt, James C. Scott, Carl Landé, and Laura Guasti. Berkeley: University of California.

Shapin, Steven 1994. *A Social History of Truth*. Chicago: University of Chicago Press.

Sharma, Ram Sharan. 1965. *Indian Feudalism: c. 300–1200*. Calcutta: University of Calcutta Press.

Sharp, James Roger. 1993. *American Politics in the Early Republic*. New Haven: Yale University Press.

Shaw, Marvin E. 1964. "Communication Networks." Pp. 111–47 in *Advances in Experimental Social Psychology*, edited by Leonard Berkowitz. New York: Academic Press.

Shefter, Martin. 1976. "The Emergence of the Political Machine: An Alternative View." Pp. 14–44 in *Theoretical Perspectives on Urban Politics*, edited by Willis Hawley et al. Englewood Cliffs, NJ: Prentice Hall.

———. 1994. *Political Parties and the State*. Princeton: Princeton University Press.

Sheley, Joseph F., Joshua Zhang, Charles J. Brody, and James D. Wright. 1995. "Gang Organization, Gang Criminal Activity, and Individual Gang Members' Criminal Behavior." *Social Science Quarterly* 76: 53–68.

Sheridan, Eugene R. 1981. *Lewis Morris, 1671–1746: A Study in Early American Politics*. Syracuse, NY: Syracuse University Press.

Short, James F. Jr., and Fred L. Strodtbeck. 1965. *Group Process and Gang Delinquency*. Chicago: University of Chicago Press.

Shorto, Russell. 2004. *The Island at the Center of the World*. New York: Doubleday.

Silberbauer, G. B. 1961. "Aspects of the Kinship System of the G/wi Bushmen of the Central Kalahari." *South African Journal of Science* 58: 353–59.

———. 1972. "The G/wi Bushmen." Pp. 271–326 in *Hunters and Gatherers Today*, edited by M. G. Bicchieri. New York: Holt.

Silver, Allan. 1985. "'Trust' in Social and Political Theory." Pp. 52–67 in *The Challenge of Social Control*. Edited by Gerald D. Suttles and Mayer W. Zald. Norwood, NJ: Ablex.

———. 1994. "Democratic Citizenship and High Military Strategy: The Inheritance, Decay, and Reshaping of Political Culture." *Research on Democracy and Society* 2: 317–49.

———. 2002. "Friendship and Sincerity." Paper presented at the Conference on Kinship and Friendship, University of Bielefeld, February 8–10.

Silverman, Sydel F. 1965. "Patronage and Community National Relationships in Central Italy." *Ethnology* 4: 172–89.

Simmel, Georg. 1950 [1908]. *Soziologie: Untersuchung uber die Formen der Vergesellschaftung*. Translated and edited by Kurt H. Wolff as *The Sociology of Georg Simmel*. Glencoe, IL: Free Press.

———. 1955 [1922]. "The Web of Group-Affiliations." Translation of "Die Kreuzung sozialer Kreise," pp. 305–44 of *Soziologie*, by Reinhard Bendix, appearing as 127–95 in *Conflict and the Web of Group Affiliations*. Glencoe, IL: Free Press.

Simon, Herbert A. 1962. "The Architecture of Complexity." *Proceedings of the American Philosophical Society* 106: 467–82.

———. 1996. *The Sciences of the Artificial*. Cambridge, MA: MIT Press.

Singer, Alice. 1973. "Marriage Payments and the Exchange of People." *Man* 8: 80–92.

Sisock, Mary. 2008. "Private Forest Owners' Communication Networks: Exploring the Structural Basis for Cross-Boundary Cooperation." Ph.D. diss., University of Wisconsin, Madison.

Skolnick, Jerome H., Ricky Bluthenthal, and Theodore Correl. 1993. "Gang Organization and Migration." Pp. 193–217 in *Gangs: The Origins and Impact of Contempo-*

rary Youth Gangs in the United States, edited by Scott Cummings and Daniel J. Monti. Albany: State University of New York Press.

Skvoretz, John, and Katherine Faust. 2002. "Relations, Species, and Network Structure." 2002. *Journal of Social Structure*. Vol. 3.

Slater, Philip E. 1963. "On Social Regression." *American Sociological Review* 28: 339–64.

Slez, Adam, and John Levi Martin. 2007. "Political Action and Party Formation in the United States Constitutional Convention." *American Sociological Review* 72: 42–67.

Sluckin, Andrew M. 1980. "Dominance Relationships in Preschool Children." Pp. 159–76 in *Dominance Relations: An Ethological View of Human Conflict and Social Interaction*, edited by Donald R. Omark, F.F. Strayer, and Daniel G. Freedman. New York: Garland.

Smith, Adam. 1937 [1776]. *An Inquiry into the Nature and Causes of the Wealth of Nations*. New York: Modern Library.

Smith, David Glenn. 1993. "A Fifteen-year Study of the Association between Dominance Rank and Reproductive Success of Male Rhesus Macaques." *Primates* 34: 471–80.

———. 1994. "Male Dominance and Reproductive Success in a Captive Group of Rhesus Macaques (*Macaca mulatta*)." *Behavior* 129: 225–42.

Smith, DeVerne Reed. 1983. *Palauan Social Structure*. New Brunswick, NJ: Rutgers University Press.

Smuts, Barbara B. 1985. *Sex and Friendship in Baboons*. New York: Aldine.

———. 1987a. "Sexual Competition and Mate Choice." Pp. 385–99 in *Primate Societies*, edited by Barbara B. Smuts, Dorothy L. Cheney, Robert M. Seyfarth, Richard W. Wrangham, and Thomas T. Struhsaker. Chicago: University of Chicago Press.

———. 1987b. "Gender, Aggression, and Influence." Pp. 400–412 in *Primate Societies*, edited by Barbara B. Smuts, Dorothy L. Cheney, Robert M. Seyfarth, Richard W. Wrangham, and Thomas T. Struhsaker. Chicago: University of Chicago Press.

Smuts, Barbara B., Dorothy L. Cheney, Robert M. Seyfarth, Richard W. Wrangham, and Thomas T. Struhsaker, eds. 1987. *Primate Societies*. Chicago: University of Chicago Press.

Sniderman, Paul M., Richard A. Brody, and Philip E. Tetlock. 1991. *Reasoning and Choice: Explorations in Political Psychology*. Cambridge: Cambridge University Press.

Snodgrass, A. M. 1965. "The Hoplite Reform and History." *Journal of Hellenic Studies* 85: 110–22.

Snyder, Frank M. 1993. *Command and Control: The Literature and Commentaries*. Washington, DC: National Defense University Press.

Sombart, Werner. 1967 [1915]. *The Quintessence of Capitalism: A Study of the History and Psychology of the Modern Business Man*. Translated and edited by M. Epstein. New York: Howard Fertig.

Somers, Margaret. 1993. "Citizenship and the Place of the Public Sphere: Law, Community, and Political Culture in the Transition to Democracy." *American Sociological Review* 58: 587–620.

Somerset, Anne. 2003. *Elizabeth I*. Garden City, NY: Anchor Books.

Sorenson, Olav, and Toby E. Stuart. 2001. "Syndication Networks and the Spatial Distribution of Venture Capital Investments." *American Journal of Sociology* 106: 1546–88.

Sorokin, Pitrim A. 1959 [1927 and 1941]. *Social and Cultural Mobility.* Glencoe, Ill.: The Free Press.

Spencer, Herbert. 1896 [1873]. *The Study of Sociology.* New York: D. Appleton.

———. 1910 [1886]. *The Principles of Sociology.* Vol. 2. New York: D. Appleton.

———. 1910 [1896]. *The Principles of Sociology.* Vol. 3. New York: D. Appleton.

Spiegel, Bernt. 1961. *Die Struktur der Meinungverteilung im Sozialen Feld.* Bern: Verlag Hans Huber.

de Spinoza, Benedict. 1930 [1677]. *Ethic.* Translated by W. Hale White and Amelia Hutchinson. London: Oxford University Press.

Sprecher, Susan. 1998. "The Effect of Exchange Orientation on Close Relationships." *Social Psychology Quarterly* 61: 220–31.

Srivastava, A. K. 1985. *Ancient Indian Army: Its Administration and Organization.* New Delhi: Ajanta.

Stacey, Robert C. 1994. "The Age of Chivalry." Pp. 27–39 in *The Laws of War: Constraints on Warfare in the Western World,* edited by Michael Howard, George J. Andreopoulos, and Mark R. Shulman. New Haven: Yale University Press.

Stahr, Water. 2005. *John Jay.* London: Hambledon and London.

Stammbach, Eduard. 1987. "Desert, Forest, and Mountain Baboons: Multilevel Societies." Pp. 112–20 in *Primate Societies,* edited by Barbara B. Smuts, Dorothy L. Cheney, Robert M. Seyfarth, Richard W. Wrangham, and Thomas T. Struhsaker. Chicago: University of Chicago Press.

Stark, David. 1996. "Recombinant Property in East European Capitalism." *American Journal of Sociology* 101: 993–1027.

Stigler, George J. 1968. *The Organization of Industry.* Homewood, IL: R. D. Irwin.

Stinchcombe, Arthur L. 1990. Chapter 16 Pp. 285–302 in *Economics and Sociology,* edited by Richard Swedberg. Princeton: Princeton University Press.

Stokes, Susan C. 1995. *Cultures in Conflict: Social Movements and the State in Peru.* Berkeley: University of California Press.

Strachan, Hew. 1984. *Wellington's Legacy: The Reform of the British Army, 1830—54.* Manchester, UK: Manchester University Press.

Strayer, F. F., and Mark S. Cummins. 1980. "Aggressive and Competitive Social Structures in Captive Monkey Groups." Pp. 85–96 in *Dominance Relations: An Ethological View of Human Conflict and Social Interaction,* edited by Donald R. Omark, F. F. Strayer, and Daniel G. Freedman. New York: Garland.

Strayer, F. F., and Janet Strayer. 1976. "An Ethological Analysis of Social Agonism and Dominance Relations among Preschool Children." *Child Development* 47: 980–89.

———. 1980. "Preschool Conflict and the Assessment of Social Dominance." Pp. 137–57 in *Dominance Relations: An Ethological View of Human Conflict and Social Interaction,* edited by Donald R. Omark, F. F. Strayer, and Daniel G. Freedman. New York: Garland.

Strier, Karen B. 1986. "The Behavior and Ecology of the Wooly Spider Monkey, or Muriqui (*Brachyteles arachnoides* E. Geoffroy 1806)." Ph.D. diss., Harvard University.

————. 2000. *Primate Behavioral Ecology.* Boston: Allyn and Bacon.

————. 2003. "Primatology Comes of Age: 2002 AAPA Luncheon Address." *Yearbook of Physical Anthropology* 46: 2–13.

Strier, Karen B., Laiena T. Dib, and José E.C. Figueira. 2002. "Social Dynamics of Male Muriquis (*Brachyteles arachnoides hypoxanthus*)." *Behaviour* 139: 315–42.

Strogatz, Steven H. 2001. "Exploring Complex Networks." *Nature* 410: 268–76.

Sunter, Ronald M. 1986. *Patronage and Politics in Scotland, 1707–1832.* Edinburgh: John Donald.

Suttles, Gerald D. 1968. *The Social Order of the Slum.* Chicago: University of Chicago Press.

Swedberg, Richard. 1994. "Markets as Social Structures." Pp. 255–82 in *The Handbook of Economic Sociology*, edited by Neil J. Smelser and Richard Swedberg. Princeton: Princeton University Press.

Sweetman, John. 1984. *War and Administration: The Significance of the Crimean War for the British Army.* Edinburgh: Scottish Academy Press.

Swidler, Ann. 2001. *Talk of Love.* Chicago: University of Chicago Press.

Syme, G. J., and L. A. Syme. 1979. *Social Structure in Farm Animals.* Amsterdam: Elsevier.

Tacitus. 1942. *The Complete Works of Tacitus.* New York: The Modern Library.

Takahata, Yukio. 1991. "Diachronic Changes in the Dominance Relations of Adult Female Japanese Monkeys of the Arashiyama B Group." Pp. 123–39 in *The Monkeys of Arashiyama*, edited by Linda Marie Fedigan and Pamela J. Asquith. Albany: State University of New York Press.

Taylor, Lilly Ross. 1968. [1949] *Party Politics in the Age of Caesar.* Berkeley: University of California.

Terwiel, Barend J. 1984. "Formal Structures and Informal Rules: An Historical Perspective on Hierarchy, Bondage and the Patron-Client Relationship." Pp.19–38 in *Strategies and Structures in Thai Society*, edited by Han ten Brummelhuis and Jeremy H. Kemp. Amsterdam: Antropologisch-Sociologisch Centrum, Universiteit van Amsterdam.

Thrasher, Feredic M. 1963 [1927]. *The Gang: A Study of 1,313 Gangs in Chicago.* Chicago: University of Chicago Press.

Thucydides. 1972 [1954]. *History of the Peloponnesian War*, translated by Rex Warner. London: Penguin.

Tiger, Lionel. 1970. "Dominance in Human Societies." *Annual Review of Ecology and Systematics* 1: 287–306.

Tilly, Charles. 1990. *Coercion, Capital, and European States, A.D. 990–1990.* Oxford: Blackwell.

————. 1998. *Durable Inequality.* Berkeley: University of California Press.

Tjon Sie Fat, Franklin E. 1990. "Representing Kinship: Simple Models of Elementary Structures." Ph.D. diss., Leiden University.

Tolz, Vera. 1990. *The USSR's Emerging Multiparty System.* New York: Praeger.

Travers, Jeffrey, and Stanley Milgram. 1969. "An Experimental Study of the Small World Problem." *Sociometry* 32: 425–43.

Travers, Tim. 2005 [1992]. *How the War Was Won.* Yorkshire: Pen and Sword Books.

Turnbull, Colin M. 1962. *The Forest People.* New York: Clarion.

Valente, Thomas W. 1995. *Network Models of the Diffusion of Innovations*. Cresskill, NJ: Hampton Press.

Van Fleet, David D., and Gary A. Yukl. 1986. *Military Leadership: An Organizational Behavior Perspective*. Greenwich, CT: JAI Press.

Varenne, Hervé. 1977. *Americans Together: Structured Diversity in a Midwestern Town*. New York: Teachers' College Press.

Varga, Nicholas. 1960. "Election Procedures and Practices in Colonial New York." *New York History* 41: 249–77.

Varley, Paul. 1999. "Warfare in Japan 1467–1600." Pp. 53–86 in *War in the Early Modern World*, edited by Jeremy Black. London: Westview.

Vaughn, Brian E., and Everett Waters. 1980. "Social Organization among Preschool Peers: Dominance, Attention, and Sociometric Correlates." Pp. 359–79 in *Dominance Relations: An Ethological View of Human Conflict and Social Interaction*, edited by Donald R. Omark, F. F. Strayer, and Daniel G. Freedman. New York: Garland.

Veblen, Thorstein. 1912. *The Theory of the Leisure Class*. London: Macmillan.

de la Vega, Garcilaso. 1961 [c. 1609]. *The Incas: The Royal Commentaries of the Inca Garcilaso de la Vega*, translated by Maria Jolas. New York: Orion Press.

Venkatesh, Sudhir Alladi, and Steven D. Levitt. 2000. "'Are We a Family or a Business?' History and Disjuncture in the Urban American Street Gang." *Theory and Society* 29: 427–62.

Vernant, Jeane-Pierre. 1995. *The Greeks*. Translated by Charles Lambert and Teresa Lavender Fagan. Chicago: University of Chicago Press.

Vigil, James Diego. 1988. *Barrio Gangs: Street Life and Identity in Southern California*. Austin: University of Texas Press.

Viveiros de Castro, Eduardo. 1998. "Dravidian and Related Kinship Systems." Pp. 332–85 in *Transformations of Kinship*, edited by Maurice Godelier, Thomas R. Trautmann, and Franklin E. Tjon Sie Fat. Washington: Smithsonian Institution Press.

de Waal, Frans. 1977. "The Organization of Agonistic Relations within two Captive Groups of Java-Monkeys (*Macaca fascicularis*)." *Zeitschrift für Tierpsychologie* 44: 225–82.

———. 1986. "Deception in the Natural Communication of Chimpanzees." Pp. 221–44 in *Deception: Perspectives on Human and Nonhuman Deceit*, edited by Robert W. Mitchell and Nicholas S. Thompson. Albany: SUNY Press.

———. 1987. "Dynamics of Social Relationships." Pp. 421–29 in *Primate Societies*, edited by Barbara B. Smuts, Dorothy L. Cheney, Robert M. Seyfarth, Richard W. Wrangham, and Thomas T. Struhsaker. Chicago: University of Chicago Press.

———. 1990. *Peacemaking among Primates*. Cambridge, MA: Harvard University Press.

———. 1998. *Chimpanzee Politics*. Rev. ed. Baltimore: Johns Hopkins University Press.

———. 2001. *The Ape and the Sushi Master*. New York: Basic Books.

Wachter, Kenneth W. 1980. "Ancestors at the Norman Conquest." Pp. 85–93 in *Genealogical Demography*, edited by Bennett Dyke and Warren T. Morrill. New York: Academic Press.

Wallace, Walter L. 1966. *Student Culture: Social Structure and Continuity in a Liberal Arts College*. Chicago: Aldine.

Wallace-Hadrill, Andrew. 1989. "Patronage in Roman Society: From Republic to Empire." Pp. 63–87 in *Patronage in Ancient Society*, edited by Andrew Wallace-Hadrill. London: Routledge.

Waller, Willard. 1937. "The Rating and Dating Complex." *American Sociological Review* 2: 727–34.

Walters, Jeffrey R., and Robert M. Seyfarth. 1987. "Conflict and Cooperation." Pp. 165–77 in *Primate Societies*, edited by Barbara B. Smuts, Dorothy L. Cheney, Robert M. Seyfarth, Richard W. Wrangham and Thomas T. Struhsaker. Chicago: University of Chicago Press.

Ward, S.G.P. 1957. *Wellington's Headquarters: A Study of the Administrative Problems in the Peninsula, 1809–1814*. London: Oxford University Press.

Ward, W. R. 1952. "The Administration of the Window and Assessed Taxes, 1696–1798." *English Historical Review* 67: 522–42.

Watts, Duncan J. 1999. *Small Worlds: The Dynamics of Networks between Order and Randomness*. Princeton: Princeton University Press.

Watts, Duncan J., Peter Sheridan Dodds, and M.E.J. Newman. 2002. "Identity and Search in Social Networks." *Science* 296: 1302–5.

Waugh, Scott L. 1986. "Tenure to Contract: Lordship and Clientage in Thirteenth-Century England." *English Historical Review* 401: 811–39.

Weber, Max. 1946 [1915]. "Religious Rejections of the World and Their Directions." Pp. 323–59 in *From Max Weber: Essays in Sociology*, translated and edited by H. H. Gerth and C. Wright Mills. New York: Oxford University Press.

———. 1946 [1918]. "Politics as a Vocation." Pp. 77–128 in *From Max Weber: Essays in Sociology*, translated and edited by H. H. Gerth and C. Wright Mills. New York: Oxford University Press.

———. 1978. *Economy and Society*. 2 vols. Edited by Guenther Roth and Claus Wittich. Berkeley: University of California Press.

Weigley, Russell F. 1967. *History of the United States Army*. New York: Macmillan.

Weimann, Gabriel. 1982. "On the Importance of Marginality: One More Step into the Two-Step Flow of Communication." *American Sociological Review* 47: 764–73.

Weingrod, Alex. 1968. "Patrons, Patronage, and Political Parties." *Comparative Studies in Society and History* 10: 377–400.

Weisfeld, Glenn E., Donald R. Omark, and Carol L. Cronin. 1980. "A Longitudinal and Cross-Section Study of Dominance in Boys." Pp. 205–16 in *Dominance Relations: An Ethological View of Human Conflict and Social Interaction*, edited by Donald R. Omark, F. F. Strayer, and Daniel G. Freedman. New York: Garland.

Weissman, Ronald. 1987. "Taking Patronage Seriously: Mediterranean Values and Renaissance Society." Pp. 25–45 in *Patronage, Art, and Society in Renaissance Italy*, edited by F. W. Kent and Patrica Simons. Oxford: Clarendon Press.

Wendel, Thomas. 1968. "The Keith-Lloyd Alliance: Factional and Coalition Politics in Colonial Pennsylvania." *The Pennsylvania Magazine of History and Biography* 92: 289–305.

White, Douglas R., and Frank Harary. 2001. "The Cohesiveness of Blocks in Social Networks: Node Connectivity and Conditional Density." *Sociological Methodology* 31: 305–59.

White, Harrison C. 1970. *Chains of Opportunity: System Models of Mobility in Organizations*. Cambridge, MA: Harvard University Press.

White, Harrison C. 1992. *Identity and Control*. Princeton: Princeton University Press.

———. 2002. *Markets from Networks*. Princeton: Princeton University Press.

White, Harrison C., Scott A. Boorman, and Ronald L. Breiger. 1976. "Social Structure from Multiple Networks, I: Blockmodels of Roles and Positions." *American Journal of Sociology* 81: 730–79.

Whitehead, Neil L. 1990. "The Snake Warriors—Sons of the Tiger's Teeth: A Descriptive Analysis of Carib Warfare, ca. 1500–1820." Pp. 146–70 in *The Anthropology of War*, edited by Jonathan Haas. Cambridge: Cambridge University Press.

———. 1992. "Tribes Make States and States Make Tribes." Pp. 127–50 in *War in the Tribal Zone*, edited by R. Brian Ferguson and Neil L. Whitehead. Santa Fe, NM: School of American Research Press.

Whiting, Charles. 1981. *Death of a Division*. New York: Stein and Day.

Whyte, William Foote. 1981 [1943]. *Street Corner Society*. 3d ed. Chicago: University of Chicago Press.

Wickler, Wolfgang. 1973 [1969]. *The Sexual Code*. Translated by Francisca Garvie. Garden City, NY: Anchor.

Wiessner, Polly, and Akii Tumu. 1998. "The Capacity and Constraints of Kinship in the Development of the Enga *Tee* Ceremonial Exchange Network (Papua New Guinea Highlands)." Pp. 277–302 in *Kinship, Networks, and Exchange*, edited by Thomas Schweizer and Douglas R. White. Cambridge: Cambridge University Press.

Wilensky, Harold L. 1967. *Organizational Intelligence: Knowledge and Policy in Government and Industry*. New York: Basic Books.

Wilentz, Sean. 2005. *The Rise of American Democracy: Jefferson to Lincoln*. New York: W. W. Norton.

Wiley, James A., and Stephen J. Herschkorn. 1989. "Homosexual Role Separation and AIDS Epidemics: Insights from Elementary Models." *Journal of Sex Research* 26: 434–49.

Willerton, John P. 1992. *Patronage and Politics in the USSR*. Cambridge: Cambridge University Press.

Williams, John Allen. 1996. "The Navy." Pp. 63–82 in *America's Armed Forces*, edited by Sam C. Sarkesian and Robert E. Connor, Jr. Westport, CT: Greenwood Press.

Williamson, Oliver E. 1967. "Hierarchical Control and Optimum Firm Size." *Journal of Political Economy* 75: 123–38.

———. 1975. *Markets and Hierarchies: Analysis and Antitrust Implications*. New York: Free Press.

———. 1981a. "The Economics of Organization: The Transaction Cost Approach." *American Journal of Sociology* 87: 548–77.

———. 1981b. "The Modern Corporation: Origins, Evolution, Attributes." *Journal of Economic Literature* 19: 1537–68.

———. 1985. *The Economic Institutions of Capitalism*. New York: Free Press.

Wills, Garry. 2002. *James Madison*. New York: Henry Holt.

Wilson, Edward O. 1975. *Sociobiology: The New Synthesis*. Cambridge, MA: Harvard University Press.

Wilson, Monica. 1957. "Joking Relationships in Central Africa." *Man* 57: 111–12.

Wilson, Peter. 1999. "European Warfare 1450–1815." Pp. 177–206 in *War in the Early Modern World*, edited by Jeremy Black. London: Westview.

Winship, Christopher. 1977. "A Distance Model for Sociometric Structure." *Journal of Mathematical Sociology* 5: 32–39.

Wolf, Eric R. 1977. "Kinship, Friendship, and Patron-Client Relations in Complex Societies." Pp. 167–77 in *Friends, Followers, and Factions: A Reader in Political Clientalism*, edited by Steffen W. Schmidt, James C. Scott, Carl Landé, and Laura Guasti. Berkeley: University of California.

Wong, Ling Heng, Philippa Pattison, and Garry Robins. 2006. "A Spatial Model for Social Networks." *Physica A: Statistical Mechanics and its Applications* 360: 99–120.

Woodward, C. Vann. 1938. *Tom Watson: Agrarian Rebel*. New York: Macmillan.

———. 1951. *Origins of the New South: 1877–1913*. Baton Rouge: Louisiana State University Press.

Wrangham, Richard W. 1987. "Evolution of Social Structure." Pp. 282–96 in *Primate Societies*, edited by Barbara B. Smuts, Dorothy L. Cheney, Robert M. Seyfarth, Richard W. Wrangham, and Thomas T. Struhsaker. Chicago: University of Chicago Press.

Yablonsky, Lewis. 1965. *The Tunnel Back: Synanon*. New York: Macmillan.

Yamagishi, Toshio, and Karen S. Cook. 1993. "Generalized Exchange and Social Dilemmas." *Social Psychology Quarterly* 56: 235–48.

Yamaguchi, Kazuo. 2002. "The Structural and Behavioral Characteristics of the Smallest-World Phenomenon: Minimum Distance Networks." *Social Networks* 24: 161–82.

Yerkes, Robert M., and Ada W. Yerkes. 1935. "Social Behavior in Infrahuman Primates." Pp. 973–1033 in *A Handbook of Social Psychology*, edited by Carl Murchison. Worcester, MA: Clark University Press.

Yeung, King-To. 2005. "What Does Love Mean? Exploring Network Culture in Two Network Settings." *Social Forces* 84: 391–420.

Young, Alfred F. 1967. *The Democratic Republicans of New York: The Origins, 1763–1797*. Chapel Hill: University of North Carolina Press.

Zablocki, Benjamin. 1980. *Alienation and Charisma: A Study of Contemporary American Communes*. New York: Free Press.

Zachary, Wayne W. 1977. "An Information Flow Model for Conflict and Fission in Small Groups." *Journal of Anthropological Research* 33: 452–73.

Zemsky, Robert. 1971. *Merchants, Farmers, and River Gods: An Essay on Eighteenth-Century American Politics*. Boston: Gambit.

Zerubavel, Eviatar. 2003. *Time Maps: Collective Memory and the Social Shape of the Past*. Chicago: University of Chicago Press.

———. 2007. "Generally Speaking: The Logic and Mechanics of Social Pattern Analysis." *Sociological Forum* 22: 131–45.

Zetterberg, Hans L. 1966. "The Secret Ranking." *Journal of Marriage and the Family* 27: 134–42.

Zhao, Dingxin. 2004. "Spurious Causation in a Historical Process: War and Bureaucratization in Early China." *American Sociological Review* 69: 603–7.

Zheng, Tian, Matthew J. Salganik, and Andrew Gelman. 2006. "How Many People Do You Know in Prison? Using Overdispersion in Count Data to Estimate Social Structure in Networks." *Journal of the American Statistical Association* 101: 409–23.

Index

Abbott, Andrew, 24
acquaintance, 32–36, 38, 41–42
action, and orders, 119–22, 131–34
action imperative, 17
action profile, 11, 21
Adams, John, 305
Adams, Simon, 294
administration, in armed forces, 274–75
adolescents, and dominance orders, 129–39
adoption, 83n17. *See also* contagion
advertising, 158n9
age, and dominance, 114
age bias, and marriage exchange, 91, 91n30
agglomeration, limits of, 68. *See also* concatenation
aggregation, 20, 30–31, 208–9. *See also* concatenation
agonism, 114, 123–24, 132–34, 139–41
AirLand Battle, U.S. doctrine of, 280
Alexander the Great, 248
Alien and Sedition laws of 1798, 312
alienation, in asymmetric relationships, 21
alignment of interests, 303, 305–7; regional, 313
"all channel" network, 236
Allee, W. C., 110
alliance, 21, 26–28, 42–45, 67–71, 121–22, 183–87
alliance formation, 291, 305–7
alpha boy, 135
alphas, role of, 119–22
alternatives, knowledge of, and equality of exchange, 79
altruism, 120
Amar, Akhil, 326
amelioration, in patronage system, 202–3
amigocracy, 213
Aminzade, Ronald, 307n32
Ammon, Harry, 304
analytic space, 34–36
anarchists, Spanish, 251–52
anarchy, 195–96
Anderson, Bo, 54n32
Anderson, Elijah, 141n49
AND formula, 39

animals: and dominance orders, 106–11, 119; ritual among, 116–19
Ansell, Christopher, 94, 94n36, 95, 95n37
anthropology, 5–6, 25n28
antiequivalence, 26, 47–48, 53; relations and classes of, 48–55
antifederalism, 302, 302n30, 303–4
anti- prefix, use of, 12n16
antistructure, 79–81
antisymmetric relationship, 12, 12n15, 21, 26, 152–53, 175, 189–90. *See also* dominance order; tree
antitransitivity, 23, 58, 211–12
apex, 190–92, 287
a- prefix, use of, 12n16
Arapaho, 48n24
Arapesh, 81–82
Archidamus, Spartan king, 253n27
architectonics, of influence structures, 173–74
armed force: and civil service, 321–27; and command hierarchy, 241–54; and command tree, 232–33; introduction of transitivity to, 270–82
armies, size of, 248, 257
army: British, 260, 278n65; medieval, 248–49; Prussian/German, 280; Roman, 246–47, 256n30, 262n40, 268; standing, 259–60; U.S., 244, 271
Arunta, 97–98
asymmetric relationship, 12, 12n15, 21, 26, 61, 73. *See also* donation
attractiveness, and choice pattern, 65–66
authoritativeness, 171
authority, 171–73, 236
authority relationship, 173–74
avoidance relations, 46–59
Azaña, Manuel, 251
Aztecs, 262n41, 323n5

baboons, 113, 115, 122, 124, 184n41
Back, Kurt, 33, 164
balance, as strong type of transitivity, 59–60
balance theory, 42–67, 292, 306, 334
Bantu, 197
Barth, Fredrik, 7–8, 82n13, 218
base, of triangle, 190